LaunchPad Solo for Journalism

News Reporting and Writing doesn't just cover the integration of print and digital media—it practices it, too, with our new *LaunchPad Solo for Journalism*. This dynamic platform combines a curated collection of tools for journalism students, including the *News Reporting and Writing* workbook, access to thousands of grammar and writing exercises in Exercise Central for AP Style, videos that compliment the material in the text and video tools that make it easy to upload, embed and collaborate on video assignments.

Throughout the book, call-outs in the margins link to a series of thought-provoking online videos that expand on the material covered in the print chapters with an insider's look at journalism. Topics include legal rights of bloggers, real news versus satirical "fake" news, citizen journalism, shield laws and more. All videos are accompanied by discussion questions.

Turn to the inside back cover for more information on how to access *LaunchPad Solo for Journalism* along with a full list of available videos.

Contemporary Design and Coverage

News Reporting and Writing, Twelfth Edition, features an eye-catching design and is in full-color for the first time. Brand new openers for every chapter relate to contemporary topics and current events.

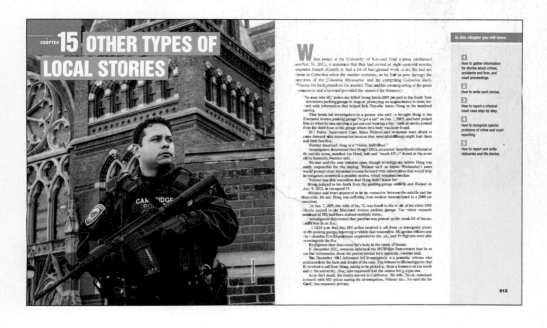

News Reporting and Writing

Twelfth Ed

The Missouri Group

Brian S. Brooks

George Kennedy

Daryl R. Moen

Don Ranly

School of Journalism
University of Missouri

bedford/st.martin's
Macmillan Learning
Boston | New York

For Bedford/St. Martin's
Vice President, Editorial, Macmillan Learning Humanities: Edwin Hill
Publisher for Communication: Erika Gutierrez
Development Manager: Susan McLaughlin
Development Editor: Linda Stern
Assistant Editor: William Stonefield
Editorial Assistant: Daniela Velez
Production Editor: Louis C. Bruno Jr.
Media Producer Content Management: Sarah O'Connor
Publishing Services Manager: Andrea Cava
Production Manager — Humanities: Joseph Ford
Marketing Manager: Kayti Corfield
Project Management: Jouve
Photo Research Manager: Martha Friedman
Photo Researcher: Julie Tesser
Permissions Editor: Linda Winters
Senior Art Director: Anna Palchik
Text Design: Korab Company Design
Cover Design: John Callahan
Composition: Jouve
Printing and Binding: LSC Communications

Manufactured in the United States of America.

1   0   9   8   7   6
f   e   d   c   b   a

For information, write: Bedford/St. Martin's, 75 Arlington Street, Boston, MA 02116
   (617-399-4000)

ISBN 978-1-319-03481-8

Acknowledgments
*Text acknowledgments and copyrights appear at the back of the book on pages 483–84, which
constitute an extension of the copyright page. Art acknowledgments and copyrights appear on the
same page as the art selections they cover.*

At the time of publication all Internet URLs published in this text were found to accurately link
to their intended web site. If you do find a broken link, please forward the information to
daniela.velez@macmillan.com so that it can be corrected for the next printing.

Preface

What does it mean to be a journalist today? The image of the print newspaper reporter wielding a trusty pen and notebook has been replaced by a journalist recording interviews on a smartphone and posting news updates on social media. How do students get their news? From a print newspaper, a network or cable news broadcast or a news blog — or from one another's Instagram pages? These are important questions in the dramatically changing world of journalism. Consider the many forms today's journalism encompasses: 24-hour channels and news sites, traditional and online newspapers, podcasts and blogs, and even satiric programs like *Last Week Tonight with John Oliver* and *The Daily Show with Trevor Noah*. What do these changes mean for today's journalism students? How can they best prepare for a successful career in this evolving industry?

The staff of today's converged newsrooms can agree on one answer: Editors want journalists who can report fully and write clearly, whether for an online news outlet, a professional blog, a cable news show or a print newspaper. The keys to being a good journalist are still as fundamental as that. We have revised the twelfth edition of *News Reporting and Writing* to reflect the ways these essential skills are applied across this changing field. To this end, we have added more — and better integrated — coverage of news reporting across various media.

When it comes to integrated media, we practice what we preach: The new edition of *News Reporting and Writing* combines print and digital media into a single accessible package. Callouts in the book's margins link to videos on *LaunchPad Solo for Journalism* that offer insider perspectives on issues of modern journalism, including the legal rights of bloggers, journalistic ethics, the common ground between real news and satiric fake news, and the power of images. Our integrated media program takes *News Reporting and Writing* beyond the limits of the printed page.

Even as we expand further into the digital realm, we continue to stress the essential reporting and writing skills that are the foundations of our profession — past, present and future — no matter the medium. We've also updated our current examples and issues, while still modeling in these examples — and in our own writing — the clear and descriptive writing that journalism students must learn. Our emphasis on these topics in the textbook, combined with robust online support and practice opportunities, ensures that students will have more opportunities than ever before to practice and refine their skills.

New to This Edition

Revisions to the twelfth edition of *News Reporting and Writing* address changes to the journalism landscape and provide additional opportunities for students to refine their reporting and writing skills in today's world. Specifically, this new edition offers the following features:

- ◉ *LaunchPad Solo for Journalism,* a dynamic new online course platform that includes the downloadable student workbook, videos with discussion questions, the huge Exercise Central for AP Style question bank, and downloadable instructor resources including lecture outlines and recommended in-class activities. The videos get students thinking critically about news media by giving them an insider's look at journalism from a variety of provocative angles.

- **A new full-color design.** For the first time, *News Reporting and Writing* is in color, with a gorgeous, modern design that reflects the text's cutting-edge approach to journalism. Updated chapter opener photos and colorful design elements make the book more visually appealing than ever.

- **An increased and strengthened focus on web writing and social media.** Chapter 11, "Writing for Digital Media," has been expanded to include more coverage of journalism on blogs and social media, from Twitter to Instagram to Snapchat, in addition to traditional news sites. The coverage of social media is integrated throughout the book, addressing social media alongside legacy media and recognizing its prominence in the journalism landscape.

- **Eleven new "On the Job" boxes that prepare students for contemporary careers.** In every chapter, a working journalist illustrates how the skills students learn in class will prepare them for careers across the media and in public relations in today's challenging and evolving job market. The journalists profiled have wide-ranging careers, from editing online articles at *The Huffington Post* to writing long-form investigative stories. Many of the newest boxes focus on new job opportunities and challenges created by a field in transition. They discuss how a journalist's role can change and expand unexpectedly because of technology, and they suggest ways journalists can embrace that change and stay engaged with their work. For example, one writer explains how she graduated with a degree in journalism but wound up working in public relations and now uses her journalism training to help her communicate effectively with clients.

- **New Grammar Check exercises.** This new margin feature expands on the grammar coverage in Appendix 1 and helps students practice writing in AP style. Each Grammar Check box includes a sample news sentence that contains a common grammar mistake. Students fix the sentence by identifying and correcting the mistake, and they can turn to Appendix 1 for more information.

- **New digital formats.** The PDF e-Book for *News Reporting and Writing* includes the same content as the print book, offering an affordable option for students. Learn more about PDF e-Books at **macmillanlearning.com/ebooks**.

Enduring Features of the Text

Users of *News Reporting and Writing* have come to expect that every new edition of our textbook will be readable and current as well as deeply focused on journalistic essentials. We are proud to continue to offer the following features:

- **Comprehensive coverage of all aspects of reporting and writing the news.** *News Reporting and Writing* teaches students the elements of good reporting and writing and provides the basic tools they need to become journalists across various media platforms, including advice on how to conduct interviews and research, employ media-enriched reporting techniques and create rich and well-crafted stories for the basic beats.

- **A focus on storytelling.** From life stories to world-news reports, local meetings to national press conferences, good journalism means good writing. We use real-life examples, up-to-the-minute news story samples and a consistent focus on writing essentials to show students how to craft rich and interesting stories. In addition, Chapter 9, "Writing to Be Read," helps students master coherence, effective language and other techniques central to captivating an audience.

- **Thorough coverage of media convergence and online journalism.** *News Reporting and Writing* ensures that students learn how to prepare stories effectively for multiple forms of media. Reflecting changes to the journalism landscape, this book covers the rising role of technology, the convergence and the emergence of integrated newsrooms, the challenges to legacy media and the future of online journalism.

- **Unparalleled discussion of legal and ethical issues.** Throughout the book, we offer students a framework for critically assessing the ethical questions they will face as journalists. In addition, we dedicate Chapters 19 and 20 to legal and ethical matters.

- **A chapter on math for journalists.** *News Reporting and Writing* includes a chapter on "Reporting with Numbers" (Chapter 7), which stresses the importance of using and understanding data—a vital skill for political and business news writers in particular.

- **Coverage of common grammar issues, Associated Press style, and proofreading and copy editing symbols—in print and with the best online tools.** The appendices provide helpful information students need to turn in polished, professionally edited copy, and an easy-to-find reference for proofreading and copy editing symbols is located at the end of the book. In addition, thousands of accompanying online exercises offer students additional opportunities to improve their grammar and AP style knowledge (**macmillanhighered.com/newsreporting12e**).

Resources for Students and Instructors

As before, *News Reporting and Writing* is supported by a range of effective resources for students and instructors. For more information, please visit the online catalog at **macmillanhighered.com/newsreporting12e/catalog**. The following ancillaries are available with this edition:

- ■ ⊚ *LaunchPad Solo for Journalism.* This new online course platform includes the downloadable Student Workbook, videos with discussion questions, the huge Exercise Central for AP Style question bank, and downloadable instructor resources including lecture outlines and recommended in-class activities. *LaunchPad Solo for Journalism* can be purchased separately or packaged together with *News Reporting and Writing,* Twelfth Edition. To order the student edition of this book packaged with *LaunchPad Solo for Journalism,* please use the ISBN 978-1-319-10581-5.

- ■ **Online Student *Workbook for News Reporting and Writing*, Twelfth Edition.** Supplementing the exercises at the end of each text chapter, the revised workbook gives students extra practice mastering the principles of journalism. The workbook is downloadable from *LaunchPad Solo for Journalism.*

- ■ **Online *Instructor's Manual for News Reporting and Writing*, Twelfth Edition.** This revised and updated manual contains a sample syllabus; additional teaching resources; and chapter-specific overviews, teaching tips, lecture outlines, classroom activities and discussion questions, as well as answers to the end-of-chapter exercises from the main text and answers to the workbook exercises. The Instructor's Manual is available for immediate download at **macmillanhighered.com/newsreporting12e/catalog**. The manual is also downloadable in modules from *LaunchPad Solo for Journalism.*

Acknowledgments

Our colleagues and students at the University of Missouri have given us invaluable feedback on the book, for which we are grateful.

We especially appreciate the contributions of our faculty colleagues who lent their expertise in revising these chapters: Sandra Davidson, law; David Herzog, investigative reporting; Marty Steffens, business; Scott Swafford, beats; and Stacey Woelfel, radio and television. We apologize to Prof. Davidson for having failed to credit her in the previous edition for her assistance with the law chapter. We are also grateful to Karl Grubaugh of American River College and Granite Bay High School for his superb work on the workbook and Instructor's Manual for this edition.

We thank all of the instructors who thoughtfully reviewed the text: Jill Adair, Arizona State University; Annie-Laurie Blair, Miami University; Debra Brenegan, Westminster College; Bettina Durant, Georgia State University; Mark Grabowski, Adelphi University; Tim Hanson, Francis Marion University; Andrew Levy, Borough of Manhattan Community College–City University of New York; Deidre Pike, Humboldt State University; Hai Tran, DePaul University; Mike Trice, Florida Southern College; Maureen Tuthill, Westminster College; and Tsitsi Wakhisi, University of Miami.

We also thank those who reviewed previous editions: Betsy B. Alderman, University of Tennessee at Chattanooga; Anne Becker, Oakland University; Mark Berkey-Gerard, Rowan University; JoAnne C. Broadwater, Towson University; Mary Elizabeth Carey, University of Massachusetts; Justin Catanoso, Wake Forest University; Betty S. Clapp, Cleveland State University; Jan Barry Crumb, Rutgers University; Helene DeGross, Lake Forest College; Dee Drummond, University of Toledo; Rory Faust, Northern Arizona University; Sandra Fish, University of Colorado; Jennifer Follis, University of Illinois; Gwen R. Fowler, Coastal Carolina University; Peter Friederici, Northern Arizona University; Eddye Gallagher, Tarrant County College; Patrick Harwood, College of Charleston; Ron Hollander, Montclair State University; Amani Ismail, California State University, Northridge; Elena Jarvis, Daytona State College; Kevin R. Kemper, University of Arizona; Alec Klein, Northwestern University; Laura Krantz, Tyler Junior College; Anup Kumar, Cleveland State University; Linda Loomis, State University of New York, Oswego; Therese Lueck, University of Akron; Kimberley Mangun, The University of Utah; Suzanne McBrice, Columbia College Chicago; Carole McNall, St. Bonaventure University; Kristi Nies, Peru State College; Jean Reid Norman, University of Nevada, Las Vegas; Carolyn Olson, Maryville University; Debra Patterson, Motlow State Community College; Richard Puffer, Coker College; Leland "Buck" Ryan, University of Kentucky; Cathy Stablein, College of DuPage; Scott A. Strain, Laney College; Margaret Tebo, Columbia College Chicago; Cynthia Thomas, Grand Valley State University; Tracy Warner, Indiana-Purdue, Fort Wayne; Thomas E. Winski, Emporia State University; and Vallorie Wood, Kennesaw State University.

We have worked with editors at Bedford/St. Martin's for more than 30 years now. With each edition, they have challenged us to improve, and we appreciate their efforts. We would like to acknowledge the expert work of our developmental editor, Linda Stern, who kept us in line and on time. Thanks are also due to Erika Gutierrez, Susan McLaughlin, Will Stonefield and Daniela Velez. We are equally grateful to the production team, which includes Lou Bruno and John Shannon and Susan McNally, both of Jouve, as well as our photo researcher, Julie Tesser. We'd like to extend further thanks to our marketing team, led by Kayti Corfield and including Gillian Daniels.

As always, we value your comments. You can reach us via email at BrooksBS@ missouri.edu; KennedyG@missouri.edu; MoenD@missouri.edu; or RanlyD@missouri.edu.

Brian S. Brooks
George Kennedy
Daryl R. Moen
Don Ranly

Brief Contents

Contents

PART TWO   REPORTING TOOLS

3 Interviewing   38

4 Quotations and Attributions   60

PART THREE STORYTELLING

8 The Inverted Pyramid 150

PART FOUR   WRITING FOR SPECIFIC MEDIA

14 Speeches, News Conferences and Meetings   296

News Reporting and Writing

CHAPTER 1 THE NATURE OF NEWS

Let's begin with the basics. This book is intended to help you learn about journalism. So we'll first answer two fundamental questions. What is news? And what is journalism? Neither answer is as simple as you might expect.

Take a look.

The Supreme Court announced its momentous decision in favor of gay marriage at 10 a.m. on a Friday. At 10:05, National Public Radio posted this report on its website:

> States cannot keep same-sex couples from marrying and must recognize their unions, the Supreme Court says in a ruling that for months has been the focus of speculation. The decision was 5-4.

That was a hard news lead on a story written just minutes after the event. Two hours later, *The Huffington Post* followed up with more information:

> The Supreme Court legalized gay marriage nationwide on Friday in a historic 5-4 decision.
>
> The justices found that, under the 14th Amendment, states must issue marriage licenses to same-sex couples and recognize same-sex unions that have been legally performed in other states.
>
> Read the Supreme Court's full decision on gay marriage below. . . .

In the time between those two hard news stories, President Barack Obama—or someone acting on his behalf—tweeted, "Today is a big step in our march toward equality. Gay and lesbian couples now have the right to marry, just like anyone else. #LoveWins."

That tweet was news too, but it wasn't journalism.

Journalism and the News

To put it simply, news is what's new. It's what happened today—or what happened earlier and was just discovered today—in your neighborhood, your city, your country, your world. News can be a speech by the president, a tornado touching down, an assault on campus. It can be as frivolous as a celebrity's latest love affair or as serious as war.

The people whose job it is to report, analyze and present the news are journalists. Of course, not everyone who writes or talks about events or personalities is a journalist. As we've just seen, one of those joining the public conversation might even be the president. So it's important to understand the characteristics of journalism that set it apart from gossip, rumor or propaganda.

It's also important to understand that many pieces of personal information that interest you as a private individual aren't necessarily relevant or interesting to the broad public. Not every celebrity Facebook post or tweet is journalism.

1
What journalism and the news are, including the presentation of news in different media and the rise of citizen journalism.

2
How consumers get the news today, including distinguishing between hard news, soft news and commentary.

3
What the elements of a good news story are.

4
How convergence and the forces of technology are reshaping journalism.

5
What roles journalism plays in a democracy, including contemporary challenges and journalists' responsibilities.

6
How to apply principles of accuracy and fairness and how to avoid bias.

7
How to think about the issue of objectivity.

8
How to distinguish news from commentary and opinion.

No one has done a better job of describing journalism and the news journalists report than Bill Kovach and Tom Rosenstiel in their book *The Elements of Journalism.*

The authors begin by explaining that "the purpose of journalism is to provide people with the information they need to be free and self-governing." Then they offer 10 principles that define journalism and distinguish it from other forms of communication:

1. Journalism's first obligation is to the truth.
2. Its first loyalty is to citizens.
3. Its essence is a discipline of verification.
4. Its practitioners must maintain independence from those they cover.
5. Journalism must serve as an independent monitor of power.
6. It must provide a forum for public criticism and compromise.
7. It must strive to make the significant interesting and relevant.
8. It must keep the news comprehensive and proportional.
9. Its practitioners must be allowed to exercise their personal conscience.
10. Citizens, too, have rights and responsibilities when it comes to the news.

In these principles, you can hear echoes of the Journalist's Creed, written nearly a century before by Walter Williams, founding dean of the world's first journalism school, at the University of Missouri. Dean Williams wrote that "the public journal is a public trust . . . (and) acceptance of a lesser service than the public service is a violation of this trust."

Getting Information Today

The journalism of Williams' day was produced in newspapers and magazines. Those still exist, but the multiplication of media today would startle and amaze anyone who hasn't been a news consumer in the past 10 years. Just think of how you keep up with the news.

Chances are good that you got some news today from a Facebook posting or a Twitter feed or from another **social media** source. The chances also are good that the news report you read originated with a newspaper, which put it up on a website, where it was grabbed by an aggregator. A friend of yours may have spotted it on her Google news feed and forwarded it to you and dozens of others. After reading, you may have added a comment and replied. This is the way the public conversation that is journalism works today.

However, while social media multiply our sources of news and other information, the content of journalism remains more important than the medium through which it reaches us. That content can include hard news, soft news and commentary.

Let's return to the conversation about that historic Supreme Court ruling. In this chapter we've already seen two hard news reports. That's probably what most of us think of as journalism. **Hard news** is the straightforward reporting of a news event.

It is usually delivered as clearly and simply as circumstances permit. Hard news is often the beginning of the public conversation, but it is only the beginning.

A close cousin of hard news is analysis, or **explanatory journalism**. In her *New York Times* story "What's at Stake," published on June 14, 2015, Tera Siegel Bernard looked ahead to the possible consequences of the Supreme Court decision. Then on the day of the ruling, *The Times* updated Bernard's story online and gave it a new headline: "What the Same-Sex Marriage Decision Means for Couples' Rights and Benefits." In her article, Bernard went beyond announcing the decision to examining its likely impact. Her analysis began with this:

> The Supreme Court's ruling that the Constitution guarantees a right to same-sex marriage means married gay couples can gain all the financial and legal rights and responsibilities of being married, regardless of which state they call home.

Analysis journalism is intended to explain what the hard news means to those who read or hear it. Of course, news is usually about people. So another important part of journalism's public conversation is the reporting that introduces or helps us understand the people who are making the news. We often call this **soft news**, or **features**.

Justice Anthony Kennedy wrote the majority decision in the same-sex marriage case. Even before the ruling was announced, Sheryl Gay Stolberg in *The New York Times* shed some light on his attitude toward the topic in a June 21, 2015,

Lucas Jackson/Reuters/Newscom

Today, more people than ever read the news on devices like smartphones and e-readers, even as many print newspapers are in decline.

piece she wrote for the online edition, a version of which was in the print edition the next day:

> SACRAMENTO – In the fall of 1987, a package arrived on the desk of Laurence H. Tribe, a Harvard law professor who had just lost a Supreme Court case on gay rights. It contained the legal opinions of Anthony M. Kennedy, a strait-laced, conservative Republican jurist from Sacramento who hardly seemed sympathetic to that cause.
>
> The package was sent by one of the most influential men in the California capital then, Gordon Schaber, a law school dean who had enlisted a young Mr. Kennedy to teach night classes and nurtured his career. Now Mr. Schaber was angling for President Ronald Reagan to elevate his friend to the Supreme Court – and he wanted the Harvard professor's support.
>
> "Gordon Schaber said that Tony Kennedy was entirely comfortable with gay friends," said Professor Tribe, who later testified to urge the Senate to confirm Justice Kennedy. "He said he never regarded them as inferior in any way or as people who should be ostracized, and I did think that was a good sign of where it was on these matters."

That is a valuable piece of soft news. It shows us something of the man who would be making the hard news.

There's more. Journalism also includes **commentary**, or opinion. There's certainly room in the public conversation for opinions from all sides, as long as those opinions are identified as commentary and not confused with either hard or soft news.

The Media Revolution

Just look, for example, at what is happening to the legacy media—newspapers and television news. The Pew Research Center's "State of the News Media 2015" reports that network television news increased its audience by 5 percent, and local TV news grew its audience by 3 percent. By contrast, cable news lost 8 percent of its prime time audience and newspapers dropped another 3 percent of subscribers. The newspaper industry's advertising revenue fell to less than half what it was 10 years earlier.

Meanwhile, many of the new digital-first journalism companies are blossoming. Washington-based Politico, for example, launched a European edition and announced plans to open bureaus in several American states. Vox.com claimed nearly 14 million unique visitors in early 2015. It was valued at $380 million.

The evolution of nonprofit digital news sites continues. One of the most successful is *The Texas Tribune*, which now has more than 40 staff members and a budget of more than $7 million. Others aren't faring that well. *The St. Louis Beacon*, for example, announced a merger with the city's public radio station. According to a consultant's report in 2013, the *Beacon*'s digital revenue was "very low, below $50,000, because there has been very little focus on this revenue stream."

New players also include aggregators such as Google and HuffingtonPost.com, which collect, reorganize and often link to work originally done by others—sometimes without full credit and usually without payment.

Then there is the phenomenon known as Facebook, which now boasts more than 1 billion users worldwide. The social network allows participants to exchange news, commentary, gossip and personal information without the involvement of professional journalists. By 2014, nearly half of all adults with web access reported seeking news of government and politics on Facebook.

Many of those Facebook regulars, of course, are in the millennial generation, which is usually defined as people aged 15 to 34. In an effort to reach millennials, *The New York Times* and other legacy organizations are now posting their content on Facebook as well as on their own sites.

Another recent attempt to reach millennials is CBSN, a free live-streamed digital news channel watchable on computers, tablets and phones. As the name suggests, this is an experiment by CBS, which is also known as the "geezer network" because of the demographics of its broadcast audience.

It is far from clear which, if any, of these responses to technological and demographic change will be effective.

One thing that is clear is that journalists today have added to their traditional tasks new roles—curator and fact checker—as they scramble to assess the accuracy and identify the sources of news that is as likely to be announced by Twitter as by the Associated Press.

Elements of a Good News Story

We've discussed what news is. Now let's consider the criteria that professional reporters and editors use to decide what's important enough to share. The standards journalists use to evaluate news can be summarized in three words:

- Relevance
- Usefulness
- Interest

Relevance, usefulness and interest for a specific audience are the broad guidelines for judging the news value of any event, issue or personality. These criteria apply generally, but each journalist and each news organization uses them in a specific context that gives them particular meaning. That context is supplied by the audience—the reader, listener or viewer. Journalists always determine newsworthiness with a particular audience in mind.

Within the broad news standards of relevance, usefulness and interest, journalists look for more specific elements in each potential story. The most important elements are these:

- **Impact.** The potential impact of a story is another way of measuring its relevance and usefulness. How many people are affected by an event or idea? How seriously does it affect them? The wider and heavier the impact, the better the story. Sometimes, of course, impact isn't immediately obvious. Sometimes it isn't very exciting. The challenge for good journalism is making such dull but important stories lively and interesting. That may require relying on the next three elements.

- **Conflict.** Conflict is a recurring theme in all storytelling, whether the stories told are journalism, literature or drama. Struggles between people, among nations

TIPS

**Elements of a
Good News Story**

- Impact
- Conflict
- Novelty
- Prominence
- Proximity
- Timeliness
- Engagement
- Solutions

or with natural forces make fascinating reading and viewing. Conflict is such a basic element of life that journalists must resist the temptation to overdramatize or oversimplify it.

■ **Novelty.** Novelty is another element common to journalism and other kinds of stories. People or events may be interesting and therefore newsworthy just because they are unusual or bizarre.

■ **Prominence.** Names make news. The bigger the name, the bigger the news. Ordinary people have always been intrigued by the doings of the rich and famous. Both prominence and novelty can be, and often are, exaggerated to produce "news" that lacks real relevance and usefulness.

■ **Proximity.** Generally, people are more interested in and concerned about what happens close to home. When they read or listen to national or international news, they often want to know how it relates to their own community. Some news organizations are turning to hyperlocal coverage as they seek to reconnect with readers; they report at the neighborhood level, sometimes by soliciting contributions from residents or citizen journalists. Independent websites devoted to this kind of extremely local coverage are springing up across the country. Increasingly, however, journalists and scholars are recognizing that communities organized around a particular interest—a sport, a hobby or an issue—are at least as important as geographic communities.

■ **Timeliness.** News is supposed to be new. With the internet and cable and satellite television, "new" means instantaneous. Events are reported as they happen, and this poses a challenge for journalists. Speed conflicts with thoughtfulness and thoroughness. Opportunities for error multiply. Perspective and context are needed today more than ever, but both are more difficult to supply with little time for thinking. Despite the drawbacks of 24/7 news coverage, it's clear that for news to be relevant and useful, it must be timely. For example, it is much more useful to write about an issue facing the city council before the issue is decided than afterward. Timely reporting can give people a chance to be participants in public affairs rather than remain mere spectators.

The digital age, with its often-confusing multitude of sources, splintering of audiences and growing complaints about negative news, has inspired most journalists to add two new criteria for assessing the value of stories:

■ **Engagement.** When news was only broadcast or printed on paper, the flow of information was one-way—from journalists to audiences. No more. Today, a news report is often just the beginning of the conversation. Audience members online respond to, correct and criticize the journalism. Many reporters and commentators maintain blogs and invite responses on social networking media such as Twitter and Facebook to encourage such involvement. Increasingly, a goal of both individual journalists and news organizations is to engage the public with the news and with the news provider.

GRAMMAR CHECK

What's the grammar error in this sentence?

The U.S., the U.K., Germany, China, Russia, and France all agreed to the historic Iran nuclear deal.

See Appendix 1, Rule 1.

■ **Solutions.** Scholars and audiences alike complain that journalists too often report problems and controversies without offering solutions. Political scientist Thomas Patterson has even argued that the negative tone of much coverage of politics and government has the effect of increasing cynicism and decreasing participation in the most basic activities of citizenship, such as voting. More and more journalists are seeking out expert sources and inviting audience members not only to explain complex problems but also to suggest solutions.

Convergence in Journalism

Convergence is the term that describes efforts to use the different strengths of different media to reach broader audiences and tell the world's stories in new ways. Convergence demands of journalists new skills and new flexibility. Print reporters find themselves summarizing their stories into a television camera and tweeting while an event unfolds before them. Videographers find themselves selecting images to be published in the partner newspaper. Both print and broadcast journalists look for web links to connect their stories to the worldwide audience and nearly infinite capacity of the internet. Smartphones provide new outlets and require new storytelling techniques.

The technological revolution also has exploded traditional definitions of just who is a journalist. Millions of people across the world have launched blogs—online journals or columns. Although one estimate is that only 5 percent of those sites include original reporting, and although most have tiny audiences, many have become influential voices in the public conversation. In an effort to add personality and encourage interactivity with audience members, traditional news organizations are encouraging staff members to write blogs.

Increasingly, members of the public are being invited to respond to stories that are published or broadcast. Citizens are even being enlisted as amateur reporters. **Crowdsourcing**, as it is called, has become a reporting tool at news organizations from North Dakota to Florida. Readers and viewers are invited to submit their own stories, photographs and video. They are sometimes asked to lend their expertise to help solve community problems.

The Public Insight Network takes crowdsourcing to the next logical step. Pioneered by public radio, the Public Insight Network is, as the name suggests, a network of citizens who agree to share their knowledge and their insights with professional reporters. National Public Radio and *The New York Times* have teamed up in a Public Insight Network. So have the investigative nonprofit ProPublica and local news organizations. Network members may be experts in any

> "Traditional newsrooms, meanwhile, are different places than they were before the recession. They are smaller, their aspirations have narrowed and their journalists are stretched thinner. But their leaders also say they are more adaptive, younger and more engaged in multimedia presentation, aggregation, blogging and user content. In some ways, new media and old, slowly and sometimes grudgingly, are coming to resemble each other."
>
> — *Project for Excellence in Journalism, "The State of the News Media, 2011"*

**macmillanhighered.com
/newsreporting12e**
Watch **"Convergence and
Essential Skills."**

- What impact does convergence
  have on journalistic quality?
  What situations call for
  a specialist, such as a
  photojournalist?
- Journalists' tweets and
  Facebook posts are not usually
  edited. How might this situation
  affect a media company's
  focus on basic writing skills?

field of public interest. Some have professional credentials; others have valuable life experience. They join the network as volunteers. Their pay is the satisfaction they derive from enriching the content and improving the accuracy of journalism.

Even the fundamentals of journalism are evolving as technology speeds up the communication process, provides new sources for both reporters and audiences, and reshapes journalism from a one-way flow of information to a give-and-take with audiences and competitors. One element that hasn't changed, however, is the importance of accuracy and fairness. And the essential role of journalism in a democratic society remains the one assigned to it by James Madison in 1822: "A popular government without popular information or the means of acquiring it is but a prologue to a farce or a tragedy, or perhaps both."

The basic skills required of every journalist haven't changed either, despite the revolution in technology. Whatever the medium, the skills of news gathering and storytelling are essential to good journalism.

The different news media give different weights to the criteria for assessing the value of news stories and require different approaches to telling those stories. For example, newspapers and magazines are better than television or radio for explaining the impact of an issue or the causes of a conflict. Scholars have learned that, although most people say they get most of their news from television, few can remember very much of what they've seen or heard on a newscast. But print can't compete with television in speed or emotional power. The differing strengths and limitations of each medium make it more likely that you'll find a lengthy explanatory story in a newspaper or magazine, while you're more likely to learn of an event from television, radio or the internet. A newspaper lets you read the details of a budget or a box score, but television shows you the worker whose job was cut or the player scoring the winning basket. The unique power of online journalism is that it brings together the immediacy of television and the comprehensive authority of print, with endless opportunities for users to pursue their interests through the web. Social media create new communities of interest and allow nonjournalists to join the public conversation.

The Role of Journalism

The First Amendment to the U.S. Constitution protects the five freedoms that the nation's founders considered essential to a democracy: freedom of speech, religion, the press, petition and assembly. In the 1830s, French aristocrat Alexis de Tocqueville came to study the U.S. and wrote his classic *Democracy in America*. He was struck by the central role played by the only journalism available then: newspapers. "We should underrate their importance if we thought they just guaranteed liberty; they maintain civilization," he wrote.

Challenges to American Journalism

More than 200 years after they were guaranteed in the Constitution, the First Amendment freedoms are still essential and still under threat. After the terrorist attacks of Sept. 11, 2001, a new emphasis on national and personal security tempted government officials and citizens alike to question just how much freedom is compatible with safety. The role of journalism in guaranteeing liberty and maintaining civilization is challenged by those who make news and those who need it.

American journalism is also under threat from growing public skepticism about how well today's journalists are fulfilling their historic roles. National surveys by the Pew Research Center for the People and the Press show, for example, that more than half the public sees bias in the news. About half say that journalists' reports are often inaccurate. Fewer than half say journalism protects democracy, and about one-third say journalism is hurting democracy. In assessing coverage of the 2012 election, voters gave journalists only a grade of C–. Views of the press increasingly vary with political affiliation. Republicans are much more critical than Democrats. And those who

> **"** If you have any message at all, in any form, that you want to convey to the world, you now have a platform to do so. . . . Your fans and supporters are never more than a click or two away, and they're ready to help you make history – or change it. **"**
>
> — *David Mathison,* Be the Media

ON THE JOB Career Crosses Media Lines

Sara Bondioli, after working at daily newspapers and a specialty publication, is now deputy politics editor at the *Huffington Post*, an online news organization that didn't exist when she graduated from journalism school. Here's her description of today's newsroom:

> One of the major differences I see working at a newer, online-only publication versus other places I've worked is that people really are jacks of all trades. Reporters and editors will help out journalists on another beat. Social media editors will step in to help out on a section of the website. Reporters will cut and edit video for their stories. Video editors will report and write a story that interests them.

> The newsroom is very collaborative, and journalists have the opportunity to learn new skills and try new things on a regular basis. I've seen situations such as when a page editor shadowed the video team for a week simply because she wanted to learn more about what they do. With that in mind, journalists interested in working in a digital newsroom like this should aim to be well-rounded with a large skill set and enthusiastic to learn new skills regularly.

> The competition to post breaking news quickly is fierce in the digital media world, and we want to have our story up and our email and mobile push alert sent first. However, we also have a process to help ensure that what we post is accurate. On the flip side, the lack of a print deadline often allows journalists to devote the time needed to do longer stories without the pressure of filling a daily newshole.

Damon Dahlen/The Huffington Post.

> Social media is a bigger focus here than at other places I've worked. We also have pushed the use of user-generated content, which we often curate via social media.

> The advantage of starting in the media world now is that young journalists fresh out of college are in tune with new digital technologies that are influencing newsrooms. That digital knowledge can translate into big opportunities for young journalists who can apply it to newsrooms looking for new ideas and energy.

get their news online rate the major internet sources—such as Google, Yahoo, AOL and Slate.com—even lower than the traditional media.

On the other hand, the same surveys show that credibility has improved, at least a little, from historic lows. Comfortable majorities say they believe all or most of what they read in newspapers and see on television news. Most people give higher ratings to the particular newspaper or TV station they use than to the news media in general. And two-thirds rate journalists as highly professional. (For regular samplings of public opinion about journalism, visit www.people-press.org, the website of the Pew Research Center.)

Journalists' Responsibilities in a Democracy

People making efforts to reform or restore journalism recognize these vital functions of journalists in a free society:

- **Journalists report the news.** News reporting, the first and most obvious function of journalists, is the foundation of the rest. Reporters cover Congress and council meetings, describe accidents and disasters, and show the horrors of war and the highlights of football games. This reporting takes many forms: tweets, live television, online bulletins, next-day newspaper analyses and long-form magazine narratives. We've already seen how that history-making Supreme Court decision was reported, analyzed and commented on.

- **Journalists monitor power.** The power that Americans most often are concerned about is the power of government. Lately, private power has become more of a worry and more of a source of news. Alexandra Berzon and her colleagues at the *Las Vegas Sun* won the Pulitzer Prize for public service for their investigation of lax inspections that led to high rates of death and injury among construction workers on the Las Vegas Strip. Monitoring is required even if power is used legitimately —when governments raise taxes or take us to war, for example, or when businesses close plants or cut health care benefits for employees. When the power is used illegally or immorally, another important function comes into play.

- **Journalists uncover injustice.** Every year the organization Investigative Reporters and Editors (IRE) rewards the work of reporters in all media who reveal abuses. For example, an unusual coalition that included the Weather Channel, the Investigative Fund, Telemundo and Efran Films reported on the failures of immigration control that resulted in hundreds of deaths of migrants trying to cross the U.S.-Mexico border.

- **Journalists tell compelling stories that delight us and some that dismay us.** For example, the husband-and-wife team of Nicholas D. Kristof and Sheryl WuDunn told the horrifying and hopeful stories of women struggling to overcome discrimination and abuse in the developing world for *The New York Times* and in a book, *Half the Sky: Turning Oppression into Opportunity for Women Worldwide*. Television's *60 Minutes* and *Frontline* tell the stories of true-life dramas. Bloggers bring firsthand experiences and often great passion to their posts.

- **Journalists sustain communities.** These communities may be small towns, cities or even virtual communities of people connected only by the internet. One important community consists of armed forces veterans. A year-long series of reports in *The Arizona Republic* documented unjustified delays and denials of medical services. Reforms were introduced and top officials were forced to resign.

- **Journalists set the record straight.** When the candidates for president met in televised debates in 2012, every television network and major newspaper deployed fact checkers whose assignment was to assess the accuracy of the candidates' claims and of the charges they exchanged. At least two national organizations, FactCheck.org and PolitiFact.com, have full-time staff members who do nothing but separate fact from fiction in political argument.

Scholars have used other terms for this combination of vital functions. One is "agenda setting," the placing of issues on the public agenda for discussion and decision. Another is "gatekeeping," the process by which some events and ideas become news and others do not. Today the function performed by so-called **gatekeepers** has largely evolved into curating or navigating, guiding readers and viewers through oceans of fact, rumor and fantasy in search of solid meaning. Bloggers such as Matt Drudge and Josh Marshall sometimes serve as agenda setters for mainstream journalists. When the entertainer Jon Stewart hosted *The Daily Show*, he served as a source not only of laughs but of information and as a media critic. Even in the internet age, however, the news you read on Google or some other website probably was first reported in one of the traditional newsrooms.

Accuracy, Fairness and Bias

The goal toward which most journalists strive has seldom been expressed better than in a phrase used years ago by Bob Woodward, then an editor at *The Washington Post*. Woodward was defending in court an investigative story published by *The Post*. The story, he said, was "the best obtainable version of the truth."

A grander-sounding goal would be "the truth," unmodified. But Woodward's phrase, while paying homage to the ideal, recognizes the realities of life and the limitations of journalism. Despite centuries of argument, philosophers and theologians are still unable to agree on what truth is. Even if there were agreement on that basic question, how likely is it that the Roman Catholic Church and the Planned Parenthood organization would agree on the "truth" about abortion, or that a president and an opposition presidential candidate would agree on the "truth" about the state of the American economy?

In American daily journalism, that kind of dispute is left to be argued among the partisans on all sides, on the editorial pages and in commentaries. The reporter's usual role is simply to find and write the facts. The trouble is, that task rarely turns out to be simple.

Sometimes it's hard to get the facts. The committee searching for a new university president announces that the field of candidates has been narrowed to five, but the names of the five are not released. Committee members are sworn to secrecy. What can you do to get the names? Should you try?

> **"The new media tools and techniques are wonderful ways to generate information much, much faster. They don't so much take away from the actual reporting as they allow the reporter to know so much more."**
>
> — *Karen Dillon, reporter,* The Kansas City Star

Sometimes it's hard to tell what the facts mean. The state supreme court refuses to hear a case in which legislators are questioning the constitutionality of a state spending limit. The court says only that there is no "justiciable controversy." What does that mean? Who won? Is the ruling good news or bad news, and for whom?

Sometimes it's even hard to tell what is fact. After a yearlong study, a presidential commission says there is no widespread hunger in America. Is that conclusion a fact? Or is the fact only what the commission said? And how can you determine whether the commission is correct?

Daily journalism presents still more complications. As a reporter, you usually have only a few hours—or at most a few days—to try to learn as many facts about an event as possible. Then, even in such a limited time, you may accumulate information enough for a story of 2,000 words, only to be told that there is space or time enough for just 1,000 words or fewer. The new media offer more space but no more time for reporting. When you take into account all these realities and limitations, you can see that reaching the best obtainable version of the truth is challenge enough for any journalist.

How can you tell when that goal has been reached? Seldom, if ever, is there a definitive answer. But there are two questions every responsible journalist should ask about every story before being satisfied: Is it accurate? Is it fair?

Accuracy and Fairness

Accuracy is the most important characteristic of any story, great or small, long or short. Every name must be spelled correctly; every quote must be just what was said; every set of numbers must add up. And that still isn't good enough. You can get the details right and still mislead unless you are accurate with context, too. The same statement may have widely different meanings depending on the circumstances in which it was uttered and the tone in which it was spoken. Circumstances and intent affect the meaning of actions as well. You will never have the best obtainable version of the truth unless your version is built on accurate reporting of detail and context.

Nor can you approach the truth without being fair. Accuracy and fairness are related, but they are not the same. Being fair requires asking yourself if you have done enough to uncover all the relevant facts and have delivered those facts in an impartial manner, without favoring one side or another in a story. The relationship between accuracy and fairness—and the differences between them—is shown clearly in this analogy from the world of sports.

The referee in a basketball game is similar, in some ways, to a reporter. Each is supposed to be an impartial observer, calling developments as he or she sees them. (Of course, the referee's job is to make judgments on those developments, while the reporter's job is just to describe them. Rendering judgment is the role of columnists, bloggers and other opinion writers.) Television has brought to sports the instant replay, in which a key play—for example, one in which a player may have been fouled while taking a shot—can be examined again and again, often from an angle different from the referee's line of sight. Sometimes the replay shows an apparent outcome different from the one the official called. Perhaps the players actually didn't make contact. Perhaps what looked like an attempted shot was really a pass. The difference may be due to human error on the official's part, or it may be due to the differences in angle and in viewpoint. Referees recognize this problem. They try to deal with it by obtaining the best possible view of every play and by conferring with their colleagues on some close calls. Still, every official knows that an occasional mistake will be made. That is unavoidable. What can, and must, be avoided is unfairness. Referees must be fair, and both players and fans must believe they are fair. Otherwise, their judgments will not be accepted; they will not be trusted.

With news, too, there are different viewpoints from which every event or issue can be observed. Each viewpoint may yield a different understanding of what is occurring and of what it means. There is also, in journalism as in sports, the possibility of human error, even by the most careful reporters.

Fairness requires that you as a reporter try to find every viewpoint on a story. Rarely will there be only one; often there are more than two. Fairness requires that you allow ample opportunity for response to anyone who is being attacked or whose integrity is being questioned in a story. Fairness requires, above all, that you make every effort to avoid following your own biases in your reporting and in your writing (Figure 1.1). However, neither fairness nor objectivity requires that every viewpoint receive the same amount of time or space.

	News Stories	Commentaries
Accuracy	• Make sure facts (events, names, dates, statistics, places, quotes) are correct. • Verify facts with multiple sources. • Use reliable sources for statistics. • Use facts as the substance of the story. • Discover and include all necessary facts.	• Make sure facts (events, names, dates, statistics, places, quotes) are correct. • Include all the facts needed to prove a point of view. • Possibly leave out facts that don't support the argument but ideally provide context or ideas that explain the facts.
Fairness	• Provide context for facts. • Give all relevant sides of a story. • Strive for balance.	• Provide context for facts. • Use facts and reason to persuade the audience of a point of view. • Appeal to emotion, but not by distorting the facts.
Bias	• Leave personal bias out of the story. • Use neutral language.	• Support personal bias with facts and reasoning. • Acknowledge and rebut other points of view. • Use civil language, not highly charged language or personal attacks.

FIGURE 1.1

Accuracy, fairness and lack of bias are essential in news stories. Writers of commentaries (editorials, blogs, written and spoken essays, reviews and letters to the editor) must also be accurate and fair in order to be credible.

Dealing with Bias

The research summarized earlier in this chapter suggests that citizens don't think journalists do enough to keep bias—conscious or unconscious—out of the news. More than eight out of 10 respondents in a national survey said they see bias at least sometimes. Of those, about twice as many said the bias seemed to be culturally and politically liberal as those who thought it conservative. A chorus of critics claims that journalists lean to the left. A smaller chorus complains of a rightward tilt. Books and cable television talk shows add heat, if not light, to the criticism. How valid is it?

One answer is that American journalism has many biases built into it. For example, journalists are biased toward conflict. War is a better story than peace. Journalists are biased toward novelty. Airplanes that don't crash are seldom reported. Journalists are biased toward celebrity. The lives and deaths of celebrities are chronicled in detail on the network news as well as in fan magazines.

There's a less obvious but even more important bias that probably accounts for much of the criticism. It is hidden in the job description of journalism. What do journalists say they do? What are they proudest of? What do they honor?

Journalists describe themselves as the outside agitators, the afflicters of the comfortable and the comforters of the afflicted. They see their job as being the watchdog against the powerful, the voice of the voiceless, the surrogate for the ordinary citizen, the protector of the abused and downtrodden. Journalists expect themselves to be forever skeptical, consistently open-minded, respectful of differences, sensitive to what sociologists call "the other." Neither patriotism nor religion should be exempt from their critical examination.

Does that job description seem more "liberal" or more "conservative"?

Consider that conservatives generally are respectful of authority and supportive of the status quo. Is it any surprise, then, that the overwhelming majority of conservatives and many liberals see a liberal bias in journalism—at least on the surface? Notice that this bias has little or nothing to do with partisan politics.

Now suppose we had a journalism that wasn't questioning, disrespectful of authority, open to new ideas, dogging the powerful and speaking for the weak. Who would benefit, and who would suffer? Would society and democracy be better or worse off?

At a deeper level, however, American journalism is profoundly conservative. Journalists seldom examine critically the foundation stones on which the American way of life is based. Among these are capitalism, the two-party system, the concepts of the ethnic melting pot and of social mobility. When was the last time you saw any of those ideas questioned seriously in the mainstream press?

One conclusion suggested by this analysis is that in societies that aren't free—such as America before independence—a free press is a revolutionary instrument. In a society such as 21st-century America, which considers itself free and is overall self-satisfied, the free press becomes, at a fundamental level, conservative.

The Issue of Objectivity

The rules that mainstream journalists follow in attempting to arrive at the best obtainable version of the truth—to report accurately, fairly and without bias—are commonly summarized in the concept of objectivity. Objectivity has been and still is accepted as a working credo by most American journalists, as well as by students and teachers of journalism. It has been exalted by leaders of the profession as an essential, if unattainable, ideal. Its critics, by contrast, have attacked objectivity as, in the phrase of sociologist Gaye Tuchman, a "strategic ritual" that conceals a multitude of professional sins while producing superficial and often misleading coverage.

In his classic *Discovering the News*, Michael Schudson traces the rise of objectivity to the post–World War I period, when scholars and journalists alike turned to the methods and the language of science in an attempt to make sense of a world that was being turned upside down by the influence of Sigmund Freud in psychology and Karl Marx in politics, the emergence of new economic forces and the erosion of traditional values. Objectivity was a reliance on observable facts, but it was also a methodology for freeing factual reporting from the biases and values of source, writer or reader. It was itself a value, an ideal.

Schudson writes, "Journalists came to believe in objectivity, to the extent that they did, because they wanted to, needed to, were forced by ordinary human aspiration to seek escape from their own deep convictions of doubt and drift."

Objectivity, then, was a way of applying to the art of journalism the methods of science. Those methods emphasized reliance on observable fact. They also included the use of a variety of transparent techniques for pursuing truth and verifying facts. In science, transparency means that the researchers explain their objectives, their methods, their findings and their limitations. In journalism, only part of that methodology is usually followed. Journalists seldom describe their methods or discuss the limits of their findings. If they did, at least some members of the public might be less suspicious and less critical.

In *The Elements of Journalism*, Kovach and Rosenstiel worry that a kind of phony objectivity has replaced the original concept. The objectivity of science does not require neutrality or the artificial balance of two sides in a dispute. Scientists are free, and expected, to state their conclusions, as long as they report how they reached those conclusions. However, as usually practiced today, journalistic objectivity employs both neutrality and balance, sometimes instead of the kind of openness that is essential in science. This misunderstanding or misapplication of the real principles of objectivity has opened the way for critics to call for its abandonment. Journalists would be more honest, these critics argue, if they were open about their biases. In much of Europe, for example, journalists practice openly biased reporting, which their audiences expect.

The problem with that approach is easy to see in European journalism or, closer to home, in the opinionated journalism of partisan publications, cable television or many blogs. One-sided reports appeal to audiences that share the writer's bias, but they repel those that don't. Fairness and accuracy too often are casualties in this journalism of assertion rather than of verification.

Properly understood, objectivity provides the journalistic method most likely to yield the best obtainable version of the truth. True objectivity, Kovach and Rosenstiel argue, would add scientific rigor to journalistic art. Without that, journalists and audiences alike can be misled.

What Is *Not* News

Though there's debate about just how objective a reporter can possibly be, journalists and scholars all agree about one thing: Reporting the news is not the same as expressing an opinion. The primary goal of a news story is to inform. Whether in print, on television or radio, or online, a reporter's job is to communicate pertinent facts, together with enough background information to help the audience understand those facts. Accuracy and fairness are paramount. By contrast, the primary goal of opinion writers and speakers is to persuade. Accuracy and fairness are still important—though they sometimes get lost in argument. A commentator is expressing a point of view rather than reporting the views of others.

To see for yourself the differences in style and substance, watch the *NBC Nightly News*. Then, later in the evening, switch to MSNBC, a sister network. Now move to Fox. The events of the day haven't changed, but their context and meaning sound very different from the viewpoints of the political left (MSNBC) and right (Fox). For another clear example of the differences between reporting and commentary, compare a front-page story in *The New York Times* with an editorial on the same subject on the newspaper's opinion page. The former is seeking to inform you, the latter to persuade you.

Because the aims are different, news stories and commentary approach accuracy, fairness and bias differently.

In 1947, the Hutchins Commission on freedom of the press concluded that what a free society needs from journalists is "a truthful, comprehensive and intelligent account of the day's events in a context which gives them meaning." The goal of this chapter is to show you how the journalists of today and tomorrow understand that need, how they are trying to meet it, and how complex the task is. The rest of the book helps you develop the skills you'll need to take up the challenge. There are few challenges as important or as rewarding.

SUGGESTED READINGS

Journalism reviews: Every issue of *Columbia Journalism Review*, *American Journalism Review*, *Quil!* and *The American Editor*, the bulletin of the American Society of News Editors, offers reports and analyses of the most important issues of contemporary journalism.

Kovach, Bill, and Tom Rosenstiel. *The Elements of Journalism: What Newspeople Should Know and the Public Should Expect*. New York: Three Rivers Press, 2007. This little book is packed with practical advice and inspiration, a kind of applied ethics for journalists in any medium.

Schudson, Michael. *Discovering the News: A Social History of American Newspapers*. New York: Basic Books, 1978. This well-written study traces the development of objectivity in American journalism.

Wurman, Richard Saul. *Information Anxiety*. New York: Doubleday, 1990. This guide for consumers of information can also serve as a guide for journalists as they seek to provide understanding.

SUGGESTED WEBSITES

www.asne.org

The American Society of News Editors is the most important of the industry's professional organizations. This website gives you access to the society's landmark credibility project, including the results of a major study of Americans' attitudes toward, and uses of, journalism. You'll find that study in the "Archives" section.

www.cjr.org

Columbia Journalism Review is the oldest of the magazines devoted to the critical analysis of journalists' performance. You'll find critiques of major stories, essays on ethics, book reviews and trade news.

www.journalism.org

The site of the Pew Research Center for Journalism & Media contains relevant research and articles on the current state of journalism. See especially the "State of the News Media" reports for the most comprehensive look at the current performance of all the major news media.

macmillanhighered.com/newsreporting12e

When you visit LaunchPad Solo for Journalism, you will find research links, exercises, and LearningCurve adaptive quizzing

to help you improve your grammar and AP style usage. In addition, the site's video collection hosts the videos highlighted in this and other chapters as well as additional clips of leading professionals discussing important media trends.

www.people-press.org

The site of the Pew Research Center for U.S. Politics & Policy is a reliable source for frequent reports on public attitudes toward journalism, as well as on topics in the news.

www.politifact.com

This site is one of the best fact-checking sites. It is operated by the *Tampa Bay Times* in Florida and staffed by professional journalists. Its analyses usually provide not only fact but context.

www.poynter.org

This site is an excellent starting point for journalism students. The Poynter Institute is the leading center of continuing professional education for journalists. On this site you'll find not only a guide to the services and resources of the institute itself but also links to the sites of every major professional organization and a variety of other useful resources.

EXERCISES

1. With a classmate, compare your sources of news. Do either of you read an actual newspaper or watch the nightly news on television? How do you assess the accuracy of news items you receive from Twitter or Facebook? Where do those items originate?

2. Choose a news event of some importance. Then compare the coverage of the event in at least three different news media—for example, on television, in the print edition of a newspaper, and in an online news source accessed through your smartphone. How does each medium cover the story? What is each medium's unique contribution? Do the media complement each other? Or does getting the news from one source render the other sources unnecessary?

3. Go to the Pew Research Center for Journalism & Media (www.journalism.org) and click on "State of the Media" to read "State of the News Media 2015." What strikes you as most important? How do the research findings compare with your own experience as a news consumer?

4. Most Americans say they get most of their news from television. Watch an evening newscast on one of the major networks. Read the print edition of *The New York Times* or *USA Today* for the same day. Compare the number of stories, the

topics covered and the depth of coverage. How well informed are television-dependent Americans?

5. Get copies or visit the websites of your local newspaper, a paper from a city at least 50 miles away and a paper of national circulation, such as *USA Today* or *The Wall Street Journal*. Analyze the front page or home page according to the criteria discussed in this chapter, and answer the following questions:

   a. What does the selection of stories on the front page or home page tell you about the editors' understanding of each paper's audience?

   b. If you find stories on the same topic on the front page or home page of two or more newspapers, determine whether the stories were written differently for different audiences.

   c. On the basis of what you've learned in this chapter, do you agree or disagree with the editors' news judgments? Why?

6. **Your journalism blog.** Create your own blog for the class (www.blogger.com is a good place to start). For your first post, write about your goals for the blog. Email the blog's name and link to your classmates and instructor. Use your blog throughout the term to discuss the issues raised in this and other chapters, especially the tricky ones such as objectivity and fairness.

CHAPTER 2

THE FUTURE OF JOURNALISM

Andrew D. Bernstein/NBAE via Getty Images

When Jenifer Langosch went to college, she was intent on covering sports journalism, probably for a newspaper. Ten years into her career, she's writing about sports, but her destination changed when she was offered a job with MLB.com—first covering the Pittsburgh Pirates and now the St. Louis Cardinals.

"It's hard to narrow down the things I like about this job," Langosch says. "The fact that I get to do so many different types of writing appeals to me. Writing a game story is quite different from writing an in-depth feature story, which is quite different from writing a hard news article. On a weekly basis, I typically have to do all of these."

Langosch urges journalists in training to immerse themselves in all forms of the craft.

"Even if you're a writer, learn how to use a camera and camcorder. Find a way to allow social networking to help you better reach out and interact with readers."

What Langosch found when she entered the job market was that newspaper sportswriting jobs were tough to find. But she also quickly learned that emerging media outlets on the web and elsewhere presented a host of new possibilities.

Working at MLB.com allowed her to combine her passion for writing with newly learned skills in audio and video editing. In her first few years with the company, she found herself covering baseball's All-Star Game as well as the World Series.

"Working at an online company has put me in a position to better weather the storm that the journalism industry finds itself in right now," she says.

We'll describe that storm in this chapter. In particular, we'll review the rapid decline of the newspaper industry—a key source of news for centuries—while examining the movement afoot to ensure that serious news is not left uncovered.

As Langosch learned, the good news is that for graduates who can write, edit or design, there is no shortage of job possibilities in journalism. Today, journalism jobs are found in a wide range of organizations, many of which did not exist 20 years ago. But there also are still thousands of jobs to be had at legacy media companies, even at newspapers. Young people right out of school who are armed with knowledge of the web and mobile communication are prime candidates for all those jobs.

Technology and Jobs in Journalism

Technology has led to huge shifts in how news is delivered to consumers, but journalism is far from the only industry to be affected by technological change. For example:

- Amazon has put a major dent in the sales of retailers like Sears and J.C Penney, and its market value has surpassed that of the world's largest retailer, Walmart. Even before that, Amazon had severely hurt bookstores and driven many out of business.

In this chapter you will learn:

1
How technology has changed journalism jobs.

2
How technology has affected newspapers.

3
Why newspapers are critical in gathering the news.

4
How technology has affected other legacy media.

5
What new models are emerging for news organizations.

6
How citizen journalism is changing the news industry.

7
How the changes in journalism affect job prospects.

- Travel agents have begun to feel the pinch of declining revenues caused by the ability of consumers to book hotels, rental cars and travel at online sites such as Expedia and Travelocity.

- TurboTax and similar tax-preparation software programs have greatly reduced the market for tax accountants.

- Ever-improving language-translation programs have decreased the need for interpreters.

New challenges to traditional industries arrive each year. Recently, for example, Uber and Lyft seemed to appear out of nowhere to become significant threats to traditional taxi companies in cities worldwide. The task for any industry is to rise to the challenge posed by new competitors.

Because of the change that technology has brought to the journalism industry, great shifts in the nature of employment are taking place. Newspapers are employing far fewer journalists than they did 25 years ago, but those losses have been offset by job gains in growth sectors of the larger media industry. There are far more cable television channels than there were 25 years ago, and employment at websites is booming. The net result is that despite a major shift in where jobs can be found, there are still plenty of jobs for graduating journalism majors.

For every newspaper job lost in the last decade, another has been created to replace it. Yes, it's tougher than ever to find a job as a sportswriter at a daily newspaper. Instead, as Langosch did, try MLB.com, the site of Major League Baseball, which has hired writers in every city where a team is located. Can't get a job at *Time* magazine? Try landing one at the magazine published for the employees of one of your local companies. There are literally thousands of such publications. Are local television reporting jobs tough to find? Try one of the many cable networks that did not exist 20 years ago. Or try any website. Video and audio editing skills are in demand at websites of all sorts—news as well as non-news sites.

CENTRAL FLORIDA POLITICAL PULSE

Rick Scott joins ranks of governors opposing Syrian refugees in U.S.

BLOG POST

TALLAHASSEE – Gov. Rick Scott announced Monday he will oppose efforts to resettle Syrian refugees in Florida, but also wants Congress to take action to ensure refugees are denied entry to the Sunshine State. Scott joined governors in seven states – Alabama, Arkansas, Texas, Illinois, Indiana, Massachusetts...

› **Some governors halt, question plan to accept Syrian refugees**

NEWS

French president says he wants coalition dedicated to fighting

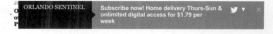

The Orlando Sentinel *is among the large-market print newspapers still doing well, yet its online version is steadily growing.*

Many media organizations, including Al Jazeera, house their online and television news reporting groups in one converged newsroom.

Thomas Koehler/Getty Images

More and more competitors are entering the news industry, and they are hiring journalists to staff their operations. In particular, they are hiring young journalists who grew up feeling comfortable with computers, social media and the web. As Caroline Little, former president and CEO of the Newspaper Association of America, notes:

> There is more demand than ever for news and journalism. There are also more competitors. There was no BuzzFeed or Facebook or *Huffington Post* 15 years ago. New digital channels offer consumers a dazzling array of options, all of which compete for time and attention.

So, if newspapers show signs of continuing their decline, journalism as a whole does not. Indeed, it is an essential ingredient in our Information Age society. Young people who can produce news and other types of information in this environment will continue to be in demand at companies of all sorts. For journalism, if not for some newspapers, the future is bright.

The Impact of Digital Technology on Newspapers

When the World Wide Web arrived in the mid-1990s, people starting migrating from print to online to get their news. Each year, more and more people move away from traditional news sources and get their news on mobile devices—cell phones, tablets and **phablets**. The Pew Research Center, in an annual report titled "State of the News Media," calls users of such devices the "mobile majority."

Decline of Newspaper Revenues

Most people still want to consume news, the newspaper's primary product. However, more and more they prefer to get it online or on

> **"**I think Twitter primarily is a news system. Early on we didn't necessarily know what it was. We thought social networks.**"**
>
> — *Evan Williams, co-founder of Twitter*

their mobile devices. Nationwide, print circulation is flat or declining even as the population continues to grow. Unfortunately for most newspaper companies, as readers migrate to online news websites and mobile devices in droves, the money simply doesn't follow. In addition, many get that news not from traditional news sites but from social media sites such as Facebook or from **content aggregators** such as Google or Yahoo. Today's daily newspaper industry is a mere shadow of what it once was. Consider these realities:

- Newsroom employment at U.S. newspapers continues to decline, dipping to an estimated 36,700 in 2013, the most recent year for which figures are available. Put another way, almost 20,000 newsroom jobs have been shed in the last decade or so. On a positive note, the pace of job losses in 2013 slowed to 3 percent, the best in a decade. So, while the decline in newspaper jobs continues, it is slowing.

- Industry revenues were down almost $26 billion in 2014 from 10 years earlier. Almost all that decline came in print advertising revenue. Online ad revenue and circulation revenue have grown steadily in the last five years but not nearly enough to offset the print losses. And the pace of increase was much slower than the likes of Google are experiencing.

- Print advertising generated 80 percent of newspaper revenue as recently as 2007. But by 2013, only about 46 percent of revenue was produced that way.

Profits at newspapers have declined so significantly that many now find it difficult to fund investments in their websites. In many ways, newspapers are burdened by their past. Too many are unwilling or unable to emphasize their digital products first, although many profess to try. Their sagging legacy products, born during the Industrial Revolution of the 19th century, drive what little profits remain, and they are reluctant to tamper with that model. Meanwhile, their competitors often have no such baggage and nimbly go about creating new online products.

The result is that the business model of newspapers is broken. Newspapers continue to derive about 85 percent of their advertising revenue from print and only

Facebook and Twitter: News Providers

Sixty-three percent of Facebook and Twitter users get their news from those social media outlets, the Pew Research Center and the Knight Foundation reported in July 2015. That was an increase from 52 percent of Twitter users and 47 percent of Facebook users just two years earlier. Clearly, the way Americans consume news and where they find it is changing.

That development makes sense. After all, most Americans these days are tethered to their mobile phones or tablets during almost all their waking hours. Those devices make it easy to find out about a breaking news story or to follow a continuing one. The two services provide news in different ways. Twitter's unfiltered feed is ideal for breaking news, and it is developing Project Lightning, an attempt to curate the Twitter experience. Facebook, meanwhile, is partnering with nine news organizations to create Instant Articles, an enhanced reading experience similar to Apple's new News app.

about 15 percent from digital ad sales, even as readers flock to consuming news digitally. *The New York Times* does much better than most, earning 28.2 percent of its ad revenue from digital sales, but that's still not good enough.

The Need for Reinvention

Still, even in these tough times, the newspaper industry has shown an amazing degree of resiliency. As difficult as things are for newspaper companies and their investors, notes NAA's Little, "There is one fact that always tends to be obscured or outright ignored—newspapers are still making money, and newspapers remain a good investment."

Newspapers *are* profitable, as Little notes, but their profit margins are a fraction of what they were as recently as 25 years ago. Then, many newspapers earned 25 to 30 cents on each dollar that came through the door. Today, most earn a meager 1 to 3 percent. That's a rate of profit common in the low-margin grocery business but one with which newspapers until recently were unfamiliar.

Why does Little believe in newspapers? Perhaps it's because in January 2015, the digital audiences of newspapers reached a record 173 million. That figure was up 4.8 percent in a single month and represented 82 percent of the total U.S. adult online population. If 82 percent of any population is consuming your product, you're doing something right.

Or perhaps it's because a savvy investor like Warren Buffett invested heavily in newspapers as recently as 2014. And, of course, there are still about 1,380 daily newspapers nationwide. Small- and medium-sized newspapers are doing relatively well, too. It's the metro newspapers in large- and medium-sized cities that are responsible for much of the industry's rapid decline.

One major problem is that little of the digital ad revenue from online news sites is flowing to the news organizations that actually *report* that news. According to Pew, five companies—Google, Facebook, Microsoft, Yahoo and AOL, all content aggregators, not sources of original news reporting—were the recipients of 61 percent of domestic digital ad revenue in 2014. Their percentage of the market is declining by only 1 percent a year. That means others, such as news companies, are not experiencing much of an increase.

There's tremendous growth in digital ad revenue, particularly in mobile, but only slightly increasing, flat or declining revenue for the **legacy media** companies that actually report and write the news. Again, Google, Facebook and similar companies don't gather the news. For the most part, they simply aggregate it or link to it. While doing so, they collect the lion's share of that growing digital revenue stream. Those who pay to create it in the first place get little of that revenue.

In the face of declining ad revenues, maintaining any profit margin at all has been difficult for print media. To achieve those meager results, newspapers have cut employment severely and moved to various pay models for their online sites. Some found new streams of revenue in commercial printing (printing other newspapers, for example) or acting as advertising agencies to place ads in various local media, not just those they own. Still others are selling their aging buildings on prime downtown land and moving to smaller, more cost-efficient offices. As a result, meager profits to date have been maintained primarily through cost-cutting or the one-time

Legacy Media Extend Their Reach

If readers are determined to consume news on mobile devices, publishers seem happy to provide it that way. Two notable shifts in ways to get news were announced recently, and one major publisher, *The New York Times*, is participating in both.

Facebook rolled out a service called Instant Articles, which allows publishers to post their stories directly into Facebook's newsfeed. Early participants, in addition to the *Times*, are *National Geographic*, *The Guardian*, BBC News, Spiegel Online, BuzzFeed, NBC News and *The Atlantic*.

Facebook engineered a design change in its mobile app that allows articles to load faster than ever before. There are new interactive features, too, including the ability to zoom in on high-resolution photos. Autoplay videos can be embedded in stories, and interactive maps, something the *Times* has handled exceedingly well on its website, also are possible. The user also can comment on an article or hear audio captions for photos.

Publishers were attracted to the service because they can keep all the revenue derived from stories they post by selling ads within them. They also can use Facebook's Audience Network to monetize unsold content. In that case, Facebook gets a cut.

Weeks after the Facebook Instant Articles announcement, Apple announced a News application it bundled with iOS9, the newest version of its operating system. It combines articles from more than 50 publishers, again including *The New York Times*. Among other publishers on board at launch were the *Daily Mail* of London, Vox Media, Condé Nast, Hearst and Time Inc.

Like Facebook, Apple said its contracts with the publishers allow them to keep 100 percent of the revenue from ads they sell themselves and 70 percent of revenue generated through Apple's iAd system.

Both ventures allow publishers to put their content in front of huge audiences. Facebook is on the mobile devices and desktops of millions of users worldwide. And Apple's News app is ubiquitous, too, because it is bundled with the operating system, also on millions of mobile devices and desktops worldwide.

"We see great potential . . . to reach very, very large groups," said Mark Thompson, president of The New York Times Co. By partnering with a social media powerhouse like Facebook and one of the world's largest companies in Apple, publishers hope to vastly increase their digital revenues.

---

sale of assets. Most of those savings have been achieved, and now comes the tough part—finding more new revenue.

Recently, however, legacy news organizations have sought ways to recoup advertising revenues. Perhaps news aggregators have begun to realize that without the work of newspapers, they would have little to aggregate. Whatever the impetus, newspapers, magazines and other legacy media have begun to enter into financial arrangements with large web companies that benefit both parties. (See the box "Legacy Media Extend Their Reach" above.)

Newspapers: Still the Source of Most News

There's an excellent reason for the media industry, the online and mobile industries and the population in general to be concerned about the health of newspapers. Newspapers are the creators of most of the news consumed in the U.S. In fact, several studies have concluded that as much as 85 percent of all U.S. news originated at newspapers. The reason? Newspapers have the largest and best news-gathering staffs in almost every city in the country. They typically employ more journalists

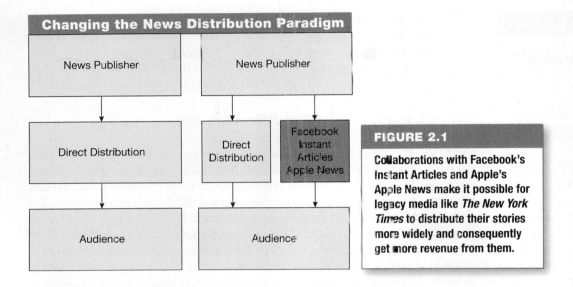

Changing the News Distribution Paradigm

News Publisher → Direct Distribution → Audience

News Publisher → Direct Distribution / Facebook Instant Articles Apple News → Audience

FIGURE 2.1

Collaborations with Facebook's Instant Articles and Apple's Apple News make it possible for legacy media like *The New York Times* to distribute their stories more widely and consequently get more revenue from them.

than all the radio and television stations in that city combined. That's still true in most places even with the recent sharp reductions in newsroom employment.

For more than a century, the legacy media, newspapers in particular, have funded the extensive news-gathering operation that exists in the U.S. and much of the rest of the world. Yet increasingly, because of the diminished audiences for print journalism, newspapers are trimming the size of their staffs in an effort to survive. Local television stations did the same in recent years as cable news channels reduced the size of their audiences.

Because newspapers are the source of most of the news we consume, if they disappear, who produces that news? Indeed, most of the information found on Yahoo, Google News or other content aggregators originated with legacy media operations, most often newspapers. The same is true with most other news websites.

As we go about the task of creating a new business model for the news media, what we must save is not specific newspapers and television programs, and not necessarily the companies that own them, but the high-quality reporting they produce.

True, replacing **spot news**—breaking news that occurred today—might not be too tough. After all, if a plane crashes, some blogger or citizen, if no one else, is bound to report it. More problematic is the potential loss of in-depth investigative journalism—what journalist Alex S. Jones calls establishing in the public a new understanding of an issue derived from intensive journalistic investigation.

Jones is the Laurence M. Lombard Lecturer in the Press and Public Policy and the director of the Joan Shorenstein Center on the Press, Politics and Public Policy at Harvard University. In his book *Losing the News: The Future of the News That Feeds Democracy*, he praises the technological changes that are altering the journalism landscape, but he fears the loss of the "iron core of news that serves as a watchdog over government, holds the powerful accountable, and gives citizens what they need." He's hopeful and optimistic that the "iron core" can be saved.

GRAMMAR CHECK

What's the grammar error in this sentence?

After arriving at the Greek island of Lesbos thousands of refugees find themselves with insufficient food and medical care.

See Appendix 1, Rule 6.

In a review of Jones' book in *The New York Times*, Harold Evans, former editor of *The Sunday Times of London* and *The Times of London*, points out what happens when this kind of news doesn't get enough attention: "the insufficiently monitored housing bubble, leading to the financial meltdown; the neglect in New Orleans, leading to the devastation after Katrina; or the formation of Al Qaeda in Afghanistan, leading to 9/11."

Other Legacy Media Are Affected, Too

Other legacy media—television and newsmagazines in particular—have been affected by changing news consumption patterns, too, but certainly not to the degree that newspapers have. For a while, it appeared that cable television news channels were cutting into the audiences and revenue of local television stations in a way that mimicked the decline at newspapers. But according to Pew, which tracks media consumption patterns, in the last few years average daily viewership of local television began increasing again (3 percent in 2014, for example) and cable audiences began to shrink (a sharp 8 percent decline during the same year). Network television news also experienced a 5 percent increase in viewership that year following years of decline.

The increasing popularity of the web and mobile news also forced television stations to add staff members who create news for those media. Television scripts were not useful on the web, so many stations hired journalists to write and edit stories that much more closely resembled those found in newspapers. That added to their costs even as revenue decreased or remained flat.

For its part, the magazine industry shares a lot of problems with newspapers, not the least of which are high production and distribution costs. In 2014, the magazine industry as a whole experienced a precipitous decline of 14 percent in total circulation. But the Pew Center is primarily interested in tracking a subset of 15 magazines that specialize in providing news or news analysis, among them *Time, The Nation, Fortune, Forbes, Vanity Fair, Rolling Stone, The Economist* and *Wired*. Those 15 experienced a decline of only 1 percent that year.

For those interested in magazine careers, the newsmagazines are not the only place to find jobs. The industry as a whole continues to provide thousands of new jobs for young journalists each year. Most who graduate from schools and departments of journalism and seek magazine jobs find employment at publications outside the news sector. Those jobs are found at places such as corporate magazines, magazines published by not-for-profits, business-to-business magazines and thousands of niche magazines catering to targeted audiences—*Boating* for powerboat enthusiasts, *Men's Health, Woman's Day* and the like.

There also are thousands of niche websites, some designed to appeal to users with common interests. Passionate football fans, for example, can follow their teams' recruiting on sites like Rivals.com, Scout.com, and ESPN.com. Then there are the magazinelike sites that have no print equivalent, including Slate.com.

Every company and every not-for-profit has a website these days, and those provide good opportunities for those with journalistic skills, just as their magazines have done for years.

Courtesy of Adam Falk.

ON THE JOB   The Lure of New Media

Adam Falk graduated with a degree in magazine journalism, but he knew he wouldn't be entering the magazine world right away. There was too much more he wanted to try.

At the University of Missouri, he'd focused on building a new-media skill set to tell stories in innovative ways. Just after graduation, he took a web design internship with the Media Policy Center, a nonprofit film company in Santa Monica, Calif.

Eventually, he found his way to the startup world. He moved to Newsy, a video news company headquartered in Columbia, Mo., for which he had worked while attending college. Then he went back to Los Angeles to start a small Newsy studio there.

"The best thing about working for a startup is that your presence makes an impact, and your work gets seen. Chances are,

I wouldn't have the same opportunities working an entry-level job at a larger media company," Falk says.

Then, *The Wall Street Journal* came calling. He now lives in New York and works as assistant mobile news editor for the *Journal.*

"I work on What's News, the *Journal*'s first-ever, mobile-first product. It is an app that takes its name from a column of news briefs in the paper, and, like the column, it is designed to catch up mobile readers on the need-to-know news quickly. Specifically, I edit copy from *Journal* stories for the app and create motion-graphic explainers to give those stories more context."

New Models for Providing the News

As newspapers and other legacy media struggle to find new revenue, some entrepreneurial journalists are trying other business models. They seek financing through various means and hope to turn a profit. Several models for these new forms of web-based journalism are emerging:

- **Financed by venture capital.** Some sites, like HuffingtonPost.com and Newsy .com, received startup financing from private investors and became nationally popular, attracting significant amounts of advertising. Some also charge for subscriptions to premium content.

- **Funded by foundations.** ProPublica.org, which seeks to do investigative reporting nationwide, and similar sites are financed by grants from foundations and operate as not-for-profit corporations.

- **Financed with hybrid models.** Some sites, like MinnPost.com, are hybrids funded by advertisers, corporate sponsors and individual donors. In St. Louis, a startup website called STLBeacon.com ended up merging its operations with the local public radio station to create a strong local news website (news.stlpublicradio.org). The funding model is basically that of public radio.

- **Financed as an old media/new media hybrid.** Politico.com and other sites sell ads to support their free web content while publishing traditional products. *Politico*

- What implications do news aggregator sites like Newsy .com have for traditional newspapers and network news shows?
- If you wanted to become an web media entrepreneur, what might you study and do in college to help you achieve that goal?

is both a website and a Washington-based political newspaper that recently expanded to Europe.

- **Financed by individual entrepreneurs.** Other sites, like WestSeattleBlog.com, were established with spare change and hope to attract enough advertising to survive.

Some of the founders of these sites don't even think of themselves as journalists; they're merely filling a perceived void in news coverage in their communities. Others, like the founders of MinnPost.com, are displaced journalists with formal training and significant experience in news gathering.

For the most part, private citizens, families or publicly traded companies own the legacy media operations in the U.S. As a result, these companies continue to exist only if they earn a profit. Traditionally, most revenue has come from advertising, with some additional revenue from newsstand sales and subscriptions. Many of the new web-based journalism sites aim to follow the same model by supporting themselves through advertising or subscriptions. Not-for-profit sites, however, seek only to support their operations—to pay staff and other costs—not to make a profit for owners or investors.

The not-for-profit models in which foundations are a key source of funding are relatively new, and in some circles they are controversial. Jack Shafer of Slate.com says, "There's also something disconcerting about wanting to divorce the newspaper [or a news website] from market pressures." Others disagree. ProPublica.org, a foundation-funded nonprofit site, produces journalism of unquestioned high quality. Its editors explain how they operate:

> The Sandler Foundation made a major, multi-year commitment to fund ProPublica at launch. . . .
> We spend more than 85 cents out of every dollar on news—almost the exact opposite of traditional print news organizations, even very good ones, that devote about 15 cents of each dollar spent to news . . . . [O]ur donors support the independence of our work, and do not influence our editorial processes.
> ProPublica also accepts advertising.

The model is working. ProPublica won a Pulitzer Prize for national reporting for a series on Wall Street bankers who enrich themselves at the expense of their clients and sometimes even their own companies. The year before, ProPublica won a Pulitzer in the investigative reporting category when it discovered that doctors at a New Orleans hospital had engaged in euthanasia following Hurricane Katrina. More recently, it won a Peabody Award, the highest honor in broadcast journalism, for a story about a mass murder in Guatemala and a prosecutor who helped bring the perpetrators to justice.

ProPublica typically offers its stories to legacy media operations, free of charge, for publication or broadcast. After a period of exclusivity for the partner organization, the story appears on the ProPublica site. The New Orleans story, for example, appeared first in *The New York Times Magazine*. This totally new model works because the credentials of ProPublica's reporters are outstanding. Without that credibility, no legacy media organization would publish or broadcast its stories.

ProPublica.org operates as a not-for-profit organization, funded by foundation grants. Other sites may combine corporate funding and individual donations to finance their operation.

MinnPost.com, formed largely by laid-off journalists in the Minneapolis-St. Paul area, accepts donations from corporations and individuals but also sells advertising. It is professionally staffed and designed, and it operates as a not-for-profit corporation. *Gotham Gazette* in New York City (GothamGazette.com) and a growing group of other sites operate similarly.

The Investigative News Network (inn.org) was formed in 2009 in an effort to promote investigative reporting, often the hallmark of such sites. More than 20 nonpartisan, nonprofit news sites gathered in New York to form the organization, and it has already grown to more than 100 members throughout North America.

As newspapers cover less news each year, there is growing concern among journalists that something replace what they produce. These experimental ventures are designed to do just that.

Embracing Citizen Journalism

The best of the legacy media companies are embracing the public's involvement in the news-gathering process and allowing readers and viewers to contribute to stories for print and broadcast products, or the web. Citizen journalists increasingly provide photos and videos, especially when they were on the scene of an event and professional journalists were not. The old "one provider to many consumers" model of newspapers and television is becoming a thing of the past, and audience participation in the process of presenting the news is now considered desirable.

Citizen journalism—gathering and reporting of the news by nonjournalists—is increasingly popular on websites around the world, much of it on sites of established media companies. For example, when the BBC asked users around the world to snap photos of scheduled anti-war protests and send them in, hundreds of photos were

Since anyone with a smartphone can post observations on social media, some media outlets are beginning to moderate what gets posted to try to combat false reports.

Ollie Millington/Getty Images

macmillanhighered.com
/newsreporting12e
Watch **"Newspapers Now: Balancing Citizen Journalism and Investigative Reporting."**

■ What are some strengths and weaknesses of citizen journalism? When are citizen journalists useful?

■ Will citizen journalism ever replace traditional journalism? Explain.

submitted. When an F-15 fighter crashed, a citizen in Virginia shot photos that she sent to a local television station. The photo taken immediately following the impact was used in the newscast along with video footage taken later.

Citizen journalists can be an asset to legacy media, particularly those with decreasing staff sizes. When terrorists planted bombs on a London subway, the first images of the disaster came from survivors who used their mobile phones to take photos and transmit them to the outside world from below ground. When an airplane struck birds during takeoff and was forced to land, nearly miraculously, on New York's Hudson River, some of the first images came from nearby apartment dwellers who took photos and video from their windows. When the Arab Spring uprisings occurred in the Middle East, citizen reporting through social media sometimes was the only source of news as repressive governments banned reporters from the scenes. Social media allowed citizens to provide eyewitness accounts, which were picked up and distributed by mainstream media.

Although most mainstream media outlets are allowing citizens to participate, they are moderating what goes onto their sites. As a result, back in the newsroom, journalists often find that their roles have changed. Not only do they perform their traditional roles, but they also edit stories, photos and videos shot by readers and viewers; moderate web-based discussion forums; write blogs; and post breaking news on Facebook and Twitter. As a result, newsrooms have begun to look different from those of the past, and the websites of traditional media companies are getting more and more attention. That means more and more journalists—even in newspaper newsrooms—are being trained in digital audio and video editing. Some find themselves in front of television cameras to create mini-newscasts that will appear on the website.

Much of the video and still footage taken by people who happen to be on the scene finds its way to **moblogs**, a form of blogging in which the user publishes blog entries directly to the web from a mobile phone or tablet. But when it finds its way onto the sites of mainstream media, as the examples above show, citizen journalists effectively serve as an extension of the media outlet's traditional reporting staff.

When Citizen Journalism Fails

Citizen journalism often works, but occasionally it goes awry, just like professional journalism. Many citizen journalists have little or no training in the profession, which means they have little sense of journalistic standards. Some journalists dismiss the idea of citizen journalism, citing the likelihood of inaccuracies. But it may be telling that some 15 years after the advent of citizen journalism, relatively few instances of major errors have been found in national media. One significant error was a false report posted in 2008 on CNN's iReport that Apple CEO Steve Jobs had suffered a heart attack. The erroneous story, which rattled investors, led to a $12 decline in Apple's stock price before the company debunked it three hours later. Jobs died in 2011, but in 2008 he was very much alive.

Forms of Citizen Journalism

While some citizen journalism finds its way onto the sites of legacy media, today's web publishing environment makes it easy for citizens to create their own sites and cut out the legacy media entirely. Anyone, it seems, can become a publisher. In an article in *Online Journalism Review*, J.D. Lasica sorted the media forms used in citizen journalism into six types:

- **Audience participation** (user comments attached to news stories, personal blogs, photos or video footage captured from mobile phone cameras, local news written by members of the community). Mainstream media outlets such as msnbc.com give readers the chance to post comments and other items on their sites.

- **Independent news or information websites** (such as the Drudge Report). These sites are published by those not normally associated with traditional media.

- **Participatory news sites** (*Northwest Voice*). Here, readers get to write, take photos and publish their work, perhaps even in newspaper format, with the assistance of professional editors.

- **Collaborative and contributory news sites** (Slashdot.org). These sites, often featuring a specific subject-matter area, are based on reader comments and contributions.

- **Thin media** (mailing lists, email newsletters). Through thin media, targeted news content is directed to those with narrowly defined interests.

- **Personal broadcasting sites**. On these sites, the operators provide news-based subject matter in a specific area of interest, such as technology. The result is downloadable audio or video.

There are more sources of information than ever before, and the public is embracing those alternatives. Many websites target specific groups of readers with great precision. Interested in knowing more about the conflict in the Middle East?

There are multiple websites for that. Interested in a nontraditional take on local politics? There may well be a blog for that. All of these new alternatives are eroding the strength of legacy media.

Prospects for Journalism Grads

The changing media environment poses a challenge to journalism schools and departments and to their students. No longer is it adequate for students to focus tightly on preparation for becoming a newspaper reporter, a magazine designer or a print photojournalist. Today, all those jobs—indeed, all jobs in journalism—also require:

- A thorough working knowledge of the web, using it as both a source of information and as a platform for extending your company's reach.
- A knowledge of the differences in web and print content.
- Video skills, both shooting and editing.
- Audio skills, including both capturing audio and editing it.
- Familiarity with mobile devices and how the public uses them.
- An understanding of audiences and how to connect with them.
- Basic familiarity with web analytics and other means of determining what users are consuming and how they are doing so.

These requirements have forced schools and departments of journalism to buy large amounts of audio and video equipment to provide practical training for all students in audio and video editing. The changes in the media industry also have necessitated a complete revision of journalism curricula. For the student new to a job, at a minimum the skillset needed almost invariably encompasses writing for print, writing for the web, audio and video editing, and basic web production.

FIGURE 2.2

Median yearly salaries for 2013 bachelor's degree recipients with full-time jobs.

Source: Lee B. Becker, Tudor Vlad, and Holly Anne Simpson, "2013 Annual Survey of Journalism and Communication Graduates," James M. Cox Jr. Center for International Mass Communication Training and Research, Grady College of Journalism and Mass Communication, University of Georgia, 2014. Available at http://www.grady.uga.edu /annualsurveys.

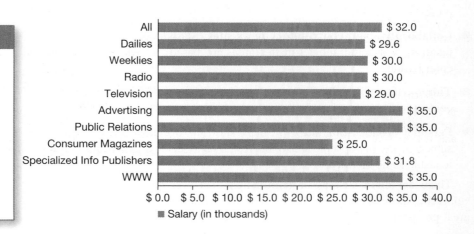

	Salary (in thousands)
All	$ 32.0
Dailies	$ 29.6
Weeklies	$ 30.0
Radio	$ 30.0
Television	$ 29.0
Advertising	$ 35.0
Public Relations	$ 35.0
Consumer Magazines	$ 25.0
Specialized Info Publishers	$ 31.8
WWW	$ 35.0

Engaging the Community

For years, newspapers, radio and television covered their communities with little or no engagement from readers, listeners and viewers. They operated as one-to-many operations that served as gatekeepers to their audiences, deciding what readers would read about and setting the public agenda. There was some feedback, of course—letters to the editor, the occasional radio caller, the compliment or complaint delivered by mail or telephone. But for the most part, there were few opportunities for the public to react to the journalist's product.

Joy Mayer, a leading expert in the community engagement movement, says the reason for that disconnect was simple: "To enhance their ability to fairly report the news, journalists needed to stand apart from their community rather than be participants." Journalists also moved from job to job and often ended up with no roots, history or context in their communities.

Mayer argues that journalists still prefer to "celebrate otherness more than they do connection." Writing for *Nieman Reports*, she says, "Ever mindful of conflicts of interest—actual or perceived—they hold themselves apart from influence and are wary of being swayed by sources or vocal readers."

Yet in conversations with her, journalists often say:

- They want community members to feel invested in and connected to the news product.
- They want as much information as they can get about what their readers want and need to know.

Mayer points out that there are a host of journalistic values to which most subscribe—obligation to the truth, loyalty to citizens, monitoring people in power and serving as a forum for public discussion.

Says Mayer:

I would argue that today's media landscape now requires an additional element—a new principle to keep us in tune with our digital times: Journalists have an obligation to identify and attempt to connect with the people who most want and need their content.

Adhering to this obligation is good for journalism's challenging bottom line. It mimics marketing, in a way—find the customer, meet the need, bring eyeballs to the product, and build brand loyalty. It's customer service, too—anticipating needs, inviting feedback, being responsive to input, and acting like a human being. It also is the right thing to do for our communities.

Toward that end, Mayer created a community involvement team at the *Columbia Missourian*. It was one of the first such efforts nationwide, and in effect it extended marketing into the newsroom, where that concept once was viewed with disdain.

The concept Mayer advocates is not only to allow readers and reporters to interact on the website but also to create forums at which they can interact face-to-face. She calls it a "take-the-party-to-the-people" philosophy.

"Let's not ignore the value that comes from those person-to-person interactions that inform coverage, encourage content sharing and foster brand loyalty."

If that means inviting the public to an open forum, do it. The *St. Louis Beacon*, an online site that evolved into a partnership with St. Louis public radio, did just that with a series of open breakfast forums it calls "Beacon and Eggs." At those sessions, readers and *Beacon* staffers discuss issues important to the community.

Another approach is to allow readers to write their own stories and take their own photographs. Newspapers print them and run them online.

Those things, Mayer argues, build reader loyalty to the publication, to the website or to the broadcast station.

"Editors ought to require that story pitches and budget lines include an engagement component reflecting community conversation, collaboration and outreach," she says. "In many cases, conversations about stories need to include these questions: Who is going to benefit most from this information? And how will reporters, editors and producers be sure those people find it?"

The good news is that students who possess those skills will have no trouble finding jobs. And many of those jobs are vastly different from those of 20 years ago. They sometimes have different names:

- **Web producer**—one responsible for creating the content of a website.
- **Web designer**—one responsible for the design of a website.
- **Web analytics specialist**—one who analyzes users of a website.
- **Audience development specialist**—one who finds ways to expand the audience of a website or mobile services.
- **Community engagement editor**—one responsible for coordinating efforts of a legacy media outlet to connect with the public (see the sidebar "Engaging the Community").

There are dozens of similar titles that simply did not exist in newsrooms 20 years ago.

The changes extend to related fields, too. Many schools and departments of journalism have majors in **strategic communication**, a combination of advertising and public relations that increasingly is in demand. These majors need the same skills today that journalists need—the ability to write and edit, the ability to produce websites, the ability to understand and analyze audiences, and the ability to edit audio and video. Why? Because even in advertising agencies, graduates find themselves working for clients who need them to produce news articles, audio, video and websites targeted to specific audiences.

SUGGESTED READINGS

Briggs, Mark. *Entrepreneurial Journalism: How to Build What's Next for News*. Thousand Oaks, Calif.: Sage, 2012. This is a good reference for starting your own news publication.

Brock, George. *Out of Print: Newspapers, Journalism and the Business of News in the Digital Age*. Philadelphia: Kogan Page, 2013. A good update on the status of the newspaper business and what it means.

Chaney, Paul. *The Digital Handshake: Seven Proven Strategies to Grow Your Business Using Social Media*. Hoboken, N.J.: John Wiley, 2009. This excellent book discusses the importance of social media in spreading the word about new websites.

Gillmor, Dan. *Mediactive*. Self-published, 2010. In this book, Gillmor discusses the changes occurring in traditional media and the democratization of new media forms.

Jones, Alex S. *Losing the News: The Future of the News That Feeds Democracy*. New York: Oxford Univ. Press, 2009.

This is a superb review of why legacy media are so critical to democracy.

Mathison, David. *Be the Media: How to Create and Accelerate Your Message . . . Your Way*. New Hyde Park, N.Y.: Natural E Creative Group, 2009. Mathison offers an excellent discussion about how to become an entrepreneur and build a circle of "true fans."

Meyer, Philip. *The Vanishing Newspaper: Saving Journalism in the Information Age*. 2nd ed. Columbia: Univ. of Missouri Press, 2009. In this excellent book, Meyer discusses the importance of newspapers in the news-gathering process.

Wollan, Robert, Nick Smith and Catherine Zhou. *The Social Media Management Handbook: Everything You Need to Know to Get Social Media Working in Your Business*. Hoboken, N.J.: John Wiley, 2011. This is a good primer on incorporating social media into a business model.

SUGGESTED WEBSITES

www.grady.uga.edu/annualsurveys
The University of Georgia issues an annual report on the employment patterns of journalism graduates nationwide.

www.huffingtonpost.com
The Huffington Post is one of the premier news sites on the web. It was founded with venture capital and designed to be free of the weight of legacy media. It is now owned by AOL.

www.journalists.org
The Online News Association was organized in 1999.

www.magazine.org
The Association of Magazine Media is the professional organization for magazine journalists.

www.naa.org
The Newspaper Association of America, a leading trade association for the industry, tracks trends in newspaper consumption.

www.nab.org
The National Association of Broadcasters is the primary trade organization of the broadcast industry.

www.people-press.org
The Pew Research Center for U.S. Politics & Policy is an excellent source that tracks the changing attitudes of the American people toward the press. Pew's research can be found here.

www.politico.com
Politico.com is an excellent example of a new politically oriented media site supported by advertising. It has a companion newspaper that is traditional in nature.

www.propublica.org
This excellent foundation-supported site brings together some of the nation's top journalists to pursue investigative reporting.

www.rtdna.org
The Radio Television Digital News Association, a leading trade group for broadcast journalists, tracks trends in that field.

EXERCISES

1. Interview two college students to determine their top three sources of news. Then do the same with two people 40 or older. Write a one-page report on the differences you found in media consumption patterns.

2. Go to www.politico.com. Choose a political story from that site, and contrast how the same story is covered on www.washingtonpost.com.

3. Research two legacy media companies, one that is primarily print-oriented and one that is broadcast-oriented. Using publicly available reports, describe any differences you find in the commitment of those companies to online news.

4. Set up a Twitter account if you don't already have one. Elect to follow at least three news sites on Twitter. Analyze the tweets you receive over a three-day period. How similar (and different) are the tweets and links from the different sites? If Twitter were your main source of news, how well-informed would you be?

5. Search online to find five job openings that might appeal to you once you become a professional journalist or a strategic communication professional. Based on the descriptions of those jobs, list the skills that you would need to land each of the five.

6. **Your journalism blog.** Find a blog or website that tries to cover local news with intensity. Interview the editor about the nature of the site. Does it make money? Does he or she care? Why? Post your findings on your own journalism blog and invite comments from your classmates.

CHAPTER 3 INTERVIEWING

Caiaimage/Robert Daly/Getty Images

ournalists get much of their information by asking people questions. Sometimes, though, the hardest part is just convincing a source to talk with you. One of the masters of getting people to open up is Mike McGraw, special projects reporter for the Hale Center for Journalism at Kansas City public television and formerly a Pulitzer Prize–winning projects reporter at *The Kansas City Star*. McGraw is a persistent reporter who has been known to work for months to convince a source to talk with him.

"I couldn't get a lawyer to talk to me for the longest time," McGraw says of his time at the *Star*. "I finally learned he was active as an adult leader in the Boy Scouts, as I was. So I brought up our common connection in an email one day. We both valued the organization, he emailed me back, and we began a dialogue that finally ended in an interview."

Persistence is just one of many techniques McGraw uses to get people to talk.

"I once wanted to talk to workers at a turkey-processing plant," McGraw says. "I put my business cards under windshield wipers in the parking lot and asked them to join me for a beer. About 12 showed up."

Often, reporters get sources to talk by first making them feel at ease. Many are not accustomed to speaking with a reporter and find the experience intimidating. "I look for pictures of grandkids on someone's desk and find other things we might have in common," McGraw says.

"Sometimes I actually start off saying (the conversation) is off the record, which puts them at ease and gets me closer to the truth. I am honest and forthright with them, and I often convince them to go on the record."

McGraw often makes it clear that he's not going to quit working on a story until he gets the interview. "I often tell them, 'Look, I'm going to be looking into this for a long time. I'm going to find the flaws and the positives. Take this journey with me—help educate me—and at the end I promise you a chance to respond to everything I write that affects you. I won't show you the story, but I'll tell you what's in it. No, you won't like all of it, but it won't be lopsided, either.'"

Interviewing—having conversations with sources—is the key to most stories you will write. Your ability to make people feel comfortable with you is often the difference between mediocre reporting and good reporting. A face-to-face interview is always preferable to a telephone interview, which in turn is preferable to having a source answer questions by email. Face-to-face interviews allow you to develop a rapport with a source that is difficult, if not impossible, to achieve over the telephone or by email or instant messaging. If you meet sources in their offices, like McGraw you might find photos or objects that give you a way to break the ice with a nonthreatening conversation.

Of course, when a deadline looms on a breaking news story, you may be forced to settle for a telephone interview. That also may be necessary if you and the source are not in the same city or area. Least desirable of all is the email interview, which does not allow any sort of rapport to be established. You'll

In this chapter you will learn:

1 How to prepare for an interview for a news story, profile or investigative piece.

2 How to conduct an audio or video interview.

3 How to evaluate the pros and cons of doing interviews by telephone, email, instant messaging or Skype.

4 How to set up an interview.

5 How to prepare your questions.

6 How to establish rapport with a source.

7 How to ensure accuracy and fairness.

8 How to end an interview.

often get dry and uninformative answers to questions posed by email, and you won't have an opportunity to ask the follow-up questions you may have asked during a face-to-face interview.

Information is a journalist's raw material. While some of it is gathered from records and some from observation, most is gathered in one-on-one conversations. You try first to talk to **primary sources**, those who witnessed the event or have authority over documents. If you can't get to a primary source, you may be forced to go to a **secondary source**, someone who talked to a witness, such as a public safety official, a lawyer or a next-door neighbor.

Even when you are doing a profile, determine how your source knows your profile subject. Does your source work with the subject? If so, he's probably not much of an authority on the subject's after-hours activities. Does she play poker with the subject? If so, she probably doesn't know the subject in the workplace. Once you know how your source knows what he or she knows, then you can start the conversation. If you're interviewing for television, broadcast or **webcast** (an audio or video report published on the web), your goals and techniques may be different from those of a print reporter, but the basics are the same.

Preparing for the Interview

How you prepare for an interview depends in part on what kind of story you intend to write. (Figure 3.1 shows a checklist you can use in doing interviews.) You may be doing a news story, a personality profile or an investigative piece. In each case, you check the newspaper library and search online databases, talk to other reporters and, if there's enough time, read magazine articles and books. Social media sites such as Facebook offer you information on some people you might not otherwise be able to contact. Don't print information off these sites without verification even though it's often tough to verify information taken from the web.

Interviews are best used to solicit reactions and interpretations, not to gather facts. Good reporters gather their facts *before* an interview. To prepare for a news story, you pay more attention to clips about the subject of the story than those about the personality of the interviewee. To prepare for a profile, you look for personality quirks and information about the subject's interests, family, friends, travels and habits. To prepare for an investigative piece, you want to know both your subject matter and the person you are interviewing. In all these stories, don't overlook other reporters and editors who know something about the person or subject. Let's look more closely at each of these types of common stories.

Interviewing for the News Story

Usually, reporters don't have much time to prepare to cover a news story. You'll be lucky if you have a few minutes to dig into your newsroom's digital archive for background on the event or the issue. With a few more minutes, you can go online to see what other reporters have written on similar topics. Those hurried searches will provide

Figure 3.1 Interviewing Checklist

Before the Interview

1. Know the topic.
   - Seek specific information.
   - Research the topic.
   - List the questions.
2. Know the person.
   - Find salient biographical information.
   - Understand the person's expertise regarding the topic.
3. Set up the interview.
   - Set the time.
     - Schedule at the interviewee's convenience, but suggest a time.
     - Estimate the length of time needed.
     - Ask about possible return visits.
   - Set the place.
     - Choose the interviewee's turf or neutral turf.
4. Discuss arrangements.
   - Will you bring a digital recorder?*
   - Will you bring a photographer or a videographer?*
   - Will you let the interviewee check the accuracy of quotes?

During the Interview

1. When you arrive:
   - If possible, control the seating arrangement.
   - Place your digital recorder at the optimum spot.
   - Warm up the person briefly with small talk.
   - Set the ground rules: Everything is on the record once the recorder is turned on.
2. During the interview itself:
   - Use good interviewing techniques.
     - Ask open-ended questions, which require the source to elaborate rather than give simple yes or no answers.
     - Allow the person to think and to speak; pause.
     - Don't be threatening in voice or manner.
     - Control the conversational flow, but be flexible.
   - Take good notes.
     - Be unobtrusive.
     - Be thorough.
   - Use a digital recorder.
     - Make sure it's on and working, but take notes, too.
     - Note the number on the digital counter at important parts in the interview so you can find quotes easily.
3. Before you leave:
   - Ask if there's anything else the interviewee wants to say.
   - Check facts: spellings, dates, statistics and quotes.
   - Set a time for rechecking facts and quotes.
   - Discuss when and where the interview might appear.
   - For a print publication, ask if the interviewee wants extra copies.

After the Interview

1. Organize your notes immediately.
2. Craft a proper lead.
3. Write a coherent story.
4. Check facts for accuracy with the interviewee.

*Some sources may feel uncomfortable being recorded, videotaped or photographed.

background and perhaps some context. And with a mobile phone or tablet, you may even be able to check more online sources en route to the interview or just before it.

There are three important mental steps you can take as you chase the news.

First, review in your head what you've turned up in your quick background research. If you're off to meet a political candidate, a public official or a celebrity, when was the person last in the news? For what? What will your audience (or your boss) most likely want to know now? If you're headed for a crime scene or a disaster, what do you know about the neighborhood? Has anything like this happened lately? With what results?

Second, plan your approach. Whom will you seek out at the scene? Who's likely to be in charge? What do you know about that person and her or his attitude toward reporters? Are you alone on this assignment and expected to capture audio or video? If so, double-check your equipment. Will you be reporting live on camera? If so, double-check your appearance.

Finally, plan out your first few questions. Sometimes, those are obvious. If the news involves a crime or disaster, you'll want to know what happened. Was anybody hurt? What's the damage? If the story is focused on an issue or a person, you'll have some choices to make. Ideally, your backgrounding has gotten you past the most basic "Who are you?" and "Why are you here?" questions. So you may want to start with something like "What are you hoping to accomplish here?" or "Why do you think this issue is so important?"

Most news interviews aren't adversarial, but if you have tough questions, save them for the end of the conversation. That way, they won't keep you from getting most of what you need.

From there, follow your instincts and your training to find the story.

Interviewing for the Profile

Lane DeGregory, a staff writer for the *Tampa Bay (Fla.) Times*, was writing a **profile** story about a Largo, Fla., city manager who was fired when he announced he was going to have sex-reassignment surgery. (The aim of a profile is to reveal the personality or character of an institution or person.) DeGregory's first hurdle was getting the city manager to talk at length with her. The next hurdle was convincing the manager's wife to talk with her. Says DeGregory, "It came to this: 12 days, 10 phone calls, a two-page letter, a note, two stories, immeasurable groveling and a lot of luck."

Sometimes, journalism is hard work. Describing to Poynter.org how she obtained the key interviews for the remarkable story, DeGregory said she typed a two-page letter to the wife to explain why she wanted to interview her and added a handwritten note and then delivered it to the house. She finally got the interview one evening when she called the former city manager, who handed the phone to the wife. DeGregory said the wife was at first reluctant. She progressed from yes and no answers to sentences. She started to relax. They talked for four hours.

Not every interview is that difficult, time-consuming or important. But every successful interview begins with establishing trust and ends with telling a story.

DeGregory says that writing previous stories on gender issues helped her establish rapport and gain the trust of the city manager. She knew the language, for one thing. She also knew the issues.

"I knew for most transgendered people, it isn't about who they want to have sex with but about who they feel they really are. So I didn't have to ask any dumb 'I-don't-get-it' questions, and I could speak with some authority on the subject."

If you don't have the background on your subject that DeGregory had on hers, you need to research the subject and the person you'll be profiling. For most profiles, you will be talking not only to your subject but also to his or her friends, family and co-workers. In many cases, you will get their names from your subject. Ask how your subject knows them: co-worker, social acquaintance, recent or lifelong friend.

ON THE JOB Getting the Tough Interview

Courtesy of David Kravitz.

Derek Kravitz has worked as a reporter for *The Washington Post* and the Associated Press, but a story he did years ago while on his first job at the *Columbia (Mo.) Daily Tribune* is a strong reminder of how important it is to be persistent to get people to open up and talk. He explains:

Alan Farha was wanted by Columbia police for scamming area churches, so he was on the move. I found a phone number for his father in Georgetown, Texas, and left a voice mail. Later that night, I got a call from Farha on my cellphone. We spent the next hour discussing why I not only shouldn't interview him (he said he had nothing to say and his case was unimportant) but why we shouldn't focus resources on a larger story on his case (it could affect his fragile sobriety, he said, and he could fall into a deeper hole with his drug addictions).

I told him that many people, not just in Columbia, but across many states and in countless churches, thought he was a con man. He said he wasn't. I gave him the opportunity to tell his story, and after laying out the Police Department's case against him, he described his addictions and how he had resorted to asking people for money to get by. That didn't make him a con man, he said. That made him a beggar. And a Columbia police detective spoke to agree.

We ran the story. Farha left Columbia and since has been charged with (but not arrested for) scamming churches . . . in Indiana, Texas and New Hampshire.

The *Tribune* story seems to follow him because every time he hits a new town, I get an email or a link from a local newspaper asking about him. He hasn't stopped, but his story is now well-known, mainly thanks to Google.

Oddly enough, I also got a "friend request" from Farha on LinkedIn recently. His profile says he's still struggling with his addictions.

Then ask the co-worker or friend how he or she knows your profile subject. With this information, you won't ask inappropriate questions—you don't want to ask about your subject's love for hunting if the interviewee only knows the person from work, for example—and you can properly evaluate the information you are getting.

Interviewing for the Investigative Story

The casual conversations you want to have for profile interviews are not always possible for the investigative reporter. An adversarial relationship determines both the preparation required for an investigative piece and the atmosphere of the interview itself. **Investigative reporting** is the pursuit of information that has been concealed, such as evidence of wrongdoing. An investigative reporter is like an attorney in a courtroom. Wise attorneys know in advance what the answers to their questions will be. Investigative reporters often do, too, but they also are open-minded enough to switch gears if sources convince them they are on the wrong track. Regardless, preparation is essential.

Lowell Bergman, a veteran investigative reporter who worked in both print and television, advises, "Learn as much about the subject before you get there, regardless of whether you play dumb because you want them to explain it to you, or whether you just want them to know that you're not going to waste their time."

Gathering Information

In the early stages of the investigation, you conduct some fishing-expedition interviews. Because you don't know how much the source knows, you cast around. Start with people on the fringes. Gather as much as you can from them. Study the records. Only after you have most of the evidence should you confront your central character. You start with a large circle and gradually make it smaller.

Requesting an Interview

DeGregory had difficulty getting her interview because she wanted to ask questions about a personal topic. Investigative reporters frequently have problems getting the interview because the information they seek is often damaging to the person. Sources who believe you are working on a story that will be critical of them or their friends often try to avoid you. Steve Weinberg, author of an unauthorized biography of industrialist Armand Hammer, had to overcome the suspicion of many former Hammer associates. Their former boss had told them not to talk to Weinberg. Instead of calling, Weinberg approached them by mail. "I sent letters, examples of my previous work, explained what I wanted to cover and why I was doing it without Hammer's blessing," Weinberg says.

He recommends that you use a letter or an email to share some of what you know about the story that might surprise or impress the source. For instance, a reference such as "And last week, when I was checking all the land records . . ." indicates the depth of your research.

In his letter to former Hammer associates, Weinberg talked about how Hammer was one of the most important people in the history of business. The letters opened doors to all seven of Hammer's former executive assistants whom Weinberg contacted.

Weinberg, like DeGregory, has shown former stories as a way of trying to gain the subject's confidence. Weinberg also offers to show the sources relevant portions of his manuscript as an accuracy check. An *accuracy check* just verifies the facts. It does not give the source the option of choosing what goes in and what stays out of a story. He makes it clear in writing that he maintains control of the content.

Requesting an interview in writing can allow you to make your best case for getting it. And an offer to allow your sources to review the story assures them that you are serious about accuracy. Email makes both the request and the offer simpler and faster.

Doing an Audio or Video Interview

When you're interviewing someone in front of a camera, the basic rules of preparation and interviewing don't change. For instance, Bob Schieffer, who retired after hosting *Face the Nation* on CBS for 24 years, says the most important preparation before every interview is to know as much about the story as possible.

Some of your objectives and techniques, however, do change. Television journalists, at least those who appear on camera, are also performers. Sure, they have to report and write, but they also have to be able to tell their stories with both words and body language to people who are watching and listening—not reading. An important part of the television reporter's performance is the interview.

Reporters who conduct interviews that will appear on radio, in a podcast or online also are performers. They must ask questions and respond to answers smoothly. (A **podcast** is a digital audio file that can be posted on a news website and downloaded by listeners to their own digital devices.)

Both print and television reporters often interview to develop information that can be used in further reporting. Interviews conducted on camera usually have a different goal. That goal is the **sound bite**, the few seconds of words with accompanying video that convey not only information but also emotion. Print is a medium that mainly provides information. Television is a medium of emotion. The best interviews for television are those that reveal how a situation feels to the participants or witnesses.

Al Tompkins, the Poynter Institute's group leader for broadcast and online journalism, offers what he calls "a new set of interviewing tools" intended to produce better storytelling for television. You can find these and other tools at www.poynter .org. Here are some tips that show both the similarities and differences between print and television interviewing:

- **Ask both objective and subjective questions.** To gather facts, ask objective questions: "When?" "Where?" "How much?" But subjective questions usually produce the best sound bites: "Why?" "Tell me more about . . ." "Can you explain . . . ?" "How did you feel about . . . ?"

- **Focus on one issue at a time.** Vague, complicated questions produce vague, complicated, hard-to-follow answers. Remember that readers can reread until they understand, but viewers often can't rewind an interview. (These days, many broadcast organizations, including PBS, are posting interviews online.) Help viewers follow the story by taking your interviewee through it one step at a time.

- **Ask open-ended questions.** For print, you occasionally want a simple yes or no. That kind of answer stops a television interview. Open-ended questions encourage conversation, and conversation makes for a good interview. (For more on this, see the section "Open-Ended Questions" later in this chapter.)

- **Keep questions short.** Make the interviewee do the talking. Tompkins points out that short questions are more likely to produce focused responses. They also keep the viewer's attention on the person being interviewed and on what she or he has to say.

- **Build to the point.** The best interviews are like the best stories; they don't give away the punch line in the first few words. Ask soft, easy questions to encourage the interviewee to relax and trust you. Then move to the heart of the issue.

macmillanhighered.com /newsreporting12e

Watch **"Radio: Yesterday, Today and Tomorrow."**

- The video talks about ways in which radio has changed over the last 80 years. What other changes can you think of?
- Will the internet (and online music sources) be the end of radio, or will radio stations still be around decades from now? What example from the video supports your view?

■ **Be honest.** Although it is as true for television as for print and online, the importance of honesty is too often overlooked by rookie reporters. You do neither your source nor yourself a favor if you lead the source to expect an interview about softball when you have an indictment in mind. Tell the source ahead of time that you'll want to ask some tough questions. Say that you want to get the whole story to be fair—and mean it. Then politely but firmly dig in. As Tompkins notes, honesty has the added benefit of helping you defend yourself against any later accusations of malice.

Using the Telephone, Email, Instant Messaging or Skype for Interviews

Interviews, as noted earlier, are always more successful if conducted in person. But when you have to interview by phone, there are at least three points to remember. These are more important for feature stories, profiles and investigative work than for standard news stories, though some news stories require more time and effort during interviews than others.

First, if this is the first time you've spoken to the source, attempt to establish rapport, just as you do in a face-to-face interview. Don't immediately start firing questions. Express your appreciation for the person's time. Explain why you are calling and how important the interviewee is to the story. If you have talked to others who know this person, mention that to help your source relax.

Second, depending on how much time is available and how important this interview is, you may want to record it. You must seek the permission of the person you are interviewing: "Is it OK to record this conversation? I want to make sure I get it accurately, and this way, I can concentrate more fully on the content." Put the request on the recording. In most states, it is illegal to record a phone conversation without the other person's consent. Remember to take notes even if you are recording an interview. If the recorder malfunctions, you'll still have material for your story.

Third, just as in any other interview, try to have a conversation rather than a Q&A session. (A Q&A—**question-and-answer**—story is more or less a verbatim transcript of an interview. The interview material isn't digested and reworked into a story.) React to what is said with affirmations. Laugh when appropriate. Admit when you don't understand, and ask for more explanation.

The phone can be a friend, but it can never replace personal contact. Neither can email, but reporters are using email more frequently because they are facing more deadline pressure than ever as they feed websites, often in addition to another medium.

Email interviews have many weaknesses. They don't permit you to establish rapport. And you need to be certain the person with whom you are corresponding is the person you think he or she is. The classic *New Yorker* cartoon shown on page 47 explains the risk.

On the other hand, email is quick and convenient as a follow-up to personal or phone interviews. Email can also be effective for a Q&A story. The email captures

"On the Internet, nobody knows you're a dog."

You can't be sure who's on the other end of an email message or that other people aren't helping the interviewee respond to your questions.

Source: © Peter Steiner The New Yorker Collection/ The Cartoon Bank.

the original questions and preserves the responses. Once you've made contact and established identity, an email interview can be useful and even surprisingly revealing. Some people will say things at a keyboard they wouldn't say face to face. Some get carried away by the power of their own prose. Some, of course, are cryptic and not forthcoming.

Instant messaging has the same strengths and weaknesses as email, but it is potentially much faster. You can best use IM for follow-up questions, clarifications and checking information to ensure accuracy.

Don't forget that email and IM are permanent. Don't ask or say anything you wouldn't want to see forwarded to others. Make your questions clear and grammatically correct. The permanence works *for* you, too. The answers are equally permanent. They can't be taken back or denied later. And it's difficult to misquote an email.

Online videoconferencing through Skype or FaceTime offers the advantages of email and eliminates one major drawback. With Skype or FaceTime, you're communicating in real time with someone you can actually see. And you're talking as opposed to typing. So, you can be more comfortable that you have the right person on the other end of the link, and you can add the visual information that's missing from an email interview. Soldiers deployed overseas use videoconferencing to stay in touch with families. Reporters can use the same technology to interview sources they might never see in the flesh.

Setting Up the Interview

All this homework is important, but something as trifling as your appearance may determine whether you will have a successful interview. You would hardly wear cutoff shorts into a university president's suite, and you wouldn't wear a three-piece suit to talk to underground revolutionaries.

Most interviews are conducted in the source's office. If the story is a profile or a feature, however, it usually is better to get the source away from his or her work. If you are doing a story about a rabbi's hobby of collecting butterflies, seek a setting appropriate to the topic. Suggest meeting where the rabbi keeps the collection.

In some interviews, it is to your advantage to get the source on neutral territory. If you have questions for the provost or a public official, suggest meeting in a coffee shop at a quiet time. A person has more power in his or her official surroundings.

It is important, too, to let the source know how much time you need and whether you expect to return for further information. And if you don't already know how the source might react to a recording device, ask when making the appointment.

This reporter dresses to fit in with the marchers he is interviewing; he gains their confidence by being friendly and attentive.

Funcrunch Photo/Alamy

Preparing Questions

You've now done the appropriate homework. You are properly attired. You've made an appointment and told the source how much time you need. Before you leave to meet your source, you may want to write down a list of questions to ask. They will guide you through the interview and prevent you from missing important topics altogether. The best way to encourage a spontaneous conversation is to have your questions prepared. You'll be more relaxed. Having questions prepared relieves you of the need to be mentally searching for the next question as the source is answering the last one. If you are trying to think of the next question, you can't pay close attention to what is being said, and you might miss the most important part of the interview.

Researching Questions

Preparing the questions for an interview is hard work, even for veterans. If you're writing for your campus newspaper, seek suggestions from other staff members. You'll find ideas in the newspaper's electronic database. If you anticipate a troublesome interview with the chancellor, you might want to seek advice from faculty members, too. What questions would they ask if they were you? Often, they have more background knowledge, or they might have heard some of the faculty talk around campus. Staff members also are valuable sources of information.

Although you may ask all of your prepared questions in some interviews, in most you probably will use only some of them. Still, you will have benefited from preparing the questions in two important ways. First, even when you don't use some of them, the work you did thinking of the questions helped prepare you for the interview. Second, sources who see that you have a prepared list often are impressed with your seriousness.

On the basis of the information you have gathered already, you know what you want to ask. Now you must be careful about how you phrase the questions.

Phrasing Questions

A young monk who asked his superior if he could smoke while he prayed was rebuked sharply. A friend advised him to rephrase the question. "Ask him if you can pray while you smoke," he said. The young monk was discovering that how questions are structured often determines the answer. Journalists face the same challenge. Reporters have missed many stories because they didn't know how to ask their questions. Quantitative researchers have shown how only a slight wording change affects the results of a survey. If you want to know whether citizens favor a city plan to beautify the downtown area, you can ask the question in several ways:

- Do you favor the City Council's plan to beautify the downtown area?
- The City Council plans to spend $3 million beautifying the downtown area. Are you in favor of this?
- Do you think the downtown area needs physical changes?
- Which of the following actions do you favor?
  - Prohibiting all automobile traffic in an area bounded by Providence Road, Ash Street, College Avenue and Elm Street.
  - Having all the downtown storefronts remodeled to carry out a single theme and putting in brick streets, shrubbery and benches.
  - None of the above.

How you structure that question may affect the survey results by several percentage points. Similarly, how you ask questions in an interview may affect the response.

Many reporters signal the response they expect or the prejudices they have with the way they phrase the question. For instance, a reporter who says, "Don't you think that the City Council should allocate more money to the Parks and Recreation Department?" is not only asking a question but also influencing the source or betraying a bias. Another common way of asking a leading question is this: "Are you going to vote against this amendment like the other City Council members I've talked to?" A neutral phrasing would be, "Do you think the City Council should allocate more money to the Parks and Recreation Department?" To avoid leading or even irritating your source, ask neutral questions.

Also ask the interviewee one question at a time. Listen to journalists at news conferences, who occasionally jump up and ask two or three questions at a time. The source then chooses the one he or she wishes to answer and ignores the rest. That can happen in one-on-one interviews, too.

In situations where you have to ask embarrassing or awkward questions, Jeff Truesdell of *People* magazine suggests demonstrating empathy. "Say, 'I'm sorry I have to ask this,' or 'I can't believe I'm asking this but here goes,' or 'My editors will want to know'—editors in absentia make for great fall guys—or 'Let me play devil's advocate here,'" Truesdell suggests. "Acknowledge that there are unpleasant questions, apologize for asking and then ask."

Sometimes the reporter's phrasing of a question unwittingly blocks a response. A reporter who was investigating possible job discrimination against women conducted several interviews before she told her city editor she didn't think the women with whom she talked were being frank with her. "When I ask them if they have ever been discriminated against, they always tell me no. But three times now during the course of the interviews, they have said things that indicate they have been. How do I get them to tell me about it?" she asked.

"Perhaps it's the way you are asking the question," the city editor replied. "When you ask the women whether they have ever been discriminated against, you are forcing them to answer yes or no. Don't be so blunt. Ask them if others with the same qualifications at work have advanced faster than they have. Ask if they are paid the same amount as men for the same work. Ask them what they think they would be doing today if they were male. Ask them if they know of any qualified women who were denied jobs."

The city editor was giving the reporter examples of both closed- and open-ended questions. Each has its specific strengths.

Open-Ended Questions

Open-ended questions allow the respondent some flexibility. People may not respond frankly when asked whether they have ever been discriminated against. The question calls for a yes or no response. But an open-ended question such as "What would you be doing at work today if you were a man?" is not as personal. It does not sound as threatening to the respondent. In response to an open-ended question, the source often reveals more than he or she realizes or intends to.

A sportswriter who was interviewing a pro scout at a college football game wanted to know whom the scout was there to see. When the scout diplomatically declined to say, the reporter tried another approach. He asked a series of questions:

- "What kinds of qualities does a pro scout look for in an athlete?"
- "Do you think any of the players here today have those talents?"
- "Who would you put into that category?"

The reporter worked from the general to the specific until he had the information he wanted. Open-ended questions are less direct and less threatening. They are more exploratory and more flexible. However, if you want to know a person's biographical data, don't ask, "Can you tell me about yourself?" That question is too general. Phrase your questions to get information about specific times and places.

Closed-Ended Questions

Eventually, you need to close in on a subject, to pin down details, to get the respondent to be specific. **Closed-ended questions** are designed to elicit specific responses.

Instead of asking the mayor "What did you think of the conference in Washington, D.C.?" you ask, "What did you learn in the session 'Funds You May Not Know Are Available'?" Instead of asking a previous employee to appraise the chancellor-designate's managerial abilities, you ask, "How well does she listen to the people who work for her?" "Do the people who work for her have specific job duties?" "Does she explain her decisions?"

A vague question invites a vague answer. By asking a specific question, you're more likely to get a specific answer. You're also communicating to your source that you have done your homework and that you are looking for precise details.

Knowing exactly when to ask a closed-ended question or when to be less specific is not something you can plan ahead of time. The type of information you are seeking and the chemistry between you and the source are the determining factors. You must make on-the-spot decisions. The important thing is to keep rephrasing the question until the source answers it adequately. Sports writer Gary Smith wrote in *Intimate Journalism*, "A lot of my reporting comes from asking a question three different ways. Sometimes the third go at it is what produces the nugget, but even if the answers aren't wonderful or the quotes usable, they can still confirm or correct my impressions."

Every reporter seeks anecdotes, and closed-ended questions help elicit them. "What is the funniest thing you've ever done?" "The weirdest?" "What's the saddest thing that ever happened to you?" When the source talks in generalities, ask a closed-ended question to get to specifics. "You say Mary is a practical joker. Can you think of an example of a practical joke she played on someone?" The answers to these types of questions yield the anecdotal nuggets that make your story readable.

Closed-Ended Questions	Open-Ended Questions
Do you like the proposal?	What are the strengths of the proposal? What are the weaknesses?
Did you have trouble coping when your child was in the car accident?	How did you cope after your child was in the car accident? Why did you attend counseling sessions?
Did you keep your promises to exercise today?	What was your exercise routine for today?
Did you give the theater teacher permission to stage that play?	What did you tell the theater teacher when she asked if her group could perform the play?
Do you use Gmail chat in your work?	How do you use Gmail chat in your work?

Establishing Rapport

The most basic requirement of any successful interview is a reasonable degree of trust between reporter and source. Usually, as a reporter you have to earn that trust. Wright Thompson, who worked for *The Kansas City Star* when he wrote this story and now works for ESPN, tells about the time he wanted to do a story about a former college football player named Ernest Blackwell, who had gone on a rampage in his neighborhood, shot a child and almost kicked another to death. He'd collapsed on a police gurney afterward and died en route to the hospital. No one could figure out what had happened. Media outlet after media outlet approached the family for an interview. All got turned down. Thompson tried a unique approach:

> When I called, I had a line. I told them I was going to talk to the cops and was going to do a story about Ernest. The police, I told them, would give me more than enough detail about the last five minutes of Ernest's life. Then I said, "I think there's a lot more to his life than the last five minutes. I think he deserves to be remembered for how he lived and not just how he died."

Thompson's reasoning won him the interview. His conclusion: "Have a plan. You must give someone a reason why it's better if they talk to you than if they don't."

Because he earned the trust of the family, he was able to develop the insights that allowed him to write this:

> Those who knew him wonder how Blackwell arrived on that day with so much rage in his heart, so much bad intent. Truth is, none of them could peer into the man's soul and see the hate that grew until it reached the breaking point.
> On Aug. 11, 2004, Blackwell could take no more.
> "Lord, why didn't I see the signs?" says his aunt Joyce Strong, who mostly raised Blackwell. "Why didn't I see he was reaching out for help? He must have been a ticking time bomb waiting to go off."

That's the payoff on the investment in building trust.

You probably won't have many assignments that difficult. It always helps, though, to have a plan. It also helps to have the honesty and empathy that lead strangers to be honest with you. Act like a human being.

Rapport—the relationship between the reporter and the source—is crucial to the success of the interview. It helps a reporter get better story information. The relationship is sometimes relaxed, sometimes strained. Often it is somewhere in between. The type of relationship you try to establish with your source is determined by the kind of story you are doing. Several approaches are possible.

Interview Approaches

For most news stories and personality profiles, the reporter can put the subject at ease by starting with small talk. Ask about a trophy, the plants or an engraved pen. Bring up something humorous you found during your research. Ask about something you know the source will want to talk about. If you think the subject might be skeptical about your knowledge of the field, open with a question that demonstrates your knowledge.

Establishing rapport with interview subjects helps a reporter get better story information.

FRANCIS SPECKER/MCT/Newscom

Rapport also depends on where you conduct the interview. Many people, especially those unaccustomed to being interviewed, feel more comfortable in their workplace. Go to them. Talk to the businessperson in the office, to the athlete in the locker room, to the conductor in the concert hall. However, if the source cannot relax at the workplace or is frequently interrupted, you may get a better interview elsewhere. Reporters have talked to politicians during car rides between campaign appearances. They've gone sailing with businesspeople and hunting with athletes. One student reporter doing a feature on a police chief spent a weekend with the chief, who was painting his home. To do a profile, which requires more than one interview, vary the location. New surroundings can make a difference.

There are times when the reporter would rather have the source edgy, nervous or even scared. When you are doing an investigation, you may want the key characters to feel uneasy. You may pretend you know more than you actually do. You want them to know that the material you have is substantive and serious. Seymour Hersh, a Pulitzer Prize–winning investigative reporter, uses this tactic. *Time* magazine once quoted a government official commenting on Hersh: "He wheedles, cajoles, pleads, threatens, asks a leading question, uses little tidbits as if he knew the whole story. When he finishes you feel like a wet rag."

In some cases, however, it is better even in an investigation to take a low-key approach. Let the source relax. Talk around the subject but gradually bring the discussion to the key issues. The surprise element may work in your favor.

> " I need to create what I call accelerated intimacy. We can't write the beautiful narrative stories that we all dream of unless we can get some things from the mouths of our sources. They must be comfortable enough to tell us *anything*. In journalism school, no one called the interactions between journalists and sources *relationships*, but that's what they are. "
>
> — Isabel Wilkerson, winner of the
> Pulitzer Prize for journalism

So may the sympathetic approach. When the source is speaking, you may nod or punctuate the source's responses with comments such as "That's interesting." Sources who think you are sympathetic are more likely to volunteer information. Researchers have found, for instance, that a simple "mm-hmmm" affects the length of the answer interviewers get.

Other Practical Considerations

Where you sit in relation to the person you are interviewing can be important. Unless you are deliberately trying to make interviewees feel uncomfortable, do not sit directly in front of them. Permit your sources to establish eye contact if and when they wish.

Some people are even more disturbed by the way a reporter takes notes. A digital recorder ensures accuracy of quotes, but it makes many speakers self-conscious or nervous. If you have permission to use a recorder, place it in an inconspicuous spot and ignore it except to make sure it is working properly. Writing notes longhand may interfere with your ability to digest what is being said. But not taking any notes at all is risky. Only a few reporters can leave an interview and accurately write down what was said. Certainly no one can do it and reproduce direct quotes verbatim. You should learn shorthand or develop a note-taking system of your own.

Be sure that you address the people you are interviewing correctly. If you are unsure how they should be addressed—*Mrs., Miss, Ms., Dr., Professor*—ask them.

If you are interviewing someone from a culture or race different from your own, recognize and avoid your own stereotypes. Perhaps you are uncomfortable in the presence of an Islamic woman wearing a veil when she attends school in the U.S. Instead of letting your feelings influence your actions, respect her beliefs. As a reporter, take pride in your ability to move among people from all cultures. This requires that you read about cultural differences. It might help you to know that in Chinese society, people are generally uncomfortable with too much eye contact. Many Arabs consider it improper for a man to look into a woman's eyes. No one knows everything about every culture, but you can prepare for some situations, and you can also recognize what you don't know. These days, it is easy enough to do a quick internet search about specific cultural differences before you conduct an interview.

Ensuring Accuracy and Fairness

Accuracy is a major problem in all interviews. Both the question and the answer may be ambiguous. You may not understand what is said. You may write it down incorrectly. You may not remember the context of the remarks. Your biases may interfere with the message.

TIPS

Personal Pronouns for Transgender People

The *AP Stylebook* recommends using the pronoun (*he, she*) the person prefers. If you don't know the person's preference, use the pronoun that reflects the way the person lives publicly.

Using a Recorder

The only way to be sure you capture the content of any interview with word-perfect accuracy is to record it. Careful listening is important, and taking good notes is essential. But using a recorder is the only way you can be certain you've got exactly what was said, both by the source and by you. That's important journalistically. As sources and audiences become increasingly skeptical, absolute accuracy adds to credibility and protects against complaints and even lawsuits. It's also increasingly common for sophisticated sources to use their own recorders as a form of self-protection from reporters they may not trust.

Today's digital recorders are so small and so powerful that it's often possible to use them while they're in your pocket, purse or briefcase. However, there's seldom a need to be secretive. Moreover, you may get a clearer recording by putting the device in full view on a nearby desk or table, or even on the floor in front of you. Putting the device on a stable surface helps eliminate transient rustling noises you might make when you move in your chair. And remember that in most states it is illegal to record someone without permission. State laws can be complicated, so make sure you understand them thoroughly beforehand.

If you're doing a phone interview, you may be able to download an app for your smartphone that will make it easy to record the call without affixing hardware to your phone. However, keep in mind that if your interviewee is in a different state, you will have to adhere to the laws of that state as well as those of your own.

Taking Notes

Knowing the background of your sources, having a comfortable relationship with them and keeping good notes are important elements of accuracy. All those were missing when a journalism student, two weeks into an internship at a major daily, interviewed the public information officer for a sheriff's department about criminal activity in and around a shelter for battered women. The reporter had never met the source. She took notes on her phone interview with the deputy and others in whatever notebook happened to be nearby. She didn't record the time, date or even the source. There were no notes showing context, just fragments of quotes, scrawled in nearly illegible handwriting.

After the story was published, the developer of the shelter sued. Questioned by attorneys, the deputy swore that the reporter misunderstood him and used some of his comments out of context. In several cases, he contended, she completed her fragmentary notes by putting her own words in his mouth. He testified that most reporters come to see him to get acquainted. Many call back to check his quotes on sensitive or complex stories. She did neither.

When the court ordered the reporter to produce and explain her notes, she had trouble reconstructing them. She had to admit on several occasions that she wasn't sure what the fragments meant.

The accuracy of your story is only as good as your notes. David Finkel, whose story on a family's TV-watching habits became a Pulitzer Prize finalist, took extra steps to be certain his material was accurate. Observing what his subjects were

T I P S

Taking Notes

Here are some helpful guidelines for taking notes during an interview:

- Write the date, the place, and the interviewee's name at the top of the page.
- Develop a consistent shorthand. For example, always use "w/" to mean "with."
- Use a spiral-bound notebook with pages that are easy to turn and that lie flat.
- Make sure you have several working pens or sharpened pencils.
- Leave a wide margin so that you can annotate your writing later on.
- Look up at the interviewee frequently as you write.
- Ask for the spellings of names.
- Always take notes, even if you are using a digital recorder.

watching, he obtained transcripts of the shows so he could quote accurately from them. If he knew transcripts would not be available, he set his recorder near the TV to record the program.

Verifying Information

Reporters should do research after an interview to ascertain specific figures when a source provides an estimate. For example, if a restaurant owner says he runs one of 20 pizza parlors in town, check with the city business-license office to get the exact number.

When you finish your interview, go back over the key points in your notes to confirm them. Read back quotes to make sure that you have them right. Realize, too, that you will need to confirm some of the information you get from other, perhaps more authoritative, sources. And if your interview produces allegations against other people or organizations, you will need to talk to those named.

Some possibilities for making errors or introducing bias are unavoidable, but others are not. To ensure the most accurate and complete reporting possible, you should use all the techniques available to obtain a good interview, including observing and asking follow-up questions. Let's examine these and other techniques.

Observing

Some reporters look but do not see. The detail they miss may be the difference between a routine story and one that is a delight to read. Your powers of observation may enable you to discover a story beyond your source's words. Is the subject nervous? What kinds of questions are striking home? The mayor may deny that he is going to fire the police chief, but if you notice the chief's personnel file sitting on an adjacent worktable, you may have reason to continue the investigation.

Wright Thompson says, "It's all about the scenes. Don't just ask questions. Be an observer." Like any good writer, he offers an example to show what he means:

> I was doing a story about former Heisman Trophy winner Eric Crouch. It was almost exactly one year since he'd won the trophy, and that year had been tough for him. He'd quit pro football and had been forced to ask some hard questions about his life. As we sat in an Omaha bar, a clip of him running the football came on the television. One of the women at the table said, "You're on TV, Eric." I remember he looked up at the screen and spat, "That's not me, man." Then he took a shot of liquor. No amount of interviewing could breathe life into the idea that he had changed like that scene.

Asking Follow-Up Questions

If you understand what the source is saying, you can ask meaningful follow-up questions. There's nothing worse than briefing your city editor on the interview and having the editor ask you, "Well, did you ask . . . ?" Having to say no is embarrassing.

Even if you go into an interview armed with a list of questions, the most important questions will probably be the ones you ask in response to an answer.

A reporter who was doing a story on bidding procedures was interviewing the mayor. The reporter asked how bid specifications were written. In the course of his reply, the mayor mentioned that the president of a construction firm had assured him the last bid specifications were adequate. The alert reporter picked up on the statement:

> "When did you talk to him?"
> "About three weeks ago," the mayor said.
> "That's before the specifications were published, wasn't it?"
> "Yes, we asked him to look them over for us."
> "Did he find anything wrong with the way they were written?"
> "Oh, he changed a few minor things. Nothing important."
> "Did officials of any other construction firms see the bid specifications before they were advertised?"
> "No, he was the only one."

Gradually, on the basis of one offhand comment by the mayor, the reporter was able to piece together a solid story on the questionable relationship between the city and the construction firm.

There are three questions that are always useful. One is "What did you mean by that?" The second is "How do you know that?" And the last is "Is there anything I haven't asked that I should?"

Using Other Techniques

Although most questions are designed to get information, some are asked as a delaying tactic. A reporter who is taking notes may fall behind. One good trick for catching up is just to say, "Hold on a second—let me get that" or "Say that again, please." Other questions are intended to encourage a longer response. "Go on with that" or "Tell me more about that" encourages the speaker to add more detail.

You don't have to be stalling for time to say you don't understand. Don't be embarrassed to admit you haven't grasped something. It's better to admit to one person you don't understand something than to advertise your ignorance worldwide online.

Another device for making the source talk on is not a question at all; it is a pause. You are signaling the source that you expect more. But the lack of a response from you is much more ambiguous than "Tell me more about that." It may indicate that you were skeptical of what was just said, that you didn't understand, that the answer was inadequate or several other possibilities. The source will be forced to react.

Ending the Interview

There are two things you should always do when you finish your questions: Check key facts, figures and quotes, and then put away your pen or recorder but keep your ears open. You're not breaching any ethical rule if you continue to ask questions

> "Today one has the impression that the interviewer is not listening to what you say, nor does he think it important, because he believes that the tape recorder hears everything. But he's wrong; it doesn't hear the beating of the heart, which is the most important part of the interview."
>
> — *Gabriel García Márquez, Colombian writer and Nobel laureate*

after you have put away your pen or turned off the recorder. Many dull interviews become interesting after they end. That's when some sources loosen up.

Quickly review your notes and check facts, especially dates, numbers, quotes, spellings and titles. Besides helping you get it right, this shows the source you are careful. If necessary, arrange a time when you can call to check other parts of the story or clear up questions you may have as you are writing. Researchers have found that more than half of direct quotations are inaccurate, even when the interview is recorded. That reflects an unacceptable sloppiness. Make sure you are the exception.

As a matter of courtesy, tell the source when the story might appear. You may even offer to send along a link to the article when it's completed. And of course, thank the source for granting the interview in the first place.

SUGGESTED READINGS

Adams, Sally, and Wynford Hicks. *Interviewing for Journalists*. 2nd ed. New York: Routledge, 2009. Adams and Hicks offer a useful description of interviewing techniques for journalists.

Chimera, Paul. *Nuts, Bolts & Anecdotes*. Amherst, N.Y.: Chimera Communications, 2015. Designed as a practical guide for journalists, this book covers interviewing, among other topics.

Kramer, Mark, and Wendy Call, eds. *Telling True Stories*. New York: Plume, 2007. This book contains excellent advice, including how to prepare for and conduct interviews.

Sedorkin, Gail. *Interviewing: A Guide for Journalists and Writers*. 2nd ed. Crows Nest, New South Wales, Australia: Allen and Unwin, 2011. This book is an excellent guide to interviewing skills for reporters and writers.

SUGGESTED WEBSITES

www.cjr.org/realtalk/the_art_of_the _interview.php
Excellent advice on interviewing appears on the site of the *Columbia Journalism Review*.

www.journalism.about.com/od/reporting/a /interviewing.htm
This site offers a discussion of basic journalism interviewing techniques.

www.poynter.org/tag/interviewing
Various articles describe interviewing techniques for journalists.

EXERCISES

1. Learn to gather background on your sources by writing a memo of up to two pages about your state's senior U.S. senator. Concentrate on those details that allow you to focus on how the senator views health care issues or another major issue. Indicate the sources of your information.

2. List five open-ended questions you would ask the senator you researched for exercise 1. Then list five closed-ended questions you would ask.

3. Interview a classmate about his or her hobbies. Then switch roles and do the interview again. Write a brief summary of what you learned, and list three additional questions you would ask if you had more time.

4. **Your journalism blog.** In your blog, describe your experience completing exercise 3. What did you learn about interviewing? Comment on the blog post of the classmate you partnered with. What can you add to each other's assessments of the exercise?

5. Interview three complete strangers and ask them about their school or work. Try to get an email address or telephone number for each. Then write a one-page summary of your experience and what you learned.

QUOTATIONS AND ATTRIBUTIONS

No one knew *Mad Men*'s Don Draper (played by John Hamm) better than show creator Matthew Weiner. Before the second half of the final season began, Weiner said to *USA Today*'s Bill Keveney, "I cannot tell you how many people, male and female, young and old, tell me that they're Don."

Later in the interview, Weiner said: "Don is at times a wish fulfillment and at times a punishment for those wishes. Part of the reason he resonated with the audience is he's a devil that lives inside us. You can't get enough of him. You want to be with him; you want to be like him." Even if you never heard of Don Draper, you now might want to meet him after reading Weiner's words. Direct quotes, good ones, have that kind of power.

Direct quotes—the exact words that a source says or writes—add color and credibility to your story. By using a direct quote, you put your readers right in touch with the speaker in your story. Like a handwritten letter, direct quotes are personal. Quotation marks, which usually enclose a direct quote, signal to the reader that something special is coming. Direct quotes provide a story with a change of pace, a breath of fresh air.

As Paula LaRocque, former writing coach and assistant managing editor of *The Dallas Morning News*, says, "The right quotes, carefully selected and presented, enliven and humanize a story and help make it clear, credible, immediate and dramatic. Yet many quotations in journalism are dull, repetitive, ill-phrased, ungrammatical, nonsensical, self-serving or just plain dumb."

Now that's a quotation worth quoting!

Not everything people say is worth quoting. You need to learn what to quote directly, when to use partial quotes and when to paraphrase. You also must learn how and how often to attribute quotations and other information. Remember, though, that attributing a remark or some information does not excuse you from a possible **libel** suit. A libelous statement, for which media organizations can be sued in court, is a false report that damages a person's reputation. Finally, you want to be fair.

Being fair is difficult especially when sources do not want to be quoted. For that reason you also must learn how to deal with off-the-record quotes and background information.

What to Quote Directly

Crisp, succinct, meaningful **quotes** spice up any story. But you can overdo a good thing. Inexperienced reporters often tend to use too many direct quotations. Even many experienced public relations practitioners use too many quotes.

You need direct quotes in your stories, but you also need to develop your skill in recognizing what is worth quoting directly. Let's look at the basic guidelines.

1

How to determine what is worth quoting directly.

2

How to ensure accuracy and fairness in quotations.

3

Whether, when and how to alter quotations.

4

When and how to attribute direct and indirect quotes.

5

How to handle both on- and off-the-record information.

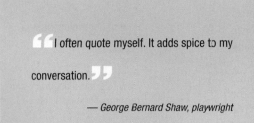

❝ I often quote myself. It adds spice to my conversation. **❞**

— *George Bernard Shaw, playwright*

Unique Material

A source sometimes tells you information you would not get in any other way. When you can say, "Ah, I never heard *that* before," you can be quite sure your readers would like to know exactly what the speaker said. Sometimes it is something surprising, something neither you nor your readers would have expected that person to say.

When singer Dolly Parton was asked how she felt about dumb-blonde jokes, she replied: "I'm not offended by all the dumb blonde jokes because I know I'm not dumb—and I also know that I'm not blond."

Use Good Judgment in Selecting Quotes

Striking statements like Parton's should be quoted, but not always. The *Arizona Daily Star* did a profile of a chef who writes a weekly column. Describing his food philosophy, the chef said, "I have a food philosophy, but it's a kind of an angry one. I'd eat a baby if you cooked it right. Yeah, that's pretty much it."

The *Star*'s reader advocate wrote that at least a half dozen readers objected. Said one, "Shame on the chef for saying it, and shame on the *Star* for printing it."

Don't Use Direct Quotes for Straight Facts

There is no reason to place simple, factual material inside quotation marks. Here is an extract from a story about similarities in the careers of a father and son that needed no quotes at all:

> "My son was born on campus," says the elder Denney.
> "In fact, he was born in the same hospital that I met my wife," he says. Since that time, his son has earned his bachelor's degree "technically in agriculture with a major in biological science and conservation."

Although the quoted material is informative, it contains nothing particularly interesting, surprising, disturbing, new or even different.

Avoid quotes that provide statistics. You can usually make a clearer, more succinct presentation by paraphrasing and attributing the information to your source. Save quotes for reaction and interpretation.

Use Quotes That Move the Story Forward

A direct quotation should say something significant, and it should not simply repeat what has been said indirectly. It should move the story forward. Here's a passage from a story in the *Columbia (Mo.) Daily Tribune* about a falconer. First the reporter sets up the quote:

> Duffee-Yates does not fly her birds during programs at parks but describes how they are used for hunting.

Then the story goes on to discuss this topic with this introduction:

> "It's all about food motivation, all weight control," Duffee-Yates said. "You get the bird down to the weight where it is hungry enough to want to eat and then reward the bird for good behavior."

The quotation is not just thrown in. It moves the story forward and serves as an introduction to the ways Duffee-Yates hunts with her birds.

Consider Using Dialogue to Tell Part of the Story

Sometimes spoken material is unique not because of individual remarks that are surprising or new but because of extended dialogue that can tell the story more effectively than writers can in their own words. Dialogue is not the same as a quotation. A quotation comes from a source speaking to the reporter. **Dialogue** occurs when two or more sources are speaking to one another.

Here's an example of how dialogue can move the story along and "show" rather than "tell." The story is about the restoration of old cars. A father is passing on a rare technique to his son:

> When the lead is smooth and the irregularities filled to his satisfaction, he reaches for his file.
>
> "How long has it been since you've done this?" his son asks.
>
> "It's been at least 20 years."
>
> "How do you tin it so it won't melt and all run off on the floor?"
>
> "Very carefully."
>
> Before the lesson is finished, a customer and two other shop workers have joined the group watching Larry at work. This is a skill few people know.
>
> "I don't like the way this lead melts," he says.
>
> "That's what it does when there's not enough tin?" his son asks.
>
> "Tin helps it stick."
>
> "Why do you pull the file instead of pushing it?"
>
> "So I can see better."
>
> "I would already have the fiberglass on and be done by now."
>
> "I know, but anything worthwhile you have to work for."

Notice the careful instruction and concerned advice from the father. His last sentence contains one of life's lessons: "Anything worthwhile you have to work for."

The Unique Expression

When you can say, "Ah, I've never heard it said *that* way before," you know you have something quotable. Be on the lookout for the clever, the colorful, the colloquial. For example, an elderly man talking about his organic garden said, "It's hard to tell people to watch what they eat. You eat health, you know."

A professor lecturing on graphic design said, "When you think it looks like a mistake, it is." The same professor once explained that elements in a design should not call attention to themselves: "You don't walk up to a beautiful painting in someone's home and say, 'That's a beautiful frame!' "

A computer trainer said to a reporter: "Teaching kids computers is like leading ducks to water. But teaching adults computers is like trying to teach chickens to swim."

Now and then even a commencement address can yield a great quote or two, especially if the speaker is the renowned historian and film documentarian Ken Burns. He said, for example, at Washington University in St. Louis in 2015:

> But the isolation of those two mighty oceans has also helped to incubate habits and patterns less beneficial to us: our devotion to money and guns, our certainty—about everything; our stubborn insistence on our own exceptionalism, blinding us to that which

> **❝**Read. The book is still the greatest manmade machine of all—not the car, not the TV, not the computer or the smartphone.**❞**
>
> — *Ken Burns, film documentarian*

needs repair, our preoccupation with always making the other wrong, at an individual as well as global level.

You might want to keep a book of classical quotations handy. Sometimes a quote from the classics fits the mood of your piece perfectly, even as a lead.

Here is Charles Lane quoting Jonathan Swift in his lead about a story on the harm reporters do when they mislead the public or rush to a story without all the facts:

> "Falsehood flies, and truth comes limping after it," wrote Jonathan Swift, "so that when men come to be undeceived, it is too late; the jest is over, and the tale hath had its effect."

Sometimes something said uniquely is a colloquialism. Colloquialisms and regional usages can add color and life to your copy. A person from Louisiana might say, "I was just fixing to leave when the phone rang." In parts of the South you're apt to hear, "I might could do that." A person from around Lancaster, Pa., might "make the light out" when turning off the lights. In some parts of the U.S., people "redd up" the dishes after a meal, meaning that they wash them and put them away.

Important Quotes by Important People

If citizen Joe Smith says, "Something must be done about this teachers' strike," you might or might not consider it worth quoting. But if the mayor says the same words, you are likely to include the quote. Generally, reporters quote public officials or known personalities in their news stories (although not everything they say is worth quoting). Remember, prominence is an important property of news.

Quoting sources whom readers are likely to know lends authority, credibility and interest to your story. Presumably, a meteorologist knows something about the weather, a doctor about health, a chemistry professor about chemicals. However, it is unlikely that a television star knows a great deal about cameras, even if he or she makes commercials about cameras. Important, knowledgeable people are good sources for quotes even if what they say is not unique or said uniquely.

Accuracy and Fairness in Direct Quotations

The first obligation of any reporter is to be accurate. You must learn how to get the exact words of the source.

It's not easy.

Scribbled notes from interviews, press conferences and meetings are often difficult to decipher and interpret. A study by Adrienne Lehrer, now professor emeritus of linguistics at the University of Arizona, found that only 13 of 98 quotations taken from Arizona newspapers proved to be verbatim when compared to recordings. Only twice, however, were the meanings of the nonverbatim quotes considered

ANNOTATED MODEL   Using Quotes Effectively

Ads Put Obese People in Spotlight

By Bruce Horovitz
USA Today, Oct. 4, 2012

Obese people are showing up in the very place that's mostly excluded them for decades: ads.

Some of the nation's largest brands—from Nike to Blue Cross Blue Shield—are featuring images of obese folks in their advertising in a bid to change consumer behavior. Obesity is considered to be anything 20% or more over ideal weight.

Note that all the attributions are in the present tense, which gives a sense of immediacy.

The move comes at a time two in three adults are overweight or obese, and diseases caused by obesity cost Americans $145 billion last year. In the past, obese folks in ads were often the butts of jokes. Now, they're increasingly visual images for change.

Why is it now acceptable to show obesity? "More of us are overweight, so it's a shared problem," says Valerie Folkes, marketing professor at University of Southern California.

This strong quote from an authority figure is nonthreatening and inviting.

It's a generational thing, too, says brand consultant Erich Joachimsthaler. "The new generation doesn't see (obese people) as different. There is a new, democratic world view: Everyone can be a star."

The different point of view expressed here is worth a direct quote.

Among those showing obesity:

• **Blue Cross Blue Shield of Minnesota.** The health provider has two new ads with obese actors. In one, an obese father with a tray full of fast food thinks twice when he overhears his large son arguing with a big friend over whose father can eat more. "We want to encourage folks to make healthier choices," says Marc Manley, chief prevention officer.

This acceptable, if unexciting, quote is from an authority figure

• **Nike.** It launched an ad this summer showing an obese runner jogging. "It's not just championship athletes that aspire to push their limits," spokesman KeJuan Wilkins says.

A more colorful and specific quote: It's important that we hear directly from industry people.

Marketers must avoid stereotypes, warns James Zervios of the Obesity Action Coalition. "So far, they're staying on the positive side of the line, but it's easy to cross over."

This is a good thought that makes for an excellent summary.

This story by *USA Today* marketing reporter Bruce Horovitz uses good quotations and excellent attributions.

> ❝I think of quotes as spices. Spices in themselves have no nutritional value. They make nutritious things taste better, but, like spices, quotes should be used sparingly.❞
>
> — *Isabel Wilkerson, Pulitzer Prize–winning reporter at* The Washington Post, *quoted in* Jack Hart, A Writer's Coach, *2006*

inaccurate. Your passion for accuracy should compel you to get and record the exact words of your sources. Only then can you decide which words to put between quotation marks.

Be sure to check the policy of your employer. Chances are, the policy is similar to that articulated by the ombudsman of *The Washington Post*, Deborah Howell: "When we put a source's words inside quotation marks, those exact words should have been uttered in precisely that form."

But no one expects reporters to insert every "huh" or "ya know," and there is almost never cause to embarrass anyone with few English skills.

Radio and television news editors can cut in and out of quotes, and they can certainly insert them out of context. Doing so is not just inaccurate because it distorts the meaning of what the source has said; it is also unethical.

Verification

When someone important says something important but perhaps false, putting the material in quotes does not relieve you of the responsibility for the inaccuracies. Citizens, officials and candidates for office often say things that may be partially true or altogether untrue and perhaps even libelous. Quotations need verification, like any other information you gather.

In the interest of balance, fairness and objectivity, many papers leave out, correct or point out the errors and inconsistencies in quotations. They do this in the article itself or in an accompanying story.

If candidate Joe Harkness says that his opponent, Jim McGown, is a member of the Ku Klux Klan, you should check before you print the charge. Good reporters don't stop looking and checking just because someone gives them some information. Look for yourself. Prisoners might have an altogether different account of a riot from the one the prison officials give you. Your story will not be complete unless you talk to all sides.

Quoting from Email, Social Media, the Internet and Chat Rooms

When you quote from email you have received personally, you can usually be sure the sender has written those words. If you have doubts, be sure to check with your correspondent. It's also a good idea to let readers know that you obtained the quote through email and did not speak with the source in person.

If you get a quote from the web, you need to be much more careful. Try to verify the quote with the source, but if you can't do that, at least be sure to tell readers that the quote comes from the web, and then cite the **URL** (internet address).

Reading what people are saying in chat rooms, blogs and tweets can be useful to reporters. However, quoting what people write in these forums is unwise because some statements might be unverifiable and even libelous. Nevertheless, if you have verified the information—and identified the person who is saying it—and if you specifically

AP Images/Michael R. Sisak

macmillanhighered.com /newsreporting12e Watch **"Computer-Assisted Reporting."**

- Computers offer research possibilities—but also challenges. What should journalists be cautious about in handling quotations?
- What experiences have you had using computers for research? Have you found information that would have been hard to locate by other methods?

state where you obtained the information, you might on occasion use such a quote. Identifying the person might well be impossible, though, because some people use screen names, aliases or pseudonyms on the internet.

Although quotes from experts and public figures are generally used to strengthen a story's authority, quotes from ordinary citizens with unique experience in a newsworthy event may also add credibility.

Using Someone Else's Direct Quotations

If you use a direct quotation that you did not personally get from a source, always indicate your source for the quote. Jessica Heslam wrote on BostonHerald.com that a *Boston Herald* review of WBZ-TV political analyst Jon Keller's book *The Bluest State* revealed "almost three dozen instances of direct quotes and other material lifted from numerous newspaper articles without any attribution."

Don't be tempted to use direct quotes you find in news releases. Don't be lazy; get your own quotes. Sources are much less likely to say things that are self-serving if they are talking to a journalist rather than a public relations person.

The Public Relations Society of America doesn't mind if you use material from a news release without attribution. Gerard Corbett, chair and CEO of PRSA, says doing so is not plagiarism, but he does recommend attribution when reporters use direct quotes, facts or figures from releases.

The Kansas City Star obviously disagrees about a reporter using material from news releases. The paper fired 32-year *Star* reporter Steve Penn for using news release materials in his columns dating back four years. Penn sued McClatchy Co., owner of the newspaper. He says this practice was always OK at *The Star*, and he was not notified of a change in policy. The case has still not gone to court.

Practicing Prepublication Review

A decade ago, you would not have had a city editor tell you to check the accuracy of your direct quotations with your source. Today, it is standard practice on many newspapers. Steve Weinberg, a former Missouri School of Journalism professor and former head of Investigative Reporters and Editors, calls it PPR—prepublication review.

Weinberg states candidly that it is not sensitivity to the feelings of his sources that motivates him to support the use of PPR. Rather, he insists that prepublication review loosens the tongues of tight-lipped sources and gets their statements on the record. Prepublication review extends also to checking the facts. Most professional journalists insist it does not make them feel compromised or make them surrender control over their stories or appear as "obsequious lapdogs." *New York Times* Associate Managing Editor for Standards Philip B. Corbett used those words and assured readers they did not apply to reporters at *The New York Times*.

The fact is, however, that too many times journalists get direct quotes wrong. Craig Silverman, an award-winning journalist and author and founder of Regret the Error, a blog that reports on media errors and corrections, has reported on mangled direct quotations from the past and the present. No paper is immune, and neither is history. He writes that while doing research for his book, *Regret the Error: How Media Mistakes Pollute the Press and Imperil Free Speech*, he found that William Randolph Hearst did not say, "You furnish the pictures; I'll furnish the war"; President Lyndon Johnson did not say, "If I've lost Cronkite, I've lost Middle America"; and Vice President Al Gore "sure as hell" never claimed to have invented the internet.

> "When you see yourself quoted in print and you're sorry you said it, it suddenly becomes a misquotation."
>
> — *Dr. Laurence J. Peter, author of* Peter's Quotations *and* The Peter Principle

If you Google "Misquotations," you will find a list of about 100 quotations under "Misquoted or Misattributed" and "Unsourced, Unverified or Other Best Guesses." You will also find a list of people who are most commonly misquoted. The name on top of the list? You guessed it. Yogi Berra.

Journalist Philip Weiss offers another reason why more journalists are practicing prepublication review: Reporters are often the subjects of stories. "They have had a taste of their own medicine and they don't like it."

Another reason for prepublication review is that it serves as a defense against libel. Jurors are less likely to find "reckless disregard for the truth" in an article that the source reviewed.

But what happens when sources want to change a quote? Weinberg says he makes it clear that the source is checking only for accuracy. He will consider comments about interpretation, phrasing or tone, but he retains the right to change or not change the quotes.

The White House/Sipa USA/Newscom

Getting good quotes in a television interview takes skill and practice.

And what happens if someone denies saying something that is in a direct quote? That possibility is why you need to have good notes, Weinberg says, even if they are in shorthand. Having the interview on tape is even better.

The issue of quote approval is far from settled. In 2012, Poynter reported that *The New York Times*, *The Washington Post*, Bloomberg and Reuters had all agreed to let politicians and campaigns have prior approval on quotations. Getting good quotes in a television interview takes skill and practice.

But policies can change in a hurry. Just two months later, *New York Times* Executive Editor Jill Abramson wrote a memo to her staff that said:

> So starting now (Sept. 20, 2012), we want to draw a clear line on this. Citing *Times* policy, reporters should say no if a source demands, as a condition of an interview, that quotes be submitted afterwards to the source or a press aide to review, approve or edit.

Note the words "review, approve or edit." What could be wrong with checking the accuracy of a quote? *The Huffington Post* admits that at times it allows sources to edit its quotes. Does "edit" mean change the wording or change the meaning? It surely means something different from checking the accuracy. The Associated Press, McClatchy Co. and *National Journal* have banned checking quotations.

Why? You certainly need to check the accuracy of the facts in your story. Doesn't it make sense to check the accuracy of the quotations? A simple reading of the quotes to the source can accomplish that.

That's a far cry from what *Washington Post* higher education reporter Daniel de Vise did when University of Texas officials were unhappy with his first draft of a story.

ON THE JOB Reinventing a Career

Courtesy of Rachel Reese.

When **Diana Reese** was a journalism student, she never imagined she would someday write for *The Washington Post.*

"Back then, I was not interested in writing news," she said, "so I was in the magazine sequence."

Her first career goal was editor of a regional publication such as *Missouri Life*—a job she had by the age of 23. She later worked in Knoxville, Tennessee, and New York City as an editor for Whittle Communications, a company founded by the young entrepreneurs who bought *Esquire* magazine.

Reese fulfilled her second career goal when she moved to Kansas City to freelance, specializing in articles on health for national consumer magazines. She soon discovered that getting and using good direct quotations were key to getting her articles accepted and read.

After taking a break to raise her children, she returned to freelancing, only to discover a different world. "Most of the magazines I'd written for were out of business," she said. She wrote for a variety of websites until a personal article she did about unemployment among the middle class in middle America landed her a spot as a regular contributor to *The Washington Post* women's blog "She the People."

She discovered she liked "the adrenaline rush" of covering or commenting on breaking news and seeing it online almost immediately.

Her Midwest location was often an advantage. The race between Sen. Claire McCaskill (D-Mo.) and challenger Todd Akin (he of "legitimate rape" fame) took place in neighboring Missouri. Reese's take on Sarah Palin's campaign speech in a you-pick blueberry patch just outside of Kansas City trended as the most-read article on the *Post* website.

Reese did more than 200 articles for "She the People" until it was discontinued in January 2015. She continues to freelance and is putting together a collection of her favorite "She the People" pieces for an e-book so she can learn how self-publishing works.

She has mixed feelings about the term "blog." "I did a lot of reporting and a lot of digging for 'She the People,'" she said. "Lively quotes always made for more interesting stories."

She offers these tips for getting great quotations:

- **Let sources talk.** Wait to ask the next question—people want to fill the silence. "I think I asked actress Mariska Hargitay one question," Reese said. "Her comment about being a 'badass' at age 50 was a great ending for the story."
- **Be ready.** "No one expected Mindy Corporon—whose son and father were killed in the shooting at the Jewish Community Center in Kansas—to show up at a vigil afterwards," Reese said. "Her comment, 'I know they're in heaven together,' was beautiful and heart-breaking."
- **Ask hard questions but stay human.** "I'm working on an article about a 20-year-old who committed suicide, and I had to say to the parents, 'Tell me about the day your son died.'"
- **Don't let physicians (or other professionals) get away with jargon.** Ask for an explanation in non-medical terms.
- **Check quotes for accuracy, if you need to, by calling sources and reading their words back to them.** Don't be tempted—or bullied—into sending a copy of the entire story.
- **Avoid email interviews.** Sources usually sound too formal.

Finally, don't forget about pulling a catchy quote to use on Twitter and other social media when promoting a story.

An email accompanying his second draft included the words, "I'd like to know of any phrases in the piece that you think are too harsh or over-hyped . . . . Everything here is negotiable."

Patrick B. Pexton, ombudsman for *The Washington Post*, writes that de Vise made a mistake. "He forgot that *Post* reporters write for readers, not for sources."

We all need to remember that we write for our readers.

Altering Quotations

By now you realize that although you should use direct quotations, they present many challenges and problems. Though there is no set number of quotations you should strive to include, a story with no quotes often lacks life and substance. Still, including lengthy quotes indiscriminately is a sign that you haven't really digested the material for your audience. Instead of quoting someone at length, look for the effective kernel within a long quotation.

Paraphrasing Quotes

Some quotations need verification; others need clarification. Do not quote someone unless you are sure of what that person means. "But that's what the man said" is not a sufficient reason (or excuse) for using an ambiguous quote. It is much better to skip a quotation altogether than to confuse the reader.

The best way to avoid confusing or wordy quotes is to paraphrase. In a **paraphrase** you use your own words to communicate the speaker's meaning. As a reporter, you must have confidence that you will sometimes be able to convey that meaning in fewer words, in better language and more clearly than the speaker did. Digesting, condensing and clarifying quotes take more effort than simply repeating them word for word. Here is a quote that could be cut drastically:

> "When I first started singing lessons I assumed I would be a public school teacher and maybe, if I was good enough, a voice teacher," he said. "When I graduated from the university, I still thought I would be a teacher, and I wanted to teach."

A paraphrase conveys the meaning more succinctly:

> When he first started singing lessons, and even after he graduated from the university, he wanted to be a public school voice teacher.

Using Partial Quotes

It is much better to paraphrase or to use full quotes than to use fragmentary or partial quotes. Partial quotes often make for choppy, interrupted sentences. Some editors would have you avoid these "orphan quotes" almost altogether. Here is an example of the overuse of partial quotes:

> The mayor said citizens should "turn off" unnecessary lights and "turn down" thermostats "to 65 degrees."

Since the quoted words are so mundane and uncontroversial, the sentence would be better with no quotation marks at all. Taking out the quotation marks would turn this sentence into an indirect quotation. In an indirect quotation, the reporter includes an attribution but doesn't use quotation marks. Indirect quotations need to meet the same test for accuracy that direct quotations require.

If a particular phrase has special significance or meaning, a partial quote may be justifiable. Sometimes you might want to put a word or phrase in quotation marks to indicate that this was precisely what the speaker said. Look at this use of a one-word quote in a story about genetic engineering in *The Atlantic*:

> **By all but eliminating agricultural erosion and runoff—so Brian Noyes, the local conservation-district manager, told me—continuous no-till could "revolutionize" the area's water quality.**

The writer thought it important that readers know that "revolutionize" was not his word but the word of his source. And he was right; "revolutionize" is a strong word.

When you do use partial quotes, do not put quotation marks around something the speaker could not have said. Suppose a speaker told a student audience at a university, "I am pleased and thrilled with your attendance here tonight." It would be incorrect to write the following:

> **The speaker said she was "pleased and thrilled with the students' attendance."**

The correct version is this:

> **The speaker said she was "pleased and thrilled" with the students' attendance.**

Partial quotes often contain an ellipsis (three periods) to tell the reader that some of the words of the quote are missing. For example:

> **"I have come here tonight . . . and I have crossed state lines . . . to conspire against the government."**

When using ellipses, you should not keep the reader guessing about what is missing. Sometimes the speaker's actual meaning is distorted when certain words are dropped. If a critic writes about a three-act play, "A great hit—except for the first three acts," an ad that picks up only the first part of that quote is guilty of misrepresentation. A journalist who uses the technique to distort the message is no less guilty.

Capturing Dialect or Accent

Using colorful or colloquial expressions helps the writer capture a person in a particular environment. The same can be true when you write the way people talk:

> **"Are you gonna go?" he asked.**
> **"No, I'm not goin'," she replied.**

In everyday speech hardly anyone enunciates perfectly. To do so would sound affected. In fiction, therefore, it is common to use spellings that match speech. But when conversation is written down in newspaper reporting, readers expect correct, full spellings. Not only is correct spelling easier to read, it is also less difficult to

GRAMMAR CHECK

What's the grammar error in this sentence?

In September 2015, Pope Francis delivered an evening prayer at St. Patrick's Cathedral, that has stood in midtown Manhattan for more than 100 years.

See Appendix 1, Rule 5.

write. Capturing dialect consistently is difficult, as these passages from a story about a Hollywood actress illustrate:

> "Boy, it's hot out theah," she started. "I could sure use a nice cold beer. How about it, uh? Wanta go get a couple beers?"

If she said "theah," wouldn't she also say "beeah"? Perhaps she said, "How 'bout it, uh?" And if she said "wanta," maybe she also said "geta."

In another passage, the writer has the actress speaking "straight" English:

> "Would you believe I used to dress like that all the time? Dates didn't want to be seen with me. I was always being asked to change clothes before going out."

It is unlikely she is that inconsistent in her speech

The writer of this story tried to show us something of the character of the actress. If he wanted to convey her speech patterns, he should have either been consistent or simply reported that she talked the same off the set as on it.

Bear in mind that writing dialect authentically is a narrative art that novelists, playwrights and screenwriters put much time and effort into learning. Be cautious about transcribing regional, ethnic and racial speech idiosyncrasies. Sometimes when a newspaper attempts to quote someone saying something uniquely, it betrays a bias. A Southern politician is more likely to have his quote spelled phonetically than an Eastern politician who says "idee-er" and "Cuber."

Some reporters seem to feel the need to write a quote like this: "And when police come in and do that kinda work, I think that's really great." How many people say "kind of" when they speak? Why would we quote someone saying he was "doin'" his homework. Do all of us say "doing"? What is the point of writing certain words in that manner?

However, you should not make everyone's speech the same. Barbara King Lord, former director of editorial training for the Associated Press, laments "our frequent inability to write other than insipid speech" and "our tendency to homogenize the day-to-day speech patterns of the heterogeneous people we write about." She acknowledges that writers worry about exposing to ridicule the immigrant's halting or perhaps unconventional speech while the stockbroker's speech appears flawless.

Lord calls the argument specious. Of course, people should not be exposed to ridicule through their speech. "The point here," she says, "is simply that when the writer's intention in writing dialects, quaint expressions, nonconventional grammar, flowery or showy speech, or the Queen's English is to make a person human, that intention is not only acceptable, it's desirable."

The only way you can make people human is to listen to them. Lord says reporters and writers usually hear but rarely listen. She advises reporters to "listen for expressions, turns of phrase, idiosyncratic talk" and to work these into their stories.

J.R. Moehringer of the *Los Angeles Times* did this in his Pulitzer Prize–winning article:

> "No white man gonna tell me not to march," Lucy says, jutting her chin. "Only make me march harder."

> " The surest way to make a monkey of a man is to quote him. "
>
> — *Robert Benchley, humorist*

Here the actual speech makes the speaker's determination and passion all the more evident.

You must be especially careful when quoting people for whom English is a second language. Nearly any attempt to quote nonfluent speakers exactly will be looked upon as making fun of their English. Better that you paraphrase their comments or, as some would advise, make them speak good English. Once again, however, if you have audio from baseball star Albert Pujols on your website and have the same quotes in perfect, fluent English in the written text, many would see the discrepancy as a serious problem. Others would say that you are hurting the uniqueness and character of the great slugger, who was born in the Dominican Republic. These problems are as old as radio and television, but convergence of the media has increased their frequency.

Mixing and Matching Questions and Answers

Writers often agonize over whether they must use quotations in the exact order in which the speaker said them.

The primary questions you must ask yourself are these: Why am I changing the order? Am I being fair? Am I distorting the meaning? Am I putting quotes together that change what the speaker intended to say?

Here are two versions of an emotional outburst in a Kansas City Chiefs' locker room after the Chiefs were defeated by Baltimore and some Chiefs fans had cheered when quarterback Matt Cassel was knocked unconscious and suffered a concussion.

> "It's 100 percent sickening," Chiefs tackle Eric Winston said. "I've never, ever—and I've been in some rough times on some rough teams—I've never been more embarrassed in my life to play football than at that moment right there. I get emotional about it because these guys, they work their butts off. Matt Cassel hasn't done anything to you people.
>
> "Hey, if he's not the best quarterback, he's not the best quarterback, and that's OK, but he's a person," Winston continued, the big offensive lineman's voice slowly rising. "And he got knocked out in a game and we've got 70,000 people cheering that he got knocked out."

Here's another version of Winston's words in the locker room:

> "But when you cheer, when you cheer somebody getting knocked out, I don't care who it is, and it just so happened to be Matt Cassel—it's sickening. It's 100 percent sickening. I've been in some rough times on some rough teams, I've never been more embarrassed in my life to play football than in that moment right there.
>
> "I get emotional about it because these guys, they work their butts off. Matt Cassel hasn't done anything to you people, hasn't done anything to you people. Hasn't done anything to the media writers that kill him, hasn't done anything wrong to the people that come out here and cheer him. Hey, if he's not the best quarterback then he's not the best quarterback and that's OK. But he's a person. And he got knocked out in a game and we have 70,000 people cheering that he got knocked out?"

It's obvious that both of these quotes cannot be correct. Neither of them is exact. Other print versions of Winston's words were equally misquoted and out of order. Does it matter?

It should.

More than 80,000 fans heard (and saw) exactly what Winston said on YouTube. In fairness to Winston, he later apologized by acknowledging that he knew that not all 70,000 fans cheered when Cassel was knocked unconscious.

Correcting Grammar in Quotes

Perhaps the most perplexing problem tied to the proper handling of direct quotations is this: When should you correct grammatical errors in a direct quotation? Should you expect people in news conferences or during informal interviews to speak perfect English?

The Case for Correcting Grammar

It is accepted practice at many newspapers to correct mistakes in grammar and to convey a person's remarks in complete sentences. None of us regularly speaks in perfect, grammatical sentences. But if we were writing down our remarks, presumably we would write in grammatically correct English.

Reporters are expected to use standard American written English.

- **Standard.** News audiences expect to read or hear the most widely and generally accepted English.

- **American.** Some words have different spellings and meanings in England, Australia and other English-speaking countries.

- **Written.** Admittedly, people often use words and expressions while speaking that they do not use when writing.

Reporters and editors differ widely on when or even whether to correct quotes. A reporter for the *Rocky Mountain News* of Denver quoted an attorney as saying, "Her and John gave each other things they needed and couldn't get anyplace else." The reporter said the quote was accurate but, on second thought, said it might have been better to correct the grammar to "She and John" in the written account. Of course, he could have corrected the grammar by paraphrasing the sentence.

The Case Against Correcting Grammar

You are most likely to find direct quotations with grammatical errors in the sports pages of daily newspapers. After the 2015 NBA playoffs, the Associated Press quoted LeBron James as saying, "If I could have gave more, I would have done it, but I gave everything I had." Nevertheless, often you can read an entire newspaper sports section and not find a single grammatical error in a direct quote.

Most papers have no written policy on correcting grammatical errors in direct quotations. Because so many variables are involved, these matters are handled on a case-by-case basis. Some argue you should sacrifice a bit of accuracy in the interest of promoting proper English—except in the speech of elected officials and public figures.

On the subject of correcting grammar in direct quotations, read what *The AP Stylebook* says under the entry "Quotations in the News":

> Never alter quotations even to correct minor grammatical errors or word usage. Casual minor tongue slips may be removed by using ellipses but even that should be done with extreme caution . . . . If there is a question about a quote, either don't use it or ask the speaker to clarify.

In this age of convergence, print reporters might also have shot video, and even if they haven't, they know someone who has. Correcting quotations is even more unwise for radio and television reporters. Writers and editors for print should remember that the quotation they use might have been heard by millions of people on radio or television or online. Changing the quote even slightly might make viewers and listeners question the credibility of print reports. Readers might also ask why print writers feel the need to act as press agents who strive to make their subjects look good.

This caution applies to celebrities of all kinds (such as actors and sports figures), but it might also apply to political candidates and elected officials. At least, some argue, news agencies should have some consistency. If a reporter quotes a farmer using incorrect grammar, then shouldn't the same be done for the mayor or for a college professor?

Removing Redundancies

Another question reporters deal with is whether to remove redundancies and other irrelevant material by using ellipses. Again, there is no agreement in the industry. For most reporters and editors, the answer to the problem of correcting quotes is to take out the quotation marks and to paraphrase. Sometimes you can just remove a phrase or a sentence. However, when you do that, you sometimes lose a lot. The value of quotes often lies in their richness and uniqueness.

When the *Columbia Missourian* quoted University of Missouri basketball star Keon Lawrence after a winning game, it dropped a sentence:

> "That felt good," Keon Lawrence said. "I look forward to doing that again."

The *Columbia Daily Tribune* wrote it this way:

> "Oh, that felt good," Lawrence said a few minutes after the game that hardly anyone thought the Tigers could win. "I didn't never do that. I look forward to doing that again."

Which version do you like better? Which version would you have written?

Deleting Obscenity, Profanity and Vulgarity

Many news organizations never allow some words that people say to be printed or broadcast—even if they are said uniquely. You won't even find examples in this chapter. Some language offends readers or listeners, and editors and producers know better than to print or broadcast it. The trouble is that few people have the same labels for these words:

- **Obscenities:** language that is in some way lewd, lascivious or indecent.

- **Profanities:** words used irreverently to refer to a deity or to beings, places or objects that people regard as divine or sacred; cursing.

- **Vulgarities:** words primarily referring to excretory matters; coarse, crude.

Of course, there are legitimate reasons to use proper sex-related terms in health stories and in some crime stories, including child molestation stories.

News stories about sexual assaults or accusations sometimes contain words such as these, especially if those involved are noted celebrities or politicians.

Terms such as "God" and "Jesus Christ" used in serious discussions of religion have always been acceptable to most people.

Nevertheless, the rules are different for what some call "swear" words in a direct quotation. Some papers follow *The Associated Press Stylebook* rule:

> **Do not use them (obscenities, profanities, and vulgarities) in stories unless they are part of direct quotations and there is a compelling reason for them . . . . If the obscenity involved is particularly offensive but the story requires making clear what the word was, replace the letters of the offensive word with hyphens, using only an initial letter:** *f---, s---.*

News is likely to reflect the sensibilities of its audience. Like it or not, language that was once considered vulgar in polite society is now tolerated more widely.

Of course, the Federal Communications Commission regulates the content of radio and television (except for cable) and can still fine a station or suspend its license for indecency. Fining is rare, but audiences are quick to let a station know that it has gone too far.

Individuals and advocacy groups try to curtail the use of profanity in the media. One such group is the Parents Television Council, a U.S.-based advocacy group founded in 1995 by conservative activist L. Brent Bozell III. This group's primary mission is to list television programs and other entertainment products it deems harmful to children. Among other measures, it counts the times profanity is used on a program.

Researchers from the University of Tennessee and Florida State University have kept track of the rapid rise of words such as "jackass" and "sucks." *New York Times* writer Edward Wyatt quotes Timothy Jay, a psychology professor at the Massachusetts College of Liberal Arts, as saying, "Vulgar slang has a way of waxing and waning, where we become desensitized to a word's earlier meanings."

The New York Times eased up a bit on its strict policy against printing vulgarities and obscenities. Managing Editor for Standards Phil Corbett told news aggregator site *The Wire* in an email, "The new version allows for a wider range of exceptions in cases where an offensive term is central to a news story." Here's what the updated *New York Times* style guide says:

> **If the precise nature of an obscenity, vulgarity or other offensive expression is essential to the readers' understanding of a newsworthy event—not merely to convey color or emotion—editors should consider using the term or a close paraphrase.**

At times you might wish to use vulgarities to show the intensity of someone's anger, terror, frustration or bitterness. Few inside the news media condone the casual, gratuitous use of vulgarities, however.

And neither do most readers and listeners.

But sometimes you just have to have a little fun. *Columbia (Mo.) Daily Tribune* sportswriter Joe Walljasper offered this wry observation when Cincinnati Reds manager Bryan Price unburdened himself for five minutes and 34 seconds to some reporters early in the 2015 season. Walljasper kept track: "Final tally: 971 words, 77 of which were the F-bombs, a 7.9 percent rate." He wrote: "That was enough to put him in elite company."

He then went on to compare Price's performance to those of Royals manager Hal McRae and Cubs manager Lee Elia—using the same method of measurement. He concluded: "Price has achieved notoriety that will last a lifetime, although, if the managerial history of McRae and Elia is a guide, it will be the only reason he is remembered."

Avoiding Made-Up Quotes

Fabricating a direct quote, even from general things that a source has said or from what the source might say if given the chance, is never acceptable. Even seasoned reporters are sometimes tempted to put quotation marks around words that their sources "meant to say" or to clarify or simplify a quote. They reason that it's more important to have a clear and concise quote for the reader than to be a slave to the verbose and unclear words of the source. That's bad reasoning. It's better to paraphrase.

Even worse is fabricating a quote that makes a source look bad or that is defamatory or perhaps even libelous. Doing so can result in a lawsuit. In 1991, in *Masson v. Malcolm*, the U.S. Supreme Court ruled that suits regarding quotations can proceed to trial if the altered quote "results in a material change in the meaning conveyed by the statement."

Libel or no libel, your credibility as a reporter demands that you be scrupulously exact when you place people's words inside quotation marks. When in doubt, paraphrase.

Attributing Direct and Indirect Quotes

Now that you've learned some of the complexities of using quotations, let's take a look at when and how to attribute them to a source.

When to Attribute

Attribution involves giving the name of, and sometimes other identifying information about, the source of a direct quotation, an indirect quotation or paraphrased material. You should almost always attribute direct quotes—with some exceptions. You would not, for example, attribute a quotation to a 7-year-old who witnessed a gang shooting. You might not wish to attribute a quote to someone who saw a homicide suspect with the victim. To do so in either case could put the source in danger.

You need a good reason to allow an entire paragraph of direct quotations to stand without an attribution. However, if you are quoting from a speech, an interview or a press conference and only the speaker is mentioned in the story, it might be excessive to put an attribution in every paragraph.

A Stirring in St. Albans
Emboldened by '08 Race to Roil Waters at Home

By Anne Barnard
The New York Times, Sept. 4, 2009

(The final paragraphs of the story are excerpted here.)

Mr. Whitehead wanted new candidates to challenge the club-endorsed officials....

The person he had in mind was Brian Simon, 27, another Obama campaigner. . . . He was eyeing a City Council seat. . . .

Mr. Whitehead recalls Mr. Simon worrying that if he challenged the incumbent, the party could sabotage his career. . . .

Now he pushed Mr. Simon hard. "He read to me about 'the fierce urgency of now,'" Mr. Simon recalled. Mr. Obama too had quoted the phrase of Dr. King.

Mr. Whitehead recalls saying, "If they could tell you to sit down for four years and be quiet, then you're finished. If you're not a warrior at 27, when are you going to be a warrior?"

Mr. Simon would not budge. He says he never feared retaliation, but thought running would be "toxic" and divisive and could deprive the district of an effective legislator. "I put my community first," he says.

Mr. Whitehead reminded him that he had nothing against Mr. Comrie, saying, "It's not the individual, it's the principle."

In February, City Comptroller William C. Thompson Jr., running for mayor, spoke in the Whiteheads' basement. The volunteers noted their new clout, and the visit attracted newcomers. One was Clyde Vanel, 35. He wanted to run for City Council.

Mr. Vanel was the son of Haitian immigrants. A lawyer in Manhattan and an owner of an East Village restaurant, Permanent Brunch, he was not an obvious partner for Donald 23X.

But they talked for hours. Both saw a one-time chance to attract new voters, and Mr. Vanel won Mr. Whitehead's highest praise: "A hard worker."

Mr. Simon pleaded with Mr. Whitehead not to deploy his network for Mr. Vanel. He wanted to run in 2013. Mr. Whitehead realized he might have to abandon the man he had nurtured.

(continued)

Annotations (left margin):

Note the quote within the quote, important because they are the words of Dr. Martin Luther King.

The final sentence of this quotation is excellent because the thought is unique and uniquely expressed.

The word "toxic" is in quotation marks to indicate that this strong word was spoken by Mr. Simon.

Again, a well-expressed thought worthy of quotation marks.

Annotations (right margin):

The attribution "recalled" is in the past tense. "Recalled" here is more descriptive than "said."

Here the attribution "recalls" is in the present tense.

Here again the attribution "says" is in the present tense in both the indirect and direct quotations.

There is no attribution here and none is necessary. It's clear Mr. Whitehead said it.

Colorful and distinctive quotations enhance the readability and interest of a story.

ANNOTATED MODEL Using Attributions *(continued)*

This unique quotation is rich and colorful. The simile is wonderful.

"It's like if you're sitting on a nail," said Ronald Summers Sr., a transit employee and an Obama volunteer. "You see an opportunity to get up off that nail, and someone says, I want you to sit back down and wait four years."

"Said" is in the past tense, but it might have been better in the present tense. Mr. Summers would still say that.

The last sentence of this quote is remarkable. Just what is it Mr. Whitehead is saying?

The deciding moment came when people walked into the Whiteheads' basement with a message from the Democratic club. Mr. Whitehead will not say who the people were, and club leaders deny sending anyone. The visitors delivered this request: Stay neutral.

A good quotation is a good way to end. The quote answers the "what's next?" in the story.

Mr. Whitehead says the club could offer him nothing: "We want a free, fair and democratic society. In other words, we don't want anything."

The next day, he called Mr. Vanel and said, "Look, let's start work."

"Says" is in the present tense; he would still say that.

"Called" is in the past tense, so "said" must also be in the past tense.

Ordinarily you should attribute **indirect quotations**. You should usually have a source for the information you write, and when you do, attribute the information to that source. The source can be a person or a written document. However, there are exceptions.

If you are a witness to damages or injuries, do not name yourself as a source in the story. Attribute this information to the police or to other authorities. But you do not have to attribute the totally obvious. If you are on the scene of an accident and can see that three people were involved, you do not have to write, "'Three people were involved in the accident,' Officer Osbord said." If you are unsure of the information or if there are conclusions or generalities involved, your editor probably will want you to attribute the information to an official or a witness. Avoid, however, attributing factual statements to "officials" or "authorities" or "sources." "Such constructions," writes journalist Jack Hart, "suggest that we are controlled by form and that we have forgotten about function."

If you are quoting from an interview conducted by someone other than yourself, be sure to note that. Do not claim that you obtained the quote yourself by writing, "In an interview, Smith said. . . ." That would make it seem as though you conducted the interview.

Not everyone agrees. Well-known journalist and commentator Fareed Zakaria, who was found guilty of plagiarism, was also found guilty of not attributing sources. In one case he justified his actions by saying that his book was "not an academic work where everything has to be acknowledged and footnoted." He did not wish to "interrupt the flow for the reader."

Zakaria says he feels the same way about attributing quotes from other people's interviews.

He's wrong.

Hart pleads for common sense regarding attributions. "Let's save them for direct quotations or paraphrased quotes laced with opinion," he writes. "Or for assertions likely to be especially sensitive. Or controversial." He says we should attribute only "if it matters."

This is good advice for the veteran. Nevertheless, although it is possible to attribute too often and although you do not always need to attribute, when you have doubts, include an attribution.

That goes for attributing anonymous sources, too. Even though you should seldom use them, you must attribute them. Try to preserve your credibility by giving as much information as you can about the sources without revealing their names. For example, you might report "a source close to the chancellor said." For the second reference to the same source, use "the anonymous source said."

Whether we like them or not, anonymous sources are common, even in the best of newspapers. The annotated model "Using Anonymous Sources" (page 82) shows a few paragraphs from an Associated Press story published in the *Columbia (Mo.) Daily Tribune*. The attributions—all anonymous—are highlighted in bold.

Notice how many quotes the story attributes to a "criminal complaint" without really saying exactly who was responsible for filing the complaint. Notice also the attribution "family members." The reporter had no reason to name them and invade their privacy.

Sometimes, as in stories about crime victims, you might have to change someone's name and follow the pseudonym with "not her real name" in parentheses to protect the source's privacy or to avoid endangering the source's life or family.

How to Attribute

In composition and creative writing classes, you may have been told to avoid repeating the same word. You probably picked up your thesaurus to look for a synonym for "to say," a colorless verb. Without much research you may have found 100 or more substitutes. None of them is wrong. Indeed, writers might search long for the exact word they need to convey a particular nuance of meaning. For example:

> **The presidential candidate announced the choice of a running mate.**
>
> **The arrested man divulged the names of his accomplices.**
>
> **The judge pronounced sentence.**

At other times, in the interest of precise and lively writing, you might write:

> **"I'll get you for that," she whispered.**
>
> **"I object!" he shouted.**

Nevertheless, reporters and editors prefer forms of "to say" in most instances, even if these are repeated throughout a story. And there are good reasons for this word choice. "Said" is unobtrusive. Rather than appearing tiresome and repetitious, it hides in the news columns and calls no attention to itself. "Said" is also neutral. It has no connotations. To use the word "said" is to be objective.

ANNOTATED MODEL Using Anonymous Sources

Terror Sting Thwarts Car Bomb Attempt
Attack was planned on Federal Reserve.

NEW YORK (AP)—A Bangladeshi man snared in an FBI terror sting considered targeting President Barack Obama and the New York City Stock Exchange before settling on a car bomb attack on the Federal Reserve, just blocks from the World Trade Center site, a law enforcement official told The Associated Press today.

The official, who was not authorized to speak publicly about the investigation and talked to the AP on condition of anonymity, stressed that the suspect never got beyond the discussion stage in considering an attack on the president.

The reporter states the reason for the source's anonymity.

In a September meeting with an undercover agent posing as a fellow jihadist, Quazi Mohammad Rezwanul Ahsan Nafis explained he chose the Federal Reserve as his target "for operational reasons," according to a criminal complaint. Nafis also indicated he knew that choice would "cause a large number of civilian casualties, including women and children," the complaint said.

The criminal complaint is a matter of public record.

The bomb was fake, but authorities said that Nafis' admiration of Osama bin Laden and aspirations for martyrdom were not.

The word "authorities" tells the reader the information was confirmed with more than one source.

FBI agents grabbed the 21-year-old Nafis—armed with a cellphone he believed was rigged as a detonator—after he made several attempts to blow up a fake 1,000-pound bomb inside a vehicle parked next to the Federal Reserve yesterday in lower Manhattan, the complaint said. . . .

Nafis is a banker's son from a middle-class neighborhood, and family members said today that they were stunned by his arrest. . . .

The reporter preserves the sources' privacy.

Sources can be anonymous for a number of reasons. Explaining those reasons improves the credibility of the story.

Some of the synonyms for "said" sound innocent enough, but be careful. If you report that a city official "claimed" or "maintained" or "contended," you are implying that you do not quite believe what the official said. The word "said" is the solution to your problem. If you have evidence that what the official said is incorrect, you should include the evidence or the correct information in your story.

In some newspaper accounts of labor negotiations, company officials always "ask" and labor leaders always "demand." "Demanding" sounds harsh and unreasonable, but "asking" sounds calm and reasonable. A reporter who uses these words in this context is taking an editorial stand—consciously or unconsciously.

Other words you may be tempted to use as a substitute for "said" are simply unacceptable because they represent improper usage. For example:

> "You don't really mean that," he winked.
> "Of course I do," she grinned.
> "But what if someone heard you say that?" he frowned.
> "Oh, you are a fool," she laughed.

You cannot "wink" a word. Similarly, it is impossible to "grin," "frown" or "laugh" words. But you might want to say this:

> "Not again," he said, moaning.
> "I'm afraid so," she said with a grin.

This usage is correct. Words like "moaning" or phrases like "with a grin" sometimes are needed to convey the speaker's meaning, but often they are not necessary or even helpful.

Learning the correct words for attribution is the first step. Here are some other guidelines to follow when attributing quotations:

■ **If a direct quote is more than one sentence long, place the attribution at the end of the first sentence.** This placement makes the copy flow better and doesn't keep the reader in the dark about the attribution for too long. For example:

> "The car overturned at least three times," the police officer said. "None of the four passengers was hurt. Luckily, the car did not explode into flames."

That one attribution is adequate. It would be redundant to write the following:

> "The car overturned at least three times," the police officer said. "None of the four passengers was hurt," he added. "Luckily, the car did not explode into flames," he continued.

Nor should you write this:

> "The car overturned at least three times. None of the four passengers was hurt. Luckily, the car did not explode into flames," the police officer said.

Although you should not keep the reader wondering who is being quoted, in most cases, you should avoid placing the attribution at the beginning of a quote. Do not write the following:

> The police officer said: "The car overturned at least three times. None of the four passengers was hurt. Luckily, the car did not explode into flames."

■ **If direct quotes from two different speakers follow one another, start the second with its attribution.** This placement avoids confusion for the reader:

> "The driver must not have seen the curve," an eyewitness said. "Once the car left the road, all I saw was a cloud of dust."
> 　The police officer said: "The car overturned at least three times. None of the four passengers was hurt. Luckily, the car did not explode into flames."

Notice that when an attribution precedes a direct quotation that is more than one sentence long, wire service style requires that a colon follow the attribution.

- **Separate partial quotes and complete quotes.** Avoid constructions like this one:

  The mayor said the time had come "to turn off some lights. We all must do something to conserve electricity."

  The correct form is to separate partial quotes and complete quotes:

  The time has come "to turn off some lights," the mayor said. "We all must do something to conserve electricity."

- **The first time you attribute a direct or an indirect quote, identify the speaker fully.** How fully you provide this identification depends on how well the speaker is known to the readers. In Springfield, Ill., it is sufficient to identify the mayor of Springfield simply as Mayor Houston. But if a story in the *Chicago Tribune* refers to the mayor of Springfield, the first reference should be "J. Michael Houston, mayor of Springfield"—unless the dateline for the story is Springfield.

- **Attribute direct quotes to only one person.** For example, don't do the following:

  "Flames were shooting out everywhere," witnesses said.

  If indeed any witnesses made statements like this, all you have to do is eliminate the quotation marks to turn this into an indirect quotation. For example:

  Several witnesses said that flames were shooting out everywhere.

- **Do not make up a source. Never attribute a statement to "a witness" unless your source is indeed that witness.** At times you might ask a witness to confirm what you have seen, but never invent quotes for anonymous witnesses. Inventing witnesses and making up quotes is dishonest, inaccurate and inexcusable.

- **In stories covering past news events, use the past tense in attributions, and use it throughout the story.** However, features and other stories that do not report on news events might be more effective if the attributions are consistently given in the present tense (see the annotated model "Using Quotes Effectively," page 65, for example). In a feature story like a personality profile, when it is safe to assume that what the person once said, he or she would still say, you might use the present tense. For example, when you write, "'I like being mayor,' she says," you are indicating that the mayor still enjoys her job.

- **Ordinarily, place the noun or pronoun before the verb in attributions:**

  "Everything is under control," the sheriff said.

  However, if you must identify a person by including a long title, it is less cumbersome to begin the attribution with the verb:

  "I enjoy the challenge," says Janet Berry, associate dean for graduate studies and research.

He Said, She Said—Punctuating Direct Quotations

"Always put the comma inside quotation marks," she said. Then she added, "The same goes for the period."

"Does the same rule apply for the question mark?" he asked.

"Only if the entire statement is a question," she replied, "and never add a comma after a question mark. Also, be sure to lowercase the first word of a continuing quote that follows an attribution and a comma.

"However, you must capitalize the first word of a new sentence after an attribution," she continued.

"Do not forget to open and close the sentence with quotation marks."

"Why are there no quotation marks after the word 'comma' at the end of the third paragraph?" he asked.

"Because the same person is speaking at the beginning of the next paragraph," she said. "Notice that the new paragraph does open with quotation marks. Note, too, that a quote inside a quotation needs single quotation marks, as around the word 'comma' in the paragraph above."

Attributing Written Sources

Do not use the word "says" when quoting from written sources. You might be general at times and write, "As *Time* magazine reported last week . . ." or "According to *Time* magazine. . . ." When you know the author of the piece, you might wish to include it: "As Katha Pollitt wrote in the June 8, 2015, issue of *The Nation*. . . ." For a report, survey or study cited in a news story, it's usually enough to identify the authors, the date of publication and the name of the journal or the issuing agency. (For guidance on avoiding unintentional plagiarism, see Chapter 20.)

Handling On- and Off-the-Record Information

Your job would be easy if all of your sources wished to be "on the record."

Some sources do not want to be named for sound reasons. You must learn to use professional judgment in handling the material they give you. If you agree to accept their information, you must honor their request to remain off the record. Breaching that confidence destroys trust and credibility and might get you in trouble with the law. But it is your obligation to take the information elsewhere to confirm it and get it on the record.

Anonymous sources helped *The New York Times* report the Bush administration's extralegal bugging of international communications. But another *Times* front-page story based on anonymous sources suggesting Sen. John McCain had an extramarital affair with a lobbyist was a great embarrassment.

Problems with Anonymous Sources

Not naming sources is dangerous for three important reasons. First, such information lacks credibility and makes the reporter and the newspaper suspect. Why should readers believe writers who won't cite the sources of their information? Who is to say that the writers didn't simply make things up to suit their stories?

Second, the source might be lying. He or she might be out to discredit someone or might be floating a trial balloon, that is, testing public reaction on some issue or event. Skilled diplomats and politicians know how to use reporters to take the temperature of public opinion. If the public reacts negatively, the sources will not proceed with whatever plans they leaked to the press. In such cases the press has been used—and it has become less credible.

Finally, once you have promised anonymity to a source, you cannot change your mind without risking a breach-of-contract suit. In 1991, the U.S. Supreme Court ruled 5-4 in *Cohen v. Cowles Media Co.* that the First Amendment does not prevent news sources from suing the press for breach of contract when the press makes confidential sources public. That's why at papers such as *The Miami Herald* only a senior editor has authority to commit the paper to a pledge of confidentiality.

Arianna Huffington said at a meeting in Boston that her site would rescind anonymity because: "I feel that freedom of expression is given to people who stand up for what they say and not hiding behind anonymity."

Disagreement About Terminology

Some reporters make these distinctions regarding sources and attribution:

- **Off the record.** You may not use the information.

- **Not for attribution.** You may use the information but with no reference as to its source.

- **Background.** You may use it with a general title for a source (for example, "a White House aide said").

- **Deep background.** You may use the information, but you may not indicate any source.

By no means is there agreement on these terms. For most people "off the record" means not for attribution. For some it means that you cannot use the information in any way. Some find no difference between "background" and "deep background." Journalists are vague about the meaning of the terms, and so are sources. Your obligation is to make sure you and your sources understand each other. Set the ground rules ahead of time. Clarify your terms. Make sure you agree on them.

Be careful not to allow a speaker to suddenly claim something is off the record. Sometimes in the middle of an interview a source will see you taking notes and try to change the rules: "Oh, I meant to tell you, that last example was off the record." With all the tact you can muster, try, without losing the source altogether, to change the person's mind. At least, tell the person to try to avoid doing that for the rest of the interview.

Background Interviews

If a city manager or police chief wishes to have a background session with you, unless it is against newspaper policy, you should not refuse. Often these officials are trying to be as open as they can under certain circumstances. Without such background sessions the task of reporting complex issues intelligently is nearly impossible. But you must be aware that you are hearing only one point of view and that the information might be self-serving.

Some sources make a habit of saying everything is off the record and of giving commonplace information in background sessions. Although you should not quote a source who asks to remain off the record, you might use the information if one or more of the following is true:

- The information is a matter of public record.
- It is generally known.
- It is available from several sources.
- You are a witness.

So as not to lose credibility with your source, it's a good idea to make it clear that you plan to use the information for one or more of the preceding reasons.

Remember these two important points:

- When possible, set the ground rules with your sources ahead of time.
- Know your newspaper's policy regarding these matters.

Knowing when and how to attribute background information is an art you should continue to develop as a reporter.

SUGGESTED READINGS

Brooks, Brian S., James L. Pinson and Jean Gaddy Wilson. *Working with Words: A Handbook for Media Writers and Editors.* 8th ed. New York: Bedford/St. Martin's, 2013. The section on quotations is excellent and follows Associated Press style.

Callihan, E.L. *Grammar for Journalists.* Rev. ed. Radnor, Pa.: Chilton, 1979. This classic text contains a good section on how to punctuate, attribute and handle quotations.

Germer, Fawn. "Are Quotes Sacred?" *American Journalism Review* (September 1995): 34–37. This article presents views from all sides on whether and when to change quotes.

King, Barbara. "There's Real Power in Common Speech." *Ottaway News Extra*, no. 137 (Winter 1989): 8, 16. The author presents an excellent discussion on using real quotes from real people.

LaRocque, Paula. "People Are Using Quotes More Often—But in Many Cases They Shouldn't Be." *Quill* (March 1, 2004): 32. LaRocque, an excellent writer, writing coach and teacher, provides good advice.

Stein, M.L. "9th Circuit: It's OK to Make Up Quotes." *Editor & Publisher* (Aug. 12, 1989): 16, 30. This article reports reactions from the press and lawyers to the court decision allowing quotes that are not verbatim.

Stimson, William. "Two Schools on Quoting Confuse the Reader." *Journalism Educator* 49, no. 4 (Winter 1995): 69–73. Strong arguments against cleaning up quotes are presented in this article.

Stoltzfus, Duane. "Partial Pre-publication Review Gaining Favor at Newspapers." *Newspaper Research Journal* 27, no. 4 (Fall 2006): 23–37. A practice long thought unconscionable among journalists gains acceptance.

Stowall, James Glen. *Writing for the Mass Media*. 9th ed. Knoxville: University of Tennessee Press, 2014. First published in 1984, this practical text was among the first that introduced students to writing for all the mass media.

Sullivan, Margaret. "In New Policy, *The Times* Forbids After-the-Fact 'Quote Approval.'" *The New York Times*, Sept. 20, 2012, The Opinion Pages. After months of discussion, a new policy states that "reporters should say no if a source demands, as a condition of an interview, that quotes be submitted afterward, to the source or a press aide to review, approve or edit."

Weinberg, Steve. "So What's Wrong with Pre-publication Review?" *Quill* (May 1990): 26–28. Weinberg answers objections to prepublication review.

Weinberg, Steve. "Thou Shalt Not Concoct Thy Quote." *Fineline* (July/August 1991): 3–4. In this article, Weinberg presents reasons for allowing sources to review quotations before publication.

SUGGESTED WEBSITES

http://owl.english.purdue.edu/owl/resource/577/1
This site provides an excellent, succinct summary of the rules for using quotation marks.

http://journalism.about.com/od/writing/a/attribution.htm
This page provides an excellent discussion of attribution, including on- and off-the-record attribution and deep background.

EXERCISES

1. **Your journalism blog.** Interview three different news reporters or editors working in online media, print, radio or television about his or her policies for handling sources regarding the following types of information:

   a. Off the record.
   b. Not for attribution.
   c. Background.
   d. Deep background.

   Write a blog post on your findings, and state which of the policies you think are the best—clearest, easiest to follow, most ethical.

2. Rewrite the following story. Pay special attention to the use of quotations and attribution. Note the sensitive nature of some of the quotations. Delete or paraphrase when you think it's necessary.

   Christopher O'Reilly is a remarkably happy young man, despite a bout with meningitis eight years ago that has left him paralyzed and brain-damaged.

   "I am happy," O'Reilly commented, as he puffed a cigarette. He has much to be happy about. Physical therapy has hastened his recovery since the day he awoke from a 10-week-long coma. He has lived to celebrate his 26th birthday.

   "I had a helluva birthday," he said. "I seen several friends. I had big cake," he added slowly.

   He lives in a house with his mother and stepfather in the rolling, green countryside near Springfield.

   O'Reilly's withered legs are curled beneath him now, and his right arm is mostly paralyzed, but he can do pull-ups with his left arm. He can see and hear.

   "When he came back, he wasn't worth a damn," his mother said. "The hack doctors told me he would be a vegetable all his life," she claimed.

   "He couldn't talk; he could only blink. And he drooled a lot," she smiled.

   Now, Chris is able to respond in incomplete sentences to questions and can carry on slow communication. "He don't talk good, but he talks," his mother commented.

   It all began when he stole a neighbor's Rototiller. His probation was revoked, and he found himself in the medium-security prison in Springfield. Then came "inadequate medical treatment" in the prison system. O'Reilly's family argued that he received punishment beyond what the Eighth Amendment of the U.S. Constitution calls "cruel and unusual."

   "Those prison officials were vicious," they said.

   As a result, he was awarded $250,000 from the state, the largest legal settlement in federal court in 10 years. "That sounds like a lot of money. But it really isn't, you know, when you consider what happened and when you consider the worth of a human life, and the way they treated him and all, we thought we should get at least a million," his mother remarked.

O'Reilly contracted the infection of the brain after sleeping "on the concrete floor" of a confinement cell his mother maintained. He had been placed in solitary confinement because he would not clean his cell. The disease went undiagnosed for eight days, leaving him paralyzed and brain-damaged, she said.

Now O'Reilly likes watching television. "I like TV," he grinned. "And smoking."

His mother said she "never gives up hope" that "one day" her son will "come out of it."

3. Attend a meeting, a press conference or a speech, and record it. While there, write down the quotes you would use if you were writing the story for your local newspaper. Then listen to the recording, and check the accuracy of your written quotations.

4. Engage a classmate in a half-hour interview about his or her life. Write a story based on the interview. Use as many direct quotes as you think are fitting. Then check the accuracy of the quotations with your classmate.

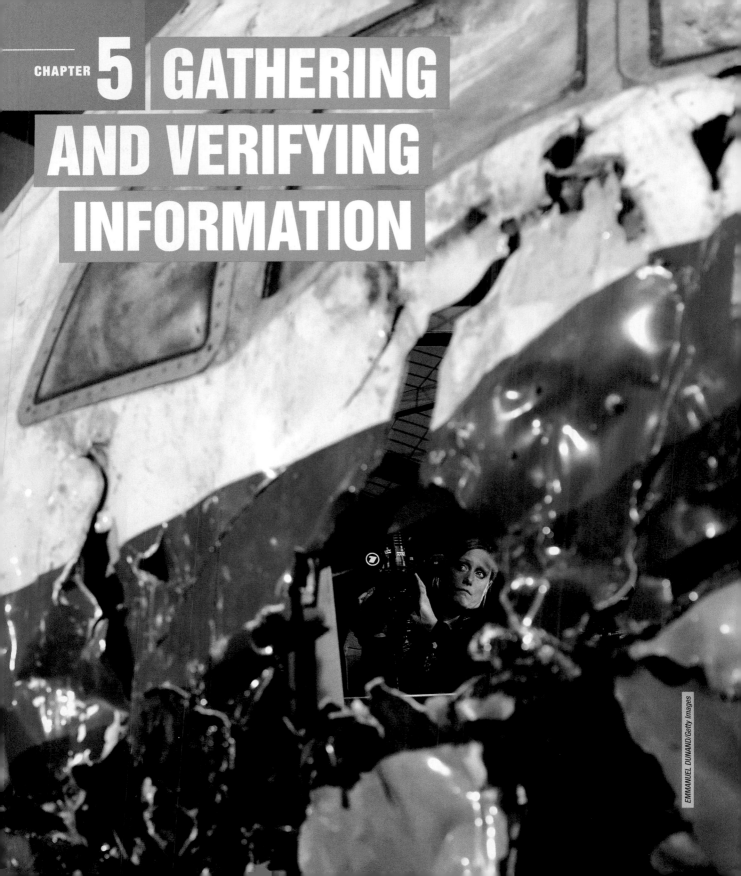

When Ukrainian separatists and their Russian backers shot down Malaysia Airlines Flight 17 in July 2014, Russian army Col. Igor Girkin claimed responsibility on VKontakte, the Russian equivalent of Facebook. He thought his separatist colleagues had used a Russian-built Buk missile to down a Ukrainian transport plane. But when it was learned that the plane was a commercial airliner, Girkin quickly erased his post. On Oct. 13. 2015, the Dutch Safety Board announced its conclusion that it was a Buk missile that was responsible for the aircraft's destruction.

Erasing the post was of no consequence. It was nicely preserved for all the world to see and surfaced on numerous social media sites as well as on those of mainstream media organizations. Girkin tried to shift responsibility to the Ukrainians by saying the incident occurred over Ukrainian airspace and that therefore the Ukrainians were responsible. But the plane crashed in separatist-held territory, which belied his claim. Intelligence photos also showed movement of the missile launcher onto separatist turf.

When a plane crashes, the site often is sealed off by authorities, who usually release only sanitized photos of the wreckage. But in this case, residents of the area posted hundreds of photos of crash debris on social media. *The Wall Street Journal* website collected the photos and mapped the locations where wreckage was found.

Both the Russian social media post and the *Journal*'s enterprising reporting show the power of social media in assisting journalists with reporting of the news. Still, the role of social media in mainstream reporting continues to evolve. Most journalists, even citizen journalists, don't want to report erroneous information, but it's easy for those who want to deceive to doctor photos and put out false reports. For journalists, the need to get breaking news quickly to readers and viewers makes it tempting to put out news that has not been verified. Speed has always been important in journalism, and in the era of Facebook and Twitter, it counts more than ever. But so does accuracy.

What social media do is useful—today, they almost always report the news first—but what matters even more is sorting through the mass of information, verifying it and making sense of what happened. That's what professional journalists do. It's their job to separate fact from fiction, the good information from the bad. Call this "curating" if you wish. Most journalists simply call it good journalism.

In this chapter, we'll explore the process of not only finding information on the web, on social media and elsewhere, but also getting it right.

Accurate Information: The Basis of a Good Story

Ask any editor whether a reporter can be a good writer without being good at information gathering, and you're likely to hear a resounding "No!" That's because good writing depends on good reporting. Reporting isn't good unless

1

How to ensure accuracy in information gathering through the disciplines of multiple sources and verification.

2

How to find and evaluate information from online sources.

3

How to use traditional sources of information to check facts.

it is thorough and accurate. To ensure reports are thorough and accurate, journalists employ two main techniques: the discipline of multiple sources and the discipline of verification.

The Discipline of Multiple Sources

Good writing is of course important, as we explore in other chapters, but the quality of writing depends in large part on good fact gathering, which we call good reporting. It's impossible to write a great story without first doing a great job of reporting. Gathering information requires skilled interviewing, as discussed in Chapter 3. It also requires knowing how to use the many sources of information readily available. Make no mistake about it: There are hundreds of places to find information.

Good reporters know that the worst kind of news story is one with a single source. Rarely is such a story worth publishing. Even a personality profile should be based on more than just an interview with the subject. To get a fuller perspective, the journalist also needs to talk with individuals who know the subject. Gathering information from several sources is one of the keys to good writing and good communication. It's also the best way to ensure accuracy because when several sources are used, information is more likely to be verified. When additional sources are checked and cross-checked, the chances of a story being accurate improve greatly.

Imagine how many sources the reporters for the *Milwaukee Journal Sentinel* used in their award-winning series about how the federal government allowed chemical manufacturers to influence the approval of potentially harmful substances in everyday products. Even in the short excerpt from the multipart series, shown in the annotated model "Integrating Multiple Sources into a Story," it's evident that the reporters used dozens of sources, including peer-reviewed research journals that most reporters seldom touch. Such reporting requires analyzing thousands of pages of data, poring over online and paper records, interviewing dozens of people, and checking, cross-checking and rechecking. Such reporting is both time-consuming and tedious, but work of this sort is exactly what journalists must do as they act as watchdogs over the actions of government agencies and others. Getting it right is of paramount importance.

The Discipline of Verification

Journalists, when operating as they should, follow the same investigative system employed by scientists. They develop a hypothesis and then seek facts to support or reject it. In the 20th century, journalists developed the concept of objectivity—an elusive idea that was often misinterpreted.

As Philip Meyer of the University of North Carolina suggests to journalists Bill Kovach and Tom Rosenstiel in their classic book, *The Elements of Journalism*: "I think (the) connection between journalism and science ought to emphasize objectivity of method. That's what scientific method is—our humanity, our subjective impulses . . . directed toward deciding what to investigate by objective means."

What objectivity isn't, Kovach and Rosenstiel argue, is blind loyalty to the concepts of fairness and balance. Fairness, they argue, can be misunderstood if it is seen as a goal unto itself. Fairness should mean that a journalist is fair to the facts

ANNOTATED MODEL   Integrating Multiple Sources into a Story

Chemical Fallout: Bisphenol A Is in You

By Susanne Rust, Cary Spivak and Meg Kissinger
Milwaukee Journal Sentinel

For more than a decade, the federal government and chemical-makers have assured the public that a hormone-mimicking compound found in baby bottles, aluminum cans and hundreds of other household products is safe. But a *Journal Sentinel* investigation found that these promises are based on outdated, incomplete government studies and research heavily funded by the chemical industry.

> *The lead hints at the large number of sources the journalists consulted to counter safety claims.*

In the first analysis of its kind by a newspaper, the *Journal Sentinel* reviewed 258 scientific studies of the chemical bisphenol A, a compound detected in the urine of 93 percent of Americans recently tested. An overwhelming majority of these studies show that the chemical is harmful— causing breast cancer, testicular cancer, diabetes, hyperactivity, obesity, low sperm counts, miscarriage and a host of other reproductive failures in laboratory animals.

> *Here the article gets specific about the wide scope of the newspaper's research.*

> *The article summarizes the main findings regarding health hazards.*

Studies paid for by the chemical industry are much less likely to find damaging effects or disease.

U.S. regulators so far have sided with industry by minimizing concern about the compound's safety.

Last week, a panel commissioned by the National Toxicology Program released a report finding bisphenol A to be of some concern for fetuses and small children. It found that adults have almost nothing to worry about.

> *The report outlines the most recent finding of toxicity in the chemical compound.*

Its recommendations could be used by the U.S. Environmental Protection Agency and other regulators to assess federal policies on how much bisphenol A is safe and may have huge ramifications for the multibillion-dollar chemical industry.

> *The story hints at a possible government change of position and its impact on the chemical industry.*

The panel said it considered more than 700 studies by university scientists, government researchers and industry-funded chemists. It picked the work it felt was best and threw out the rest.

The *Journal Sentinel* found that panel members gave more weight to industry-funded studies and more leeway to industry-funded researchers.

> *The newspaper's investigation finds fault with previous claims of safety.*

• The panel rejected academic studies that found harm—citing inadequate methods. But the panel accepted industry-funded studies using the same methods that concluded the chemical does not pose risks.

> *Faulty methodology in government studies is reported.*

(continued)

Using summaries, bulleted lists and quotes, the writers integrated research from a range of sources seamlessly into the story.

ANNOTATED MODEL Integrating Multiple Sources into a Story *(continued)*

More reliable university research differs with federal conclusions.

• The panel missed dozens of studies publicly available that the *Journal Sentinel* found online using a medical research internet search engine. The studies the panel considered were chosen, in part, by a consultant with links to firms that made bisphenol A.

• The panel accepted a Korean study translated by the chemical industry's trade group that found bisphenol A to be safe. It also accepted two studies that were not subjected to any peer review—the gold standard of scientific credibility. Both studies were funded by General Electric Co., which made bisphenol A until it sold its plastics division earlier this year.

"This undermines the government's authority," said David Rosner, professor of history and public health at Columbia University. "It makes you think twice about accepting their conclusions."

An expert finds fault with the government position.

Panel chairman Robert Chapin, a toxicologist who works for Pfizer Inc., the pharmaceutical giant, defended his group's work.

The chairman of the government panel defends his group's work.

"We didn't flippin' care who does the study," said Chapin, who worked as a government scientist for 18 years before joining Pfizer.

If the studies followed good laboratory practices and were backed with strong data, they were accepted, Chapin said. . . .

and to the public's understanding of them. It should not mean, "Am I being fair to my sources, so that none of them will be unhappy?" or "Does my story seem fair?" Those are subjective judgments that lead the journalist away from the task of independent verification.

Similarly, balance should not mean that it's necessary to get an equal number of scientists speaking on each side of the global-warming debate, for example, if an overwhelming number of scientists in fact believe that global warming is a reality.

Kovach and Rosenstiel argue that sharpening the meaning of verification and resisting the temptation to simplify it are essential to improving the credibility of what journalists write. So, while citizen journalists may rush to get out information quickly on Twitter and Facebook without much regard for accuracy, professional journalists seek to get it right—while also producing news as quickly as possible.

The journalistic process of layered editing also helps get facts right. At a good newspaper, magazine, radio or television station, or website, once the reporter writes a story, it may be subjected to extensive review by several editors. Each may find facts to correct or language to clarify in the quest for a story that is as compelling—and accurate—as possible. Thus, as a story flows through the editorial process (Figure 5.1), the goal is to make it as nearly perfect as possible.

INDIVIDUAL	ACTION
Reporter	Gathers facts, writes story, verifies its accuracy, forwards to city editor.
City Editor*	Edits story, returns to reporter for changes or additional detail (if necessary), forwards story to news editor.
News Editor*	Decides on placement of story in newspaper, forwards story to copy desk chief for implementation of instructions.
Copy Desk Chief	Prepares page design that accommodates the story's length, setting and headline size, forwards to copy editor. At some large newspapers, a separate design desk may play this role.
Copy Editor	Polishes writing of story, checks for missing or inaccurate detail, writes headline, returns to copy desk chief for final check.
Copy Desk Chief	Verifies that story is trimmed as necessary and that correct headline is written, transmits page to typesetting equipment.

FIGURE 5.1

Editing and producing a newspaper is a fast-paced and complex process in which editors at different levels review stories. Shown here is a typical copy-flow pattern for a daily newspaper.

* Or assistant

Note: At any point in the process, a story may be returned to an earlier editor for clarification, amplification or rewriting.

Editors talk about the need to look at a story on both the micro and macro levels. *Microediting* is the process of paying attention to detail:

- Are the facts correct?
- Are the names spelled correctly?
- Is the grammar sound?

Macroediting, on the other hand, looks at the big picture:

- Will readers understand this?
- Are there unanswered questions or inconsistencies in the story?
- Does this agree with what I know from previous stories on the subject?

All of this, and much more, goes into the editorial process of verification. In the end, the goal is to get the story right.

As they strive to get it right, journalists use all types of sources, including interviews, source documents and a variety of other sources ranging from the obvious, such as a Google search, to online sites, computer databases and traditional sources like printed almanacs and encyclopedias. Good reporters make frequent use of all these sources.

Online Sources of Information

Reporters and editors today have a wealth of information available at their fingertips. In addition to making raw data available, computers help reporters organize and analyze information.

From the news library in your local office to national databases of published newspaper, magazine, radio and television stories, the amount of online information is staggering. Primary sources of online information include the following:

- The news archive, or **morgue**, maintained digitally by your own publication, radio or television station or website. When you're hired, one of the first things you must do is learn to use your organization's archive. The background material you find there will help you provide context for the stories you cover.
- Search engines (Google, Bing, Yahoo, Dogpile, DuckDuckGo). Anyone can use Google, right? Well, learning to use search engines wisely is important to a journalist. Some of the tools we use to search the web have as their main purpose selling advertising. Page-rank algorithms and filters that personalize search results can yield misleading material. In Google, Bing and Yahoo, search results are ranked based not on quality but on several factors related to audience targeting. These three search engines filter information and rank their results accordingly. One of the newer search engines, DuckDuckGo, claims not to filter or personalize results.
- Wikipedia. The online encyclopedia's content at its best is well-documented with footnotes showing where the information originated. Wikipedia is especially valuable for gaining an overview of a topic. But because anyone can post a change to an article there, be careful before using material from it. It's good practice to verify Wikipedia information with another source.

- News sites, social media and content aggregators (USAToday.com, NYTimes.com, msnbc.com, CNN.com, Yahoo News, Google News).
- Other sites on the web. Millions of organizations maintain websites with useful information. Learning to evaluate their accuracy is important, and later in this chapter we'll give some tips to assist you in doing that.
- Mobile apps (applications for mobile phones and tablets). News apps are available for *The New York Times*, the Associated Press, NPR, CNN, Reuters and Newsy as well as for most other prominent media outlets.
- Commercial database services (Factiva, LexisNexis, NewsBank, ProQuest and others).
- Government databases (city, county, state and federal).
- Special-interest databases (those created by organizations with a cause).
- Custom databases and spreadsheets.

Let's explore the usefulness of some of these.

News Archives: The Place to Start

Digital archives are a marvel that good reporters and editors cherish. Before they were available, doing research for a story was a laborious process that involved a trip to the newspaper, magazine or television station library to sift through hundreds or even thousands of tattered, yellowed clippings or old scripts or sometimes even microfilm or microfiche. Too often, clippings and scripts had disappeared, were misfiled or had been misplaced, which made such research a hit-or-miss proposition. Despite those shortcomings, the library was considered a valuable asset. Reporters were routinely admonished to check there first.

You still hear that advice in newsrooms today, but most of today's news libraries are online or are in the process of being digitized. This almost ensures that an item will not disappear and will be easy to locate. Typically, you can do a check of the archive from your own computer, sometimes even from a remote location. This makes it easier than ever to do good background work on a story. Your ability to search online databases is limited only by your skill with search techniques and your access to the databases you need.

Digital news archives are full-text databases. All words in the database have been indexed and are searchable. Such capability gives you great flexibility in structuring searches using Boolean search commands. Boolean operators such as AND, OR and NOT allow you to structure the search to find the material most closely related to the subject being researched. For example, if you are interested in finding articles in Factiva, a Dow Jones database, on German Chancellor Angela Merkel's visits to the U.S., you might issue this command on the search line:

Merkel AND U.S.

That search command pulls all articles in which both "Merkel" and "U.S." appear, generating almost 30,000 hits. Obviously, that's too many. You need to narrow your search. Try:

Merkel SAME U.S.

TIPS

Ten Sources of Story Ideas

- Other people.
- Other publications.
- News releases.
- A social services directory.
- Government reports.
- Stories in your own newspaper.
- Advertisements.
- Wire copy.
- Local news briefs.
- You.

That search generates more than 6,000 articles in which both terms appear in the same paragraph. You can then narrow further:

> **Merkel w/3 U.S.**

That command asks for the Merkel-U.S. combination occurring within three words of one another. This yields more than 300 articles, closer to a manageable number. The next step is to narrow by date, region or source to find what you really need.

There are limitations. Some digital archives do not allow you to see photos, nor can you see articles as they appeared in the newspaper or magazine. PressReader.com, however, provides PDF files of thousands of newspapers from about 100 countries. (A **PDF file** preserves the formatting of the original document.) Some radio and television stations, including NPR and PBS, have podcasts or vodcasts—downloadable audio or video files—stored on their websites. Factiva also contains audio and video interviews and news clips along with transcripts.

Search Engines and Wikipedia

Google is the first stop for many journalists. Indeed, Google and other search engines, such as Yahoo, Bing, Dogpile and DuckDuckGo, can be helpful journalistic tools. The key to using them successfully is recognizing whether the information contained on the website to which the search takes you is accurate and therefore usable. Journalists also need to be aware that many search engines like Google, Yahoo and Bing filter information, personalizing it based on the information that they have gathered about the user's previous searches and online purchase history. Good journalists supplement these well-known search engines with newer ones that do not filter, like DuckDuckGo.

Information from well-known sites may be reliable; information from websites advocating a cause may not be. Be wary of Wikipedia, a user-written and user-edited social encyclopedia. Although much of the information on Wikipedia is excellent, anyone can enter erroneous information into it. Errors or misrepresentations are usually corrected quickly by others, but beware of depending on information from only that source. We discuss how to evaluate such information later in this chapter.

News Sites, Social Media and Content Aggregators

Some might consider it strange to think of news websites, social media and content aggregators as useful sources of information for reporters. Don't tell that to the reporters who use them.

Such sites are accessible to anyone with a computer and an internet connection. News sites are those published by established media outlets such as *The New York Times*, Microsoft's MSN and CNN.

While mainstream media offer blogs, those found on blog sites such as Google's Blogger or WordPress are usually classified as social media. In part, they are different because their writers answer only to themselves, not to editors. Social media also include Twitter, Instagram, Facebook and other "friending" sites. Twitter has become so important to journalists that it now has its own journalism and news manager. Many journalists now "tweet their beat." They tweet events live and seek to grow followers for their company's website. Twitter is just one of the social media tools that journalists use to increase engagement with their audience.

Not only do journalists often learn about breaking news from tweets—such as airplane crashes, fires and shootings—but they also communicate with readers through social media. They post links to their stories on Facebook, and they ask Twitter readers to suggest story ideas and sources.

The most popular content aggregators include Yahoo News, Google News and Newsy.com. An aggregator is a website that summarizes a story and links to the originating media for the full report. Newsy does so with the additional benefit of video.

Commercial Database Services

Commercial databases make it easy to see what has been written about a subject in other newspapers and magazines. But there are potential problems with using excerpts from those stories:

- **Copyright laws must be obeyed.** Take care not to use too much material without obtaining permission. Courts have ruled that small amounts of text can be incorporated into your story under *fair-use* provisions, but just what constitutes a small amount is not clear. As a result, be cautious, and credit anything you use to its source.

- **Not all articles that appeared in a newspaper can be found in a database.** Wire-service and market reports, death notices, box scores, social announcements and items written by freelancers often are excluded.

- **Publication doesn't ensure accuracy.** History is littered with incidents of newspapers quoting each other's inaccuracies.

- **The reporter might not be credible.** The reporter who wrote the story may not have any real knowledge of the subject matter. Using information from that reporter may introduce an inaccuracy into your story.

- **Databases aren't infallible.** The information is entered by humans, who are susceptible to mistakes. Also, databases are occasionally doctored in an attempt to prove a position or promote a cause.

On many topics, searching your own digital archive will not be sufficient. If U.S. Rep. Steve Cohen is making his first appearance in your community, your archive probably won't help; little will have been written about the Memphis, Tennessee, Democrat in your city. It probably will be much more useful to search the web or commercial databases for articles published both in Tennessee, where he resides, and nationally. This research will arm you with questions to ask about recent events. In such situations, the national commercial databases are invaluable.

macmillanhighered.com /newsreporting12e
Watch **"Media Effects Research."**

- Why are media researchers so concerned with the effects of marketing on children? Is it a useful focus? Explain.
- How useful could media research be for bloggers and other web journalists? Why?

The three leading commercial database services are Factiva (Figure 5.2), NewsBank and ProQuest Newsstand, all of which provide full-text access. If your employer does not subscribe to any of these, see if your local library does. Of course, while you are a student, you have access to many databases through your school's library.

Government Databases

For years, government agencies have maintained large databases of information as a means of managing the public's business. These databases cover almost every conceivable service that government offers, from airplane registration and maintenance records to census data to local court records. They are maintained not only by the federal and state governments but also by even the smallest of city and county agencies.

Now, any reporter with a computer and training can find stories in the numbers. Among those taking advantage of the technology is Penny Loeb, who now writes books after a 30-year reporting career. When she worked for *New York Newsday*, she used a computer analysis of tax and property records to reveal an astounding story: New York City owed $275 million to taxpayers as a result of overpayments on real estate, water and sewer taxes. To get that story, Loeb had to analyze millions of computer records. Doing that by hand would have consumed a lifetime, but with the assistance of a computer, she accomplished the task in a matter of weeks. Still, Loeb cautions against expecting instant stories:

> Don't just (use a computer) and expect a great story. You need a tip that there is a problem that computerized data can confirm. Or you may have seen a problem occur repeatedly, such as sentencing discrimination. The computer can quantify the scope.

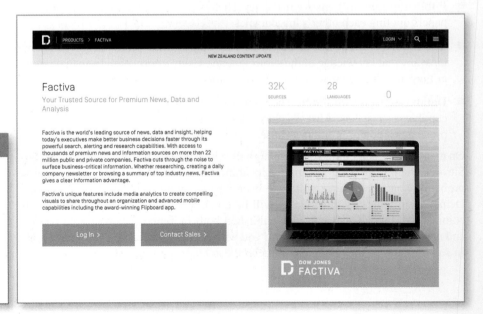

FIGURE 5.2

Factiva, owned by Dow Jones & Co., the parent company of *The Wall Street Journal*, allows subscribers to perform in-depth research on "more than 35,000 global news and information sources from 200 countries in 28 languages," according to www.dowjones.com.

Analyses of this type usually are done with relational database programs. **Relational database programs**, unlike simpler **flat-file databases**, permit you to compare one set of data to another. A classic example would be to compare a database of a state's licensed school-bus drivers to another database of the state's drunken-driving convictions. The result would be a list of school-bus drivers found guilty of such offenses.

After the introduction of this technology, investigative reporters were among the first to use it. Reporters can use database programs in their day-to-day work just as easily. For example, you might want to analyze federal records on airplane maintenance to produce a story on the safety record of a particular airline. If the records are maintained in an easily accessible format, the next time an airplane crashes it will be possible to call up the complete maintenance record of the aircraft merely by entering its registration number. Such information can be extremely useful, even in a deadline situation.

ON THE JOB Use All Available Tools

Right after graduation, **Eric Dundon** decided to jump at the chance to become a top-ranking editor at a small newspaper rather than becoming a reporter at a large one. He's enjoying his experience as managing editor of the *Hannibal* (Mo.) *Courier-Post*.

At the local level, he says, engagement with the community can often lead to stories. "Key in to social media—particularly Facebook and Twitter—to discover possible issues that pose problems to people in the community," Dundon says. "These tools are particularly beneficial because ideas found here can often impact a wide circle of people and elicit strong feedback. Participation in and knowledge of social, civic and charity organizations can also provide an endless array of story ideas."

But whether you're working at a large paper or a small one, Dundon says, verification of information is essential.

In a small-town environment, a boots-on-the-ground mentality is the strongest way to effectively verify information. The community is your newsroom. Don't assume that all information can be verified from behind a reporter's desk. A reporter must rely on the power of observation, which means seeing a situation in person, talking to a witness or neighbor at the scene, or going to the site of an event. Writing will improve from having first-hand experiences.

Dundon believes that some of the most underused tools for a journalist in a small-town setting are Sunshine Laws, or open meetings and records laws.

Courtesy of Laken McDonald.

Because municipalities with smaller populations generally have fewer media outlets to serve as a watchdog, the Sunshine Law can illuminate and verify information like few other tools. The Sunshine Law, in brief, allows anyone to request public documents from government agencies or sit in on a public meeting.

Already in his career, Dundon has used Sunshine Law requests to get:

- Emails between county commissioners discussing a highly controversial construction project.
- Full police reports detailing an officer-involved shooting.
- Closed-session minutes from a school board meeting where a well-liked principal was placed on leave.

"Knowing and using your state's Sunshine Law can help you get information that will best serve and inform the public," says Dundon.

Evaluating Digital News Sources

Journalists must differentiate carefully between fact and fiction on the web. Lately, journalists have assumed the task of curating citizen contributions, particularly when citizens are the first to break the news. When two bombs exploded at the Boston Marathon, the first reports came on Twitter from those at the scene. It took another 10 minutes before CNN and NPR reported the blasts. Associated Press and the cable news networks were next.

That shows just how important Twitter has become in breaking news stories, but it's important for journalists to verify such information before blasting it out to the world. In Twitter Best Practices, produced by Twitter itself, Jennifer Preston, a writer for The Lede blog at *The New York Times*, suggested a cautious approach:

> I consider most posts on Twitter a "tip," not a fact. We seek to apply the same good judgment and reporting practices to information on Twitter as we would anywhere else. It's not difficult to find official sources and/or whether user-generated content has been actually produced by an eyewitness.

Evaluating digital media sources is not a guessing game. You won't always be correct in your assessment of a report's credibility, but you can dramatically improve your chances.

Journalists have developed methods of gathering and editing news that help ensure, though they don't guarantee, accuracy. Those methods are described in several other chapters in this book. The web presents its own problems and solutions. How do you differentiate between a credible website and one that has a hidden agenda? Wikipedia is more popular than reputable print encyclopedias, but is it as credible? How do you know if a tweet or a Facebook posting is true? The answer lies in the discipline of verification.

A traditional method of verification relies on the journalistic process of layered editing. At most news media, print and digital, once the reporter writes a story, it is subject to extensive review by one or more editors. Each may find reporting inadequacies, facts to correct or language to clarify. Individual bloggers and those who post on social media outlets aren't edited. That's why curating and editing news posted on social media have become important new functions in newsrooms.

The web is a great resource for reporters, but determining the credibility of online information can be problematic. If the source is a respected media organization such as *The New York Times* or *The Washington Post*, chances are the information is solid. But if the information was published by an organization promoting a cause, there is ample reason to be wary.

Stan Ketterer, a journalist and journalism professor at Oklahoma State University, tells reporters to evaluate information on the web by following the same standard journalistic practices they would use for assessing the credibility and accuracy of any other type of information:

- **Before using information from a website in a story, verify it with a source.** There are exceptions to this rule, including taking information from a highly credible

Another common use of computers has been to compare bank records on home mortgages to census data. By tracking how many mortgages are issued to homeowners in predominantly black or Hispanic areas, reporters have been able to document the practice of *redlining*, through which banks make it difficult or impossible for minorities to obtain loans.

Again, such records are useful even after the investigation is complete. Access to census data, bank records and other forms of data can be used daily to produce news stories, charts, maps and other graphic devices. Numbers can be valuable in helping to tell a story. They can be particularly effective as the basis for charts that illustrate the impact of the numbers.

government site like the U.S. Census Bureau. Sometimes you can't contact the source on a breaking story because of time constraints. An editor must clear all exceptions.

- **In most cases, information taken directly from the web and used in a story must be attributed.** If you have verified the information on a website with a source, you can use the organization in the attribution, for example, "according to the EPA" or "EPA figures show." If you cannot verify the information after trying repeatedly, attribute unverified information to the website—for example, "according to the Voice of America's website." Consult your editor before using unverified information.

- **If you have doubts about the accuracy of the information and you cannot reach the source, get it from another source, such as a book or another person.** When in doubt, omit the information.

- **Check the extension on the site's web address to get clues as to the nature of the organization and the likely slant of the information.** The most common extensions used in the U.S. are *.gov* (government), *.edu* (education), *.com* (commercial), *.mil* (military), *.org* (not-for-profit organization) and *.net* (internet administration). Most government and military sites have credible and accurate information. In many cases, you can take the information directly from the site and attribute it to the organization. But consult your editor until you get to know these sites.

- **Treat the sites of colleges and universities as you would other sites.** If college and university sites have source documents, such as the Constitution, attribute the information to the source document. But beware. Personal home pages can have .edu extensions, and the information on them is not always credible.

- **In almost all cases, do not use information directly from the websites of commercial and not-for-profit organizations without verification.**

- **Check the date when the site was last updated.** The date generally appears at the top or bottom of the first page of the site. Although a recent date does not ensure that the information is current, it does indicate that the organization is paying close attention to the site. If no date appears, if the site has not been updated for a while or if it was created some time ago, do not use the information unless you verify it with a source.

- **Check to see if the website is what it appears to be.** The www.martinlutherking.org website was registered in 1999, but if you search its domain registration (whois.net), you'll find it is registered to a white supremacy organization, not the King family. The site ranks high in search results based on its longevity on the web, its domain name (which includes Martin Luther King's name) and external links to the site. It has not been endorsed by the King family, and in fact, family members have tried many times to have the site removed. However, the domain was registered legitimately, and copyright doesn't protect website domain names. This is an excellent example of poor-quality or fraudulent sites ranking high in search results.

Special-Interest Databases

Numerous special-interest groups have discovered the usefulness of placing information in computerized databases, and they are eager to introduce journalists to that information. Some of their material may be quite useful; indeed, it may be unobtainable from other sources. For instance, OpenSecrets.org has databases on campaign contributors that list who is spending what to lobby to whom, among other things. It has proved to be a credible source for news organizations. But other special-interest databases are designed to promote a particular perspective on a topic. Check the "About Us" link, and do a web search to see how often the group's material appears in other media.

Custom Databases

Journalists Tracy Weber, Charles Ornstein and Maloy Moore had reason to believe the California Board of Registered Nursing was failing in its duty to ensure that nurses are competent, sober and law-abiding. To find out for sure, they had to build their own analysis tool.

Using a database manager, they entered and analyzed all the accusations filed and all the disciplinary actions taken by the board over a six-year period. The printouts involved more than 2,000 nurses.

The team, representing the online news organization ProPublica and the *Los Angeles Times*, described the task as an enormous amount of work. But in the end, the database enabled the reporters not only to flag the best cases to use as examples but also to highlight a number of weaknesses in the board's oversight. Among the problems they uncovered were nurses involved in multiple disciplinary cases and those with multiple criminal convictions.

The project had immediate impact. The day after their first story appeared, California's governor replaced a majority of the nursing board's members. A day later, the board's longtime executive director resigned.

Traditional Sources of Information

Accessing information through computerized sources is quick and easy, but more traditional reference sources also are valuable. In some cases, the sources listed in this section cannot be found on computers.

The Traditional Newsroom Library

Every working reporter gets this advice from an editor early in his or her career: Check the morgue. The morgue, or newsroom library, is often more than a digital archive. Indeed, at most publications and some broadcast stations it's also a physical place with a real librarian. We list it here because many such libraries house bound volumes of old printed editions and clippings of news stories that predate the publication's digital archive. The digital archive is usually the first stop for a reporter on any kind of assignment, but the traditional library also may be of great help, particularly when a reporter needs to understand the historical background of a story.

Covering a speech? Look up background information on the speaker. Covering a sports event? What are the teams' records? Who are the coaches? What's the history of the rivalry? Reporters answer questions like these, and many others, by checking the library, both the digital and analog versions.

One other note on the print or broadcast archive: Here you can find photos of a speaker or coach you haven't met. You'll also find historic photos. A contemporary photo might help you recognize that person for a possible one-on-one interview before the speech or game begins. An old photo may show readers a sports hero who set a record decades ago.

Other Traditional Sources

Traditional sources of information—such as reference books, dictionaries and encyclopedias—still play an important role in the production of the daily news product. Good reporters and editors make a habit of checking every verifiable fact. Here is a list of commonly used references. An increasing number of these are now available online, as noted below, but some are still available only in print form.

- **City directories.** You can find these directories, not to be confused with telephone books, in most cities. They provide the same information as a telephone book but also may include information on the occupations of citizens and the owners or managers of businesses. Useful street indexes provide information on the names of next-door neighbors. City directories usually are found in print form only.

- **Local and area telephone directories.** Use telephone books for verifying the spelling of names and addresses. They usually are reliable, but they are not infallible. Remember that people move and have similar names. Almost all landline telephone numbers in North America are now listed on various web-based services, including Switchboard.com.

- **Maps of the city, county, state, nation and world.** Local maps usually are posted in the newsroom. Google Maps and Google's street views can help direct you around town. So can MapQuest.com.

- **State manuals.** Many state governments publish directories that provide useful information on various government agencies. These directories, most of which are online, sometimes list the salaries of state employees.

- *Bartlett's Familiar Quotations* (Little, Brown). This writing resource is now available for free at Bartleby.com.

- *Congressional Directory* (Government Printing Office). The directory provides profiles of members of Congress. It's available electronically at www.congress .gov/members.

- *Congressional Record* (Government Printing Office). The complete proceedings of the U.S. House and Senate are published in the *Congressional Record*. The *Record* is available at www.congress.gov/congressional-record.

- *Dictionary of American Biography* (Scribner's). There are several such biography sources, and this one lists famous deceased people up through 1995. There is no comparable online source for biographies of living people. LexisNexis has a "research people" function that provides biographies from newspapers, magazines and biographical directories.

- *Facts on File World News Digest* (Facts on File Inc.). The digest is a weekly compilation of news from metropolitan newspapers. It is available by subscription online at www.infobasepublishing.com/.

- *Guinness Book of World Records* (Guinness Superlatives). World records in countless categories are listed here. These are also available online at www.guinness worldrecords.com.

- *InfoPlease Almanac.* This resource includes biographies and almanac information. It is available at www.infoplease.com.

- *Readers' Guide to Periodical Literature* (EBSCO). This index to magazine articles on a host of subjects is available online for a fee.

- *Webster's Biographical Dictionary* (Merriam-Webster). This dictionary is a good resource for historical biographical information.

- *Webster's New World College Dictionary*, Fifth Edition (Houghton Mifflin Harcourt). This is the primary reference dictionary recommended by both the Associated Press and United Press International.

- *Webster's Third New International Dictionary* (Merriam-Webster). AP and UPI recommend this edition of the unabridged dictionary as a backup to *Webster's New World Dictionary*.

- *Who's Who* (Various publishers). Several companies produce biographical information on prominent people, generally organized by geographic region or topic. There is also a Who's Who Online at www.whoswho.com.

- *World Almanac and Book of Facts* (Simon & Schuster). This almanac is published annually.

These useful publications, and many others like them, enable reporters to verify data and to avoid the embarrassment caused by errors in print. Traditional printed sources of information include government records, business documents, pamphlets published by government and nongovernment agencies, books, newspapers and magazines.

Be careful when using material from a source with which you are not familiar. Some publications come from biased sources promoting a cause. It's the reporter's job to determine whether the information is unbiased and reliable. A good way to do that is to balance information from one source with information from another source with an opposing viewpoint. It may not always be possible for you to determine who's correct. Ensuring balance between two viewpoints is the next best thing.

SUGGESTED READINGS

Associated Press Stylebook and Briefing on Media Law. New York: Associated Press, 2016. This definitive work on stylistic matters in journalistic writing is published annually. It is also available as an online subscription.

Brooks, Brian S., James L. Pinson and Jean Gaddy Wilson. *Working with Words: A Handbook for Media Writers and Editors.* 9th ed. New York: Bedford/St. Martin's, 2016. This handbook is a comprehensive work on the correct use of language in journalistic writing and editing.

Callahan, Christopher, and Leslie-Jean Thornton. *A Journalist's Guide to the Internet: The Net as a Reporting Tool.* Boston: Allyn & Bacon, 2007. Journalists will find this a useful guide to using the internet as a reporting resource.

IRE Journal. This quarterly magazine is available from Investigative Reporters and Editors in Columbia, Mo. It offers regular articles on the use of computers in the news-gathering process.

SUGGESTED WEBSITES

www.ire.org
Investigative Reporters and Editors maintains an excellent website for anyone interested in investigative reporting.

www.journalism.org
Research reports of the Pew Research Center for Journalism & Media may be found here.

macmillanhighered.com/newsreporting12e
When you visit LaunchPad Solo for Journalism, you will find research links, exercises, and LearningCurve adaptive quizzing to help you improve your grammar and AP style usage. In addition, the site's video collection hosts the videos highlighted in this and other chapters as well as additional clips of leading professionals discussing important media trends.

EXERCISES

1. Do an internet search on material in a story from your local newspaper. Write a 500-word explanation of how the story could be improved by using online sources. List all your sources, or use links.

2. If you needed to determine where Apple Inc. is located and the name of its chief financial officer, where would you look? What other sources of information about the company are available?

3. **Your journalism blog.** On your blog, post a one-page biographical sketch of your congressional representative based on information from your library or a database. Send a tweet or a short email to your classmates highlighting a recent important action by the representative.

4. Using the internet, find the following information:

   The census of Rhode Island (or your home state) in 2010.
   The size of Rwanda in land area.
   The latest grant awards by the U.S. Department of Education.
   The name of a website that contains the complete works of Shakespeare.
   The name of a website that contains federal campaign contribution data.

5. Go to Google News and attempt to determine where the top three stories originated. Are any of them from the wire services or newspapers?

CHAPTER **6** USING NEWS RELEASES AS SOURCES

Sometimes you hear editors say that they pay no attention to news releases. Either they are lying, or they are not good journalists. They would have been foolish to ignore a release if they saw this on top of it:

Courtesy of the City of Ferguson.

Ferguson, Missouri, a suburb of St. Louis with a population of 21,000 people, had been in the news since Officer Darren Wilson, a white police officer on the suburban police force, shot and killed Michael Brown, an unarmed 18-year-old African-American. Protests arose immediately, but when a grand jury declined to indict Wilson, demonstrations spread to at least 170 cities. International leaders and foreign news organizations joined in, and Amnesty International sent a team to Ferguson, the first time it had ever sent a team to the U.S.

What came out of Ferguson was news.

The citizens of Ferguson were determined to do something about their city, which was 67 percent African-American but had a white mayor, a white chief of police, and a city council with six of its seven members being white. Moreover, the Ferguson school board, with six white members and one Hispanic, had suspended the African-American superintendent for no apparent reason. Protesting citizens had already succeeded in getting the city manager and the police chief to resign.

The U.S. Department of Justice had reported that the city's municipal court had become, in effect, a collection agency amassing money from citizens, mostly the poor and African-Americans. People held the mayor accountable for much of what was wrong with their city. He had to go, so they staged a recall petition. Here's the news release announcing the petition.

NEWS RELEASE
Media Relations: Jeff Small, 314-801-8540
City of Ferguson Receives Notification Concerning Recall Efforts of Mayor James Knowles III

(FERGUSON, Mo.) – The City of Ferguson received notification today that the recall petition submitted for Mayor James Knowles III lacks the required number of valid signatures according to the St. Louis County Board of Election Commissioners. The petitioners turned in signatures to the City of Ferguson on Wednesday, May 28, 2015. The St. Louis County Board of Election Commissioners began verifying all signatures on that same day.

1
How to explain the importance of news releases.

2
How to recognize the types of news releases.

3
How to deal with news releases.

4
How to use a news release as a starting point for a story.

According to the Ferguson Charter Section 8.4 the Ferguson city clerk must complete a certificate specifying the insufficient number of valid signatures and provide notice to the petitioners' committee. The committee has two days after receiving the certificate to file its intent to file an amended petition with additional signatures. Those additional signatures must be filed within ten days.

"We understand the rights of the petitioners and their recall efforts," said Ferguson Mayor James Knowles III. "But for as long as I am Mayor, I will continue to work with Council and Staff to bring together the citizens of Ferguson, and to move our community forward with the many reforms and initiatives that we have been working on for several months," added Knowles.

According to the City Charter, if a petition is certified insufficient and the petitioners' committee does not elect to amend the petition with additional signatures, the clerk shall promptly present the certificate to council and the certificate shall be a final determination as to the sufficiency of the petition.

The release assumes that readers knew that a recall petition was taking place. It also assumes that readers knew about the sizable dissatisfaction with the mayor.

The release leaves some questions for the reporter. How many signatures were required? By how many signatures did the petitioners fall short? (The release doesn't say the number was 27.) Will they continue to seek more?

The mayor's statement is what you would expect: It is self-serving. If you can get a chance to talk to him, you could ask him what those "many reforms and initiatives" are that they have been working on.

You (and your editors) would be most remiss if you did not follow up on this release in what has been called by many "post-Ferguson America."

The Importance of News Releases

Reporters do not go out and dig up all the ideas for stories they write. Many, like the ideas in this City of Ferguson news release, come to them. They are mailed, telephoned, sent via Twitter or another social networking service, faxed or hand-delivered by people who want to get something in "the news"—though today email is the preferred method of delivery. They come from people or offices with different titles: press agents, press secretaries, public relations departments, public information offices, community relations bureaus and publicity offices. The people who write these call them news releases, press releases or handouts. They are well-attuned to the social media and use Facebook, LinkedIn, Twitter and similar sites to spread their messages.

Because good publicity is so important, private individuals, corporations and government agencies spend a great deal of money to obtain it. Much of the money pays the salaries of skilled and experienced personnel, many of whom have gained valuable experience working in the news business. Part of their job is to write news releases that newspapers, radio and television stations, websites and syndicated public relations wire services will use and that will appear on websites perhaps throughout the world.

A significant development today is that organizations now are their own publishers. They can publish their news on their websites. That means the public has access to their messages when and how they wish to present them. The media are no longer their gatekeepers.

As a journalist, you need to know the value of, and problems with, news releases for news organizations. But also, you might very well want to be among the people who write news releases for universities, corporations and organizations of all kinds. If that's your goal, studying news releases and how news organizations handle them will help you be successful in public relations or in offices of public information. Knowing how reporters are taught to deal with news releases will help you write better releases.

Skilled public relations or public information practitioners know how to write news stories, and they apply all the principles of good news writing in their news releases. A good news release meets the criteria for a good news story.

Nevertheless, news releases are not intended to take the place of reporters. In *On Deadline: Managing Media Relations*, Carole Howard, formerly with *Reader's Digest*, and Wilma Mathews, formerly with AT&T and Arizona State University, write that news releases simply acquaint an editor with the basic facts of potential stories. Those who write news releases accept that their carefully crafted sentences will be checked and rewritten by reporters.

As a reporter, you must recognize that news releases, regardless of how they are delivered, are both a help and a hindrance to news agencies of all kinds. They are a help because without them, news organizations would need many more reporters. They are a hindrance because they often contain incomplete, self-serving or even incorrect information. Because they are intended to promote the interests and favorable reputation of the individuals and organizations that disseminate them, news releases, by their very nature, are not objective.

Nevertheless, wise editors do not discard news releases, whether they are sent by mail or email or appear on the internet, without reading them. These editors often give them to reporters, often the newest ones, as starting points for stories.

When your editor hands you a news release, you are expected to know what to do with it, regardless of which of the media you are employed in. You must be able to recognize the news in the release and apply all that you have learned about news values. The release may lead you to a good story. Your resourcefulness might improve your chances of being assigned to bigger things.

Types of News Releases

After you have read a number of news releases, you will notice that generally they fall into three categories:

- Announcements of coming events or of personnel matters: new hires, promotions, retirements and the like.
- Information about a cause.
- Information that is meant to build someone's or some organization's image.

Recognizing the types and purposes of news releases (and recognizing that some are hybrids and serve more than one purpose) will help you determine how to rewrite them.

GRAMMAR CHECK

What's the grammar error in this sentence?

Ballot selfies, which may reveal who a person voted for, could prompt the return of vote-buying, according to a prominent elections expert.

See Appendix 1, Rule 13.

**macmillanhighered.com
/newsreporting12e**
Watch **"Filling the News Hole:
Video News Releases."**

- How might a video news release interview differ from an interview conducted by a journalist?
- Would you want to see video news releases on televised news broadcasts? What rules should television news stations follow when airing a video news release?

Announcement Releases

Organizations use the news media to tell their members and the public about coming events. For example:

> The Camera Club will have a special meeting at Wyatt's Cafeteria at 7 p.m. on Wednesday, March 20. Marvin Miller will present a slide program on "Yellowstone in Winter." All interested persons are invited to attend.

Although the release promotes the Camera Club, it also serves as a public service announcement. Community newspapers and websites that offer such announcements are serving their readers. They might choose to present the information in a calendar of coming events. Depending on the topic, they might also want to assign a reporter. Here is another example:

> The first reception of the new season of the Springfield Art League will be on Sunday, Sept. 8, 3 to 5 p.m. in the Fine Arts Building.
>
> Included in the exhibition will be paintings, serigraphs, sculpture, batiks, weaving, pottery and jewelry, all created by Art League members who, throughout the summer, have been preparing works for this opening exhibit of the season.
>
> The event also will feature local member-artists' state fair entries, thus giving all who could not get to the fair the opportunity to see these works.
>
> The exhibition continues to Friday, Sept. 13. All gallery events and exhibitions are free.

Other news releases concern appointments, promotions, new hires and retirements. The announcement of an appointment might read like this:

> James McAlester, internationally known rural sociologist at Springfield University, has been appointed to the board of directors of Bread for the World, according to William Coburn, executive director of the humanitarian organization.
>
> McAlester attended his first board meeting Jan. 22 in New York City. He has been on the university faculty since 2005. Prior to that, he served as the Ford Foundation representative in India for 17 years.
>
> The 19,000-member Bread for the World organization is a "broad-based interdenominational movement of Christian citizens who advocate government policies that address the basic cause of hunger in the world," says Coburn.

The occasion is the appointment of McAlester, but the release also describes the purpose of the Bread for the World organization. By educating readers about the organization's purpose, the writer hopes to publicize its cause. A reporter, of course, would simply report the information.

Companies often send releases when an employee has been promoted. For example:

> James B. Withers Jr. was named senior vice president in charge of sales of the J.B. Withers Co., it was announced Tuesday.
>
> Withers, who has been with the company in the sales division for two years, will head a sales force of 23 people.
>
> "We are sure Jim can do the job," James B. Withers Sr., company president, said. "He brings intelligence and enthusiasm to the job. We're pleased he has decided to stay with the company."
>
> Founded in 1936, the J.B. Withers Co. is the country's second-largest manufacturer of dog and cat collars.

ON THE JOB Reading News Releases: Sweat the Small Print

Lara Jakes began covering politics and national security at the Associated Press in 2002. From 2006 to the end of 2008, she covered the Justice Department. She later covered the Pentagon and State Department for AP and also worked as an AP correspondent and bureau chief in Baghdad, Iraq. In January 2015, she began working for the bimonthly magazine *Foreign Policy* and its sister daily website ForeignPolicy.com as deputy managing editor for news.

She has covered fighting in Iraq, Afghanistan, Israel, the West Bank and Northern Ireland. Her reporting has won a number of awards, including a homeland security fellowship at the Knight Center for Specialized Journalism at the University of Maryland's Philip Merrill College of Journalism.

Once on a quiet day in her Justice Department pressroom office, Lara Jakes went back to a release handed out weeks earlier about new penalties for fraud, waste and abuse in government contracts. Attached to the release was the language of regulations outlining the kinds of abuses that would be prosecuted. And buried within that language was a multibillion-dollar loophole that specifically exempted penalties for overseas government work by private companies—despite U.S. contracts in Iraq and Afghanistan that had cost taxpayers more than $102 billion over five years.

None of the other Justice Department reporters who had gotten the release had written about the exemption, and at first she assumed she had misread or misunderstood the small print in the rules' language.

"So I called the prosecutor who was in charge of the program," she says. "He somewhat sheepishly agreed there was a major loophole in the regulations and blamed the White House (under President George W. Bush) for the wording of the new rules."

J. Scott Applewhite / The Associated Press.

Her stories caught the attention of Congress, sparking House of Representatives hearings and an investigation into how the loophole was quietly slipped into rules that were supposed to punish abusive contractors. One congressman called it an "egregious and flagrant disregard of taxpayer rights." Five months later, Congress passed a law to close the loophole and force stricter oversight of overseas contracts.

Justice Department prosecutors later jokingly referred to the rules that closed the loophole as "L.J.'s law." Lara says it was one of those stories that just seemed too good to be true—especially since it was initially handed over in a press release.

"I would have never found it if I'd not read the text of the regulations," she says. The prosecutor who confirmed that the loophole was in the rules seemed surprised only that she'd found it—not that it was there. "It was almost like they were daring us to not read the release or pay attention to what was going on," Lara says.

The moral: Sweat the fine print—even in news releases.

A release like this one is an attempt by the company to get its name before the public and to create employee goodwill. Written in the form of an announcement, unlike reporting, it is an attempt at free publicity.

Cause-Promoting Releases

News releases in this category seek to further a cause. Some of these releases come from organizations whose worthwhile causes are in need of funds or volunteers. The letter reprinted here is from a county chairman of the American Heart Association to the editor of a newspaper. It is not written in the form of a release, but its effect is meant to be the same:

> The alumnae and collegiate members of the Alpha Phi Sorority have just completed their annual Alpha Phi "Helping Hearts" lollipop sale. This year Valerie Knight, project chairwoman, led sorority members to achieve record-breaking sales. The lollipop sale is a national project of the Alpha Phi Sorority.
>
> Sunday, March 5, Valerie Knight presented a check for $1,800 to the American Heart Association, Shelby County Unit. The contribution was presented during a reception at the Alpha Phi house. This contribution is an important part of the annual fundraising campaign of the American Heart Association.

Heads of organizations attempt to alert the public to their message in any way they can. Any release, notice or letter they can get into the media for free leaves money for the cause that they represent.

Image-Building Releases

Another kind of news release serves to build up the image of a person or organization. You can see an example of an image-building release below. This Mayo Clinic news release seeks to enhance the images of the medical facility and also two local NBA teams.

Courtesy of Mayo Clinic News Network

Courtesy of Mayo Clinic News Network

NEWS RELEASE
Celebrating Grand Opening Today for Mayo Clinic Square: Mayo Clinic, Minnesota Timberwolves, Minnesota Lynx

MINNEAPOLIS – Dignitaries from the worlds of medicine, sports, business and politics hit the court today, Wednesday, June 17, to dedicate Mayo Clinic Square in downtown Minneapolis.

The event was the first in a series of grand-opening events marking the strategic collaboration of Mayo Clinic, the Minnesota Timberwolves and Minnesota Lynx.

"At Mayo Clinic we pride ourselves in teamwork," said John Noseworthy, M.D., president and CEO of Mayo Clinic. "We are proud to be part of the team that made this day possible."

Mayo Clinic Square is home to Mayo Clinic Sports Medicine and the new headquarters of the Minnesota Timberwolves and Minnesota Lynx. Mayo Clinic Sports Medicine provides medical services to the teams and is located just across from their training facility and practice court.

"I've never seen anything like this," said Adam Silver, commissioner of the NBA. "It's the gold standard."

"I couldn't be prouder to be a partner of the Mayo Clinic," said Laurel Richie, president of the WNBA.

Guests at Wednesday's dedication ceremony got a behind-the-scenes look at Mayo Clinic Sports Medicine, a 22,000-square-foot facility that opened in October 2014. It serves players and the public alike.

MEDIA CONTACT: Rhoda Madson, Mayo Clinic, 507-284-5005, madson.rhoda@mayo.edu

What happens at the Mayo Clinic is often news and when professional basketball gets involved, you probably ought to pay attention. All the quotes in the release are self-inflated, self-serving and non-news, but if you pursue the people involved, you might be able to get some better ones.

The release is also vague about just how Mayo Clinic Sports Medicine serves "players and the public alike." You need to dig up some examples. The news release is just a starting point.

Organizations and government agencies at all levels often try to build their public image. Many of them persuade local mayors to proclaim a day or a week of recognition for their group, as in the following:

> **Mayor Juanita Williams has proclaimed Saturday, May 11, as Fire Service Recognition Day. The Springfield Fire Department in conjunction with the University Fire Service Training Division is sponsoring a demonstration of the fire apparatus and equipment at the Springfield Fire Training Center. The displays are from 10 a.m. to 5 p.m. at 700 Bear Blvd. All citizens are urged to attend the display or visit their neighborhood fire station on May 11.**
>
> **Our PRODUCT is your SAFETY.**

An editor who hands you a release like this has probably decided that you should find a story here.

You can start by finding the names of the people in charge or at least their public information people. Just what will the "demonstration" involve? What kinds of equipment will be there? Will people, even children, be allowed to climb onto or even into the equipment? Will the demonstration be live; that is, will the equipment be up and running? You should be able to get some good quotes from the fire chief of the city and of the university.

You need to know, too, if this is the first such Recognition Day and if this will be an annual event. See if you can get a photographer to accompany you. You should be able to get a good story.

Handling News Releases

Regardless of the type of news release, be sure to read the information that appears at the top (see the news release in Figure 6.1 on the following page). All that information might be useful to you. Even so, many news releases leave unanswered questions. You will probably want to contact people other than the director of information or even the contact person if you have doubts about some of the data given. But for routine accuracy checks, the people listed on the release can do the job. They might lead you to other helpful sources, too. Sometimes you might have sources of your own. And sometimes you might uncover the real story only from people who are neither connected to nor recommended by the director of information.

You might have to consult your editor regarding the release date. As a courtesy, most news media honor release dates. However, sometimes waiting would render the information useless. Also, once a release is public knowledge, editors feel justified in

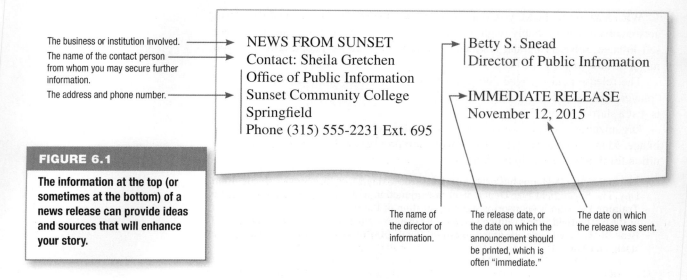

The business or institution involved. ⟶

The name of the contact person from whom you may secure further information. ⟶

The address and phone number. ⟶

NEWS FROM SUNSET
Contact: Sheila Gretchen
Office of Public Information
Sunset Community College
Springfield
Phone (315) 555-2231 Ext. 695

Betty S. Snead
Director of Public Infromation

IMMEDIATE RELEASE
November 12, 2015

The name of the director of information.

The release date, or the date on which the announcement should be printed, which is often "immediate."

The date on which the release was sent.

FIGURE 6.1

The information at the top (or sometimes at the bottom) of a news release can provide ideas and sources that will enhance your story.

releasing whatever information it contains, even prior to the suggested release date. A release date is broken for all when it is broken by one.

Using an Announcement Release

Sometimes directors of information want nothing more than a listing on the record or calendar page of a newspaper or news site. Here is an example of an announcement release:

> FOR THE CALENDAR
> Elisabeth Bertke, quiltmaker and designer from Salem, Massachusetts, will discuss her work at 7:00 o'clock P.M. Tues., February 7, in Charters Auditorium, Hampton College. Two quilts designed and constructed by Bertke are included in the exhibit "The New American Quilt," currently on display at the Smith Art Gallery.
> "This is an exciting display," Betty Martin, president of the Smith Art Gallery board of directors, said. "You simply can't afford to miss it."

This simple release might go directly to the news desk or to a special calendar editor.

If it is given to you, rewrite it. Some news organizations insist that you rewrite every news release if for no other reason than to avoid the embarrassment of running the same story as a competing news outlet. For some, it is a matter of integrity and professionalism.

After reading carefully through the release, check all the facts. Confirm the spelling of Bertke's name, and see if there is an apostrophe in "Charters Auditorium." The Smith Gallery might or might not be on the Hampton campus.

Next, if time allows, do some additional reporting. Call the gallery to ask how long the exhibit will be there. Are quilts made by local people included in the exhibit? Perhaps your questions will lead to a feature story on local quilting.

Then do your rewrite. Drop Martin's quotation: It is self-serving and promotional. But you might call Martin, Bertke or someone else connected to the event to try for a better quote. Reread your story to make sure the lead works and the writing is tight and clear.

Finally, correct any violations of AP style. In the preceding example:

- A hyphen should be inserted in "quilt-maker."
- "7:00 o'clock P.M." should be "7 p.m."
- "Tues." should be spelled out "Tuesday."
- "February" should be abbreviated "Feb."

Avoid relying on the copy desk to do your work if the rewrite is given to you.

Here is another example of an announcement release:

> Mr. Richard G. Hernandez has been selected as the Outstanding Biology Teacher of the Year by the National Association of Biology Teachers. He was previously selected as Nevada Science Educator of the Year.
>
> As an outstanding representative of good high-school biology teaching Hernandez will receive a certificate and a series 50 binocular microscope with an engraved citation. Hernandez has been teaching at Hickman High School since 1980.

The story is far from earthshaking, but the honor is statewide. In large markets the release might not get much **play**—that is, it might not be prominently displayed. Smaller markets, however, will use it and perhaps enlarge upon it.

A first reading of the release tells you that it is wordy and leaves many questions unanswered. Hernandez might be an interesting fellow, but the release tells us little about him. You should approach this release in the same way you approach any news release: Finish the reporting, and then rewrite it. News style demands a new lead to the release:

> A Hickman High School science teacher has been named Outstanding Biology Teacher of the Year by the National Association of Biology Teachers.
>
> Richard G. Hernandez, a Hickman teacher since 1980, will receive a certificate and a series 50 binocular microscope with an engraved citation.
>
> Previously selected as Nevada Science Educator of the Year, Hernandez . . .

There the story runs out of information. You need to ask the following questions:

- Age?
- Degrees from where?
- Local address?
- Spouse? Family?
- Annual award? One teacher selected from each state?
- Any previous Hickman winners? Any from other local high schools?
- Year he received Nevada Science Educator award?
- Nominated for the award by whom?
- Date and place of bestowal? Public ceremony?
- Value of series 50 binocular microscope?

Then call Hernandez, and find out how he feels about the award. Talk to the principal, to fellow teachers and to some of Hernandez's students. Good quotations will spice up your story. The length of the story will ultimately depend on how much space your editor wishes to give it.

Using a Cause-Promoting Release

News media generally cooperate with causes that are community-oriented. News releases like the following get attention, and well they should. This one comes from the giant soap maker, Cincinnati-based Procter & Gamble. Among its best-selling detergents are Tide and Gain. In February 2012, Tide became the first detergent to come out in pod form. Gain and other soaps followed Tide's example quickly; none thought of a possible danger to young children.

Emerging Health Risk: Every Day More Than 30 Children Get into Liquid Laundry Packets
Simple precautions can prevent serious harm
Wednesday, June 24, 2015 6:03 am EDT
Dateline: WASHINGTON
Public Company Information: NYSE: PG

WASHINGTON (BUSINESS WIRE) – With liquid laundry packets gaining in popularity, now used by 20 percent of U.S. households, parents need to be aware of this emerging risk for children. Between 2012 and 2013, more than 700 children 5 and under experienced serious effects as a result of liquid laundry packets, with the impact greatest among 1- and 2-year-olds. In fact, the poison centers received more than 33,000 calls from 2012 through May 2015.

Safe Kids Worldwide, and Tide and Gain, have teamed up to teach parents about keeping kids safe around liquid laundry packets.

"Young children are explorers, and as they develop, often learn by touch and by putting things into their mouths," said Kate Carr, president and CEO of Safe Kids Worldwide. "With the increasing popularity of liquid laundry packets, it's especially important to make parents aware of the importance of keeping them out of the reach and hands of children."

These packets are a concentrated, single-dose product designed to dissolve in water, so when they come in contact with wet hands or mouths, they start to dissolve and might release the concentrated liquid inside.

If children get into laundry packets, the health risk can be significant. According to the U.S. Consumer Product Safety Commission, children can experience loss of consciousness, difficulty breathing, excessive vomiting, severe eye burns, and temporary vision loss.

"Fortunately, the solution to protect children in the home against potential poisoning is simple," said Carr. "It's making sure that families and caregivers know what to do to ensure a serious incident doesn't happen in the home, and what to do if help is needed."

To prevent poisoning, Safe Kids, and Tide and Gain, offer simple tips to keep children safe:

- Keep liquid laundry packets out of children's reach and sight.
- Keep packets in their original container and keep the container closed.
- If a child gets into them, call the Poison Help number immediately, 1-800-222-1222.

"At P&G, safety is our number one priority," said Shailesh Jejurikar, P&G's North America Fabric Care and New Business Development President. "Most of us are parents too, and we want families to use our products safely. Our Up, Up, and Away campaign and our partnership with Safe Kids Worldwide will support families with information and tools to create safe home environments. We deeply respect and admire the work that Safe Kids Worldwide does in helping reduce the amount of preventable injuries and know that they will be great partners in equipping families with laundry safety information and tools."

The release prompts a host of questions for the reporter. You note that this 2015 release is written as if it is reporting on the first time Procter & Gamble has dealt with this important subject on its website. You try to verify this with P&G, but you find no one who can or will give you a confirmation.

You might check "soap pods" in *Consumer Reports*. There you would find that the consumer magazine first warned about soap pods in May 2012, three years before the release on the P&G website. The highly concentrated detergent in the pods is more dangerous than regular detergent; it can cause vomiting, breathing problems and even death.

In October 2012, the Centers for Disease Control and Prevention reported cases from various poison centers around the country dealing with exposures to laundry detergent pods, and *Consumer Reports* again reported on the issue, saying that the CDC called exposure to the pods "an emerging public health hazard."

In March 2013, the Consumer Product Safety Commission issued a safety alert. About the same time, a *Consumer Reports* story credited P&G with planning the design of a new triple latch and an opaque container that hid the appealing brightly colored pods inside. However, it called on the industry to do much more.

Additional research shows you that *The New York Times* did a story on the pods on June 27, 2012, and again on Nov. 10, 2014, both before the P&G release. The November story ends grimly with the story of a 16-month-old boy who died from ingestion of a pod. His parents had the emptied packet with his teeth marks on it.

Though no one can say that the P&G news release was the cause, after it appeared, you find that all the networks (CBS, NBC, ABC and CNN) covered the issue as did *USA Today*, the *Orlando Sentinel*, the *New York Daily News*, the *Palm Beach Post*, the *Globe and Mail* and many others.

The American Association of Poison Control Centers website tells you that through June 30, 2015, poison centers received reports of 6,046 exposures "to highly concentrated packets of laundry detergent by children 5 and younger." The site explains that "exposure" means contact in some way. It also says that people should contact a poison center immediately if a child has had any exposure to a soap packet.

A June 23, 2015, *USA Today* headline reads: "More Child Poisonings Prompt New Liquid Laundry Pod Warnings." The newspaper contacted Kate Carr, the president and CEO of Safe Kids Worldwide, referred to in the P&G release. NBC's *Today* show ran a story about the danger of pods and why children were so attracted to them.

The P&G website the following week, June 30, 2015, reports that the company has added a bitter taste to the outer layer of its Tide, Gain and Ariel pods. It also spoke of more secure and opaque closures and a TV, print and digital advertising campaign about safe storage and usage. The site claims a 28 percent drop in pod accidents with children.

Now with all this background, you are ready for some local reporting.

Have children in the community experienced these serious effects from liquid laundry packets? A check on the local hospitals and clinics would be a good first step.

Then perhaps you can find a child's parents who will talk about their child's horrible experience. You can also ask parents how they protect their children from getting into the soap-pod bin.

The P&G release notes that 12,000 of the 2,200,000 calls to U.S. Poison Control Centers every year are related to laundry packets. So you could call the closest poison center and ask if there have been any cases of pod-soap poisoning in the local area.

Of course, other soap companies make pods. Which are they? You could try calling one or two and asking the public information person whether the company has had any lawsuits or serious complaints about the small packets.

Now you can develop a major story from a news release.

Using an Image-Building News Feature

In March 2015, Merck published on its website another profile in its "Featured Stories" collection. The story, shown below, is typical of image-building news features and puts an engaging human face on the company.

EMPLOYEE PROFILE
Name: Ayesha Sitlani
Title: Executive Director, Bioanalytical Development and Vaccines Clinical Access
Education: B.A., Smith College; M.A., Columbia University; Ph.D., California Institute of Technology
Favorite Downtime Activity: Watching "Downton Abbey"

Early on in her career, after completing her postdoctoral fellowship at Yale as a Jane Coffin Childs Fellow in Biophysical Chemistry, Ayesha had to make a choice: Continue in the world of academics or look elsewhere.

Merck & Co., Inc., Kenilworth USA

"I interviewed at Merck thinking, "Would I really like to be here? And I was just blown away by the company's mission," she remembers. "We're here to find medicines for people. I get to apply the basic research that I have spent so many years doing to such a good cause. I try to solve some of the unmet medical needs out there. It's just an amazing, amazing opportunity."

In her 16 years at Merck, Ayesha has made an impact—as a scientist and as a leader.

"For a drug to make it, it involves people from many different strengths and experiences to come together and work as a team," she says. "You can't do it on your own. You shouldn't think you can do it on your own. It takes true collaboration between people, trying to find the best out of everyone, because drug discovery and development is really hard and truly takes a team to act as the champion."

As for the future, Ayesha wants to continue focusing her energy on those medicines that will help people the most. "Discovering new things and using that discovery to help people inspires me," she says. "I look around and see there is so much need. There are people who are dying at very young ages, at older ages, and families suffer as a result. At Merck, there's an opportunity for scientists to help change that. To use their hearts and minds to come up with solutions. That is what motivates me to come to work every morning."

This profile on the Merck website fulfills two purposes: First, it introduces us to one of Merck's brilliant veteran scientists, and by telling us what she does, tells a lot about the aims, purposes and work of the company. Second, in building the scientist's image, it also substantiates the image of the company for which she works.

Nevertheless, the profile is vague and full of generalities. It says that Sitlani has made an "impact." How? What has she done? Could she elaborate on why "drug discovery is really hard and truly takes a team"? She says that people are dying at "young ages, at older ages." What does she mean by that? Is this really something new?

Ayesha Sitlani sounds like a good person for a story. You could ask her the above questions after finding out more about her: her country of origin, her marital status, and her college studies, for example.

Using a News Release as a Starting Point—An Example

Sometimes a news release can lead to an interesting story with broad implications for the community, even if the actual release is self-serving—or misleading. Suppose you were given the following news release.

NEWS RELEASE
Springfield Community Teachers Association
Lillian A. Briggs, President
Contact: Tom Monnin, SCTA Salary Committee Chairman
Phone: 555-555-6794 (Central High School)
        555-555-2975 (home)

For Immediate Release

SPRINGFIELD—Police officers and firefighters in Springfield earn a greater starting salary than Springfield teachers, as discovered in a recent survey by the Springfield Community Teachers Association. According to their research, a new teacher in the Springfield public school system makes $40,000, while a firefighter starts at $40,725, $725 more than a new teacher. "This is a shameful situation for an educational community," said Tom Monnin, SCTA Salary Committee chairman.

The statistics gathered by the SCTA Salary Committee indicate that police officers with a bachelor's degree make $42,758. A dogcatcher with no college education earns just $6,536 less a year than a beginning teacher. Following is a comparison of starting salaries of some Springfield city employees and of public school teachers for the school year:

Occupation	Starting Salary
Police officer with bachelor's degree	$42,758
Firefighter with bachelor's degree	40,725
Meter reader	32,402
Animal control officer	33,464
Bus operator	32,402
Teacher with bachelor's degree	40,000

"Springfield teachers do not think city employees are overpaid but that teachers are underpaid," Monnin said.

Even though teachers work under a 9¼-month contract, the workweek is not 40 hours. When the hours for preparing and grading, attending sports events, musical concerts, dances, other after-school activities and PTA meetings are considered, a teacher's workweek is much longer than 40 hours. Summer break is used by many teachers for advanced preparation at the university, at their own expense.

The SCTA Salary Committee will present the salary proposal at the next meeting of the Springfield Board of Education.

The SCTA represents approximately 523 members in the public school system.

Read the News Release Carefully

Your first task is to read the release, including the information at the top of the form, closely a couple of times, making notes in the margin about items that stand out for you. For example, the second paragraph cleverly suggests that dogcatchers make nearly as much money as teachers do, but you notice it speaks only of starting salaries. The more you read the release, the more uncomfortable you start to feel with it. No one can blame teachers for wanting more money, but there are other factors to consider.

Check for Accuracy and Fairness

You should ask yourself what information is missing and what other viewpoints need to be considered. For example, you might wonder, What about working conditions? Teachers in Springfield's schools certainly don't have to put their lives on the line the way police officers and firefighters do. And most people do not want to spend their lives chasing stray dogs.

Take special care when news releases cite studies, polls or surveys. Check the source of the figures for accuracy and possible bias. If you can't confirm the figures and their reliability, don't use them.

The fact that teachers work for a little more than nine months a year is down in the fourth paragraph. The release fails to mention a two-week break over Christmas and a week off in the spring semester. Most police officers and firefighters get two weeks off per year.

Is the release trying to suggest that because teachers actually spend more than 40 hours a week working, they should not have to work more than 9 1/4 months? Not all teachers spend their summers going to school. You probably know several who have summer jobs or who take long vacations.

Do Additional Research and Interviews

Before you turn in a rewrite of this release, you have a lot of checking to do. But you also decide to go beyond checking to do some of your own reporting.

You begin by calling the city of Springfield's personnel office. The person answering the phone refers you to the department's website. Here you can gather all of the salary information you need, but you still have some questions. You call the personnel office again. When asked about the $40,725 starting salary of a firefighter, the personnel officer replies: "You wouldn't begin at that salary. Everyone is hired at

$39,225 for a trial period of at least six months. If you work out OK, you might jump up to $40,725. Again, there are a lot of considerations besides the college degree."

Now you know you are on to something. Comparing starting salaries is one thing. But how much can a person eventually earn in a position?

You then ask about the starting salary for a police officer. "Yes," the director of personnel says, "$42,758 is the beginning salary for a police officer with a B.S. degree."

You then ask whether anyone with a B.S. degree can get hired at that salary.

"Most people wouldn't stand a chance of being hired," he says. "We have more than 100 applicants for every position, so we can be quite choosy. Unless a person has had some real experience as a police officer, I don't think he or she would make it."

Further questioning reveals that a top salary for a police officer is $54,712 after six years of service.

You also find the website of the Springfield public school system and check its salary schedule for teachers. Then you call a high school teacher. You ask her if she has to put in more than 40 hours a week at her job.

"Oh, yes," she says. "I teach a section of English composition, and I have a lot of papers to grade. I used to spend a lot of evenings preparing for classes, but once you've taught a course, it gets easier. And then I have to go to all those football games and basketball games."

You discover that she is indeed required to attend the games, but only because she is in charge of the cheerleaders. When you express sympathy, the teacher replies, "No, I really don't mind. After all, I get $3,500 a year extra for being in charge of the cheerleaders."

You then learn from someone at the Springfield schools' personnel office that quite a few teachers receive compensation for after-school activities—coaching, directing plays and musical activities, advising the staffs of the school newspaper and senior yearbook, and chaperoning dances. Teachers sponsoring class and club activities can earn from $1,000 to $4,000; a sponsor of the pep squad can earn up to $2,300. The top teacher's salary without any of these extras is $67,214.

You note that top pay for a city dogcatcher is $37,626, so you think it might be interesting to interview one. You find Luis Gonzalez, an animal control officer. It doesn't take much prodding to get Gonzalez to talk. "I sure wish I got summers off like those teachers," he says. "I got nothing against teachers. But most of them make more money than I'll ever make. . . . Besides, students don't bite many teachers."

Get Back to the News Release Contact with Questions

Now you are ready to call Tom Monnin, the man whose name is on the release, for additional information. Here's how your interview might go.

Q: Is it fair to compare a new teacher's salary with a new police officer's salary when the top pay for a police officer is $54,712 and the top teacher's salary is $67,214?

A: Well, it takes 17 years for a teacher with a master's degree plus 75 hours of continuing education classes to reach that top salary. A teacher with a bachelor's degree can make $54,219 after 11 years of teaching

ANNOTATED MODEL   Integrating News Release Information

The Springfield Community Teachers Association said Tuesday that new ← Lead gives SCTA claim.
police officers can earn over $2,000 more than new teachers.

Info from research adds → What the teachers did not say was that a teacher eventually can earn
a differing point of view. $12,502 more a year than a police officer can.

The SCTA statement was included with a survey that lists starting teach- ← Incorrect info about
ers' salaries at $40,000. Other figures listed as starting salaries are these: firefighters' starting
police officer with a bachelor's degree, $42,758; animal control officer, salary is omitted.
$33,464; meter reader, $32,402; bus operator, $32,402.

Quotes from news → "This is a shameful situation for an educational community," said Tom
release give teachers' Monnin, the SCTA Salary Committee chairman. "Springfield teachers do
point of view. not think city employees are overpaid but that teachers are underpaid."

The association officers said that even though teachers work under ← Info from the release
a nine-month contract, extracurricular activities extend the workweek is paraphrased
beyond 40 hours. Summer break, they said, is used for advanced study at and attributed to
the teachers' own expense. association officers.

Source of quote from → "I figure I work a 60-hour week," Monnin said in an interview. "That
interview is included. means I work 51 weeks of 40 hours each a year."

Some extracurricular activities, such as coaching, directing plays and ← Common knowledge
supervising cheerleaders, earn extra compensation. is confirmed by two
sources.

Quote clarifies info in → Teachers are not compelled to attend after-school functions, but "we do
earlier paragraphs. feel the responsibility to attend," Monnin said.

Teachers also feel compelled to continue their education. Top pay for a ← Facts verified by
teacher with only a bachelor's degree is $54,219 after 11 years of teaching. government sources
A teacher with a master's degree plus 75 hours of classes can earn $67,214 are common
after 17 years of teaching. knowledge.

A police officer with a bachelor's degree can reach a top salary of
$54,712 after six years of police work. But a person with a bachelor's
Paraphrased opinion is → degree and no police work experience is not likely to be hired, said Phil
attributed to source. James, the Springfield director of personnel. James also said all firefighters
are hired at $39,225. If a person has a bachelor's degree and stays on, he or
she could make $40,725 after a six-month trial period.

Top pay for a dogcatcher is $37,626. "I sure wish I got summers off ← Quote adds color to the
like those teachers," Luis Gonzalez, an animal control officer, said. "I got story.
nothing against teachers. But most of them make more money than I'll ever
make. . . . Besides, students don't bite many teachers."

The "so what" appears → The SCTA Salary Committee will present its salary proposal at the next
at the end. meeting of the Springfield Board of Education.

Journalists can do their own research to build a story prompted by a news release.

Q: What about summers off and other vacations?

A: I figure I work a 60-hour week. That means I work 51 weeks of 40 hours each year.

Q: Aren't teachers paid extra for after-school activities?

A: Many are paid. But not all of them are, and there are many activities we do feel the responsibility to attend.

Q: Teachers don't have to put their lives on the line the way police and fire officials and even dogcatchers do. Isn't that a factor?

A: It's debatable who has to put their lives on the line. We're not as bad off as some schools, but we often have to restrain students physically. We read about school shootings all of the time, and we can't help but wonder whether that could happen here.

Write the Story

You've checked for accuracy, found out the important facts, and taken all the viewpoints into account. Only now are you ready to write the story. Write a lead that communicates the news, make sure your writing is tight, and check for AP style.

The annotated model "Integrating News Release Information" on page 124 shows one possible story resulting from the news release. This story does with a news release what you should do with many of them. You should not be satisfied with the way a news release is written or with the information it contains. By asking some important questions, you can often put together an informative and more accurate story. Without saying that the news release was dishonest or misleading, a good reporter can correct or clarify some of the information it contains. Here, the plight of the teacher is told clearly and objectively, but it is placed in a much better perspective than that of the news release.

Like many news releases, this one was the basis for a story the news outlet otherwise would not have had. That is why editors pay attention to news releases and why reporters look for the real story.

SUGGESTED READINGS

Bivins, Thomas H. *Public Relations Writing: The Essentials of Style and Format.* 8th ed. Lincolnwood, Ill.: NTC/Contemporary Publishing Group, 2013. This book explains how public relations professionals approach a wide variety of writing tasks.

Howard, Carole, and Wilma Mathews. *On Deadline: Managing Media Relations.* 5th ed. Prospect Heights, Ill.: Waveland Press, 2013. This practical book offers suggestions on how organizations should deal with the news media.

Wilcox, Dennis L., and Lawrence W. Nolte. *Public Relations Writing and Media Techniques.* 7th ed. New York: HarperCollins, 2013. The authors cover the writing, production and distribution of a variety of public relations materials. The book has real-world examples and tells how to distribute them through traditional and social media.

SUGGESTED WEBSITES

www.odwyerpr.com

This is the website of the hard-hitting *O'Dwyer's*. It does a thorough job doing what it says it does, getting "Inside News of Public Relations and Marketing Communications."

www.pressflash.com/resources_anatomy.php

On this website for a news release distribution service, you will find a terse description of a good news release.

http://press-release-writing.com/10-essential-tips -for-writing-press-releases

These 10 essential tips for writing news releases demonstrate how serious professionals approach this type of writing.

http://prwatch.org

This website is run by the nonprofit Center for Media and Democracy. According to the website, the CMD "is a national watchdog group that conducts in-depth investigatoins into corruption and the undue influence of corporation on media and democracy."

EXERCISES

1. Read the following release. Then interview people in three households, and ask these questions:

   a. When did you last change the batteries in your smoke alarms and carbon monoxide detectors?

   b. Do you test your alarms on a regular day or time each year?

   c. Do you replace them every 10 years?

   d. Do you and those you live with have an evacuation plan in case of a fire?

   Write your story.

   SPRINGFIELD FIRE DEPARTMENT
   News Release
   For Immediate Release
   Reminder: Change Smoke Alarm Batteries and Clocks

   The Springfield Fire Department is reminding residents to change the batteries in their smoke alarms and carbon monoxide detectors when they turn their clocks back this weekend.

   Working smoke alarms cut in half the risk of dying in a home fire, yet Springfield Fire Department data shows less than half of Springfield homes have a working smoke alarm. Worn or missing batteries are the most common cause of a smoke alarm or carbon monoxide detector malfunction. Changing the batteries is one of the simplest, most effective ways to prevent tragic deaths and injuries.

   In addition to changing the batteries, smoke alarms should be tested monthly and replaced at least every 10 years.

   This weekend also serves as an ideal time for families to review their home evacuation plans. All family members should plan two ways to escape from each room and practice escape routes with the entire family at least twice a year.

   For information on how you can receive a free smoke alarm, call the Springfield Fire Department at 555-1500.

   Media Only: For more information, contact: Fire and Life Safety Educator Cara Restelli Erwin.

2. Read each of the following news releases. First, indicate the type of news release it is. Second, list questions you would have if you were to rewrite it, including the facts you would check and the sources you would turn to for the answers. Third, suggest ideas for visuals or videos that would accompany a web story. Finally, correct all departures from Associated Press style rules.

   a. NEWS RELEASE
       For Further Information, Contact:
       Humane Society of Missouri Media Center
       314-802-5712

   Humane Society of Missouri Confirms: Guilty Pleas Entered in Federal Court to Charges from Largest Dog Fighting Raid and Rescue in U.S. History
   Photos and Video of Dogs at Rescue Sites and Emergency Shelter Now Available

   ST. LOUIS, Mo., September 14, 2015 – The Humane Society of Missouri today confirms guilty pleas have been entered in connection to the July 8, 2015 multi-state federal dog fighting raid that resulted in the rescue of more than 500 fighting dogs. Federal agents made 26 arrests and dogs were rescued in 8 states.

   This rescue operation is the largest dog fighting raid in U.S. history. The Humane Society of Missouri participated in the 18-month investigation and led the subsequent rescue and shelter operations, working in partnership with the Federal

Bureau of Investigation, the Missouri State Highway Patrol, the United States Department of Agriculture's Office of the Inspector General, the U.S. Marshals Service and the United States Attorney.

Four eastern Missouri men, Robert Hackman of Foley, Teddy Kiriakidis of Leasburg, Ronald Creech of Leslie and Michael Morgan of Hannibal pled guilty today in U.S. District Court in St. Louis to charges connected to the dog fighting raid. Another man arrested in connection with the dog fighting raid, Jack Ruppel of Eldon, pled guilty to charges on September 4 in federal court in Jefferson City.

"We can confirm that five of the individuals charged with this gruesome form of animal abuse are being brought to justice," said Kathy Warnick, president of the Humane Society of Missouri. "Today's guilty pleas raise awareness that dog fighting is unacceptable, inhumane and illegal and will not be tolerated. The unprecedented scale of this investigation and rescue operation should alert the entire nation to what a horrible crime dog fighting is and what a dangerous and serious affect it can have on animals and communities.

Warnick continued, "We sincerely hope these guilty pleas will result in sentencing that sends the message that this form of animal abuse will no longer be tolerated. Humane Society of Missouri staff and our many partners have selflessly sacrificed much of their personal lives in the pursuit of this investigation and the care of these dogs. We fervently desire that this historic effort marks the beginning of the end to dog fighting in the United States."

"This was the largest dog fighting raid in U.S. history, but it will not be the last," warned Michael Kaste, Assistant Special Agent in Charge of the FBI in St. Louis. "This case sets precedents for the FBI along with our local, state and federal partners to aggressively root out underground dog fighting rings where people have absolutely no qualms about torturing man's best friend for money and entertainment."

b. NEWS RELEASE
Concussion Assessment Tool Wins Notre Dame Business Plan Competition
By University Alliance on June 18, 2013

Speech-based technology that can help diagnose concussions was named the grand prize winner in the University of Notre Dame's 13th annual McCloskey Business Plan Competition.

The Contect technology was selected from among six finalists for the $25,000 prize. Its developers, Patrick Flynn and Christian Poellabauer, are members of the university's computer science faculty.

Contect analyzes an individual's voice for evidence of concussion or traumatic brain injury, such as indistinct consonants and distorted vowels. The assessment can be administered via tablet.

The technology, which was tested on participants in student boxing tournaments, is seen as having particular poten-

tial in diagnosing concussions among athletes and military personnel. Flynn and Poellabauer estimate that about 90% of concussions are undetected.

According to the Centers for Disease Control and Prevention, traumatic brain injuries (TBI) account for up to 3.8 million sports injuries annually, with about 300,000 diagnosed in young, nonprofessional athletes.

Additionally, a study published in the medical journal JAMA Psychiatry in May 2013 found that military personnel who had suffered multiple TBIs were at greater risk for committing suicide.

Brain injuries can produce numerous symptoms, including memory loss, diminished cognitive functioning, headaches and depression. Diagnosing such injuries has typically required the use of MRIs, X-rays or CT scans. The Contect technology offers greater portability and lower costs compared with more traditional diagnostic tools.

"This project is a great example of how mobile computing and sensing technologies can transform healthcare," Poellabauer told Notre Dame News in March 2013.

3. Assume you are a reporter for the Springfield paper. Rewrite the following release as a news story. Your instructor will be your news source for any questions you have.

NEWS RELEASE
Nearly 11,000 seat belt violation warnings were issued to motorists by the State Highway Patrol during the first month the new seat belt law was in effect.

Colonel Howard J. Hoffman, Superintendent of the State Highway Patrol, reported today that 10,908 warnings were issued to motorists in passenger vehicles for not wearing their seat belts as required by State Law.

Colonel Hoffman also noted that during this same reporting period, 50 persons were killed in traffic accidents investigated by the Highway Patrol. Only two of the persons killed in these mishaps were found to be wearing seat belts.

"The value of wearing a seat belt cannot be overemphasized," Hoffman said. "We don't know how many of these investigated traffic deaths could have been avoided by the use of seat belts. It is known, however, that seat belts have saved lives and prevented serious injuries to others. We will continue to vigorously enforce the State seat belt law and hopefully more and more motorists will make it a habit to buckle their seat belts."

4. Assume you are the editor of a news website. Write an email to the staff explaining why you read every news release.

5. **Your journalism blog.** Explain in a blog to a nonjournalism student the clear difference between a news story and a news release. Send a tweet to your classmates asking them to read your blog and comment.

OUR NATIONAL DEBT:
14,398,865,774,588.
YOUR *Family share* 121,951

THE NATIONAL DEBT CLOCK

Numbers surround us. They inform us, explain things and sometimes confuse us. As a journalist whose job it is to inform and not confuse, you need to understand how to use numbers. You need to understand those numbers whether you are reporting on your local school board's spending or on the national debt.

Tyler Dukes, an investigative reporter at WRAL News in Raleigh, North Carolina, had read dozens of news releases from the governor's office announcing new jobs. Like other states, North Carolina offered companies financial incentives to locate there. Dukes wondered whether these jobs actually got created.

Dukes went through more than 200 news releases to record the number of jobs that were promised, the wages to be paid and the value of the incentives. All that information went into a spreadsheet he created. He calculated the number of jobs actually created.

Starting from that data, the WRAL reporters were able to report on television and in more detail on the station's website that only 38 percent of the promised jobs had been created. The investigation also found that the wealthiest counties benefited from the grants and that the poorest counties, which needed new jobs the most, were left behind.

These numbers were the foundation for this and other stories that journalists gather. This chapter covers the basics that will help you deal with numbers correctly in daily stories.

Proportion

One of the most important services journalists perform for their readers is to give **proportion** to numbers in the news—explaining things relative to the size or the magnitude of the whole. A municipal budget that is going up by $500,000 would be a windfall for a small town in New Hampshire but a minor adjustment for a metropolis such as New York, Chicago or Minneapolis. For example, Louisiana had to deal with a $1.6 billion deficit in order to balance its budget in 2015.

Other figures might mean a lot or a little, depending on the context. If you know little or nothing about baseball, you might think that Babe Ruth's career batting average of .342—34.2 hits for every 100 times at bat—indicates that Ruth wasn't a good hitter. After all, he failed almost two out of three times at bat. But when you look at the context—other players' averages—you realize that Ruth was exceptional. For instance, in the 2014 regular season, no major league player had a higher average than Ruth's career average.

Percentages and Percentage Change

Percentages are basic building blocks used to explain proportion. Batting averages explain the number of hits compared with the number of times at bat. The political strength of a public official is partly reflected in the percentage

To Calculate a Percentage

- Portion ÷ whole = .xxx.
- Move decimal point two places to the right: .xxx = xx.x percent.

of votes won at the polls. Stories about budgets, taxes, wages, retail sales, schools, health care and the environment all are explained with percentages.

To calculate a percentage, take the portion that you want to measure, divide it by the whole and then move the decimal two places to the right. For example, suppose you want to know what portion of the city's budget is allocated to police services. Divide the police budget by the city budget, move the decimal point two places to the right, and you get the percentage of the budget that pays for police services.

To calculate a percentage:

Step 1   Portion (police budget) ÷ whole (city budget) = .xxx
$30,000,000 ÷ $120,000,000 = .25

Step 2   Move the decimal point two places to the right: 25%

Precision in the use of numbers requires that you ask some basic questions. Reporters need to be careful of percentages that might be misleading or that tell only part of a story.

Populations, Samples and Margins of Error

If someone is giving you percentages, you must ask what **population** the figures are based on. For instance, suppose a juvenile officer tells you that 70 percent of the juvenile offenders do not have to return to his program. Your first question should be, "What population was used to figure the percentage?" Was it all the juveniles in the program during the last calendar year? If so, perhaps the success rate is high because the period being measured isn't long enough to take less successful years into account. And how has your source counted juveniles who are old enough now to be certified as adults? How does he account for juveniles who may have committed a crime in another jurisdiction?

The officer might explain that the figure is based on a sample of the population in the program over 10 years. A **sample** is a small number of people picked at random to represent the population as a whole. Using common statistical tables, researchers draw a sample of the names of all juveniles who were in the program over 10 years and contact them. From those contacts, they can determine the success rate of the program. If the figure is based on a scientific sampling like the one just described, there will also be a **margin of error**, which will be expressed as "plus or minus x points." Say that the margin of error for this sample is 4 percentage points. That means that the success rate for the juvenile offender program is between 66 and 74 percent.

The base on which a percentage is calculated is significant. Say a colleague is making $40,000, and you make $30,000. The salary is the base. Your employer decides to give your colleague a 4 percent increase and to give you a 5 percent increase. Before you begin feeling too good about your raise, consider that your colleague's raise is $1,600, and yours is $1,500. Your colleague won a bigger raise, and the gap between the two of you grew. Hence, if you have different bases on which to figure the percentages, the comparisons are invalid.

In one investigative report, the *St. Louis Post-Dispatch* recognized it had percentages with different bases, and it handled them correctly. The newspaper examined repeat drunken-driving offenders in seven jurisdictions in its circulation area. In Missouri, drivers convicted two times of driving while intoxicated are supposed to be charged with a felony on the third offense. In reporting on the results, the reporters carefully gave the percentages and the base for each jurisdiction. That was important because the base ranged from seven cases in the city of St. Louis to 120 in St. Louis County. The percentages of cases handled correctly ranged from 29 to 51 percent.

Percentage Change and Percentage Points

Confusion often occurs when people talk about the difference between two percentage figures. For example, say the mayor won the election with 55 percent of the vote and had only one opponent, who received 45 percent. The mayor won by a margin of 10 **percentage points**. The percentage points, in this case, equal the difference between 55 and 45. However, the mayor won 22 percent more votes (10 divided by 45 equals .22, or 22 percent). Because the 55 and 45 percentages are based on the same whole number—in this case, the total number of votes cast—the percentages can be compared. But if you compare the percentage of a city budget devoted to law enforcement in consecutive years, you will need to include the actual dollar amounts with the percentages because total spending probably changed from one year to the next.

Another important aspect of percentages is the concept of **percentage change**. This number explains how much something goes up or down. In the city budget summary shown in Figure 7.1 (page 140–141), for example, look under "Appropriations" and then under "Revised Fiscal Year 2015." Total spending in 2015 was $18,654,563. The proposed budget for 2016 ("Adopted Fiscal Year 2016") is $19,570,518. What is the percentage increase? You find a percentage change by dividing the increase or decrease by the old budget.

To calculate a percentage change:

Step 1   Find the change.
$19,570,518 − $18,654,563 = $915,955 (increase)

Step 2   Change ÷ base amount = .xxx
$915,955 ÷ $18,654,563 = .049

Step 3   Move the decimal point two places to the right: 4.9 percent

Rounded off, this is a 5 percent increase in spending.

If the 2016 budget is increased 4.9 percent again in the following year, that will be a $958,955 increase, or $43,000 more, because of the bigger base.

When changes are large, sometimes it is better to translate the numbers into plain words rather than using a percentage figure. That $1.6 billion deficit in Louisiana amounted to $344 for every person living there.

GRAMMAR CHECK

What's the grammar error in this sentence?

The Alaskan peak known as Mount McKinley was officially restored to it's original Koyukon name, Denali.

See Appendix 1, Rule 12.

TIPS

To Calculate Percentage Change

- (New number) – (old number) = change.
- Change ÷ old number = .xxx.
- Move decimal point two places to right: .xxx = xx.x percent.
- Percentage change can be a positive or a negative number.

Averages and Medians

Averages and medians are numbers that can be used to describe a general trend. For any given set of numbers, the average and the median might be quite close, or they might be quite different. Depending on what you are trying to explain, it might be important to use one instead of the other or to use both.

The **average**—more technically called the *arithmetic mean*—is the number you obtain when you add a list of figures and then divide the total by the number of figures in the list. The **median** is the midpoint of the list—half the figures fall above it, and half the figures fall below it.

To calculate an average:

Step 1   Add the figures.

Step 2   Divide the total by the number of figures:
Total ÷ number of figures = average

To find the median:

Step 1   Arrange the figures in rank order.

Step 2   Identify the figure midway between the highest and lowest numbers. That figure is the median.

Note: When you have an even number of figures, the median is the average of the two middle figures.

As a general rule, you are safe using averages when there are no large gaps among the numbers. If you took an average of 1, 4, 12, 22, 31, 89 and 104, you would get 37.6. The average distorts the numbers because the average is higher than five of the seven numbers. The mean, or midpoint, is 22. On the other hand, if you had numbers ranging from 1 to 104 and the numbers were distributed evenly within that range, the average would be an accurate reading.

"Average" Can Mean Different Things to Different People

Although most people understand "average" to refer to "arithmetic mean," the word is sometimes used for other types of statistical results, including "median" and "mode."

In reporting statistics, be certain you know the "average" involved. All of the following are averages.

- **Mean.** The arithmetic average, found by adding all the figures in a set of data and dividing by the number of figures. The mean of 2, 4 and 9 is 5 (2 + 4 + 9 = 15; 15 ÷ 3 = 5).

- **Median.** The middle value in a set of figures. If there is no middle value because there is an even number of figures, average the two middle numbers. The median of 2, 4 and 9 is 4. The medians of 5, 7, 9 and 11 and of 3, 7, 9 and 15 both are 8 (7 + 9 = 16; 16 ÷ 2 = 8).

- **Mode.** The most frequent value in a set of figures. The mode of 2, 5, 5, 5, 15 and 23 is 5.

When Averages Distort

Take a set of scores from a final exam in a class of 16 students. The students scored 95, 94, 92, 86, 85, 84, 75, 75, 65, 64, 63, 62, 62, 62 and 62. Both the average (that is, the arithmetic mean) and the median are 75.

The picture can look quite different when the figures bunch at one end of the scale. Consider this example from professional baseball: In 2015 the Washington Nationals had a payroll of $163 million. With a range of salaries from $503,000 to $17 million, the median income was $3.5 million. However, the average, or mean, was $7.4 million ($163 018,658 ÷ 22 players). Much of the payroll went to a few players at the high end of the pay scale.

Rates

A **rate** is used to make fair comparisons among different populations. One example of a rate comparison is *per capita*, or per person, spending. Per capita calculations can be useful in crime reporting too. A team of reporters at the *Tampa Bay Times* created a spreadsheet to record all marijuana arrests in its two primary counties. They translated the main finding this way: "Black people in Pinellas and Hillsborough counties are at least six times as likely to be arrested for marijuana possession as white people on a per capita basis."

The counties do not have equal populations, so by using a per capita calculation, they were able to compare the numbers correctly.

When it comes to spending, even though a big-city school budget looks incredibly large to someone in a small community, the money has to stretch over more students than it would in a smaller district. As a result, spending per capita provides a better comparison between districts with different enrollments. Suppose your school district (district A) has 1,000 students and spends $2 million. You want to compare spending in your district with spending in district B, which has 1,500 students and a budget of $3 million. You would use the following formula to calculate per capita spending.

To calculate per capita spending:

Budget in dollars ÷ number of people = dollar amount per capita
District A: $2,000,000 ÷ 1,000 = $2,000 per capita
District B: $3,000,000 ÷ 1,500 = $2,000 per capita

School district B spends $1 million more a year than district A, but both districts spend the same amount per pupil.

To compare crime incidents or spending amounts among municipalities with varying populations, use per capita figures.

TIPS

To Calculate Per Capita Spending

Divide the budget by the number of people:
- Budget ÷ population = per capita spending.

Interest and Compounding

Interest is a financial factor in just about everyone's life. Consumers pay interest on home mortgages, car loans and credit card balances. Individuals and businesses earn interest when they deposit money in a financial institution or make a loan.

TIPS

To Calculate Simple Interest and Total Amount Owed

- Express the interest rate as a decimal by moving the decimal point two places to the left.
- Multiply the principal by the interest rate: $1,000 × .05 = $50
- Add the principal to the interest owed: $1,000 + $50 = $1,050

The same result can be obtained another way.

- Multiply the principal by 1 plus the interest rate expressed as a decimal: $1,000 × 1.05 = $1,050

TIPS

To Calculate Compound Interest

- Add 1 to the interest rate expressed as a decimal: 1 + .05 = 1.05
- Using a calculator, multiply the principal by $(1.05)^n$ (the superscript n represents the number of years of the loan).

The result is the total amount owed.

Federal regulations require the interest rates charged by or paid by most institutions be expressed as an **annual percentage rate (APR)**, so that interest rates are comparable from one institution to another.

There are two types of interest: simple and compound. **Simple interest** is interest that is paid on the **principal**, the amount borrowed. It is calculated by multiplying the amount of the loan by the annual percentage rate.

Suppose a student borrows $1,000 from her grandfather at a 5 percent annual rate to help cover college expenses. She needs only a one-year loan, so the cost is figured as simple interest.

To calculate simple interest:

Multiply the principal by the interest rate.
$1,000 × .05 = $50

To find the amount the student will repay her grandfather at the end of the year, add the principal to the interest. The student will owe $1,050.

If the loan is made over a period longer than a year, the borrower pays **compound interest**. Compound interest is interest paid on the total of the principal and the interest that already has accrued.

Suppose the student borrows $1,000 at an annual percentage rate of 5 percent and pays her grandfather back four years later, after graduation. She owes 5 percent annual interest for each year of the loan. But because she has the loan for four years, each year she owes not only simple interest on the principal but also interest on the interest that accrues each year.

At the end of year one, she owes $1,050. To see how much she will owe at the end of year 2, she has to calculate 5 percent interest on $1,050: $1,050 × .05 = $52.50.

Here is how to calculate the interest for all four years. (Note that 1.05 is used instead of .05 to produce a running total: principal and interest. If you multiply 1,000 by 1.05, you get 1,050; if instead you multiply 1,000 by .05, you get 50, which you then have to add to 1,000 to get the principal and interest.)

$1,000 × 1.05 × 1.05 × 1.05 × 1.05 = $1,215.51

Because most consumers pay off student loans, car loans, mortgages and credit card debt over a period of time, and because interest is compounded more often than once a year, calculations usually are far more complicated than those in the example. Many financial websites and computer programs offer calculators for computing interest. Simply search for calculators.

Student loans taken out through federal programs administered by banks, credit unions and universities are a prime example of more complicated transactions. Suppose a student has a $5,000 guaranteed student loan with an interest rate of 8 percent per year. After finishing school, the student has 10 years to repay, and each year she pays 8 percent interest on the amount of the original principal that is left unpaid. If the student makes the minimum payment of $65 on time each month for the 10-year life of the loan, she will pay the bank a total of $7,800. She pays $2,800 in interest on top of the original principal of $5,000. If she does not pay the balance down each month, the interest she owes will be even higher

Consumers get the benefits of compounding when they put money in interest-bearing accounts, because their interest compounds. The same effect takes place when people make good investments in the stock market, where earnings are compounded when they are reinvested.

Inflation

Inflation is an increase in the cost of living over time. Because prices rise over time, wages and budgets also have to increase to keep up with inflation. A worker who receives a 2 percent pay increase each year will have the same buying power each year if inflation rises at 2 percent. Because of inflation, reporters must use a few simple computations to make fair comparisons between dollar amounts from different years.

Let's say the teachers in your local school district are negotiating for a new contract. They claim that their pay is not keeping pace with inflation. You know that the starting salary for a teacher in 2010 was $50,000 and that the starting salary in 2016 was $55,000. To determine whether the teachers' claim is true, you convert 2010 dollars to 2016 dollars. You will find that the starting salary in 2016 would have been $54,369 if the district had been keeping up with inflation. In other words, in constant dollars, first-year teachers earned slightly more in their first year than they earned in 2010. (Numbers that are adjusted for inflation are called *constant*, or *real*, *dollars*. Numbers that are not adjusted for inflation are called *nominal*, or *current*, *dollars*.)

The most common tool used to adjust for inflation is the Consumer Price Index, which is reported each month by the U.S. Bureau of Labor Statistics, an agency of the Labor Department. You can get current CPI numbers on the web at www.bls.gov/cpi.

Taxes

Reporters not only pay taxes but also have to report on them. Governments collect taxes in a variety of ways, but the three major categories are sales taxes, income taxes and property taxes. Tax rates are expressed as percentages.

Sales Taxes

State, county and municipal governments can levy sales taxes on various goods and services. Sales taxes—also known as *excise taxes*—are the simplest to figure out.

To figure a sales tax, multiply the price of an item by the sales tax rate. Add the result to the original price to obtain the total cost.

Take the example of a student buying an $1,800 computer before beginning school at the University of Florida. If he shops in his home state of Delaware, he will

---

TIPS

To Calculate Sales Tax

- Multiply the price of the item by the sales tax rate.
- To obtain the total cost, add the result to the price of the item.

pay no state sales tax. If he buys the computer after arriving in Florida, where the state sales tax is 6 percent, he will pay a state sales tax of $108 and another $13.50 in county sales tax, for a total of $1,921.50.

Sales taxes are an excellent way for you to track sales in your city, county or state. The appropriate government unit—a finance or comptroller's office, for instance—will have sales tax revenues, which are a direct reflection of sales and, therefore, an excellent resource for reporting on the economy in your area.

Income Taxes

Governments tax your income to support such services as building roads, running schools, registering people to vote and encouraging businesses to grow. Income taxes are paid to the federal government, to most state governments and to some municipalities.

Calculating income taxes can be tricky because many factors affect the amount of income that is subject to the tax. For that reason, the only way to figure a person's income tax is to consult the actual numbers and follow tables published by the Internal Revenue Service (www.irs.gov) or the state department of taxation.

Governments use tax incentives to encourage people to undertake certain types of economic activities, such as buying a home, saving for retirement, and investing in business ventures. By giving people and businesses tax deductions, the government reduces the amount of income that is taxable.

A tax deduction is worth the tax rate times the amount of the tax deduction. The most common tax deduction is for the interest people pay on their home loans. Tax deductions are worth more to people with higher incomes. Take the example of two families who own homes. Both pay $2,500 in interest on their home mortgage in a year, the cost of which is deductible for people who itemize deductions on their income tax forms. The lower-income family is in the lowest federal income tax bracket, in which the tax rate is 10 percent, so that family saves $250 on its tax bill ($2,500 × .10 = $250). The higher-income family, which is in the federal income tax bracket of 33 percent, saves $825 on its tax bill ($2,500 × .33 = $825). In fact, the family in the 33 percent tax bracket probably owns a more expensive home and probably pays much more than $2,500 in mortgage interest a year. The impact is that the family saves even more on its income tax.

Income tax rates are based on your *adjusted gross income*. For example, if you are single and make between $8,350 and $8,400 after deductions, you will pay $838, or 10 percent. If you make between $40,000 and $40,050 after deductions—enough to move you into the 15 percent bracket—you will pay $6,036.

Property Taxes

City and county governments collect property taxes. When people talk about property taxes, they usually mean taxes on the value of houses, buildings and land. In some places, people also are taxed each year on the value of their cars, boats and other personal property.

ON THE JOB Working with Numbers

Courtesy of Rachel de Leon, The Center for Investigative Reporting.

From city budgets to election results to the economic meltdown, today's important stories frequently involve numbers. Too often, unfortunately, reporters avoid them or leave their interpretation to officials.

But understanding how to interpret and present numbers in a news story can make a big difference. As the computer-assisted reporting editor for three newspapers and as training director for Investigative Reporters and Editors, **Jennifer LaFleur** saw that reporters who had these skills were able to break important stories. For instance, at *The Dallas Morning News*, math skills led education reporters to uncover millions of dollars in misspending in the Dallas Independent School District. At the nonprofit investigative newsroom ProPublica, many of LaFleur's first stories involved the nation's economic crisis and the nearly $800 billion federal stimulus package. ProPublica reporters have used math skills to uncover problems in many areas from health care to campaign finance. Now senior editor for data journalism at the Center for Investigative Reporting, she says, data and math help reporters dig into environmental and public safety issues.

Over the years, LaFleur has noticed these common problems:

- Love for the superlative leads some reporters to use phrases such as "Texas has the most hunting accidents" or "California has the most cars" without putting the numbers in perspective. Big states have lots of everything, so the numbers should be adjusted for the population.
- Things cost more today than in the past, but too often reporters fail to adjust the figures for inflation. A dollar in 1950 was worth a lot more than it is today.
- In striving for precision, some reporters give readers a false message. A poll of just 400 people can't be that precise, so we shouldn't report that 43.25 percent of those respondents said something.

"In a time when every reporter is asked to do more, no reporters should be without the basic skills to interpret the numbers they run across every day," LaFleur says. "They should know how to compute a percentage change, percent of total and per capita and know what all those things mean."

The two key factors in property taxes are the assessed value and the millage rate. The **assessed value** is the amount that a government appraiser determines a piece of property is worth. The **millage rate**—the rate per thousand dollars—is the tax rate determined by the government.

To calculate property taxes:

Step 1 Divide the assessed value by 1,000.
$140,000 ÷ 1,000 = 140

Step 2 Multiply the result by the millage rate.
140 × 2.25 = $315 in taxes

Counties and cities hire professional appraisers to assess the values of land and buildings in their jurisdiction, and typically their assessments have been far lower

TIPS

To Calculate Property Tax

- Divide the assessed value by 1,000:
$140,000 ÷ 1,000 = 140
- Multiply that result by the millage rate:
140 ×2.25 = $315

than the actual market value of the property. Because of abuses and public confusion, most states in recent years have ordered revaluations to bring assessments into line with market values, and they have adjusted millage rates accordingly, though assessments can vary widely from appraiser to appraiser.

Appraisals are based on complicated formulas that take into account the size, location and condition of the property. Still, the government might say your house is worth $160,000, even if you know you could sell it for $180,000.

When you are reporting tax rate changes, you should find out how they affect houses in different value brackets to help explain the impact. By talking to the assessor or tax collector, you should be able to report, for instance, that the taxes for a house valued at $140,000 would be $315 and that taxes for a house valued at $250,000 would be $562.50.

Budgets

The budget is the blueprint that guides the operation of any organization, and a reporter must learn to read a budget just as a carpenter must learn to read a set of blueprints. It's not as difficult as it appears at first glance.

In many cases today, you'll be able to get the budget (and other financial information as well) for your city or school district in an electronic file. You might also be able to view it on a local website, but you probably cannot download that file into a spreadsheet database. However, once you have the budget in an electronic file, you can create your own spreadsheet and perform analyses that not long ago only the institution's budget director could perform. This is one of many ways the computer has become an essential newsroom tool. However, with a computer or without, first you need to know the basics of budgeting.

Budget Basics

Every budget, whether it's your personal budget or the budget of the U.S. government, has two basic parts—*revenues* (income) and *expenditures* (outgo). Commercial enterprises earn their income primarily from sales; not-for-profit organizations depend heavily on contributions from public funding and private donors. Government revenues come from sources such as taxes, fees and service charges, and payments from other agencies (such as state aid to schools). The budget usually shows, in dollar amounts and percentages, the sources of the organization's money. Expenditures go for such items as staff salaries, supplies, utility bills, construction and maintenance of facilities, and insurance. Expenditures usually are listed either by line or by program. The difference is this: A **line-item budget** shows a separate line for each expenditure, such as "Salary of police chief—$150,000." A **program budget** provides less detail but shows more clearly what each activity of the agency costs—for example, "Burglary prevention program—$250,000."

Finding Stories in Budget Changes, Trends and Comparisons

Now let's see what kinds of stories budgets might yield and where to look for those stories. Take a minute to scan Figure 7.1, a summary page from the annual budget of a small city. You can apply the skills of reading a city's annual budget to similar accounting documents on other beats—for example, annual reports of businesses and not-for-profit organizations.

The most important budget stories usually deal with changes, trends and comparisons. Budget figures change every year. Generally, as costs increase, so do budgets. But look under "Department Expenditures" in our sample budget at the line for the parks and recreation department. There's a decrease between Revised Fiscal Year 2015 and Adopted Fiscal Year 2016. Why? The summary page doesn't tell you, so you'll have to look further. Sometimes that information will be in the detail pages; other times, you'll have to ask the department director. You might discover, for example, that the drop resulted from a proposal by the city staff to halt funding of a summer employment program for teenagers. That's a story.

Another change that may be newsworthy is the increase in the police department budget. In 2015 spending totaled $4,139,055, and the budget adopted for 2016 is $4,375,336. In this case, it turned out that most of the increase was going to pay for an administrative reorganization that would add new positions at the top of the department. The patrol division was actually being reduced. Another story.

Look again at the police department line. Follow it back to Actual Fiscal Year 2014, and you'll see that the increase the year before was even bigger. In two years, the expenditures for police increased by nearly one-third, from $3.3 million actually spent in 2014 to nearly $4.4 million budgeted for 2016. That's an interesting trend. The same pattern holds true for the fire department. More checking is in order. With copies of previous budgets, you can see how far back the growth trend runs. You can also get statistics on crimes and fires from the individual departments. Are the budget-makers responding to a demonstrated need for more protection, or is something else at work behind the scenes?

More generally, you can trace patterns in the growth of city services and city taxes, and you can compare those with changes in population. Are the rates of change comparable? Is population growth outstripping growth in services? Are residents paying more per capita for city services than they paid five or 10 years ago? More good story possibilities.

Another kind of comparison can be useful to your readers. How does your city government compare in cost and services with the governments of comparable cities? Some professional organizations have recommended levels of service—such as the number of police officers or firefighters per 1,000 inhabitants—that can help you help your readers assess how well they're being governed.

The same guidelines can be applied to the analysis of any budget. The numbers will be different, as will the department names, but the structures will be much the same. Whether you're covering the school board or the statehouse, look for changes, trends and comparisons.

General Fund   Summary

PURPOSE

The General Fund is used to finance and account for a large portion of the current operation expenditures and capital outlays of city government. The General Fund is one of the largest and most important of the city's funds because most governmental programs (Police, Fire, Public Works, Parks and Recreation, and so on) are generally financed wholly or partially from it. The General Fund has a greater number and variety cf revenue sources than any other fund, and its resources normally finance a wider range of activities.

APPROPRIATIONS

	Actual Fiscal Year 2014	Budget Fiscal Year 2015	Revised Fiscal Year 2015	Adopted Fiscal Year 2016
Personnel services	$9,500,353	$11,306,619	$11,245,394	$12,212,336
Materials and supplies	1,490,573	1,787,220	1,794,362	1,986,551
Training and schools	93,942	150,517	170,475	219,455
Utilities	606,125	649,606	652,094	722,785
Services	1,618,525	1,865,283	1,933,300	2,254,983
Insurance and miscellaneous	1,792,366	1,556,911	1,783,700	1,614,265
Total operating	15,101,884	17,316,156	17,579,325	19,010,375
Capital additions	561,145	1,123,543	875,238	460,143
Total operating and capital	15,663,029	18,439,699	18,454,563	19,470,518
Contingency	—	200,000	200,000	100,000
Total	**$15,663,029**	**$18,639,699**	**$18,654,563**	**$19,570,518**

DEPARTMENT EXPENDITURES

	Actual Fiscal Year 2014	Budget Fiscal Year 2015	Revised Fiscal Year 2015	Adopted Fiscal Year 2016
City Council	$75,144	$105,207	$90,457	$84,235
City Clerk	61,281	70,778	74,444	91,867
City Manager	155,992	181,219	179,125	192,900
Municipal Court	164,631	196,389	175,019	181,462
Personnel	143,366	197,844	186,247	203,020
Law Department	198,296	266,819	248,170	288,550
Planning and Community Development	295,509	377,126	360,272	405,870

(continued)

DEPARTMENT EXPENDITURES

	Actual Fiscal Year 2014	Budget Fiscal Year 2015	Revised Fiscal Year 2015	Adopted Fiscal Year 2016
Finance Department	893,344	940,450	983,342	1,212,234
Fire Department	2,837,744	3,421,112	3,257,356	3,694,333
Police Department	3,300,472	4,007,593	4,139,085	4,375,336
Health	1,033,188	1,179,243	1,157,307	1,293,362
Community Services	50,882	74,952	74,758	78,673
Energy Management	—	—	54,925	66,191
Public Works	2,838,605	3,374,152	3,381,044	3,509,979
Parks and Recreation	1,218,221	1,367,143	1,400,334	1,337,682
Communications and Information Services	532,153	730,129	742,835	715,324
City General	1,864,200	1,949,543	1,949,543	1,739,500
Total Department Expenditures	15,663,028	18,439,699	18,454,563	19,470,518
Contingency	—	200,000	200,000	100,000
Total	**$15,663,028**	**$18,639,699**	**$18,654,563**	**$19,570,518**

Financial Reports

Another document that is vital to understanding the finances of local government or of any organization is the annual financial report. The report explains the organization's financial status at the end of a fiscal year, which often is not the same as the end of the calendar year. (For example, a fiscal year might end on June 30.) In the report you will find an accounting of all the income the organization received during the year from taxes, fees, state and federal grants, and other sources. You'll also find status reports on all the organization's operating funds, such as its capital improvement fund, its debt-service fund and its general fund.

Making sense of a financial report, like understanding a budget, isn't as hard as it may look. For one thing, the financial officer usually includes a narrative that highlights the most important points, at least from his or her viewpoint. But you should dig beyond the narrative and examine the numbers for yourself. The single most important section of the report is the statement of revenues, expenditures and changes, which provides important measures of the organization's financial health. Depending on the comprehensiveness of the statement, you may have to refer to the budget document as well. You can check:

- Actual revenue received compared with budgeted revenue.
- Actual spending compared with budgeted spending.
- Actual spending compared with actual revenue.
- Changes in balances available for spending in years to come.

> *Get your facts first, and then you can distort 'em as much as you please.*
>
> — *Mark Twain*

Lies, Damned Lies and Statistics

Here are some of the ways statistics can deceive:

- **Bias can influence the credibility of a survey.** For example, a national survey on sexual behavior indicated that 1 percent of 3,321 men questioned said they were gay, compared with the 10 percent commonly accepted as constituting the gay population. When reporting the survey results, *Time* magazine pointed out that people might be reluctant to discuss their sexual orientation with a "clipboard-bearing stranger."

- **One year does not a trend make.** A large increase in the number of rapes merits a story, but it might represent a fluctuation rather than a trend. Depending on the subject matter, you need to study at least five to 10 years of data to determine whether there is a significant shift.

- **The way organizations compile figures can differ, and that can distort comparisons.** The Scripps Howard investigation of sudden infant deaths, for example, found what one expert called a "deeply muddled approach" of wide variations in reporting from one state to the next, distorting real results and making accurate comparisons impossible. Jurisdictions with inadequately trained medical examiners report many times as many "unexplained" deaths as do jurisdictions with more rigorous standards. Inadequately trained journalists unknowingly spread misinformation.

- **Conclusions that sound credible might not hold up under the scrutiny of cause and effect.** Advocacy groups that call for less violence on television say studies show TV violence causes violence in children. They cite research at Yale University showing that prolonged viewing of violent programs is associated with aggressive behavior among children. But the association could be that children who tend to be aggressive watch more violent programming, not the other way around.

macmillanhighered.com /newsreporting12e
Watch **"Freedom of Information."**

- What effect might freedom of information laws have on using statistical information?
- Should governments ever be allowed to keep secrets from the public? Explain.

The guidelines offered here should help you shape your questions and understand the answers. With financial statements, as with budgets, look for changes, trends and comparisons, and ask for explanations.

Public Opinion Polls

Surveying is a powerful journalistic tool. It is also a tool that is often misused. For every election, many commentators and some candidates misread them and many media misreport them. Despite the problems, many journalists, politicians, businesses and scholars today are using poll results because they show more reliably than anecdotes or ordinary interviews what the public thinks about important issues. Many news organizations now go beyond reporting the findings of national polling firms such as Gallup and Harris Interactive and conduct or commission their own surveys. Some pollsters are described as "Democratic" or "Republican." That's really a shorthand way of saying they usually work for candidates of one or the other party. It doesn't mean the polls' results are slanted, though they could be. An accurate sense of the public mood is at least as important to politicians as to journalists. Of course, if you report the results of one of these one-party pollsters, make sure you explain the connection.

Every day, new poll results illustrate what people think about various topics in the news. And just about every day, journalists confuse readers when they try to interpret the results.

The Margin of Error

The most important thing to keep in mind about polls and surveys is that they are based on samples of a population. Because a survey reflects the responses of a small number of people within a population, every survey has a *margin of error*—the difference between the entire population and the random sample. The results must be presented with the understanding that scientific sampling is not a perfect predictor for the entire population.

Suppose your news organization buys polling services that show that Candidate Hernandez has support from 58 percent of the people surveyed, Candidate Jones has support from 32 percent, and 10 percent are undecided. The polling service indicates that the margin of error of the poll is plus or minus 3 percentage points. The margins separating the candidates are well beyond the margin of error, so you can write that Hernandez is leading in the poll.

Candidate	Percentage of Support	Percentage of Support Adjusted for Margin of Error (+/− 3%)
Hernandez	58%	55–61%
Jones	32%	29–35%
Undecided	10%	7–13%

Now suppose Hernandez has 52 percent support and Jones has 48 percent. The difference between them is within the margin of error, less than plus or minus 3 percentage points. That margin of error means that Hernandez could have as little as 49 percent and Jones could have as much as 51 percent. Seldom would results vary that much, but caution is the best guide. Report that the results are too close to call.

Candidate	Percentage of Support	Percentage of Support Adjusted for Margin of Error (+/− 3%)
Hernandez	52%	49–55%
Jones	48%	45–51%

When polls are conducted properly and reported carefully, they can tell us something we could not know otherwise and perhaps even lead to wiser public policies. But when they are badly done or sloppily reported, polls can be bad news for journalists and readers alike.

The chances are good that sometime in your reporting career you will want to conduct an opinion poll or at least help with one your employer is conducting. The Suggested Readings listed at the end of the chapter will tell you much of what you need to know for that. Even if you never work a poll, you almost certainly will be called on to write about polling results. What follows will help you understand what you are given and will help you make sure your readers understand it, too.

Poll Information to Share

The Associated Press Media Editors prepared a checklist of the information you should share with your audience about any poll on which you are reporting. Several of their points require some explanation.

- **Identity of the sponsor.** The identity of the survey's sponsor is important to you and your readers because it hints at possible bias. Most people would put more trust in a Gallup or Harris poll's report that, for instance, Hernandez is far ahead of Jones in the presidential campaign than they would in a poll sponsored by the Hernandez for President organization.

- **Exact wording of the questions.** The wording of the questions is important because the answers received often depend at least in part on how the questions were asked. (See Chapter 3 on interviewing for more detail.) The answer might well be different, for example, if a pollster asks, "Whom do you favor for president, Jones or Hernandez?" rather than "Wouldn't Jones make a better president than Hernandez?"

- **Population sampled.** In science, the *population* is the total number of people—or documents or milkweed plants or giraffes—in the group being studied. For an opinion survey, the population might be, for example, all registered voters in the state, black males under 25 or female cigarette smokers. To understand what the results of a poll mean, you must know what population was studied. The word *sampled* refers to the procedure in which a small number—or sample—of people is picked at random so as to be representative of the population.

- **Sample size and response rate.** The sample size is important because—all other things being equal—the larger the sample, the more reliable the survey results should be. The response rate is especially important in surveys conducted by mail, in which a low rate of response may invalidate the poll.

- **Margin of error.** The margin of error, or sampling error, of any survey is the allowance that must be made for the possibility that the opinion of the sample might not be exactly the same as the opinion of the whole population. For large populations, such as the size involved in an election, the margin of error depends mainly on the size of the sample. For instance, all other things being equal, a sample of 384 would have a margin of error of 5 percentage points, and a sample of 1,065 would have a margin of error of 3 percentage points.

- As we saw earlier, if a poll with a margin of error of 3 percentage points has Hernandez with 58 percent of the votes and Jones with 32 percent, you can be confident that Hernandez actually has between 55 and 61 percent and Jones actually has between 29 and 35 percent. The laws of probability say that the chances are 19 to 1 that the actual percentages fall within that range. Those odds make the information good enough to publish.

■ **Which results are based on part of the sample.** The problem of sampling error helps explain why it is important to know which results may be based on only part of the sample. The smaller that part is, the greater the margin of error. In political polls, it is always important to know whether the results include responses from all eligible voters or only from individuals *likely* to vote. The opinions of the likely voters are more important than the opinions of others.

■ **When the interviews were collected.** When the interviews were collected may be of critical importance in interpreting a poll. During campaigns, for example, the candidates themselves and other events may cause voters' preferences to change significantly within a few days. Think of presidential primaries. As candidates join or drop out of the race, support for each of the other candidates changes. A week-old poll may be meaningless if something dramatic happened after it was taken. Candidates have been known to use such outdated results to make themselves appear to be doing better than they really are, or their opponents worse. Be on guard.

Polling voters is an excellent way to forecast election results. Random digit dialing includes cellphones, but cellphone users are less likely to take a call from an unknown number than landline owners. In the general population, about 25 percent of people who own cellphones do not own a landline. Pollsters must be careful to get a proper proportion of cellphone users.

Caution in Interpreting Polls

Whether you are helping conduct a survey or only reporting on one produced by someone else, you must exercise caution. Be on guard for the following potential problems.

■ **The people interviewed must be selected in a truly random fashion if you want to generalize from their responses to the whole population.** If the selection wasn't randomized, you have no assurance that the interview subjects are really representative. The old-fashioned people-in-the-street interview is practically worthless as an indicator of public opinion for this reason. The man or woman in the street probably differs in important ways from all those men and women who are not in the street when the questioner is. Also invalid are the questionnaires members of Congress mail to their constituents. Only strongly opinionated—and therefore unrepresentative—people are likely to return them. For the same reason, the "question-of-the-day" feature that some newspapers and broadcast stations ask you to respond to online tells you nothing about the opinions of the great mass of people who do not respond. Even worse are the TV polls that require respondents to call or send a text message to a number to register their opinions. Because there is a charge for

Cautions About Using Poll Data

- The people interviewed must be selected in a truly random fashion if you want to generalize from their responses to the whole population. Random means that any person in the population has as much chance as any other of being selected.
- Beware of polls that claim to measure opinion on sensitive, complicated issues.

such calls, these pseudopolls produce not only misleading results but profits that encourage their use.

■ **Beware of polls that claim to measure opinion on sensitive, complicated issues.** Many questions of morality, or on social issues such as race relations, do not lend themselves to simple answers. Opinions on such matters can be measured, but only by highly skilled researchers using carefully designed questions. Anything less can be dangerously oversimplified and highly misleading.

Polling—like field experiments, systematic analysis and participant observation—can help you as a reporter solve problems you could not handle as well with other techniques. But these are only tools. How effectively they are used—or how clumsily they are misused—depends on you.

"*Next question: I believe that life is a constant striving for balance, requiring frequent tradeoffs between morality and necessity, within a cyclic pattern of joy and sadness, forging a trail of bittersweet memories until one slips, inevitably, into the jaws of death. Agree or disagree?*"

Some pollsters' questions seem designed to elicit a desired response.

© George Price/The New Yorker Collection/The Cartoon Bank

Mixing Numbers and Words

Whatever the story and whatever the subject, you probably can use numbers to clarify issues for readers and viewers. All too often, however, numbers are used in ways that muddy the water. Many journalists have some trepidation about working with numbers, and they create confusion unwittingly when they work with the volatile mixture of numbers and words.

Jennifer LaFleur, featured in the "On the Job" box in this chapter, says she has seen numerous reports from government agencies with math errors that a quick double check by a reporter would find. "Reporters background-check sources. They verify anecdotes with documents. But seldom do we double-check numbers," she reminds us.

One website that does check numbers regularly is PolitiFact.com. Many of the statements they check are from politicians, but one time, they checked facts from Leonard Pitts Jr., a national columnist.

Using data from a Pew Research Center survey, Pitts wrote of Rush Limbaugh, the radio commentator, and Fox News that "America's least-trusted news sources are also its most popular."

PolitiFact confirmed the statement about Limbaugh but noted that more people say they trust Fox News than distrust it. Pitts had neglected to subtract the percentage of people who trust Fox from the percentage of people who distrust Fox in order to get a "net value" for Fox. Once that calculation was done for all the news outlets in the survey, Fox rated higher in trustworthiness than 21 other sources.

The reporters there also pointed out another fallacy with numbers: Although Fox News has the largest audience *among cable news outlets,* the CBS news audience is three times larger. NBC, CBS and ABC all draw much larger audiences for their nightly news programs than the cable stations.

Sometimes, journalists encourage misunderstandings by describing large increases in percentage terms. For example, when gasoline prices increased from about $2 to nearly $4 a gallon, some in the media reported, accurately, that the price had doubled. Others, however, incorrectly called it a 200 percent increase instead of a 100 percent increase: $2 + (100\% \times \$2) = \$4$.

Another trouble spot for mixing numbers and words occurs when reporters calculate how much larger or more expensive something is. For example, a class that grew from 20 students to 100 students is five times bigger than it was ($5 \times 20 = 100$), but it has four times as many students as it had before: $(4 \times 20) + 20 = 100$.

The lesson to be learned from these examples is not to avoid numbers, but rather to use great care to ensure accuracy. Picking the right numbers to use and using them wisely will help your news stories have the biggest impact.

SUGGESTED READINGS

Blastland, Michael, and Andrew Dilnot. *The Commonsense Guide to Understanding Numbers in the News, in Politics, and in Life*. New York: Penguin, 2009. You can laugh as you learn more about handling numbers.

Cohen, Sarah. *Numbers in the Newsroom: Using Math and Statistics in News*. Columbia, Mo.: Investigative Reporters and Editors, 2001. This book includes helpful, readable information on how to do basic math, graphs and polls.

Cuzzort, R.P., and James S. Vrettos. *The Elementary Forms of Statistical Reason*. New York: St. Martin's Press, 1996. Non-mathematicians in the humanities and social sciences who must work with statistics will appreciate this basic guide.

Meyer, Philip. *Precision Journalism: A Reporter's Introduction to Social Science Methods*. 4th ed. Lanham, Md.: Rowman and Littlefield, 2002. This step-by-step guide explains how to use social science research methods in news reporting.

Paulos, John Allen. *A Mathematician Reads the Newspaper*. New York: Anchor Books, 1997. Structured like the morning paper, this book investigates the mathematical angles of stories in the news and offers novel perspectives, questions and ideas.

Silver, Nate. *The Signal and the Noise*. New York: Penguin Press, 2012. The creator of the FiveThirtyEight blog explains how to evaluate predictions in fields ranging from politics to the weather.

SUGGESTED WEBSITES

www.bankrate.com
Bankrate offers calculators to figure everything from interest rates to currency conversions.

www.bls.gov/data/inflation_calculator.htm
The Bureau of Labor Statistics has a calculator that enables you to adjust dollar amounts for inflation. In addition, the website provides Consumer Price Index information for the entire nation, broken down by region and type of spending.

www.math.temple.edu/~paulos
John Allen Paulos, a professor at Temple University, is the author of *Innumeracy: Mathematical Illiteracy and Its Consequences*. At this site you can read more from the master of numbers.

www.minneapolisfed.org
The Federal Reserve Bank of Minneapolis maintains a great website that helps you calculate inflation. It also has clear and simple explanations of how inflation is calculated and how to use the Consumer Price Index.

www.robertniles.com/stats
Robert Niles, who worked at newspaper internet sites in Denver and Los Angeles, is a self-described "math and computer geek." His explanations of statistics are simple and clear.

EXERCISES

1. Go to PolitiFact.org and select an item the site checked involving numbers. Write a succinct report on the statement and the findings.

2. Your local school board sets the tax rate at $3.33 per thousand valuation, up from $3.21. Explain to readers the impact on a typical home.

3. Find a national survey released by any of the national media or by one of the major polling firms, such as Gallup or the Pew Research Center. Report the margin of error and whether the main results are within that margin or exceed it.

4. The federal minimum wage began in 1938 at 25 cents an hour. In 1968, it was $1.60. Calculate how much $1.60 in 1968 is worth today. Compare those numbers with the present minimum wage in the state where you attend school. Determine the percent your state is above or below the federal minimum wage of $7.25. Suggest a story idea based on the result. (Consult www.dol.gov/whd/minimumwage.htm for the current federal minimum wage and www.dol.gov/whd/minwage/america.htm for the current state minimum wages.)

5. If one candidate gets 48 percent of the vote and another gets 52 percent, what is the percentage difference? What is the difference in percentage points?

6. Search for the payrolls by player of all the teams in the NFL. Choose three and calculate the average salary and the median salary. Which is the fairest comparison for each of the teams?

7. If a city budgets $186,247 for personnel one year and $203,020 the next, what is the percentage increase?

8. A city of 219,000 had 103 murders last year. Another city of 88,812 in the same state had 48 murders. How many murders were there per 1,000 residents in each city?

9. **Your journalism blog.** Find out how much your college charged for tuition in 1995, 2005 and 2015. Adjust those numbers for inflation so they can be compared. (Use an inflation calculator like the one at www.minneapolisfed.org.) Write a blog post about the cost of going to college, and use figures adjusted for inflation. Remember to keep your readers in mind. Are you writing for students? Parents? University officials? All of these?

The **inverted pyramid**—a news story structure that places all the important information in the first paragraph—has been used to write the "first draft of history" in the U.S. for generations. Here is the Associated Press lead on the first use of the atomic bomb in 1945:

> An atomic bomb, hailed as the most destructive force in history and as the greatest achievement of organized science, has been loosed upon Japan.

Twenty-four years later, here is how the AP started its story of the first moon landing:

> Man came to the moon and walked its dead surface Sunday.

And in 2015, when a man joined a prayer service in Charleston, South Carolina, then killed all but one of the participants, the local newspaper used the inverted pyramid:

> Nine people were shot, some fatally, inside one of Charleston's oldest and most well-known black churches tonight. A bomb threat complicated the investigation and prompted police to ask nearby residents to evacuate.

The lead reporting the moonwalk would work well as a short post on social media such as Twitter. In fact, citizens who are suddenly thrust into reporting what's happening around them are tweeting in inverted pyramid style. The brevity of a tweet neatly reflects the goal of the traditional inverted pyramid news lead: Report the most important news succinctly. For Twitter, the church tweet probably would be something like this:

> 9 shot, some fatally, inside the Emanuel African Methodist Episcopal Church in Charleston tonight. Police are searching for the suspect.

With that goal, citizen journalists have joined specialized financial news services such as Bloomberg News, which relies on the inverted pyramid. So do newspapers, despite many editors' encouragement of new writing forms. So do radio, television, the internet and newsletters. Businesspeople often use the inverted pyramid in company memos so their bosses don't have to read to the end to find the main point. Public relations professionals use it in news releases to get the attention of news editors.

Importance of the Inverted Pyramid Story

Frequently misdiagnosed as dying, the inverted pyramid has more lives than a cat—perhaps because the more people try to speed up the dissemination of information, the more valuable the inverted pyramid becomes. In the inverted pyramid, information is arranged from most important to least important. The King of Hearts in *Alice in Wonderland* would never succeed in the electronic news service business. When asked where to start a story, he replied, "Begin at the beginning and go on till you come to the end: then stop." Reporters, however, often begin a story at its end.

In this chapter you will learn:

1
Why the inverted pyramid story is important.

2
How to translate news values into leads.

3
How to create variations on the inverted pyramid lead.

4
How to organize a story using the inverted pyramid.

5
How to use the inverted pyramid across media platforms.

6
How to improve your accuracy.

> **" Because a story is important, it doesn't follow that it must be long. "**
>
> — *Stanley Walker,* City Editor

Subscribers to financial services such as Reuters, Dow Jones Factiva and Bloomberg, for instance, react instantly to news about the financial markets to get an edge over other investors. They don't want narration; they want news. This is a typical Bloomberg lead:

> **More first-time homebuyers took the plunge in May, helping catapult U.S. sales of previously owned properties to their highest level since 2009.**

Many newspaper readers, on average, spend about 15 minutes a day reading the paper. Online readers, who skip around sites as if they were walking barefoot on a hot stove, spend even less time. Both prefer very short stories with the news on top. If a reporter were to write an account of a car accident by starting when the driver left the house, many readers would never read far enough to learn that the driver and a passenger had been killed. Instead, such a story starts with its climax:

> **Two people died Thursday when a backhoe fell off a truck's flatbed and sliced the top off an oncoming vehicle near Fairchild Air Force Base.**

In the inverted pyramid, the lead, which can consist of one or two paragraphs, sits atop other paragraphs arranged in descending order of importance. These paragraphs explain and provide evidence to support the lead. That's why print editors can quickly shorten a story by cutting from the bottom; the paragraphs at the end are the least important. On the internet, space is not a consideration, but readers' time is. That's why the same inverted pyramid that is used in newspapers is the most common story structure found on such news websites as CNN.com, msnbc.com, CBSNews.com and ABCNews.com. For instance, msnbc.com used the inverted pyramid to report this breaking news:

> **DNA from at least one of the two escaped New York prisoners was found at a burglarized cabin in a rural town about 20 miles from the prison, sources told NBC News on Monday.**

The inverted pyramid has yet another attribute that endears itself to websites. Because the keywords are in the first couple of paragraphs, you increase your chances of showing up high in an internet search.

The inverted pyramid does have some shortcomings. Although it delivers the most important news first, it does not encourage people to read the entire story. Stories stop; they don't end. There is no suspense. In a Poynter Institute study, researchers found that half of the 25 percent of readers who started a story dropped out midway through. Interest in an inverted pyramid story diminishes as the story progresses. But the way people use it attests to its value as a quick form of information delivery. Readers can leave a story whenever their needs are met, not when the writer finishes the story. In an age when time is golden, the inverted pyramid still offers value.

The day when the inverted pyramid is relegated to journalism history is not yet here and probably never will be. Perhaps 80 percent of the stories in today's newspapers and almost 100 percent of the stories on news services for target audiences

TIPS

The Inverted Pyramid

- Requires the writer to rank the importance of information.
- Puts the most important information first.
- Arranges the paragraphs in descending order of importance.

such as the financial community are written in the inverted pyramid form. That's changing, but it's changing slowly. Some of the new media highlight other forms of writing, such as narratives, lists and chunks, which are stories broken into smaller parts. Still, as long as newspaper, electronic and television journalists continue to emphasize the quick, direct, simple approach to communications, the inverted pyramid and its variations will have a role.

There are many other ways to structure a news story. However, before you explore the alternatives, you should master the inverted pyramid. As you do, you will master the art of making news judgments. The inverted pyramid requires you to identify and rank the most newsworthy elements in each story. This is important work. No matter what kinds of stories you write—whether obituaries, accidents, speeches, press conferences, fires or meetings—you will be required to use the skills you learn here.

Finding the Lead

To determine a **lead**—a simple, clear statement consisting of the first paragraph or two of a news story—you must first recognize what goes into one. As you read in Chapter 1, you begin by determining the story's relevance, usefulness and interest for readers. One way to measure these standards is to ask "So what?" or "Who cares?" So what if there's a car accident downtown? If it's one of hundreds a month, it may not be news. Any holdup in a community of 5,000 may be news because the "so what" is that holdups are uncommon and some residents probably know the victim. It's unlikely newspapers, radio or television stations would report the holdup in a metropolitan area where holdups are common. But if the holdup appears to be part of a pattern or if someone is killed, the story becomes more significant. One holdup may not be news, but a holdup that authorities believe is one of many committed by the same person may be news. The "so what" is that if the police catch this robber, they stop a crime spree.

To determine the "so what," you have to answer six basic questions: who, what, where, when, why and how. The information from every event you witness and every story you hear can be reduced to answers to these six questions. If the answers add up to a significant "so what," you have a story. Consider this example of an incoming call at fire headquarters.

> **"Fire Department," the dispatcher answers.**
>
> **"Hello. At about 10 o'clock, I was lying on my bed watching TV and smoking," the voice says. "I must have fallen asleep about 10:30 because that's when the football game was over. Anyway, I woke up just now, and my bedroom is on fire. . . ."**

That dialogue isn't informative or convincing. More likely, our sleepy television viewer awoke in a smoke-filled room, grabbed his cellphone and punched in 9-1-1. The conversation with the dispatcher would more likely have gone like this:

> **"9-1-1 call center."**
> **"FIRE!" a voice at the other end yells.**
> **"Where?" the dispatcher asks.**
> **"At 1705 W. Haven St."**

When fire is licking at their heels, even nonjournalists know the lead. How the fire started is not important to the dispatcher; that a house is burning—and where that house is located—is.

The journalist must go through essentially the same process to determine the lead. Just as the caller served himself and the fire department, reporters must serve their readers. What is most important to them?

After the fire is over, there is much information a reporter must gather. Among the questions you would routinely ask are these:

TIPS

The Six Basic Questions

1. Who?
2. What?
3. Where?
4. When?
5. Why?
6. How?

More questions:

- So what?
- What's next?

- When did it start?
- When was it reported?
- Who reported it?
- How was it reported?
- How long did it take the fire department to respond?
- How long did it take to extinguish the fire?
- How many fires this year have been attributed to smoking in bed?
- How does that compare with figures from previous years?
- Were there any injuries or deaths?
- What was the damage?
- Who owned the house?
- Did the occupant or owner have insurance on the house?
- Will charges be filed against the smoker?
- Was there anything unusual about this case?
- Who cares?

With this information in hand, you can begin to write the story.

Writing the Inverted Pyramid Lead

Start by looking over your notes.

Who? The owner, a smoker, Henry Smith, 29. The age is important. Along with other personal information, such as address and occupation, the age differentiates the subject from other Henry Smiths in the readership area.

What? Fire caused damage estimated by the fire chief at $2,500.

Where? 1705 W. Haven St.

When? The call was received at 10:55 p.m., Tuesday. Firefighters from Station 19 arrived at the scene at 11:04. The fire was extinguished by 11:30. Those times are important to gather even if you don't use them. They show whether the fire department responded quickly.

Why? The fire was started by carelessness on the part of Smith, according to Fire Chief Bill Malone.

How? Smith told fire officials that he fell asleep in bed while he was smoking a cigarette.

If you had asked other questions, you might have learned more from the fire department:

- This was the eighth fire this year caused by smoking in bed.
- All last year there were four such fires.
- Smith said he had insurance.
- The fire chief said no charges would be filed against Smith.
- It was the first fire at this house.
- Smith was not injured.

Have you figured out the "so what"?

Assume your city editor has suggested you hold the story to about six paragraphs. Your first step is to rank the information in descending order of importance. There are lots of fires in this town, but eight this year have been caused by smoking in bed. Perhaps that's the most important thing about this story. You begin to type:

> A fire started by a careless smoker caused an estimated $2,500 in damage to a home Tuesday.

Only 17 words and 91 characters. That's even shorter than a tweet. You should try to hold every lead to fewer than 25 words unless you use more than one sentence. Maybe it's too brief, though. Have you left anything out? Maybe you should include the time element—to give the story a sense of immediacy. Readers would also want to know where the fire occurred. Is it near their house? Is it someone they know? You rewrite:

> A Tuesday night fire started by a careless smoker caused an estimated $2,500 in damage to a home at 1705 W. Haven St.

Just then the city editor walks by and glances over your shoulder. "Who said it was a careless smoker?" she asks. "Stay out of the story."

You realize you have committed a basic error in news writing: You have allowed an unattributed opinion to slip into the story. You have two choices. You can attribute the "careless smoker" information to the fire chief in the lead, or you can omit it. You choose to rewrite by attributing the opinion. You also revise your sentence to emphasize the cause instead of the damage. You write:

> Fire that caused an estimated $2,500 in damage to a home at 1705 W. Haven St. Tuesday was caused by smoking in bed, Fire Chief Bill Malone said.

Now 28 words and only 144 characters have answered the questions "what" (a fire), "where" (1705 W. Haven St.), "when" (Tuesday) and "how" (smoking in bed). And the opinion is attributed. But you have not answered "who" and "why." You continue, still ranking the information in descending order of importance.

> The owner of the home, Henry Smith, 29, said he fell asleep in bed while smoking a cigarette. When he awoke about 30 minutes later, smoke had filled the room.
>
> Firefighters arrived nine minutes after receiving the call. It took them about 26 minutes to extinguish the fire, which was confined to the bedroom of the one-story house.
>
> According to Chief Malone, careless smokers have caused eight fires this year. Smith, who was not injured, said the house was insured.

TIPS

When Writing the Lead, Remember

- Always check names.
- Keep the lead to fewer than 25 words.
- Attribute opinion.
- Find out the who, what, where, when, why and how.
- Tell readers what the news means to them.
- Gather basic information even if it's routine.

You take the story to the city editor, who reads through the copy quickly. As you watch, she changes the lead to emphasize the "so what." The lead now reads:

> A smoker who fell asleep in bed ignited a fire that caused minor damage to his home on West Haven Street Tuesday, Fire Chief Bill Malone said. It was the city's eighth fire caused by smokers, twice as many as occurred all last year.

The lead is 44 words, but it is broken into two sentences, which makes it more readable. The importance of the "so what" changed the direction of the story. The fire was minor; there were no injuries. However, the increase in the number of fires smokers caused may force the fire department to start a public safety campaign against careless smoking. The city editor continues:

> The owner of the home, Henry Smith, 29, of 1705 W. Haven St., said he fell asleep in bed while smoking a cigarette. When he awoke about 30 minutes later, smoke had filled the room.

Too many numbers bog down a lead. Focus on the impact of the figures in the lead, and provide details later in the story.

When the editor checks the telephone listings and the city directory, she uncovers a serious problem. Both the telephone listings and the city directory give the man who lives at 1705 W. Haven St. as Henry Smyth: S-m-y-t-h. City directories, telephone lists and other sources can be wrong. But at least they can alert you to possible errors. Confirm spellings by going to the original source, in this case, Mr. Smyth.

Never put a name in a story without checking the spelling, even when the source tells you his name is Smith.

Look at the annotated model "A Sample Inverted Pyramid Story" on page 158 to see the completed fire story. There are several lessons you can learn from this example:

- Always check names.
- Keep the lead short, usually fewer than 25 words, unless you use two sentences.
- Attribute opinion. (Smoking in bed is a fact. That it was careless is an opinion.)
- Find out the who, what, where, when, why and how. However, if any of these elements have no bearing on the story, they may be omitted.
- Write a sentence or paragraph telling readers what the news means to them.
- Report information basic to the story even if it is routine. Not everything you learn is important enough to be reported, but you'll never know unless you gather the information.

When you are learning to write an inverted pyramid story, the process is deliberate. You'll check your notes to be certain you have the six basic questions answered. Eventually, though, you will mentally check off those questions quickly. Of course, you will not always be able to find answers immediately to "how" and "why." Sometimes, experts need time to analyze accidents, crimes, fires and so on.

After you've checked your notes, ask yourself, "What else do readers need to know?" Using the news values of relevance, usefulness and interest and figuring out the "so what," decide which answers are the most important so you can put them in the lead. The rest go in the second and third paragraphs. In the Annotated Model "A Sample Inverted Pyramid Story," the news values and "so what" are these:

Relevance	Eight similar fires are more relevant than one minor fire.
Usefulness	Highlighting the number of fires also establishes usefulness by pointing out the bigger problem.
Interest	Multiple fires attract more interest than one minor one.
The "so what"	One minor fire lacks impact, but the fact that eight fires this year were caused by smoking suggests a public safety problem.

In what order are the key questions answered in the fire story? What does that order say about news values?

Emphasizing Different News Values

In the lead reporting the house fire, the "what" (fire) is of secondary importance to the "how" (how the fire started). A slightly different set of facts would affect the news value of the elements and, consequently, your lead. For instance, if Smyth turned out to have been a convicted arsonist, you would probably emphasize that bizarre twist to the story:

> A convicted arsonist awoke Tuesday to find that his bedroom was filled with smoke. He escaped and later said that he had fallen asleep while smoking.
> Henry Smyth, 29, who served a three-year term for . . .

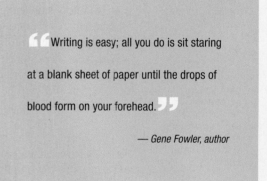

> Writing is easy; all you do is sit staring at a blank sheet of paper until the drops of blood form on your forehead.
>
> — *Gene Fowler, author*

That lead emphasizes the news value of novelty. If Smyth were the mayor, you would emphasize prominence:

> Mayor Henry Smyth escaped injury Tuesday when he awoke to find his bedroom filled with smoke. Smyth said he had fallen asleep while smoking in bed.

What, So What and What's Next

You know that the answer to "what" is often the lead. The preceding example also illustrates the "so what" factor in news. A $2,500 fire is not news to many people in large communities where there are dozens of fires daily. Even if you crafted a tightly written story about it, your editor probably would not want to print or broadcast it.

In small communities, the story would have more impact because there are fewer fires and because a larger proportion of the community is likely to know the victim.

The "so what" factor grows more important as you add other information. If the fire occurred during a fire-safety campaign, the "so what" would be the need for

ANNOTATED MODEL A Sample Inverted Pyramid Story

The identification of "who" is delayed until the next paragraph because the person is not someone readers would recognize and because his name would make the lead unnecessarily long. Also in the lead are the "what," "when," "how" and, most significantly here, the "so what."

A smoker who fell asleep in bed ignited a fire that caused minor damage to his home on West Haven Street Tuesday, Fire Chief Bill Malone said. It was the city's eighth fire caused by smokers, twice as many as occurred all last year.

The owner of the home, Henry Smyth, 29, of 1705 W. Haven St., said he fell asleep in bed while smoking a cigarette. When he awoke about 30 minutes later, smoke had filled the room.

The "who" is identified. More details on the "how" are given.

The performance of the fire department is monitored.

The fire department, which received the call at 10:55 p.m., had the fire out by 11:30.

Malone said the damage, estimated at $2,500, was confined to the bedroom. The house was insured.

Careless smokers caused only four fires last year in the city. Malone said that he is considering a public awareness campaign to try to alert smokers to the hazards. Those four fires caused total damages of $43,000. This year, fires started by careless smoking have caused total damages of $102,500, Malone said.

Details on the "so what" are given. The impact question is answered with the possible campaign.

Least important: If someone else had been endangered and charges had been filed, this information would move higher in the story.

No charges will be filed against Smyth because no one other than the smoker was endangered, Malone said.

The inverted pyramid structure dictates that the most important information goes in the lead paragraphs. It is the job of the writer and the editor to decide what that information is.

fire safety even in a community where awareness of the problem had already been heightened. If the fire involved a convicted arsonist or the mayor, the "so what" would be stronger. Oddity or well-known people increase the value of a story. If someone had been injured or if the damage had been $1.2 million instead of $2,500, the "so what" factor might even push the story into the metropolitan press. As discussed, once you have answered all six of the basic questions, it's important to ask yourself what the answers mean to the reader. That answer is your "so what" factor.

In many stories, it is also important to answer the question "What's next?" The city council had its first reading of its budget bill. What's next? *Members will vote on it next month.* Jones was arrested Monday on suspicion of passing bad checks. What's next? *The prosecuting attorney will decide whether there is enough evidence to file charges.*

Kip Hill (see "On the Job" on p. 161) wrote about defendants in a marijuana case. One of his subheads asked "What's next?" Then he answered:

> The sentencing hearing for Firestack-Harvey and the Greggs is scheduled for June 10. None of the defendants are in custody. Telfeyan has asked for more time to review the

trial transcript before that hearing takes place and the government hasn't objected, meaning the hearing could be pushed back. Zucker, who pleaded guilty to growing more than 100 marijuana plants, faces a potential prison sentence of 63 months to 78 months. He is scheduled to be sentenced July 24.

A reader in a focus group once told researchers that she just wants to be told "what," "so what" and "what's next." That's a good guideline for all journalists to remember.

Variations on the Inverted Pyramid Lead

No journalist relies on formulas to write inverted pyramid leads, but you may find it useful, especially in the beginning, to learn some typical types of leads. The labels in the following sections are arbitrary, but the approaches are not.

The "You" Lead

Regardless of which of these leads journalists use, they are trying to emphasize the relevance of the news to the audience. One good way to highlight the relevance is to speak directly to readers by using "you." This informal, second-person lead—the **"you" lead**—allows the writer to tell readers why they should care. For instance:

> **You will find the lowest rates in two years if you are buying a home.**
> **Most Springfield banks yesterday lowered the 15-year loan rate to 2.85 percent, down from 3.9 percent a year ago.**

Readers want to know what's in it for them. The traditional approach is less direct:

> **The real estate mortgage rate hit a two-year low yesterday.**

As with any kind of lead, you can overdo the "you" lead. You don't need to write "You have another choice in the student president's race." Just tell readers who will be running. However, you may use those words in writing for radio or television news as a setup for the story to come. And in tweets and on Facebook, where you are talking to readers one-on-one, "you" is usually appropriate.

The Immediate-Identification Lead

In the **immediate-identification lead**, one of the most important facts is "who," or the prominence of the key actor. Reporters often use this approach when someone important or well-known is making news. Consider the following example:

> **Taylor Swift appears to have prompted a policy change at Apple, after threatening to withhold her album "1989" from the company's streaming music service over royalty payments.**

Names make news.

When writing for your campus newspaper or your local newspaper, you would use names in the lead that are known locally but not necessarily nationally. The name of your student body president, the chancellor, the mayor or an entertainer who has a local following would logically appear in the lead. None of these names would be used in a newspaper 50 miles away.

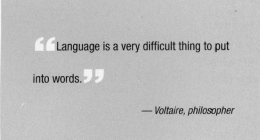

In small communities, names almost always make news. The "who" involved in an accident is usually in the lead. In larger communities, names are not as recognizable. As a rule, if the person's name or position is well-known, it should appear in the lead.

The Delayed-Identification Lead

Usually a reporter uses a **delayed-identification lead** because the person or organization involved has little name recognition among readers. Thus, in fairly large cities, an accident is usually reported like this:

> MADISON, Wis.—A 39-year-old carpenter was killed today in a two-car collision two blocks from his home.
> William Domonske of 205 W. Oak St. died at the scene. Mary Craig, 21, of 204 Maple Ave., and Rebecca Roets, 12, of 207 Maple Ave., were taken to Mercy Hospital with injuries.

However, in a smaller community, names almost always make news. Unless a name is nationally recognized, it often appears in the second paragraph:

> ALFRED, Maine (AP)—A man accused of beating his grandmother with a golf club, stabbing her dozens of times and setting fire to the house they shared has been convicted of murder in Maine.
> A jury returned the verdict Friday in the trial of Derek Poulin, of Old Orchard Beach.

The name Derek Poulin was not widely known except in his local area, so his identification was delayed until the second paragraph.

The Summary Lead

Reporters dealing with several important elements may choose to sum up what happened in a **summary lead** rather than highlighting a specific action. This is one of the few times when a general statement is preferable to specifics.

The Associated Press chose a summary lead to give the overall view of the weather in Arizona:

> PHOENIX (AP)—Arizona is in the midst of a prolonged heat wave that has produced record-high temperatures in Phoenix, prompted dozens of daily calls to the Humane Society about overheated pets, and sparked triple-digit temperatures in typically cooler mountain locations.

Likewise, if a city council rewrites city ordinances, unless one of the changes is of overriding importance, most reporters will use a summary lead:

> MOLINE, Ill.—The City Council replaced the city's 75-year-old municipal code with a revised version Tuesday night.

Summary leads do not appear only in reports of board meetings. A Spokane, Washington, reporter used a summary lead to report a neighborhood dispute:

> An Idaho farmer's fence apparently was cut last week. It set off a chain of events Friday night that landed three people in the hospital, killed a cow and totaled a vehicle in the eastern Spokane Valley.

The basic question you must answer is whether the whole of the action is more important than any of its parts. If the answer is yes, use a summary lead.

The Multiple-Element Lead

In some stories, choosing one theme for the lead is too restrictive. In such cases, you can choose a **multiple-element lead** to work more information into the first paragraph. But you should write the lead within the confines of a clear, simple sentence or sentences. Consider this example:

> PORTLAND, Ore.—The City Council Tuesday ordered three department heads fired, established an administrative review board and said it would begin to monitor the work habits of administrators.

Notice that the actions are parallel, as is the construction of the verb phrases within the sentence. Parallel structures also characterize the following news extract, which presents a visual picture of the scene of a tragedy:

> BAY CITY, Mich.—A flash fire that swept through a landmark downtown hotel Saturday killed at least 12 persons, injured 60 more and forced scores of residents to leap from windows and the roof in near-zero cold.

ON THE JOB   Advice to a Beginning Journalist

Kip Hill graduated with a master's degree in journalism in May 2013. Since that time, he's worked at *The Spokesman-Review* newspaper in Spokane, Washington, as a cops, courts and county government reporter. Here is his advice to a beginning journalist:

If you were at a bar (or coffee shop), how would you start a story to your friends?

All journalists writing for the web should ask themselves that question. You're vying for the attention of readers whose attention span can be measured in 140 characters. That's how long you have to hook readers glancing at your story before they're off to another picture of kittens or the latest GIF du jour.

With breaking news, this is often an easy proposition. Prominently place the subject, then the verb, then the most important detail. You can worry about filling in the details in a later version of the story, or put them lower in the story. If your readers don't immediately connect to what you're telling them, they're already reading someone else.

But what if the story is about government, where the verb can be elusive? "The City Council discussed Tuesday the possibility

Courtesy of Colin Mulvaney.

of testing sewage in town for remnants of marijuana." This could have been the lead of a story I wrote for *The Spokesman-Review* in Spokane. But the first four words are all wrong. While there's a subject and verb prominent, it's a vague subject and a weak verb. There's the nugget of a great story here, but the fact that some elected officials are jawing isn't how you'd introduce it at a bar.

You'd make a joke, right?

So here's the lead sentence that I ran with: "The most important numbers to Spokane city officials looking for accurate data about residents' marijuana use may be one and two."

Remember that your first sentence isn't the only thing that draws readers into a story. They've clicked the headline; they know you're going to write about sewage and marijuana. So why not have a little bit of fun with it? You would if you were talking to friends. And isn't that the relationship you should have with your readers?

We are told what happened, where it happened and how many were killed and injured.

Some multiple-element leads consist of two paragraphs. This occurs when the reporter decides that several elements need prominent display. For example:

> The Board of Education Tuesday night voted to lower the tax rate 12 cents per $100 valuation. Members then approved a budget $150,000 less than last year's and instructed the superintendent to decrease the staff by 25 people.
>
> The board also approved a set of student-conduct rules, which includes a provision that students with three or more unexcused absences a year will be suspended for a week.

This story, too, could emphasize the "so what" while retaining the multiple elements:

> The Board of Education lowered your real estate taxes Tuesday. Members also approved a budget $150,000 less than last year's and instructed the superintendent to decrease the staff by 25 people.

Simpler leads are preferable. But a multiple-element lead is one of your options. Use it sparingly.

Many newspapers are using graphic devices to take the place of multiple-element leads. They use summary boxes to list other actions. Because the box appears under the headline in type larger than the text, it serves as a graphic summary for the reader who is scanning the page. The box frees the writer from trying to jam too many details into the first few paragraphs. On the web, such methods are even more common. When news breaks, organizations like CNN often post stories with multiple elements like videos and highlights lists. (See Figure 8.1 for an example of this approach).

FIGURE 8.1

A list, such as CNN's "Story highlights" on the left, allows the writer to simplify the lead.

Another approach is to break the coverage of a single event into a main story and a shorter story called a **sidebar**. This approach offers the advantage of presenting the information in short, palatable bites. It also allows the writer to elevate more actions into lead positions. Researchers have found that breaking stories into small segments increases readers' comprehension and retention. For instance, in the Board of Education lead above, the angle about the superintendent's having to decrease staff could be spun off into a short sidebar.

On the web, there is an additional advantage. The more stories with separate headlines, the better chance you have to increase the **click-through rate**, the measurement of how many people open the stories.

> **"**The lead should be a promise of great things to come, and the promise should be fulfilled.**"**
>
> — *Stanley Walker,* City Editor

Danger Signals

Here are some leads that understandably raise red flags to editors:

- **Question leads.** Readers don't know the subject, don't know why they are being asked a question and probably couldn't care less. So the next time you are writing a weather story and are tempted to begin with "So, how hot was it yesterday?" lie down until the temptation passes. Either tell readers the temperature or open with an anecdote of a specific roofer sweating on the job. That's showing how hot it is.

- **Leads that say what might happen or what might have happened.** News organizations try to report what happened. Stay away from leads like this: "Springfield residents might be looking forward to warmer weather." Or they might not. Talk to people. Don't speculate.

- **Leads that overreach.** Report what you know. You might think it's harmless to write, "Springfield residents warmly greeted spring yesterday," but you don't know that all Springfield residents were happy about it. Maybe the guy who runs a snow-removal business would rather see winter last longer.

Leads with Flair

Although the inverted pyramid tells readers the news first and fast, not all stories begin with the most important statement. When the news value you want to emphasize is novelty, often the lead is unusual.

> CASTLE SHANNON, Pa. (AP)—This deer wasn't caught in the headlights. It was called on the carpet.
>
> A Pittsburgh-area carpeting store has been cleaning up after the wild animal smashed into the store and ran amok Tuesday.

A less imaginative writer might have written:

> A deer ran through the window of a Pittsburgh-area carpeting store Tuesday.

That approach is like slapping a generic label on a Mercedes-Benz. The inverted pyramid approach is not so rigid that it doesn't permit fun and flair.

Story Organization

Like a theater marquee, the lead is an attention-getter. Sometimes the movie doesn't fulfill the promises of the marquee; sometimes the story doesn't fulfill the promises of the lead. In either case, the customer is dissatisfied.

The inverted pyramid helps you put information in logical order. It forces you to rank, in order of importance, the information you will present.

The One-Subject Story

As we have seen in this chapter, constructing an inverted pyramid news story involves a series of judgments based on classic news values and the specific news outlet. A fire or an accident in a small community is bigger news than a fire or an accident in another, larger area. Earlier events will also influence how you write a story.

The annotated model "A Single-Subject Inverted Pyramid Story" on page 165 shows a story about the arrest of a suspect in an assault case. Police say drugs were involved. If there had been a string of assaults or a pattern of drug-related violence, the writer probably would have emphasized different aspects of the story. For instance, the writer could have emphasized the suspect's criminal record with this lead:

> **A Columbia man who was convicted of assault three times was arrested again Thursday night for an attack on his girlfriend.**

The Memo-Structure Story

The memo structure (as illustrated in the annotated model "A Memo-Structure Story" on page 166) is one of many hybrid forms journalists are experimenting with as they transition to the web. It is an effective way to organize information that has no narrative and few voices. You can use it to write an **advance** about upcoming meetings and to update developing stories. The categories can follow the standard who, what, where, when, why, how and so what, or you can create your own subject categories. Reporters can write memo-structure stories quickly, and readers can scan them quickly—a convenient feature for readers using a small-screen device such as a smartphone.

The Multiple-Element Story

Multiple-element stories are most commonly used in reporting on the proceedings of councils, boards, commissions, legislatures and courts. These bodies act on numerous subjects in one sitting. Frequently, their actions are unrelated, and more than one action is often important enough to merit attention in the story. You have four options:

1. **You can write more than one story.** This, of course, requires permission from your editor. There may not be enough space.
2. **You can write a story highlights list.** The list would be displayed along with the story either in print or on the web. In it you would list the council's major actions or the court's decisions.

Man Arrested in Attack, Charged with Child Endangerment

By Elizabeth Phillips
Columbia Missourian

The arrest, not the assault, is the latest development, so it is emphasized.

Police arrested a Columbia man in connection with an attack on his girlfriend Thursday night.

The lead gives "who," "what" and "when."

Details of the charges are in the second paragraph because the list is too long to put in the lead.

Darrell Vanness Johnson, 37, was arrested on suspicion of second-degree domestic assault, unlawful use of a weapon, felony possession of a controlled substance, misdemeanor possession of a controlled substance and endangering the welfare of a child at about 9 p.m. Thursday in the 1500 block of Greensboro Drive.

The name is not in the lead because most readers would not recognize it.

"Where" is identified. "When" is made more specific than in the lead.

The writer adds details, attributed to the police, on how the assault occurred. This information includes the "why."

Johnson and his girlfriend began arguing over drugs Thursday evening, Columbia Police Sgt. Ken Hammond said. Johnson choked her and held a revolver to her head before she was able to escape and call 911 from a neighbor's house, Hammond said. Three children, two 9-year-olds and a 4-year-old, were in the home during the attack, Hammond said.

Information about the children is pertinent because it adds to the "so what"—the children were also endangered.

This paragraph continues the chronology of the assault and capture.

When Columbia police arrived, Johnson was driving away from the Greensboro Drive home with the three children in the car, Hammond said. When police arrested Johnson, they found marijuana and cocaine, Hammond said.

The victim was taken to an area hospital by ambulance for treatment of bruises and scratches to the hands, neck and back, Hammond said. Her injuries were not life threatening.

The writer offers evidence of the injuries and attributes this information.

Now that the basic facts are established, the writer adds background on the suspect, attributed to a public safety website.

According to Missouri Case.net, Johnson has pleaded guilty to third-degree domestic assault three times in the past four years in Boone County Circuit Court, serving close to seven months in jail for those charges. He has also pleaded guilty to theft, first-degree trespass and second-degree property damage in Boone County Circuit Court, serving 75 days in Boone County Jail for the theft charge and receiving two years of unsupervised probation for the trespass and property damage charges.

Johnson violated his probation on the trespass and property damage charges and was scheduled to appear in Boone County Circuit Court for a probation violation hearing in December. He was charged with theft last October in Boone County Circuit Court.

Writer gives the "what's next."

He faces up to 40 years in prison and up to a year in jail in connection with the attack.

This typical one-subject story written in the inverted pyramid form features a delayed-identification lead.

ANNOTATED MODEL   A Memo-Structure Story

Parks and Recreation, City Council Discuss Plans for Parks Tax

By Asif Lakhani
Columbia Missourian

The multiple-element lead gives basic facts—the "who," "what" and "when." → COLUMBIA—Earlier this month, Columbia voters approved the extension of the park sales tax. On Monday night, the Columbia City Council and the Parks and Recreation Department attended a work session where they discussed where the tax revenue would go.

← Subsequent paragraphs organize information by categories, not necessarily by importance.

Subheadings introduce the paragraphs. → **What happened:** Mike Hood, director of parks and recreation, presented a proposed five-year plan to council members.

Cost: During the next five years, the one-eighth-cent sales tax is expected to garner about $12 million for Columbia's parks. ←

The writer has chosen categories that are relevant to the reader.

Timetable: The proposed plan divides projects into four categories: land acquisition and annual park funding, new facility and park development, improvements to existing parks, and trails and greenbelts. . . .

Projects: The five-year plan would be front-loaded with construction projects over a four-year fiscal period between 2011 and 2015, which would leave more room for land acquisition later on, Hood said. Most of the construction projects are listed under new facility and park development and improvements to existing parks. . . .

Comments: First Ward Councilman Paul Sturtz and Sixth Ward Councilwoman Barbara Hoppe voiced concern about front-loading the plan with construction. Both said land acquisition is more important because its value could increase over the next five years. . . .

The last paragraph wraps up the story. → **What's next:** The proposed plan now goes to the Parks and Recreation Commission. After, it will go to the City Council for consideration. The council plans to discuss the suggested land acquisition at an upcoming council meeting.

In a memo-structure story, subheads can reflect the answers to essential questions.

3. **You can write a multiple-element lead and story.** Your lead would list all the major actions at the board meeting. The remainder of the story would provide more detail about each action.

4. **You can write a single-element lead and cover the other elements further on in the story.** Your lead would focus on the element you believe readers would find most interesting, relevant and useful.

Let's go back to a multiple-element lead we saw earlier:

> The Board of Education Tuesday night voted to lower the tax rate 12 cents per $100 valuation. Members then approved a budget $150,000 less than last year's and instructed the superintendent to decrease the staff by 25 people.
>
> The board also approved a set of student-conduct rules, which include a provision that students with three or more unexcused absences a year will be suspended for a week.

Four newsworthy actions are mentioned in those two paragraphs: (1) changing the tax rate, (2) approving a budget, (3) cutting staff, (4) adopting student-conduct rules. In stories that deal with several important elements, the writer usually highlights the most important. When this is the case, it is important to summarize the other, lesser actions after the lead.

If you and your editor judge that changing the tax rate was more important than anything else that happened at the school board meeting, you would approach the story like this:

Lead	The Board of Education Tuesday night voted to lower the tax rate 12 cents per $100 valuation.
Support for lead	The new rate is $1.18 per $100 valuation. That means that if your property is assessed at $300,000, your school tax will be $3,540 next year.
Summary of other action	The board also approved a budget that is $150,000 less than last year's, instructed the superintendent to cut the staff by 25 and approved a set of rules governing student conduct.

Notice that the lead is followed by a paragraph that supports and enlarges upon the information in it before the summary paragraph appears. Whether you need a support paragraph before summarizing other action depends on how complete you are able to make the lead.

In every multiple-element story, the first two or three paragraphs determine the order of the rest of the story. To ensure the coherence of your story, you must describe the elements in the order in which you introduce them.

Writing a Story Across Media Platforms

The inverted pyramid can serve you throughout the news reporting and writing process, from tweets to online updates. Most breaking news stories are first tweeted and then put on the web before they are printed in a newspaper or broadcast on television. In fact, the story may never even be printed or broadcast.

The story in the annotated model "The Classic Inverted Pyramid Story" on page 168 appeared in print. Let's follow its progress from what the first tweet might possibly look like.

TIPS

Checklist for Assembling the Rest of the Inverted Pyramid

- Introduce additional important information you were not able to include in the lead.
- If possible, indicate the significance or "so what" factor.
- Elaborate on the information presented in the lead.
- Continue introducing new information in the order in which you have ranked it by importance.
- Develop the ideas in the same order in which you have introduced them.
- Generally, use only one new idea in each paragraph.

ANNOTATED MODEL   The Classic Inverted Pyramid Story

The lead identifies the "what," "where" and "when." The "so what" is that people were killed.

The second paragraph provides details to support the lead and answers "who."

This paragraph shows impact beyond deaths and injuries.

What's next? This would be higher if the driver, rather than a tire, appeared to be the cause of the accident.

A four-vehicle accident on eastbound I-70 near Stadium Boulevard ended in two deaths on Sunday.

Barbara Jones, 41, of St. Louis died at the scene of the accident, and Juanita Doolan, 73, of St. Joseph died at University Hospital, according to a release from Springfield police. Two other people, William Doolan, 73, of St. Joseph and Theodore Amelung, 43, of Manchester, Missouri, were injured in the accident.

Both lanes of traffic were closed on the eastbound side and limited to one lane on the westbound side as rescue workers cleared the scene.

Authorities said a westbound late-model Ford Taurus driven by Lan Wang of Springfield was traveling in the right lane, developed a tire problem and swerved into the passing lane. A Toyota pickup truck in the passing lane, driven by Jones, was forced over the grassy median along with the Taurus. The two vehicles entered eastbound traffic where the truck struck an Oldsmobile Delta 88, driven by Juanita Doolan, head on.

Wang and the one passenger in his car, Kenneth Kuo, 58, of Springfield, were not injured.

John Paul, a tractor-trailer driver on his way to Tennessee, said he had to swerve to miss the accident.

"I saw the red truck come across the median and hit the blue car," Paul said. "I just pulled over on the median and called 911."

Jones, who was wearing a seat belt, died at the scene, Officer Stan Williams said. Amelung, a passenger who had been in the truck, was out of the vehicle when authorities arrived, but it was unknown whether he was thrown from the truck or was pulled out by someone else, Williams said.

No charges have been filed, but the investigation continues.

The "how" is less important than the "what," "where" and "when," so it appears later in the story.

An eyewitness account adds sensory details that make the scene more vivid.

Note how this story, typical of the inverted pyramid structure, delivers the most important news in the lead and provides less essential details toward the end. It also reflects more complete reporting than an earlier web version.

Breaking-News Tweets

If you can write a lead, you can write a tweet. The limitation of 140 characters is not much of a problem for journalists. The lead on the accident story is only 95 characters. The difference between writing a lead and writing a tweet is that the journalist often does not know as many details when tweeting. A journalist at the scene of an accident might send this tweet:

EMT crews are working 4-car accident on I-70 near Stadium Blvd. Exit Missouri 41 to avoid traffic backup.

After the reporter has had a chance to talk to an officer at the scene, she could send the next tweet:

> Police: 4 injured in accident on I-70 near Stadium Blvd. No IDs yet. Exit Missouri 41 to avoid traffic backup both directions.

Initial Online Story

When the reporter is able to get more information, she might post the first blast for online and mobile devices:

> Two people were killed and two others were injured today in a four-car accident on I-70 near Stadium Boulevard, Springfield police said.
>
> Names of the victims were being withheld pending notification of relatives. All four were state residents.
>
> The two injured were taken to Springfield Hospital.
>
> Authorities said a westbound Toyota pickup truck swerved across the median and collided with an Oldsmobile in the eastbound lane.

Full Story with Ongoing Updates

The next version, shown in the annotated model above, would appear both in print and on the web. Most publications post the story on the web immediately, even before the newspaper is printed or the news report is aired. The next day, the reporter may be able to update the web version:

> Two people injured in a four-car accident Sunday were released from Springfield Hospital today. The accident claimed the lives of two others.
>
> William Doolan, 73, of St. Joseph, and Theodore Amelung, 43, of Manchester, were released. Barbara Jones, 41, of St. Louis, and Juanita Doolan, 73, of St. Joseph, died as a result of the collision.

This new lead would replace the first three paragraphs of the existing story. In all versions for all platforms, it is essential to answer and rank the questions that are basic to any inverted pyramid story.

Checking Accuracy

All of us can improve our accuracy. Some improvement comes with experience, but most of the errors journalists make involve routine facts. In Chapter 3, you learned the importance of accurately capturing the words that you quote. Here are additional procedures you should use to produce more accurate stories.

These four habits will help you become more accurate:

1. **Go over your notes at the end of every interview.** Read back the quotes and the facts as you have written them down. Don't assume anything. As you read earlier in the chapter, if someone tells you his name is Smith, ask him how to spell it.

> "Selecting the quotes isn't so hard; it's presenting them that causes the trouble. And the worst place to present them is at the beginning. Quote leads deserve their terrible reputation. Yet they still appear regularly in both print and broadcast journalism.
>
> "We can make three generalizations about quote leads. They're easy, lazy and lousy. They have no context. The readers don't know who's speaking, why, or why it matters. Without context, even the best quotations are wasted."
>
> — *Paula LaRocque, former assistant managing editor,* The Dallas Morning News

2. **Carefully check your story against your notes and the documents you have collected to be certain you didn't introduce any errors while writing.** We all make typing errors. We make errors because of background noise and commotion. If you recognize that you are not infallible, you will be a more accurate journalist.

3. **When sources give you facts, check them if possible.** During an interview, the mayor may tell you that the city has 50 police officers. Check with the police department. The mayor may have the number wrong.

4. **Do a prepublication check.** Some journalists object to prepublication checks because they believe it gives the source too much opportunity to argue over what they will print. Some are afraid sources may approach other media to get their version of the story out even before publication, but those situations are rare.

In a study published in the *Newspaper Research Journal*, researcher Duane Stoltzfus found that more newspapers than formerly believed permitted their reporters to check stories or portions of stories with sources before publication. In all cases, sources are told that they are being asked to check the accuracy of the information. No journalist should cede authority for decisions about what goes in and what does not. But no journalist should be afraid to take every step possible to ensure accuracy. Some read back quotes; some read back facts gathered from that source. Some even describe information obtained from other sources. *USA Today*, among many other newspapers, permits its reporters to decide whether to check with sources before publication.

If your publication permits prepublication checks, you will do yourself and your profession a favor by performing them. Verify everything you intend to publish or broadcast. In the online world, where speed is king, verification often is sacrificed in the rush to be first. But being first and wrong is never right, as bloggers will tell you. In an effort to be transparent, some news sites put a note on stories that have been corrected.

SUGGESTED READINGS

Brooks, Brian S., James L. Pinson and Jean Gaddy Wilson. *Working with Words: A Handbook for Media Writers and Editors.* 8th ed. New York: Bedford/St. Martin's, 2013. This must-have book provides excellent coverage of grammar and word usage and has a strong chapter on "isms."

Gillman, Timothy. "The Problem of Long Leads in News and Sports Stories." *Newspaper Research Journal* (Fall 1994): 29–39. The researcher found that sentences in leads were longer than sentences in the rest of the story.

Kennedy, George. "Newspaper Accuracy: A New Approach." *Newspaper Research Journal* (Winter 1994): 55–61. The author

suggests that journalists do prepublication accuracy checks with proper safeguards in place.

Maier, Scott R. "Accuracy Matters: A Cross-Market Assessment of Newspaper Error and Credibility." *Journalism and Mass Communications Quarterly* (Autumn 2005): 533–51. This study documents the error rates of journalists and the impact on credibility.

Stoltzfus, Duane. "Partial Pre-publication Review Gaining Favor at Newspapers." *Newspaper Research Journal* (Fall 2006): 23–37. The researcher surveyed the 50 largest newspapers to determine their policies toward prepublication review and found that the trend is to permit it.

SUGGESTED WEBSITES

**www.documentcloud.org/documents/1995453
-graves-nyhan-reifler-mpsa15.html**
"Why do journalists fact-check?" is a research study that found the practice of fact checking is spreading.

www.poynter.org/tag/regret-the-error/
Regret the Error, housed on the Poynter.org website, chronicles errors made in all media. The site reports how and when they are corrected.

www.public.wsu.edu/~brians/errors/index.html
Paul Brians, a professor of English at Washington State University, will answer your questions about the English language.

www.stateofthemedia.org
The Pew Research Center's Project for Excellence in Journalism produces an annual "State of the News Media" report that examines journalistic trends and economic trends.

EXERCISES

1. Choose a story that is being widely reported and compare how the Associated Press, CNN.com, Foxnews.com and *The New York Times* cover it. Do they use inverted pyramid leads? Are they straight news, leads with a flair, summary leads or multiple-element leads?

2. Identify the who, what, where, when, why and how, if they are present, in the following lead:

   > The United Jewish Appeal is sponsoring its first-ever walkathon this morning in Springfield to raise money for the Soup Kitchen, a place where the hungry can eat free.

3. Identify the who, what, where, when, why and how, if they are present, in the following story. Would you move any information higher in the story? If so, why?

   > COLUMBIA—A Missouri man died Sunday afternoon after his car hit a utility pole in the 300 block of William Street.
   >
   > Police believe the driver had a medical condition prior to the crash that caused the accident, according to a news release from the Columbia Police Department.
   >
   > The driver, a 72-year-old man, was not identified in the release because police still have to notify his family.
   >
   > According to police, the driver veered off the right side of the road around 2 p.m. and then hit the pole. Medical personnel removed the driver from the car and took him to University Hospital, where he was later pronounced dead.
   >
   > Speed, drugs and alcohol were not considered a factor in this crash, the release said.
   >
   > Source: "Man Dies in Afternoon Car Accident," June 21, 2015. http://www.columbiamissourian.com/news/local/update-man-dies-in-afternoon-car-accident/article_3c7b35d0-1875-11e5-9595-33961a762765.html

4. Rewrite the lead in exercise 2 as a "you" lead. Which are better, the third-person or second-person leads? Why are they better?

5. From the following facts, write a tweet of 140 characters or fewer that you could send to tell the story and promote it for a website.

Who: A nuclear weapon with a yield equivalent to 150,000 tons of TNT

What: Detonated

Where: 40 miles from a meeting of pacifists and 2,000 feet beneath the surface of Pahute Mesa in the Nevada desert

When: Tuesday

Why: To test the weapon

How: Not applicable

   Other information: Department of Energy officials are the source; 450 physicians and peace activists were gathered to protest continued nuclear testing by the U.S.

6. **Your journalism blog.** Collect three leads from different internet news sites. Write a blog post in which you identify each type of lead used and determine what questions each lead answers and what questions it does not. Give your opinion of the effectiveness of each lead. Then review the blog post of at least one other classmate and post a comment in response.

7. From the following facts, write the first two paragraphs of a news article.

Who: 40 passengers

What: Evacuated from a Delta Airlines jet, Flight 428

Where: At the LaCrosse, Wis., Regional Airport

When: Monday following a flight from Minneapolis to LaCrosse

Why: A landing tower employee spotted smoke near the wheels.

How: Not applicable

   Other information: There was no fire or injuries; the smoke was caused by hydraulic fluids leaking onto hot landing brakes, according to Bob Gibbons, an American Airline spokesman.

8. Describe picture and information-graphic possibilities for the story in Exercise 5.

Diana Marcum wanted to see the impact of the drought in the Central Valley of California, which she covers for the *Los Angeles Times*. After talking to dozens of the people affected, she produced a story, full of facts and figures but told through the people who were out of work, losing their businesses and trying to feed their children and themselves. This is how it started:

> Beneath this small farm town at the end of what's left of the Kings River, the ground is sinking.
>
> Going into the fourth year of drought, farmers have pumped so much water that the water table below Stratford fell 100 feet in two years. Land in some spots in the Central Valley has dropped a foot a year.
>
> In July, the town well cracked in three places. Household pipes spit black mud, then pale yellow water. After that, taps were dry for two weeks while the water district patched the steel well casing.
>
> In September, the children of migrant farmworkers who usually come back to Stratford School a few weeks late, after the grape harvest, never came back at all.
>
> By October, there were new faces in the drought relief line in front of the school, picking up boxes of applesauce, canned tomatoes, peanut butter, rice.
>
> If rain doesn't come soon to California, cities and suburbs will survive, with maybe fewer flowerbeds or more expensive lettuce.
>
> But in Stratford—where the school has had some of the same teachers for 40 years, the auto parts store doubles as a coffeehouse and first names change but last names don't—survival isn't a given.
>
> Even above ground, the town is sinking.

"The *LA Times* has this umbrella that allows storytelling," Marcum told Lois Kiernan of the website Nieman Storyboard. "I mean real storytelling, where you take somebody into a world and keep them there from the beginning to the end, and the main thing is about the characters and the feelings."

A good story told well is important to readers—and to writers such as Diana Marcum, who won a Pulitzer Prize for this work. Notice Marcum's expressive use of several important narrative techniques: vivid description—pipes "spit black mud, then pale yellow water"; keenly observed detail—"boxes of applesauce, canned tomatoes, peanut butter, rice" and "the auto parts store doubles as a coffeehouse"; and narrative tension—"the children of migrant farmworkers . . . never came back at all." Readers don't see this type of writing as often as they should, but when they do, they appreciate it. Marcum said readers wrote her notes telling her the stories made them feel better.

Writing to inform and entertain is as important for journalists as it is for novelists. Just because newspapers and broadcast reports are finished and gone in a day doesn't mean that we should accept a lower level of skill. Comparing the temporal nature of newspapers to a beach, syndicated columnist James Kilpatrick challenged writers: "If we write upon the sand, let us write as well as we can upon the sand before the waves come in."

If Kilpatrick's challenge to your pride is not enough, then the demands of readers and listeners—and of the editors and news directors who are hiring—should be. Editors are looking for those unusual people who can combine reporting and writing talents. The journalist whose prose jerks around the page like a mouse trapped in a room with a cat has no future in the business.

1

How the skills of reporting make good writing possible.

2

How to add accurate, specific details.

3

How to write a coherent story.

4

How to write with conciseness and simplicity.

5

How to use correct and effective language.

6

How to create scenes, use dialogue and anecdotes and create a sense of person.

The American Society of News Editors has made the improvement of writing one of its principal long-range goals. Each year, it honors the reporting and writing of journalists in several categories. Some of them go on to win Pulitzer Prizes. Many well-known writers—among them Daniel Defoe, Mark Twain, Stephen Crane, Ernest Hemingway and Alex Haley—began their careers as journalists. Carl Bernstein and Bob Woodward of *The Washington Post* wrote *All the President's Men*, Mark Bowden of *The Philadelphia Inquirer* wrote *Blackhawk Down*, later made into a movie. Rebecca Skloot, a freelance journalist, correspondent and contributing editor, wrote *The Immortal Life of Henrietta Lacks*. George Hodgman wrote *Bettyville*. All were bestsellers.

At media organizations around the country today, small but growing numbers of journalists are producing literature daily as they deal with everything from traffic accidents to affairs of state. If you have respect for the language, an artist's imagination and the dedication to learn how to combine them, you, too, may produce literature.

We should all attempt to bring quality writing, wit and knowledge to our work. If we succeed, our work will be not only informative but also enjoyable, not only educational but also entertaining, and not only bought but also read.

Good Writing Begins with Good Reporting

Marcum and a photographer traveled through the drought-stricken farmland to see the cracked soil and talk to the people trying to make a living. Her story, which opened this chapter, is a testament to the power of reporting and writing. (See the link to the full story at the end of this chapter in "Suggested Websites.") Without the proper use of participant accounts, personal observation and detail, the best journalist's stories land with a thud. Good writing begins with good reporting. You can settle for a dry police report, or you can go to the scene and gather details. In Chapter 8 we introduced you to this lead:

> **Two people died Thursday when a backhoe fell off a truck's flatbed and sliced the top off an oncoming vehicle near Fairchild Air Force Base.**

Now let's look at some of the detail writer Alison Boggs of *The (Spokane, Wash.) Spokesman-Review* collected by being there:

> **The top of the Suburban, from about hood height, was shorn off by the backhoe's bucket. The front seats were forced backward, and the dashboard, roof and steering wheel were torn off.**
>
> **Parts of the car lay in a heap of crumpled metal and glass under the overpass. The silver Suburban was identifiable only by a 1983 owner's manual lying in the dirt nearby.**
>
> **Both victims wore seat belts, but in this case, that was irrelevant, (Sgt. Jeff) Sale said. Both suffered severe head injuries.**
>
> **Sleeping bags, a Coleman cooler and fishing equipment scattered on the highway and in the back of the Suburban suggested a camping trip. Unopened cans of Pepsi were jammed behind the front seat of the car.**

Notice that the writer built every sentence on concrete detail. Good reporting makes good writing possible.

ON THE JOB Setting the Hook in the Opening

Courtesy of Amanda Heckert.

Justin Heckert, who lives in Indianapolis and has written for national publications such as *Grantland, Esquire* and *The New York Times Magazine*, believes one of the most important elements of any story is the first few sentences:

> The experience of reading and being hooked can be because of word play, or rhythm, or a particular style or device. I can recite the first sentences to some of my favorite stories. That's just how they stick with me.
>
> "The madness of an autumn prairie cold front coming through." That's Jonathan Franzen. "It was a pleasure to burn. It was a special pleasure to see things eaten, to see things blackened and changed." That's Ray Bradbury. "Aye, that face. There's a story about that face, you know. About what he was willing to do with it." That's Tom Junod. "Sometimes the silence gets inside of you." That's Gary Smith. "They don't count calories at Fausto's Fried Chicken." That's Wright Thompson. These books/stories are nowhere near me as I write this, but I can remember those sentences, and I know I got them right.
>
> This idea has been a huge part of my own writing. I've done it, or tried to, in pretty much every single story I've ever written, be it a success or failure. A recent example: A few years ago, I reported and wrote a story for *Men's Journal*. I was sitting on top of amazing material. I could've, honestly, probably just written it out like I was talking to a third grader, and it still would've been an interesting story. But after I talked to my editor and sat down to write it, I sweated forever about how to begin. I sat on the porch and thought about it. I thought about it driving the car. I thought about how to begin while I was watching a football game, before I was going to bed.
>
> The story was about two people who had been pulled out to the sea and had treaded water for hours. The ocean has been written about more than anything since the beginning of time. It was hard to try and think of something new to say about it, to tie it in to the experience of this guy and his son, victims of the ocean, even though they didn't die. How this situation resolved itself is as esoteric as the nature of writing itself: It just came to me.
>
> "The ocean at night is a terrible dream. There is nothing beyond the water except the profound discouragement of the sky, every black wave another singular misfortune." I had stared at the ocean for hours, had thought about how it affected the characters of the story, thought about everything they said about it. I knew it when the words appeared—they came to me the way ideas come to people, inexplicably. I think those are two good sentences. So did my editor. So have a lot of other people who read it. They were that important to me because I wanted them to hook the readers and then keep them with me.

Accurate, Specific Details

Good writing is accurate when it is built on concrete details. When you use language to communicate those details precisely, you inform and entertain your readers.

Use Concrete Examples

For lawyers, the devil might be in the details, but for writers, clarity is in the details. Echoing your bureaucratic sources, you can write of infrastructures or facilities or learning pods. But try actually touching any of these. By contrast, you ride on a highway, sit in an arena and learn in a reading group.

Be specific. You might write that the speaker is big, but compared with what? Abstractions are ambiguous. To someone who is 6 feet tall, someone big might be 6 feet 6 inches tall. To someone who is 5 feet 2 inches tall, 6 feet is huge.

Note how the concrete details in the following lead from *The Boston Globe* about an employee who killed five co-workers make the story more informative:

> He was an accountant who had a chip on his shoulder and a bayonet on his kitchen table. He lived with his parents across from a llama farm in a small beige house with a sign informing visitors: "Trespassers will be shot; survivors will be shot again."
>
> As dawn broke over Ledyard yesterday, Matthew Beck, 35, left his folks' home—across town from the casino—got in his car, and drove 1 1/2 hours to his job at Connecticut Lottery headquarters. At some point, he strapped a bandolier of bullets across his chest, over his gray pinstriped shirt but concealed by a brown leather jacket. He carried a 9mm pistol and a knife.

Almost every sentence contains specific, concrete detail: "accountant," "bayonet," "across from a llama farm," and so on.

Marcum, whose story opens this chapter, packed concrete details into her story to create this scene at the only local store left in town:

> A man put two packages of hot dog buns and a roll of paper towels on the counter.
>
> "Hey, Kenny, OK if I pay for these after Friday?" he asked, lowering his voice.
>
> Alrihimi nodded. But his stomach dropped. This was a man who had never asked for credit before.
>
> The store owner had 29 receipts that constituted the week's IOUs. On the backs of two torn-up cigarette cartons, he wrote the running accounts: the ones where they owed $34, paid $12, then charged $8.
>
> "It's too sad to say no. I think of their kids," said Alrihimi, a father of five.
>
> "They don't have any money. I don't have any money. We're all trying to get through, little-by-little-bit."
>
> When he has to run errands, Darlene Lacey watches the store. She's been helping out since her husband died 13 years ago.
>
> Alrihimi worries about her.
>
> "I think that when people can't pay, she takes money out of her own pocket and puts it in the cash register," he said. "She is a very good-heart lady. But she has too little money."
>
> Later that afternoon, when Alrihimi was at the bank, Lacey rang up two sodas for an elderly couple who asked for credit. Then she slipped $2 in the cash register.
>
> "Kenny is hanging on by a thread," she said. "And, oh my gosh, our little town needs him."

The scene *shows* the economic impact of the drought.

To be concrete, you must have facts. And you must describe those facts in a way that makes readers able to touch, feel or smell them. Lazy reporters create puffballs. Poke their stories, and you'll stick your finger clear through them. Instead of saying "some council members," say "five council members." Instead of writing that a business is "downsizing," report that 150 workers will lose their jobs. Avoid abstractions; covet concrete details.

Show, Don't Just Tell

As you chauffeur the reader through the scenes in your story, you can drive down the road or over the green-laced, rolling hills of Kentucky. You can report that a car hit a skunk, or you can convey the nauseating smell. A word here, a phrase there, and you can hear the plane ripping the tin roof off a house, smell the acrid stench of burning tires, feel the boxing glove's leather rasp against the skin. Good writing appeals to one or more of our five senses: sight, hearing, smell, taste and touch.

Reporting for *The Oregonian*, Steve Duin talked to voters standing in the rain while waiting to vote. He observed: "They arrived in wool hats and sweatpants, in Chuck Taylors and hospital scrubs, with borrowed umbrellas and voter guides and 18-month-olds in their arms."

In addition to the years of anecdotal experience journalists have, there is also statistical support for the common advice to show rather than just tell. For instance, researchers constructed 10 sentences telling information and 10 showing information. College students were divided into two groups and asked to read one of the groups of sentences. Then they were asked to rate the sentences on such qualities as interesting–dull, clear–unclear and engaging–unengaging. The researchers concluded, "The experiment found strong evidence that, as many experts have implied, show sentences are seen as more interesting and engaging than tell sentences."

A student writing about a swim class for young children took readers to the pool to watch and listen:

> Aleena is working on putting her face in the water. The instructor has thrown a group of rings across the bottom of the shallow end, but Aleena continues to pick them up with her feet. The instructor tries another method.
> "You guys want to blow bubbles for me? This time we're looking for fish."
> "I see one, I see one!" Aleena exclaims.
> "You do? Blow bubbles at it!"

Another student writer used her sense of touch to gather information: "After 40 years of working outside, his skin is as leathery as an alligator's." Did she actually touch the tree farmer? "Yes," she says. "I kept looking at his skin. Finally, even though I was embarrassed, I asked him if I could touch his face. He laughed. 'You can tell I don't use no fancy lotions, can't you?'"

The writing is better because the reporters didn't just ask questions and record answers. They looked; they listened; they touched. Readers can see and feel along with the reporters.

Use Words Precisely

Words should mean exactly what you intend them to mean. You should never use "uninterested" when you mean "disinterested." Nor should you use "allude" for "refer," "presume" for "assume," "endeavor" for "try," "fewer" for "less," "farther" for "further." If you report that fire destroyed a house, you mean the home needs rebuilding, not repair. If you say firefighters donned oxygen masks to enter a burning building, you are either impugning their intelligence or revealing your ignorance. (Oxygen is dangerous around fire; firefighters use air tanks.) You can make the mayor "say," "declare," "claim" or "growl"—but only one is accurate.

> "There's a time to sow and a time to reap, but there's never a time for seasonal agricultural activities."
>
> — *Jack Cappon, Associated Press senior writer and writing coach*

Coherence

When you write coherently, your writing is understandable. Coherence is built by following a logical order, by matching the content to the appropriate sentence structure, by using the correct coordinating conjunctions and by guiding readers with transitions.

Decide on the Order of Elements

Chronology is the most easily understood of story structures. You start at the beginning and go to the end. A story in the aftermath of Hurricane Sandy began 48 hours before the storm hit and continued until the storm passed and the "sun makes a welcome appearance." It was told chronologically. (For more on story structure, see Chapter 10.) Journalists, however, often don't have the luxury of readers' time or publication space to use chronology. That's why it is important to outline a story, even if your outline merely lists the three or four points you expect to make. Your outline is your map. If you know where you are going, your readers will be able to follow.

Here's a list you might make about what happened at a city council meeting:

1. Approved one-way streets.
2. Raised parking fines.
3. Bought snowplows.
4. Agreed to study downtown parking facilities.
5. Hired audit firm.

To outline the story, first you rank the actions in order of importance. Then you decide whether to focus on one element or to write a summary lead or a multiple-element lead. (See Chapter 8 for more on leads.) Once you have done that, you add detail to your outline:

1. Single-element lead: one-way streets
2. Summary of other actions
   a. Parking fines
   b. Snowplows
   c. Parking study
   d. City audit
3. Support for lead
   a. The vote
   b. Jones quote
   c. Opposition
4. Support for other actions (in order introduced in second paragraph)
   a. Parking fines
      (i) Amount; (ii) reason; (iii) no opposition
   b. Snowplows
      (i) Cost; (ii) when delivered

   c. Parking study
      (i) Define problem; (ii) when study is due; (iii) who will do it;
      (iv) Dehaven quote; (v) Chamber of Commerce request
   d. City audit
      (i) Who will do it; (ii) cost; (iii) when due

Although outlining might take five minutes, it will save you much more time. The outline also creates a structure that flows logically from one idea to the next. Here's how you could start the story outlined above:

> **The Springfield City Council voted Tuesday to make four streets in the downtown area one-way.**
>   **The council also raised parking fines to $5, voted to buy two snowplows, ordered a study of downtown parking facilities and hired a firm to audit the city.**
>   **Effective March 1, the four streets that will be one-way are . . .**

Select the Proper Sentence Structure

Within each sentence, you must express the proper relationships between ideas. One way to do this is to think about your sentence structure. Simple sentences express one idea. Compound sentences express two or more ideas of equal importance. Complex sentences subordinate one idea to another. Here are some examples.

> **Simple**   The mayor scolded the council.
>
> **Compound**   The mayor scolded the council, and she insisted on a vote.

Compound sentences equate two or more ideas without commenting on them. Complex sentences allow you to show sequence and cause and effect, among other things:

> **Complex**   After the mayor scolded the council, she insisted on a vote. (Shows sequence.)
>
> **Complex**   Because the mayor was angry, she insisted on a vote. (Shows cause and effect.)

Both sentences are correct, but the meaning of each is slightly different.

Use the Precise Conjunction

Subordinating conjunctions—such as "if," "since," "while," "after" and "until"— each carry a different and precise meaning. Choose the subordinating conjunction that expresses the idea you want.

Coordinating conjunctions ("and," "or," "but," "for," "nor," "so," "yet") also require careful selection. Observe how the meaning changes with the conjunction in these examples:

> **The mayor insisted that the council vote, and the members ignored her.**

> **The mayor insisted that the council vote, but the members ignored her.**

The second example is more coherent because it expresses the council members' reaction more logically.

TIPS

Six kinds of transitions

1. Time.
2. Direction and/or place.
3. Repetition of words or phrases.
4. Numbers.
5. Demonstrative adjectives: *this, that, these, those.*
6. Relationship connectors: coordinating conjunctions, subordinating conjunctions, and conjunctive adverbs.

Use Transitions

Transitions are words, phrases, sentences or paragraphs that show the logical progression of the story structure and the ideas within the structure. Transitions are road signs directing readers through a story. The annotated model "Using Transitions" (see page 181) shows how transitions can be used in a story.

The reference to memory in the next example directs us from the first to the second paragraph:

> Mr. and Mrs. Lester Einbender are using their memory to project life as it might have been.
> *That memory* centers around a son named Michael, a rheumatic disease called lupus and a desire to honor one while conquering the other.

The use of the word "That" at the beginning of the second paragraph is subtle, but its impact is dramatic. If you wrote "A memory," you would not link the reader to the memory already mentioned. If you wrote "The memory," you would be more specific, but by writing "That memory," you point directly to the memory mentioned in the preceding paragraph. Because "a" is good only for general references, "a" is called an *indefinite modifier*. Because "the" is more specific, "the" is called a *definite modifier*. Because "that" is most specific, it is a *demonstrative adjective*; it demonstrates precisely the word or phrase to which you are referring when you couple it with the noun ("memory"). Other demonstrative adjectives include "this," "these" and "those." When you move from indefinite to definite modifier and then to demonstrative adjective, you climb the ladder of coherence.

Another way to write clearly is to use relationship connectors. There are three types:

1. Coordinating conjunctions are "and," "but," "for," "nor," "or," "so" and "yet." Choose them carefully to express the relationship.
2. Subordinating conjunctions include "although," "because," "since" and "while." Each means something different.
3. Conjunctive adverbs include "however," "therefore," "accordingly" and "consequently."

> "But I obsess during writing to the point where I can lose sleep over the right word."
>
> — *Madeleine Blais, writer*

Transitions help you achieve coherence, the logical connection of ideas. They guide you from one sentence to the next, from one paragraph to the next. Writers unfamiliar with transitions merely stack paragraphs, like pieces of wood, atop one another. Transitions keep the story, if not the woodpile, from falling apart.

Repeating a word or phrase also helps to keep the story from falling apart. In the preceding example, the writer used a demonstrative adjective and repeated a word.

Parallelism, repetition of a word or grammatical form, is another way to guide readers through a story. Writers frequently use parallelism to achieve coherence.

ANNOTATED MODEL　　Using Transitions

The first four paragraphs focus on Billman, which makes the story easy to follow. Billman's name or a pronoun links the paragraphs.

On a Monday afternoon, Dr. Glenn Billman pulled back from the autopsy he was performing on a dead girl and stared at the sight before him.

In his seven years at Children's Hospital, he had never seen anything like it. The girl's colon was severely hemorrhaged, ravaged by bacteria that normally lived in a cow's intestine.

Puzzled and quietly alarmed, Billman notified local health officials. It was the first indication that the lethal strain of bacteria E. coli 0157:H7 was on the loose.

"But" is a transition that shows the writer is introducing another angle.

But Billman didn't make his discovery at Children's Hospital in Seattle. He made it at Children's Hospital in San Diego, and he made it three weeks before the E. coli epidemic struck the Northwest, killing three children and sickening about 500 people.

In December, San Diego was hit by a small E. coli outbreak that killed the 6-year-old girl and made at least seven other people sick.

Time reference used as a transition: "It is now . . ." links the Northwest outbreak to the earlier San Diego outbreak ("In December . . .").

It is now being linked to the Seattle outbreak, but in its early stages, San Diego health officials were slow to recognize the crisis, and they have been sharply criticized for failing to notify the public about the E. coli death and illnesses.

"I really believe we need to be safe and not sorry, and the fact is, a girl died in San Diego," said San Diego County Supervisor Dianne Jacob. "I was outraged. The only way I found out was by reading it in the newspaper" after the Northwest outbreak.

Time references ("after the Northwest outbreak" and "When the first . . .") link these paragraphs.

When the first Washington cases were reported in mid-January, authorities there immediately queried neighboring states, including California, but were not told about the E. coli death of the San Diego girl. That information would have alerted them about the bacteria's severity and might have pointed them sooner to the source of the contamination.

The phrase "Like the patients here" links this paragraph to the preceding one.

Like the patients here, the San Diego girl had eaten a hamburger at a Jack in the Box restaurant days before she got sick and died. The seven other E. coli patients had all eaten hamburgers at fast-food restaurants, among them Jack in the Box.

The word "that" is a demonstrative adjective that points to the preceding paragraph.

That information was available in early January, according to Dr. Michele Ginsberg, San Diego County epidemiologist. She would not say how many of the seven patients had eaten at Jack in the Box.

"A variety of restaurants were mentioned," she said. "Naming any one of them would create public reaction and perhaps avoidance of those restaurants."

"That" again creates a transition from the preceding paragraph.

That reticence angers Jacob, the San Diego County supervisor. "I had a follow-up meeting with county health officials, and I have to tell you, very honestly, I was not pleased with their attitude," she said. . . .

Transitions, like road signs, help readers understand where they have been and where they are going.

Writing about the complicated subject of nuclear-waste disposal in America, Donald Barlett and James Steele, then of *The Philadelphia Inquirer*, relied on parallelism for coherence and emphasis. Notice the parallel use of "They said . . ." to start sentences—and the repeated variations of "It cannot."

> This assessment may prove overly optimistic. For perhaps in no other area of modern technology have so many experts in the government, industry and science been so wrong so many times over so many years as have those involved in radioactive waste.
>
> They said, repeatedly, that radioactive waste could be handled like any other industrial refuse. It cannot.
>
> They said that science had most of the answers, and was on the verge of getting the few it did not have, for dealing with radioactive waste permanently. It did not, and it does not.
>
> They said that some of it could be buried in the ground, like garbage in a landfill, and that it would pose no health hazard because it would never move. It moved.
>
> They said that liquid radioactive waste could be put in storage tanks, and that rigorous safety systems would immediately detect any leaks. The tanks leaked for weeks and no one noticed.

Barlett and Steele's use of parallelism sets up the story. In the following case, the writer, Amy Ellis Nutt, in a story about Hurricane Sandy, a storm that devasted parts of the East Coast in 2012, repeated the word "waiting" for emphasis:

> Realized or not, we live in constant anticipation. We're always waiting. Waiting to drive. Waiting to turn 21. Waiting for winter break. Waiting to graduate. Waiting for a significant other to come along.

Chronology and references to time provide other ways to tie a story together. Words and phrases such as "now," "since then" and "two days later" are invaluable in helping readers understand where they have been and where they are going. Chronology is important in everything from reports of automobile accidents (which car entered the intersection first?) to recaps of events that occurred over months or even hours.

Conciseness and Simplicity

Conciseness is a virtue, particularly in newspapers and broadcasting where space and time constraints are severe—as well as on Twitter and Facebook feeds. However, even when you write longer online stories, you have to respect readers' time. No one has unlimited time or attention to give you.

Be Concise

Being concise means saying what you need to say in as few words as possible. Some subjects require more details than others. Here are four ways to shorten your stories. (See also the annotated model "Editing for Conciseness" on page 184.)

1. **Eliminate some subject areas.** Always ask yourself whether all of the subjects need to be included. No doubt, your editor will have a more dispassionate view of what's needed than you will.

2. **Eliminate redundancies.** One way to achieve conciseness is to rid your sentences of cabooses, unneeded words or phrases that hitch themselves, like barnacles, onto other words. Delete the barnacles in italics: remand *back*; gather *together*; consensus *of opinion*; *totally* destroyed; *excess* verbiage; open *up*; fall *down*; my *own personal* favorite; strangled *to death*.

3. **Challenge intensive and qualifying adverbs.** Your job is to select the right word so you don't need two or more. Instead of "really unhappy," perhaps you mean "sad." Instead of "very cold," perhaps you mean "frigid." "Really" and "very" are examples of intensive adverbs. When you say "almost there," you are using a qualifying adverb. You might be near, or you might be a mile away. Be specific.

4. **Train yourself to value brevity.** Some of the most notable writing in history is brief: Lincoln's Gettysburg Address contains 272 words; the Ten Commandments, 297; and the American Declaration of Independence, 300.

You will use fewer words when you figure out what you want to say and then express it positively. Enter the following negatively phrased thicket of verbiage at your own risk:

> The Missouri Gaming Commission has 30 days to appeal a judge's temporary order reversing the commission's decision not to grant a gaming license to a firm that wanted to dock a riverboat casino in Jefferson City.

The writer is lost in a maze of reversals of negative findings. The lead tries to cover too much territory. Express it in the positive and strip it to its essential information:

> The state has 30 days to persuade a judge it should not have to license a firm that wants to open a riverboat casino in Jefferson City.

The writer of this sentence also failed to think clearly.

> Amtrak, formally the National Passenger Railroad Corp., was created in 1970 to preserve declining passenger train service.

The writer did not mean that Amtrak was created to preserve *declining* passenger train service. It was created to increase passenger train service.

Keep It Simple

The readers of one newspaper confronted the following one-sentence paragraph:

> "Paradoxically, cancer-causing mutations often result from the repair of a cell by error-prone enzymes and not the 'carcinogenic' substance's damage to the cell," Abe Eisenstark, director of biological sciences at the university, said at a meeting of the Ad Hoc Council of Environmental Carcinogenesis Wednesday night at the Cancer Research Center.

"Short is beautiful. Short and simple is more beautiful. Short, simple and interesting is most beautiful.**"**

— *Don Gibb, educator*

ANNOTATED MODEL   Editing for Conciseness

"Currently" is usually redundant because the verb tense implies it.

"With" is unnecessary.

The plural form gets around the wordy "his or her."

"Season" isn't required in either sentence in this paragraph.

"Strong" and "too" are unnecessary intensifiers.

Change "has plans" to "plans" to strengthen the verb.

"In the future" is already implied in the verb.

No information is lost by eliminating "serve as a way to."

"Traveling" says "taking a trip" in one word.

"Up" is an unnecessary caboose on "baking." Treats are delicious. Whom else do you bake treats for?

Bartholow is ~~currently~~ working on other projects, but he ~~has~~ plans to continue ~~with~~ his video game research. ~~In the future~~, he hopes to recruit female subjects—a difficult task because far fewer women than men play violent video games. He's also interested in examining how ~~a person's prior~~ *people's* gaming history affects ~~his or her~~ *their* response to a single exposure to a violent video game.

Pumpkins are everywhere ~~during the fall season~~ *in fall*. They ~~serve as a way to~~ help families and friends ~~to get closer~~ *bond* during the ~~holiday season~~ *holidays*. Whether you're ~~taking a trip~~ *traveling* to the local pumpkin patch ~~to search for the perfect pumpkin~~, or baking ~~up some delicious~~ treats ~~for people to enjoy~~, pumpkins are a ~~strong~~ reminder that comfort isn't ~~too~~ far away.

To be concise, challenge every word or phrase you write. These examples show how to eliminate 36 of the 127 words. (The replacement words are in italics.)

If there is a message in those 52 words, it would take a copy editor, a lexicologist and a Nobel Prize–winning scientist to decipher it. The message simply is not clear. Although the sentence is not typical of newspaper writing, it is not unusual either.

The scientist is using the vocabulary of science, which is inappropriate for a general audience. The reporter should say, "I don't understand that exactly. Can you translate it for my readers?" The response may produce an understandable quote, but if it doesn't, paraphrase the statement and check back with your source to be sure you have paraphrased it accurately.

Too much of what is written is mumbo jumbo. For instance:

> Approximately 2 billion tons of sediment from land erosion enters our nation's waters every year. While industrial waste and sewage treatment plants receive a great deal of attention, according to the Department of Agriculture the No. 1 polluter of our waterways is "non-point" pollution.

The writer of that lead contributed some linguistic pollution of his own. The message may have been clear in his mind, but it is not clear in print. Here's another way to approach this story:

> Soil carried into the water by erosion, not industrial waste or sewage from treatment plants, is the No. 1 polluter of U.S. waterways, according to the Department of Agriculture.

One remedy for unclear writing is the short sentence. The following examples introduce the same subject:

> From measurements with high-precision laser beams bounced off reflectors left at three lunar sites by Apollo astronauts, plus one atop an unmanned Soviet lunar vehicle, scientists believe that the moon is still wobbling from a colossal meteorite impact 800 years ago.

> Scientists believe the moon is still wobbling from a colossal meteorite impact 800 years ago.

The writer of the first example drags the reader through some prickly underbrush full of prepositional phrases. The writer of the second has cleared the brush to expose the flowers.

Correct and Effective Language

Writing to be read is not easy. Reporters become writers by the sweat of their brows. John Kenneth Galbraith, a best-selling author who was able to make economics understandable to the lay reader, commented on the difficulty of writing well. "There are days when the result is so bad that no fewer than five revisions are required," he wrote. "In contrast, when I'm inspired, only four revisions are needed."

Trying the techniques discussed in this chapter is the first step. Mastering them will be the result of repeated practice.

Figures of Speech

Good writers understand how to use literary devices known as figures of speech. Similes and metaphors, two common figures of speech, permit writers to show similarities and contrasts. *Similes* show similarities by comparing one thing to another, often using the word "like" or "as." Describing her roommate's reaction to the news that she was moving, one writer said, "She stared into space for a few moments, scowling, *as if she were squaring large numbers in her head*." From a profile of a CEO: "There's barely a picture on the wall or a paper on the desk. It's as clutter-free as a monk's quarters."

Metaphor is the first cousin of simile. A simile says one thing is *like* another, but a metaphor says one thing *is* another: "Michael is a lion with gazelle legs." A metaphor is a stronger analogy than a simile. Describing the radio personality and writer Garrison Keillor, a reporter once wrote, "And there he is. A sequoia in a room full of saplings." The metaphor works on two levels. Keillor is tall enough to tower over most others in the room. Because he is known internationally, his work towers over that of others, too.

With similes and metaphors, writers draw word pictures. These techniques turn the pages of a scrapbook of images in each reader's mind.

GRAMMAR CHECK

What's the grammar error in this sentence?

Formerly flying outside the State House in Charleston, S.C., state troopers took down the Confederate flag after a vote in the state assembly.

See Appendix 1, Rule 10.

> ❝The real problem is that misplaced modifiers and similar glitches tend to distract readers. Introduce blunders to an otherwise smoothly flowing story and it's as though a drunk stumbled through a religious procession.
>
> "What's more, while those errors due to carelessness may not permanently damage the language, they can damage a paper's credibility. Botching a small job sows mistrust about the larger enterprise.❞
>
> — Jack Cappon, Associated Press
> senior writer and writing coach

Careful Word Choice

Freedom in word choice is exhilarating when the result is a well-turned phrase. Here's how one student described the weather in fresh terms: "I rushed off the bus into a downpour of beaming sunlight." Here's Julie Sullivan of *The Spokesman-Review*: "Hand him a soapbox, he'll hand you a homily."

Freedom in word choice is dangerous when it results in nouns masquerading as verbs (*prioritize, impact, maximize*) or jargon masquerading as respectable English (*input, output, throughput*).

Precision, however, means more than knowing the etymology of a word; it means knowing exactly what you want to say. Instead of saying, "The City Council wants to locate the landfill three blocks from downtown," to be precise, you say, "Some members of the City Council . . ." or, better yet, "Five members of the City Council want to located the landfill three blocks east of downtown. . . ."

Precision also means using the conditional (*could, might, should, would*) when discussing proposals:

> **Incorrect** The bill will make it illegal . . .
>
> **Correct** The bill would make it illegal . . .

The use of "will" is imprecise because the legislation has not been passed. By using "would," you are saying, "If the legislature passes the bill, it would. . . ."

Bias-Free Language

Even when used innocently, sexist and racist language, besides being offensive and discriminatory, is imprecise. Doctors aren't always "he," nor are nurses always "she." Much of our language assumes people are male unless they are identified as female. Precise writers avoid "policeman" ("police officer"), "ad man" ("advertising representative"), "assemblyman" ("assembly member") and "postman" ("postal worker"). In some situations, you can use the plural to eliminate the need for a gender-specific word: "Doctors treat their patients."

Check *The Associated Press Stylebook* to see whether to identify a person's race or ethnicity. Then try to follow the person's own preference and be as specific as possible: "Asian-American" is acceptable but "Chinese-American" may be preferable. "Black" is acceptable for any nationality, but use "African-American" only for an American black person of African descent.

Some words, perfectly precise when used correctly, are imprecise when used in the wrong context. "Boy" is not interchangeable with "young man," and "girl" is not

---

TIPS

Avoiding Carelessness in Word Choice

- Know precisely what you want to say.
- Use the conditional ("could," "might," "should," "would") when discussing proposals.
- Choose the correct sentence structure to communicate explicitly what you mean.

interchangeable with "young woman." Not all active retired people are "spry," which implies that the writer is surprised to find that the person is active. "Grandmotherly" fails when you describe people in their 40s who are grandmothers. It also fails when you use it indiscriminately. When Nancy Pelosi became the first female speaker of the U.S. House of Representatives, many accounts identified her as a grandmother. While it is true that she's a grandmother, accounts of new male leaders seldom mention that they are grandfathers. When Hillary Clinton was running for president, many of the news stories included references to her clothing and hair style. You seldom see that in stories of male candidates.

"Dumb," as in "deaf and dumb," is imprecise and derogatory. Instead, use "speech-impaired." When the terms are used in tandem, use "hearing-impaired and speech-impaired" for parallelism. Because alcoholism is a disease, use "recovering alcoholic" instead of "reformed alcoholic." "Handicapped" is imprecise; "disabled" is preferred.

The Associated Press recommends "gay" and "lesbian" and sometimes allows "homosexual" but does not permit "queer" and other derogatory terms. AP suggests consulting the National Lesbian and Gay Journalists Association "Stylebook" and "Journalists Toolbox" (www.nlgja.org) for background on this other similar issues. For example, according to the NLGJA, the preferred term for a person who was identified as female at birth but subsequently came to express a male gender identity is "transgender man."

The battle over abortion extends to the terms used in news. One side wants to be described as "pro-life"; the other wants to be described as "pro-choice." The Associated Press prescribes the terms "anti-abortion" and "pro-abortion rights" in an attempt to be neutral.

Some dismiss this concern for language as overly zealous political correctness. That attitude implies that we are afraid to tell the truth. What is the truth about ethnic slang? The truth is that many words historically applied to groups of people were created in ignorance or hate or fear. During the world wars, American citizens of German descent were called "krauts" to depersonalize them. Over the years, pejorative terms have been applied to immigrants from Ireland, Poland, China and Africa. We see the same thing happening to more recent immigrants from Latin America, the Caribbean and the Middle East. The adjective "Muslim" is seldom seen or heard in news reports except to modify "terrorists" or "fundamentalists." In reality, "Muslim" refers simply to an adherent of Islam. As writers concerned with precision of the language, we should deal with people, not stereotypes.

Words are powerful. When used negatively, they define cultures, create second-class citizens and reveal stereotypical thinking. They also change the way people think about and treat others. Writers have the freedom to choose precisely the right word. That freedom can be both exhilarating and dangerous.

> " I like to say to writers: Write to save your life. Revise to give a gift to the reader. That gift may be insight, entertainment, illumination—better still, let it be all three. The pact between writer and reader is one of trust and generosity. "
>
> — *Carol Edgarian, cofounder and publisher of* Narrative Magazine

Correct Grammar and Punctuation

Far too often, grammar and punctuation errors obscure meaning. Consider this example:

> **Watching his parents struggle in low-paying jobs, a college education looked desirable to him.**

Because the first noun following the participial phrase ("Watching . . .") is "college education," the sentence seems to mean that the college education did the watching. Write the sentence this way:

> **Watching his parents struggle in low-paying jobs, he realized he wanted a college education.**

No one who aspires to be a writer will succeed without knowing the rules of grammar. Dangling participles, subject-verb disagreement, pronoun-antecedent disagreement and misplaced modifiers are like enemy troops: They attack sentences and destroy their meaning, as the authors of a survey discovered.

The personnel director of an Inglewood, California, aerospace company had to fill out a government survey form that asked, among other things, "How many employees do you have, broken down by sex?" After considering the sentence for a few moments, she wrote, "Liquor is more of a problem with us."

Here are some typical errors and ways to correct them:

Pronoun-antecedent disagreement	Each of the boys brought *their* sleeping bags.
Correct	Each of the boys brought *his* sleeping bag.
Subject-verb disagreement	The *mayor* together with the city council *oppose* collective bargaining by the firefighters.
Correct	The *mayor* together with the city council *opposes* . . .
	The *mayor and city council oppose* . . .
Misplaced modifier	*Despite his size*, the coach said Jones would play forward.
Correct	The coach said that Jones, *despite his size*, would play forward.

Improper punctuation creates ambiguities at best and inaccuracies at worst. For instance:

> **Giving birth to Cynthia five years earlier had been difficult for Mrs. Davenport and the two parents decided they were content with the family they had.**

Without the required comma before "and," the sentence can easily be misunderstood. A person reading quickly misses the pause and sees this: "Giving birth to Cynthia had been difficult for Mrs. Davenport and the two parents." That's a lot of people in the delivery room. (For more examples of common grammar and punctuation errors, see Appendix 1.)

Most newsrooms used to have two or three people read each story to catch these and other errors. Now, almost all media have reduced the number of copy editors. It is even more important these days for the writer to get it right in the first place.

The Tools of Narration

The tools of narration allow you to build interest in stories. When we use scenes, dialogue and anecdotes, or create a sense of person and place, we are using narrative tools that help make our stories as informative as they are interesting. In exposition, the writer clearly stands between the reader and the information. Journalists have sources, who tell them things. Journalists then tell the reader what they heard and saw. Scenes, dialogue and anecdotes allow the reader to see the action.

Scenes

Gene Roberts, former managing editor of *The New York Times*, tells about his first job at a daily newspaper. His publisher, who was blind, had someone read the newspaper to him each morning. One day, the publisher called Roberts into his office and complained, "Roberts, I can't see your stories. Make me see."

We should all try to make readers see, smell, feel, taste and hear. One way to do that is to write using scenes as much as possible. To write a scene, you have to be there. You need to capture the pertinent details. Think of yourself as a playwright, not as a narrator standing on a stage. Leave the stage and let your readers see the action and hear the dialogue. You can see and hear what is happening in the following excerpt. Put yourself in a theater watching the actors on stage:

> **" The most important thing to any writing, and especially profile writing, is the telling detail. "**
>
> — *Jacqui Banaszynski, Pulitzer Prize winner*

> She was in her office getting ready to attend a doctoral candidate's prospectus defense when the call came that would turn her life upside down. The surgeon told her she was very sorry, but it was invasive breast cancer.
> "Am I going to die?" Carver asked her.
> "Well, I certainly hope not," the surgeon said.
> She hung up the phone in a daze but refused to go home. Somehow, she managed to get through the defense. Then she went to see her husband, Bill Horner, an MU political science professor. She walked into his office and shut the door. Horner knew before she had uttered a word.

A student reporter at South Dakota State University was on a farm to capture this opening scene:

> Don Sheber's leathery, cracked hands have been sculpted by decades of wresting a living from the earth.

David Bacon / The Image Works

"Don Sheber's leathery, cracked hands have been sculpted by decades of wresting a living from the earth." Use descriptive language to paint a vivid picture for readers and to bring a story to life.

> But this year, despite work that often stretches late into the evening, the moisture-starved soil has yielded little for Sheber and his family.
>
> Sheber's hands tugged at the control levers on his John Deere combine last week as rotating blades harvested the thin stands of wheat that have grown to less than a foot high.

The writer allows the reader to visit Sheber on the farm. We can see and feel the farmer's hands. We can touch the John Deere combine and the stunted wheat.

To create such scenes, you must use all your senses to gather information, and your notebook should reflect that reporting. Along with the results of interviews, your notebook should bulge with details of sights and smells, sounds and textures. David Finkel, winner of the American Society of News Editors Distinguished Writing Award in 1986 and a Pulitzer Prize in 2006, says, "Anything that pertains to any sense I feel at any moment, I write down." Gather details indiscriminately. Later, you can discard those that are not germane. Because you were there, you can write the scene as if you were writing a play.

Because Bartholomew Sullivan of *The (Memphis) Commercial Appeal* was observing and listening closely at a trial, his readers were able to sit in the courtroom with him:

> Helfrich banged an index finger on the rail of the jury box as he recalled Thursday's testimony in which a string of Bowers's Jones County friends testified that he was a solid businessman, a Christian—"a gentleman." One of the witnesses was Nix, who called Bowers a "real, real nice man."

"They talk of gentlemen," Helfrich whispered. Then, shouting, he said: "These people don't have a gentle bone in their bodies. They were nightriders and henchmen. They attacked a sleeping family and destroyed all they owned."

Analyze the detail: the banging of an index finger, the whisper, the shout. We can see and we can hear. By creating a scene, the writer transported us to the courtroom rather than just telling us what he saw.

To write a scene, you must be able to capture a sense of place. Show us where the action is taking place. Take us to the courtroom, the basketball court or the city.

Dialogue

The use of *dialogue*—conversation between two or more people, not including the reporter—allows the reporter to recede and the characters to take center stage. When you use quotations, you—the writer—are repeating for the reader what the source said, and the reader listens to you relating what was said. But when you use dialogue, you disappear, and the reader listens directly to the characters. Dialogue is a key element in creating scenes. Compare these examples:

> During the public hearing, Henry Lathrop accused the council of wasting taxpayers' money. "If you don't stop voting for all this spending, I am going to circulate a recall petition and get you all kicked off the council," he said.
> Mayor Margorie Gold told Lathrop he was free to do as he wished. "As for us," she said, "we will vote in the best interests of the city."

That is the traditional way of presenting quotations. The reporter uses quotes but also paraphrases some of what was said. That's telling readers instead of taking them to the council chambers and letting them listen. Here is how that account would sound handled as dialogue:

> When Henry Lathrop spoke to the City Council during the public hearing, he pounded on the podium. "You folks are wasting taxpayers' money. If you don't stop voting for all this spending, I am going to circulate a recall petition and get you all kicked off the council."
> Mayor Margorie Gold slammed her gavel on her desk.
> "Mr. Lathrop," she said as she tried to control the anger in her voice. She looked at him directly. "You are free to do as you wish. As for us, we will vote in the best interests of the city."

At the hearing, Lathrop and Gold were speaking to each other. The second version captures the exchange without the intercession of the writer.

Here's another example of dialogue. This conversation took place between Cindy Martling, a rehabilitation nurse, and Mary Jo, a patient's wife, after Martling scolded the patient for feeling sorry for himself:

> She wandered around a bit, then saw Mary Jo standing in the hallway. The two women went to each other and embraced. "I'm sorry," Martling said through more tears. "I didn't mean to lose control. I hope I didn't offend you."
> "What you did was wonderful," Mary Jo said. "He needed to hear that. Dan is going to work through it, and we're all going to be OK."

Anecdotes

The ultimate treats, **anecdotes**, are stories embedded in stories. They can be happy or sad, funny or serious. Whatever their tone, they should illustrate a point. Readers are likely to remember the anecdotes more readily than anything else in a story. You probably remember the stories that your professors tell regardless of whether you remember the rest of the lecture. Long after you've forgotten this chapter, you will probably remember some of the examples from it. Facts inform. Anecdotes inform and entertain.

> "If history were taught in the form of stories, it would never be forgotten."
>
> — *Rudyard Kipling, English writer*

As befits something so valuable, anecdotes are hard to obtain. You can't get them by asking your source, "Got any good anecdotes?" But you can get them by asking for examples so you can re-create the scene. To do this, be alert to the possibilities that an anecdote might be lurking in the details. One reporter gathered this quote:

> "We had one of those coaching nights where we sat up until I don't know when trying to figure it out," Richardson says. "We refer to that as the red-letter day in Spartan football, and since that day, we are 33-15, with three district titles and a conference championship."

The editor pointed out to the reporter that if it was a red-letter day, the reporter should have asked more questions about that coaching meeting. He did, and he ended up with an anecdote about how the coaches figured out a new strategy that turned out to be successful.

Here's another example. Your source says: "Darren is like a one-man entertainment committee. He's always got something going on. And if nothing is going on, he'll hike up his pants really high and dance to Fetty Wop."

To turn this dry quote into an anecdote, you need to ask, "Can you give me an example of when he acted like an entertainment committee?" or "Tell me about the time he danced to Fetty Wop."

Some anecdotes come from phrasing questions in the superlative: "What's the funniest thing that ever happened to you while you were standing in front of an audience?" "What's the worst case you've ever seen come into this emergency room?" "People tell me Rodney is always the first one they call when they need help on a project. Has he ever helped you? Can you give me an example?"

A source told a student reporter Sara Trimble that the funeral home owner was one of the most compassionate people she had met. She was doing a profile on the man, so she asked for examples of his compassion. She turned the answer into this anecdote:

> Opportunity would take Millard away from close friends yet again when he moved to Jefferson City to buy his own funeral home after graduating, but it wouldn't be long before his charm would win over another community.
>
> "You're just as cute as can be. What are you doing here on a Friday night?" Peggy Talken asked a man sitting across from her. She was attending a fundraiser at her children's school.
>
> "Well, you're here too," Millard said.
>
> "I've got kids. You don't!" Talken said.

That was the first time Talken made Millard blush, and she took great pleasure in doing so. They became great friends after that, but she had no idea just how important his friendship would be until one fateful day in June 2013.

"Your daughter's dead. She didn't make it," an ER nurse said.

The words a parent never wants to hear, followed by a sight she should never have to see: her daughter, Corrie, in the hospital bed, her hair still matted down with blood and her neck fractured and gashed.

Pools of blood stained the floor, and Talken considered taking off her shirt to mop it up herself. She couldn't bear to say her last goodbye to her baby like this.

Like an answered prayer, Millard showed up at the hospital.

He asked the hospital staff for 15 minutes alone in the room. That's all he needed. In that time, he cleaned the blood off Corrie's face, put a sheet over her neck to cover up the gash and turned the lights down just a little bit.

Four days later, over 2,000 people showed up for Corrie's funeral services. How everyone found parking in the small funeral home's lot, Talken still doesn't know. Millard took care of it.

He also took care of Corrie's body.

"I told him that if even one of her eyelashes looked out of place, I would make them close the casket," Talken says.

The casket remained open.

Her neck? Still fractured, but covered with a scarf Millard had found to match the bridesmaid's dress she was buried in. Her fingernails? Cleaned, filed and polished. Her skin? Covered with natural makeup, as if she were attending her cousin's wedding as planned.

Doves were released at the gravestone—something else Talken wasn't expecting. But one dove in particular stood out to her. It was dyed pink, Corrie's favorite color.

Use anecdotes to entertain while you are informing. If the relevance of the anecdote to the larger story isn't obvious, establish the connection in the transition into the anecdote or at the end of it.

Sense of Person

To turn sources into characters, offer your readers a sense of person. Describe the subjects physically and tell us what's in their minds. A student offered this physical description: "Meinke, 48, has the build of Jason Alexander and the voice of Nathan Lane."

Student Megan Farokhmanesh offers both a physical sense and helps explain the character's personality:

But Overeem is more than a music fanatic. As a literature teacher at Hickman High School, he sponsors programs like Science Olympiad, Battle of the Bands and Academy of Rock. He helps with the Speak Your Mind forum, Amnesty International and the True/False film festival. He strives to offer his students something more than just an education, but some key component that will open their eyes to their own life.

It's Tuesday. The class is discussing Jonathan's Swift's "A Modest Proposal." Some students sit up straight, bright-eyed and attentive, while the eyelids of a few others here and there droop under the weight of their adolescent exhaustion. Overeem, a man of solid build, slowly paces around the room, his steps slow and sure. His Chuck Taylors hit the ground in a smooth, rhythmic pattern. One. Two. One. Two. His glasses zoom repeatedly into his hands and back to his nose as he gestures, continually taking them on and off. Each statement he makes is punctuated with a sharp jump of his eyebrows, as he crumples his forehead in earnest. His voice is level without being monotone, deep without being booming. Even in his excitement he is cool and collected.

In a particularly vigorous wave of his hands, his glasses fly off once more as he addresses the class. He opens the discussion to the purpose of existence. The question of whether life is worth living. Some students shift in their seats at the idea. He tells them, "I'd never kill myself. I'm afraid one of the greatest records in the world would be released the next day, and I'd never get to listen to it. And my wife would be left alone." Perhaps his students don't realize it, but Overeem has just bared his soul for them. Just like that, the two loves of his life are out in the open.

SUGGESTED READINGS

Hart, Jack. *Storycraft: The Complete Guide to Writing Narrative Nonfiction*. Chicago: The University of Chicago Press, 2011. This is as complete a how-to book on writing narrative nonfiction as exists. It practices what it preaches: it is informative and entertaining.

Osborn, Patricia. *How Grammar Works: A Self-Teaching Guide*. New York: John Wiley, 1999. This book will do for you what it promises: It will guide you, step by step, through the basics of English grammar. Its goal is to make you feel comfortable with grammar and the way words work.

Strunk, William, and E.B. White. *The Elements of Style*. 3rd ed. Boston: Allyn & Bacon, 1995. This little book practices what it preaches. For the beginner, it is a good primer; for the pro, it is a good review of writing rules and word meanings.

Tankard, James, and Laura Hendrickson. "Specificity, Imagery in Writing: Testing the Effects of 'Show, Don't Tell.'" *Newspaper Research Journal* (Winter/Spring 1996): 35–48. The authors found that participants in a test said that examples of "show" writing were more interesting and believable.

SUGGESTED WEBSITES

www.papyr.com/hypertextbooks/comp1/coherent.htm
Daniel Kies of the Department of English at the College of DuPage explains how to achieve coherence in your writing.

www.niemanstoryboard.org
This site often interviews the authors of great narrative nonfiction.

www.pulitzer.org/files/2015/feature-writing/marcum
/03marcum2015.pdf
Go to this website to see the full version of the drought story that opens this chapter.

EXERCISES

1. Underline and count the number of prepositional phrases in the following. Then rewrite to reduce the number of prepositions:

   I also thought it was interesting that the teacher mentioned that the number of prepositions used in a sentence can also determine the rhythm of your story. We've just gone over the use of prepositions in magazine editing, and they can hurt your work more than they can help it. I've never really paid attention to my use of prepositions before last week's magazine editing lecture, but I will try to limit my use as much as possible.

2. **Your journalism blog.** In the following paragraph, identify the concrete details and the similes. Evaluate what they add to your understanding of the scene. Then list and evaluate the verbs. Write a blog post about your analysis of the paragraph.

   Boyd is in his truck with Fire Chief James Samarelli, who is at the wheel. They turn right onto Sampson Avenue and are nearly hit by a wooden lifeguard boat slicing through the floodwater. A wall of water is headed directly for them, bringing a second lifeguard boat. Samarelli jerks the truck to the right. A large piece of the boardwalk, ripped away by the waves, slams into the front of the flatbed truck. Boyd looks down at his suddenly cold feet. Seawater is rushing into the cab and a 6-foot-tall swell lifts the truck and begins pushing it sideways, into a telephone pole.

3. Choose precisely the right word:

    a. We need to (ensure, insure) a victory.
    b. Stop (annoying, irritating) your friend.
    c. The attorney won because she (refuted, responded to) the allegations.
    d. The prisoner was able to produce (mitigating, militating) evidence.

4. Write a paragraph in which you give readers a sense of a particular person in your class or a local celebrity. Can your classmates identify him or her?

5. Write a paragraph in which you give readers a sense of a particular place on your campus or in the immediate neighborhood. Can you classmates identify the place?

6. Punctuate the following sentences:

    a. Government officials have come under a newly enacted censorship system and several foreign speakers have been denied permission to enter the country.

    b. It was a Monday night and for the next two days he teetered between life and death.

    c. The council approved the manager's proposals and rejected a tax increase.

7. Use a simile to explain the following numbers:

    The student council's budget is $350,000. The university has 19,000 students. The local city budget is $3 million. The city has 70,000 residents.

8. Calculate the readability levels for a couple of paragraphs you have written and for stories from *The New York Times* and the Associated Press. Compare the readability scores, and account for scoring differences and similarities. You can get the calculation at https://readability-score.com.

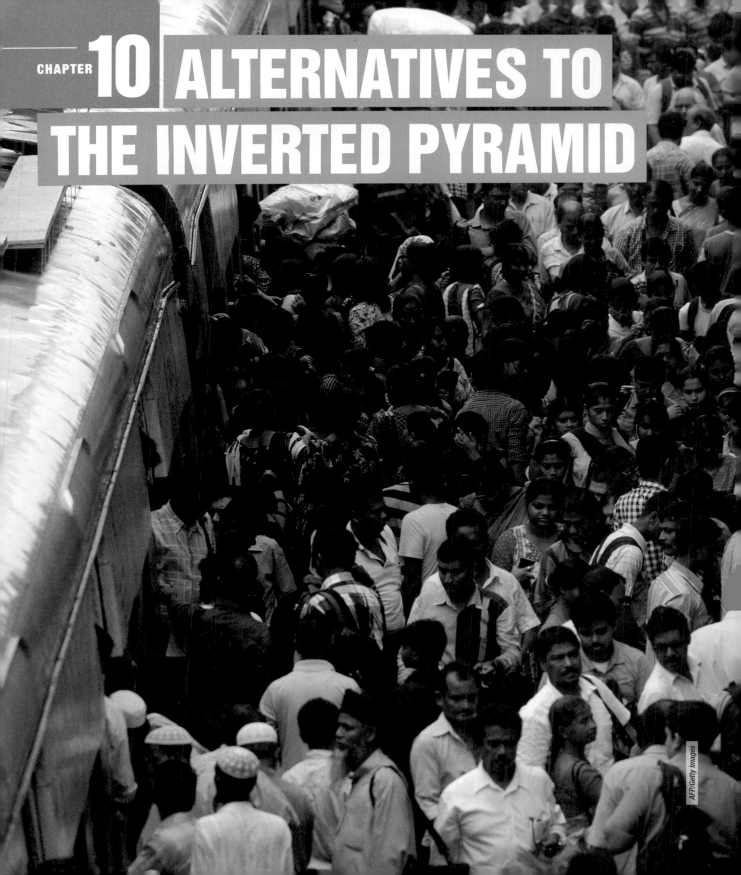

AFP/Getty Images

For all its strengths, the inverted pyramid doesn't serve all stories well. That's why journalists use other structures to tell stories in newspapers, magazines, television and websites. Increasingly, journalists are developing new structures to tell stories by taking advantage of the special strengths of the web. We'll look at those alternative structures in this chapter, but first, let's look at how a story with characters, complications and a resolution is structured:

Ill-Fated Train Ride Tears Indian Boy from Mother, Sparks 25-Year Worldwide Hunt for Home

By Kristen Gelineau and Ravi Nessman

KHANDWA, India—Saroo's eyes snapped open and everything was suddenly, horribly, wrong.

The 5-year-old's tiny body was still curled up on the hard wooden seat of the Indian train, just as it was when he'd drifted off to sleep. The rattle of the train was loud and steady, just as it always was when he rode home with his big brother, Guddu.

But Guddu was not there. And the alien landscape flashing past the window looked nothing like home.

Saroo's heart began to pound. The train car was empty. His brother should have been there, sweeping under the seats for loose change. Where was Guddu?

Where was Saroo?

It was 1987 and Saroo knew only that he was alone on the train.

Soon, he would find himself alone in the world. He wouldn't know for decades that this fateful train ride was setting into motion a chain of events both fantastic and horrific—events that would tear him away from his family and join him with a new one. Events that would spark the determined hunt of a mother for her son and a son for his mother, brought together only to realize that you can never really go home again.

In the beginning, though, all Saroo knew was that nothing was as it should be. "MA!" he screamed, wild with fear as he ran up and down the empty compartment, tears streaming down his face. "GUDDU!"

Only the relentless hum of the train answered his cries. Outside the window, the remains of his old life had faded into the distance. The train was thundering down the track toward a destination—and a destiny—unknown.

Fatima Munshi was frantic. When she returned to her cramped house after a hard day of work on a construction site, her two young sons still hadn't arrived. They should have been back hours earlier.

Fatima lived for her children. She had little else to live for. . . .

When night fell and her boys still weren't home, Fatima panicked. She took a neighbor she called Uncle Akbar to the station to look for them, but most of the trains had already come and gone. They searched the nearby market where the boys would beg. She went to the fountain where they liked to play.

By morning, her body felt like it was on fire. Her mind raced.

Maybe they had been kidnapped.

Maybe they were lost.

Maybe they were dead.

She had never been on a train before, but she and Uncle Akbar rode to Burhanpur and Bhusawal, asking police if they had seen her sons. She widened her search to bigger and further cities.

She cried and prayed for their safe return at the holy crypt of the Sufi Muslim saint Tekri Wale Baba. She approached another mystic said to channel the dead saint's spirit.

1

How to construct a chronology.

2

How to construct a news narrative story.

3

How to construct a focus structure story.

4

How to deliver information in service journalism formats.

5

How journalists are using structured journalism techniques.

"There are no longer two flowers," he said. "One flower has fallen, the other has gone to a far off place. He doesn't remember where he is from. He will come back, but only after a long, long time."

She didn't believe him. Her boys were going to be fine.

Then she ran into a police officer she knew.

Guddu was dead, he said.

The boy had either fallen off the train or been pushed. Police took photos of the mangled but still identifiable body found by the tracks, and then cremated him.

Fatima fainted.

AP writers Gelineau and Nessman used chronology to reconstruct the story of a young boy's separation from his family and his search, which ended successfully 25 years later. In Chapter 8 you learned how to rank information from most important to least important. That inverted pyramid structure serves news, particularly breaking news, well. Other structures support other types of stories better. Like the standard formula for telling fairy tales, chronology works best when characters encounter complications in bringing the story to a resolution. Writers focus on the people involved in issues to tell important stories—health care, cancer research, prayer in schools—in an interesting and informative way.

If time, detail and space are available, consider the alternative structures we describe in this chapter and summarize in Figure 10.1 on pages 200–201. Whether you are writing about a car accident, the Boy Scouts' jamboree or the drought in the western part of the U.S., writing the story will be easier if you know how to use some of the alternative story forms: the chronology, news narrative, focus structure and service journalism formats. Then we'll look at a new development in story structure.

Chronology

Stories that work best as a chronology are those that have complications or tension and a resolution worth waiting for. Saroo Brierley was separated from his family. That's one complication. Fortunately, he ended up in an orphanage, was adopted by a family in Australia and grew up healthy and educated. That's a resolution. But there was another complication. Brierley wondered about his family in India. So the next complication is how to find his family when he didn't know his Indian name or the city in which he lived. That part of the story reaches a resolution when he returns to India and finds his mother.

Complications are present even in events like meetings. When a city council faces a contentious issue, such as a proposed smoking ban in public places, you are presented with controversy (supporters and opponents testifying), tension (balancing health and economic interests) and a resolution (the vote). Time constraints and tradition often dictate an inverted pyramid structure. But you have other options:

- You could summarize the vote in a sidebar and use chronology to tell the story of the meeting.

GRAMMAR CHECK

What's the grammar error in this sentence?

Rowan County clerk Kim Davis refused to issue marriage licenses to same-sex couples, she spent five days in jail for contempt of court.

See Appendix 1, Rule 2.

■ You could write an inverted pyramid version of the story for both the website and the newspaper and then write a chronological version for the web to replace the earlier version.
■ You might use news narrative (see the next section) to report the results and then move to chronology.

Where to Start

Oddly enough, when you use chronology, you don't have to begin at the beginning. Instead, you look for a key moment you can use in the lead to engage readers. To get started, writers often jot down a timeline. In the case of the council meeting, it might look like this:

7:00 p.m.	Opponents and supporters of the smoking ban begin testifying before the council.
	Jones, an opponent, angrily denounces the proposal.
	Smith, a supporter, relates a story about her cancer.
8:15	Council members begin debate.
	Mayor pounds the gavel to break up an out-of-control argument between two council members.
	Council member Rodriguez is nearly in tears as he urges the council to pass the ordinance.
	Council member Jackson says merchants will face financial ruin.
8:47	Solinski, a member of the audience, interrupts the debate and is escorted out of the chambers by city police. Several in the audience boo, but some cheer.
9:10	During a recess, no council members mingle with the public, which irritates several of those who are attending.
9:30	The council votes 5-4 in favor of the smoking ban. There are both jeers and cheers.

A Sample Outline

You could begin at the beginning of the timeline given above, with the chamber filling with members of the public, but this lead would not attract much attention. You need a dramatic scene that captures emotion, is short and does not give away the outcome. The removal of a member of the audience has potential; so does the heated argument within the council. Here is a typical outline for a story using chronology:

1. The lead (the scene with Rodriguez).
2. The nut (theme) paragraph.
3. Foreshadowing.
4. A transition back to the beginning of the meeting to pick up the story from that point.
5. The body, highlighting key events found in the timeline. (As with any news story, much of the action is left out; this is a news story, not a secretary's report.)
6. An ending that highlights the vote and the audience reaction.

News Story Structures

	Inverted Pyramid	Chronology
What is it?	The lead paragraphs have the most important information, and succeeding paragraphs give details in descending order of importance.	Starting at a particular point of interest, the paragraphs tell a story in chronological order.
When should it be used?	It's best used for hard news, when timeliness is essential and the reader wants to know the important facts right away.	It's good for reporting a detailed sequence of events in a story with controversy or tension and resolution, especially as a follow-up to a news story.
How is it structured?	**Traditional news lead** • Give who, what, when, where, why and how. • Frame the story. **Body: support paragraphs in descending order of importance** • Give additional details about the lead. • Summarize other significant actions or elements relevant to the lead. • Give the impact or effect of the event. • Give the "so what"—the story's importance to the reader. • Give background and history. • Describe relevant physical details. • Narrate relevant sequences of events. • Use quotations from relevant sources. • Give sources of additional information, including links to websites. **Ending** • End with the least significant information, *not* with a conclusion, summary or tie-back to the beginning. The story can be cut from the bottom up without compromising its effectiveness.	**Narrative lead** • Describe a dramatic point in the story. • Create narrative suspense with foreshadowing. **Nut paragraph** • Give the theme of the story. **Body: narrative support paragraphs** • Use foreshadowing. • Pick up story with a transition back to the beginning of the narrative. • Tell the story in chronological order, highlighting key events found in the timeline. • Describe relevant physical details. • Use narrative techniques like dialogue, flashback and foreshadowing. **Ending** • Give a conclusion to the story. • Resolve the tension or conflict in the story.

FIGURE 10.1

Different structures are useful for different types of news stories.

The Nut Paragraph, Foreshadowing and the "To Be Sure"

Like the lead in an inverted pyramid story, a **nut paragraph** (or *nut graf*) is a paragraph that gives the theme of the story and summarizes the key facts. Unlike the lead in the inverted pyramid format, however, the nut paragraph is not the first paragraph in the story. For the council story, after the first (or lead) paragraph describing the scene with Rodriguez, the nut paragraph might look like this:

News Narrative	Focus Structure
The story combines elements of inverted pyramid and chronology formats, with an emphasis on either news or narrative.	The story follows one individual as a representative of a larger group.
It's useful for stories when timeliness is somewhat important but the hard news element is not prominent.	It's useful for making complex or abstract stories meaningful to readers.

News Narrative

Narrative lead
- Open with an interesting scene or twist that teases the story.
  or

Traditional news lead
- Give who, what, when, where, why and how.

Support paragraphs
- Briefly add whatever helps the reader understand the story summarized in the lead.

Body: narrative support paragraphs
- Go back to the beginning, and tell the story in chronological order.

Ending
- Give a conclusion to the story.
- Resolve the tension or conflict in the story.

Focus Structure

Narrative lead
- Introduce the subject and describe the person's problem.

Transition
- Create a bridge from the subject to the theme of the story.

Nut paragraph
- Give the theme of the story.

Support paragraphs
- Foreshadow.
- Give the "so what"—the story's importance to the reader.
- Give the "to be sure"—opposing perspectives.

Body: narrative and expository support paragraphs
- Interweave narrative about the subject with facts about the theme to tell the story.

Ending
- Conclude the story, with a summary or with a tie-back that refers to the beginning of the story.

In a meeting filled with emotional, sometimes angry testimony, citizens and the City Council debated the proposed smoking ban for nearly three hours. Citizens urged—sometimes threatened—council members. The mayor pounded his gavel to bring the council to order several times when some members engaged in heated, personal arguments. In the end, council members voted on the landmark legislation amid jeers and cheers and then left through a back door.

From the beginning, it was clear that emotions were running high. . . .

The nut paragraph both defines the story and foreshadows the heated debate. Even though readers will know the results, many will want to read the blow-by-blow account. It also establishes the "so what": This is a divisive issue, involving landmark legislation,that people care about. Notice that the last line, "From the beginning . . . ," creates a transition back to the start of the story narrative.

In the story that opened this chapter, the nut paragraph and foreshadowing start in paragraph 5:

> Where was Saroo?
>
> It was 1987 and Saroo knew only that he was alone on the train.
>
> Soon, he would find himself alone in the world. He wouldn't know for decades that this fateful train ride was setting into motion a chain of events both fantastic and horrific—events that would tear him away from his family and join him with a new one. Events that would spark the determined hunt of a mother for her son and a son for his mother, brought together only to realize that you can never really go home again.

In some stories, you might also need to include a **"to be sure" paragraph**. This paragraph, which gives opposing points of view, is a must when you are focusing on one side of an issue. Before the council vote, you could do a story about a restaurant shift from the perspective of a server. You could follow that with a story from the perspective of a smoker at a bar. In both cases, you would include a paragraph acknowledging that others disagree, especially if that opposing viewpoint is not included elsewhere in the story. For instance:

> Not everyone agrees with Megan Addison that smoking should be banned. Others, including smokers and business owners, believe that the proposal infringes on their right to smoke or to run their business as they please. But Addison and her fellow servers at the Sports Grill want to work in a smoke-free environment.

You do not need a "to be sure" paragraph in the council meeting story because all sides are represented in the debate.

The Ending

Stories written chronologically need strong endings. After the tearful reunion with his family, Saroo Brierley returned to Australia, where he had another family, a girlfriend and a job. His Indian mother wanted him to live in India. The resolution is not a simple, happy ending. Instead, both parties accept the separation reluctantly:

> Saroo doesn't want to overthink it. He wants to revel in the joy of their remarkable reunion. For him, it has been a miracle punctuated by a happy ending.
>
> "It's sort of taken a weight off my shoulders," he says. "Instead of going to bed at night and thinking, 'How is my family? Are they still alive?' I know in my head now I can let those questions rest."
>
> He hopes to visit India once or twice a year, but he cannot move back. He has other responsibilities, other family and a whole other life in Tasmania.
>
> He is Australian now.
>
> "This is where I live," he says. "When I come back, whether it's sooner or later, then we can start building our relationship again."
>
> Fatima is confused and frustrated.

She doesn't want him to move back here, where there is nothing. But she wants to be with him. Maybe she can move to Australia, she says. She adds sternly that she would ban all girlfriends from his house.

A few minutes later she softens. She couldn't really move away from her life here to an unfamiliar place where no one can talk with her, she says.

At least, and at last, Saroo's return has brought her "mental peace," she says. She tries to understand that he has new parents, new expectations and a new life a world away.

She just wants him to see her once in a while, to call her occasionally, even if they can only speak a few sentences to each other.

"For the moment," she says, "it's enough for me that I went to him. And he called me Amma."

Mother.

For both the hypothetical council story and the real story of the reunion, readers want to know the outcome of the narrative. In the council story, how did the meeting end? How heated was it? The reunion story was framed through the eyes of Saroo, searching for his mother, and Fatima, searching for her son. Readers read a chronology to the end because they want to see how the complications are resolved.

News Narrative

In Chapter 8, you saw examples of inverted pyramid stories that didn't have the news in the first paragraph (see "The 'You' Lead" and "Leads with Flair") but as soon as the writer teased the reader, the news lead appeared. Then the writer arranged the rest of the story in the traditional descending order of importance. Further modification, though, offers writers more choices. The **news narrative** structure combines the inverted pyramid and chronology. Here is an outline of its basic elements:

1. An opening with an interesting scene or twist that teases the story.
2. A traditional news lead.
3. Brief paragraphs that add whatever help readers need to understand the story summarized in the traditional lead.
4. A transition back to the beginning to tell the story in chronological order.

The "news" in "news narrative" implies that the story has a time element and that the story is not a feature. Features, sometimes called "soft stories," are those that can run nearly any time, such as a profile of a stamp collector, a story on a volunteer at the local food bank or an article about riding with a police officer for a shift. A story with a time element usually has to be tweeted, posted on the web and broadcast on the next television news show or published in the next issue of the newspaper. The "narrative" in "news narrative" means that you can use chronology, one of the most important tools of narrative writing. In the news narrative, you will often find other narrative tools, such as those discussed in Chapter 9: scenes, dialogue, anecdotes and sense of person.

ANNOTATED MODEL   News Narrative with News Emphasis

The opening paragraphs set the scene with information that informs and is interesting. →

PALM HARBOR—They carried knapsacks and bags to tote loot. They had a screwdriver to pry open doors and windows.

They used latex gloves.

They acted like professional criminals, but officials say they were teenage burglars coached and directed by a Palm Harbor woman whose son and daughter were part of her gang.

A traditional news lead gives "who," "what" and "when." →

Pinellas County Sheriff's deputies arrested Rovana Sipe, two of her children and two other teens Wednesday after a series of home burglaries.

"She was the driver," said Sheriff's Sgt. Greg Tita. "She pointed out the houses. She's the one who said 'Do these.'" ← *The writer supports the lead with a quote.*

The story continues with the breaking news for the next four paragraphs. →

Sipe, 38, of 2333 State Road 584, was charged with two counts of being a principal in burglary. She was held Thursday in lieu of $20,000 bail.

Her daughter, Jackie Shifflet, 16, was charged with grand theft. Her son, Ryan Shifflet, 15, was charged with two counts of burglary.

Charles Ruhe, 17, of 1600 Ensley Ave., in Safety Harbor, and Charles Taylor, 16, of 348 Jeru Blvd. in Tarpon Springs, also were held on four counts of burglary each.

"They were very well-prepared to do burglaries, especially with the guidance they were given," Tita said. "We recovered thousands of dollars of stolen items. Anything that could be carried out, was."

The burglary ring unraveled Tuesday, Tita said. A Palm Harbor woman saw a large, yellow car driven by a woman drop off three boys, he said. The three went to the back of her house. ← *Now that the news has been established, instead of continuing to present the information in order of importance, the writer presents the rest of the story in chronological fashion. Note the important transition from inverted pyramid to chronology: "The burglary ring unraveled Tuesday, Tita said."*

They put on gloves and started to pry open a window with a screwdriver, she said. When she tapped on a window, they ran.

She called 911. As she waited for deputies, other neighbors saw the boys walk through a nearby neighborhood carrying bags.

Deputies chased the boys and caught two. The third got into a large yellow car driven by a woman.

The bags contained jewelry, a shotgun and other items deputies say were taken from another house in the neighborhood.

Tita said the boys, later identified as Taylor and Ruhe, told detectives about other burglaries in Dunedin and Clearwater and who else was involved.

At Sipe's house, detectives found stolen VCRs, televisions, camcorders and other valuables. They arrested the other two teens and Sipe.

The story ends with a quote rather than a tie-back or summary. →

"We're very familiar with this family and its criminal history," Tita said. "We have found stolen property at the house in the past and made juvenile arrests."

In news narratives with a news emphasis, the writer needs to establish the facts before giving the chronology. This format is associated with breaking news of significance, such as crime.

Source: Jane Meinhardt, "Mother Accused of Being Criminal Ringleader," *St. Petersburg Times*, Oct. 21, 1994.

News Narrative with News Emphasis

When the local sheriff's department broke an unusual burglary ring, Jane Meinhardt of the *St. Petersburg (Fla.) Times* elected to use the news narrative structure. In the annotated model "News Narrative with News Emphasis" (page 204), you can read her story, which follows the outline above. Notice that the story is a news narrative with news emphasis. This format works well for news that is significant but not earth-shattering. You probably wouldn't use it to report during the first few hours or perhaps even the first couple of days after a major news event like a mass shooting. You need to be able to get all the details of how something happened to relate the chronology. Immediately following a disaster or other major event, the authorities don't have all the information, and the reporter might not have access to witnesses or documents.

News Narrative with Narrative Emphasis

When the news is less important, the news narrative structure is also useful, but the emphasis is on narrative rather than news. John Tully, a reporter for the *Columbia Missourian*, was asked to look for a story at a horse-riding competition one Sunday afternoon. Because most of the competitors were not from the newspaper's local area, reporting the results of the competition was not as important as finding a good story.

Tully knew nothing about horse-riding competitions, so he first found people who could explain the judging. He also asked people to suggest interesting competitors. A youth coordinator told him that Cara Walker was competing for the first time since her accident. After gathering more information from the coordinator, Tully found Walker and her mother—and a story that lent itself to news narrative. Through Tully's story (see the annotated model "News Narrative with Narrative Emphasis" on page 206), readers learned that Walker, who had been seriously injured in a car accident, was able to recover enough to ride again. What they didn't find out until the end was that she won the competition. Because he had less news to report, Tully was able to go to the chronological format more quickly than Meinhardt, who was reporting the newsier story about the burglary ring. He used the outcome of the competition to reward readers who completed the story.

Focus Structure

For centuries, writers have used the focus structure to tell the story of an individual or a group that represents a bigger population. This approach allows the writer to make large institutions, complex issues and seven-digit numbers meaningful. Not many of us can understand—let alone explain—the marketing system for wheat, but we could more easily do so if we followed a crop of wheat from the time it was planted until a consumer bought a loaf of bread.

ANNOTATED MODEL   News Narrative with Narrative Emphasis

The first two paragraphs reveal the news of the injury and the twist that even though doctors were unsure, she recovered enough to compete. The horse show is the news event that generated the story. Note that the second paragraph reveals that she competed but only foreshadows how she did.

About five months ago, Cara Walker, 17, was lying in a hospital recovering from the spinal injury she received when she lost control of her car, rolled the vehicle and was thrown halfway through the side window.

Doctors weren't sure she would ever ride again. On Sunday, in a remarkable turnaround, Walker competed in the Midway Fall Classic Quarter Horse Show at the Midway Expo Center. The results were surprising.

Last July, Walker, a junior at Rock Bridge High School, was taking a lunch break from riding in preparation for the Fort Worth Invitational, where she qualified in five events. Driving with three passengers on a back road near Moberly, she rolled her car at 50 mph where the paved road turned to gravel without warning. Walker was the only one not wearing a seat belt. Her head and upper body smashed through the side window.

"Last July" is the transition to chronology after the news lead.

Fortunately, she was still in her riding boots. Her spurs got caught on the bar under the seat, which Walker says may have saved her life.

At the time of the accident, Walker was nationally ranked in the trail-riding event.

Note that there are no quotes to break the narrative flow. "My spurs got caught on the bar under my seat" and "She first started walking, and going to the mailbox wore her out" (paragraph 8) are paraphrased to stay in storytelling mode.

Doctors fused her neck in surgery. During the next couple of weeks, she was able to shed her full upper-body cast. Walker returned home to her parents and twin sisters two days after surgery, but her mother, Jane Walker, said doctors told her to stay away from her sport for a few months until she healed.

This background helps establish that she isn't just any rider and that she had more to lose in this accident than most riders.

For Walker, the top all-around youth rider in Missouri and the president of the American Quarter Horse Youth Association, the four months following the accident was her first time away from riding.

After returning home she worked to regain strength and mobility from the accident that initially left her right side paralyzed. She walked short distances. Going to the mailbox at the end of the driveway wore her out, her mother recalls.

The story has a surprise ending, which is possible in a chronology. In a straight news story, this would have been the lead.

Walker had to work almost every muscle in her body back into shape. After the accident, the family brought her 10-year-old quarter horse to their barn in Columbia. That motivated Walker to at first walk to the barn and then to start caring for the horse and eventually ride again.

Sunday, the rehabilitation was complete. With ramrod posture and strict horse control, she won first place in the horsemanship class.

In news narratives with a narrative emphasis, less space is devoted to the news, and more narrative techniques are used than in the inverted pyramid format. These types of narratives use fewer quotes and save important information for a strong ending.
Source: John Tully, "Horse Power," *Columbia Missourian*, Nov. 27, 2006.

The Wall Street Journal knew that not many of us would be attracted to a story about the interaction between pesticides and prescription drugs. That's why a reporter focused on one person to tell a story of pesticide poisoning:

> Thomas Latimer used to be a vigorous, athletic man, a successful petroleum engineer with a bright future.
> Then he mowed the lawn.

Does this opening make you want to read on?

In a quip attributed to him, the Soviet dictator Josef Stalin summed up the impact of focusing on a part of the whole: "The death of one man is a tragedy; the death of millions is a statistic." Think about that the next time you hear that a plane crash killed 300 people. Some events, such as mass shootings or earthquakes, are horrific enough to attract attention in and of themselves. However, when readers have digested the news, you can reach them again by creating a narrative told through the eyes of participants.

Writing the Lead

Issues like health care, budget deficits and sexual harassment don't have much emotional appeal in the abstract. You make them relevant if you discuss the issue by focusing on someone affected by the issue. For instance, the college student who wrote the following story spoke to Karen Elliott, who willingly told her story to help others with the same disease. The key word is "story." You write articles about diseases; you write stories about people. The lead paragraphs focus on one person in an anecdote that shows her as a character we can relate to:

> Karen Elliott, 44, remembers the phone call from Dr. Jonathen Roberts, a general surgeon, as if it had happened yesterday. Dr. Roberts' nurse called one afternoon two years ago and told Karen to hold the line. She froze. She had just had a biopsy on her right breast because of a new lump. It's never good news when the doctor calls at home. Dr. Roberts cut to the chase.
> "You have atypical hyperplasia," he said.
> Being a nurse, Karen knew exactly what he meant. No number of breast self-exams could have detected this. Atypical hyperplasia is a life-long condition characterized by abnormal cells. Affecting only 4 percent of the female population, it puts Karen and others at an increased risk for breast cancer. With her family history of the disease, her risk of breast cancer jumps sky-high.

Reporters working on local stories have just as many opportunities to apply the focus structure as those writing national and international stories. For example, instead of keeping score on the United Way fund drive, focus on the people who will benefit—or will fail to benefit—from the campaign. If the streets in your city jar your teeth when you drive, write about the problem from the point of view of a driver. If a disease is killing the trees in your city, concentrate on a homeowner who has lost several. The focus structure offers the writer a powerful method of reducing institutions, statistics and cosmic issues to a level that readers can relate to and understand.

TIPS

Applying the Focus Structure

- Focus on the individual.
- Transition to the larger issue.
- Report on the larger issue.
- Return to the opening focus.

Advertising agencies use the technique, too. That's why instead of being solicited for money to help the poor and starving, you are asked to support one child for only pennies a day. The technique gives poverty and hunger a face. A starving population is an abstraction; one starving child is a tragedy.

Writing the Setup

Once you've completed the opening, you must finish the setup to the story. The **setup** consists of the transition to the nut paragraph, foreshadowing, the "so what" and the "to be sure." Let's look at each of these elements.

The Transition and the Nut Paragraph

When you open with a scene or an anecdote, you must construct a transition that explicitly makes the connection to the nut, or theme, paragraph. "Explicitly" is the key word. If you fail to help readers understand the point of the opening, however interesting it is, you risk losing them. The transition in this example is in italics:

> Anita Poore hit the rough pavement of the parking lot with a thud. She had never felt such intense, stabbing pain and could barely lift her heavy head. When she reached for the car door, a police officer stared at her and asked her husband, "Is she drunk?" A wave of nausea swept over her, and she vomited.
>
> "That's it. Get her out of here!" the officer demanded.
>
> Poore was not drunk. She avoided jail, but she faces a life sentence of pain.
>
> Now 25, she has suffered migraine headaches since she was in seventh grade.
>
> *Not that it is much comfort, but she's not alone.* Health officials estimate that Americans miss 157 million workdays a year because of migraines and spend more than $2 million a year on over-the-counter painkillers for migraine, tension and cluster headaches. Researchers haven't found a cure, but they have found methods to lessen the pain.

The italicized transition explicitly places Anita Poore among those who miss work, buy painkillers and are waiting for a cure. The material that follows the transition is the theme.

Here's an example of a nut paragraph that follows an opening showing the subject tutoring students. In this one, there is a transition that also works as foreshadowing at the end:

> She's 73 and has been teaching for 53 years. Lindquist supposedly works part-time, but she doesn't plan on slowing down anytime soon. The Lord hasn't told her it's time to quit just yet.
>
> So she goes on, taking her therapy dogs to hospitals and rehab centers to see patients, crocheting afghans for those in nursing homes with no families, cooking meals for people she knows are going through a rough time.
>
> Lindquist is as reliable as the tides. Her faith gives her endless reserves of empathy. She offers herself as a crutch for those who need it. She cooks meals because it makes life just a smidge easier for others. She knows how gray life can be. *She's been there.*

Those last three words—"She's been there"—are the writer's promise that she will explain Lindquist's experience in a "gray life."

The nut paragraph, says Jacqui Banaszynski, Pulitzer Prize–winning writer, "is like a secret decoder ring—it lets the hapless reader know what your story is about

macmillanhighered.com /newsreporting12e

Watch **"Narrowcasting in Magazines."**

- Which magazines are good examples of narrowcasting? Why? Do you consider these magazines successful?
- What role might service journalism play in niche publications?

and why they should read it." When you have involved the reader and successfully written the explicit transition to the nut paragraph, you are ready to build the rest of the setup.

Foreshadowing

Foreshadowing can be done in a single line: "The killing started early and ended late." Or you can foreshadow events over several paragraphs. The goal is to assure readers you will reward them if they continue reading.

Moviemakers tease you with the scenes they think will encourage you to buy a ticket. Broadcasters use foreshadowing to keep you from leaving during a commercial: "Coming up, there's a burglar prowling your neighborhood." Every lead foreshadows the story. The leads that not only tell but promise more good stuff to come are the most successful. Tom Koetting, then of *The Wichita (Kan.) Eagle*, spent nine months observing the recovery of a doctor who had nearly lost his life in a farm accident. He produced a story of about 100,000 words. The simple lead promised great things to come: "Daniel Calliendo Jr. had not expected to meet death this calmly."

In the next example, the long opening is packed with promises of great things to come:

> Deena Borman's relationship with her roommate, Teresa, during her freshman year in college had shattered long before the wine bottle.
>
> Weeks had gone by with Teresa drawing further and further away from Deena. Finally, after repeatedly hearing Teresa talk about suicide, Deena says, "I kept telling her how silly she was to want to die."
>
> That made Teresa angry, so she threw a full wine bottle at Deena. It shattered against the wall and broke open the simmering conflict between them. That was when Deena tried to find out what had gone wrong with Teresa's life, and that was when Teresa told Deena that she wanted to do something to get rid of her.
>
> And that was when Deena began to be scared of her own roommate.

The writer is promising a great story. What is wrong with Teresa? Does Teresa really try to hurt Deena? Does Deena really have something to be scared about? There is a promise of great things to come. Would you keep reading?

The "So What"

The "so what" tells readers explicitly why they should care. Thomas Latimer was poisoned when he mowed his lawn. Anita Poore almost got arrested for having a migraine headache. Interesting, but so what? Reporters and editors know the "so what" or they wouldn't spend time on the story. Too often, however, they fail to tell it to readers. Latimer's story is interesting, but it's much more important because the writer added the "so what" (in italics):

> The makers of the pesticide, diazinon, and of Tagamet firmly deny that their products had anything to do with Mr. Latimer's condition. The pesticide maker says he doesn't even believe he was exposed to its product. And in fact, Mr. Latimer lost a lawsuit he filed against the companies. *Even so, the case intrigues scientists and regulators because it illustrates the need for better understanding of the complex interactions between such everyday chemicals as pesticides and prescription drugs.*

> *Neither the Food and Drug Administration nor the Environmental Protection Agency conducts routine tests for such interactions. Indeed, the EPA doesn't even evaluate the synergy of two or more pesticides commonly used together. "We have not developed ways to test any of that," says an EPA spokesman. "We don't know how to do it." And a new congressional report says the FDA lacks both the resources and the enforcement powers to protect Americans from all kinds of poisons.*

The "so what" is the impact—the relevance—for people who have no warning that pesticides and prescription drugs may interact to poison them.

In other cases, the "so what" may be included in the theme statement. Let's look at the migraine story again:

Sentence 1: Not that it is much comfort, but she's not alone.

Sentence 2: Health officials estimate that Americans miss 157 million workdays a year because of migraines and spend more than $2 million a year on over-the-counter painkillers for migraine, tension and cluster headaches.

Sentence 3: Researchers haven't found a cure, but they have found methods to lessen the pain.

Sentence 1 is the transition. Sentence 2 is the "so what." The reporter is writing about Anita Poore, but the problem is widespread. Sentence 3 is the theme, which includes foreshadowing. The search for a cure, and the intermediate discovery of ways to lessen the pain, will be the focus of the story. The "so what" establishes the dimensions of the problem. When you define the "so what," you are establishing the story's impact.

The "To Be Sure"

To maintain an evenhanded approach, writers must acknowledge that there are two or more sides to a story. We call this the "to be sure," as in "to be sure, there are other opinions." We've seen in the pesticide story that the drug and pesticide makers "firmly deny that their products had anything to do with Mr. Latimer's condition." We see the technique again in an article about the impact of gambling on Tunica, Mississippi. Writer Jenny Deam opens with a scene in the mayor's store. The mayor

Types of Journalistic Writing

News Writing
- News stories emphasize facts and current events.
- Timeliness is especially important.
- Typical news stories cover government, politics, international events, disasters, crime, important breakthroughs in science and medicine, and sports.

Feature (Soft News) Writing
- Feature stories go into depth about a generally newsworthy situation or person.
- Timeliness is relevant but not critical.
- Typical feature stories are profiles, day-in-the-life stories, how-to stories, and background stories.

says gambling is the best thing that ever happened to the town. At the front counter, a woman is asking for the $85 back she paid on furniture last week because she lost her grocery money gambling. What comes next is a combination theme and "to be sure" statement, highlighted in italics:

> And so is the paradox of this tiny Mississippi Delta county, now that the casinos have come to call.
>
> On the one hand, unemployment in a place the Rev. Jesse Jackson once called "America's Ethiopia" has dropped from nearly 24 percent to a low last fall of 5 percent. Anyone who wants a job has one with the casinos. There are more jobs than people to fill them. In a county of about 8,100 people, the number of food stamp recipients fell from 4,218 before the casinos to 2,907 now.
>
> *But there is another side. New problems never before seen.*

Now that you have constructed the setup, you are ready to enter the body of the story.

Writing the Body

Think of readers as people antsy to do something else. To maintain their interest, offer them frequent examples to support your main points. Use anecdotes, scenes and dialogue to move the story line. Mix *exposition* (the facts) with *narration* (the story line). Let's look in on Karen Elliott, who just learned that she has atypical

---

ON THE JOB Just Relax and Tell a Story

Wright Thompson, a senior writer at *ESPN The Magazine*, concentrates on long-form stories built around characters, complications and resolutions in both print and television documentaries. This is how he describes his approach:

In his book *Writing for Story*, Jon Franklin details the most important element in storytelling: conflict and resolution. Every story has characters, is laced through with a strong sense of place, and the character faces a challenge that reveals something. That's such a standard definition that now that I've typed it, I'm sure it's stolen from somewhere. It's that essential and universal. There must be conflict, and there must be resolution. So how do you turn the theory of characters facing challenges into an actual story?

For me, it's through religious and detailed outlining, whether you're doing a 10,000-word profile for print or an hour-long documentary for television. Stories are all about arc, and when there are multiple and supportive arcs in a story, it has more muscle and driving force. So when you're outlining, make sure you see that your story moves with determined but steady pace.

Figure out the micro arc of chronology, and the macro arc of understanding. We go from, say, Monday to Tuesday, or 1980 to 2015, while we are also going from nothing to something, mystery to knowledge, light to dark.

Remember to ask a question in the beginning that is answered at the end. Use scenes as the engine of a story. Use backstory as the mechanism to give the action meaning, not as the story itself. Remember, the facts are the tool for the job, not the job itself.

When I'm outlining, thinking about these principles of asking a question and answering it, and about scenes, I start by reading through the notes with a pen and a highlighter. I do this once or twice. Then I transfer these notes to note cards, laying them out so I can see them visually, and see the story start to take shape. I read and reread the cards. Then when I know where everything goes, I begin to write, hopefully without notes. I want to know the story, know the scenes and the characters and the setting, know the conflict and the resolution, and just relax and tell a story.

hyperplasia. The writer, Tina Smithers, has been dealing in exposition for a few paragraphs, so she shares an anecdote set in the following scene to keep the readers' interest:

> Karen was walking downstairs to get the beach ball out of the summer box for Bethany's Hawaiian swim party at Kindercare. Suddenly, Karen fainted and fell down the stairs. She knew she had broken something. Coming to, she blindly made her way upstairs and lay on the bed.
>
> "The cat was staring me in the eyes," she mumbled as Bob, fresh from the shower, grabbed ice and a pillow.
>
> Karen noticed Bethany crying in the doorway. At this point, Karen realized she had been shouting, "Call 9-1-1! Call 9-1-1!" She didn't want her daughter to see her lose control. She quieted down and told Bethany to come to her bed.
>
> "It's okay, honey. Mommy broke her arm, but they'll be over soon to fix it." Later, in the ambulance, one of the paramedics tried to cut off her yellow Tommy Hilfiger sweater.
>
> "It's brand new," Karen shouted. "Can't you pull it off?"
>
> They gave one small yank, and Karen immediately changed her mind. Every bump along the way was agonizing. Karen pleaded for more morphine. Her wrist, it turned out, was broken in 20 places.

Writing the Ending

As in the chronology structure, you need a strong ending in the focus structure. The difference is that in chronology, you end with the resolution or outcome. In the focus structure, one device is the **tie-back**, a reference to something that appears at or near the beginning of the story. In this profile of a young gay man who performs as a drag queen, writer Kevin Dubouis starts with his subject entering the bar to prepare for his performance. Then he moves back in chronology to retrace his life. Notice that when "he" arrives, the pronoun is masculine; while in costume as a drag queen, the pronoun is feminine.

> Paul Reeves hadn't been on stage in five months when he arrives at the relocated SoCo Club on a Friday mid-afternoon. He is carrying a large dark handbag and uses his other hand to roll a small wheel suitcase full of his persona's tricks. His gestures convey his excitement. Reeves doesn't know yet what he'll be wearing at night, but he has five hours to figure it out. His eyebrows are already covered with glue stick—just the first step in the long process of disguise.
>
> Reeves walks in and greets the staff members he knows.
>
> "He is a performer," the hostess says to the man who is standing by the large wooden door. "Let him in."

The ending ties back to the beginning, where the performer arrived. Now, the performance is over. In between, we have learned about his life.

> Reeves doesn't think about his future when he is Houston-Boheme. He enjoys the stage and his relationship with the audience. After five months off stage and an eating disorder that still haunts him, the night proved to be a well-deserved break.
>
> When the performance is over, Houston-Boheme gets off stage and meets with friends on the rooftop. "It was a good one," she thinks to herself, sipping another cocktail. At the last stroke of midnight, Houston-Boheme knows that she doesn't have to rush home like Cinderella. Now that society is becoming more tolerant and welcoming

of her lifestyle, she knows that the magic she has on stage could follow her off-stage. Plus, she gets to keep the shoes.

The goal in the focus structure is to summarize the theme of the story or tie back to the top of the story. Anecdotes, dialogue, scenes and good quotes can all end the story. Don't just stop writing; construct an ending.

Service Journalism

In Chapter 1, you read that one of the criteria for news is usefulness. Many, if not most, magazines you find on the racks appeal to readers by presenting information they might find useful. More than that, they attempt to present this useful information in the most usable way. This approach to presenting information has been called **service journalism**. You often see it labeled "news you can use." One way to think of this is "refrigerator journalism," information presented in such a way that people can cut it out and put it on their refrigerator or bulletin board. (See Figure 10.2, pages 214-215.)

When a young man walked into a church in Charleston, South Carolina, and killed nine people, the local news media swung into action. Not only did journalists follow the police investigation but they also told people how and where to donate, where and when vigils were being held and how to help the victims' families. Readers and listeners could act on that type of information.

A pioneer in service journalism, James Autrey of the Meredith Corp., liked to call service journalism "action journalism." Its goal is to get readers to use the information. Magazine publishers know that people are more likely to re-subscribe to a magazine if they do some of the things the magazine suggests they do.

All media produce service journalism. Providing tips on how to save money on travel is service journalism. A recipe is service journalism. Telling people when and where an upcoming event is and how much tickets are is service journalism. Front-page news stories, too, often contain elements of service journalism, even if it's just a box listing a sequence of events or directing readers to more information. Service journalism is even easier to do on the web. You can provide links to lists, how-to information, time-date-place of events, and relevant websites.

In this textbook, you see examples of service journalism in the marginal elements that list the learning objectives for each chapter or that highlight important points. The techniques of service journalism require that you think about content and presentation even as you are reporting. Ask yourself, "What do readers need so they can act on this information?" The answer might range from a web address to a phone or fax number to instructions on how to fix a lawnmower or make a loaf of bread. It might include directions on how to travel to a festival or information on where and when to buy tickets. As these examples illustrate, you move from simply talking about something to providing the information the reader needs to act on your story.

FIGURE 10.2

Employing the common presentation devices of service journalism, such as boxes and sidebars, this example shows how to highlight information so readers can easily find it and use it.

Service Journalism

In today's digital world, in-a-hurry readers want practical information presented in the most efficient and effective way.

What this means is that you must think not just of a message—the words. You also must think of how those words will appear on the page or screen—the presentation.

• •

Basics

Service journalism is:

- **Useful.** You must inform people, but if you also find ways to demonstrate how your audience can use the information, you will be more successful. Emphasize WIIFM: "What's in it for me?" See how often you can get "you" in the first sentence of your copy.

- **Usable.** Whenever you can, make a list. Lists get more attention and are better understood and more easily retained. You don't have to write sentences. "Tips" is a magical word.

- **Used.** People stop paying attention to information they never use. You should be able to prove that your audience acts on information. To get people to respond, promise them something. Offer a prize; give them something free.

Refrigerator Journalism

10 tips to serve audiences today

1. **Save them time.**
2. **Help them make more money, save money or get something free.**
3. **Address different levels of news interest.**
4. **Address niche audiences more effectively.**
5. **Become more personally useful.**
6. **Make information more immediately usable.**
7. **Become more accessible.** Give people your name, phone number, fax number, web address and email address.
8. **Become easier to use.** Learn to layer the news, use cross-references and links, put things in the same place, color-code, tell people where to find things, use page numbers on contents blurbs, use glossaries and show readers where to find more information.
9. **Make effective use of visuals and graphics.** Use photos, videos, slide presentations, interactive graphics, maps, cartoons, comics and other visuals.
10. **Become more engaging and interactive.** Use contests, quizzes, crosswords, games. People remember better if they do something. Give awards to those who send in answers. Give a coffee mug to the person with the best tip or post of the month.

Refrigerator journalism—giving people printouts they can post in a handy place—invites access and participation.

Other Devices of Service Journalism

1. Use blurbs. After a title and before the article begins, write a summary/contents/benefit blurb. David Ogilvy says no one will read the small type without knowing the benefit upfront. Use the same benefit blurb in a table of contents or menu or briefs column. The best word in a benefit blurb is "how." How to, how you, how I do something. Be personal. Use people in your messages. Also use internal blurbs, little summaries, pull quotes and tips to tease and coax readers into the story.

2. Use subheads. Before you write, outline. Put the main points of the outline into the copy. Perhaps a better word than subhead is "entry point." Let readers enter the copy where they find something interesting.

3. Have a FAQ page or question-and-answer column. A Q&A format allows readers to skip over things they already know or are not interested in.

4. Repeat things in different ways for different people. Don't be afraid to say something in a box or a graphic that you have said elsewhere. Reinforcing a message aids retention.

5. Think more visually. Include pictures and graphics that contain information and are not purely decorative. Remember, being effective and efficient is the only thing that matters. We used to write articles and then look for graphics or photos to enhance the message. Now we put the information in the graphic (where it will get more attention and have more impact) and write a story to enhance the graphic.

"Never be above a gimmick." —Dave Orman, ARCO

The power of the box

When you can, put some information in a box. Like lists, boxes or sidebars (1) get more attention, (2) increase comprehension, and (3) aid retention. On the web, these kinds of boxes can be linked from the main story:

1. **A reference box.** "For more information, see, read, call, click . . ."

2. **A note box.** Take notes from your articles as if you were studying for an exam. Give them to your readers to complement your message.

3. **A glossary box.** Put unfamiliar or technical terms in a glossary box. Use color or another graphic treatment to indicate which words are defined. Also, teach your audience how to pronounce difficult words.

4. **A bio box.** When you need to say something about where a person lived, went to school and worked, put this information in a box or on a separate linked web page so that your main story is not interrupted.

The 4 goals of the service journalist:

In a nutshell

1. Attention
2. Comprehension
3. Retention
4. Action

PR Tip

Newspapers, magazines, newsletters and websites are doing more and more service journalism. "News You Can Use" and "Tips & Tactics" have become familiar heads. Both newspapers and magazines are becoming more visual. Yet most news releases sent out by PR professionals look the same as they did five and 50 years ago. Why not try refrigerator journalism techniques in your next news release, whether it's sent by mail or digitally?

Much of the basic service journalism information can be presented as sidebars or lists or boxed material. Figure 10.2 uses common service journalism devices to present more information about this topic.

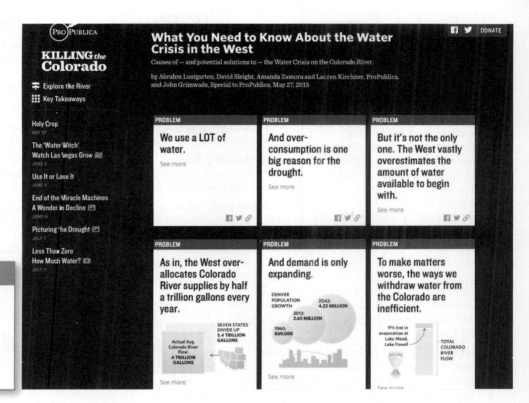

FIGURE 10.3

To break down the complex issue of water usage for readers, ProPublica used boxes to clearly outline problems and solutions.

Evolving Story Forms—Structured Journalism

Many people now access information from smartphones more often than from any other device. That is forcing news companies to think about new ways to reach these consumers. For all its strengths, narrative does not fit well on phones.

Some media are advocating a new approach, which they call structured journalism. The idea is that the journalist tries to think of information in bits and pieces and organizes the material in shorter bursts, manageable for smartphones.

■ **"Play-by-Play" Blogging.** The forerunners of this approach can be seen in the play-by-play approach journalists started at sports events but have extended to any event: a political debate, a meeting, a devastating storm. Blogging small bits of information as they are gathered is one way to implement structured journalism; essentially, that's a step above sending briefer tweets.

- **Enhanced Captions.** Another approach to structured journalism can be seen in the many examples of stories that consist only of photos and short copy blocks. For example, a viewer of *The New York Times* iPhone app on Oct. 5, 2015, would have seen a link to a video of the Coast Guard Capt. Mark Fedor giving an update on the latest search and rescue efforts concerning the cargo ship El Faro accompanied by a 32-word caption introducing the video clip. (For other examples, see OpEdNews online, listed under "Suggested Websites" at the end of this chapter.)

- **Q and A's.** ProPublica, a nonprofit that concentrates on investigative reporting, often produces long, text stories. But the site is also experimenting with new ways of telling stories, as it did by clearly and simply breaking down the basic questions about the recent drought in the western U.S. ProPublica listed 12 boxes with problems and six more with solutions. (Figure 10.3.)

More ambitious forms of structured journalism can be found in stories full of links and sidebars. You can get the essential information quickly, but you can dive deeply into nearly any of the related material. (See the link to the *Washington Post* example under "Suggested Websites" at the end of the chapter.)

Each day, journalists are experimenting with new ways to structure stories for the web and, increasingly, for smartphones and tablets.

SUGGESTED READINGS

Franklin, Jon. *Writing for Story: Craft Secrets of Dramatic Nonfiction by a Two-Time Pulitzer Prize Winner*. New York: Plume, 1994. If you want to write nonfiction narratives, this book will show you the structure and explain all the elements.

Harrington, Walt, and Mike Sager, eds. *Next Wave: America's New Generation of Great Literary Journalists*. The Sager Group at Smashwords, 2012. E-book. This is a collection of literary journalism written by authors under 40. They are practicing what we describe in Chapters 9 and 10 of this textbook.

LaRocque, Paula. *The Book on Writing: The Ultimate Guide to Writing Well*. Oak Park, Ill.: Marion Street Press, 2003. This great book for new writers covers three main topics: mechanical and structural guidelines; creative elements of storytelling; and grammar, usage and punctuation.

Stewart, James B. *Follow the Story: How to Write Successful Nonfiction*. New York: Touchstone, 1998. Stewart, formerly of *The Wall Street Journal*, won a Pulitzer Prize in 1988 for his reporting on the stock market crash and insider trading. He uses his work to illustrate how to write narration.

SUGGESTED WEBSITES

www.longreads.com
Longreads offers a selection of stories using the structures described in this chapter.

www.niemanstoryboard.org/2012/07/20/the-aps -kristen-gelineau-ravi-nessman-and-mary-rajkumar -on-the-saroo-brierley-saga
This site gives an interview with the writers and editor of the story of Saroo Brierley, which opens this chapter. It also contains a link to the complete story.

www.opednews.com/articles/Sassy-Femmes-Still -Rock-th-by-Vicki-Leon-Artistic_Artists_Creativity _Lifestyle-150127-255.html
Reporting on the work of creative women in New Mexico, the website uses short copy blocks and photos of their work.

www.washingtonpost.com/world/national-security /islamic-states-embrace-of-social-media-puts-tech -companies-in-a-bind/2015/07/15/0e5624c4-169c -11e5-89f3-61410da94eb1_story.html?kmap=1&pr=1
This site is an example of deep-dive structured journalism. It combines fast-read and slow-read approaches to produce information in layers.

EXERCISES

1. From the first few paragraphs of the following story, identify:

   a. The nut paragraph.
   b. Foreshadowing.
   c. A sense of person.

   In a story full of sadness, that's another bitter truth. Her name suits her perfectly, summing up her innocence and kind nature. It's a refreshing name, one you don't hear often. But she is a foster child, and the state of Missouri asks us to protect the identities of foster children, so we cannot use her name here.

   So, for this story, she chose a different name: Ariana.

   Her dad lives somewhere in Mexico—not the one in Missouri—and he has never spoken to her. When she was born, he punched a wall in the Boone Hospital Center delivery room. Then, he rushed out. He wanted a boy. Soon afterward, he left the country.

   In the 14 years since, her family has been fractured in other ways. Ariana has five siblings: one older sister, two younger brothers and two younger sisters. Ariana's mom, who we'll call Jane, lives about five hours away. Her mom's life is improving, but it's still nearly as messy now as it was in the early 2000s, when she was in and out of relationships and battling legal trouble. Her struggles hit their worst in July 2013, when the state took Ariana and one of her sisters, who chose the name Justice, away. Jane has lived without them for the past year and a half. The oldest sister ran away. Her mom still has custody of the other children. They weren't under her care when the state intervened on Ariana and her sister's behalf.

   Ariana and Justice are in limbo, stuck in the foster care system.

   But no matter how bad home was, Ariana still loves her mom and family. Because she loves them, she also suffers.

   Two years ago, when Ariana first came to Coyote Hill, a foster care facility in Harrisburg, she was a hopeless case. She fought every rule and quit in the face of every challenge at school. Then, last summer, she discovered horse riding and, from there, football, cheerleading, quiz bowl and competitive cheer. And she found hope. A girl who never attended school went from failing all her classes to earning As and Bs in her final semester at Harrisburg Middle School.

   She became a new person.

   Ariana has shoulder-length, naturally wavy dark brown hair and rosy cheeks. A seventh-grade boy has a crush on her, and she's not exactly sure what to do about that. She has a few crushes of her own, too, and she got to go to the Harrisburg Middle School dance this spring with one of them. Ariana giggles every time Justice brings that boy up—but, Ariana's quick to point out, Justice has a crush on that boy, too.

2. Journalist Kathy Dobie's story "The Undefeated Champions of Defeat City" appeared in *GQ* on May 12, 2014. Do an internet search for the story (www.gq.com/story/camden -new-jersey-little-league-baseball?src=longreads). You will see an opening of several paragraphs. Identify the nut paragraph and the so-what.

3. **Your journalism blog.** Re-create a scene from one of your classes. For example, you could write about the first day of class or a time when an outside expert visited. Provide the transition into the body of the story, and then stop. Invite your

classmates to comment on your story—how closely does it match their recollection of events?

4. Using a chronology, write about eight paragraphs of a story on some aspect of your experience in a journalism class.

5. Write a two-to-four paragraph "sense of person" description of a faculty member known to most in your class.

6. Write a two-to-four paragraph "sense of place" description about some location on your campus.

7. Find two examples of service journalism from newspapers, magazines or websites, and analyze them. Find an example of a story that would have benefited from service journalism techniques. Tell what you would have done to make the information more usable for readers.

8. Report on an event live while it is happening by blogging short bursts at a time or tweeting.

CHAPTER 11 WRITING FOR DIGITAL MEDIA

EGYPTIANS
EGYPTIAN
PRESS
(Nile TV, EL-Masriya,...)
PLZ STOP
DECEIVING US
80 million people want this.
EGYPT
MUBARAK
GET OUT
MUBARAK!
GAME IS
OVER..

Ron Haviv/VII/Corbis

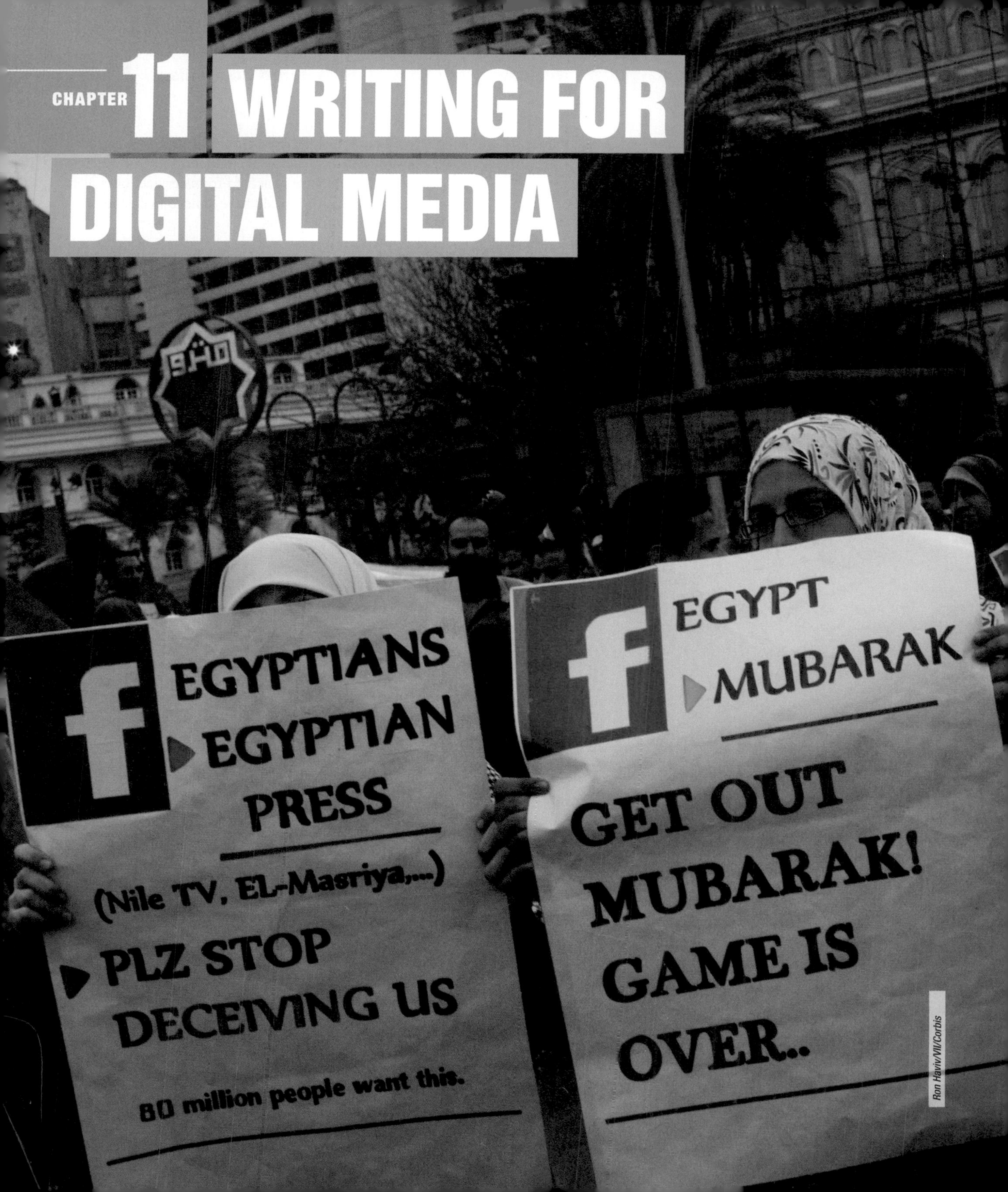

After war broke out in Syria in 2011, it quickly became evident that two wars were being fought—one the traditional way with rifles, bombs and missiles, and another on the web and in social media with news reports, photos and videos from citizen journalists. By four years into the war, both sides had become adept at taking advantage of the near-total absence of experienced journalists in the war-torn area to present partisan views of the conflict. The views of those would-be journalists were often distorted based on their "side" in the conflict.

International news media were banned from the conflict area by both sides. People in the war-torn area knew that with social media they could still tell the world their side of the story. The result was that videos taken on mobile phones became a primary source of information available to the outside world, although the accuracy of that information was often suspect. Some television stations aired videos that eventually were determined to have been made in earlier conflicts in Lebanon and Iraq.

Since the start of the Syrian war, millions of videos have been uploaded by both sides to YouTube and similar sites. *The Wall Street Journal* observed that the "unprecedented confluence of two technologies—cellphone cams and social media—has produced, via the instant upload, a new phenomenon: the YouTube war."

When Russia directly entered the conflict in support of the Syrian regime in 2015, the presence of Russian troops in the country was confirmed when those troops began posting selfies on social media sites. So, while traditional media may have found it difficult to cover the war in Syria, social media made it possible to provide at least some coverage.

Similarly, when hundreds of thousands of Egyptians flocked to Tahrir Square in 2011, they came determined to overthrow the government of President Hosni Mubarak. Through Facebook, organizers directed followers to Tahrir and other protest sites for the rallies. The word spread via Twitter, and massive demonstrations followed. The government figured out what was happening and, on Jan. 24, 2011, blocked access to the two websites and their mobile phone applications.

That might have been the end of it, but web-savvy Egyptians found a way to circumvent the blockage by using sites like HootSuite, which allowed them to reach Facebook and Twitter indirectly. As a result, the Egyptian uprising arguably became the first revolution engineered through social media, although scholars continue to debate the impact of those media.

Such events show both the power of social media and, in the hands of nonjournalists, the ability of social media to inform as well as to misinform. Harnessing the power of the web and social media and ensuring that power is used to convey truth, not fiction, is becoming more important than ever to journalists and society.

That's true of journalists in local communities, too, as well as for journalists covering the big international stories like those in the Middle East. Car accidents, fires, shootings and similar events must be covered accurately, not just quickly.

1

Why the web is a unique media form.

2

What readers expect from digital media.

3

How to write for the web.

4

How to write with search engines in mind.

5

How to write for blogs.

6

How to use social media.

The power of the web and social media in the hands of citizens is a great asset to journalists in reporting the news. Assuring that such information is accurate before disseminating it is vital to your reputation and that of your company. In this chapter, we'll discuss these relatively new media forms and how to write for them. We'll also discuss how to evaluate the veracity of news produced by nonjournalists.

The Web as a Unique Media Form

When it first appeared, web journalism followed a familiar pattern—one established when radio began to yield to television. As television emerged as a major medium in the post–World War II era, news reports consisted almost entirely of someone sitting at a desk reading written-for-radio news. Similarly, when the web appeared in the mid-1990s, media organizations quickly adopted this same pattern. This was merely regurgitated news written for traditional media in copy that came to be known as **shovelware.** Sites operated by legacy media—newspapers, magazines, radio and television—contained little more than that morning's stories, which had already appeared in print or on the air.

As the web evolved, that began to change. News organizations started to write web-exclusive, or at least web-first, stories. Also, citizen journalism began to flourish and to challenge the dominance of traditional media in disseminating news. Anyone, it seemed, could now become a journalist or even a publisher.

Those developments have slowly led editors and publishers of legacy media to the conclusion that the web is an entirely new medium that demands a fresh approach. In this age of consumer choice, people want information when they want it and how they want it. Traditional publishers have now embraced blogs, news alerts on social media networks such as Twitter, Facebook, Instagram and Snapchat, and even citizen journalism itself.

Some readers receive the news on their smartphones, others on their desktops or tablets. Publishers have developed apps for smartphones and tablets. These devices put pressure on news disseminators to deliver breaking news instantly and in bursts. In addition, the news media now provide links to other sites, link people with two-way communication and provide not only text, photos and graphics but also audio and video on demand to users with high-speed connections.

When the web first came along, no one knew how to make money with it, an essential ingredient in a country such as the U.S. in which most media are not state-supported. All that has changed. By 2019, online advertising revenue is expected to exceed $240 billion worldwide. No other medium in recent years has experienced revenue growth even approaching that.

Just as writing for television evolved from its early iterations, so too is writing for the web evolving. The web is clearly a unique medium that requires a new approach, but that approach is still changing as journalists learn new ways to communicate online. Let's look at the latest techniques on writing for the web as practiced by some of America's top journalists. (See Figure 11.1 for a comparison of print and digital media news stories.)

Comparison of Print and Digital Media Stories

	Print Stories	Web Stories
Audience	Communication is one-way: from writer to reader. All readers get the same stories.	Communication is two-way: Readers expect to be able to respond online through blogs, forums and so on. Readers customize their reading by using links and specifying preferences.
Structure	Inverted pyramid predominates, but writers use other structures too. All of a news event is covered in one major story.	Inverted pyramid, with the key facts up front, is standard; use of suspense is rare. Coverage is layered so that readers can choose how much of a story to read.
Style	Writers sometimes use literary techniques to enhance stories. Stories are mostly written paragraphs with some breakers.	Readers expect stories to be straightforward, crisp and clear, without much use of literary techniques. Writers use a lot of bullets and lists.
Length	Important stories may be lengthy to accommodate in-depth coverage.	Stories are usually short; additional info is "chunked" into linked sidebar stories that readers can click on if they want to know more.
Sidebars	Writers might add short sidebars on one aspect of a story; newspapers may print the text of a speech.	Stories provide links to past stories that are of possible interest and to information on other sites that readers might want.
Visual Appeal	Newspapers use photos, charts, graphs and drawings. Readers expect to see columns of print.	Websites use photos, charts, graphs and drawings, as well as audio, video and animation. Readers expect sites to be colorful, well-designed, interesting and easy to navigate.
Timeliness	Newspapers are published on a regular schedule, and writers have set deadlines for stories. Readers get news from one medium—the printed newspaper.	Websites are updated throughout the day, and breaking news is posted immediately. Readers get the news at any time on devices such as smartphones.

FIGURE 11.1

Writing for digital media is different in many respects from writing for print newspapers.

Readers' Expectations of Digital Media

Before you start to write for the web, you need to understand readers' expectations of the medium. Even if you plan to work at a print newspaper or magazine, or at a radio or television station, you will need to know how to write for the web. Every company has a website. At a growing number of newspapers, for example, journalists are being asked to turn in two versions of their stories, one for the newspaper and one for the paper's website.

To be sure, there are readers who want the stories as they appear in the newspaper and not rewritten in some other form. Those readers want to know what readers of the print edition are seeing. Many worldwide readers of *The New York Times*' online edition undoubtedly want to see what the print readers of the New York, National, Europe and Asia editions have read. *The Times* and many other newspapers now produce downloadable PDF versions that look exactly like the print edition. So, there's a market for that. But most readers want stories tailored to take advantage of the web's considerable power. They want links, and they want graphics, audio and even video to accompany the text.

To write effectively for the web, you need to learn a unique way of thinking about writing. Let's begin with these realities about the nature of the web and what readers expect online:

- Readers want the news right away.
- Readers want to have their say.
- Readers want multimedia variety.
- Readers want the news upfront.
- Readers want to customize content.
- The audience is international.
- Structure is all-important.

Readers Want the News Right Away

At the St. Paul *Pioneer Press*, all print reporters must file a web story for TwinCities .com (see Figure 11.2) within 30 minutes after witnessing an event or learning about the news. Typically, this story is accompanied by Twitter news bulletins or Facebook posts designed to drive traffic to the story on the newspaper website. Other news sites have similar rules.

FIGURE 11.2

Reporters for the St. Paul *Pioneer Press* file their first stories for TwinCities.com, the newspaper's website and the site's smartphone app.

One of the first expectations of web-based journalism is immediacy. In the old days, newspapers printed several editions a day and occasionally came out with an "extra." Today, cyberspace has turned newspapers into 24-hour competitive news machines, and print-only reporters are rapidly becoming a disappearing species. Television reporters, too, post stories to their companies' websites throughout the day, and the stories they write for the website are much more like those of the newspaper reporter than those they write for the nightly newscast. Web-based journalism is all about getting out the story as quickly as possible. For today's journalist, the message is this: mobile and web first, print and broadcast second. Readers expect to get the news as soon as it breaks.

Readers Want to Have Their Say

A major reason readers are increasingly abandoning legacy media in favor of digital media is that readers want to be active consumers of news, which for the most part is what digital media, as opposed to legacy media, offer. Many web users expect to be active participants in the discussion, proposing their own take on the news, arguing about the impact of the news with their peers and with writers, and perhaps even adding significant information or perspective to the discussion. Indeed, some readers want to provide content by sending in written accounts, photos or videos of things they have witnessed. Citizen journalism, as that phenomenon is called, is alive and well.

The one-way communication paths of the past are increasingly giving way to the two-way communication path the web provides. Journalists must understand that changing dynamic and adjust to it.

One social media platform that news organizations are using to build community is Snapchat, a video messaging application. With Snapchat, users can send photos, videos, text and drawings to friends or acquaintances. *The Washington Post* used Snapchat to gather photos during a major snowstorm; NPR used the app to gather creative selfies from readers. According to Masuma Ahuja, digital editor of the *Post*, the advantage of using Snapchat is not to drive traffic to the website, which is the main goal of using Twitter and Facebook. Instead, Ahuja says, Snapchat helps reporters forge personal connections with people in their communities.

Readers Want Multimedia Variety

The most successful writers understand that reading news on the web or on a smartphone is a much different experience compared with reading it in a print newspaper or magazine. The best writers know that the digital media excel when they present news using a full spectrum of assets—not only text but also links, photos, graphics, audio and video. Online readers expect more than text, and that's just what they're getting.

Writing for the digital media is about determining the best way to tell a story and then using a variety of media tools—text, audio, video, photographs and graphics—to deliver it. This requires an understanding of audio and video production and the

use of information graphics. Even *The New York Times* recognizes that and delivers an incredible amount of multimedia on its website. So, too, do ESPN, CNN and a host of local news sites. Over the years, the way news is written and packaged for these websites has changed, and it continues to change as technology evolves.

Writing for the web also requires us to think about changes in the ways media messages are consumed. No longer is the web something you navigate only on a desktop or laptop computer. Today's readers use smartphones, tablets and e-readers to consume news. Many media organizations have created applications for consuming news on smartphones and tablets. Other organizations do not have

FIGURE 11.3

The *Columbia Missourian* is one of many newspapers that publishes an online edition, updated 24/7.

FIGURE 11.4

Viewed on a smartphone, the *Missourian* uses a different layout that is designed for greater readability on mobile devices. This layout includes a menu button in the top left corner that users can tap to easily navigate to other areas of the site.

mobile apps but have websites that are "mobile-friendly"—that is, when viewed on a mobile device, the websites display in a different layout that is ideal for small touchscreens.

Readers Want the News Upfront

On occasion, print journalists writing for newspapers and magazines build a story with a suspenseful ending. Online news writers, on the other hand, should keep no secrets from readers. With rare exception, they should not try to withhold information until later in the story. When you're writing online, it's important to surrender control of the story's sequence to the reader.

In Chapter 8, you were introduced to the most traditional news writing form, the inverted pyramid, which places the most important information in the first paragraph. That technique is exactly what's needed for most web stories because the lead is even more important in an online story than it is in print. It literally may be all that appears on the screen, and readers may have to click to get more of the story. In addition, for most search engines the lead will be the only information provided for the link to the story. It's smart to include keywords such as "Maine" and "governor" in the lead or headline of a story concerning the Maine governor to help interested readers find it. The lead must nail the "what" or the "so what" to get the full attention of the reader. In fact, it is similar to the anchor's introduction to a television news story.

But as we learned in Chapter 10, even on the web there is sometimes a place for writing formats other than the inverted pyramid. It would be difficult to argue that a superbly written eight-part series should be condensed for the web. Here's what we would suggest: For most daily news stories, write briefly in the inverted pyramid format for the digital media. But at the same time, don't be afraid to give online readers the full measure of your best newspaper or magazine writing—writing that takes advantage of the power of the web by adding multimedia and links.

Readers Want to Customize Content

Every reader is different; every reader has different needs. Every reader, therefore, not only will select and choose what to read but also will choose a path that best meets those needs.

Think of ways to present different information for different people at different times. Unlike newspapers and magazines, which must decide how long to make a story, digital media should present information so that readers can choose the amount they need. Not many websites have completely mastered this concept, but it's important.

Note also that the online reader is active, not passive. Reading a first-rate website that has depth requires the user to click from place to place, to launch videos, to explore photos and to click on photo galleries. Navigating a website is not linear, as is the reading of newspapers and magazines where a reader begins reading a story and either reads to the end or drops out. On a good website with rich media offerings, the reader can jump to related stories, to previous stories on the same subject, to a photo gallery or to a video. The reader becomes much more actively engaged.

Even higher levels of engagement are possible on the web. Allowing users to navigate databases of property values allows them to compare their home values and taxes to those of their neighbors. Interactive maps allow users to see where crime is occurring in their communities. Such engagement makes the media organization more valuable to the reader's life and therefore builds loyalty to the website.

The Big Story: An Alternative Approach

At the start of this chapter, we mentioned coverage of the uprisings in Egypt and the role played by citizens using Facebook and Twitter. Unlike in Syria, the world's mainstream media outlets had access to the streets of Cairo. During that period, the BBC's website told a complex story using multiple short stories, audio, video, still photographs and information graphics. All of it was teased on Facebook and Twitter in an attempt to drive readers to the coverage.

The editors hoped that the video, picture packages and other material would convince readers to plunge into the site's longer textual material. While it's tough to tell if this worked, the approach seems to be a sensible one.

The Audience Is International

Few websites of U.S. media companies are bilingual or multilingual, but the fact is that many website users do not speak English, Spanish or French as a first language. Ideally, our websites would be multilingual, but hiring a large translation staff is usually too costly. Fortunately for the English-speaking world, English has become the most commonly used language in international commerce and interaction, so if a site must have only one language, English is usually the best choice.

Still, it's important to remember that the web is a worldwide medium, not a local one. Writers can help users around the world understand their content by using plain language and avoiding colloquialisms. Simple writing also allows international users to more accurately run a story through online translation programs, such as Google Translate, and make sense of it.

With the growth of Spanish as a second language in the U.S., news outlets need to consider providing content in that language. In the southern tier of states, it's already essential.

Structure Is All-Important

Some who write online forget entirely about structure. That's a huge mistake. Even though web stories have a unique structure, they still must be organized in a logical, coherent way. Digital media readers do not revel in chaos. Even though a story may appear on the screen as a mosaic, the way that mosaic is composed will attract readers, keep them and help them follow what for them is the most logical path.

Web writers should consider presenting information in layers (see the annotated model "Layering Content on the Web" on page 230). Remember: No two readers are alike. You can present the same information with different degrees of detail and support. Writing for the web in layers works like this:

Layer 1. Give readers a lead paragraph or several paragraphs—enough so they can understand the basic story. This first layer is information that is immediately available to readers. No action or effort is demanded of them.

Layer 2. Provide a way for readers to click to continue reading the story. Alternatively, readers should be able to easily access more information by moving the cursor or by scrolling.

Layer 3. Provide links to earlier stories on the same subject or to related written material.

Layer 4. Complement the story with video, photos, graphics or audio, or make the video or photo the centerpiece of the story and subordinate the text. This layer may require readers to click on a link that opens up still more information—perhaps audio, video or a source document.

When you write for print, you are concerned with continuity, with themes, with working into the narrative all aspects of the story while keeping the writing clear and coherent. When you write for the web, you need not worry much about the structure or flow of the whole piece but rather about the relationships of the layers and parts. It's all about understanding what readers want and helping them navigate from place to place to get the information they seek. In print, a writer seldom if ever wants to provide an exit point for the reader. But when writing for the web, it's important to offer clear entry and exit points using the layering approach.

Sometimes you may want to take readers down a path that branches into several other paths. Some call this technique *threading*. The story of a plane crash can lead to various threads: the airline and its safety record, the plane itself and the record of that type of plane, the place of the accident, the people involved, and so forth.

Don't be too concerned about repetition. Remember readers choose what parts to read. Besides, a certain amount of repetition or of stating things in different ways, perhaps visually, increases retention. All readers—whether on the web or elsewhere—process information differently.

So, because most people don't think linearly, writing done for the digital media is more in line with the way people think. It's even more in line with the way today's readers read. For the web, break the story into short, digestible pieces. Rather than stringing together a long story and trying to get readers to read the whole thing in the order in which you present it, keep in mind that many readers don't want to read everything you have to tell them. You must give them choices and let them decide what to read and in what order.

The website of the BBC (BBC.co.uk) presents information for the web in the most desirable way. The brevity of its stories, even in reporting a major event like the uprisings in Egypt, is ideal for a website. Perhaps the BBC's history of writing concisely for radio and television helps. Perhaps that's why readers increasingly

ANNOTATED MODEL   Layering Content on the Web

Readers click on a link on the home page to get the full story and a photo, shown here.

Readers can click on links in the article's sidebar to view videos about other environment-related issues.

More links encourage readers to investigate additional articles on the *Miami Herald* website.

The article includes the author's e-mail address so that readers can contact her with questions and comments.

Icons for Facebook, Twitter, e-mail, and other social media (including LinkedIn, Google+, Pinterest, and Reddit) allow readers to easily share and comment on the story.

Miami Herald

☼ 81°
Sign In | Subscribe

≡ FULL MENU   NEWS   SPORTS   BUSINESS   REAL ESTATE   Search the site 🔍

ENVIRONMENT   MARCH 19, 2015

Study suggests pythons gobbling up Everglades' critters

HIGHLIGHTS
Two years after scientists first linked the explosion of Burmese pythons in Everglades National Park to a drop in small mammals, a new study further suggests pythons are dominating the food chain.

VIDEOS

▶

about 2 months ago
Yellow fog spreads across Florida Bay

about 3 months ago
Florida vs. the giant African land snail

about 3 months ago
Bear-proof trash cans key to preventing encounters

about 3 months ago
Invasive mangroves on the run in South Florida

VIEW MORE VIDEO ➔

This Burmese python was captured in the Everglades in 2011 after it consumed a full-sized deer. **South Florida Water Management D** - South Florida Water Management District

BY JENNY STALETOVICH
jstaletovich@MiamiHerald.com

Burmese pythons munch marsh rabbits in Everglades National Park faster than any native predator, confirming what biologists already suspected: The invasive snake is changing the balance of the park's food chain.

Two years ago, researchers determined that as the python population climbed in the park, the number of small mammals declined. But they couldn't prove for sure that one caused

MORE ENVIRONMENT

Blame El Niño for South Florida's soggy winter

Deal could move power lines to edge of Everglades National Park

Mock U.N. climate summit engages students in global warming debate

The Miami Herald uses layering to draw a reader into a story. Here, the photo and text are complemented by links to additional content.

POLITICO.

Nick Gass began work at Politico in November 2012, first as a web producer and most recently as a reporter covering breaking news. The young company has grown rapidly, setting up shop in Europe's power capitals and branching out to state-level coverage in Florida and New Jersey. It also acquired the online news site Capital New York. At Politico, Gass reports on everything from the latest polls on presidential contenders to congressional figures and all the relevant political news of the day in between. It's fast-paced, demanding and rewarding.

"There are a lot of opportunities for young journalists in places like Washington, D.C., particularly if you are willing to work as a web producer," Gass says. "I produced and packaged stories for the website in my first two years at Politico, writing and reporting pieces when I had free time, including on weekends."

One particularly memorable moment came when Republican presidential candidate Donald Trump read out the personal cellphone number of South Carolina Sen. Lindsey Graham, one of his GOP primary rivals. "Upon hearing the number, I called it, and Sen. Graham actually picked up. Every other reporter from all the other major outlets just got his voicemail message. So, it pays to be fast. And it doesn't hurt to be a little lucky sometimes."

At a large and growing online company like Politico, Gass says it's important—essential, even—to go the extra mile to stand out among equally driven and accomplished colleagues: "The most exciting part about working at a place like Politico is how we as journalists are constantly encouraged to break with tradition and experiment with new workflows and processes."

In addition to his work as a web producer, Gass also has researched issues ranging from the plight of the drug trade in central Asia to the burgeoning social media scene: "News online moves at lightning speed, so it is essential to have a sharp eye and to learn how to proofread quickly and accurately."

favor television station websites over newspaper websites in many cities. Newspaper stories tend to be longer, and they too often are not tightened for the web.

Stories that require multiple continuous screens turn off many readers immediately. Many readers hate to scroll on screen. Some exit even before they get to the bottom of the screen. Few will take the time to read a lot of text in one clump. Note, of course, that this is not true of highly motivated readers who crave your information or sites like *Slate* magazine where readers expect long-form stories. It's important to know your audience and what your readers expect.

Guidelines for Writing for the Web

Those who read the digital media are surfers or scanners much more so than readers of print, perhaps because it takes 25 percent longer to read online than it does in print. Researchers Jakob Nielsen and John Morkes found that 79 percent of those they tested scanned a new page they came across; only 16 percent read the copy word for word.

Web expert Shel Holtz says you want readers to dive, not surf. Surfing is what frustrated readers do. Here are nine ways to turn surfers into divers—or at least to hold their attention long enough to get your message across.

Think Immediacy

Speed in handling breaking news is essential. Keeping readers with you means keeping them up-to-the-minute. You must expect to update breaking stories quickly and to add depth whenever it is available. But just because you can easily correct your mistakes does not mean you are allowed to make them. Posting news too quickly could sacrifice quality and damage credibility.

Save Readers Time

Readers' time is precious. Whatever you can do to save readers time is worth *your* time. It's been said by various people in different ways since the philosopher Blaise Pascal first said it: "I would have written a shorter letter, but I did not have the time." For many stories, if not most, perhaps your chief concern should be this: Have I presented this information in such a way as to cost readers the least amount of time?

The best way to save readers time is to be clear. Choose the simple word. Vary the length of sentences, but keep them short. Write short paragraphs. Help readers. Emphasize key words by highlighting them.

Another reason to write simply, using simple words and simple sentences, is to enable automated translation programs to translate the text. The simpler the words and sentences, the more likely it is that a foreign-language translation of the story will be accurate and understandable.

Provide Information That's Quick and Easy to Get

The organization of your story must show readers they can get information quickly and easily. Digital media readers have zero tolerance for confusion and no time at all to be led astray. It's too easy for them to click on something else.

Don't get carried away by your own eloquence. Be guided by what your readers want or need to know. Make it easy for them. Write short paragraphs with one idea per paragraph.

Think Both Verbally and Visually

In the past, writers for print thought little about how their stories were going to appear. Their job was to write the story—period. The designer's job was to make the story fit on the page in some meaningful way. Writers usually did not worry about headlines, subheads, summary quotes, photos, illustrations or anything but the story.

Television news writers know that they must write to the pictures. Good television has good video, so the visual medium tries to show rather than to tell. Words complement pictures and say what the pictures do not. Many times, of course, the writer does not make the pictures and is not responsible for getting them. But the writer still must consider the best way to tell the story, and sometimes visuals convey the story as no amount of text could possibly do.

As a web journalist, you may or may not have to do it all by yourself, but you definitely must *think* both verbally and visually. From the outset, you must be concerned about the most effective and efficient way for the information to appear on

TIPS

Web Writing Guidelines in a Nutshell

- Get the news online fast.
- Write shorter stories, with subheads if necessary.
- Use sidebars to keep the main story short.
- Include keywords in your lead or introductory blurb.
- Add links, still photographs and video.
- Design a visually appealing and well-organized package.
- Use social media to drive traffic to the website.

the screen. You have to think not only about the organization of the material but also about ways to use graphics and audio, to be interactive and to use online tools.

No one doubts that photos and graphics grab readers' attention. That's why you see icons and information graphics in magazines and newspapers, and that's why you must think, perhaps with the help of graphic designers, of ways to use graphic elements online.

Cut Your Copy

Many digital media readers simply will not read long stories. In the not-so-distant past, some experts advised getting the whole story on one screen. Because some screens are small, they advised not writing more than 20 lines of text.

Now, because of the proliferation of larger and less-irritating screens, some readers are finding it easier and less frustrating to scroll for more information. But as home and office screens have grown larger, smaller screens on smartphones and tablets have also grown popular. Fortunately, computer programmers are increasingly adept at designing web content that easily converts to viewing on tablets and phones.

Still, as in broadcast news writing, there's little room online to be cute or even literary. When writing for the web, your goal should always be to create something that is crisp and clear.

Use Lots of Lists and Bullets

In a now classic study, Jakob Nielsen of the Nielsen Norman Group tested five versions of the same information for usability. He concluded that web pages are most readable when they contain, among other features, bulleted lists. Often you can cut copy by putting information into lists. Whenever possible, make a list. Lists get more attention and allow for better comprehension and more retention than ordinary sentences and paragraphs. (The web-friendly memo-structure story format, illustrated in Chapter 8, has listlike features.)

An entire article structured like a list is sometimes called a **listicle.** Bulleted or numbered lists are scannable. Readers can grasp them immediately. Think of information on the web as a database. That's how people use their digital media. Besides, it's also quicker for the writer to make lists than to write paragraphs.

Mark Deuze and Christina Dimoudi of the Amsterdam School of Communications Research conclude in a study that web-based journalism is really a fourth kind of journalism after print, radio and television. Its main characteristic is "empowering audiences as active participants in the daily news." Web journalists have "an interactive relationship with their audience" and a "strong element of audience orientation" and are "more aware of their publics and service function in society than their colleagues elsewhere."

Write in Chunks

When you can't put material into lists, you can still organize it into chunks of information. Put information into sidebars or boxes. Readers will read more, not less, if you break up the information into small bites. Research has also shown that putting

Producing Video for the Web

Website users expect multimedia presentation of news, particularly in the case of important news stories. Many web producers are relatively new to video production and editing, so here are some tips for beginners:

- **Get instruction from someone who has professional video production skills.** You can learn a lot in a day or two.
- **Use good equipment.** You won't need cameras and microphones capable of producing a Hollywood movie or a CNN broadcast, but the quality of the equipment is still important.
- **Eliminate background noise as much as possible.** Some background sound is good for an on-site video, but don't record in an atmosphere where the background noise will drown out your message.
- **Use digital compression rates that are optimized for the web.** For audio, use a sample rate of 22.5 Hz and 16-bit mono or stereo at 56 Kbps. For video, save the video in uncompressed AVI format for editing and then upload it to the web in WMV or FLV format.
- **Employ search-engine optimization techniques so that your video can be found on the web.** Use important keywords in metadata and even in the name of the file itself.
- **Use video to complement other material on your site.** Video is best used in conjunction with text, photos, information graphics, links and other material.
- **Keep videos short, no more than two to three minutes.**
- **Brand your videos with your logo, and make it easy for social media users to link to them.** Facebook, Twitter, Instagram and other social media networks can drive plenty of traffic to your video and consequently to your website.
- **Consider allowing users to rate your video.** This, too, can drive more users to the video and to your site.

some information in a sidebar can give readers better comprehension of the subject. But the main objective here is to write for diverse readers who want to get only the information they want in the order in which they want it.

Think of your story as having parts. When writing a story for a newspaper, you need to think of ways to join the various parts of the story. You craft transitions carefully, and you may even add subheads. When writing a story for the digital media, use subheads if necessary. Better yet, make each segment a separate story. Be sure that each part can stand on its own well enough to be comprehensible and to make your point. Again, remember the importance of a strong lead in the inverted pyramid form.

Use Links

Users of the internet like to feel connected. If you want them to read your copy and come back for more, you must satisfy and enhance that sense of connection.

Jakob Nielsen says that websites must employ scannable text using these elements:

- Highlighted key words, including links.
- Meaningful subheads.
- Bulleted lists.
- One idea per paragraph.
- Half the word count of conventional writing.

Being connected means being interactive. Web users want to be actively involved in what they are reading. They are not passive observers. Like video game players, they want to be in control of where they are going and how they get there. Both individual stories and whole pages must be internally and externally interactive.

Internal Connections

The most challenging and necessary aspect of writing for the web is making the copy interactive. You begin that process by streamlining your copy and not including everything. Create links (also called **hyperlinks**) that allow readers to access information elsewhere on your site, earlier stories on the same subject or even information on another site.

One of the most perplexing problems writers face is deciding when to include the definition of a word. Will you insult some readers by defining a term they know? Will you leave others behind if you do not define the term? A similar problem is whether to tell who a person is. Many readers may wonder how stupid you think they are for telling them that actor Arnold Schwarzenegger was the Republican governor of California. Other readers may need or want that information.

The web writer can simply make the word or name a link to a different page. Readers need only click on a linked word to find its meaning or to read more about it. No longer do writers have to write, "For more information, see. . . ." Academic writers use footnotes. **Hypertext** and **hypermedia** linking, which connects readers directly to text on the one hand or audio, video and pictures on the other, are much more convenient.

Other techniques can also save space while reducing visual clutter on the screen. Some sites display information only when an interested reader rolls the cursor over an item on the page.

Writing concisely has never been easier. You can stick to the essentials and link to the rest. A story about a homicide can link to a map of where the crime took place, to a chart showing the number of homicides this year compared with last year, to a piece about friends of the victim, to information about violent crimes nationally, and so forth.

Remember, too, that unlike the newspaper, where you may be short of space, and unlike radio and television, where you may be short of time, online you have unlimited space and time to run photos and aspects of stories that could be of real interest to some readers. Sports fans, for example, would probably enjoy seeing a whole gallery of photos from Saturday's championship game, and they would enjoy reading or watching interviews with the stars of the game.

External Connections

Don't forget the power of links to different websites. Academic writers include bibliographies. Print journalists often identify sources in their stories. Other writers simply say to readers: "That's all I know about the subject, I'm not going to tell you where I obtained my information, and I'm not telling you where you can find more information." Linking has changed all that. Readers now expect links to source material, and you should provide them when writing for the digital media.

You are not expected to lead readers away from your site to a competitor's, especially on a breaking story. Nevertheless, readers will come to rely on your site to help them find more information about subjects that interest them greatly. And many news sites post supporting documents to buttress their stories.

The New York Times made terrific use of an external link when it reported on the death of singer Scott Weiland of the band Stone Temple Pilots on its website. It provided a link to YouTube videos of several of Weiland's hit songs, including "Plush" and "Creep." Even those not familiar with his music were able to hear a sample of his talent.

To find appropriate external links, use search engines like Google, Bing and Yahoo! Search. Google News is a master of providing links for readers to peruse.

Give Readers a Chance to Talk Back

A big part of providing interactive content is allowing readers to talk back. The web has leveled the playing field. Everyone can be an owner or a publisher. Everyone feels the right, and often the need, to talk back—if not to the writer of the piece, then to other readers in blogs or simply in the comments section at the end of a story. The wonderful thing about allowing readers to talk back is that they do. When they do, they will revisit the site again and again. Web readers want to be part of the process. Readers love it when newspapers like *The Miami Herald* include the reporter's email address in the byline, and many of them respond.

Never has it been easier to find out what is on the minds of your readers. Print and broadcast have mainly been forms of one-way communication. Now, not only can you get opinions easily and quickly, but you also can incorporate them into your story or include links to them. Letters to the editor have always been among the best-read sections in newspapers and magazines. Many readers, especially those reading on the web, not only want to express their own opinions but love to read the opinions of others. Be sure, however, that you use the same strict standards for publishing others' remarks on your website that you use for publishing in your newspaper or magazine. Even email polls can and have been flooded by advocacy groups. Reporting their results can be meaningless, misleading and certainly unprofessional unless the polls are monitored carefully.

Writing with Search Engines in Mind

It's almost impossible to overemphasize one major consideration in writing for the digital media: If your online story cannot be found, it won't be read. That's why editors of websites place great emphasis on *search-engine optimization*, or SEO, the process of making sure your story will be found when someone searches for its topic on sites such as Google, Bing or Yahoo! Search. Generally, the better job you do getting keywords into the lead, the more likely your story will appear near the top of the search results for that topic.

In fact, search engines are more likely to rank the story higher if those keywords are repeated in the headline and in the first couple of paragraphs—something newspaper and magazine editors often try to avoid. How does that work with a story in which the lead obviously was not written with search-engine optimization in mind? A good solution is to place a summary blurb at the top of the web story for indexing purposes.

Another way to accomplish the same thing is to craft a lead in the form of an extended headline, followed by two or three statements that also read as headlines. If you link the headlines, readers can click on them to read the full version of the story on another page within the website.

Newspapers and magazines are notorious for writing baseball stories that never mention the word "baseball" and hockey stories that never use the word "hockey." That's not a problem if users search for the team name, such as Atlanta Braves. They'll find your story even if it doesn't include the word "baseball." But what if users search for "baseball"? Your story will not be found unless it contains metadata—that is, tagging information—that includes that search term. Understanding how search engines work is the key to making sure that all possible search terms appear either in the metadata accompanying the story or in the story itself.

Remember, again, that search engines are more likely to rank your story higher if keywords are repeated in the headline and in the first couple of paragraphs. Making these specific search-engine changes may require some extra attention at newspapers and magazines that try not to repeat words in the headline and lead.

Many websites have protocols for ensuring that the proper keywords are used, and several companies now offer services that ensure content is optimized for search engines. These services can be a wise investment for any site looking to increase its readership.

Writing for Blogs

Media organizations use blogs as a great way to allow users to interact with reporters, columnists and even guest writers who don't work for the company. Blogs are analogous to newspaper editorials and columns in many ways because they allow the writer to express opinions. But unlike those traditional forms of persuasive writing, blogs give readers the chance to answer back and even engage in online discussions with the writer.

Blog entries range from short, inverted pyramid stories, often written quickly by beat reporters, to essays. Whereas traditional journalism is formal, blogging is informal. Whereas traditional journalism is dispassionate, much of blogging is passionate. Whereas traditional journalism is third person ("he," "she," "they"), much of blogging is first person ("I," "we"). Whereas much of traditional writing is vetted by layers of editors, much of blogging goes straight from the writer to the reader.

Wide-Ranging Subject Matter

Political and sports bloggers capture a disproportionate amount of the attention, but there are respected bloggers, some of them independent, many of them working for startups or the traditional media, who blog on everything from travel to technology. Even some heads of companies are blogging, and public relations professionals are doing it on behalf of their companies or organizations. The best blogs are conversational, based in specifics, full of comparisons, explanations, turns of phrase and links. While some web writers do not distinguish between fact and fiction, professional journalists must be meticulous about the facts in their blogs. Here are a few examples of good blogging.

First, a blog about women's networking from the excellent *Huffington Post* blog section. This one is by Eleanor Beaton, and facts are there to back up her opinion that networking groups are failing women. Notice the link to Beaton's source material.

> In the 2014 Global Gender Gap Report, the World Economic Forum suggests the gender gap won't close for another 81 years. When I look at the trials our world is facing (economic disparity, environmental degradation and war), it's clear that the world needs more women's influence, not less. Powerful networking is a great way to expand our influence, close that gap, and enhance our world outlook quicker.

That one citation from the World Economic Forum, which links to the actual report, adds credibility to the blog that otherwise would be missing. Good bloggers in the journalism arena back up their opinions with facts.

Then there are blogs that help readers with popular subjects such as parenting or personal development. Here's an excerpt from "The Art of Manliness," an award-winning blog that in some ways is written like a newspaper column but clearly is based on plenty of research. Here's how one entry began:

> Do you sometimes feel like you spend all your time managing crises? That your life is basically spent putting out one proverbial fire after another?
> At the end of the day do you feel completely sapped and drained of energy, and yet can't point to anything you accomplished of real significance?
> Yes?
> Then you, my friend, are probably confusing the urgent with the important.
> We've talked before about the many leadership lessons that can be gleaned from the life of Dwight D. Eisenhower. Today we're going to talk about another—a principle that guided him through his entire, hugely successful career as general and president:
> "What is important is seldom urgent and what is urgent is seldom important."

In this case, the blog gives a link to an earlier blog post mentioned in the current post.

Great blog examples can be found in many places, not just on the sites of newspapers and other traditional media organizations. But wherever it is found, if a blog is to have credibility, it must be fact-based.

Professional Standards

Dan Steinberg, who is a full-time sports blogger for *The Washington Post*, has two gripes about blogs. In an interview with *Gelf* magazine (gelfmagazine.com), he says bloggers shouldn't steal good stuff from journalists who are doing the reporting. He also chafes at the traditional restrictions of taste imposed upon him by his

LaunchPad **Solo**
macmillan learning

Jonathan Adelstein

macmillanhighered.com /newsreporting12e
Watch **"Net Neutrality."**

■ Why do some people believe net neutrality is important? What are the arguments against net neutrality?

■ Do you support net neutrality? Explain.

newspaper. Steinberg, a former beat reporter, spends a lot of time in locker rooms. He would like to reflect some of the off-color talk, but his editors impose the same standards on his blog as they do on the rest of the paper.

Other bloggers have more freedom. Steinberg is one of the few journalists working for the traditional media who are full-time bloggers. Most are beat reporters who drop news tidbits or humorous observations into a blog about their beats. *The New York Times*, for instance, offers more than 60 blogs, all written by staff writers or columnists. Some bloggers are primarily mini-aggregators. They monitor the web for news of whatever specialty they cover and provide the links for readers. From bursts to full-blown essays, bloggers use a variety of writing styles. There may not be rules or even best practices for bloggers, but there are two worthwhile guidelines: Be interesting, and be accurate.

The Role of Social Media

Earlier in this chapter, we learned of the tremendous power of the web and social media to assist professional journalists in reporting the news. (Figure 11.5 shows a tweet that alerts a newspaper's readers to an important story.) Citizen journalists armed with mobile phones have become significant contributors to our understanding of the news. But as we also learned, in the hands of biased or unscrupulous people, those tools can be a vehicle for disinformation as well as information.

Verifying Information

As a journalist, your challenge is to embrace audience participation in the news-gathering process while remaining ever skeptical of information provided by non-journalists. Our advice is to treat tweets as tips, not fact. Find ways to independently verify the information. Similarly, view videos offered to you with a healthy dose of skepticism. Did this really occur where the person submitting it suggested? Is it real or staged? Does it accurately reflect what occurred at the scene?

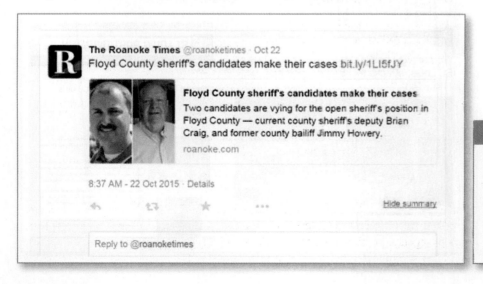

8:37 AM - 22 Oct 2015 · Details

Reply to @roanoketimes

FIGURE 11.5

Tweets can alert readers to important stories as they evolve. A tweet can include photos, links to videos and most importantly links to the reporter's story on the web, as this *Roanoke Times* tweet does.

> "In retrospect, the 'Big Bang' inflation of the World Wide Web already looks like a less complicated time, given the meteoric expansion of social media sites like Facebook, Twitter and Instagram and second-generation crowd sourcing sites like Reddit, Newsvine or Wikinews (with Wikipedia being everyone's granddaddy)."
>
> — James Klurfeld and Howard Schneider

Asking such questions is essential to ensuring that your reputation and that of your company are protected. Reporting an unsubstantiated tweet as fact or posting a staged video on your site or on the air can not only be harmful to your company but also can endanger your future in the business. Embrace user-generated content, but be ever suspicious of its accuracy.

Reaching Readers

While social media can be useful as a source of news or tips, they also play an important role in driving traffic to your company's website. Most journalists today are asked to promote their stories on Facebook, Twitter or Instagram—or maybe all these. Before or after a writer's article goes live on the website, he or she tweets followers with a tease or link to the piece. This helps drive traffic to the news organization's website. Building the size of the audience enables the organization to charge more for advertising on the site.

Facebook is used in a similar way. Many newspapers, magazines, and radio and television stations have Facebook sites on which reporters post links to their stories and readers comment on them. Facebook's Subscribe button allows readers to subscribe to the public updates of a journalist on Facebook without having to add that journalist as a friend. Both *The New York Times* and *The Washington Post* are heavy users of this service.

Journalists use Twitter primarily to promote their stories, according to a Pew Research Center study, much as television anchors use teases before they break for commercials: "After the break, we'll find out when the snowstorm will arrive." An effective tease gives enough information to pique the reader's interest but does not give away the key elements of the story. A tweeted story will get prominent play on a newspaper's site (see Figure 11.6).

FIGURE 11.6

A tweet from a *St. Louis Post-Dispatch* reporter leads readers to a breaking news story posted on the newspaper's website. Today's reporters are expected to tease their stories on Twitter and other social media sites such as Facebook. A more complete version of the story followed on the website and in the next day's newspaper.

Journalists also use Twitter to solicit reader suggestions, to talk about the process of news gathering and to break news before they are able to write even a short story for the web.

In March 2015, *The New York Times* launched an account on Instagram, a photo- and video-sharing social network. According to Katie Hawkins-Gaar, a faculty writer at the Poynter Institute, news organizations are using Instagram to showcase exceptional photography, alert readers to upcoming stories and invite viewers to participate in projects. Instagram almost seems tailor-made for delivering news in a new format—for example, on NowThisNews, "the first and only video news network built for people who love their phones and love social media," according to the site's YouTube channel. NowThisNews also integrates its news coverage with Facebook, Snapchat, Twitter, Vine, and Tumblr.

Writing Effectively and Correctly

Because tweets don't go through the editing process, it is important that you reread and edit your own tweet before sending it. Journalists who send tweets with spelling, grammar and factual errors are damaging their reputations and those of their employers.

Writing at Poynter.org, Jeff Sonderman reported on research by Dan Zarrella, who studied thousands of tweets to determine what led to the highest click-through rates. Zarrella's advice:

- Write between 120 and 130 characters.
- Place links about a quarter of the way through the tweet (not always at the end).
- Tweet only once or twice an hour.

Zarrella also confirmed earlier research that advised using more verbs and determined that tweets are most effective at night or on weekends.

Benefiting as a Journalist

Today's journalists spend a lot of time on social media sites. They do so in part to tease stories they write for websites, newspapers and magazines. No longer are deadlines daily, weekly or monthly. Social media and websites have made the delivery of news instantaneous, and every minute of the day may provide an occasion to tweet about a breaking news event.

A reporter covering a sporting event might issue as many as 40 tweets during the course of a game, which allows followers who are away from the television to learn what's happening in real time. All the while, that reporter might be crafting a story for the web and perhaps yet another for the next day's newspaper.

Social media also allow that reporter to keep in touch with an editor or colleagues covering the same story or even different ones. And because anyone can follow tweets, there's also an opportunity to see what competitors are reporting. Social media, it's safe to say, have become essential to today's journalists.

SUGGESTED READINGS

Foust, James C. *Online Journalism: Principles and Practices of News for the Web*. Scottsdale, Ariz.: Holcomb Hathaway, 2011. This excellent book has valuable material on writing for the web.

Friend, Cecilia, and Jane Singer. *Online Journalism Ethics: Traditions and Transitions*. Armonk, N.Y.: M.E. Sharpe, 2007. Friend and Singer have written an excellent treatise on the ethics of online sites.

Hill, Steve, and Paul Lashmar. *Online Journalism: The Essential Guide*. Thousand Oaks, Calif.: Sage Publications, 2014. This book is a good source of information about writing for the web.

Morkes, John, and Jakob Nielsen. "Concise, Scannable, and Objective: How to Write for the Web." Available from http://www.nngroup.com/articles/concise-scannable-and-objective-how-to-write-for-the-web. This article contains a summary of the authors' classic research regarding effective online writing.

Nielsen, Jakob. "How Users Read on the Web." Available from www.nngroup.com/articles/how-users-read-on-the-web. The site includes research on the usability of online copy.

SUGGESTED WEBSITES

blogs.spjnetwork.org/freelance
The Independent Journalist is a blog for freelancers started by the Society of Professional Journalists.

www.bbc.co.uk
Arguably, no news site on the web does a better job than the BBC of presenting news in ideal ways for the medium.

www.espn.go.com
ESPN.com, one of the best sites on the web, is probably the most extensive internet site for sports fans. It was an early leader in the use of audio and video.

macmillanhighered.com/newsreporting12e
When you visit LaunchPad Solo for Journalism, you will find research links, exercises, and LearningCurve adaptive quizzing to help you improve your grammar and AP style usage. In addition, the site's video collection hosts the videos highlighted in this and other chapters as well as additional clips of leading professionals discussing important media trends.

www.mercurynews.com
MercuryNews.com, one of the first comprehensive local news websites, includes area news courtesy of the *San Jose Mercury News*.

www.miamiherald.com
Like many daily newspapers, *The Miami Herald*'s online edition includes most of the stories from its print edition, along with additional online-only posts.

www.newsy.com
This innovative, video-heavy site compares the coverage of major stories by various media around the world.

PRESSthink.org
Journalist Jay Rosen writes this blog, which covers all facets of journalistic practice. It's entertaining and thorough.

EXERCISES

1. Visit your local newspaper or television station and interview journalists who do the news online. Find out how they were trained and what major challenges they face.

2. Your instructor will assign you a newspaper story. Rewrite it for online use, and indicate any links that you might include.

3. **Your journalism blog.** Compare the websites of three similar news companies. For example, compare three newspaper sites or three broadcast sites. In your blog, describe the differences you see in how well news is presented on the web. Invite comments from your classmates.

4. Find a website that does a good job of linking readers to original source material. In an email memo to your "managing editor," evaluate the use of that technique, and explain why it works for the website.

5. From the BBC website (www.bbc.co.uk), choose one of the major stories of the day. In a one-page memo, outline how the BBC took advantage of different types of media to tell the story.

6. List five differences in how information is conveyed in a newspaper versus how it is conveyed on a website.

7. For each of the following web stories, list multimedia elements, links and sidebars you would use.

   a. A local merchant's group invites kids from a homeless shelter to paint store windows for the holidays.
   b. A star athlete returns to give your college team a pep talk at the beginning of the season.
   c. An explosion of unknown origin destroys a bookstore and café not far from campus.

FLUCTUAT
NEC MERGITUR

As terrorists coordinated attacks in Paris and Saint-Denis, France, on November 13, 2015, many Americans first heard the news on social media. It was mid-afternoon on the U.S. East Coast when the attacks started, so those at school or work caught glimpses of what was happening through Twitter posts and Facebook links. But the powerful draw of being able to watch live and breaking news via broadcast or streaming video showed through as evening arrived. Cable news channels saw spikes in ratings as Americans arrived home from work and tuned in to watch the video to see for themselves what was going on. Nielsen reports that eight of the top 10 highest-rated broadcasts that evening were live news coverage of the attacks abroad.

Radio and television play a critical role in getting accurate information to the public when time is of the essence—warning folks of the coming dangers, helping them prepare and get to safety and connecting them with aid after the immediate crisis is past. But perhaps just as crucial is their role in helping the nation take a breath and feel good about itself. It was President George H.W. Bush who said at his inauguration, "We meet on democracy's front porch." That is one answer why we go through the time and expense of a second inauguration for two-term presidents. Author Sally Quinn explains, "We want to see the flags wave and the bands play, the parades march along and the leader of the free world standing before our Capitol dome."

Television and online media help us do that.

What Radio and Television Do Best

During major news events, radio and television journalists deliver breaking news and then update their audiences as the news develops. If you tune in to CNN or other news channels, not only do you see what's happening and listen to details from journalists, you also see additional headlines streaming below the picture on a ticker. The ticker gives the viewer the chance to find other news and seek that out, either by continuing to watch CNN or by going online to find more.

Of course, much of the time journalists must write and report news after it has occurred. Nearly every radio and television station provides at least some news that is written by journalists working for the wire services, such as the Associated Press or Reuters.

In addition, radio and television journalists are expected to publish updates all day on social media, using Twitter, Facebook, Instagram, Periscope and other platforms to provide round-the-clock details and updates on their stories. Conversely, most broadcast newsrooms routinely take content found online or sent in by audience members and incorporate it in traditional newscasts.

Even if your primary emphasis is not radio or television news, you will probably find yourself producing content that involves the use of audio and video. And if you are writing for radio or television news, almost certainly you

In this chapter you will learn:

1

What radio and television do best.

2

How the story selection criteria for radio and television news differ from those for print news.

3

How to write radio and television news.

4

How social media can supplement radio and television content.

5

How to prepare radio and television news copy.

**macmillanhighered.com
/newsreporting12e**
Watch **"Going Visual: Video,
Radio and the Web."**

■ Why are some radio stations
shooting and sharing videos
online? What do they hope to
accomplish with this?
■ Do you visit radio station
websites and watch videos?
If not, will you do so in the
future? Explain.

will be required to contribute to the station's website, writing in a style more associated with print journalism.

Radio and television stations also use the web and social media to deliver the news and information they are gathering but which cannot find a place on air in the regular newscasts. Rather than interrupt programming with new facts about a developing story, stations publish first on their websites and social media platforms. Nearly all local stations, network and cable news operations use this "push" method of delivering the news around the clock, 24 hours a day. That way, audiences do not have to wait for a scheduled news broadcast or hope a broadcaster interrupts regular programming. Instead, the information finds them wherever they are, be it on the web, on social media or on mobile devices.

Criteria for Selecting Radio and Television News

Four criteria specifically distinguish the selection of radio and television news from that of print news: timeliness, emphasis on information rather than explanation, audio or visual impact, and emphasis on people rather than concepts.

Timeliness

The radio and television news writer emphasizes one criterion of news value more than any other: timeliness. *When* something happened often determines whether a news item will be used in a newscast, as well as where it will be placed in the news lineup of stories to appear in the newscast, known as a **rundown**. The breaking story receives top priority and often leads the newscast.

Because timeliness is so important, a sense of immediacy influences everything in radio news, from what is reported to how it is reported. Often this is true of television news as well. Even with radio and television air documentaries or in-depth segments, the producers typically try to infuse the program with a sense of urgency, a strong feeling of the present, an emphasis on what's happening now.

Information Rather Than Explanation

Because airtime is so precious, radio and television reporters are generally more concerned with delivering facts and information rather than spending a great deal of time on explanations of why things are happening. Broadcast stories can be as short as 10 or 12 seconds; they tend to average only 60 seconds or so and seldom run longer than two minutes. A minute of news read aloud is only 15 lines of copy, or about 170 to 180 words. After you subtract time for commercials, a half-hour newscast has only 20 to 22 minutes of **news hole**, which includes time for weather and sports. So the typical newscast's content equates to about one-half of the front page of a newspaper.

That lack of depth on the air used to be a broadcast news weakness that left audience members to turn to newspapers or newsmagazines for further background and details. But the internet now allows newscasters to send viewers and listeners to the station's website to find expanded information on the story and get an extra perspective. Viewers no longer have to turn to a different news outlet.

Because of their relatively low production costs compared with the costs of producing prime-time scripted dramas and comedies, television newsmagazine formats such as *60 Minutes*, *20/20* and *Dateline NBC* continue to be successful. These programs represent a somewhat different challenge to television news writers, but even so, writing for a newsmagazine format resembles writing for television news.

Audio or Visual Impact

Some news is selected for radio because a reporter has recorded an on-the-scene audio report. Some news is selected for television because it is visually appealing or exciting. For this reason, news of an accident or fire that might get attention only in the records column of a newspaper might get important play on a television newscast. If a television crew returns with good video of an event, that event often receives prominent placement in the next newscast.

A good example occurred in Las Vegas in 2015. A fire at the luxury Cosmopolitan hotel in the Vegas Strip sent thick black smoke billowing into the air. Network and cable news, along with many local stations, featured the story prominently in their newscasts that day. Despite the towering smoke and flames, the fire was limited to the pool deck. It did not damage any structural part of the hotel. Firefighters had it out in 30 minutes.

Emphasis on People

Radio and television tell the news using people affected by the news as central characters more often than print does. Radio and television writers follow the classic focus structure formula of making a problem come alive by finding someone who is dealing with the problem and showing the audience how he or she is doing. (See Chapter 10 for more on the focus structure.) That "someone" can be a representative person or family, a person affected by the story or a chief player. Thus, rather than using abstract concepts, television in particular humanizes the story. You can't shoot video of an issue, but you can show the impact the issue has on people. When Don Hewitt, legendary creator of *60 Minutes*, was asked why he didn't do a segment on AIDS, his response was quick and simple: "AIDS is not a story; it's an issue."

Radio and television news writing emphasizes certain characteristics that newspaper and online news writing do not, and because of that, story structure may vary.

Writing Radio and Television News

While visuals are tops for television and audio rules on radio, writing is the foundation of both media. Broadcast writing varies greatly from other forms of journalism, both in length and in style. Successful broadcast journalists know and follow the rules to make their writing a key part of their stories.

Characteristics of Radio and Television News Writing

Because of the focus on timeliness, radio and television news writers, like journalists writing for digital media, must emphasize immediacy and write conversationally, tightly and clearly.

Immediacy

Radio and television news writers achieve a sense of immediacy in part by using the present tense as much as possible. Note the use of the present, present progressive and present perfect tenses (italicized) in this Associated Press story.

GREENVILLE, S.C. (AP)—Sheriffs in five South Carolina counties *are offering* people a chance to turn in explosives, no questions asked.

Officials in Abbeville, Anderson, Greenville, Oconee and Pickens counties *have set* aside this week as Explosives Amnesty Week.

People in those areas *can call* their sheriff's office to have any explosives, ammunition, weapons, bomb materials or military ordnance removed from their property. Certified bomb technicians will respond to remove and destroy the hazardous materials.

Dispatchers will request information about the materials to be collected, including the address where the materials *are stored.*

Callers *aren't* required to give their names and no criminal charges related to hazardous materials reported or collected will be filed against people who *participate.*

TIPS

Radio and Television News Writing

- Emphasizes immediacy.
- Has a conversational style.
- Is tightly phrased.
- Is clear.

Checklist for Writing Radio and Television News

Does My Writing Have Immediacy?
- Uses the present, present perfect and present progressive tenses.
- Uses the word "today" as high in the lead sentences as possible.
- Avoids the past tense but includes the time element if it must be used.
- In a follow-up story, leads with a new development or a new fact.
- Pushes a "today" angle in the lead of next-day stories.

Does My Writing Feature a Conversational Style?
- Uses simple, short sentences instead of complex sentences.
- Uses active, rather than passive, verbs.
- Uses contractions to add a conversational tone, but avoids any that could be misunderstood.
- Uses fragments sparingly and with effect.
- Doesn't use slang, colloquialisms or vulgar or off-color expressions.
- Uses correct grammar.

Does My Writing Employ Tight Phrasing?
- Uses as few words as possible.
- Uses few adjectives and adverbs.
- Includes carefully selected facts.

Does My Writing Have Clarity?
- Uses familiar words—not jargon or technical terms.
- Avoids unnecessary or confusing synonyms.
- Repeats words or phrases for greater comprehension.
- Avoids foreign words and phrases.
- Avoids phrases like "the former" and "the latter."
- Repeats proper names rather than using pronouns.
- Keeps the subject close to the verb, without many intervening words.
- Avoids clever figures of speech.
- Avoids lists of numbers.
- Breaks down statistics so they are understandable.

For accuracy, the past tense is sometimes necessary. But radio and television writers like to use the progressive form of the verb ("are offering") to show continuing action, and the present perfect tense ("have set") more than the past tense because the present perfect indicates past action that is continuing (see the annotated model "Use of Verb Tenses in a TV Story" on page 251).

Writers want to emphasize the immediacy of stories by indicating the event covered happened today by including the word "today" as high in the lead sentence as possible. That will sometimes yield copy that loses some conversational tone in order to gain immediacy. For example, this lead seems perfectly fine to indicate a today event:

Seattle police caught the man they say is the so-called "Handsome Robber" today.

But you can move today much higher in that sentence to increase immediacy:

Seattle police today caught the man they say is the so-called "Handsome Robber."

Sometimes reporters stress immediacy by saying, "just minutes ago" or, on a morning newscast, "this morning." If there is no danger of inaccuracy or deceit, though, you can omit references to time. For example, if something happened yesterday, you might report it like this:

The latest rash of fires in Southern California is under control.

But if you use the past tense in a lead, you should include the time element:

The legislature sent a welfare reform bill to the governor late last night. It finished just in time before the spring recess.

The best way to avoid the past tense is to avoid yesterday's story. You can do that by updating yesterday's story. By leading with a new development or a new fact, you might be able to use the present tense. So the fire example from above becomes:

Firefighters are mopping up this morning after bringing the latest rash of fires in Southern California under control.

Remember, radio and television newscasts are "live." Your copy must convey that important characteristic.

Conversational Style

Although "write the way you talk" is questionable advice for most kinds of writing, it is an imperative for radio and television news writing. "Read your copy aloud" is good advice for most kinds of writing; for radio and television news writing, that's what it's all about. You should read and re-read your copy aloud as you write to be sure it's as conversational as possible.

Write so that your copy *sounds* good. Use simple, short sentences, written with transitive verbs in the active voice. Transitive verbs do things to things; they demand an object. People rarely use verbs in the passive voice when they talk; it usually sounds cumbersome and awkward. You don't say, "Guess what I was just told by somebody." "Was told" here is in the passive voice; the subject is being acted upon. The preposition "by" also tells you the verb is in the passive voice. "Guess what

ANNOTATED MODEL   Use of Verb Tenses in a TV Story

Present and Present Perfect Tenses

The lead is in the present progressive tense ("are investigating"). The reporter wants to indicate the investigation is continuing.

The attribution "says" is in the present tense to make the report more alive and current. "Getting" is a present participle, again signifying continuing action.

"Reports" and "do not believe" are again in the present tense, even though the event happened in the past.

"Are looking" is present progressive, indicating continuing action. "Is" indicates the man is still a person of interest.

"Do not believe" is a form of the present emphatic, again indicating continuing action.

Police: Jefferson City Couple Found Shot to Death

JEFFERSON CITY, Mo. (AP)—Jefferson City police **are investigating** the shooting deaths of a man and woman.

Jefferson City police Capt. Michael Smith **says** police went to an apartment complex about 3:30 a.m. Monday after **getting** calls from neighbors.

KRCG **reports** that police **do not believe** anyone other than the couple **was** in the apartment.

Police **are looking** for a man who **is** a person of interest in the case.

Authorities **do not believe** the killings **were** drug- or gang-related.

Past Tense

"Was" is simple past tense. No one is presently in the apartment.

"Were" is past tense, indicating that the killings took place in the past.

To convey a sense of immediacy, radio and television news writers use the present or present perfect tense whenever possible.

> Good television journalism presents news in the most attractive and lucid form yet devised by man.
>
> — *Bill Small, author, veteran broadcaster, former president of CBS News*

somebody just told me" is active and more natural, less wordy and stronger. "Told" is in the active voice; the subject is doing the acting.

Because casual speech contains contractions, you should use contractions to give your story a more natural, conversational feel—so long as the person who voices the copy pronounces each contraction clearly. One exception is the negative "not," which is more clearly understood when you use the whole word rather than a contraction. For instance, saying that investigators "did not" question the suspect will be much clearer to the listener than saying they "didn't" question the subject. Avoiding the contraction also avoids the risk the listener will mistake "didn't" for "did."

Conversational style also permits the use of occasional fragments. Sentences are sometimes strung together loosely with dashes. They sometimes begin with the conjunction "and" or "but," as in the following example:

BEAVER FALLS, Pa. (AP)—Police don't plan to cite the drivers of a truck and school bus that crashed in western Pennsylvania.

But only because neither vehicle had a driver when they wrecked.

Writing in conversational style does not mean that you may use slang, colloquialisms or incorrect grammar. Nor does it mean that you may use vulgar or off-color expressions. Remember that your audience includes people of all ages, backgrounds and sensitivities.

Tight Phrasing

You must learn to write in a conversational style without being wordy. This means you must condense. Use few adjectives and adverbs. Reduce the use of the passive voice to save a couple of words. Make each word count.

Keeping it short means selecting facts carefully because often you don't have time for the whole story. Radio and television newscasters want good, tight writing that is easy to follow. Let's examine how a wire story written for newspapers can be condensed for radio and television. Look at this Associated Press newspaper wire story.

> KABUL, Afghanistan (AP)—Two massive attacks in Kabul on Friday, one near a government and military complex in a residential area and the other a suicide bombing outside a police academy, killed at least 35 people, sending the strongest message yet to Afghan President Ashraf Ghani—that militants are still able to strike at his heavily fortified seat of power.
>
> No one claimed responsibility for the attacks, though officials indicated they blamed the Taliban.
>
> The implications of the assaults, however, undermine claims by security services and the government that the capital is immune from devastating attacks. They also pose a major challenge to Ghani, who has made the peace process with the Taliban the hallmark of his presidency since taking office last year.
>
> In the evening hours, a suicide bomber dressed in a police uniform struck outside the gates of a police academy in Kabul, killing at least 20 recruits and wounding 24, Afghan officials said.
>
> The attacker walked into a group of recruits waiting outside the academy and detonated his explosives-laden vest, said a police officer, who goes by the name of Mabubullah. Many Afghans use only one name. A security official, who spoke on condition of anonymity because he was not authorized to talk to reporters, said there were at least 24 wounded among the recruits.
>
> Later on Friday evening, insurgents launched an attack on a NATO military base near Kabul's international airport, according to the coalition spokesman, Col. Brian Tribus. Two insurgents were killed in the assault, he added, without giving further details.
>
> No one claimed responsibility for that attack and it was not immediately clear if there was any damage to the NATO base.

The print story has 276 words. Here's how it appeared on the Associated Press broadcast wire in its entirety:

> KABUL, Afghanistan (AP)—Militants in Afghanistan are letting the country's president know that they are still able to strike in the heavily fortified capital. Two massive bomb attacks in Kabul left at least 35 people dead. One attack took place near a government and military complex in a residential area. The other was a suicide bombing outside a police academy. Security services and the Afghan government have said that the capital is protected from devastating attacks.

The broadcast version has just 72 words. Listeners are given just the bare facts. They must turn to print or online news sources for the details, and more and more newscasts send their audiences to the station's website for additional content. One newspaper story is often the same length as two or three broadcast stories. An online story can be and often is much longer than a broadcast story or a newspaper story.

In radio and television news, tight writing is important even when time is available. Broadcast writers usually strive to waste no words, even in documentaries, which provide in-depth coverage of events.

Clarity

Unlike readers, radio and television news audiences can't go back to re-read a passage they didn't quite comprehend. They see or hear it only once, and their attention waxes and wanes. So you must be clear and precise.

> **"Short words are best, and old words, when short, are best of all."**
>
> — *Winston Churchill, British politician*

Write simply, in short sentences filled with nickel-and-dime words. Don't look for synonyms. Don't be afraid to repeat words or phrases. Oral communication needs reinforcement. Avoid foreign words and phrases. Avoid phrases like "the former" and "the latter," which are hard for listeners to follow. Repeat proper names in the story rather than use pronouns. The listener can easily forget the name of the person to whom the pronoun refers, or be confused about which person the pronoun references if there are multiple subjects in the story.

When you are tempted to write a dependent clause in a sentence, make it an independent clause instead. Keep the subject close to the verb. Close the gap between the doer and the activity. This version doesn't do that:

> A man flagged down a Highway Patrol officer near Braden, Tenn., today and told him a convict was hiding in his house. The prisoner, one of five who escaped from the Fort Pillow Prison on Saturday, surrendered peacefully.

The second sentence contains 12 words between the subject, "prisoner," and the main verb, "surrendered." By the time the broadcaster reaches the verb, many listeners will have forgotten what the subject was. The story is easier to understand when written this way:

> A man flagged down a Highway Patrol officer near Braden, Tennessee, today and told him a convict was hiding in his house. The prisoner surrendered peacefully. He's one of five who escaped from the Fort Pillow Prison on Saturday.

The third sentence is still a complex sentence ("who escaped . . ." is the dependent clause), but it is more easily understood than the original version.

Clarity also requires that you resist a clever turn of phrase. Viewers and listeners are probably intelligent enough to understand it, but a good figure of speech takes time to savor. If listeners pause to savor it, they will not hear what follows. For that reason, clever columnists often fail as radio commentators.

Even more dangerous than figures of speech are numbers. Don't barrage the listener or viewer with a series of numbers. If you must use illustrative numbers or comparative statistics, first round off numbers so they are easier to comprehend. If a school budget is approved at $47,925,345, call that a "48 million dollar budget." Look for ways to break down numbers so that they are understandable. For example, it is better to say that one of every four Americans smokes than to say there are 46 million smokers in the United States. You might be tempted to say how many billions of dollars a federal program will cost, but you will help listeners understand if you say that the program will cost the average wage earner $73 for each of the next five years. Television reporters often supply an on-air graphic illustrating the data given orally to help the audience visually understand the information they are hearing.

Story Structure

Writers must craft radio and television leads somewhat differently from the way they cast print and online leads. They also must construct special introductions and conclusions to video or audio segments and synchronize their words with recorded segments.

Writing the Radio and Television Lead

Like newspaper reporters, radio and television reporters must grab the attention of their audience. Much of what you learned in Chapter 8, on writing the inverted pyramid lead, applies to radio and television leads. But be aware that people tend to be doing other things when listening to radio or watching television, so you must strive to attract their attention in different ways.

One way is by preparing your audience for what is to come. You cue listeners to make sure they are tuned in. You introduce the story with a general statement, something that will pique the interest of the audience, then you go to the specifics. For example:

> **General statement** Things are far from settled for Springfield's teacher strike.
>
> **Specifics** School officials and union representatives did not agree on a contract yesterday. They will not meet again for at least a week.

Sometimes the opening sentence will cover a number of news items:

> **First responders were busy today working several accidents across the Springfield region.**

"Cuing in" is only one method of opening a radio or television story. Other leads go immediately into the "what" and the "who," the "where" and the "when." In radio or television news, the "what" is most important, followed by "who" did the "what." The time and place may be included in the lead, but seldom is the "why" or the "how." If time permits, the "why" and the "how" may come later in the story, but often they are omitted.

The first words of the lead are the most important. Don't keep the listener guessing as to what the story is about. Don't begin with a dependent clause or with a prepositional phrase, as in this example:

> *In strong and urgent language,* New Mexico Gov. Susana Martinez Wednesday asked her administration to remove language about "forcible rape" from a new state policy.

The opening words are meaningless without what comes later. The listener may not know what you are talking about. Here is a better way to introduce this story:

> New Mexico Gov. Susana Martinez strongly urged her administration to remove language about "forcible rape" from a new state policy Wednesday.

Be sure to "tee up," or identify, an unfamiliar name to prepare listeners for a name they otherwise may miss. Do it this way:

> *Veteran Kansas City, Kansas, businessman and civic leader* Kenneth Durban died yesterday in a nursing home at age 83.

Don't mislead. The opening words must set the proper tone and mood for the story. Attract attention; tease a little. Answer questions, but don't ask them. Lead the listener into your story.

Writing Lead-Ins and Wrap-Ups

Radio and television journalists must learn how to write a **lead-in** that introduces a recorded segment from a news source or from another reporter, or a live report from a journalist in the field. The functions of a lead-in are twofold: to set the scene by briefly telling the "where," the "when" and sometimes the "what," and to identify the source or reporter. The lead-in should contain something substantive. Here's an example:

> A grand jury decided today not to charge a Springfield teenager in the killing of his father. Jan Morrow reports the panel believes the death was an accident.

Lead-ins should generate interest. Sometimes several sentences are used to provide background, as in the following:

> It's a long comeback, indeed, and a slow one at that. But as Bill McKinney reports, some economists continue to be optimistic about the future.

Be careful not to include in the lead-in what is in the story. Just as a headline should not steal word-for-word the lead of a newspaper story, the lead-in should not parrot the opening words of the correspondent. The writer must know the contents of the segment in order to write a proper lead-in.

After the segment is over, you may want to wrap up the story before going on to the next item. The wrap-up or tag is especially important in radio copy because there are no visuals to identify the person that listeners just heard. If the story reported by Evelyn Turner was about a meeting to settle a strike, you might tag Turner's report by adding this information:

> Turner reports negotiations will resume tomorrow.

A tag like this gives the story an ending and clearly separates it from the next story.

Writing to the Video

Writing for a video report begins with the selection of the subject and deciding how it is to be shot. The writing continues through the editing process and is done with the video clearly in mind.

Words and video must be complementary, never interfering with each other, never ignoring each other. Your first responsibility is to relate the words to the video. If you do not, viewers will not get the message because they will be wondering what the video is about.

There is a danger, however, in sticking too closely to the video by pointing out the obvious, giving your report a "play-by-play" feel. You need to avoid both extremes and use what is commonly called the "touch and go" method. This means that at the beginning of a scene or when a scene changes, you must tell the viewer where you are or what is happening by making the words and video "touch." Once you are into the scene, the script may be less closely tied to the video.

Suppose the report concerns the continuation of a hospital workers' strike and the opening scene shows pickets outside the hospital. You can explain the video by saying:

> **Union members are still picketing Mercy Hospital today as the hospital workers' strike enters its third week.**

Viewers now know three things that are not obvious on the video: who is picketing, where and how long they've been picketing. If the video switches to people sitting around a table negotiating, you must again set the scene for viewers:

> **Meanwhile, hospital administrators and union leaders are continuing their meetings—apparently without success.**

Once you have related the words to the video, you may add other details of the strike. Not only must you comment on the video, but you must complete it as well. Part of completing it is giving the report a wrap-up or a strong ending. Don't be cute and don't be obvious, but give the story an ending. Here's one possible ending for the strike story:

> **Strikers, administrators, patients and their families agree on one sure effect of the strike—it's a bad time to be sick.**

Ziv Koren/Polaris

Christiane Amanpour is CNN's anchor and chief international correspondent and the host of Amanpour, *a nightly foreign affairs program on CNN International. She also serves as Global Affairs Anchor of ABC News. Her authoritative reports from around the world have informed millions.*

Finding the Visuals for TV News

Visuals are the most important element of television news. The medium is strongest when it attracts viewers to watch moving images and listen to accompanying audio. These elements:

- Deliver a sense of presence to the story, putting the viewers on the scene of the news.
- Allow viewers to better understand what happened—or is happening now.
- Allow sources to appear in front of viewers and speak in their own words and voice.
- Provide visual context for what has transpired.
- Make long-lasting memories for viewers.
- When live, give viewers the ability to remotely view big stories as they happen.

Television journalists use a variety of visuals, not all of which are limited to video:

- *Recorded video* of news from the place where the event happened is the most common visual on TV news. While TV journalists themselves capture most video shown on newscasts, video can also come from witnesses who saw and recorded the event or come from social media.
- *Live video* of news as it is happening provides an even more immediate news experience for viewers. Live video is almost exclusively captured by television stations with their live equipment.
- A *photo* can put a face to a name in a story or show news that video cameras were not yet there to capture. Photos can come from official sources like police, from eyewitnesses to news events or even from social media.
- A *graphic illustration* can take many forms on air, from showing documents to displaying quotes from someone who does not appear on camera to displaying data in a table. TV stations have their own tools to create these graphics. Some have a graphics department with artists to build the graphics for use in the daily newscasts, while others expect producers or other journalists to create their own.
- A *map* is often used to show the scene of a news event and typically appears before the station cuts to a reporter

on site or a video of the scene of the story. Many stations have mapping software to allow producers to build these maps on their own.

- An *animation* can be used to explain the news through motion, showing more than what a single graphic image can show. For instance, a newsroom might use an animated graphic to show the course of a tornado through a city.

Each type of visual comes with special needs for journalists to verify accuracy and authenticity:

- For any video not shot by the news organization itself, it pays to be skeptical. You should ask questions about who shot the video and under what circumstances.
- Video from social media or other online sources can often be faked. If you're unable to verify a video's authenticity, you should refrain from using it on the air. At the very least, if the decision is made to air unverified video, it is essential to inform the viewers of the lack of verification.
- While enhancing an image to make it easier to see is certainly allowable, you should never alter an image in a way that changes its meaning or what it depicts.
- Typos and other text errors are far too common in on-air graphics. Be sure to check and double-check all text before airing. Do *not* rely on spell checkers to do that work.
- In the same way, journalists often make errors in arithmetic, mathematics and statistics. Any graphics with numbers should be checked for accuracy twice before being aired.
- Video and images that belong to someone else are not always available for newscasts to use without permission of the rightsholder. Learn the elements of fair use and discuss the situation with an editor if you're unsure of your legal right to use a visual in your story.

Visuals properly crafted or chosen can greatly enhance the impact of a news story, so being able to think creatively about the best use of visuals can be a valuable skill to cultivate.

Courtesy of Brian Emfinger.

ON THE JOB   Successful Reporting Means Watching the Clock

Charged with a coverage area that blankets an entire state, **Alexis Rogers** is a general assignment reporter for KATV, the ABC affiliate in Little Rock, Arkansas. The job is Rogers' first since graduating from college, where she studied radio and TV journalism.

Rogers says her days are long.

Before the station's formal morning assignment meeting at 9:30, Rogers has already been making calls as early as 8 a.m. Once she gets her assignment confirmed, she's on her way to a story that could be as much as three hours away. At the same time, she launches into what will be a day-long barrage on social media. When the story is shot and she's going back to the station or to her live shot location, Rogers is writing and working with a photographer or editor on her story. Even after she's finished delivering her story at 5 and 6 p.m., she's back on the web posting her story video and making more calls to set up stories for the next day.

Rogers says she is always watching the clock and timing her day: "You might think it's all going to go right, but there are so many things that go wrong."

Successful reporters leave enough time and have workable back-up plans so they can be sure to make deadline even when problems crop up, she says.

The single most important trait she wants the audience to recognize in her is that she is committed to being an expert on the region, Rogers says: "Our viewers are constantly questioning. They don't hesitate to ask you a question to see if you know the area and know what you are talking about."

Rogers' advice to young journalists entering their first jobs is to be the person the newsroom sees as the most dependable employee there.

"In college, you're used to working with a lot of people your own age who work hard. But when I got here, I was the youngest person on air in the market. So the people I worked with questioned whether I could do it," she says.

Her final tip, simply put, is "Grow your skills." She urges young journalists to learn the skills of the investigative reporter, including computer-assisted and data reporting and visualization.

"I probably use the Arkansas Freedom of Information Act for stories five times a week," Rogers says.

She also suggests reporters quickly learn their local court and government structure so that they can go directly to the best sources to find and cover stories.

Using Social Media in Radio and Television

Nearly all newsrooms are merging the traditional "small-screen" delivery of news via television with the even smaller screens of computers and smartphones. This technique, called "second-screen viewing," presents an opportunity for broadcast outlets to deliver additional news content.

Blending Online with On-Air

After an African-American man named Freddie Gray died while in the custody of Baltimore police in the spring of 2015, protestors took to the streets to demand action by city and state leaders. News organizations across the country quickly began using

**macmillanhighered.com
/newsreporting12e**
Watch **"Television Networks
Evolve: Cable, Satellite,
Broadband."**

- What technological changes
  have challenged the
  dominance of the broadcast
  networks and cable news
  for the past several years?
  How are the latest cellphone
  technologies again changing
  the game?
- What is a "broadcaster" and
  how might different definitions
  fit in the realm of new digital
  media?

the Twitter hashtag #Baltimore on their own coverage to be sure it was featured in the stream of social media posts about the protests. The use of a **hashtag** puts broadcast stories into the news stream of social media users. It's a crucial strategy for legacy media to reach an audience that might not consume something as traditional as a television newscast.

Along with real-time interactivity during a live broadcast, radio and television newsrooms use social media as a way to do crowdsourcing (collaborate with the audience to gather information) and collect additional perspectives on daily and long-term projects. The second screen is growing as a way to maintain and increase audience involvement. WTHR-TV in Indianapolis, like many local television stations, has its own iPhone and Android apps that allow users to watch video, interact on social media, interact with weather radar and more. Local stations continue to build the second-screen experience for their audiences. Efforts now focus on giving viewers the chance to use their tablets and laptops to consume value-added content while watching the traditional broadcast on their televisions.

As news consumers continue to explore new places to learn about the news, it is increasingly important for all journalists to think about sharing news across many different platforms, no matter for what type of newsroom they work.

Guidelines for Using Social Media

When a newsroom gathers content from viewers and social media, it must follow these strict guidelines:

1. All information gathered from social media must be verified before being published.
2. Stations should be digital first, meaning stories and information should be published online and on social media and not held for broadcast newscasts. However, stations may make exceptions for certain promoted or investigative reports designed to deliver audiences to newscasts first.
3. Reporters should not use social media posts just to entice audience members to tune in later. Instead, "teaser" posts should contain vital bits of the story being reported and naturally give audience members a reason to watch the later broadcast.
4. Stations should actively seek out user-generated content from audience members, thus giving viewers a way to supply their own video, stills audio via the station's website and social media. Any sharing should include terms of service giving the station the right to use the supplied content. Submissions must require contact information in case the newsroom needs additional information about the content.

Whether she's analyzing data for an investigative piece, field producing during breaking news or engaging with viewers on social media, **Michelle Flandreau** has a passion for in-depth journalism across all platforms.

After graduating with a degree in broadcast journalism, she began her career as a producer at WBIR, the NBC affiliate in Knoxville, Tennessee. She started off producing the weekday 5 p.m. newscast. A few months into her career at WBIR, her responsibilities expanded when she became the producer for the investigative team.

"My news director approached me about launching an investigative unit at our station. I had a background in computer-assisted reporting but had never done anything quite like this. However, I knew I was ready for the challenge," Flandreau said.

"When I look back on my time in Knoxville, the story I'm most proud of was a five-month investigation into a local tourism non-profit funded primarily by taxpayer dollars. We uncovered legal questions surrounding the president and CEO's employment contract. Our reporting ultimately led to a company reorganization that saved thousands in taxpayer dollars."

After two years at WBIR, Flandreau moved to KING 5 in Seattle, where she served as the multiplatform producer for KING 5 Morning News. She spent her mornings focused on the show's social and digital efforts. Once the show was over, she focused on long-term, special projects for KING 5 Morning News. During her time at KING 5, she also had the opportunity to work in the field to produce major news stories, such as the Oso landslide and the Seahawks' trips to the Super Bowl.

"Each day is a different challenge, but that's what keeps me coming back," Flandreau said.

Flandreau says she believes one of the most gratifying things about journalism is knowing your work can have a tremendous impact on people's lives.

Courtesy of Michelle Flandreau.

Preparing Radio and Television News Copy

When you prepare copy to be read by a newscaster, your goals are to make the copy easy for the newscaster to read and easy for the audience to understand.

Format

Nearly every station uses newsroom computer system software, commonly called "NRCS," to prepare rundowns, write copy and produce its newscasts. Details such as line spacing are built into the templates of the NRCS software. But some details are still in the hands of the writers.

In radio copy, the portion read live is separated from any prerecorded elements (Figure 12.1). Quotes are italicized. When printing, the system puts each story on a separate piece of paper. That way, the order of the stories can be rearranged, and stories can be added or dropped easily.

> " Writing a silence is as important as writing words. We don't rely on video enough. "
>
> — *John Hart, prize-winning TV news anchor*

Date	Slug	Reporter's name

09/06/12   SOBOCO0906a   Ryan Schmidt

The Southern Boone County Library in Ashland will move to a new
location next fall, pending the approval of the Daniel Boone Regional
Library board. KBIA's Ryan Schmidt tells us why officials say they need a
new library, and how they will use the new space.

SOBOCO0906a   TRT 1:06   SOC

Daniel Boone Regional Library System associate director Elinor
(ELEANOR) Barrett says the library in Ashland is outgrowing the current
building.

Barrett0906a   TRT: 20   OC: *"five years or so."*

*"Based on the population growth in the Southern Boone area, as well as the size
of collection that we need to have to adequately serve that population, we need
to increase the space that will be available to us, over the course of the next five
years or so."*

Barrett thinks library goers will appreciate the new multipurpose room
included in the plan. . . .

*Prerecorded elements
are separated from live
portions.*

*Quotations are typed in
italics.*

FIGURE 12.1

In this radio copy, the name
Elinor is also spelled ELEANOR,
in case the announcer is
unfamiliar with the first, less
common spelling.

In television copy, the stories and pages are numbered, and each story starts on
a separate page. Television copy is formatted to put anchor and reporter copy on the
right half of the page (Figure 12.2), while director instructions appear on the left of
the page. Each line averages four words, and newscasters average 40 lines per minute. The copy that is read live generally appears in all caps, while recorded audio is
in normal upper and lower case. Stations vary with scripting basics.

At most stations, copy is prepared for a **teleprompter**, an electronic device that
projects the copy over the camera lens in the studio so the newscaster can read it
while appearing to look straight into the camera.

The newscast producer determines the **slug**, or identifying name, for a story and
its placement. Some producers insist that the slug contain the time of the broadcast
to keep track of content when multiple newscasts are in production at the same time.
Newsroom computer systems help number the pages and can estimate how long a
script might run on the air on the basis of an anchor's read rate.

Names and Titles

In radio and television style, full names are typically used on first reference, with
just the surname used in subsequent references. Don't use middle initials unless they
are a widely recognized part of someone's name (Edward R. Murrow) or unless they
are necessary to distinguish two people with the same first and last names, as with
former Presidents George W. Bush and George H.W. Bush.

A title that explains a person's connection to a story should be used during the
first reference to that person, and it should precede the name so that listeners are

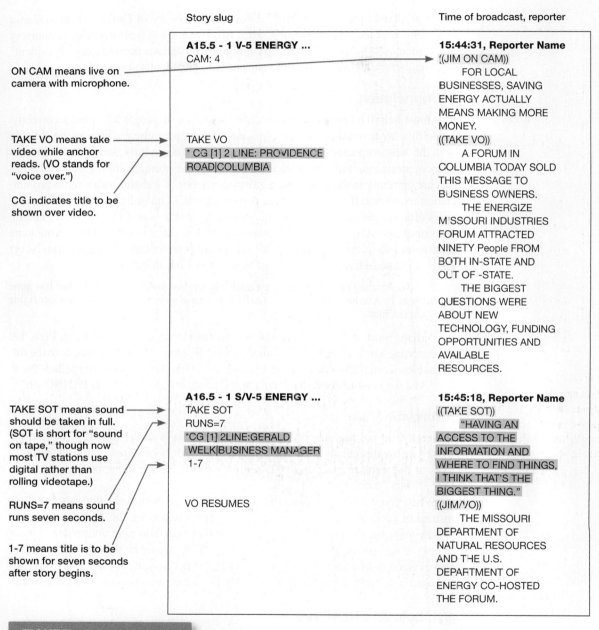

Story slug   Time of broadcast, reporter

ON CAM means live on camera with microphone.

TAKE VO means take video while anchor reads. (VO stands for "voice over.")

CG indicates title to be shown over video.

TAKE SOT means sound should be taken in full. (SOT is short for "sound on tape," though now most TV stations use digital rather than rolling videotape.)

RUNS=7 means sound runs seven seconds.

1-7 means title is to be shown for seven seconds after story begins.

A15.5 - 1 V-5 ENERGY ...
CAM: 4

TAKE VO
* CG [1] 2 LINE: PROVIDENCE ROAD|COLUMBIA

A16.5 - 1 S/V-5 ENERGY ...
TAKE SOT
RUNS=7
*CG [1] 2LINE:GERALD
 WELK|BUSINESS MANAGER
1-7

VO RESUMES

15:44:31, Reporter Name
((JIM ON CAM))
       FOR LOCAL BUSINESSES, SAVING ENERGY ACTUALLY MEANS MAKING MORE MONEY.
((TAKE VO))
       A FORUM IN COLUMBIA TODAY SOLD THIS MESSAGE TO BUSINESS OWNERS.
       THE ENERGIZE MISSOURI INDUSTRIES FORUM ATTRACTED NINETY People FROM BOTH IN-STATE AND OUT OF -STATE.
       THE BIGGEST QUESTIONS WERE ABOUT NEW TECHNOLOGY, FUNDING OPPORTUNITIES AND AVAILABLE RESOURCES.

15:45:18, Reporter Name
((TAKE SOT))
       "HAVING AN ACCESS TO THE INFORMATION AND WHERE TO FIND THINGS, I THINK THAT'S THE BIGGEST THING."
((JIM/VO))
       THE MISSOURI DEPARTMENT OF NATURAL RESOURCES AND THE U.S. DEPARTMENT OF ENERGY CO-HOSTED THE FORUM.

FIGURE 12.2

Television copy is typed in two columns—one for text to be read and the other for audio and video directions.

better prepared to hear the name: for example, Secretary of Defense Ashton Carter at first occurrence, and then just Carter. Broadcast copy typically avoids courtesy titles, such as "Mr." or "Ms." One exception: Most stations prefer to use "President" or "Mr." before all mentions of the current U.S. president's surname.

Pronunciation

You must help the newscaster pronounce the names of people and places correctly. To do this, write out difficult names phonetically in parentheses, putting the syllable with the most emphasis in all capital letters. Many stations have their own handbooks of local pronunciations, the Associated Press offers a pronunciation guide for names that are currently in the news, and a growing number of websites offer audio pronunciation examples. If you can't find a person's name in an online guide, call the person's office to get the proper pronunciation. If the name is of a U.S. town, try calling someone in that town. There is no rhyme or reason to the way some people pronounce their names or to the way some place names are pronounced. Never assume. Never guess. Find out. Here's an example of how to write out difficult names:

> **BAKU, Azerbaijan (AP)—An investigative journalist jailed since December has gone on trial in Azerbaijan (ah-zur-by-JAHN') in a case widely criticized by human rights organizations.**

Perhaps most people would know how to pronounce Lima (LEE-mah), Peru, but not everyone would correctly pronounce Lima (LIE-mah), Ohio. You must note the difference between NEW-erk, New Jersey, and new-ARK, Delaware, both spelled "Newark." And who would guess that Pago Pago is pronounced PAHNG-oh PAHNG-oh?

Abbreviations

Generally, do not use abbreviations in your copy. It is easier to read a written-out word than an abbreviation. Do not abbreviate the names of states, countries, months, days of the week or military titles. You may, however, use the abbreviations "Dr.," "Mr.," "Mrs." and "Ms," and "a.m." and "p.m."

When you use abbreviations that contain singly pronounced letters, use hyphens instead of periods to prevent the newscaster from mistaking the final period in the abbreviation for the period at the end of the sentence. You may abbreviate "United States" when you use it as a noun or adjective; "U-S" would be the correct form. If an abbreviation is well-known—"U-N," "G-O-P," "F-B-I"—you may use it. Hyphens are not used in acronyms like "NATO" and "HUD," which are pronounced as one word.

Symbols and Numbers

Do not use symbols—not even $, % and # (for number)—in your copy because newscasters can read a word more easily than a symbol. So "$4,000,000" becomes "four million dollars" in broadcast copy. Use the word "hashtag" for the # symbol in references to Twitter.

Numbers can also be a problem. As in newspaper style, write out numbers one through nine. Also write out eleven, because 11 might not be easily recognized as a number. Use figures for 10 and from 12 to 999, but write out the words "thousand," "million" and "billion"—for example, "3,800,000" becomes "three million, 800 thousand." Write out fractions ("two-and-a-half million dollars") and decimals ("three-point-two percent").

Some stations have exceptions. Figures often are used to give the time ("3:20 a.m."), sports scores ("ahead 5 to 2") and statistics, market reports ("an increase in the Dow Jones Industrial Average of 2-point-8 points") and addresses ("3-0-0-2 Grand Street").

As stated earlier in this chapter, you may round off big numbers. Thus, for 48.3 percent, write "nearly half." But when talking about human beings, don't say "more than one hundred" if you know that 104 people died in an earthquake; be precise.

Use "st," "nd," "rd" and "th" after dates: August 1st, September 2nd, October 3rd, November 4th. Make the year easy to pronounce by using numerals: June 9th, 1973.

Quotations and Attributions

Because it is difficult and awkward to indicate to listeners which words are being quoted, use indirect quotes or a paraphrase instead of direct quotations.

If it is important for listeners to know the exact words of a quotation (as when the quoted words are startling, uncomplimentary or possibly libelous), introduce the quote by saying "in his words," "with these words," "what she called" or "he put it this way." Most writers prefer to avoid the formal "quote" and "unquote," though "quote" is used more often than "unquote." Here's an example:

> **In Smith's words, quote, "There is no way to undo the harm done."**

When you must use a direct quotation, the attribution should always precede the quotation. Because listeners cannot see the quotation marks, they will have no way of knowing the words are a direct quote. If by chance they do recognize the words as a quote, they will have no idea who is being quoted. For the same reason, the attribution should precede an indirect quote as well.

If you must use a direct quotation, keep it short. If it is important to use all of a long quote, use a video of the person saying it. If you wish to use a quote of more than one sentence, break it up with phrases such as "Smith went on to say" or "and still quoting the senator." For television, put a longer or more complicated quote on a full-screen graphic display as it is read.

Punctuation

In radio and television copy, less punctuation is best. The one exception is the comma. Commas help the newscaster pause at appropriate places. Use commas, for example, after introductory phrases referring to time and place, as in these examples:

> **In London, three Americans on holiday met their death today when their car overturned and caught fire.**

> **Last August, beef prices reached an all-time low.**

Some newsrooms prefer using three periods in place of a comma. An anchor is less likely to overlook ellipses than commas. Three periods can also take the place of parentheses and the semicolon. They signal a pause and are easily visible. The same is true of the dash—typed as two hyphens in most word-processing programs. Note the dash in the following example:

> **But the judge grumbled about the news coverage, and most prospective jurors agreed— saying the news coverage has been prone to overstatement, sensationalism and errors.**

To make the copy easier to read, add hyphens to some words even when the dictionary and Associated Press do not use them: "anti-discrimination," "co-equal," "non-aggression."

Stations vary in writing style and in the preparation of copy. But if you learn the guidelines presented here, you will be prepared to work in radio or television. Differences will be small, and you will adapt to them easily.

SUGGESTED READINGS

Bliss, Edward, Jr., and James L. Hoyt. *Writing News for Broadcast.* 3rd ed. New York: Columbia Univ. Press, 1994. A classic text, often called the Strunk and White of broadcast news writing, this book excels in good writing and sets a superb example for students to do the same.

Block, Mervin. *Writing Broadcast News: Shorter, Sharper, Stronger.* 3rd ed. Washington, D.C.: CQ Press, 2010. This excellent book, written by a former network news writer, is considered the last word in broadcast copy writing.

Burum, Ivo, and Stephen Quinn. *MOJO: The Mobile Journalism Handbook: How to Make Broadcast Videos with an iPhone or iPad.* Boston: Focal Press, 2016. This book explores the explosion of mobile workflows in the newsgathering process and includes hands-on exercises to train reporters in best practices.

Freedman, Wayne. *It Takes More Than Good Looks to Succeed at Television News Reporting.* 2nd ed. San Francisco: Wayne Freedman, 2011. Freedman has been called "the best local TV news feature reporter in the country." His book is packed with practical, down-to-earth advice.

Wenger, Deborah Halpert, and Deborah Potter. *Advancing the Story: Broadcast Journalism in a Multimedia World.* 2nd ed. Washington, D.C.: CQ Press, 2011. This text continues to be updated online.

White, Ted, and Frank Barnas. *Broadcast News Writing, Reporting, and Producing.* 6th ed. Boston: Focal Press, 2013. This book has excellent coverage on all aspects of broadcast news writing.

SUGGESTED WEBSITES

www.advancingthestory.com
Be sure to check out this excellent website companion to Wenger and Potter's textbook.

macmillanhighered.com/newsreporting12e
When you visit LaunchPad Solo for Journalism, you will find research links, exercises, and LearningCurve adaptive quizzing to help you improve your grammar and AP style usage. In addition, the site's video collection hosts the videos highlighted in this and other chapters as well as additional clips of leading professionals discussing important media trends.

www.nab.org
The website of the National Association of Broadcasters is a wonderful resource for all kinds of radio- and TV-related information. It includes a career center.

www.newscript.com
This site's purpose is to help radio journalists improve their skills as writers and anchors.

www.rtdna.org
The Radio Television Digital News Association promotes excellence in electronic journalism through research, education and professional training. The site features excellent reports and useful links.

www.rtdna.org/article/social_media_blogging _guidelines
This RTDNA site will help you answer questions about sharing user-generated content. It offers detailed guidelines for newsrooms and journalists to follow when considering the use of social media.

EXERCISES

1. Your instructor will divide your class into five groups. Each group will watch an evening television newscast on your local ABC, CBS, NBC, FOX or PBS affiliate. With the members of your group, make a simple list of the news stories. Then find those stories in the next day's print-edition newspaper, and compare the coverage. Be prepared for a good class discussion.

2. **Your journalism blog.** Write a blog post about a complicated local news event. Then boil down the issue and write a 45-second television piece to present in front of your class. Finally, write a tweet that tells part of your story in 140 characters or less.

3. Check to see if the following story, written for broadcast, follows acceptable broadcast style. Is it technically correct? Does it emphasize immediacy? Change the copy where you think it's necessary.

   Catholic Priest Goes Online to Vow Innocence in Sex Abuse Case
   WORCESTER, Mass.—A Massachusetts priest has gone on the record to say he is innocent of the allegations against him and will fight to clear his name.

   Sixty-four-year-old Father John L. Runnickem was accused by three former altar boys of sexual touching and taking naked pictures.

   Runnickem spoke out in a short, recorded video posted online Wednesday, saying he had done nothing wrong and that God was "on his side."

   Boston archdiocese officials have removed Runnickem from his pastor duties at Our Lady of Snows parish church in Worcester, Massachusetts, and have pledged to cooperate as law enforcement investigates the allegations.

   The three alleged victims are now adults, but ranged in age from nine to 13 years old at the time they say the assaults took place.

   They came forward in October, speaking to media about Runnickem.

   The men said the group Survivors Plus One has helped guide their cases.

4. Rewrite the following newspaper story in broadcast writing style. Assume that the news is current.

   Airplane Makes Emergency Landing, Clogs Interstate
   ORLANDO, Fla.—The pilot of a single-engine Cessna airplane made an emergency landing on busy Interstate 4 Friday,

saving those on board the aircraft but stalling busy Walt Disney World traffic for hours.

   Rodney Berwalden, an amateur pilot and owner of a small electronics company in Savannah, Georgia, was flying with his girlfriend Joan Eldishay and her two children en route to Lakeland, Florida, to visit family. The plane was on the last leg of its trip when, Berwalden says, the engine on the 2011 model Cessna Skylane began to fail. Berwalden was following Interstate 4 from Daytona Beach to Lakeland at the time and decided to use the wide swath of concrete as his landing strip.

   "I knew we didn't have much time left in the air, so the interstate seemed like the best option," Berwalden said Saturday. "I saw some open lanes, so I went for it."

   Berwalden put the plane down in the rightmost two lanes of westbound I-4, just east of the Apopka-Vineland Road exit, near the Walt Disney World resort. The highway was clogged with weekend travelers headed for the theme park. Westbound traffic backed up for approximately four miles toward downtown Orlando.

   Orange County Sheriff's deputies and Florida State Highway Patrol troopers responded to check on the well-being of the aircraft's occupants and to try to restore traffic flow.

   "This was a first for all of us," said Cpl. Alice Lowellian of the Florida State Highway Patrol. "Seeing an airplane right in the middle of the road takes some getting used to."

   Officers were able to keep the two leftmost lanes of the interstate open while crews came to load the airplane on a flatbed, but gawkers slowed traffic to a walk. It took crews about two hours to clear the plane from the scene and get traffic back to normal.

   "I'm sorry to cause so many people to be late for their Disney World plans, but I had three people on this plane I had to protect," Berwalden said.

   The National Transportation Safety Board and Federal Aviation Administration have been called in to investigate the cause of the emergency landing. Early reports point to a fuel system problem on the plane, but the agencies said they would not have an official cause for some time.

   "We've just begun the process," said Varda Geister, a spokesperson for the NTSB. "These investigations typically take 90 to 120 days."

   As for Berwalden, he said he and his fellow travelers rented a car at Walt Disney World to finish their trip.

5. Write three paragraphs explaining how learning to write for radio and television makes you a better writer for print.

A beat is a reporter's assigned area of responsibility. That might be an institution, such as city hall. It might be a geographic area, such as a school district or a county. It might be a topic, such as politics or sports. In any news organization, there are few assignments more important, both to the newsroom and to the public.

Sara Bondioli, whom you met in Chapter 1, covers politics. As lead reporter on the Cardinals beat for the *St. Louis Post-Dispatch*, Derrick Goold covers baseball. David Nakamura (see "On the Job" in this chapter) covers the White House.

Nakamura explains the essential reporting skills that are common to all beats: "Even as the nature of coverage shifts to multimedia, including graphic elements and embedded tweets, along with a healthy dose of aggregation, there remains a significant advantage to maintaining what some might consider old-fashioned beat reporting techniques—developing sources, examining documents, observing scenes, embedding on assignments and making phone calls."

As Goold puts it, "The species of journalist known as beat reporter has two habitats: on deadline and online. For those of us out in the field, spending the day wired has taken on an entirely new and noncaffeinated meaning. Beat writers have become the on-call educated experts, especially in sports and politics."

Explaining how a reporter on his beat acquires that expertise, Nakamura says:

> Developing sources inside and outside the White House is essential. Inside sources include White House aides, as well as bureaucrats and appointed officials at federal agencies. Talking with these people can be difficult and subject to strict controls, such as not quoting them by name or clearing quotes before publication.
>
> Outside the White House, sources include lawmakers and their aides, issue advocates deeply involved in policy proposals, think tank experts, former administration officials and even people who worked for previous presidents.

The payoff for that reporting:

> I was able to write a long accountability story about the administration's failure to anticipate the surge of tens of thousands of Central American minors who crossed into the United States illegally in 2014, catching federal border control stations off guard and swamping resources.
>
> The White House was unhappy with that story, and the press secretary accused us of relying on unnamed sources, a wildly inaccurate characterization that we fought back against.
>
> There is no short cut for old-fashioned reporting that can take time and be frustrating but can pay off in the end with an exclusive, impactful story.

Importance of Beat Reporting

The goal of any beat reporter, as Nakamura has learned, is to hold accountable those who occupy positions of power and privilege. That accountability in journalism is vital to the health of the democracy, whether the beat is the White House or the courthouse.

In this chapter you will learn:

1
Why beats are important.

2
Basic principles for covering any beat.

3
How to use social media in covering beat stories.

4
How to apply the basic principles to some of the most common beats.

LaunchPad **Solo**
macmillan learning

macmillanhighered.com
/newsreporting12e
Watch **"Agenda Setting &
Gatekeeping."**

■ What does it mean to say
major television networks
and national newspapers are
responsible for agenda setting?

■ Some feel the rise of the
internet cancels out the
agenda-setting effect. Do you
agree?

Few beat reporters become media stars, as many White House reporters do, but none have escaped the changes brought by technology and economics. Additionally, as you saw in Chapter 1, the definition of news itself is getting broader. That change extends the range of beats. Along with such standard beats as local government, police, business and sports, cultural beats reflect the interests and activities of a changing America. Some beat reporters cover shopping malls. Some cover commuting. Some cover spiritual life. Some cover cyberspace or, more specifically, technology.

Covering beats is among the most important work in journalism. Economic pressures have cut the staffs in most newsrooms, print and broadcast, leaving fewer reporters and stretching their assignments over multiple beats. Often, today's reporters are trying to do more, on several platforms, in less time. That's true on the White House beat, too.

No matter the locale, beat reporters today are expected to tell their audiences not only what is happening but also how to get involved. Stories include telephone numbers, email addresses and often Twitter handles along with the names of decision-makers. Much of the most useful reporting is done in advance of public meetings, with the goal of enabling citizens to become participants instead of passive onlookers. Readers are regularly invited to use email or online bulletin boards to speak up on public issues. Journalists and officials alike encourage Twitter followers and Facebook friends. Even President Barack Obama has a Twitter account (@POTUS). With all these changes, though, beat reporters remain the eyes and ears of their communities. Surrogates for their readers, they keep track of government, education, police, business and other powerful institutions that shape readers' lives.

The principles of good reporting apply to the coverage of any beat. The same principles also apply to specialized publications, including those aimed at particular industries, professions or ethnic groups. A reporter for *Women's Wear Daily* may cover fashion designers. A reporter for *Diario Las Américas* in Miami may cover Cuban exile politics. But each is doing the same job: discovering and writing news that's relevant and useful to the publication's readers.

Editors and audiences expect reporters on these specialized beats, like those in more traditional assignments, to provide information and understanding that will help readers improve the quality of their lives. That's important work, and it's rewarding work. But it's not easy.

Principles for Reporters on a Beat

Whether you cover the public library or the Pentagon, the county courthouse or the White House, the principles of covering a beat are the same.

As David Nakamura points out, "Ultimately, that's where the White House beat is similar to any other—reporters must be dogged asking the right questions and relentless in demanding answers. They must be observant and able to identify important shifts in message and tactics, and they must be willing to challenge authority, even at the highest levels."

TIPS

**The Successful Beat
Reporter Is**

• Prepared
• Alert
• Persistent
• There
• Wary

If you want to succeed as a reporter, you must be prepared, alert, persistent and wary. And, on any beat, you must be there. These qualities will help you win the trust of your sources, keep up with important developments on your beat and avoid the trap of writing for your sources instead of your readers. Let's take a closer look at what each of those rules means in practice.

Be Prepared

Where should preparation begin? For you, it has already begun. To work effectively, a journalist needs a basic understanding of the workings of society and its various governments. You need to know at least the rudiments of psychology, economics and history. That is why the best education for a journalist is a broad-based one, providing exposure to the widest possible sampling of human knowledge. But that exposure will not be enough when you face an important source on your first beat. You will need more specific information, which you can acquire by familiarizing yourself with written accounts or records or by talking to sources.

Reading for Background

In preparing to cover a beat, any beat, your first step is to learn as much as possible about the issues and personalities you'll be covering. Google is your friend. General and specialized search engines allow you to read not only the material that has been produced by your own organization but the relevant stories from other outlets worldwide. Create Google alerts that will automatically update your email about news coming out of your beat. You can often access the contents of major newspapers, magazines, research publications and other reference libraries without regard to physical distance. Use the internet to acquire background and to understand the context of local events and issues. Of course, you'll want to double-check anything you learn from unfamiliar online sources. For example, if your new beat is medicine, you might begin with the website of the Association of Health Care Journalists (healthjournalism.org). Television and web-only newsrooms are less likely to have their own libraries. Online sources make that less of a handicap. Your local public and university libraries are also valuable resources, with their online catalogs and generally good collections of recent local periodicals.

In your local research, make notes of continuing issues, questions left dangling in previous stories or ideas for stories to come. Go back several years in your preparation. History might not repeat itself, but knowledge of it helps you assess the significance of current events and provides clues to what you can expect.

Library research is only the start of your preparation. You must become familiar with the laws governing the institution you cover. If a governmental organization is your beat, find the state statutes or the city charter that created the agencies you will be covering. Learn the powers, duties and limitations of each official. You might be surprised to discover that someone is failing to do all that the law requires. Someone else might be doing more than the law allows.

Look at your state's open-meetings and open-records laws, too. Every state has such laws, although they vary widely in scope and effectiveness. Knowing what

TIPS

Preparing to Cover a Beat

- Use the internet to acquire background information and understand context.
- Make note of continuing issues or ideas for stories to come.
- Become familiar with the laws governing the institution you cover.
- Look at your state's open-meeting and open-records laws.

information is open to the public by law can be a valuable tool for a reporter dealing with officials who may prefer to govern privately. (White House internal documents, as David Nakamura has learned, are exempt from the federal Freedom of Information Act.)

Mining Social Media

Today's beat reporters must recognize the value of social media not only as a tool for reporting the news but also as a way of monitoring and communicating with their sources. Once you've been assigned a beat, it's important that you follow the newsmakers on that beat on Twitter, Facebook, Instagram, Snapchat, Pinterest, Vine and LinkedIn. Reporters on the city government beat, for example, should seek out and follow the mayor, city council members, the city manager and other department heads on Twitter and add them as "friends" on Facebook. Many government entities (police and public works departments or school districts, for example) have Facebook pages and Twitter accounts that they use to convey information important to the publics they serve. If you're covering state government, be sure to watch legislators, the governor and other officeholders on social media. If you're a sports reporter, you'll quickly learn that athletes frequently break news through Twitter feeds or Facebook posts. No matter the beat you're working, it's a good idea to also follow competing news outlets and journalists so you can keep pace with their reporting.

Journalists should be cautious about how they interact with their sources on social media. Adding people as "friends" on Facebook isn't an act of bias that suggests you agree with their positions or ideologies, but "liking" their posts or "favoriting" their tweets is much different. Journalists must be careful not to cross those lines.

It's also important that journalists newly assigned to a beat clean up their social media presence to eliminate any indication of bias or opinion that might undermine their credibility, and to ensure that they project a professional image online. That photo of you campaigning for a Republican Senate candidate or attending a rally of abortion rights supporters becomes inappropriate once you begin a career as a journalist. Photos that depict you drinking at a party should be removed. (Be aware, of course, that simply deleting photos from any site does not actually permanently eradicate the photos; it removes them from the site for the cursory viewer.) Some journalists choose to have a dual presence on social media, creating one personal and one professional Twitter account or separate Facebook pages, for instance. That's an individual decision. Either way, be aware of the public nature of your social media activity and act accordingly. Consider also how privacy settings on your social media platforms can work for or against you.

Talking to Sources

Now you're ready to start talking to people. You should conduct your first interviews in the newsroom with your predecessor on the beat, your assignment editor and any veterans who can shed light on the kinds of things that rarely appear in statute books or newspaper stories. Who has been a good source in the past? Who will lie to you? Who drinks to excess? Who seems to be living extravagantly? Whose friends are big land developers? Who wants to run for national office? Who has been hired, fired or promoted? Who has moved to a competing company? Remember that you are hearing gossip, filtered through the biases of those relating it. Be a little skeptical.

Some understanding of the workings of your own newsroom won't hurt, either. Has your predecessor on the beat been promoted? Has he or she been transferred because of unsatisfactory performance? Will an introduction from your predecessor help you or hurt you with your sources? And what are your boss's expectations? Is your assignment to report almost every activity of government, or will you have time to do some investigative work and analysis? Living up to your boss's expectations is easier if you know in advance what they are.

Only after gaining as much background as possible are you ready to face the people you will be covering. A quick handshake and a superficial question or two might be all you have time for in the first encounter, but within a week you should arrange for sit-down conversations with your most important sources. These are get-acquainted sessions. You are trying to get to know the sources, but don't forget that they need to know you, too, if they are going to respect and trust you.

You might have noticed that the preparation for covering a beat is similar to the preparation for an interview or for a single-story assignment. The important difference is that preparing for a beat is more detailed and requires more time and work. Instead of just preparing for a short-term task, you are laying the foundation for an important part of your career. A beat assignment nearly always lasts at least six months and often two years or more. Understanding that will help shape your first round of meetings with sources.

A story might emerge from those first interviews, but their purpose is much broader. You are trying to establish a relationship, trying to convert strangers into helpful partners in news gathering. To do that, you should demonstrate an interest in the sources as people as well as officials. Ask about their families, their interests, their philosophy, their goals. Make it clear with your questions that you are interested rather than ignorant. (Don't ask if the source is married. You should already know. Say, "I understand your daughter is in law school. Is she going into politics, too?" Similarly, don't ask if your source has any hobbies. Find out beforehand.)

And be prepared to give something of yourself. If you both like to fish, or you both went to Vassar, or you both have children about the same age, seize on those ties. All of us feel comfortable with people who have something in common with us. This is the time, too, to let your sources know that you know something about their work and that you're interested in it.

Be Alert

Sometimes, being alert means thinking fast and seizing an opportunity. Sometimes, it means recognizing an important story when others don't. Important stories are seldom labeled as such. In many cases, the people involved might not realize the significance of what they are doing. Probably more often they realize it but hope nobody else will. The motivation for secrecy might be dishonesty, the desire to protect an image or a conviction that the public will misunderstand.

TIPS

Talking to Sources

- Talk to your predecessor on the beat, your assignment editor and veterans in the newsroom for background.
- Understand your boss's expectations.
- Establish a relationship with sources; demonstrate interest in them.

ON THE JOB His Beat: The White House

You've already met **David Nakamura**, who covers the White House for *The Washington Post*. He didn't begin with that assignment, of course. Fresh from journalism school, he took an internship at *The Post*. He has been there ever since, first in sports, then as a suburban reporter, then covering Washington city government, then a stint in Afghanistan. Here's how he describes the challenges and benefits of his current job:

In the social media era, online tools have given journalists the ability to expand their reach and talk directly to their audience. It has given those same opportunities, however, to the subjects of their stories—including, or perhaps especially, the White House, which already enjoys the most powerful bully pulpit.

Although the Obama White House has been ahead of the game in employing the tools of social media since the president's first campaign in 2008, it has ramped up its approach in recent years. For example, in the first three months of 2015, President Obama granted exclusive interviews to a trio of news outlets that did not exist just five years earlier and that aim to exploit social sharing to advance their journalism: Vox, BuzzFeed News and Vice. Vox started in 2004, Buzzfeed added a news division in 2011, and Vice morphed into an investigative online documentary site starting in 2013.

By contrast, the president has not sat down one-on-one with a news side reporter at *The New York Times* since 2013 and has not given an exclusive interview to *The Washington Post* since 2009.

These three websites have broad reaches that go beyond those of traditional outlets like the *Times* and *Post*, or even the wire services. It's not just a reach measured in traffic but also in the type of audience the White House was targeting—young people, especially millennials, who are driving the changes in how news is consumed.

Courtesy of David Nakamura.

If anything, the White House has expanded its strategy to employ nontraditional means to get the president's message past the filter of the traditional gate keepers.

For White House beat reporters, the challenge in countering this strategy is to offer additional context to readers and to parse the president's answers for nuance, as well as to hold the administration accountable by emphasizing areas where the president has not lived up to his promises or where he has changed his stance on an issue.

If your beat is a government agency, you will find that many public officials and public employees think they know more about what is good for the public than the public does. The theory of democratic government is that an informed citizenry can make decisions or elect representatives to make those decisions in its own best interests. If you are the reporter assigned to city hall, the school board or the courthouse, you carry a heavy responsibility for helping your audience put that theory into practice. To discharge that responsibility, you must probe beneath the surface of events in search of the "whys" and "hows" that lead to understanding.

When you are presented with a news release or hear an announcement or cover a vote, ask yourself these questions before passing the event off in a few paragraphs:

■ **Who will benefit from this, and who will be hurt?** If the tentative answer to the first part suggests private interests, or the answer to the second part is the public, some digging is in order.

- **How important is this?** An event that is likely to affect many people for good or ill usually deserves more explanation than one affecting only a handful.

- **Who is for this, and who is against it?** Answers to these questions are often obvious or at least easy to figure out. When you know them, the answers to the first two questions usually become clearer.

- **How much will this cost, and who will pay?** An architect's design for renovating downtown may look less attractive when the price tag is attached. A drive by the chamber of commerce to lure new industry may require taxpayers to pay for new roads, sewers, fire protection, and even schools and other services for an increased population.

The answers to these questions allow you to judge that most important element of news value—impact.

Be Persistent

Persistence means two things to a reporter on a beat. First, it means that when you ask a question, you do not give up until you get an answer. Second, it means that you must keep track of slow-developing projects or problems.

Insisting on a Responsive Answer

One of the most common faults of beginning reporters is that they give up too easily. They settle for answers that are unresponsive to their questions, or they return to the newsroom not sure they understand what they were told. In either case, the result is an incomplete, confusing story.

"Why is it that our fourth-graders score below average on these reading tests?" you ask the school superintendent.

He might reply, "Let me first conceptualize the parameters of the socioeconomic context for you."

The real answer probably is "I only wish I knew."

Your job is to cut through the jargon and the evasions in search of substance. Often that is not an easy task. Many experts, or people who want to be regarded as experts, are so caught up in the technical language of their special field that they find it almost impossible to communicate clearly. Many others seek refuge in gobbledygook or resort to evasion when they don't know an answer or find the answer embarrassing. Educators and lawyers are particularly adept at such tactics.

Listen politely for a few minutes while the school superintendent conceptualizes his parameters. Then, when he finishes or pauses for breath, lead him back toward where you want to go. One way is to say, "It sounds to me as if you're saying . . ." and rephrase what he has told you in plain English. At those times when you simply are in the dark—and that may be often—just confess your puzzlement and ask for a translation. And keep coming back to the point: "But how does all that affect reading scores?" "How can the problem be solved?" "What are you doing about it?"

TIPS

Insisting on a Responsive Answer

- Cut through the jargon and evasions in search of substance.
- Rephrase technical language in plain English.

All the while, you must ask yourself, "Does that make sense to me?" "Can I make it make sense to my readers?" Don't quit until the answer is yes. You should not be obnoxious, but you do have to be persistent.

Following Up on Slow Developments

Persistence is also required when you are following the course of slow-developing events. Gardeners do not sit and watch a seed germinate. They do, however, check every few days, looking for the green shoots that indicate that growth is taking place as it should. If the shoots are late, they dig in to investigate.

Beat reporting works much the same way. Officials announce a downtown redevelopment plan, say, or a revision in a school's curriculum. The story covers the plans and the hoped-for benefits. The seed is planted. If it is planted on your beat, make a note to yourself to check on it in a week or two. And a week or two after that. And a month after that. Start a file of reminders so you won't forget. Such a file often is called a **tickler** because it serves to tickle your memory. Your phone and your laptop will have apps for that.

Like seeds, important projects of government or business take time to develop. Often what happens during the long, out-of-public-view development is more important than the announcements at the occasional news conferences or the promises of the promotional brochures. Compromises are made. Original plans turn out to be impractical or politically unpalatable. Consultants are hired. Contracts are signed. Public money is spent. The public interest may be served, or it may not.

Sometimes the story is that nothing is happening. At other times the story might be that the wrong things are happening. Consulting contracts might go to cronies of the mayor. Redevelopment might enhance the property values of big downtown landowners. Curriculum revisions might be shaped by influential pressure groups.

Even if nothing improper is taking place, the persistent reporter will give readers an occasional update. At stake, after all, are the public's money and welfare.

Be There

In beat reporting, there is no substitute for personal contact. Trying to do it all by telephone or email won't work. The only way to cover a beat is to be there—every day, if possible. Joking with the secretaries, talking politics with council members and lawyers, worrying over the budget or trading gossip with the professional staff—you must make yourself a part of the community you are covering.

Sometimes, being there provides opportunity beyond the obvious story. Jim Yardley, who reports on the Vatican for *The New York Times,* decided to use Twitter and Instagram to take his readers along when Pope Francis traveled to his native South America. Yardley even shared some tricks of the reporter's trade:

> It's 5:15 a.m. in Quito, Ecuador, and still dark outside as a group of journalists gather outside a room in the Hilton Colon. This is how the work of covering Pope Francis begins. Reporters collect the texts of proposed remarks for the pope's speeches today in the Ecuadorian city of Guayaquil.
>
> One of the pope's press aides, Matteo Bruni, wins the task of handing out the speeches. The agreement is that no one can publish anything until after Pope Francis

has delivered the speeches. Getting the texts is critical because journalists need to get a sense of what the pope is going to talk about so that they can begin drafting stories—or at least parts of them—in advance. Having the prepared remarks means that reporters, especially for the wire services, are ready to put something up almost immediately after a papal speech. For the Vatican, it is intended to ensure that the articles are accurate.

But there are risks, especially with this pope. Atop the advance copies is the word EMBARGO and the phrase "check against delivery." Pope Francis likes to go off script, and often these off-script remarks are especially interesting, or even the most telling.

So the advance text becomes a guide . . . .

The final challenge is language. The pope usually speaks Italian at appearances in the Vatican and in some other countries. But in Latin America, he speaks Spanish. Most members of the news media corps who write about the pope can follow in Italian, but not everyone can in Spanish, especially if he uses Argentine colloquialisms. So fluent speakers of Spanish flag the pope's diversions from the prepared remarks and help everyone else.

By using social media, Yardley was able to give his readers a sense of immediacy and involvement—a feeling of being with him at the pope's side—in real time. This is an increasingly common approach, at the *Times* and elsewhere, as reporters try to share with readers not only what the story is but how it was obtained.

Remember that the sources who are most important to you probably are in great demand by others, too. They have jobs to do. Maneuver to get as much of their time as you need, but don't demand too much. Do your homework first. Don't expect a school superintendent to explain basic concepts of education. You can learn that information by talking with an aide or by reading. What you need to learn from the superintendent is how he or she intends to apply those concepts, or why they seem to be inapplicable here. Find out what a class I felony is before asking the police chief why they are increasing. You will get the time you need more readily if busy sources know their time will not be wasted.

There are other simple techniques you can use to build and maintain good relationships with the people on your beat. Here are some of them:

■ **Do a favor when you can.** As a reporter, you spend much of your time asking other people to do favors for you—giving you their time, sharing information they need not share, looking up records and figures. If a source needs a favor in return, don't refuse unless it would be unethical. The favors asked are usually small things, like getting a daughter's engagement picture or a club announcement in the paper, procuring a print of a picture taken with the governor to decorate the official's wall, bringing in a few copies of a favorable feature you wrote.

■ **Don't shun good news.** One ill-founded but common complaint is that news media report nothing but bad news. Admittedly, there is usually no story when people are doing what they are supposed to do. Sometimes there should be, if they do their duty uncommonly well or have done it for a very long time or do it under the burden of some handicap. Sources like these "good news" stories, and so do readers.

■ **Protect your sources.** Many people in government—politicians and bureaucrats alike—are willing to tell a reporter things they are not willing to have their names attached to in print or otherwise. The same is true of people in private business, who might fear reprisals from their employers, co-workers or competitors. Sometimes such would-be anonymous sources are trying to use you to enhance their own positions. You have to protect yourself and your audience against that possibility. Confer with an editor if you have doubts. Most news organizations are properly wary of relying on unnamed sources. Sometimes, though, the requests for anonymity are valid, necessary to protect the source's career. Once you have agreed to protect a source, you must do it. Don't tell anyone but your editor. An inability to keep your mouth shut can cost you more than a source. It can cost you your reputation. (The protection of sources has legal as well as ethical implications. So-called shield laws in some states offer limited exemptions for journalists from legal requirements to disclose sources; see Chapter 19. But there are no blanket exemptions.)

■ **Above all, be accurate.** Inaccurate reporting leads first to loss of respect from sources, then to loss of the sources themselves and finally to loss of the job. If you are a good, tough reporter, not all of the contacts on your beat will love you. But if you are an accurate reporter, they will respect you.

Remember, beat reporting is a lot like gardening. Both require you to be in the field every day, cultivating. And in both, the amount of the harvest is directly proportional to the amount of labor invested.

Be Wary

The point of all this effort—the preparation, alertness, persistence and personal contact—is to keep your audience informed. That is an obvious statement, but it needs to be made because every beat reporter is under pressures that can obscure the readers' importance. You must be wary of this problem.

Even with the interactivity offered by online, mobile and social media services, you will have little to do with most of your audience. They will not write you notes when you have done a story they like or call you when they dislike what you have said or written. They will not offer to buy you a cup of coffee or lunch, or stop you in the hall to urge you to see things their way. But your sources will.

If you report that city council members are thinking about raising the property-tax rate, you will probably hear complaints from council members about premature disclosure. If you report that the police department is racked by dissension, expect a less-than-friendly reaction from the chief. If you report that the CEO of a major business is looking for a new job, the chances are that he or she will deny it even though the story is true.

All sources have points of view, programs to sell, careers to advance, opponents to undercut. It is likely that they will try to persuade you of the merit of their viewpoint, try to sell their programs through your reporting, try to shape the news to help their careers.

Be wary of sources' efforts to use you. You can lose the critical distance a reporter must maintain from those being covered. When that happens, you start thinking like a participant rather than an observer. You begin reporting for your sources rather than your audience. This is a real danger. No one can spend as much time with sources as a beat reporter does or devote as much effort to understanding them without becoming sympathetic. You may forget that you are a surrogate for the outsiders when you associate so closely with the insiders.

Beat Reporting Across Media Platforms

Online media offer the opportunity for instant reporting. With smartphones, digital cameras and laptop computers, reporters can and do file short reports and even photographs and video for posting on the web as the story unfolds. For newspaper reporters, this is a high-tech return to the distant days of multiple editions, when instead of one deadline a day journalists had many. For radio and television reporters, the online opportunities match those of live reporting over the air. Research shows that increasing numbers of online readers rely on websites to stay in touch with news as it happens.

The Benefits and Challenges of Reporting Across Platforms

The internet, and social media in particular, give journalists the ability to be immediate in their coverage. That ability, however, creates an expectation among audiences that their news sources will provide this immediacy. Rather than wait until an entire city council meeting unfolds to begin writing a report, journalists today can file Twitter feeds from the council chamber as the news unfolds. When big news breaks, it can be reported immediately not only in the form of a news burst or bulletin on your news outlet's website, but also on its Twitter account and Facebook page. Increasingly, newspapers and broadcast outlets have turned to rolling reports, in which they continuously update the news online as it's happening and as they learn about it. This in many ways mirrors the longstanding "write-through" practices of wire services—rewriting an original story again and again as information becomes available—the primary difference being that updates today are immediately shared with readers and viewers.

The need and desire for speed, however, cannot trump the imperative of accuracy. Before you post breaking news on Twitter or Facebook, you have to take the time to verify it. Refrain from retweeting information from social media sources without first making sure it's true. There's no place in journalism for rumor or speculation.

With that opportunity, of course, comes obligation. As you see in the example of David Nakamura (see "On the Job" earlier in this chapter) beat reporters at all levels are expected to blog, send Twitter messages and post instant updates to Facebook and other social networking sites throughout the day. All that takes time and energy, often cutting into the reporter's opportunity for in-depth research or even the conversations that are important in developing sources.

Also, reporters are expected to gather and present to audiences more information, more detail and more points of view online than print, television or radio permit. Citizens who care enough to follow an issue online want and expect to see the

ANNOTATED MODEL   A Crime Story Across Media Platforms

A tweeted news flash contains only bare-bones facts, with the promise of follow-up.

Twitter feed (2 p.m.):
@COPSBEAT Another "bear hug" just reported; this @ Springfield College campus. More soon.

Twitter feed (2:30 p.m.):
@COPSBEAT Suspect described as white man in 20s, reddish beard, bad breath. Composite being circulated @Springfield College and university campuses.

Developing facts are added to the Twitter feed.

A Facebook post gives additional background to the breaking news and reports a police request.

Facebook post, shared on relevant campus Facebook pages (2:40 p.m.):
Springfield police are searching for a white man in his early 20s with a reddish beard and bad breath. He is a suspect in three "bear hug" assaults that have occurred in the past two days on the Springfield College and university campuses. Composite sketches of the suspect are being circulated at both schools. Police are asking that anyone with information contact them immediately.

Web report (3 p.m.):
Springfield College campus police report that a female student was grabbed from behind by an unknown assailant at 1:25 p.m. on the college campus.

The reporter follows her social media accounts with an online report that includes as many details as are immediately available.

This is the third such assault to be reported in the past two days. The first two both occurred on the university campus. Police suspect the same man is involved.

The suspect is described as a strongly built white male, in his 20s, with a reddish beard and bad breath. Police have produced a composite sketch, which is being circulated on both campuses.

In all three instances, the victim was walking alone in a relatively secluded area of the campus during daylight hours. None of the victims was seriously injured. None knew the assailant.

Tweets continue the updates even after the first web report.

Twitter feed (7:30 p.m.):
@COPSBEAT Police arrest Thomas Albright as suspect in "bear hug" assaults @Springfield College and university campuses.

(continued)

A reporter on the crime beat starts reporting instantly via Twitter, follows up with Facebook posts and then revises the story online and in print. Then she writes a blog post highlighting issues raised by the story.

Facebook post, shared on relevant campus Facebook pages (7:45 p.m.):
Thomas Albright has been arrested as the suspect in the Springfield College and university campus "bear hug" assaults.

Important updates can be repeated on several social media platforms.

Web update (8 p.m.):

The web report is updated with important information.

A university student has been arrested and charged with being the "bear hug" assailant who assaulted women on both the university and Springfield College campuses.

University police gave the suspect's name as Thomas Albright. He is identified as a 20-year-old sophomore from Chicago.

Springfield College campus police reported earlier that a female student was grabbed from behind by an unknown assailant at 1:25 p.m. on the college campus.

It was the third such assault to be reported in the past two days. The first two both occurred on the university campus.

Police suspect Albright was the culprit in all three assaults. He was arrested after police circulated a composite sketch of the suspect on both campuses and then received an anonymous tip identifying Albright as the assailant.

In all three instances, the victim was walking alone in a relatively secluded area of the campus during daylight hours. None of the victims was seriously injured. None knew the assailant.

Newspaper story (following morning):
A university student has been arrested and charged with being the "bear hug" assailant who assaulted women on both the university and Springfield College campuses.

With the benefit of extra time, the reporter is able to wrap up the story, with additional background and detail. This more complete account will also be posted on the newspaper's website.

University police gave the suspect's name as Thomas Albright. He is identified as a 20-year-old sophomore from Chicago.

A police spokesman said that, after sketches of an unknown suspect were circulated on both campuses, police received an anonymous call naming Albright as the perpetrator. He was taken into custody about 8 p.m. and was identified by at least one of the victims.

The spokesman said Albright denied the accusations but admitted to having tried to find a former girlfriend he believes to be a Springfield College student.

The first incident took place Monday afternoon near the university's recreation center. The victim, a university senior, told police she screamed

(continued)

ANNOTATED MODEL   A Crime Story Across Media Platforms (*continued*)

and the man who had grabbed her around the waist from behind turned and fled.

The second assault was later that day, in the Hitt Street parking garage. In that incident, the victim told police the assailant asked her if she was someone whose name she didn't recognize. When she said she wasn't, he mumbled something and released her, she said.

The third assault was Tuesday afternoon on the Springfield College campus. That victim had much the same experience as in the second incident.

None of the victims was seriously injured.

Albright is in city jail awaiting a preliminary hearing.

The blog is where a conversation between reporter and readers can begin. So blog posts can and should be more conversational, more informal than news stories. Notice that a bit of opinion sneaks in, which also would be out of place in a news story. And notice that the reporter, after checking with her editor, is soliciting reader reaction.

"Cops Beat" blog (later that day):

The cops are trying to downplay this case of the Bear-Hug Bandit so as to avoid frightening any more women. At least one officer told me as much, but since the comment was anonymous, we didn't use it in the news story. It seems to me and my editor, though, that students and administrators on both campuses should use this as a take-off point for an examination of security, especially in more secluded areas, such as parking garages. Could have been much worse. What do you think?

source documents reporters use—and that policymakers use. Document Cloud is a free online tool that makes it easy for journalists to share those documents with their readers. Audiences also want and expect links to other websites that offer related information or further background.

But what really sets online and social media apart is interactivity. Social media such as Twitter and Facebook both facilitate interactivity—with sources as well as readers. It's common for a reporter to start covering a beat story with on-site tweets that give the basic facts in 140 characters or fewer. Facebook posts offer a little more space and another platform for quickly reporting the news. It's also important that the journalist monitor—and, when appropriate, respond to—any social media conversations that ensue from his or her work.

After taking some—but not much—time for research, the reporter might follow up with a web story that gives more detail, and then update that story as more information becomes available. By the next morning, she or he will have written a print story for the newspaper that contains even more detail and background. Finally, later that day, the reporter might return to the story, this time to write a post for the beat blog that readers respond to. See the annotated model "A Crime Story Across Media Platforms" beginning on page 278 for an example of how a beat story can progress across media platforms.

Writing Professional Tweets

Because Twitter is such an immediate and informal-feeling medium, it's easy to allow professional standards to slip. Make it a habit to treat your tweets with as much care you do your lengthier texts. Before sending a tweet, check that:

- **The information is important, accurate and timely.** Journalists should refrain from flooding readers with unnecessary or repetitive tweets. And while Twitter is an indispensable tool for instant reporting, it's paramount that reporters verify information before sharing it with followers. Don't let the desire for immediacy cause you to hastily send out reports that you later will have to correct.
- **Links in the tweet work.** Use a URL shortener such as Goo.gl (https://goo.gl) or Bitly (https://bitly.com) to avoid using too many of your limited characters.
- **Any photos you include have meaning.** Photographs, even if they're not of the highest professional quality, can convey lots of information without eating up characters. Don't, however, include a photo just for the sake of doing so. Be certain it's of value to your audience.

- **Your writing is clear, unambiguous and free of bias and innuendo.** The language of Twitter is casual, but journalists should maintain a professional tone and avoid snarky messages. Occasional humor is acceptable, so long as it doesn't undermine the news you're attempting to convey or stray into the realm of opinion.
- **Your spelling and grammar are correct. Proofread tweets at least twice.** With a 140-character limit, it's common for journalists to use understandable abbreviations or shortcuts in their tweets that they wouldn't normally use in news reports. Do so sparingly, however.
- **You have used logical hashtags to help audiences follow the subject at hand.** If you're tweeting about the tornado that just swept through town, for example, use #springfieldtwister to convey the news so that others can find it quickly. Refer your website and Facebook audiences to the Twitter hashtag so they can follow along.

This fast-paced use of new media brings its own hazards. It's impossible to be nuanced in 140 characters, so a reporter in a hurry can easily overstate or misstate something that then comes back to bite painfully. In the midst of a breaking news story, authorities don't always have the facts straight, yet the reporter often can't wait for information to be confirmed before getting it out. Finally, tweets are unedited, so the reporter has no editorial "safety net" to catch errors and questionable information. So rereading your tweets at least twice before hitting "Send" is critical. All these hazards make it critical for reporters to be as thorough as possible at every stage of a story.

Using Social Media to Find Sources—and Audiences

Social media is useful not only for conveying information but also for going beyond the usual suspects to find additional and interesting sources or to gather information. Search hashtags to see who's posting on Twitter about the news that's occurring and follow up with those who appear to know what they're talking about or who have been directly affected by the events of the day. Visit the Facebook pages of people in the news to see what sorts of conversations they're having with others. Many newspapers use online services such as Storify or RebelMouse to easily aggregate social media posts and share them with their audiences as a complement to traditional reporting.

GRAMMAR CHECK

What's the grammar error in this sentence?

Since the U.S. Supreme Court's decision in Obergefell v. Hodges, *federal law requires that every state issues marriage licenses to same-sex couples.*

See Appendix 1, Rule 18.

Many news organizations, including the *Columbia Missourian,* use Instagram to gain readers and add another dimension to their stories. In October of 2015, University of Missouri students formed an activist group known as Concerned Student 1950 to protest against perceived racism on campus. Their protests ranged from public marches to boycotts of campus activities, including football games. The president of the university, Tim Wolfe, facing pressure from the student protesters and faculty, resigned that November. The same month, the *Missourian* posted a photo on Instagram of a Concerned Student 1950 marcher, giving visibility and context to the movement (see Figure 13.1).

Finally, social media can be a powerful tool for promoting a journalist's work and ensuring the right audiences find it. If you've written a story about a rare sighting of the golden-cheeked warbler in your area, it makes sense to share a link to your story on the Facebook pages of the local chapter of the Audubon Society and the state conservation department. You can also mention the story on your Twitter account, tweet it directly at interested groups and use a hashtag that bird-watchers will quickly discover. If the school board voted to change the attendance zones for your city's elementary schools, posting that story on school and PTA Facebook pages makes a lot of sense. Once the story is in front of the most relevant audiences, it's likely to be shared and read by scores of readers who otherwise would not have found it on your web page or in your newspaper or broadcast.

Clearly it pays for journalists in the digital age to be nimble in the myriad uses of social media. Those who ignore its potential do so at their own peril.

FIGURE 13.1

The *Columbia Missourian* uses Instagram to post photos related to important local events, such as the University of Missouri student protests of 2015.

comissourian   FOLLOW

61 likes   8w

comissourian Tyler Riley, an MU sophomore, makes a heart with her hands as she marches in support with Concerned Student 1950 on Friday. The group led a "We're Not Afraid March" in response to threats made to black students on MU's campus.

Photo by Ellise Verheyen/Missourian (@ellisenichol)

#concernedstudent1950 #notafraid #march #mizzou #mu #como #students #mucampus #heart #support

Log in to like or comment.   ∘ ∘ ∘

Covering the Most Important Local Beats

Your political science courses will introduce you to the structure of government, but from a reporter's viewpoint, function is usually even more important than structure. You must learn who holds the real power, who has the most influence on the power-holders and who are the most likely sources of accurate information. The specifics vary from city to city, but there are some general principles that will help you when covering any type of state or local institution.

■ **Information is power.** The holder of information may be a professional administrator (the city manager, school superintendent, police chief or court clerk) or an elected official (the mayor, chair of the county commission or chair of the school board). The job title is unimportant. Find the person who knows in detail how an organization really works, where the money goes and how decisions are made. Get to know that person because he or she will be the most important person on your beat.

■ **The budget is the blueprint.** This principle is a corollary of the first. Just as detailed knowledge of how an organization works is the key to controlling that organization, a budget is the blueprint for the organization's activities. The budget tells where the money comes from and where it goes. It tells how many people are on the payroll and how much they are paid. It tells what programs are planned for the year and how much they will cost. Over several years' time, the budget tells where the budget-makers' priorities are, and what they see as their organization's role in the community.

   So, find copies of the last two or three years' budgets for your beat. Try to decipher them. Learn all you can from your predecessor and from newspaper clips. Then find the architect who drew up this blueprint—the budget director or the clerk or the assistant superintendent—and get a translation. Ask all the questions you can think of. Write down the answers.

   When budget-making time arrives, follow every step. Attend every public hearing and every private discussion session you can. In those dollar figures are some of the most important stories you will write—stories of how much your readers will be paying for schools and roads and garbage pickup, stories of what they will get for their money.

■ **Distributing power and money is politics.** While looking for your beat's power centers and unraveling its budget mysteries, you will be absorbing as well the most interesting part of beat reporting: politics.

   At any level in any type of organization, power and money go hand in hand with politics. Politics provides the mechanisms through which limited resources are allocated among many competing groups. Neither elections nor political parties are necessary for politics. You will have to learn to spot more subtle forms of political maneuvering.

   If you are covering city hall, for example, pay close attention as the city budget is being drafted. You may find the mayor's pet project being written in

by the city manager. Nobody elects the city manager, but it is good politics for him or her to keep the mayor happy. Are the builders influential in town? If so, you will probably find plenty of road and sewer projects in the budget. Are the city employees unionized? Look for healthy wage and benefit increases if they are. Is there a vocal retirees' organization? That may account for the proposed senior citizens' center. None of those projects is necessarily bad just because it is political. But you and your readers ought to know who is getting what and why.

Now suppose an election is coming up, and the builders' campaign contributions will be heavy. A councilman who is running for mayor switches his vote from money for parks to money for new roads. Has a deal been made? Has a vote been sold? That's politics, too. Some digging is in order.

Power, money and politics are the crucial factors to watch in any beat reporting. With this in mind, let's take a closer look at the most important local beats.

City and County Government

Most medium-sized cities have council-manager governments. The mayor and council members hire a professional administrator to manage the day-to-day affairs of the city. The manager, in turn, hires the police and fire chiefs, the public works director and other department heads. Under the city charter, the council is supposed to make policy and leave its implementation to the manager. Council members are usually forbidden to meddle in the affairs of any department.

Some cities, such as New York and Chicago, have governments in which the mayor serves as chief administrator.

Whatever the structure of your city, you will have a range of good sources to draw on:

- **Subordinate administrators.** They know details of budgets, planning and zoning, and personnel matters. They are seldom in the spotlight, so many of them welcome a reporter's attention as long as the reporter does not get them into trouble. Many are bright and ambitious, willing to second-guess their superiors and gossip about politics, again providing you can assure them that the risk of getting into trouble is low.

- **Council members.** Politicians, as a rule, love to talk. What they say is not always believable, and you have to be wary of their attempts to use you, but they will talk. Like most of us, politicians are more likely to tell someone else's secret or expose the other guy's deal. So ask one council member about the political forces behind another member's pet project while asking the other about the first's mayoral ambitions. This improves the odds that you will learn all there is to know.

- **Pressure groups.** You can get an expert view of the city's land-use policies from land developers and a different view from conservationists. The manager or the personnel director will tell one side of the labor-management story. The head of the employees' union will tell the other. How about the city's record in hiring minorities? Get to know the head of the NAACP or of the local Urban League chapter.

Public officials respond to pressure. As a reporter, you need to understand those pressures and who applies them.

■ **Public citizens.** Consumer advocate Ralph Nader made the term "public citizens" popular, but every town has people—lawyers, homemakers, business executives, retirees—who serve on charter commissions, head bond campaigns, work in elections and advise behind the scenes. Such people can be sources of sound background information and useful assessments of officeholders.

■ **Opponents.** The best way to find out the weaknesses of any person or program is to talk with an opponent. Seek out the board member who wants to fire the school superintendent. Look up the police captain demoted by the new chief. Chat with the leader of the opposition to the new hospital. There are at least two sides to every public question and every public figure. Your job is to explore them all.

Once you have found the sources, keep looking, listening and asking for tips, for explanations, for reactions, for stories. The fun is just starting.

Covering a county government is very much like covering a city government. In both cases you deal with politicians, with administrators, with budgets, with problems. The similarities may be obscured by differences in structure and style, however.

Cities are more likely to have professional administrators, for example. The administration of county governments is more likely to be in the hands of elected commissioners, supervisors or judges. Counties, too, are more likely to have a multitude of elected officials, from the sheriff to the recorder of deeds. City governments are more likely to be bureaucracies. One way to generalize about the differences is to say that city governments are often more efficient and county governments are more responsive.

These differences frequently mean, for a reporter, that county government is easier to cover. More elected officials means more politicians. That, in turn, can mean more talkative sources, more open conflict, more points at which constituents and reporters alike can gain access to the governmental structure.

The principles and the problems of reporting are the same. The budget remains the blueprint whether it is drafted by a professional administrator or an elected officeholder. Knowledge is power whether it is the city manager or the elected county clerk who knows where the money goes. Politics is politics.

The Schools

No institution is more important to any community than its schools. None is worse covered. And none is more demanding of or rewarding to a reporter. The issues that arise on the school beat are among the most important in our society. If it is your beat, be prepared to write about racial tensions, drug abuse, obscenity versus free speech, religious conflict, crime, labor-management disputes, politics, sex—and yes, education.

The process of learning and teaching can be obscured by the furor arising from the more dramatic issues. Even when everyone else seems to have forgotten, though,

Writing for Readers

What does it mean to write for your audience instead of your sources? It means that you must follow several important guidelines.

Translate

The language of bureaucrats, educators, scientists and lawyers is not the same language most people speak. You need to learn the jargon of your sources, but you also need to learn how to translate it into standard English for your audience.

Think of the Public Pocketbook

If the tax rate is going up 14 percent, how much will that cost the average homeowner? If teachers are seeking a 10 percent raise, how much will that cost the school district?

Get Out of the Office

City council or school board votes are important, but many more people will have personal contact with government in the form of a police officer, a clerk or a bus driver than with a council member. Go to where government meets its constituents. Ride a bus. Visit a classroom. Patrol with a police officer. Not only will you get a reader's-eye view of your beat, but you may also find some unexpected stories.

Ask the Audience Members' Questions

Ask "Why?" "How much will it cost me?" "What will I get out of it?" You are the public's ombudsman.

Remember, a good beat reporter has to be prepared, alert, persistent and wary. If you always keep in mind the people you are writing for, you'll keep the customers—and the editors—satisfied.

---

you must not forget that those are only side issues. The most important part of the school beat is what goes on in the classroom.

Whether those classrooms hold kindergartners or high school students, the principles for covering education remain the same. For the most part, the issues are the same, too. When the schools are private rather than public, you have fewer rights of access.

The classroom is not an easy place to cover. You may have trouble getting into one. Administrators frequently turn down such requests on the grounds that a reporter's presence would be disruptive. It would be, at first. But a good teacher and an unobtrusive reporter can overcome that drawback easily. Many papers, at the start of the school year, assign a reporter to an elementary school classroom. He or she visits frequently gets to know the teacher and pupils, and becomes part of the furniture. And that reporter captures for readers much of the sight and sound and feeling of education.

There are other ways, too, of letting readers in on how well—or how badly—the schools are doing their job. Here are some of them:

- **Examine standardized test scores.** The federal No Child Left Behind law has forced testing to the core of every conversation about school quality. The Obama administration's Race to the Top program in education has added complications. Every school system administers standardized tests designed to measure how well its students compare either with a set standard or with other students. The results of such tests are or ought to be public information. Insist on learning about them. Test scores are an inadequate measure of school quality, but they are good indicators.

The frequency and importance of standardized testing has become big news. Make sure you know the context of the controversy and what the experts say. When you base a story on test scores, be sure you understand what is really being compared and what factors outside the schools may affect the scores. Find out what decisions are made on the basis of standardized test scores. For example, do schools with relatively low average scores get additional faculty? Do they get special-education teachers?

■ **Be alert to other indicators of school quality.** You can find out how many graduates of your school system go to college, how many win scholarships and what colleges they attend. You can find out how your school system measures up to the standards of the state department of education. Does it hold the highest classification? If not, why not? National organizations of teachers, librarians and administrators also publish standards they think schools should meet. How close do your schools come?

■ **Understand that in education, as in anything else, you get what you pay for.** How does the pay of teachers in your district compare with pay in similar-sized districts? How does the tax rate compare? What is the turnover rate among teachers?

■ **Get to know as many teachers, administrators, parents and students as possible.** You can learn to pick out the teachers who really care about children and learning. One way to do that is to encourage them to talk about their jobs. A good teacher's warmth will come through. Parents often are tapped into emerging issues or activities at the schools and can be invaluable sources of information.

One reason schools are covered poorly is that the school beat often does not produce the obvious, easy stories of politics, personalities and conflict that the city hall and police beats yield. School board meetings usually produce a spark only when a side issue intrudes. Most school board members are more comfortable talking about issues other than education itself, which is often left to the professionals. The stories that matter most are those that touch on the most sensitive issues. The ongoing controversy over testing is one. Another is the politically charged question of charter schools versus traditional open-enrollment schools. And you can't ignore the classroom complications of race and poverty.

The politics and the budgets of schools are very much like those of other institutions. The uniquely important things about schools are the classrooms and what happens inside them. Your reporting will suffer if you forget that fact. So will your audience.

Higher Education

Look around you. Relevant and useful stories are everywhere. From the next meeting of the governing board to the classroom of a popular professor, the same principles that apply to coverage of primary and secondary schools can be applied on the campus.

Politics, economics and pedagogy—all included as subjects in the course catalog—are also prime prospects for examination. Politics may be partisan, especially in public universities with elected or appointed governing boards, or it may

---

TIPS

Keeping Up with Issues on the Education Beat

- Subscribe to trade newsletters and magazines.
- Remember the most important part of the beat: what goes on in the classroom.
- Understand what standardized test scores mean.
- Get to know teachers, administrators and students.
- Get acquainted with the parent associations at the schools on your beat.
- Follow relevant organizations and government agencies on social media.

be bureaucratic, as individuals or departments compete for power and prestige. The economics of higher education translates to budgets, salaries and tuition costs. Pedagogy, the art and science of teaching, is often overlooked by reporters, but it is really the point of the enterprise.

The Chronicle of Higher Education and campus newsletters are required background reading—the former for insights into national issues and trends, the latter for the nitty-gritty of local developments.

Suppose, for example, that *The Chronicle* reports a nationwide increase in the average cost of tuition. The obvious local story is what's happening on your campus and how that compares with the situation at peer institutions. A less obvious story may be how students are scraping up that tuition money. And an even better, though more difficult, story would be how rising costs affect who can afford to attend, and therefore the composition—by race, ethnicity, social class, even geography—of the student body.

To cover your campus, you'll have to overcome the natural hesitancy of many students to challenge professors, administrators and other authority figures. Try to think of them not as superior beings, but as sources and possible subjects of stories. Then treat them respectfully but not obsequiously, as you would any public official. If your campus is state-supported, they are public officials, after all. That means, among other things, that state laws governing open meetings and records apply.

Here are a few of the issues that should yield good stories on most campuses:

■ **Politics.** Who are members of the governing board, and how are they chosen? What's their agenda? Within the campus, which are the favored departments? How strong is the fraternity and sorority system? How much clout does the athletic department wield with the campus administration or alumni? In an institution founded on free inquiry, just how free is speech for students, faculty and staff?

■ **Finances.** How much does the president get paid? The faculty? The janitors? Where does the money to support the institution really come from? The state? Tuition? Alumni giving? Research grants and contracts? Where does that money go? How much is spent on intercollegiate athletics? How much on the English and history departments?

■ **Pedagogy.** Who are the best (and worst) teachers on campus? Is good teaching rewarded as much as research is? Among the faculty, who gets tenure and who doesn't? Who does the teaching, anyway? Senior faculty? Graduate students? Part-timers?

You can practice good reporting without leaving your campus.

Police

The police beat probably produces more good, readable stories per hour of reporter time than any other beat. It also produces some of the worst, laziest reporting and generates many of our most serious legal and ethical problems. It is the beat many cub reporters start on and the beat many veterans stay on until they have become

TIPS

Covering the Police Beat

• Educate yourself in police lore.
• Try to fit in.
• Lend a sympathetic ear.
• Encourage gossip.
• Talk with other police watchers.

almost part of the police force. It offers great frustration and great opportunity. All these contradictions arise from the nature of police work and of reporting.

If you are going to be a police reporter—and nearly every reporter is, at least briefly—the first thing you have to understand is what police officers are and what they do. We hire police officers to protect us from one another. We require them to deal every day with the dregs of society. Abuse and danger are parts of the job, as is boredom. For the most part we pay police officers mediocre wages and accord them little status. We ask them to be brave but compassionate, stern but tolerant. Very often what we get is not what we ask for but what we should expect. Police work seldom attracts saints. Police officers are frequently cynical, often prejudiced, occasionally dishonest.

When you walk into a police station as a reporter for the first time, expect to be met with some suspicion, even hostility. Police officers often perceive young reporters as being radical, unkempt, anti-authority. How closely does that description fit you and your classmates?

Police departments are quasi-military organizations, with strict chains of command and strong discipline. Their members are sworn to uphold the status quo. The reasons that police and young reporters are mutually suspicious should be clear by now.

Then how do you cover the police?

- **Educate yourself in police lore.** Take a course in law enforcement, if you can, or take a course in constitutional law. You also might read Joseph Wambaugh's books for a realistic portrait of the police.

- **Try to fit in.** Keep your hair neat, dress conservatively and learn the language. Remember that police officers, like the rest of us, are usually quicker to trust people who look and act the way they do.

- **Lend a sympathetic ear.** You enjoy talking about yourself to somebody who seems to be interested; so do most police officers. They know they have a tough job, and they like to be appreciated. Open your mind, and try to understand even the points of view with which you may disagree strongly.

- **Encourage gossip.** Police officers may gossip even more than reporters do. Encourage such talk over a cup of coffee at the station, while tagging along in a patrol car or over a beer after the shift. The stories will be one-sided and exaggerated, but you may learn a lot. Those war stories are fascinating, besides. Just don't print anything you haven't verified.

- **Talk with other police watchers.** Lawyers can be good sources, especially the prosecutors and public defenders who associate every day with the police. Other law enforcement sources are good, too. Sheriff's deputies, for example, may be eager to talk about dishonesty or inefficiency in the city police department, and city police may be eager to reciprocate.

One important reason for all this work is that little of the information you need and want as a police reporter is material you are entitled to see under public-records laws. By law, you are entitled to see only the *arrest sheet* (also called the *arrest log* or **blotter**). This record tells you only the identity of the person arrested, the charge and when the arrest took place. You are not entitled by law to see the arrest report or to interview the officers involved.

Writing a story depends on securing more than the bare-bones information. Finding out details depends on the good will you have generated with the desk sergeant, the shift commander and the officers on the case.

Sometimes the police themselves are the story. More frequent use of cellphone videos by bystanders and the increasing use of body cams by police have led to more questions than answers. For example, the director of the FBI suggested that sensitivity to the presence of video might be inhibiting police from cracking down on violent crime. But he had to admit that there was really no evidence to support that hypothesis. In another case, a black educator wrote an opinion piece complaining that local police had accused her of "walking while black." In response, the police released a video of the encounter that seemed to show a calm and respectful encounter. Seeing isn't always believing. On the other hand, police body cams and dashboard cams have played a central role in stories about police shootings of young African American men and the consequent Black Lives Matter movement. Like all other information, videos need to be vetted for accuracy by journalists before they are used in a story.

The dangers—of being unfair, of damaging your reputation and that of your organization—are ever-present. Good reporting requires that you know what the dangers are and how to avoid them.

Sports

A good sports reporter is a good reporter. That's not always obvious, especially to beginners, because the love of sports lures them to the field in the first place. Most sports reporters were sports fans before they were journalists. That's not typical of other specialties. Reporters who cover government seldom attend city council meetings for fun. Medical reporters don't usually spend their days off observing operations. (Instead, they may watch a sports event.)

As a sports reporter and writer, you are likely to find your workplace organized in much the same way as the news department. Typically, in the sports department of a newspaper, there will be reporters, copy editors and an editor. The difference is likely to be the scale. On small papers, the sports editor may double as writer and may even take the photographs, too. On medium-sized papers, the sports reporters usually don't specialize as the news reporters may. One day you may be covering high school swimming; the next, football or a visiting rodeo.

At small and medium-sized broadcasting stations, a "sports department" is likely to consist of one person who serves as writer, photographer and sports anchor at various times of the day or night. The big crews, the "guys in the truck" you hear mentioned on ESPN, are at the network level. At most local stations, you'll be expected to report, to write, to shoot video and to deliver your work on camera. Sometimes, when time pressure is great or the game is big, you'll go on the air live, summarizing a game that has just ended or that may even be in progress. Then your skills at ad-libbing will be tested, a challenge print reporters don't face.

In the multiplatform world, of course, you should be prepared to do it all, including tweeting during the event and engaging with your audience during and after.

One more thing: Don't confuse sports reporters with play-by-play announcers. The latter may be reporters in a literal sense, but they usually aren't journalists. Their skill is in instant description, not the behind-the-scenes digging or the after-the-fact analysis expected of print and broadcast reporters. Often they are hired by the teams they follow or the sponsors they serve instead of by the station carrying their work.

To get to the "why" and "how" of a game's outcome, reporters need to dig beneath the mere results. They can bring a story to life by getting out of the press box to find an interesting story angle or to secure compelling quotes from players and coaches.

Sports Reporting *Is* Beat Reporting

Before you even thought about sports reporting, chances are good that you were reading, watching and playing sports. In that sense, at least, preparing to be a sports reporter is easier than preparing to cover city hall. But there is more to preparation than immersing yourself in sports. Competition pushes people to their limits, bringing out the best and worst in them. So you need to know some psychology. Sports has played a major role in the struggles of blacks and women for equality. So you need to know some sociology and history. Sports, professional and amateur, is big business. So you need a background in economics. Some of our greatest writers have portrayed life through sports. So you need to explore literature. And you need to know the law, especially Title IX of the federal code. This law forbids discrimination and abuse based on gender. Too often, the headlines today show prominent athletes, especially at the college and professional levels, being accused of or punished for violations. Life in sports is real life.

Meet T.J. Quinn, who reports for ESPN: "The myth of the job is that sports writers sit in the press box, eat hot dogs, live on expense accounts and get to travel all over the country. Mostly true. But covering a beat means keeping track of which players are doing what, who's injured, what a team needs to get better and where they might get it, who wants a contract, who's going to be a free agent, which pitcher is experimenting with a new grip on his slider, which coach is feuding with the owner, which power forward is angry with the point guard because she doesn't pass to the low post enough."

And here's the top of a story that resulted from Quinn's paying close attention:

Mike Hampton was already a professional athlete the first time he beat his father at basketball.

Until that day, as an 18-year-old minor leaguer, he was oh-for-life against Mike Sr., never walking off the driveway of their Homosassa, Florida, home with so much as a gift win.

When Little Mike was 8 years old, Big Mike blocked his shots. When Little Mike tried to drive the lane, Big Mike would put his body in front of the boy and put him on the ground. The boy bled often but learned to cry less and less. His eyes puffy, his breath short, he would sometimes storm off, but he always came back to play the next day.

"It was gross how tough he was," the new ace of the Mets pitching staff said. "You fall down, get a scratch. 'Get up. It'll stop hurting. Get up; let's go.'"

Big Mike knew it was cruel, and wonders still whether he pushed the boy too hard. But the boy needed to learn that winning meant taking something, not waiting for a handout.

This is a story that entertains while it informs. It shows readers something of the character of an athlete and the meaning of tough love.

Here are a few tips to help you be alert to stories that go beyond the cliché:

- **Look for the losers.** Losing may not—as football coaches and other philosophers like to assert—build character, but it certainly bares character. Winners are likely to be full of confidence, champagne and clichés. Losers are likely to be full of self-doubt, second-guessing and surliness. Winners' dressing rooms are magnets for sports writers, but you usually can tell your readers more about the game and those who play it by seeking out the losers.

- **Look for the benchwarmers.** If you follow the reporting crowd, you'll end up in front of your local version of Alex Rodriguez or Venus Williams every time. Head in the other direction. Talk to the would-be football player who has spent four years practicing but never gets into a game. Talk to the woman who dreams of being a professional golfer but is not yet good enough. Talk to the baseball player who is growing old in the minor leagues. If you do, you may find people who both love their sport more and understand it better than do the stars. You may find less press agentry and more humanity.

- **Look beyond the crowds.** Some of the best and most important sports stories draw neither crowds of reporters nor crowds of fans. The so-called minor sports and participant sports are largely untapped sources of good stories. More Americans watch birds than play football. More hunt or fish than play basketball. More watch stock-car races than watch track meets. But those and similar sports are usually covered—if at all—by the newest or least talented reporter on the staff. Get out of the press box. Drop by a bowling alley, a skeet-shooting range, the local college's ultimate frisbee tournament. Anywhere you find people competing—against each other, against nature, against their own limits—you can find good stories.

Developing Contacts

Being there, of course, is half the fun of sports reporting. You're there at the big games, matches and meets. You're there in the locker rooms, on team buses and planes, with an inside view of athletics and athletes that few fans ever get. If you are to answer your readers' questions, if you are to provide insight and anecdote, you must be there, most of the time.

TIPS

Contacts for the Sports Beat

- Players, coaches, administrators.
- Trainers.
- Equipment managers.
- Alumni (for high school and college sports).
- Business managers and secretaries who handle money.
- Former players.
- People who are disgruntled.

Sometimes you should try being where the fans are. Plunk down $20 (of your boss's money) for an end-zone seat and write about a football game from the average fan's point of view. Cover a baseball game from the bleachers. Cold hot dogs and warm beer are as much a part of the event as is a double play. Watch one of those weekend sports shows on television and compare the way a track meet or a fishing trip is presented to the way it is experienced in person. Join a city league softball team or a bowling league for a different kind of inside view.

Be sure to follow the social media activities of athletes and coaches on your beat. College and professional athletes, in particular, are among the most prolific users of Twitter as they seek to connect with their fans. They can tip you off to stories you might not find anywhere else.

A sports reporter must develop and cherish sources just as a city hall reporter must. You look for the same kinds of sources on both beats. Players, coaches and administrators—like city council members and city managers—are obvious sources. Go beyond them. Trainers and equipment managers have insiders' views and sometimes lack the fierce protectiveness that often keeps players, for example, from talking candidly.

Alumni can be excellent sources for high school and college sports stories. If a coach is about to be fired or a new fund drive is being planned, important alumni are sure to be involved. You can find out who they are by checking with the alumni association or by examining the list of major contributors that every college proudly compiles. The business managers and secretaries who handle the money can be invaluable for much-needed but seldom-done stories about the finances of sports at all levels. Former players sometimes will talk more candidly than those who are still involved in a program. As on any beat, look for people who may be disgruntled—a fired assistant coach, a benched star, a big contributor to a losing team. And when you find good sources, cherish them. Keep in contact, flatter them and protect them. They are your lifeline.

Digging for the Real Story

It is even harder for a sports reporter than it is for a political or police reporter to maintain a critical distance from the beat. The most obvious reason is that most of the people who become sports reporters do so because they are sports fans. To be a fan is precisely the opposite of being a dispassionate, critical observer. In addition, athletics—especially big-time athletics—is glamorous and exciting. The sports reporter associates daily with the stars and the coaches whom others, including cynical city hall reporters and hard-bitten managing editors, pay to admire at a distance. Finally, sports figures ranging from high school coaches to owners of professional baseball teams deliberately and persistently seek to buy the favor of the reporters who cover their sports.

We are taught from childhood that it is disgraceful to bite the hand that feeds you. Professional teams and many college teams routinely feed reporters. Major league baseball teams even pay reporters to serve as official scorers for the game. In one embarrassing incident, the reporter-scorer made a controversial decision that preserved a no-hit game for a hometown pitcher. His story of the game made little mention of his official role. The reporter for a competing paper wrote that if it had been his turn to be scorer, he would have ruled the other way.

Sports journalism used to be even more parasitic toward the teams it covered than it is now. At one time, reporters routinely traveled with a team at the team's expense. Good news organizations pay their own way today.

Even today, however, many reporters find it rewarding monetarily as well as psychologically to stay in the favor of the teams and athletes they cover. Many teams pay reporters to write promotional pieces for game programs. And writing personality profiles or "inside" accounts for the dozens of sports magazines can be a profitable sideline.

Most sports reporters, and the editors who permit such activities, argue that they are not corrupted by what they are given. Most surely are not. But temptation is there for those who would succumb. Beyond that, any writer who takes more than information from those he or she covers is also likely to receive pressure, however subtle, from the givers.

Anywhere athletics is taken seriously, from the high schools of Texas to the stadiums of the National Football League, athletes and coaches are used to being given special treatment. Many think of themselves as being somehow different from and better than ordinary people. Many fans agree. Good reporters, though, regard sports as a beat, not a love affair.

Those sports reporters maintain their distance from the people they cover, just as reporters on other beats do, by keeping their readers in mind. Readers want to know who won, and how. But they also want to know about other sides of sports, sides that may require some digging to expose. Readers' questions about sports financing and the story behind the story too often go unanswered. Accountants have become as essential to sports as athletes and trainers. Talk to them. Readers have a legitimate interest in everything from ticket prices to the impact of money on the actual contests.

When a key player is traded, as much as when a city manager is fired, readers want to know the real "why." When athletes leave school without graduating, find out why. When the public is asked to pay for the expansion of a stadium, find out why. One of the attractions of sports is that when the contest is over, the spectators can see who won and how. Often that is not true of struggles in government or business. The whys of sports, however, frequently are as hard to discover as they are in any other area.

Sports figures often appear to their fans, and sometimes to reporters, to be larger than life. In fact, athletics is an intensely human activity. Its participants have greater physical skills, and larger bank accounts, than most other people, but they are people. Sports reporters know that their audience is interested in the real "who" behind the headlines.

SUGGESTED READINGS

Houston, Brant, and Investigative Reporters and Editors, Inc. *The Investigative Reporter's Handbook*. 5th ed. New York: Bedford/St. Martin's, 2009. This comprehensive guide to using public records and documents, written by members of Investigative Reporters and Editors, is a must for serious reporters. See also the suggested readings at the end of Chapter 17. They'll be useful in beat reporting, too.

Royko, Mike. *Boss: Richard J. Daley of Chicago*. New York: New American Library, 1971. This is a classic, brilliantly written study of urban machine politics.

Silverman, Craig, ed. *Verification Handbook: An Ultimate Guide on Digital Sourcing for Emergency Coverage*. European Journalism Center. This work is licensed under a Creative Commons Attribution-NonCommercial-NoDerivatives 4.0 International License. You can download this manual free of charge at http://verificationhandbook.com/downloads/verification.handbook.pdf. Edited by the author of the Poynter Institute's "Regret the Error" blog, the manual offers comprehensive guidelines for how to crowdsource during emergencies and verify information coming from the public through social media.

Sports Illustrated. This magazine—print and online—features some of the best examples of how sports should be reported and written about

SUGGESTED WEBSITES

www.espn.go.com

As every sports fan knows, here you'll find multimedia reporting, commentary, statistics and lots of good story ideas.

media.twitter.com/news

Twitter provides useful guidelines for how journalists and newsrooms can best use the popular social media platform to cover their beats and inform their audiences.

www.pewstates.org/projects/stateline

This site, a service of the Pew Charitable Trusts, provides story tips and background information on state government and state-level issues.

www.poynter.org

We recommend this site repeatedly because it is useful in many ways. One feature is its links to nearly every professional journalism organization.

stevebuttry.wordpress.com

Steve Buttry is the director of student media at Louisiana State University's Manship School of Mass Communication. His blog offers valuable tips for how journalists can use Twitter and other social media platforms to do their work.

EXERCISES

1. In most communities, the local newspaper is likely to have reporters assigned to specific beats. By following the news, identify one of those beat reporters. Interview her or him. How do the principles outlined in this chapter seem to apply in the reporter's real life?

2. Once you have met a beat reporter, stay in touch. Get yourself invited to accompany your new friend on part of her or his daily rounds. What do you learn?

3. With your classmates, form the class into a newsroom. Decide on the essential beats to cover. Assign a pool of reporters to each beat. Working with the other members of your group, take the necessary first step toward successful coverage by producing a background memo that identifies key issues and sources for your beat. Be sure to include relevant sources' Twitter handles and Facebook pages. Present your memo for class discussion. Listen to and comment on other groups' work.

4. Now get out of the classroom and spend some time actually covering one of these beats. Get acquainted with some of the sources your group has identified. Write a beat memo that describes several story ideas, with likely sources.

5. Complete the job by reporting and writing one of the stories you've identified. This would be a good opportunity for peer critiquing of one another's work.

6. **Your journalism blog.** Spend some time exploring the coverage of one specific beat on a news website. In a blog post, compare the news coverage and the features of the website with the content of the newspaper and the television outlet that cover the same beat. Which of the three is more useful, more satisfying, more fun?

With more than a year to go before the 2016 presidential election, the Republican field already had 15 announced candidates. None of them was as instantly well-known or as internationally controversial as billionaire and political outsider Donald Trump. In what would become a pattern, his announcement speech became big news. The coverage of that speech illustrates how the same public event can generate strikingly different stories. FoxNews.com, for example, posted this lead:

> New York real estate mogul and reality TV star Donald Trump on Tuesday declared himself a candidate for the Republican nomination for president, launching his against-the-odds campaign after teasing one for years.
>
> "I am officially running for president of the United States," he said from inside his signature Trump Tower in midtown Manhattan. "We are going to make our country great again."
>
> In a strong pro-business, pro-military speech, the unabashed Trump vowed to stop the Islamic State, keep Iran from building a nuclear weapon, repeal ObamaCare, build a wall along the U.S.-Mexico border, repeal President Obama's executive orders on immigration and spend more on infrastructure.

USA Today took a similar approach:

> This time, Donald Trump says, he really is running.
>
> The real-estate magnate and reality TV star—who has toyed with presidential campaigns before—announced Tuesday that he would seek the Republican nomination for president in 2016.

The Guardian of Great Britain, however, focused on the controversial content that made news in ways the speaker certainly didn't intend.

> Donald Trump, the 69-year-old businessman best known for his "You're fired" catchphrase on *The Apprentice,* announced he was running for president on Tuesday with an eccentric speech attacking Mexican immigrants and promising to build a great wall along the US's southern border.

In the fifth paragraph, the correspondent provided the specifics:

> Most of his wrath was directed at Mexico, which he accused of "bringing their worst people" to America, including criminals and "rapists."
>
> "They're sending us not the right people," he said, adding: "The US has become a dumping ground for everyone else's problems."

A month later, you could do a Google search for "Donald Trump Mexican comments" and you would find 81,900,000 results.

All three reports were accurate. It was the *Guardian*, however, that focused on the specific content that made the speech, and the candidate, memorable. The best reporters identify content that is really news and build their speech stories around that content.

To write these stories, reporters have to be knowledgeable about the topic and to be there. Whatever beat you are covering, you must be prepared to cover three basic assignments: speeches, news conferences and meetings.

1

How to distinguish among speeches, news conferences and meetings.

2

How to prepare to cover speeches, news conferences and meetings.

3

What's involved in covering these events.

4

How to structure and write stories about them.

macmillanhighered.com
/newsreporting12e
Watch **"What Makes Public
Television 'Public'?"**

- Are public television and
  radio at an advantage or
  disadvantage in covering
  speeches, news conferences
  and meetings? Why?
- Now that people can tune in
  to hundreds of commercial
  channels, is there still a role for
  public systems like PBS? Explain.

TIPS

**Preparing for the
Speech Story**

- Be sure you have the
  right person.
- Contact the group
  sponsoring the speech
  and ask for the topic
  and a copy of the pre-
  pared speech, if there's
  one available.
- Check your newspa-
  per library and online
  sources for background
  on the speaker.
- If the speech is impor-
  tant enough, contact
  the speaker for a brief
  interview.

Distinguishing Among Speeches, News Conferences and Meetings

A *speech* is a public talk. Someone speaks to an audience in person or through the media, often reading from a prepared text. Regardless of the medium, a speech is one-way communication. The speaker speaks, and the audience listens, although sometimes a question-and-answer session follows.

Speakers are usually invited and sometimes paid to address an audience. That is not the case with those who hold a *news conference*. People "call" or "hold" news conferences. They do not send invitations to the general public, but they do alert members of the news media. Journalists respond because of the importance of the person calling the news conference and because the person might have something newsworthy to say. The person holding the news conference often begins with an opening statement or announcement and usually accepts questions from reporters. A news conference is meant to be two-way communication. Many politicians, who often would rather not take questions, are using social media, particularly their web-sites and Twitter, to make announcements.

Unlike speeches and news conferences, *meetings* are not held with an audience in mind, although an audience might be present and allowed to participate. A meet-ing is primarily for communication among the members of a group or organization, whether a local parent-teacher association or the U.S. Congress. Reporters who are permitted to witness a meeting tell the public what is of interest and importance. This task of the news media is especially important if the participants are members of a governmental body that spends or allocates taxpayers' money.

Getting Ready to Cover the Story

Good reporters know that preparation makes covering a story much easier, and they always do their homework. The preparation for speeches, news conferences and meetings is similar. Because these events are usually announced in advance, you often have time for thorough preparation.

Preparing for the Speech Story

Not every speech will demand a great deal of research. Many speakers and speeches will be dry and routine. The person giving the speech will be someone you know or someone you have covered before. If you are working for campus media, it could be a university official. If you are working for the professional press, it could be the mayor or the director of the local United Way. At other times you might get an assignment on short notice and be forced to find background information after hear-ing the speech. In either case, never take the speaker or the topic for granted. Failure to get enough background on the speaker and on the speech almost guarantees fail-ure at writing a comprehensive speech story.

If you have not covered the speaker before, the first step in your research is to identify the person correctly. Middle initials are important, but sometimes even they are not enough. *USA Today* had to print a "clarification" after reporting that Larry King had made a $1,000 donation to a presidential campaign. The donor was Larry L. King, author and playwright, not Larry King the former CNN show host.

Then, before doing research on the speaker, contact the group sponsoring the speech and ask for the topic. You might find you need to do some reading to prepare yourself to understand the subject. If you are lucky, you may get an advance copy of the speech. Next, check your organization's own library to see what other reporters have written previously about the speaker. Or you can, and most reporters do, just go online and do a simple search, by name or topic or both. You may find more useful background than you expected.

If the speech is important enough, you might want to contact the speaker ahead of time for a brief interview. If he or she is from out of town, you might plan a meeting at the airport. You might also arrange ahead of time to interview the speaker after the speech. You might have questions or points to clarify.

Not every speech demands this much effort. But even the most routine speech assignment requires preparation. Sooner or later you may be called on to cover speeches by major political figures, perhaps even the U.S. president. For this task, too, you will need background—lots of it. Doing a good job demands that you read the news and know what is going on. You must keep up with current events by regularly reading or listening to the news. Subscribe to an RSS feed from one of the major news organizations, such as CNN or *The New York Times*. If you are on Facebook frequently, "like" the page of any of the big news organizations so you get postings from them. You can also sign up for one of the online aggregators of articles from a variety of sources.

Preparing for the News Conference Story

Preparing for a news conference is similar to preparing for a speech. You need up-to-date background on the person giving the news conference, and you must learn why the news conference is being held. Often the person holding the news conference has an announcement or an opening statement. Unless that statement is leaked to the press, you will not know its content ahead of time, but you can make some educated guesses. Check out any rumors. Call the person's associates, friends or secretary.

Consult your editor and other staff editors about specific information they want. Then draw up a list of questions to ask at the news conference. Once the news conference begins, you will not have time to think of questions; recording responses to other reporters' questions will keep you too busy. The better prepared you are, the better chance you will have of coming away with a coherent, readable story.

It may be impossible to arrange an interview before or after the news conference. If the person holding the news conference wanted to do interviews with individual reporters, he or she probably would not have called the news conference. But you can always ask—you might end up with some exclusive information.

TIPS

Preparing for the News Conference Story

- Get up-to-date background on the person holding the news conference.
- Learn why the conference is being held.
- Check out any rumors beforehand.
- Try to arrange an interview before or after the news conference.

Preparing for the Meeting Story

Often the meetings of important organizations are preceded by an agenda or an advance, a report outlining the subjects and issues to be covered during the upcoming meeting. With nongovernmental, and even some governmental, meetings, you often do not know what to expect, so you must do your best to prepare. Who is holding the meeting? What kind of organization is involved? Who are the key figures? Again, the news library should be your first stop, and online research will yield more information. Then contact some of the key figures.

If there is no agenda, find out what the meeting is about. Talk to the organization's president. If you know the main subject to be discussed, you will be able to study and investigate the issues before arriving. Knowing what to expect and being familiar with the issues will make covering the meeting much easier. A reporter with a regular beat—an assigned area of responsibility—usually covers meetings of the most important organizations and groups on that beat, such as the city council, the school board or the county commission. (Beat reporting is discussed in detail in Chapter 13.) Beat reporters are most familiar with the organizations and issues involved.

Covering Speeches, News Conferences and Meetings

Preparing to cover an event is only the beginning. Knowing what to do when you get there is equally important. You must cover the entire event—the content of the speech, news conference or meeting; the time, place, circumstances and number of people involved; and the possible consequences of what was said or of the actions taken.

A news conference is the most challenging of the three events. That's true because reporters become participants rather than just observers. So you must be prepared to ask questions as well to capture the answers. Sometimes the question— or the reporter—becomes the story.

President Barack Obama held a news conference in July 2015 to discuss an important and controversial agreement just reached to deter Iran from acquiring nuclear weapons. Major Garrett, the White House correspondent for CBS, was prepared with a question he intended to be provocative.

He probably wasn't prepared for the president's response.

Garrett reminded Obama of four Americans held hostage in Iran. Then he asked, "Can you tell the country, sir, why you are content, with all the fanfare around this deal, to leave the conscience of this nation and the strength of this nation unaccounted for in relation to these four Americans?"

The president paused, looked at Garrett, and replied, "I got to give you credit, Major, for how you craft those questions. The notion that I'm content as I celebrate with American citizens languishing in Iranian jails—Major, that's nonsense, and you should know better."

The provocation and the president's reaction to being provoked became news so important that Garrett was immediately interviewed on CBS' own news streaming network. "Sometimes you have to take a scolding from a president to get to an answer," he said. "That's part of my job."

Getting answers is certainly part of the job. Becoming part of the story? Probably not.

The Medium Matters

What you need to do at a speech, press conference or meeting depends on your final distribution medium. If you're writing a story for print, simply taking good notes, using an audio recorder and getting audience reaction might suffice. If you are shooting video, you have to consider the lighting and find a good place from which to shoot. (For tips on shooting video for the web, see Chapter 11.)

If the event is of enough interest, you probably will also be tweeting or posting texts and photos to your organization's mobile users. Tweeting gets the public conversation started while the event is underway. You might be charged with writing a web story, providing an audio clip and then writing yet another story for the newspaper. If you are working for a television station, you might be shooting coverage of the event, interviewing people afterward, tweeting some important lines during the event, editing the video and writing a web version.

More and more non-television news organizations are adding video to their websites, which means you might have to learn something about videography. This makes reporting more challenging today than ever. Print, web and video

> "Clearly it struck a nerve. That was my intention. . . . Was it provocative? Yes. Was it intended to be as such? Absolutely."
>
> — Major Garrett, CBS White House correspondent, about a question he asked President Obama during a press conference

REUTERS/Keith Bedford

A story about a speech, news conference or meeting often requires direct quotes.

coverage require different approaches, and doing all of them at the same time isn't easy. With today's many ways of distributing news information, you need to learn to become a multimedia journalist. Doing so will make you more valuable to your employer.

Getting the Content Correct

You may find a digital audio recorder or video camera useful for covering the content of speeches, news conferences and meetings. Be aware, though, that audio recorders and video cameras often intimidate people who aren't accustomed to being interviewed, so always ask permission to record any interviews you get. Practice using the recorder or video camera until you are familiar with its idiosyncrasies. Make sure you know how sensitive the microphone is. Get to know the camera's operation as best you can.

When someone says something newsworthy, note the counter on the recorder so you can find the quote quickly. Even if you record an event, take notes. Malfunctions can occur, even with the best recorders, at the most inopportune times. (See Chapter 3 for more on recording audio and video interviews.)

Sooner or later every reporter adopts or creates some note-taking shortcuts. You will have to do the same, perhaps expanding on the note-taking shortcuts you've used in college lectures. Learn to abbreviate (*wh* for "which," *th* for "that," *bk* for "book," *st* for "street," *bldg* for "building," etc.) and use signs (*w/* for "with," *w/o* for "without," *acc/* for "according to"). Taking notes is most crucial when you wish to record direct quotes.

As you learned in Chapter 4, putting someone's words in quotation marks means only one thing: You are quoting the exact words the person spoke. Speeches, news conferences and meetings all demand that you be able to record direct quotes. Your stories will be lifeless and lack credibility without them. A speech story, for example, should contain many direct quotes.

Whether covering a speech, a news conference or a meeting, be careful to quote people in context. For example, if a speaker gives supporting evidence for an argument, you would be unfair not to report it. Quotes can be misleading if you carelessly or deliberately juxtapose them. Combining quotes with no indication that something was said in between them can lead to inaccuracies and to charges of unfairness. Suppose, for example, someone says:

> **"Cutting down fuel costs can be an easy thing. If you have easy access to wood, you should invest in a good wood-burning stove. With little effort, you can cut your fuel bills in half."**

A reporter who omits the middle sentence of that quote, even inserting an ellipsis, makes the speaker look ridiculous:

> **"Cutting down fuel costs can be an easy thing. . . . With little effort, you can cut your fuel bills in half."**

Describing the Participants

An audio recording does not capture a speaker's facial expressions and gestures. These are sometimes more important than the words themselves.

Simply reporting the words of a speaker (or of the person holding a news conference or participating at a meeting) does not indicate the volume and tone of voice, inflections, pauses, emphases and reactions to and from those in attendance. You might note that a speaker deliberately winked while reading a sentence. Or you might notice unmistakable sarcasm in the speaker's voice.

Even if you're not taking photos for publication, consider using your smartphone camera to help you record details you'll want to write about later.

Regardless of who the speaker is or where the speech is taking place, you should always note the speaker's background. A person's words must often be measured against that individual's background. For example, if a former Communist is speaking on communism, this fact might have a bearing on what he says. If a former CIA agent is speaking about corruption in the CIA, you cannot adequately report her message if you do not mention her background.

Sometimes, purely physical facts about the speaker are essential to the story. A blind person pleading for funds to educate the blind, a one-armed veteran speaking about the hell of war, a gray-haired person speaking about care for the elderly—these speakers must be described physically for the story to be complete, accurate and understandable. Beware, however, of including gratuitous descriptions; it's problematic to include the information that a state senator advocating for gun control is black, for example.

You also should note what the person who introduces a speaker says. This may help you understand the significance of the speaker and the importance of what he or she has to say.

Being Observant

Keep an eye on the audience and on what's happening around the edges. Measure the mood of the audience by noting the tone of the questions. Are they sharply worded? Is there much laughter or applause? Perhaps members of the audience boo. Does the speaker or the person holding the news conference or the person presiding over the meeting remain calm and in control? Is there casual bantering or joking with the audience? Is the audience stacked with supporters or detractors?

Sometimes the real action takes place outside in the form of a picket line or protest. Sometimes police manage to keep protesters away from the site. Sometimes who is *not* there is news.

Don't overlook the obvious. For example, you should note the size of the audience. Reporting a "full house" means little unless you indicate the house capacity. One way to estimate attendance is to count how many people are sitting in a row or in a typical section. Then you multiply that number by the number of rows or sections in the hall. Use good judgment and common sense to adjust for some sections being more crowded than others. In large venues, you can find out the seating capacity ahead of time. In some locations, the fire department requires all public venues to post the maximum capacity of the space.

Arriving, Positioning Yourself and Staying On

Most reporters arrive early. At some events, special seating is set aside for reporters, but you should probably not count on that unless you know for sure.

At a speech, sitting in the first row is not necessarily best. Instead, choose a location that lets you see the reaction of the audience. If there is a question-and-answer period, you might want to be able to see the questioner. And you certainly want to be in a good position to ask questions yourself.

At a news conference, your location might help you get the attention of the person holding the conference. You should have your questions prepared, but preparing them is not enough. You have seen presidential news conferences on television, and you know how difficult it is to get the president's attention. Indeed, sometimes there is even a list showing the order in which reporters will be recognized. All news conferences present the reporter with similar difficulties, though on a smaller scale. You have also seen how difficult it is for reporters to follow up on their own questions. At some news conferences you will not be called on twice.

But you must do more than try to get your own questions answered. You must listen to others' questions and be able to recognize the making of a good story. Too often a good question is dropped without follow-up because reporters are not listening carefully or are too intent on pursuing their own questions. Listen for what is newsworthy and pursue it. Sticking with an important subject will make the job of writing the story easier. Remember, when the news conference is finished, you will have a story to write. Piecing together notes on dozens of unrelated topics can be difficult, if not impossible.

At a meeting you should be able to see and hear the main participants. Ordinarily, a board or council will sit facing the audience. Before the meeting starts, you should know which members are sitting where. You might want to assign each participant a number so you do not have to write the person's name each time he or she speaks. You also can draw a sketch or take a cellphone photo of where members are sitting. In this way you will be able to quote someone by number and if necessary find out his or her name later. Know who the officers are. The president or the secretary might distribute handouts before the meeting. After a meeting, the secretary might be able to help you fill in missing words or information.

As a general rule, when the speech, news conference or meeting is over, do not rush off unless you are on deadline. Some of the best stories happen afterward. You might have some questions to ask. You might need clarification or want to arrange an interview with a key spokesperson. Listen for reactions from those in attendance.

Getty Images News/Getty Images

Speeches, such as this one given by Hillary Clinton, require the reporter to be alert not only to what is said but also to the audience's reaction.

Structuring and Writing Your Story

Writing the lead for the speech, news conference or meeting story is no different from writing the lead for any other story. All of the qualities of the inverted pyramid news lead discussed in Chapter 8 are important here as well

You must be careful not to emphasize something about the event that is of great interest or curiosity but does not lead into the rest of your story. It's tempting, for example, to lead with a striking quote. But rarely does a speaker or someone holding a news conference highlight the content or the main point in a single, quotable sentence. As always, there are exceptions. As a lead for one of Dr. Martin Luther King Jr.'s most famous addresses, a good reporter might have begun with "I have a dream."

Because of the nature of the inverted pyramid news story, rarely should you follow the chronology of the event you are covering. But the flow of your story might demand *some* attention to chronology (see Chapter 10). If you pay no attention to chronology, you might distort, or cause readers to misinterpret, the meaning of the event.

ANNOTATED MODEL   Analyzing a Speech Story

Pushback on Obama's Plan to Stem Gun Violence

By Dana Bash, Jessica Yellin and Tom Cohen, CNN

Summary lead →

Washington (CNN)—President Barack Obama on Wednesday proposed background checks on all gun sales and bans on military style assault weapons and high-capacity magazines as part of a package of steps to reduce gun violence in the wake of the Newtown school massacre last month.

Additional details summarize the speech. →

With relatives of some of the 20 children killed in the Connecticut rampage looking on, Obama signed 23 executive actions—which don't require congressional approval—to strengthen existing gun laws and take related steps on mental health and school safety.

← Transition sentence describes the environment of the speech.

Third paragraph offers specifics of the plan. →

He also called on Congress to reinstate an assault weapons ban that expired in 2004, to restrict ammunition magazines to no more than 10 rounds, and to expand background checks to anyone buying a gun, whether at a store or in a private sale at an auction or convention.

← Though long, the sentence is clear because it contains items in a series.

Hyperlink → Senate Democrats hold key to passage of gun legislation

With proposals outlined, the story starts to give Obama's rationale. →

Referring to the young students killed in the Newtown shootings on December 14 and other victims of gun violence, Obama said the nation must do a better job of protecting its children, especially when they are in schools, shopping malls, movie theaters and other public places.

While some of the steps he proposed are given little chance of winning congressional approval in the face of the nation's powerful gun lobby, Obama said all efforts must be made to reduce chronic gun violence in the country.

"This is our first task as a society—keeping our children safe," the president said, adding that saving even one life would make the changes he seeks worth the effort.

← Reporters decided this was the most important quote in the speech.

Hyperlink → Read Obama's proposals

Political speeches often require opposition response for fairness. →

Republicans immediately rejected the Obama proposals as an attack on the constitutional right to bear arms.

"Nothing the president is proposing would have stopped the massacre at Sandy Hook," said a statement by Sen. Marco Rubio, R-Florida, considered an up-and-coming GOP leader. "President Obama is targeting the Second Amendment rights of law-abiding citizens instead of seriously addressing the real underlying causes of such violence."

CNN's coverage of President Obama's gun control speech illustrates a typical approach to speech stories. Because this story appeared on CNN's website, it has links.

Source: Dana Bash, Jessica Yellin and Tom Cohen, "Pushback on Obama's Plan to Stem Gun Violence," CNN, Jan. 17, 2013. www.cnn.com/2013/01/16/politics/gun-laws-battle/

Writing the Speech Story

Although you might not soon be called upon to cover the speeches of well-known politicians, you can learn a lot from the way the pros handle important political addresses. The annotated model "Analyzing a Speech Story" on page 306 shows the first 300 words of CNN's coverage of a speech in which President Barack Obama proposed new gun control laws. CNN accompanied this web story with five video excerpts and background material.

The approach for a video reporter is somewhat different. For television or video on the web, you'll introduce the subject and the speaker and then cut in video snippets of the speech itself. You might well end the piece with an interview of someone who attended and in the process get some audience reaction.

Writing the News Conference Story

Writing the news conference story might be a bit more challenging than writing the speech story. Because you will go to the conference with different questions in mind from those your fellow reporters want to ask, you might come away with a different story. Your lead, at least, might be different from the leads of other reporters.

A news conference often covers a gamut of topics. Often it begins with a statement from the person who called the conference.

For example, when the mayor of Springfield holds a news conference to announce her candidacy for a second term, you can be sure that she will begin with a statement to that effect. Although her candidacy might be news to some people, you might want to ask her questions about the location of a new landfill that the city is rumored to be planning. Most citizens will admit the need for landfills, but their location is always controversial. And then there's that tip you heard about the city manager possibly resigning to take a job in a larger city.

Other reporters will come with other questions. Will there be further cuts in the city budget? Will the cuts mean that some city employees will lose their jobs? What happened to the plans to expand the city jail?

After you leave a news conference that covered many topics, you have the job of organizing the material in some logical, coherent order. You can choose to write a multiple-element lead (see Chapter 8). But usually you will treat the most newsworthy subject first and deal with the other subjects in the order of their importance. Rarely would you report on them in the chronological order in which they were discussed.

Suppose you decide the location of the landfill is the most important item of the news conference—especially if the mayor revealed the location for the first time. You might begin your story this way:

> The city will construct its new landfill near the intersection of State Route 53 and Route E, four miles north of Springfield, Mayor Juanita Williams said today.
>
> "After nearly a year of discussion and the best advice we could obtain, we are certain the Route E location is best for all concerned," Williams said at a news conference.
>
> The mayor admitted there would be continued opposition to the site by citizens living in the general area, especially those in the Valley High Trailer Court. "No location will please everyone," Williams said.

Technical Concerns for Television Journalists

Speeches, news conferences and meetings present several technical challenges. Here are three to keep in mind:

- **Think visuals.** What will your backdrop be? Will there be signs, photos, samples, logos or flip charts to help tell the story?
- **Think sound.** Will there be one microphone or a multi-box in which you can insert your mic, or will you be free to set up your own microphone?
- **Think light.** Will the event take place outdoors or in a well-lit room, or must you bring your own lighting? How far is the camera throw (the distance from the event to your camera)? Will there be a camera platform or a set space, or will you be free to set up your camera anywhere?

Williams called the news conference to make the expected announcement of her candidacy for a second term.

Now you have to find a way to treat the other topics of the conference. You might want to list them first in a series of bullet points:

In other matters, Williams said:

- City Manager Diane Lusby will not be resigning to take another post.
- Budget constraints will not permit any new construction on the city jail this year.
- Budget cuts will not cost any city employees their jobs. However, positions vacated by retiring personnel will not be filled.

After this list, you will either go back to your lead, giving more background and quoting citizens or other city officials on the subject, or go on to discuss, one at a time, the matters you listed. Pay particular attention to making proper transitions from paragraph to paragraph so your story is coherent. "On other subjects, the mayor said . . . ," "The mayor defended her position on . . . ," "Again she stressed. . . ."

If one of the subjects is of special interest, you may want to write a sidebar, a shorter piece to go with your main story. For this story, you could do a sidebar on the mayor's candidacy, her record, her possible opponents and the like.

With a longer or more complicated story, you may want to make a summary list of all the main topics covered and place the list in a box or sidebar. Items in the list could be links to other stories or to additional source material.

You probably wrote a story before the news conference to say the mayor was expected to announce her candidacy. You tweet the announcement when she makes it. You probably also tweet the location where the city plans to locate the landfill.

Remember, your job is to give readers the news, as simply and clearly as possible. Remember, too, to cover the event itself as well as the content. Perhaps some picketers protested the mayor's remarks about a local abortion clinic. Sometimes what happens at a news conference is more newsworthy than anything the person holding the conference says. What happens there might well be the lead of your main story, or you may want to place it in a sidebar.

Writing the Meeting Story

Readers want you to take their place at the meeting you are covering. Let's look at a simple meeting story—in this case, a meeting of a local school board:

The decision of three national corporations to protest a formula used to compute their property taxes is causing more than $264,000 to be withheld from the Walnut School District's operating budget for the 2009–10 school year.

Superintendent Max Schmidt said at Monday's school board meeting that International Business Machines Corp., ACR Corp. and Xerox are arguing that the method used in computing their property taxes was no longer valid. Nine California counties are involved in similar disputes.

The taxes, totaling $264,688, are being held in escrow by the county until the matter is resolved. Some or all of the money eventually may be returned to the district, but the administration cannot determine when or how much.

"If we take a quarter million dollars out of our program at this time, it could have a devastating effect," Schmidt said. "Once you've built that money into your budget and you've lost it, you've lost a major source of income."

Mike Harper, the county prosecuting attorney, and Larry Woods, the school district attorney, advised board members to take a "wait-and-see attitude," Schmidt said. He said that one alternative would be to challenge the corporations in court. A final decision will be made later.

The board also delayed action on repayment of $30,000 to IBM in a separate tax dispute. The corporation claims the district owes it for overpaid 2007 property taxes. The county commission has ruled the claim is legitimate and must be repaid.

A possible source of additional income, however, could be House Bill 1002, Schmidt said. If passed, this appropriations bill would provide an additional $46 million for state education, approximately $250,000 of which could go to the Walnut School District.

Charles Campbell, the district architect, said plans for the area's new vocational technical school to be built on the Rock Bridge High School campus will be given to contractors in February. Bids will be presented at the March 15 board meeting.

The board voted to have classes on Presidents Day, Feb. 15, to make up for time missed because of the teachers' strike.

ON THE JOB   Reporting in the Era of Social Media

Darren Samuelsohn.

Darren Samuelsohn, a senior policy reporter at Politico, covers plenty of speeches, news conferences and meetings. He takes his work seriously but himself less so. Here he shares some of what he has learned about Washington reporting in the era of social media:

Golden Journalism Rule No. 1: Post your stories on Facebook so your mom knows what you're writing about.

Yes, it can be a bit embarrassing when she forwards those posts to her friends with ALL CAPS declarations of how awesome her son or daughter is. But still, she's your mom. And Facebook for me (and I bet most journalists) has become the best way yet to share my work with my No. 1 fan.

Depending on what you're writing about, Facebook can also be a great way to make all your old high school classmates jealous. All joking aside, social media have become a routine part of my daily journalism life.

At various moments over the day, I check the feeds on my phone or with a dashboard like Hootsuite to see what people are talking about. What have I found? A small sample: On-the-record comments, press releases, story ideas, details on where a lawmaker or agency official is speaking at a public event.

Twitter, Facebook and Snapchat are no substitute for phone calls, physically going to the Capitol for a hearing, meeting sources for coffee or lunch and interviewing lawmakers. But all of these platforms have become another source of information to help with reporting out stories.

I can't stress enough this important reminder that *any information you find on social media—especially during breaking big big big news moments—must be verified.*

We have some basic rules at Politico on social media that I don't mind sharing. Post away when it comes to links to your own work or of your colleagues. Pull out the best quotes and other nuggets and give them their own separate posts to make sure they get noticed. On Twitter, it never hurts to post the same item a couple of times considering how fast streams move.

Tweeting about a live event in real time is kosher too. But there's a hard and fast rule that I live by and think other journalists should too: Don't scoop yourself. If you have something exclusive, publish it first with your news organization. Get the byline and the link. And then share away on social media and take a brief victory lap for the scoop.

The issue of the meeting was money problems—a subject that concerns every taxpayer. The writer jumped right into the subject in the lead, giving the "what" in the first paragraph, and then in the second paragraph giving us the "who," "when" and "where." The reporter then dealt with specifics, naming names and citing figures, and quoted the key person at the meeting. In the last two paragraphs the writer dealt with other matters discussed in the meeting.

The issues discussed at a meeting are not your only considerations in covering a meeting story. Remember, too, to cover the event. Who was there? Who represented the public? How did people react after the meeting was over?

One reporter began her meeting story in this way:

> **Even though they are footing the bill, only one of Boone County's residents cared enough to attend a Tuesday night hearing on the county's 2010 budget.**
>
> **With an audience of one citizen plus two reporters, County Auditor June Pitchford presented her official report on the $21 million budget to the Boone County Commission in a silent City Council chamber.**

Even when covering routine, boring events, you are allowed to use your creativity. In addition to getting all the facts, your job is also to be interesting, to get people to read the story. Remember, two of the criteria for news are that it be relevant and useful. Another is that it be interesting.

If you're a video reporter, your approach to a meeting story will be quite different. There's almost nothing as boring as video of a city council meeting, so telling the story creatively is important. If you know the council will be debating increased garbage pickup rates, get some video of garbage trucks to show while you're narrating the gist of the story. Then, of course, interviews with council members or members of the public can be used to complete the story.

No matter which medium you work for, you will be expected to write well—even for a common event like a speech, news conference or meeting.

SUGGESTED READINGS

Biography and Genealogy Master Index. Detroit, Mich.: Gale Research, 1981 to present. This compilation of biographical directories lists people whose biographies have been written and indicates which date and volume of those reference books to consult for the actual biography.

Biography Index. Bronx, N.Y.: H.W. Wilson, 1946 to present. This reference helps you locate biographical articles that have appeared in 2,000 periodicals and journals, as well as in biographical books and chapters from collective biographies.

Current Biography. Bronx, N.Y.: H.W. Wilson, 1940 to present. This monthly publication about people in the news includes a photo of each subject. It is an excellent source for people not included in more formal biographical sources.

SUGGESTED WEBSITES

http://journalism-education.cubreporters .org/2010/08/how-to-cover-speeches.html
A former reporter offers tips on how to cover speeches.

www.journalism.about.com/od/reporting/a /pressconf.htm
Tony Rogers offers some easy-to-remember tips for covering a news conference.

macmillanhighered.com/newsreporting12e
When you visit LaunchPad Solo for Journalism, you will find research links, exercises, and LearningCurve adaptive quizzing to help you improve your grammar and AP style usage. In addition, the site's video collection hosts the videos highlighted in this and other chapters as well as additional clips of leading professionals discussing important media trends.

EXERCISES

1. Find out when your university's faculty council or similar faculty representative group is having its next meeting. Plan the steps you will take to prepare for the meeting. Then cover the meeting, taking notes. Write the story. If classmates are covering the same event, it would be interesting to compare their work with yours. How similar are the leads and the story structures? How do they differ? Are direct quotations used effectively? How could the stories be improved?

2. An official transcript of President Obama's second inaugural speech is available on an official White House website (https://www.whitehouse.gov/the-press-office/2013/01/21 /inaugural-address-president-barack-obama), but a transcript also appears in a story on Politico (www.politico.com/story /2013/01/president-barack-obamas-2013-inaugural-address-full -text-86497.html). What differences do you find between the two? What has Politico done to enhance the value of the transcript? Discuss in class what you would use for your lead and why.

3. The site that contains the text of the inaugural speech also contains the video, which is also available on YouTube. After watching the video, decide what observations about the president's demeanor or delivery, audience reaction, or the setting you would add to your story.

4. A few weeks after his speech announcing his candidacy for the Republican presidential nomination, Donald Trump said that he was surprised by the reactions to his immigration comments. Did journalists exaggerate the importance of those comments? How would you have written the story about his speech? A transcript of the speech is available at http://time .com/3923128/donald-trump-announcement-speech/ or here

http://blogs.wsj.com/washwire/2015/06/16/donald-trump -transcript-our-country-needs-a-truly-great-leader/.

5. Reread the material in this chapter about Major Garrett's coverage of President Obama's news conference. Garrett said later that he had intended to be provocative at that news conference. Is that a good attitude for a news reporter to hold? Could he have asked about the American hostages in a less confrontational way? How?

6. Find out when a public figure in your area—a government official or a college administrator, for example—plans to give a speech on a specific topic. Prepare for and cover the speech, using a digital recorder. Send at least two tweets from the speech itself. Then write two versions of your news story: one for immediate posting on a website and one for the print edition of a newspaper. For the web version, what specific links would be useful? Suggest at least one possible sidebar.

7. **Your journalism blog.** Attend a speech, news conference or meeting—preferably one occurring at the school you are attending. Then on your blog, post a 300-word item about the event, including its content. Be sure to include links to pertinent social media and other sites. Invite your classmates to comment on your blog.

8. Prepare for and cover a meeting of a local government agency or committee—the school board, the city council, or a similar group. Try to interview one of the participants before or after the meeting. Then write your story in two versions—one for a website specializing in local events and one for a local radio news broadcast. How do the two stories differ? How does each story meet the criteria of usefulness, relevance and interest?

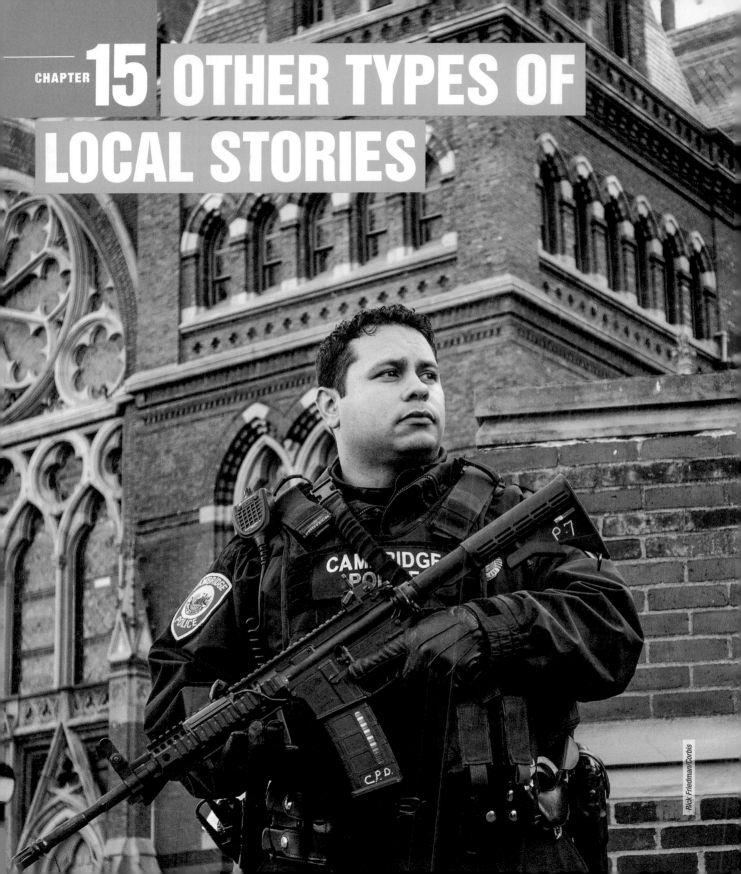

When police at the University of Missouri held a press conference on Jan. 31, 2013, to announce that they had solved an eight-year-old murder, reporter Joseph Vozzelli Jr. had a lot of background work to do. He had not been in Columbia when the murder occurred, so he had to pore through the archives of the *Columbia Missourian* and the competing *Columbia Daily Tribune* for background on the murder. That and his own reporting at the press conference and afterward provided the material for this story:

> The man who MU police say killed Jeong Im in 2005 jumped to his death from a downtown parking garage in August, prompting an acquaintance to come forward with information that helped link Timothy Aaron Hoag to the unsolved slaying.
>
> That break led investigators to a person who said he brought Hoag to the Maryland Avenue parking garage "to get a car" on Jan. 7, 2005, and later picked him up when he was carrying a gas can and wearing a face mask as smoke poured from the third floor of the garage where Im's body was later found.
>
> MU Police Department Capt. Brian Weimer said witnesses were afraid to come forward with information because they were afraid Hoag might hurt them and their families.
>
> Weimer described Hoag as a "violent individual."
>
> Investigators determined that Hoag's DNA, extracted from blood collected at the suicide scene, matched the blood, hair and "touch DNA" found at the scene of the homicide, Weimer said.
>
> Weimer said the case remains open, though investigators believe Hoag was solely responsible for the slaying. Weimer said he hoped Wednesday's news would prompt other witnesses to come forward with information that would help investigators determine a possible motive, which remained unclear.
>
> Weimer was able to confirm that Hoag didn't know Im.
>
> Hoag jumped to his death from the parking garage at Fifth and Walnut on Aug. 9, 2012, at the age of 35.
>
> Weimer said there appeared to be no connection between the suicide and the homicide. He said Hoag was suffering from medical issues related to a 2008 car accident.
>
> On Jan. 7, 2005, the body of Im, 72, was found in the trunk of his white 1995 Honda Accord in the Maryland Avenue parking garage. The retired research assistant at MU had been stabbed multiple times.
>
> Investigators determined that gasoline was poured on the trunk lid of the car, and it was lit on fire.
>
> At 12:24 p.m. that day, MU police received a call from an emergency phone at the parking garage, reporting a vehicle that was on fire. MU police officers and the Columbia Fire Department responded to the call, and firefighters were able to extinguish the fire.
>
> Firefighters then discovered Im's body in the trunk of his car.
>
> In December 2012, someone informed the MU Police Department that he or she had information about the person behind Im's homicide, Weimer said.
>
> The December 2012 informant led investigators to a potential witness who could confirm the facts and details of the case. The witness told investigators that he received a call from Hoag, asking to be picked up from a business on the north end of the university. Hoag also requested that the person bring a gas can.
>
> After Im's death, his family moved to California. His wife, Tesuk, remained in touch with MU police during the investigation, Weimer said. He said the Im family has requested privacy.

1

How to gather information for stories about crimes, accidents and fires, and court proceedings.

2

How to write such stories.

3

How to report a criminal court case step-by-step.

4

How to recognize special problems of crime and court reporting.

5

How to report and write obituaries and life stories.

The family did release a statement through MU: "We are very relieved and grateful for the resolution of the case. This brings closure on the tragedy, to our family, as well as the University of Missouri and Columbia communities as a whole.

"We are deeply grateful to the MU Police Department, university administration and all the other law enforcement agencies involved, for their dedication, professionalism, and tireless commitment over the last eight years, which have resulted in solving the case. We also thank the community for all of their support."

Seungkwon You, an assistant professor of Korean studies at MU, who knew Im for 10 years, said: "I am a native Korean, and the Korean community is quite close, and he was my neighbor. He had a big garden and he brought lettuce and other things to our house."

Mark Foecking, who worked with Im in the microbiology and immunology lab at the time of Im's death, said he was happy—especially for Im's family—that they found his colleague's killer.

"I'm glad to see that (MU Police) kept working on the case and that they kept adding evidence," he said.

"It's a huge relief for the department," Weimer said. "I mean, this is something that has literally been on our mind for eight years. Sgt. (Shawn) Spalding had Im's picture behind his desk, along with the timeline for this. So, it's something he saw every day. We didn't think about it occasionally; we thought about it daily."

He continued: "We fully believed all along that we would solve this case."

Weimer expressed some frustration about the criticism the department received for failing to solve the 8-year-old case earlier.

"Too many people watch TV and think, evidently, you don't have evidence because if you put evidence in the computer it automatically shows you a photo and tells you (who did it)," he said. "But that's not how it is."

Vozzelli's story is rich with detail, some of it gleaned from prior reporting and some of it developed with solid reporting on the day the story broke about the perpetrator of the crime. Good reporters know that you can never gather too much information for a story. The idea is to gather as much detail as possible and then decide what to include and what to exclude. Vozzelli also does a good job of using quotations to break up what otherwise could be a monotonous story.

Early in their careers, most reporters are assigned to cover bread-and-butter stories of this type that represent the worst of the human condition—crimes, accidents and fires, and court proceedings. They also are asked to chronicle the lives of a community's citizens, and they write obituaries that serve as the final chapters in those citizens' lives. So, as an aspiring journalist you are likely at some time to find yourself covering crime, chasing fire trucks or trying to make sense of court proceedings. This chapter will help. You also are likely to be assigned to tell the life story of someone who has died. This chapter will help with that, too.

Your Preparation

When news breaks, you won't have much time to prepare before rushing out the door or picking up the phone. However, there is some instant research you can do, even if it requires using your smartphone on your way to the scene (preferably with someone else driving). Begin as you would with any other story—by checking your newsroom's electronic library. There you'll learn whether a similar crime has occurred before, whether accidents are common at the location of the latest one, whether similar suspicious fires have occurred or whether the person charged with the crime has been in trouble before.

Preparing for the Crime Story

Meetings, news conferences, speeches and court proceedings are usually scheduled events, so on most occasions you should have ample time beforehand to do background research on the individual or topic to be covered. Obituaries also call for a first stop in the television station or newspaper library, but crime reporting may be different. If the police radio reports a murder in your area, you may be dispatched to the scene as the story is breaking. At that point, no one will know who is involved or what happened. There will be no time to check the library, and you will have to do your initial reporting at the scene.

Most information about crimes comes from three sources:

- Police officials and their reports.
- The victim or victims.
- The witness or witnesses.

The circumstances of the crime may determine which of the three is most important, which should be checked first or whether they should be checked at all. If the victim is available, as a reporter you should make every effort to get an interview. If the victim and witnesses are unavailable, the police and their reports become primary sources.

In the era of convergence, you'll need more than a pencil and notebook to gather information at the scene of a crime. A digital recorder will allow you to record your interviews for publication on your news organization's website, and a smartphone camera might help record what happened at the scene. That's particularly true if you are covering the event alone without the help of a photojournalist or videographer. A smartphone will make it possible for you to tweet instant updates from the scene.

The point at which your editor assigns you to a crime story is important. If you are dispatched to the scene of the crime as it happens or soon afterward, you should attempt to interview the victim and witnesses first. The police report probably hasn't even been written yet. But if you are assigned to write about a crime that occurred the night before, the police report should be your starting point.

The timing also affects what kinds of material you will be able to gather and which medium might be used for your information first. A major breaking story might warrant a mobile phone news bulletin or a television report. Something that happened the night before might require more sophisticated work, such as gathering information for a detailed information graphic of a crime scene.

A police officer investigating a crime covers much of the same ground as you. The officer is interested in who was involved, what happened, when, where, why and how. Those details are needed to complete the official report of the incident, and you need them for your story. When you write about crime, always check the police report. It is often the source of basic information, such as:

- A description of what happened.
- The location of the incident.
- The name, age and address of the victim.
- The name, age and address of the suspect, if any.
- The offense police believe the suspect has committed.
- The extent of injuries, if any.
- The names, ages and addresses of witnesses, if any.

If you arrive at the scene of a crime as it is taking place or immediately afterward, you have the advantage of being able to gather much of the required information firsthand. When timely coverage is impossible, however, the police report allows you to catch up quickly. The names of those with knowledge of the incident usually appear on the report, and the reporter uses that information to learn the story.

Reporters sometimes write crime stories from the police report alone. Good journalists, however, demand more because police reports are frequently inaccurate. Most experienced reporters have read reports in which the names of those involved were misspelled, ages were wrong and other basic information was inaccurate. Sometimes such errors are a result of sloppy reporting by the investigating officer or mistakes in transcribing notes into a formal report. Occasionally, the officer may lie in an attempt to cover up shortcomings in the investigation or misconduct at the scene of the crime. Whatever the reason, you should do your own reporting and not depend solely on a police officer's account. Remember that editors frown on single-source stories of any kind. It's your job to do solid reporting, and you are expected to consult multiple sources.

Often, you will want to post the police report itself on your organization's website. The public has a right to see primary sources of this type. But be careful to protect the privacy of victims where appropriate. After a newspaper posted the police account of interviews with the victim of a sexual assault, editors were horrified to discover that the police had failed to remove the victim's name in several places. (Nearly all news organizations protect the identities of sex crime victims.) Another thing to remember is that police reports often contain graphic details some civilians find offensive.

For crime stories, you will usually do a background check in the newsroom's morgue after you return to the office. Check whether the morgue contains relevant information about those involved in the crime, for example. Has the suspect been arrested before? Has the store been robbed before? The morgue might help answer those kinds of questions.

Preparing for Accident and Fire Stories

If you are assigned to cover an accident or fire, you can expect some of the same problems you'd encounter in covering a crime. Much depends on whether the police or fire report is available before you are assigned to the story. If the accident or fire

TIPS

What to Do at the Scene of an Accident

- Question the person in charge of the investigation.
- Try to find and interview witnesses.
- Try to find friends or relatives of the victims.
- If possible, interview the victims.
- Talk with others at the scene.
- Be sensitive to victims and their families.

took place overnight, the official report is the place to start. It will give you most of the basic information you need. It will also lead you to other sources.

If you are sent to the scene of an accident or fire, your job is to collect much of the basic information yourself. As for crimes, the basic information you'll need includes:

- A description of what happened.
- The location of the incident.
- The name, age and address of the victim or victims.
- The extent of injuries, if any.
- The names, ages and addresses of witnesses, if any.

Preparing for the Court Story

Most court stories you are likely to cover will be follow-ups to earlier stories. If a murder suspect is appearing for a preliminary hearing, details of the crime probably were reported earlier, and a check of the newsroom's library may give you ample background information as you prepare for your visit to the courtroom. Otherwise, a chat with the district attorney or the police chief or one of their assistants might provide ample background for writing the story.

Court stories are often difficult for beginners who do not understand the complex process used in criminal prosecutions. In addition, reporters might be asked to cover civil court proceedings, which are lawsuits that charge an individual or company with harming another. Here's our best advice on how to approach court stories: Ask plenty of questions of the judge and attorneys before or after the court proceeding or during recesses. It's much better to admit your lack of knowledge about the court process than to make a serious error in a story because you didn't understand what was happening.

Writing the Story

Rex Huppke, a general assignment reporter and columnist for the *Chicago Tribune* (see "On the job" in this chapter), offers useful suggestions that apply to reporting crimes, fires or any other breaking news:

> First make sure you nail down the essential information you'll need. This is, in essence, the classic "who, what, when, where and why." At the very least you need to be able to write a simple story that details whatever has happened. Once you've got the basics covered, assuming you have time, open your eyes and ears and start taking notes. Capture a mental picture of the scene and put it in your notepad.
>
> When you sit down to write the story, take a quick moment to consider what you've just witnessed. Is there an anecdote that jumps out? Is there a scene you can recreate that gets at the heart of the story?
>
> If nothing comes to you, just start writing the straightforward story—lay out the basics. You have a deadline looming and you must at least make sure you've got a story in place. Once that's done, if there's still time, take another moment. Look at the simple house you've built. What can you do to jazz it up? Is there a more interesting way to

get into the story, one that tells the news more vividly? Are there some details you can sprinkle in among the facts and quotes, tidbits that will boost the reader's mental image of the scene? If so, get them in there.

Once you've done this several times, you'll start to relax more. Knowing that you've got the basics that you need for a story provides a calm, and that calm allows you to soak in more of the surroundings. The soaking part usually will yield the best material.

Notice that Huppke emphasizes the role of revision. Often, under the pressure of a deadline, you won't come up with details, quotes and anecdotes that really engage a reader and set a story apart. Only after you've written a first draft and have the chance to review what you've gotten down will interesting "tidbits" come to mind. If that happens, don't hesitate to revise to make your story more effective.

The Crime Story

Solid reporting techniques pay off for crime stories just as they do in other types of reporting; then it is a matter of writing the story as the facts demand. Sometimes the events are most effectively told in chronological order, particularly when the story is complex (see Chapter 10). More often, a traditional inverted pyramid style works best. The amount of time the reporter has to file the story also influences the approach. Let's take a look at how two accounts of a crime were developed over time and why a different writing style seemed appropriate for each.

Gathering facts from the many sources available and sorting through conflicting information can be time-consuming tasks. Sometimes, especially when you are posting online, you may have to write the story before all the facts are gathered. The result is a bare-bones account. The breaking news story shown at the top of the annotated model "Comparison of a Breaking News Story and a Follow-Up Story," on starting on page 320 illustrates this kind of treatment.

After meeting the web deadline, the reporter had enough time to gather material for the follow-up story, also shown in the annotated model. That second story uses a chronology structure with a narrative emphasis to give a fuller picture of the sequence of events.

If a number of people witnessed or were affected by a crime, you can supplement the main story with a sidebar that deals with the personal impact of the crime—the "so what." The writer of the "Follow-Up Story" shown in the annotated model also decided to write a separate story on nearby residents who had little to add to the main story but became a part of the situation nonetheless:

> In the grass at the edge of a woods near Pierpont Friday afternoon, the only remaining signs of James Phipps were a six-inch circle of blood, a doctor's syringe, a blood-stained button and the imprints in the mud where Phipps fell after he was shot by a Highway Patrol officer. Elsewhere in the area, it was a quiet, sunny, spring day in a countryside dotted by farms and houses. But inside some of those houses, dwellers still were shaken by the morning's events that had forced a police order for them to evacuate their homes.
>
> Mrs. James G. Thorne lives on Cheavens Road across the clearing from where Phipps was shot. Mrs. Thorne had not heard the evacuation notice, so when she saw area officers crouching with guns at the end of her driveway, she decided to investigate.
>
> "I was the surprise they weren't expecting," she told a Highway Patrol officer Friday afternoon. "I walked out just before the excitement."

When the officers saw Mrs. Thorne. "they were obviously very upset and shouted for me to get out of here," she said. "I was here alone and asked them how I was supposed to leave. All they said was, 'Just get out of here.'"

Down the road, Clarence Stallman had been warned of the situation by officers and noticed the circling airplane and helicopter. "I said, 'Are they headed this way soon?' and they said, 'They're here,'" said Stallman.

After Stallman notified his neighbors, he picked up Mrs. Thorne at her home and left the area just before the shooting.

On the next street over, Ronald Nichols had no intention of running.

"I didn't know what was happening," Nichols said. "The wife was scared to death and didn't know what to do. I grabbed my gun and looked for them."

Another neighbor, Mrs. Charles Emmons, first was alerted by the sound of the surveillance plane. "The plane was flying so low I thought it was going to come into the house," she said. "I was frightened. This is something you think will never happen to you."

Then Mrs. Emmons flashed a relieved smile. "It's been quite a morning," she said.

The techniques of writing in chronological order and separating the accounts of witnesses from the main story worked well in this case. More often, however, crime stories are written in the classic inverted pyramid style because of time and space considerations.

Accident and Fire Stories

When you are assigned to cover an accident or a fire, many of the facts and all of the color are gathered at the scene. If the accident has just taken place, a visit to the scene is essential. Being there will give you the best picture of what happened, and you will be able to write a solid story. Too many reporters cover accidents and fires as purely passive observers. Indeed, you must observe. But you must also actively solicit information from those who are present. Many of them, including those directly involved, you may never be able to find again. Keep a digital recorder and smartphone at hand. You may be asked to prepare stories for multiple media.

When you are dispatched to the scene of an accident, move as quickly as possible to collect this information:

- The names, ages, addresses and conditions of the victims.
- Accounts of witnesses or police reconstructions of what happened.
- When the accident occurred.
- Where it occurred.
- Why or how it happened or who was at fault, as determined by officials in charge of the investigation.

If that list sounds familiar, it should. You could simplify it to read "who, what, when, where and why." As in any news story, that information is essential. You must gather it as quickly as possible after being assigned to the story.

Just as important is knowing what to do when you arrive on the scene of an accident. These suggestions will help:

- **Question the person in charge of the investigation.** This individual will attempt to gather much of the information you want. A police officer, for example, needs to know who was involved, what happened, when it happened and who was at fault. If

ANNOTATED MODEL   Comparison of a Breaking News Story and a Follow-Up Story

Breaking News Story

A short, inverted pyramid story may be posted online immediately after the news breaks.

A Highway Patrol marksman shot and killed a Kansas man in a rural area south of Springfield this morning after the victim threatened to blow off the head of his apparent hostage.

> *The summary lead captures the action and some of the drama.*

A hitchhiker reportedly told police earlier this morning that his "ride" had plans to rob a service station on Interstate 70. That tip apparently followed an earlier report of a van leaving a station at the Millersburg exit of I-70 without paying for gasoline.

An ensuing hour-long chase ended at 9:30 a.m. in an isolated meadow in the Pierpont area when Capt. N.E. Tinnin fired a single shot into the stomach of the suspect, identified as Jim Phipps of Kansas City, Kansas.

Phipps, armed with a sawed-off shotgun, and his "hostage," identified as Anthony Curtis Lilly, 17, also of Kansas City, Kansas, eluded police by fleeing into a rugged, wooded area at the end of Bennett Lane, a dead-end gravel road off Route 163.

> *Then comes a chronological reconstruction, but without much detail or background.*

Tinnin said he fired the shot with a .253-caliber sniper rifle when it appeared Phipps was going to shoot Lilly. Two troopers' efforts to persuade Phipps to throw down his weapon and surrender were unsuccessful, Tinnin said.

Follow-Up Story

With more time to learn the full story, the reporter can give readers a more complete account, either online or in print.

James Phipps and Anthony Lilly, a pair of 17-year-olds from Kansas City, Kansas, were heading west on Interstate 70 at 7:30 a.m. Friday, returning from a trip to Arkansas.

> *The reporter can use narrative to bring interest to an ongoing story.*

Within the next hour and a half, Phipps had used a sawed-off shotgun stolen in Arkansas to take Lilly hostage, and, after holding that shotgun to Lilly's head, was shot and killed by a Highway Patrol captain on the edge of a rugged wooded area south of Springfield.

As the episode ended, local officials had only begun to piece together a bizarre tragedy that involved a high-speed chase, airplane and helicopter surveillance, a march through a wooded ravine and the evacuation of several frightened citizens from their country homes.

> *After the lead (the first two paragraphs) comes a paragraph of scene-setting and foreshadowing.*

One attribution (underlined) allows the reporter to narrate the story without repeating the source.

<u>As police reconstructed the incident,</u> Phipps and Lilly decided to stop for gas at the Millersburg exit east of Columbia at about 7:30 a.m.

With them in the van was Robert Paul Hudson Jr., a San Francisco-bound hitchhiker.

Hudson was not present at the shooting. He had fled Lilly's van at the Millersburg exit after he suspected trouble.

With breaking news, a reporter might post the basic facts online immediately in an inverted pyramid story. Once the basic news is posted, the reporter has some time to gather additional facts and craft a chronological narrative that gives readers the full story.

ANNOTATED MODEL Comparison of a Breaking News Story and a Follow-Up Story (continued)

The trouble began when Lilly and Phipps openly plotted to steal some gasoline at Millersburg, Hudson told police. He said the pair had agreed to display the shotgun if trouble arose with station attendants.

Here is a necessary bit of explanation.

Hudson said he persuaded Phipps to drop him off before they stopped for gas. He then caught a ride to Springfield and told his driver of the robbery plans he had overheard. After dropping Hudson off near the Providence Road exit, the driver called Springfield police, who picked up Hudson.

Then the narrative begins.

Meanwhile, Phipps and Lilly put $8.90 worth of gas in the van and drove off without paying. The station attendant notified authorities.

As he approached Springfield, Phipps turned onto U.S. 63 South, where he was spotted by Highway Patrol troopers Tom Halford and Greg Overfelt. They began a high-speed chase, which ended on a dead-end gravel road near Pierpont.

Transitions orient the reader and keep the story moving.

During the chase, which included a U-turn near Ashland, Phipps bumped the Highway Patrol car twice, forcing Halford to run into the highway's median.

Upon reaching the dead end, the suspects abandoned the van and ran into a nearby barn. At that point, Phipps, who Highway Patrol officers said was wanted in Kansas for escaping from a detention center, turned the shotgun on Lilly.

When Halford and Overfelt tried to talk with Phipps from outside the barn, they were met with obscenities. Phipps threatened to "blow (Lilly's) head off," and vowed not to be captured alive.

The reporter uses a direct quote to add color to the narrative.

Phipps then left the barn and walked into a wooded area, pressing the gun against Lilly's head. Halford and Overfelt followed at a safe distance but were close enough to speak with Phipps.

While other officers from the Highway Patrol, the Lincoln County Sheriff's Department and Springfield police arrived at the scene, residents in the area were warned to evacuate their homes. A Highway Patrol plane and helicopter flew low over the woods, following the suspects and the troopers through the woods.

The four walked through a deep and densely wooded ravine. Upon seeing a partially constructed house in a nearby clearing, Phipps demanded of officers waiting in the clearing that his van be driven around to the house, at which time he would release his hostage. Halford said, "They disappeared up over the ridge. I heard some shouting (Phipps' demands), and then I heard the shot."

Another direct quote lends authenticity while giving the story a dramatic conclusion.

After entering the clearing from the woods, Phipps apparently had been briefly confused by the officers on either side of him and had lowered his gun for a moment.

The story is wrapped up in the final paragraph.

That was long enough for Highway Patrol Capt. N.E. Tinnin to shoot Phipps in the abdomen with a high-powered rifle. It was about 8:45 a.m. Phipps was taken to Boone County Hospital, where he soon died.

you are able to establish a good relationship with the investigator, you may be able to secure much of the information you need from this one source, though single-source stories are usually inadequate.

Remember that the spellings of names, addresses and similar facts must be verified later. Any veteran reporter can tell you that police officers and other public officials are notoriously bad spellers and often make errors in recording the names of victims. To avoid such errors, call relatives of the victims or consult the city directory, telephone book or other sources to check your information.

- ■ **Try to find and interview witnesses.** Police and other investigators may lead you directly to the best witnesses. The most accurate account of what happened usually comes from witnesses, and the investigators will try to find them. You should, too. A good way to do that is to watch the investigators. Listen in as they interview a witness, or approach the witness after they are finished. If there is time, of course, try to find your own witnesses. You cannot and should not always rely on investigators to do your work for you. Social media may reveal the identity and contact information of some witnesses.

- ■ **Try to find friends or relatives of the victims.** These sources are helpful in piecing together information about the victims. Through them you often get tips about even better stories.

- ■ **If possible, interview the victims.** Survivors of an accident may be badly shaken, but if they are able to talk, they can provide firsthand details that you won't find in an official report. Make every attempt to interview those involved.

- ■ **Talk with others at the scene.** If someone died at the scene of the accident, an ambulance paramedic or the medical examiner may be able to give you some indication of what caused the death. At the least you can learn where the bodies or the injured will be taken. That may help, because later the mortician or hospital officials may be able to provide information you need for your story.

- ■ **Be sensitive to victims and their families.** You have a job to do, and you must do it. That does not mean, however, that you can be insensitive to those involved in an accident or fire.

- ■ **Sketch elements of the scene on a piece of paper or take photos with your phone.** The sketch or photos may be useful in helping an information graphics artist re-create the scene.

- ■ **Record your interviews.** You might need a recording for your website or to help you make sure the information is correct.

Of course, your deadline will have a major impact on the amount of information you are able to gather. If you must meet a deadline soon after arriving at the scene, you will probably be forced to stick to the basics of who, what, when, where, why and how. Thus it is important to gather that information first. Then, if you have time, you can concentrate on more detailed and vivid information to make the story highly readable.

Accidents and fires present similar problems for the reporter, but at a fire of any size you can expect more confusion than at the scene of an accident. One major difference, then, is that the officer in charge will be busier. At the scene of an accident, the damage has been done and the authorities are usually free to concentrate on their investigation. At a fire, the officer in charge is busy directing firefighters and probably will be unable to talk with you. The investigation will not even begin until the fire is extinguished. In many cases, the cause of the fire will not be known for hours, days or weeks. In some cases, it may never be known. Seldom is that so in an accident, except perhaps for airplane accidents.

Another problem is that you may not have access to the immediate area of the fire. Barriers often are erected to keep the public—and representatives of the news media—from coming too close to a burning structure. Such barriers, erected to ensure safety, may hamper your reporting. You may not be able to get close enough to firefighters to learn about the problems they are having or to obtain the quotes you need to improve your story.

These problems usually make covering a fire more difficult than covering an accident. Despite the difficulties, you cover a fire in much the same way, interviewing officials and witnesses at the scene. You also should try to interview the property owner. Moreover, because the official investigation will not have begun, you must conduct your own. When covering a fire, you must learn:

- The location of the fire.
- The names, ages and addresses of those killed, injured or missing.
- The name of the building owner or, in the case of a grass fire or forest fire, the landowner.
- The value of the building and its contents or the value of the land.
- Whether the building and contents were insured for fire damage. (Open land seldom is.)
- When the fire started, who reported it and how many firefighters and pieces of equipment were called to the scene.
- What caused the fire, if known.

As in any story, the basics are who, what, when, where, why and how. But the nature of the fire will raise other questions that must be answered. Of primary importance is whether life is endangered. If it is not, the amount of property damage becomes the major emphasis of the story. Was arson involved? Was the building insured for its full value? Was there an earlier fire at the same location? Did the building comply with fire codes? Were any rare or extremely valuable objects inside? Did explosives inside the structure complicate fighting the fire and pose an even greater threat than the fire itself?

Your job is to answer these questions for your readers or viewers. You may be able to obtain some of this information later on from official fire reports if they are ready before your deadline. But most information will come from interviews that you conduct at the scene with the best available sources. Finding your sources may not be easy, but you can begin by looking for the highest-ranking fire official. Large departments may have a designated press officer whose job is to deal with you and other reporters.

> " The news is no longer the news. . . . It's all about luridness. Body bags will be seen at 7, chasing ambulance at 8, victim's family at 9. "
>
> — *Oliver Stone, film director*

Another important source is the fire marshal, whose job is to determine the cause of the fire and, if arson is involved, to bring charges against the arsonist. You should make every effort to talk with the fire marshal at the scene, if he or she is available.

Note that it is important to verify information received at the scene to the maximum extent possible. One way to do that is to see if two sources agree on the same version of what happened. Remember, when news is breaking, confusion reigns. Be cautious, especially if you are tweeting immediate events from the scene. Even official sources can be mistaken about what happened. Verify to the extent possible, and attribute all information to the source from whom you received it.

The Court Story

Criminal justice proceedings can be very complicated, with a case moving through a number of stages, from occurrence of the crime, to police investigation, to actions by prosecutors and defense attorneys, to actual criminal trials, to legal punishments like incarceration and execution.

Throughout this cycle of events, a reporter has numerous opportunities to write stories. The extent to which the reporter does so depends on the importance of the case and the amount of local interest in it. In a major case, the filing of every motion may prompt a story; in other cases, only the verdict may be important. As in any type of reporting, news value is the determining factor.

Avoiding Libelous Statements

Accuracy also is important, as in any form of reporting. Perhaps no other area of writing requires as much caution as the reporting of crime and court news. The potential for libel is great.

Libel is damage to a person's reputation caused by a written statement that brings the person into hatred, contempt or ridicule or that injures a person's business or occupational pursuits (see Chapter 19). Reporters must be extremely careful about what they write. One of the greatest dangers is the possibility of writing that someone is charged with a crime more serious than is the case. Suppose that after checking clippings in the newsroom library, for example, a reporter were to write the following:

> The rape trial of John L. Duncan, 25, of 3925 Oak St. has been set for Dec. 10 in Jefferson County Circuit Court.
>
> Duncan is charged in connection with the June 6 rape of a Melton High School girl near Fletcher Park.

Duncan had been charged with rape following his arrest. However, the prosecutor later determined that the evidence was insufficient to win a rape conviction, the charge was reduced to assault and the newspaper had to print a correction that identified the correct charge.

Many courts handle both civil and criminal cases. Media coverage often focuses on criminal cases, although civil actions—lawsuits involving disputes of one type or another—are often excellent sources of stories.

ON THE JOB "Every Story Is Important"

Earlier in this chapter, we introduced you to **Rex Huppke**, a reporter and columnist for the *Chicago Tribune* and chicagotribune.com. This isn't the job he landed fresh from school. In fact, he majored in chemical engineering, only to discover six months into his first job that he had made a big mistake. Eventually, he returned to graduate school, this time in journalism. His first reporting job was in Colorado. Then later on in Indiana, he joined the Associated Press while his wife earned her law degree. He has never forgotten a lesson learned on his first assignment in Colorado Springs:

I was dispatched to a county fair with the mission of finding something "cute" to put in the next day's paper. There was, without question, a part of me that felt I was above such a simple assignment. I was a journalism school graduate, after all.

But I went and found two sisters prepping their goats for a 4-H competition, and wound up spending about an hour with the girls and their mother learning the intricacies of goat upkeep

and show prep. The family was so excited to have a reporter in their midst that the mother insisted I pose for a picture with the girls and their goats.

Courtesy of Rex Huppke.

I did, then went back to the newsroom and, charmed by the family, put together a nice feature story that ran inside the next day's feature section. About a week later, I received a letter and opened it to find a copy of the picture the mother took with a note that gushed about how much the article meant to those girls. It was something, the mother wrote, that they would keep forever.

I have kept that photo, and I look at it now and then to remind myself what matters in this business. Every story is important. You are never greater than the people who let you into their lives, whether it's at a time of triumph or tragedy or simple day-to-day existence.

Start each story with that one truth—every story is important—and you will do fine.

Any story involving arrests should raise caution flags. You must have a working knowledge of libel law and what you can and cannot write about an incident. Any reporter who writes the following, for example, is asking for trouble:

John R. Milton, 35, of 206 East St. was arrested Monday on a charge of assaulting a police officer.

It would be safer, and more accurate, to write that he was arrested "on suspicion of" the assault. Only a prosecutor, not a police officer, may file charges. In many cases, a police officer may arrest a person with the intent of asking the prosecutor to file a certain charge, but the prosecutor may find that the evidence warrants only a lesser charge. For that reason, many journalists prefer to release the name of an arrested person only after the charge has been filed.

Reporters who cover court news encounter many such pitfalls. They are not trained as attorneys, and it takes time to develop a working knowledge of legal proceedings. The only recourse is to ask as many questions as necessary when a point of law is not clear. It is far better to display ignorance of the law and ask questions than to commit a serious error that harms the reputation of the accused and exposes the newspaper to costly libel litigation.

However, it is also important to know that anything said in open court is fair game for reporters. If, in an opening statement, a prosecutor says the defendant is "nothing but scum, a smut peddler bent on polluting the mind of every child in the city," then by all means report the comment in context in your story. But if a spectator makes that same statement in the hallway during a recess, you probably would not report it. Courts do not extend the qualified privilege to report court proceedings beyond the context of the official proceeding.

Types of Courts and Cases

The U.S. has two main court systems: federal and state. Federal district courts handle violations of federal crime statutes, interpretation of the U.S. Constitution and matters dealing with civil rights, election disputes, commerce and antitrust laws, postal regulations, federal tax laws and similar issues. They also handle actions between citizens of different states when the disputed amount exceeds $50,000.

Each state has its own system, with many similarities from state to state. The average citizen is most likely to encounter city or municipal courts, which have jurisdiction over traffic and other minor violations. News from these courts is handled as a matter of record in many newspapers.

Violations of state statutes usually are handled in the state trial courts. These *courts of general jurisdiction* (often called *circuit* or *superior courts*) handle civil cases, such as contract disputes, as well as criminal cases.

Most state crimes are either misdemeanors or felonies. A *misdemeanor* is usually punishable by a fine, a county jail term not to exceed one year, or both. *Felonies* are punishable by a fine, a state prison sentence of more than one year, or death.

Reporting a Case Step-by-Step—An Example

Let's trace a sample criminal case from the time of arrest through the trial to show how a reporter might cover each step.

A Breaking-News Tweet

When arrested, a suspect is taken to a police station for fingerprinting, photographs and perhaps a sobriety test or a lineup. The police may take statements as evidence only if the person is informed of and waives the Miranda rights, which include the right to have an attorney and the right to remain silent. A charge must be filed, or the person must be released, usually within 24 hours.

The first report of a story could come as a tweet as soon as the arrest is confirmed:

Arrest made in Springfield murder. More to come.

A Typical First Story

Next would come a more detailed version of the story for the web. You'll notice that unanswered questions remain. This bare-bones story, however, provides a glimpse of several key points in covering arrest stories:

> An unemployed carpenter was arrested today and charged with the Aug. 6 murder of Springfield resident Anne Compton.
>
> Lester L. Rivers, 32, of 209 E. Dillow Lane was charged with first-degree murder, Prosecuting Attorney Mel Singleton said.
>
> Chief of Detectives E.L. Hall said Rivers was arrested on a warrant after a three-month investigation by a team of three detectives. He declined to comment on what led investigators to Rivers.
>
> Compton's body was found in the Peabody River by two fishermen on the morning of Aug. 7. She had been beaten to death with a blunt instrument, according to Dr. Ronald R. Miller, the county medical examiner.

Notice that the reporter carefully chose the words "arrested . . . and charged with" rather than "arrested for," a phrase that may carry a connotation of guilt.

Another important element of all crime and court coverage is the tie-back sentence. This sentence relates a story to events covered in a previous story—in this case, the report of the crime itself. It is important to state clearly—and near the beginning of the story—which crime is involved. It is also important to provide enough information about it so that the reader recognizes it. In this story, the reporter identifies the crime in the lead and then at the end gives more detail to help the reader recall the event. Clarification of the crime is important even in major stories with ready identification in the community. This story does that by recounting when and where Compton's body was found and by whom. It also tells that she died after being hit with a blunt instrument.

Follow-Up Story: First Court Appearance

After the prosecuting attorney, who argues for the state, files charges, the defendant is usually brought before a judge, informed of the charges and reminded of the Miranda rights. Bail may be set.

For a *misdemeanor*, if the defendant pleads guilty, the judge usually handles the case immediately with a sentence or fine. If the plea is not guilty, a trial date is set.

For a *felony*—a much more serious offense—the defendant does not enter a plea. The judge sets a date for a preliminary hearing, unless the defendant waives the right to such a hearing. A defendant who waives this hearing is bound over to the general jurisdiction trial court; that is, the records of the case are sent to the trial court.

In the Rivers case, the following morning the suspect was taken to Magistrate Court for his initial court appearance. Here is part of the story that resulted:

> Lester L. Rivers appeared in Magistrate Court today charged with first-degree murder in connection with the Aug. 6 beating death of Springfield resident Anne Compton.
>
> Judge Howard D. Robbins scheduled a preliminary hearing for Nov. 10 and set bail at $10,000. Robbins assigned Public Defender Ogden Ball to represent Rivers, 32, of 209 E. Dillow Lane.
>
> Rivers said nothing during the 10-minute session as the judge informed him of his right to remain silent and his right to an attorney. Ball asked Robbins to set the bail at

TIPS

Writing the Court Story

- Possess a strong working knowledge of libel law.
- Ask questions when a point of law is unclear.
- Know that anything said in open court is fair game.
- Early in the story, state clearly which crime is involved and provide enough information so the reader recognizes it.
- Don't overstate facts.
- Take good notes. Trial coverage is greatly enhanced with direct quotations of key exchanges.

a "reasonable amount for a man who is unemployed." Rivers is a carpenter who was fired from his last job in June. Despite the seriousness of the charge, it is essential that Rivers be free to help prepare his defense, Ball said.

Police have said nothing about a possible connection between Rivers and Compton, whose body was found in the Peabody River by two fishermen on the morning of Aug. 7. She had been beaten to death.

The reporter clearly outlined the exact charge and reported on key points of the brief hearing. Again, the tie-back helps readers recognize and remember details of the crime.

Follow-Up Story: Preliminary Hearing

Next comes the *preliminary hearing*, in which the evidence linking the defendant to the crime is first revealed.

The hearing is usually held before a magistrate or a lower-level judge. The prosecutor tries to convince the judge that there is *probable cause* to believe the defendant committed a crime. The defendant can cross-examine the state's witnesses and present evidence, but normally does not. Because preliminary hearings are thus often one-sided reporters must be careful to write a well-balanced story.

If the judge finds probable cause, the prosecuting attorney must file, within a short time period (usually 10 days), what is called an "information" based on the judge's finding.

Here's the story that resulted from Rivers' preliminary hearing:

> Lester L. Rivers will be tried in Jefferson County Circuit Court for the Aug. 6 murder of Springfield resident Anne Compton.
>
> Magistrate Judge Howard D. Robbins ruled today that there is probable cause to believe that a crime was committed and probable cause that Rivers did it. Rivers was bound over for trial in Circuit Court.
>
> Rivers, 32, of 209 E. Dillow Lane is being held in Jefferson County Jail. He has been unable to post bail of $10,000.
>
> At today's preliminary hearing, Medical Examiner Ronald R. Miller testified that a tire tool recovered from Rivers' car at the time of his arrest "could have been used in the beating death of Miss Compton." Her body was found floating in the Peabody River Aug. 7.
>
> James L. Mullaney, a lab technician for the FBI crime laboratory in Washington, D.C., testified that "traces of blood on the tire tool matched Miss Compton's blood type."

In reporting the testimony, the reporter is careful to use direct quotes and not to overstate the facts. The medical examiner testified that the tire tool *could have been used* in the murder. If he had said it *had been used*, the reporter would have needed a stronger lead.

Defense attorneys usually use preliminary hearings to learn about the evidence against their clients and do not present any witnesses. This apparently was the motive here because neither the police nor the prosecutor had made a public statement on evidence in the case. They probably were being careful not to release prejudicial information that could be grounds for a new trial.

In most states, a person can also be brought to trial by a grand jury indictment. In federal courts, the Constitution requires indictment by a grand jury in felony cases.

In some states, grand jury hearings are secret, and potential defendants are not allowed to be present when testimony is given. The prosecuting attorney presents evidence that determines whether there is probable cause to prosecute.

A grand jury returns a "true bill" if it finds probable cause and "no true bill" if not. The jury foreman or forewoman and the prosecuting attorney must sign the indictment, which then is presented in open court to a trial judge.

If the defendant is not already in custody, the judge orders an arrest warrant. Arraignment in the trial court follows.

Follow-Up Story: Arraignment

Arraignment, conducted in open court, is the first formal presentation of the information or the indictment to the defendant. The defendant enters a plea to the charge: guilty, not guilty, or not guilty by reason of mental disease or defect.

In the Rivers case, the prosecutor filed an information, as state law required. The defendant was arraigned in Circuit Court, and the result was a routine story that begins as follows:

> Circuit Judge John L. Lee refused today to reduce the bail of Lester L. Rivers, who is charged with first-degree murder in the Aug. 6 death of Springfield resident Anne Compton. Rivers pleaded not guilty. Repeating a request he made earlier in Magistrate Court, Public Defender Ogden Ball urged that Rivers' bail be reduced from $10,000 so he could be free to assist in preparing his defense.

The not-guilty plea was expected, so the reporter concentrated on a more interesting aspect of the hearing—the renewed request for reduced bail.

At this point in criminal proceedings, *plea bargaining* sometimes occurs. A defendant changes a plea from not guilty to guilty in return for a lighter sentence, typically pleading guilty to a lesser charge. A charge of premeditated murder, for example, might be reduced to manslaughter. To save the time and expense of a trial, prosecutors often agree to this if they believe justice is served.

If the defendant enters a guilty plea, the judge may impose a sentence immediately, or a *presentencing investigation* of the defendant's background may be ordered to help the judge set punishment. Many jurisdictions require presentencing investigations, at least in felony cases. A sentencing date may be set.

If the defendant enters a plea of not guilty, the judge sets a trial date. Most jurisdictions require speedy trials.

As the prosecutor and defense attorney prepare for trial, they may file motions for disclosure of evidence, suppression of evidence and similar rulings. A defense attorney who feels that pretrial stories in the local media may prejudice potential jurors will often ask for a **change of venue**, which moves the trial to a county other than the one in which the crime occurred.

Follow-Up Story: First Day of the Trial

On the first day of a trial, a jury, usually 12 jurors and at least one alternate, is selected during a process called *voir dire* (vwar DEER). The prosecutor and defense attorney question the prospective jurors to identify jurors they hope will be sympathetic to their positions. In the federal system the judge often asks questions, but the prosecutor and defense attorneys may suggest questions for the judge to ask.

Each attorney can eliminate a certain number of people as jurors without having to state a reason and also dismiss an unlimited number *for cause* (if, for example, the prospective juror is related to the accused).

In the Rivers case, after a series of motions was reported routinely, the trial began. Here's the story written on the first day:

> Jury selection began today in the first-degree murder trial of Lester L. Rivers, who is charged with the Aug. 6 beating death of Springfield resident Anne Compton.
>
> Public Defender Ogden Ball, Rivers' attorney, and Prosecuting Attorney Mel Singleton both expect jury selection to be complete by 5 p.m.
>
> The selection process started after court convened at 10 a.m. The only incident occurred just before the lunch break as Singleton was questioning prospective juror Jerome B. Tinker, 33, of 408 Woodland Terrace.
>
> "I went to school with that guy," said Tinker, pointing to Rivers, who was seated in the courtroom. "He wouldn't hurt nobody."
>
> Singleton immediately asked that Tinker be removed from the jury panel, and Circuit Judge John L. Lee agreed.
>
> Rivers smiled as Tinker made his statement, but otherwise sat quietly, occasionally conferring with Ball.

The testimony is about to begin, so the reporter sets the stage here, describing the courtroom scene. Jury selection is often routine and becomes newsworthy only in important or interesting cases.

Once the jurors are sworn in, the prosecutor makes an opening statement that outlines how the state expects to prove each element of the crime. The defense attorney may follow with a statement, may wait until after the prosecution has introduced its evidence to make a statement, or may waive an opening statement altogether.

Follow-Up Story: Trial Testimony

A basic tenet of criminal law is that the prosecution must prove the defendant guilty beyond a reasonable doubt. The defendant is not required to prove anything or even to testify.

To establish what happened and to link the defendant to the crime, the state calls witnesses to testify. First, the prosecutor asks questions, and the witness responds. The defense attorney then cross-examines the witness. Frequently, one attorney will object to questions posed by the other, and the judge must rule on the objection.

When the defense attorney finishes cross-examination, the prosecutor conducts *re-direct examination* to clarify certain points or to bolster a witness's credibility. Cross-examination and re-direct examination continue until both sides have asked the witness all their questions.

Trial coverage can be tedious, but when the case is interesting, the stories are easy to write. As the Rivers trial progressed, the reporter picked the most interesting testimony to use in leads:

> A service station owner testified today that Lester L. Rivers offered a ride to Springfield resident Anne Compton less than an hour before she was beaten to death Aug. 6.
>
> Ralph R. Eagle, the station owner, was a witness at the first-degree murder trial of Rivers in Jefferson County Circuit Court.
>
> "I told her I'd call a cab," Eagle testified, "but Rivers offered her a ride to her boyfriend's house." Compton had gone to the service station after her car broke down nearby. Under cross-examination, Public Defender Ogden Ball, Rivers' attorney, questioned whether Rivers was the man who offered the ride.
>
> "If it wasn't him, it was his twin brother," Eagle said.

"Then you're not really sure it was Mr. Rivers, are you?" Ball asked.

"I sure am," Eagle replied.

"You think you're sure, Mr. Eagle, but you really didn't get a good look at him, did you?"

"I sold him some gas and got a good look at him when I took the money."

"But it was night, wasn't it, Mr. Eagle?" Ball asked.

"That place doesn't have the best lighting in the world, but I saw him all right."

The reporter focuses on the key testimony of the trial by capturing it in the words of the participants.

After the prosecution witnesses have testified and the state rests its case, the defense almost always makes a motion for acquittal, arguing that the state has failed to prove its case beyond a reasonable doubt. Almost always, the motion is denied.

The defense then calls witnesses to support its case, and the prosecutor cross-examines them. Finally, when all witnesses have testified, the defense rests.

At this point, the prosecutor calls *rebuttal witnesses* in an attempt to discredit the testimony of the defense witnesses. The defense then has the right to present even more witnesses, called *surrebuttal witnesses*.

Follow-Up Story: Verdict

After these witnesses have testified, the judge instructs the jury about possible verdicts and key points of law. The prosecutor makes a closing argument, usually an impassioned plea for a guilty verdict addressed directly to the jury. The defense attorney's closing argument follows, and the prosecutor is allowed a final rebuttal. In the federal system, closing arguments precede the judge's instructions to the jury. The jury then retires to deliberate.

For the journalist covering the trial, there is eventually the verdict story, which is usually one of the easiest to write. Here's the verdict story in the Rivers case:

> Lester L. Rivers was found guilty of first-degree murder today in the Aug. 6 beating death of Springfield resident Anne Compton.
>
> Rivers stood motionless in Jefferson County Circuit Court as the jury foreman returned the verdict. Judge John L. Lee set sentencing for Dec. 10.
>
> Rivers, 32, of 209 E. Dillow Lane could be sentenced to death in the electric chair or life imprisonment in the State Penitentiary.
>
> Public Defender Ogden Ball, Rivers' attorney, said he will appeal.
>
> After the verdict was announced, Mr. and Mrs. Lilborn O. Compton, the victim's parents, were escorted from the courtroom by friends. Both refused to talk with reporters.

Because a criminal trial requires a unanimous verdict, deliberations often are protracted. If jurors fail to agree (a *hung jury*), the judge may order a mistrial; then the entire case will be retried with a new jury. If a verdict is reached, the jury returns to the courtroom, where the verdict is read.

Sentencing and Appeals

In some states, juries may recommend sentences in guilty verdicts. But the final decision is always made by the judge unless a crime carries a mandatory sentence. Sentencing may be done immediately, but more likely a presentencing report will be ordered and a sentencing date set. For a really important criminal trial, reporters might be assigned to cover a sentencing hearing.

The defense often files a motion asking that a guilty verdict be set aside or requesting a new trial. These motions, though usually denied, are often prerequisites to the filing of an appeal. Appeals often follow guilty verdicts. Except in cases involving serious crimes, judges often permit a defendant to be released on bail pending the outcome of appeals.

Many other types of stories can be written about a trial. Lengthy jury deliberations, for example, might prompt stories about the anxiety of the defendant and attorneys and their speculations about the cause of the delay.

Covering court news requires care and good reporting. As in any kind of reporting, you must be well-prepared. If you understand the language of the courts and how they are organized, your job is simplified.

Other Issues in Crime and Court Reporting

Covering crime and the courts is not a simple matter. While the complexity of court proceedings can be baffling to a beginning reporter, there are other pitfalls as well.

The Free Press/Fair Trial Controversy

The 1954 murder trial of Dr. Samuel Sheppard in Cleveland was the landmark case involving the perceived conflict between a defendant's right to a fair trial and the public's right to know. Sheppard was accused of murdering his wife. News coverage in the Cleveland newspapers, which included front-page editorials, was intense. In 1966, the U.S. Supreme Court said the trial judge had not fulfilled his duty to protect the jury from the news coverage that saturated the community and to control disruptive influences in the courtroom. The judge overturned his conviction.

That case, more than any other, ignited what is known as the **free press/fair trial controversy**. This controversy raged during the O.J. Simpson case in the mid-1990s. On numerous occasions, Judge Lance Ito threatened to end television coverage of court proceedings to protect Simpson's rights during his criminal trial. Lawyers charged that the media were threatening the Sixth Amendment right of the accused to an impartial jury. The media countered with charges that lawyers were threatening the First Amendment.

Editors realize that coverage of a crime can make it difficult to impanel an impartial jury, but they argue that courts have available many remedies other than restricting the flow of information. In the Sheppard case, for example, the Supreme Court justices said a change of venue, which moves the trial to a location where publicity is not as intense, could have been ordered. Other remedies suggested by the court in such cases are to "continue" (delay) the trial, to grant a new trial or to head off possible outside influences during the trial by sequestering the jury. Editors also argue that acquittals have been won in some of the most publicized cases in recent years.

> "To make inroads into the mind-set that 'if the press reported it, it must be true' is the lawyer's most challenging task."
>
> — *Robert Shapiro, attorney*

Gag Orders and Closed Trials

Despite the remedies the Supreme Court offered in the Sheppard case, trial judges continued to be concerned about impaneling impartial juries. Judges issued hundreds of gag orders in the wake of the Sheppard case. Finally, in 1976, in the landmark case of *Nebraska Press Association v. Stuart*, the Supreme Court ruled that a gag order was an unconstitutional prior restraint that violated the First Amendment to the Constitution. The justices did not go so far as to rule that all gag orders are invalid. But in each case, the trial judge has to prove that an order restraining publication would protect the rights of the accused and that no other alternatives would be less damaging to First Amendment rights.

That ruling, of course, did not end the concerns of trial judges. Rather than issue gag orders restricting the press from reporting court proceedings, some attempted to close their courtrooms. In the first such case to reach the U.S. Supreme Court, *Gannett v. DePasquale*, the press and public suffered a severe but temporary blow. On July 2, 1979, in a highly controversial decision, the justices said, "We hold that members of the public have no constitutional right under the Sixth and Fourteenth amendments to attend criminal trials." The case itself had involved only a pretrial hearing.

As a result of the decision and the confusion that followed, the Supreme Court of Virginia sanctioned the closing of an entire criminal trial. The accused was acquitted during the second day of the secret trial. The U.S. Supreme Court agreed to hear the appeal of the trial judge's action in a case known as *Richmond Newspapers v. Virginia*. On July 2, 1980, the court said that under the First Amendment "the trial of a criminal case must be open to the public." Only a court finding of an "overriding interest," which was not defined, would be grounds for closing a criminal trial.

Covering Sex Crimes

The reporting of sex crimes often causes controversy. Most news executives think of their products as family newspapers or broadcasts and are properly hesitant about reporting the lurid details of sex crimes.

Sex Crime Victims

One problem in reporting on sex crimes is the question of how to handle rape victims. Too often, rapes are not reported to police because victims are unwilling to appear in court to testify against the suspects. Defense attorneys sometimes use such occasions to attack the victim's moral character and imply that she or he consented to sexual relations. Many victims decline to press charges because of fear that their names will be made public in the media. Both of these things happened to the woman who accused basketball star Kobe Bryant of rape. There is, after all, still a lingering tendency to attach a social stigma to the rape victim, despite increasing public awareness of the nature of the crime. In some states, "rape shield" statutes prohibit a defendant's attorney from delving into the rape victim's prior sexual activity unless some connection can be shown with the circumstances of the rape charged.

Sex Crime Offenders

In Massachusetts, a judge excluded the public and press from the entire trial of a man accused of raping three teenagers. A Massachusetts law provided for the mandatory closing of trials involving specific sex offenses against minors. In 1982, the U.S. Supreme Court held in *Globe Newspaper Co. v. Superior Court* that the mandatory closure law violated the First Amendment right of access to criminal trials established in the Richmond Newspapers case. The justices ruled that when a state attempts to deny the right of access in an effort to inhibit the disclosure of sensitive information, it must show that the denial "is necessitated by a compelling governmental interest." The court indicated in the opinion that in some cases *in-camera proceedings* (proceedings that take place in a judge's chambers outside the view of the press and public) may be appropriate for youthful witnesses.

In *Press-Enterprise v. Riverside County Superior Court*, the U.S. Supreme Court ruled in 1984 that a court order closing the jury-selection process in a rape-murder case was invalid. The court ruled that jury selection has been a public process with exceptions only for good cause. In a second *Press-Enterprise v. Riverside County Superior Court* case, the U.S. Supreme Court said in 1986 that preliminary hearings should be open to the public unless there is a "substantial probability" that the resulting publicity would prevent a fair trial and there are no "reasonable alternatives to closure." In 1993, the Supreme Court continued its emphasis on the importance of open court proceedings. It struck down a Puerto Rican law that said preliminary hearings "shall be held privately" unless the defendant requests a public preliminary hearing.

Press-Bar Guidelines

These cases appeared to uphold the right of the press and the public to have access to criminal proceedings. Judges, however, have a duty to protect the rights of the accused. The Supreme Court of the State of Washington, in *Federated Publications v. Swedberg*, held in 1981 that press access to pretrial hearings may be conditioned on the agreement of reporters to abide by the voluntary press-bar guidelines that exist in some states. The decision involved a preliminary hearing in a Bellingham, Washington, murder case tied to the "Hillside Strangler" murders in the Los Angeles area. The state Supreme Court ruled that the lower-court order was "a good-faith attempt to accommodate the interests of both defendant and press." The lower court had required reporters covering the hearing to sign a document in which the reporters agreed to abide by press-bar guidelines. The state Supreme Court said the document should be taken as a moral commitment on the part of the reporters, not as a legally enforceable document.

The U.S. Supreme Court in 1982 refused to hear an appeal of that case. Fortunately, many states have statutes to the effect that "the setting of every court shall be public, and every person may freely attend the same." When such statutes are in place, the closed-courtroom controversy appears to be moot. In states that have no such statute, the result seems to be that:

- A criminal trial must be open unless there is an "overriding interest" that requires some part of it to be closed.
- Judges must find some overriding interest before closing pretrial hearings.

One effect of the Washington decision is that many media groups are withdrawing from state press-bar agreements in the few states that have such guidelines. Their reasoning is that the voluntary guidelines in effect could become mandatory.

Cameras in the Courtroom

In 1994, the U.S. Judicial Conference ended its three-year experiment with cameras in federal courts by banning them. Two years later, the Judicial Conference agreed to permit cameras in some lower federal courts. And 47 states do allow cameras in at least some state courtrooms. Only Indiana, Mississippi, South Dakota and the District of Columbia ban courtroom cameras.

The fact remains that there are many ways for judges to protect the rights of the accused without trampling on the right of the press and public to attend trials and pretrial hearings. Indeed, most editors are sensitive to the rights of the accused. Most exercise self-restraint when publishing or broadcasting information about a crime. And most have attempted to establish written policy on such matters, although others insist that individual cases must be judged on their merits.

Coverage of Minority Groups

Reporters and editors must share with judges the burden of protecting the rights of the accused. They also must ensure that certain groups within our society are not treated unfairly, either by the courts or in the media. In a study of crime reporting at the Gannett Center for Media Studies, Robert Snyder discovered that minorities tend to be covered by the media mainly in the context of crime news. Crime reporting is a staple of urban news, and urban areas are where minorities are concentrated. In large cities like New York and Los Angeles, some areas of the city often make news only because of crime. As it is reported now, Snyder says, crime is almost always a conversation about race. He concludes that if the media are to change that perception, they must cover minorities more broadly and sympathetically. The real story of crime, Snyder says, should be the "breaking down of communities and the real weakening of the social structure."

Many editors are concerned about the way minorities are portrayed in crime stories. In fact, many newspapers and broadcast stations studiously avoid gratuitous mentions of race. Their reporters are allowed to mention the race of a suspect only as part of the complete identification of a fugitive. For many years, it was common to read or hear references to a "six-foot-tall black man" wanted for a crime. Today such a description would be considered unacceptable. Too many men fit that description, and the racial reference merely reinforces the stereotype of blacks as criminals. However, if a complete description of a fugitive might help lead to an arrest, it is appropriate to mention race as a part of that description. Only when race becomes the central theme of a story should it be emphasized.

Similarly, most editors consider a person's sexual orientation off limits unless the story focuses on heterosexuality or homosexuality. Increasingly, though, gays and lesbians are willing to talk openly about their sexual orientation as a means of advancing the cause of gay rights. Such issues cannot and should not be ignored by the media. But tastefully handling crime news involving homosexual crimes often proves to be difficult. This was never more true than in the sensational murder trial

**macmillanhighered.com
/newsreporting12e**
Watch **"Fake News/Real News:
A Fine Line"**

- *Onion* editor Joe Randazzo suggests that fake news outlets like *The Onion* do better at getting at "the truth" than traditional media companies do. Do you agree? Explain.
- Think about the ways you get your news. How do you decide which sources to consult? How much do you trust what they tell you?

of Milwaukee's Jeffrey Dahmer, convicted of sexually molesting young boys and men, killing them and eating parts of their bodies. In such cases, the press walks a fine line between responsibly informing the public and pandering to its seemingly insatiable appetite for sensational crime news.

Coverage of Terrorism

Since the 2001 attacks on the World Trade Center and the Pentagon—and, more recently, the 2015 Paris attacks—much has been written about the rights of those arrested as alleged terrorists. Suspects have been held for years without charge at the U.S. naval base at Guantánamo Bay, Cuba, and interrogated by U.S. officials in foreign countries. Rights activists and the suspects' attorneys have challenged such actions as unconstitutional, and the courts have agreed. This ongoing battle is likely to be a matter of contention for the foreseeable future.

Crime and Social Media

Citizens who witness a crime or come upon a crime scene after the fact are prone to post about it on social media. It's important to remember that such reports can be and often are wildly inaccurate. Make sure not to quote information from social media reports without verifying that information with better sources.

Issues of Taste and Ethics

News editors ponder a number of major issues involving taste and ethics in crime and court reporting:

- When should the media reveal details of how a murder or another crime was committed?
- When should the media reveal details about sex crimes or print the names of sex crime victims?
- When should the media reveal a suspect's confession or even the fact that the suspect confessed?
- When should the media reveal a defendant's prior criminal record?
- When should the media reveal the names of juveniles charged with crimes?

None of these questions can be answered to everyone's satisfaction, and it is doubtful whether rules can be established to apply in all such situations.

Reporting Details of a Crime

There have been charges that when the media reveal details of a murder, some people use the techniques described to commit additional murders. This charge is directed most frequently at television, but newspapers have not been immune, and online media may also face this issue.

Reporting Confessions and Prior Convictions

Many editors will not publish or broadcast details of a suspect's confession in an effort to protect the suspect's rights. Revealing such information blocks the way for a fair trial perhaps more than anything else the media can do. Some newspapers and broadcast stations, however, continue to reveal assertions by police or prosecutors that a confession was signed. Many critics question whether such information isn't just as prejudicial as the confession statement itself.

Occasionally, journalists question whether to suppress an unsolicited confession. After a youth was charged with a series of robberies and was certified to stand trial as an adult, a newspaper reporter phoned the youthful defendant, who was free on bail, for an interview. The result was interesting. The defendant admitted to two other robberies in what amounted to a confession to the newspaper and its readers. The editor, who would not have printed a simple statement by police that the defendant had confessed to the crimes, printed this one. Why? The editor reasoned that information about a confession to police amounts to secondhand, hearsay information. The confession to a reporter, however, was firsthand information obtained by the newspaper directly from the accused.

Lawyers also view as prejudicial the publication of a defendant's prior criminal record. Even if authorities refuse to divulge that information, much of it may be in the morgue. Should it be reported? Most journalists believe it should be, particularly if a prior conviction was for a similar offense. Most attorneys disagree.

Identifying Juveniles

Whether to use the names of juveniles charged with crimes is a troublesome issue as well. Most states prohibit law enforcement officers and court officials from releasing the names of juveniles. The reasoning of those who oppose releasing juveniles' names is that the publicity marks them for life as criminals. Those who hold this view argue that there is ample opportunity for these individuals to change their ways and become good citizens—if the media do not stamp them as criminals. Others argue that juveniles who commit serious offenses, such as rape and armed robbery, should be treated as adults.

Questions such as these elicit divergent views from editors, some of whom regularly seek the advice of their lawyers. Little guidance for the reporter can be offered here. Because the decision to publish or not to publish is the editor's, not the reporter's, consultation is necessary. Each case must be decided on its merits.

Obituaries and Life Stories

In the online world, obituaries are big business. Newspaper websites sell advertising to funeral homes and auxiliary services because they have found that readers search for obituaries frequently. Even former residents of a city monitor obituaries. Some websites are devoted to obituaries and provide resources for readers and advertisers. One, legacy.com, which is partially owned by a newspaper, provides links and a searchable database to hundreds of newspapers, and it sells advertising to the funeral industry. It also allows readers to post memorials to friends and family members who have died.

Newspaper editors have known about the drawing power of obituaries for years. Chuck Ward, publisher of the *Olean (N.Y.) Times Herald*, once told his readers about the time his editor asked whether they should do a special obituary on the father of one of their employees: "My response was that unless the father (or any relative) of the employee met the criteria for a glorified obituary, the obituary should be treated as 99 percent of our obituaries are."

He then recounted that when he went to the visitation that evening, the line extended 50 yards outside the mortuary. He returned in an hour, and the line was still long. That got Ward thinking about his question earlier in the day: "What did he do?"

"All he did, apparently, was live a wonderful, loving life with a splendid family. During the course of that life, he must have touched the lives of countless people in our community. And they all were there to say goodbye."

Ward learned that people don't have to be public figures to deserve well-reported obituaries. Too many obituaries read as if they were written by a computer program—efficient but lifeless. This tendency persists despite readership surveys that show that about 50 percent of readers look at obituaries, about twice as many as those who look at most other features.

And obituaries are read critically. If the deceased belonged to the Shiloh Baptist Church, count on a phone call if you say she was a member of Bethany Baptist. Reporting and writing obituaries is important work, and you must get it right.

Despite this importance, many newspapers do not publish a news obituary unless the person who died was well-known. Television news generally follows the same policy. However, you're more likely to find staff-written obituaries in local publications, in print and online. Jim Nicholson of the *Philadelphia Daily News*, who wrote obituaries full-time and won the American Society of News Editors Distinguished Writing Award, explained why. Readers want to know, he said, "How did someone live a good life? How did they get through this world?"

An obituary is a news story. You should apply the same standards to crafting a lead and building the body of an obituary as you do to other stories.

Crafting a Lead

You begin by answering the same questions you would answer in any news story: who (Michael Kelly, 60, of 1234 West St.), what (died), where (at Regional Hospital), when (Tuesday night), why (heart attack) and how (while jogging). With this information, you are ready to start the story.

The fact that Kelly died of a heart attack suffered while jogging may well be the lead, but the reporter does not know this until the rest of the information essential to every obituary has been gathered. You also must know:

- Time and place of funeral services.
- Time and place of burial.
- Visitation time (if any).
- Survivors.
- Date and place of birth.
- Achievements.
- Occupation.
- Memberships.

Any of these items can yield the nugget that will appear in the lead. However, if none of these categories yields notable information, the obituary will probably start like this:

Michael Kelly, 60, of 1234 West St., died Tuesday night at Regional Hospital.

Another standard approach could be used later in the news cycle:

> Funeral services for Michael Kelly, 60, of 1234 West St., will be at 2 p.m. Thursday at St. Catherine's Roman Catholic Church.

However, good reporters often find distinguishing characteristics of a person's life. It may be volunteer service, an unusual or important job, service in public office or even just having a name of historical significance. Whatever distinguishes a person can be the lead of the obituary.

Building the Story

You will find most of the obituary information on a standard form from the mortuary. When the reporter relies only on the form, this is usually what results:

> Michael Kelly, 60, of 1234 West St. died Tuesday night at Regional Hospital.
> Kelly collapsed while jogging and died apparently of a heart attack.
> Services will be at 2 p.m. Thursday at St. Catherine's Roman Catholic Church. The Rev. Sherman Mitchell will officiate. Burial will be at Glendale Memorial Gardens in Springfield.
> Friends may visit at the Fenton Funeral Chapel from 7 to 9 p.m. Wednesday.
> Born Dec. 20, 1956, in Boston to Nathan and Sarah Kelly, Kelly was a member of St. Catherine's Roman Catholic Church and a U.S. Navy veteran. He had been an independent insurance agent for the last 25 years.
> He married Pauline Virginia Hatfield in Boston on May 5, 1974.
> Survivors include his wife; a son, Kevin, of Charlotte, North Carolina; and a daughter, Mary, who is a student at the University of North Carolina at Chapel Hill.
> Also surviving are a brother, John, of Milwaukee, Wisconsin, and a sister, Margaret Carter, of Asheville, North Carolina.

Writing Life Stories

The Kelly obituary is a dry biography, not a story of his life. There is no hint of Kelly's impact on friends, family or community. Good reporting produces stories of life, such as this one:

> Frank Martin loved to garden and loved to share.
> "When the ground began to thaw, he'd try to figure out how to grow things," friend and co-worker Walter Begley recalled.
> Another friend, Caroline Newby, said he would come to her home to help take care of her small vineyard. He made wine from the grapes to share with his family during the holidays. When she had problems with her crop, Mr. Martin would drive over and open the trunk of his old Dodge to reveal a nursery of soil and gardening tools.
> On the back of that car was a bumper sticker that read "Practice Random Acts of Kindness and Senseless Acts of Beauty." Newby said Mr. Martin lived by that phrase. . . .

The more traditional biographical information, along with information about visitation and funeral services, appears later in the story.

When writing a life story, you ask people what was important to the deceased and what the evidence for that is. If the subject volunteered, find out where and why and talk to the people served. Your goal is to capture the theme of the person's life. If family members and friends recognize the deceased in your story as the person they knew, you have done your job.

Sources of Information

Writing an obituary or life story is like writing a feature story. You seek anecdotes that reveal the person. Your sources include the mortuary form, your publication's own library, and family and friends of the deceased (and possibly their paid funeral notices).

The Mortuary Form

For many reporters, the standard form from the mortuary is the primary source of information. The mortuary can be of further help if you need more information. Does your city editor want a picture of the deceased? Call the mortuary. They can usually obtain one quickly from the family. Is there some conflicting or unclear information on the form? Call the mortuary for clarification.

Writing obituaries from the mortuary's information alone is a clerk's work. As a reporter, you should go beyond the form. You should also confirm every fact on the sheet. Mortuary forms are notoriously inaccurate.

Sometimes, what the mortuary form doesn't tell you is as important as what it does. For the writer of the following obit, the first clue that the death notice was unusual was the age. The deceased was 12. That alone was enough for the reporter to start asking questions. The result was an obituary that moved from the records column to the front page:

Sandra Ann Hill, 12, lost her lifetime struggle against a mysterious muscle ailment Wednesday night. The day she died was the first day she had ever been admitted as a hospital inpatient.

Although they knew it was coming, the end came suddenly for Sandra's family and school friends, said her father, Lester, of 1912 Jackson St.

Just last Friday, she attended special classes at the Parkdale School. "She loved it there," Hill said. "Like at recess, when the sixth graders would come in and read to her. She always wanted to be the center of attention."

"Bright as a silver dollar" was the way one of Sandra's early teachers described her. In fact, no one will ever know. Sandra couldn't talk.

"We didn't know what she knew or didn't know," her father said. Sandra's only communication with the world around her came in the form of smiles and frowns—her symbols for yes and no.

"There were times when I'd come around the corner and kind of stick my head around and say 'boo,'" her father recalled. "She smiled. She liked that."

The care and attention Sandra demanded makes the loss particularly hard for her family to accept, Hill said. "I can't really put it into words. You cope with it the best you can, keep her comfortable and happy. We always took her with us."

Sandra came down with bronchitis Friday. Complications forced her to be admitted Wednesday to Lincoln County Hospital, where she died later that night.

Sandra's fight for life was uphill all the way. It started simply enough when she was 4 months old. Her mother, Bonnie, noticed she "wasn't holding up her head" like her other children.

Although her ailment was never firmly diagnosed, doctors found Sandra's muscles held only half the tissues and fibers in a normal child's body. The diagnosis: a type of cerebral palsy. The prognosis: Sandra had little chance to live past the age of 2. Medical knowledge offered little help.

Sandra was born in Springfield on Jan. 15, 1984. She is survived by her parents; one brother, Michael Eugene Hill; one sister, Terrie Lynn Hill, both of the home; and her grandparents, Gordon Hill of Seale, Alabama, and Mrs. Carrie Harris of Phoenix, Arizona.

TIPS

Sources for Obits

- Mortuary forms.
- Paid funeral notices.
- The newsroom's library.
- Interviews with family and friends of the deceased.

Services will be at 3:30 p.m. today at the Memorial Funeral Chapel with the Rev. Jack Gleason conducting. Burial will follow at the Memorial Park Cemetery.

The family will receive friends at the Memorial Funeral Home until time for the service.

The reporter who wrote this obituary clearly did a great deal of research beyond what was on the mortuary form. Because the girl was not a public figure, the reporter could not simply do an internet search or consult a national publication. But the reporter did have access to the newspaper library and could interview the girl's family and friends.

The Newsroom Library

In the newsroom library, you may find an interview with the deceased, an interesting feature story or clips indicating activities not included on the mortuary form. In an interview or feature story, the person may have made a statement about a philosophy of life that would be appropriate to include in the obituary. The subject also may have indicated his or her goals in life, against which later accomplishments can be measured. You can find the names of friends and co-workers in the clips as well. These people are often the source of rich anecdotes and comments about the deceased.

Your newsroom files are not the only source for information on people who have state or national reputations. You or your librarian should also search electronic databases for stories that have appeared elsewhere.

Interviews with Family and Friends

Journalists treat public figures in more detail than private citizens not only because they are newsworthy but also because reporters know more about them. Even though private citizens are usually less newsworthy, many good stories about them are never written because the reporter did not—or was afraid to—do the reporting. The fear is usually unfounded.

Cause of Death

If the person who died was not a public figure and the family does not wish to divulge the cause of death, some news organizations will comply. That is questionable news judgment. The reader wants to know what caused the death. A reporter should call the mortuary, the family, the attending physician and the appropriate medical officer. Only if none of these sources will talk should you leave out the cause of death.

A death certificate must be filed for each death, but obtaining it often takes days, and some states do not make the cause of death part of the public record. Even if the state lists the cause of death and the reporter has timely access to the death certificate, the information is often vague.

If the deceased was a public figure or a young person, most newspapers insist on the cause of death. If the death is the result of suicide or foul play, reporters can obtain the information from the police or the medical examiner. Some newspapers

TIPS

Policy Options for Handling Obits

- In an obituary, ignore any embarrassing information, and if necessary, omit the cause of death. If circumstances surrounding the death warrant a news story, run it separate from the obituary.
- Include embarrassing details and the cause of death in all obituaries.
- Include embarrassing details and the cause of death in an obituary only for a public figure.
- Put a limit on how far back in the person's life to use derogatory information such as a conviction.
- Print everything thought newsworthy that is learned about public figures but not about private figures.
- Print everything thought newsworthy about public and private figures.
- Decide each case as it comes up.

> **"** I don't write about death, I write
>
> about life. **"**
>
> — Michael Best, *The Detroit News*

include suicide as the cause of death in the obituary, others print it in a separate news story, and still others ignore it altogether. This is one way to report a suicide:

> Services for Gary O'Neal, 34, a local carpenters' union officer, will be at 9 a.m. Thursday in the First Baptist Church. Coroner Mike Pardee ruled that Mr. O'Neal died Tuesday of a self-inflicted gunshot wound.

Private or Embarrassing Information

Another newspaper policy affecting obituaries concerns private or embarrassing information. When the *St. Louis Post-Dispatch* reported in an obituary that the deceased had been disbarred and that he had been a key witness in a bribery scandal involving a well-known politician 13 years earlier, several callers complained. The reader's advocate for the paper defended the decision to include that history in the obituary:

> One who called to complain about the obit told me it reminded her of the quotation from Shakespeare's *Julius Caesar*, about how the good a man does is often buried with him and forgotten.
>
> Yes, I said, and the first part of that quotation could be paraphrased to say that the news a man makes often lives after him.

When author W. Somerset Maugham died, *The New York Times* reported that he was a homosexual, even though the subject generally had not been discussed in public before. Yet many years later, when Susan Sontag died, few publications included the fact that she had acknowledged her bisexuality in a newspaper interview, even though Sontag herself clearly wasn't embarrassed by this information.

Most editors believe that a person's sexual orientation really isn't news in the era of same-sex marriages. While that's generally true for everyday citizens, it still often becomes big news when a celebrity like Olympic medalist Bruce Jenner goes through sexual reassignment and becomes known as Caitlyn Jenner. That story was big news throughout the country.

When Bill Mauldin, a Pulitzer Prize–winning editorial cartoonist, died in 2003, the *Chicago Sun-Times*, where he had worked for years, wrote, "In his last years, Mr. Mauldin battled alcoholism and Alzheimer's." Alzheimer's is often reported as a cause of death, but describing someone as an alcoholic in an obit is unusual. The *Sun-Times*, of course, was in a position to know, and its reporting was brutally honest.

The crucial factor in determining the extent to which you should report details of an individual's private life is whether the deceased was a public figure or a private person. A public figure is someone who has been in the public eye. A participant in civic or social activities, a person who spoke out at public meetings or through the mass media, a performer, an author, a speaker—these all may be public figures. A public official, an individual who has been elected or appointed to public office, is generally treated like a public figure.

Whether the subject is a public figure or a private citizen, the decisions newspapers must make when dealing with the obituary are sensitive and complicated. It is your obligation to be aware of your organization's policy. In the absence of a clear policy statement, consult an editor.

TIPS

Choosing Your Words

- Avoid euphemisms; such terms are out of place in a news story. People don't "pass away." They die. If a "lingering illness" was cancer, say so.
- Watch your language as you report the cause and circumstances of the death.
- Be careful with religious terms.

SUGGESTED READINGS

Center on Crime, Communities and Culture and *Columbia Journalism Review. Covering Criminal Justice.* New York: Graduate School of Journalism, Columbia University, 2000. This manual lists resources that will help reporters cover crime and the courts.

Giles, Robert H., and Robert W. Snyder, eds. *Covering the Courts: Free Press, Fair Trials and Journalistic Performance.* Piscataway, N.J.: Transaction, 1999. This book provides useful guidance from professional journalists.

Pulitzer, Lisa Beth. *Crime on Deadline: Police Reporters Tell Their Most Unforgettable Stories.* New York: Boulevard, 1996.

Real stories from nine of the nation's top crime reporters are featured in this book.

Siegel, Marvin, ed. *The Last Word:* The New York Times *Book of Obituaries and Farewells: A Celebration of Unusual Lives.* New York: Quill, 1998. Examples abound of well-written and compelling obituaries from *The New York Times.*

Singer, Eleanor, and Phyllis M. Endreny. *Reporting on Risk: How the Mass Media Portray Accidents, Diseases, Disasters and Other Hazards.* New York: Russell Sage Foundation, 1993. The authors take a critical look at media reporting of accidents and disasters.

SUGGESTED WEBSITES

www.fbi.gov

The FBI website provides useful information about crime.

www.fema.gov

The Federal Emergency Management Agency, part of the U.S. Department of Homeland Security, provides assistance during major emergencies. This site provides useful background information and contacts.

www.ntsb.gov

The National Transportation Safety Board website is an excellent source of accident information.

www.ojr.org

The *Online Journalism Review* has useful tips, articles and information about tools and techniques for reporting and storytelling online.

www.supremecourtus.gov

The U.S. Supreme Court is the nation's highest court. The Supreme Court's website outlines its operation.

EXERCISES

1. Working in teams, analyze the coverage of a major national crime, accident or fire story. Each team member should scrutinize the coverage of the story by a different news organization—print, online or broadcast. Then meet with the other members of your team to compare notes and discuss which stories are most satisfactory and why.

2. **Your journalism blog.** Monitor a day of local news. Take note of how many of the stories are the types covered in this chapter. Do they provide an accurate picture of your town? Do these stories meet the standards you've just learned? If not, how could they be improved? Write a blog entry of at least 500 words to report your conclusions.

3. Find an accident story in a local newspaper. List all the sources the reporter used in obtaining information for the story. List additional sources you would have checked.

4. Talk with a firefighter in your local fire department about the department's media policy at fire scenes. Using what you learn, write instructions for your fellow reporters on what to expect at fires in your city or town.

5. Cover a session of your local municipal or circuit court. Write a story based on the most interesting case of the day.

6. Research the coverage of constitutional rights as they pertain to terrorism suspects. Evaluate whether the media have done an adequate job of covering this issue. If you find fault with the coverage, describe what you would do differently.

7. Research and write the life story of a resident of your city.

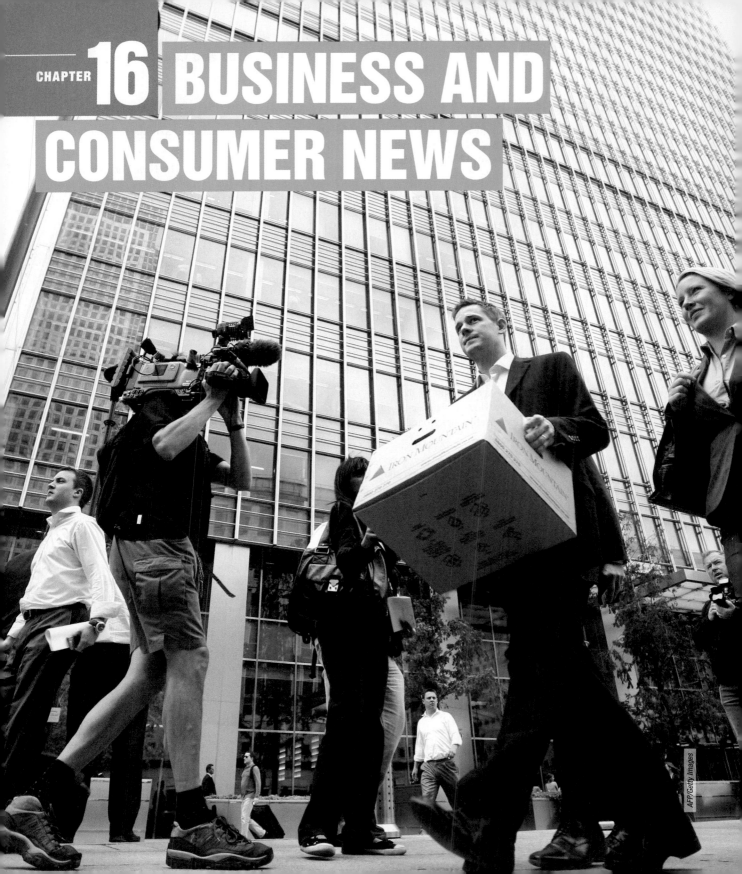

Business news is now big news. Stories about job creation or the latest tech invention lead local and national newscasts. Turn on satellite or cable television in any country around the world, and you'll find 24-hour channels like CNBC or Bloomberg following the world stock markets and broadcasting that information in English, Chinese, Arabic, Spanish, Portuguese and German. The speed of the internet and TV complicates an already hard-to-understand topic.

Many young business journalists soon find themselves at the center of the world's most important stories. One night in September 2008, a mere 14 months after graduating from journalism school, FoxBusiness.com reporter Ken Sweet found himself collaborating with editor Kathryn Vasel to piece together a story that would become one of the biggest in the financial world. The investment bank Lehman Brothers had collapsed. Says Vasel: "It was a Sunday night, and there were so many moving parts—we had Lehman collapsing and then the news broke that Bank of America was buying Merrill Lynch—any other day it would have been a huge story, but it was sidelined by Lehman, and then the problems at AIG came into the mix."

"First you have to get the straight news story out, but it doesn't end there—you have to add in company statements, reaction and what this means for the average consumer and other companies. You have to constantly massage the story to make sure it still flows with the latest add-ins while making sure the latest news is still in the lead," she says. On a major story, Vasel knew she had to get details precisely right, making sure she didn't overstate or mislead. "It was hard to swallow such a big story, but I also had to make sure to do the mundane tasks of double-checking names and titles to get it right." Vasel went on to write and produce web shows for FoxBusiness, and now works for CNNMoney.

Despite woes in many sectors of journalism, business news has seen growth, and knowledgeable young journalists have attractive job prospects. Christopher Dieterich, a 2010 graduate, now covers mutual funds and exchange-traded funds for *Barron's*, a magazine aimed at investors. Victoria Craig found work soon after graduation in 2012 at Fox Business, a network that grew rapidly after its founding in 2007. Austin Alonzo, another 2012 graduate, is back in his hometown of Kansas City, covering transportation logistics and the construction industry for the *Kansas City Business Journal*.

Business has broadened to include a featurized approach. Websites such as thepointsguy.com, which is a digital-only publication, cater to business travelers who want to maximize all those frequent flyer and credit card miles. Recent graduate Matt Zuzolo covers the travel industry for the small web publication, which operates out of start-up, shared space in New York's financial district. Zuzolo's supervisor is Zach Honig, a former tech reporter who now reports on the business of air travel. One of Honig's assignments was to cover the inaugural flight of a new A350 Airbus plane for Qatar Airways. After the plane automatically aborted its first takeoff on December 10, 2015, because it determined

In this chapter you will learn:

1
Why business journalism is growing in importance.

2
How to report business stories.

3
Where to find business stories.

4
How to understand business numbers.

5
How to find and report consumer news.

FIGURE 16.1

Zach Honig tweeted the news in real time for thepointsguy.com, his business travel website.

Zach Honig

the runway was too short, Honig tweeted: "Wow wow wow . . . Our A350 violently aborted takeoff at JFK. Got the whole thing on video" (Figure 16.1).

And even though the airline executives asked him to stop tweeting and shooting video, Honig persisted and uploaded the takeoff video to thepointsguy.com.

So, how do you get started covering business news? First, you need to understand basic business terminology and basic math. You also need to learn how to read financial statements, which is surprisingly easy. Beyond that, you need the skills of any journalist: perseverance, curiosity and an ability to ask questions and get answers.

The Importance of Business Journalism

It's clear that government intervention into markets and business is here to stay, so it's especially important for political reporters to learn the basics of business. In 2015, business news focused on the health of China's and Europe's economies and whether the declines abroad would unsettle the post-recession economy in the United States.

All stories have some sort of business angle. A quick glance at an edition of *The Wall Street Journal* shows the breadth of news with an economic component—from admissions policies at Ivy League schools to how Apple iPhone sales affect the gross domestic product of the U.S., to the latest technology employed by Procter & Gamble scientists in the $1.3 billion home hair-coloring industry.

With the passage of the Affordable Care Act, health issues are also becoming increasingly related to economics. Reporters covering health care reform need to understand the business side of medical care so they can explain these changes to their audiences. Influenza epidemics sideline workers, costing millions of dollars every flu season. The 2014-2015 measles outbreak that was started by an infected visitor to Disneyland soon spread to 121 people in 17 states, according to the U.S. Centers for Disease Control. That incident caused considerable losses to Disneyland, as well as millions in costs to local governments that tried to stop the spread of the outbreak.

But even more financially concerning was the 2014 Ebola scare. Two patients treated in Nebraska ran up a tab of $1.2 million. And *USA Today* reported that New York Sen. Charles Schumer asked the federal government to reimburse New York City for $20 million in costs for caring for one Ebola patient, including monitoring hundreds of travelers from West Africa, where the infection originated.

Yet many news directors and editors still struggle with the focus of business news. Who is their audience? Is it consumers, investors, local business executives or people looking for work? When oil prices drop, should reporters in Houston emphasize how much motorists are saving on gasoline and the rise in the number of miles driven? Or should they focus on how low prices translate into layoffs in the oil industry? Or should they focus on the politics of changing restrictions to allow the U.S. to export more oil? This array of ways to focus business stories provides an opportunity in the field of business journalism.

Business journalism has adapted to the digital world very rapidly because the internet delivers news faster, which is of high importance to traders. Financial news, including up-to-the-second stock prices, is available on mobile devices. Today's business journalists must know the ins and outs of using Twitter, Instagram, Facebook, Snapchat and LinkedIn to do their job well.

Business executives use Twitter to communicate directly to customers, and the number of business-related Facebook, Instagram and Snapchat sites continues to grow. When oil superconglomerate BP settled with the U.S. government in 2012 over its role in the Deepwater Horizon oil spill, the company took to Facebook, YouTube and Twitter to post information about its restoration effort. In 2015, the digital-only news organization *Business Insider* tweeted out a story about a boss in Texas who gave a $100,000 bonus to each of his 1,381 employees. The story was retweeted 613 times and was "liked" by more than 400 readers (Figure 16.2).

These types of public exchanges give journalists a glimpse inside the customer service operations of major companies. And that has business journalists taking to social media to cover stories, as well as monitoring social media for important trends.

FIGURE 16.2

This tweet from *Business Insider* was retweeted at least 613 times.

Business Insider

The increasing number of business news outlets, in print, online and broadcast, is just one reason why business-trained journalists are in high demand. Even in a troubled newspaper industry, these specially trained journalists often command a 20 percent premium in salary, according to Joe Grimm, a college instructor who blogs for the Poynter Institute.

Business journalism training is also important for those who seek jobs in corporate communications. About 55 percent of Americans own stock, according to Gallup, mostly through 401(k) retirement plans, and corporate communications divisions employ journalists to write about investor and consumer issues.

Specialized Business News

Local newspapers are shedding business staff members as part of a major employment decline, but those reporters are finding job opportunities at the weekly business journals that have grown and expanded in all major U.S. cities—from Fresno to Louisville to Hartford. American City Business Journals, based in Charlotte, N.C., publishes profitably in about 40 cities, with a total readership in both print and digital of about 13 million.

Pick an industry and there is a magazine, internet news site, newsletter or newspaper that specializes in covering it. Far from sleepy operations, these publications often are in the midst of breaking news. *CFO* magazine—whose audience is made up of chief financial officers in a wide range of industries—doesn't shy away from covering the scandals that have rocked the finance industry. Watt Global Media, based in Rockford, Ilinois, has covered agribusiness for nearly a century. Its *Poultry USA* publication has covered the bird flu epidemic and the resulting rise in egg prices. Its *Poultry International* publication, also available digitally, is sent to 41,000 professionals in 160 countries and includes a Chinese-language edition.

As hacking has rocked businesses worldwide, from Sony Pictures to Chick-fil-A to Staples, reporters like Sean Sposito of the *San Francisco Chronicle* write about cybersecurity and hacking. Other publications have created beats in tourism. Recent battles with the car-sharing service Uber have generated stories on the sharing economy for Allison Prang, who covers tourism and technology for *The Post and Courier* in Charleston, South Carolina. Madeline O'Leary writes about the intricacies of business deals for Dealreporter, a global digital service that reports on the minutiae of mergers and acquistions. Since its founding in 2002, Dealreporter has grown to operate digital publications in North America, Europe, Asia and Latin America.

Global Reach

Business journalism is a growing global industry. Business newspapers are now prevalent in China's major cities. *Shanghai Securities News*, founded in 1991, focuses on covering the Shanghai and Hong Kong stock exchanges as well as Asian economic news. American business media outlets have bureaus in major Asian cities and often employ multilingual reporters. It was a team of Chinese and American reporters for Dow Jones

Newswires, the fee-based industry wire service, that broke the China copper-trading scandal in 2005. Those stories won several distinguished journalism prizes.

Business journalists who work for mainstream organizations must acknowledge the often-conflicting outcomes of economic events. A story about an outbreak of mad cow disease in Washington state could have multiple effects—depressing the earnings of McDonald's but boosting the price of Brazilian beef and leading to trade restrictions from a nervous Taiwan.

And business journalists must be able to see the big picture. While many Americans have lost jobs that went to workers in India or Mexico, an increasing number of Americans now work for global employers. It surprises many that the U.S. has often led the world in foreign direct investment; funds from other countries are building businesses in every state. Workers in South Carolina make small refrigerators for Chinese-owned Haier Group. Autoworkers in southern Indiana learn Japanese manufacturing techniques while manufacturing SUVs and minivans for Toyota. And though the Great Recession was blamed on the mortgage crisis in the U.S., problems in eurozone countries like Greece and Spain, and even China's economic stall, have sent world stock markets on an up-and-down roller coaster ride.

Wide Range of Topics

The range of possible business stories is as broad as business itself. Some business stories are about a company's promotions and retirements, and some concentrate on company profits, which are of interest to investors and potential investors in that company. Other business stories cover personal finance issues that are of interest to lay readers rather than investment community insiders. Such stories explore issues such as, Which is a better choice, a 15- or 30-year mortgage? Is art a good investment? Which mutual funds are high performers? Personal finance news is so popular that there are scores of websites devoted to this topic, like money.cnn.com and the venerable Kiplinger, which started as a newsletter and now is a robust website. A business story might also be about new products, like the array of tablets or smartwatches released before every holiday season. These stories interest not just shareholders of the company but potential consumers as well. How does the latest smartphone stack up against its competitors? And what does that mean for investors? Interest in Apple products pushed the company's stock to record highs and made the Cupertino, California–based tech firm one of the world's most valuable companies.

Many stories are both global and local. A story about a decision by the Federal Reserve Board's Open Market Committee to expand or tighten the money supply may seem far removed from your audience. But that decision can affect the rate your readers pay for a car or mortgage loan. A sizable trade deficit for the U.S. may weaken the value of the dollar and increase the price of a Korean-made TV, a Volkswagen car or a bottle of Cutty Sark Scotch whiskey. It takes skill, but a good business journalist can make these seemingly esoteric stories clear and relevant to the audience.

Many important corporate and economic decisions that affect us all are made in Washington, New York, Chicago and a few other major metropolitan centers. But those cities do not have a monopoly on the creation and coverage of business news.

Even in towns of a few thousand residents, businesses will be opening or closing, and manufacturing plants will be increasing or decreasing production, hiring or firing employees. Local residents will be spending money for houses, cars, vacations or tablets, or socking it away in local banks or savings and loan associations. There is a business story in every such development.

Increasingly, economics plays a strong role in disaster coverage, second only to coverage of the loss of life. Hurricane Katrina caused at least $125 billion in economic damage when it swamped coastal areas in Louisiana, Mississippi, Alabama and Florida in 2005. Only half of that was covered by insurance. Hurricane Sandy, which devastated coastal areas in New Jersey, New York and Connecticut in 2012, cost that region more than $50 billion. The most expensive natural disaster in world history was the 2011 Tohoku earthquake and tsunami, which resulted in more than $235 billion in losses to the Japanese economy, according to the World Bank. The disaster, including the related meltdown of three nuclear reactors at the Fukushima Daiichi power plant, rocked manufacturing in Japan, caused parts shortages in Toyota plants worldwide and affected investment in the Japanese economy.

In fact, the economic risk of natural disaster is of paramount interest to investment professionals, who abide by the investing wisdom "Buy on rumor and sell on news." Two days before Katrina hit, financial news outlets like Bloomberg News and Dow Jones Newswires were already reporting the potential impact on oil drilling and gasoline refineries in the Gulf of Mexico.

Taxes are also a mainstay in business coverage, including stories aimed at consumers filing taxes each spring. But taxes are a big part of every business. Reporter Zachary Mider of Bloomberg News won a Pulitzer for explanatory reporting in 2015 for his "explanation of how so many U.S. corporations dodge taxes and why lawmakers and regulators have a hard time stopping them." It was the first Pulitzer for Bloomberg News, which was established in 1990 with just six employees and now employs more than 2,300 in offices around the globe.

How to Report Business Stories

Business stories use the same structures as other types of stories: inverted pyramid, chronology, news narrative and focus. The preparation is the same as for any other beat, but business writers also have some unique challenges.

Finding the "So What" and Avoiding Jargon

What separates a business story from a soccer story—or, for that matter, a soccer story from a story about atomic particles—is the knowledge and language required to ask the right questions, to recognize the newsworthy answers and to write the story in a way that readers without specialized knowledge will understand. A reporter who understands the subject can explain what the jargon means.

Business reporters must use understandable language. Oversimplification can turn readers off. *The Wall Street Journal* avoids both traps by shunning jargon as much as possible, explaining any technical terms essential to the story, and linking to more detailed explanations. In one story, for example, *The Journal* explained the terms "Federal Open Market Committee," "federal funds rate," "M1" and "M2." Sophisticated readers might know what those terms mean, but many of the paper's readers would not. Those interested could also find more detailed explanations through online links.

When business meets government, the jargon only increases. ProPublica reporter Cezary Podkul tackled a complex subject when state governments turned to Wall Street to convert years of payouts from tobacco settlements into instant cash, but at a steep discount. His lead:

> In November 1998, attorneys general from across the country sealed a historic deal with the tobacco industry to pay for the health care costs of smoking. Going forward, nearly every cigarette sold would provide money to the states, territories and other governments involved—more than $200 billion in just the first 25 years of a legal settlement that required payments to be made in perpetuity.
>
> Then, Wall Street came knocking with an offer many state and local politicians found irresistible: Cash upfront for those governments willing to trade investors the right to some or all of their tobacco payments. State after state struck deals that critics derided as "payday loans" but proponents deemed only prudent. As designed, private investors—not the taxpayers—would take the hit if people smoked less and the tobacco money fell short.
>
> Things haven't exactly worked out as planned.
>
> A ProPublica analysis of more than 100 tobacco deals since the settlement found that they are creating new fiscal headaches for states, driving some into bailouts or threatening to increase the cost of borrowing in the future.
>
> One source of the pain is a little-known feature found in many of the deals: high-risk debt that squeezed out a few extra dollars for the governments but promised massive balloon payments, some in the billions, down the road.
>
> These securities, called capital appreciation bonds, or CABs, have since turned toxic. They amount to only a $3 billion sliver of the approximately $36 billion in tobacco bonds outstanding, according to a review of bond documents and Thomson Reuters data. But the nine states, three territories, District of Columbia and several counties that issued them have promised a whopping $64 billion to pay them off.

Podkul started with a narrative that walked readers through the series of events. He explained the nature of the "high-risk debt"—massive balloon payments that would come due in the future. Then he stated the bottom line—"a whopping $64 billion" to be paid off. Throughout, Podkul kept the language lively and interesting—and the technical talk to a minimum.

Rather than imposing on busy readers, business reporters should develop the expertise to translate or explain technical terms. You may even have to do some math. For example, if banks change lending rates, the personal finance reporter might be the person to write the story explaining that an increase of 1 percentage point could result in higher interest rates for car or home loans.

If West Coast longshoremen go on strike, one reporter covering local corporations might explore the impact on the supplies for a local manufacturer, while a retail reporter might talk to store owners about whether they'll have the latest, hot toy on their shelves in time for Christmas.

Putting Sources at Ease

Sourcing presents a challenge for business reporters: How do you get information from someone who does not legally have to tell you anything? It often takes more creative reporting skills to coax a story from a business source than from a government official. Almost all government information is public. Many business records are not.

The mistrust that many businesspeople have of the press can make it difficult to cover stories adequately, even when it would be in the business's interest to see that the story is told. If executives are willing to talk, they may become angry if the reporter quotes an opposing point of view or points out a flaw on the corporate visage. And of course, businesses know they can often sell their "spin" on a story by reaching the public directly through their websites and social media outlets.

The best antidote a reporter can use against this attitude is to report fairly and accurately what a business is doing and saying. By always being fair, you can win the trust and confidence of businesspeople—or at least their grudging respect.

Because business executives tend to be cautious when talking with reporters, it may help you to dress more like a business manager than a concert reviewer. Appearances count. Businesspeople, like reporters, feel more comfortable with their own kind. The more you demonstrate that you understand their business, the more likely you are to generate trust. Public relations people are often helpful in providing background information and directing you to executives who can provide other comments and information, but you should try to get to know as many company executives as you can. Sometimes you can do this best through a background interview, one not generated by a crisis but intended simply to provide information about what the company is doing. Perhaps you can arrange to have lunch to see what the managers are thinking about and to give them a chance to see that you are probably not the demon that they may have thought you were.

Watching Out for Biases and Conflicts of Interest

Always remember that a company, government agency or pressure group may be trying to use you to plant stories that serve some special interest. Companies want stories that make them look promising to investors with the hope of driving up the price of their stock or that make them appear to be attractive merger partners. If you are suspicious, do some digging; talk to competitors and analysts, and ask detailed questions. Just because a company or some other group is pushing a story does not mean you have to write it.

Business journalists face conflict-of-interest challenges because they often write stories, some of which are unfavorable, about companies that buy advertising dollars from their media companies. Business editors across the country have become increasingly concerned as advertisers threaten to pull advertising over unfavorable coverage. For instance, a 2003 story in the *Orlando Sentinel* on the shoddy practices of homebuilders cost the newspaper $700,000 in canceled advertisements.

Because business news can affect market prices, business journalists must adhere to a strong code of ethics to avoid the appearance that their stories are

Nik Deogun didn't set out to be a business reporter. It took an internship with *The Wall Street Journal* to change his mind. True, he had studied economics as an undergraduate, but his reporting courses in his master's program in journalism school had emphasized government and education. He sought the internship not because of *The Journal*'s niche in business coverage but because he hoped for the chance to do the kinds of news features that appear on its front page.

He got hooked on business. "This is where the power lies, and not many people are writing about it," he says. "Money is the source of all power, the source of all evil"—and the source of good stories.

Deogun, now senior vice president at CNBC Business News Network, thinks his generalist background, both in liberal arts and in journalism, prepared him well. Business writers need to understand the social and political context in which their subjects operate.

"I use here the same reporting skills you'd use on any beat," he says. Deogun understands he must be able to speak the technical language without falling into the trap of also writing it. "Most of your readers don't know that much about business," he observes.

Clear thinking and clear writing remain essential.

Jeannine Levine.

being influenced. In addition, business journalists can be fined or even jailed if they violate U.S. securities laws and face jail time if they trade stocks based on inside information uncovered during the reporting process. In a famous case, R. Foster Winans, a former reporter for *The Wall Street Journal*, was convicted of illegal insider trading and mail fraud for tipping off a stockbroker to information he would later publish in his "Heard on the Street" columns. He served nine months in federal prison.

Where to Find Business Stories

The starting point in writing a business story is similar to the first step in reporting any story: understanding the subject you're writing about. For the business reporter, that almost always means some basic research into the subject. For openers, check your organization's archives to learn what's been written locally about your topic or company.

A broad spectrum of internet-accessible databases provides lists and summaries of stories published on a wide range of subjects. The truly adept can plumb raw data, including stock market transactions, to track the impact of announcements, mergers and personnel changes on stock prices. But everyone can use simple internet searches to access annual reports, stock analyses, press releases and other announcements. And now, many of these resources are available on mobile phone

Where to Find Business Stories

- Conduct some basic research into the subject. Check the electronic and paper archives to learn what's been written about the topic or company.
- Turn to your computer. From a broad spectrum of databases you can obtain lists and summaries of stories published on a wide range of subjects. LinkedIn, the social media site, provides autobiographical employee profiles. You can even search Facebook, as users often disclose their workplace.
- Read print sources to find stories about your business or industry. Many trade journals are available online.

apps. Journalists can use Yahoo! Finance's app to find stock quotes and business statistics in the field, or grab national or international economic statistics from the upgraded app from the Federal Reserve Economic Data (FRED)—the branch of the U.S. Federal Reserve Bank based in St. Louis, Missouri.

Any internet search of news sites will help you find stories you need for research. Reuters, Dow Jones Factiva and Bloomberg Business News provide more detailed and extensive databases of background information on companies and securities, historical prices and real-time news on business and economic issues. In addition, companies like Business Wire and PR Newswire handle thousands of news releases daily from companies and nonprofit organizations, pumping out public relations news and videos through the internet and social media. Sometimes that information causes investors to sell or buy stocks or bonds, even before journalists have the time to check that news for accuracy or "spin."

Journalists now rely on an array of aggregation websites focused on information for investors. Two examples are Yahoo! Finance and MarketWatch, which compile news on companies and provide links to government-required Securities and Exchange Commission filings and charts of historical stock prices.

Records and Reports

Here are some sources of information that you will find invaluable when writing business stories. Remember, many of these can be accessed through various online databases, so you can log on and get the information you need right away.

Corporate Data

Basic information on corporations can be found online, either on the company's own website or through government filings. Independent sources include Dun & Bradstreet Credibility Corp., which provides online information on large and small businesses. D&B also owns Hoovers.com, another business database. Standard & Poor's investigates the creditworthiness of companies and issues analysts' reports. To find suppliers and product news, check out ThomasNet.com's database of American manufacturers.

Investment Data

To get specific information about the financial performance of a company or an industry, check reports prepared by Standard & Poor's, as well as ratings competitors Moody's Investors Service and Fitch Ratings. Thomson First Call, Morningstar and Value Line discuss company prospects, forecast earnings and predict major trends. Also helpful are annual corporate scoreboards prepared by *Fortune*, Bloomberg and *Forbes*, such as their information on the wealth of individuals, Forbes World Billionaires.

Financial Ratios

To assess a company's financial picture and management, compare your subject's financial data with averages for other firms in the same industry. Industry ratios and averages can be found in reports prepared by Dun & Bradstreet, Moody's, and S&P, in a number of trade journals, and on Yahoo! Finance.

Company Filings

The U.S. Securities and Exchange Commission (SEC) mandates that companies that sell shares to the public must file detailed financial performance records. You should start with the annual report, which gives an overview of the company's operations and finances. The 10-K, a more detailed version of the annual report required by the SEC, will also give you the number of employees, a list of major real estate and equipment holdings, and information on any significant legal proceedings. Many other important documents, such as labor contracts, are listed by reference and can be acquired through the company, a Freedom of Information Act request or a private service such as Disclosure Inc. Annual reports often show up on the nightstands of business reporters. Carol Loomis, the now-retired prize-winning reporter for *Forbes* magazine, read 50 years' worth of company annual reports while researching a story on Bethlehem Steel.

Most filings are available free of charge through the SEC's online EDGAR system, but journalists often use the pay service DisclosureNet. or the newer Intelligize. Other outlets, such as MarketWatch and Yahoo! Finance, will let you set up "alerts" notifying you of news and filings on companies of interest, and are free.

Another SEC filing, the *proxy statement,* which goes to shareholders before the annual meeting or other important meetings, provides an outline of issues to be voted on, as well as executive salaries and information on the company's board of directors. The proxy also sometimes contains leads about the company's business dealings. Interesting nuggets are found under mundane headings such as "Other Matters" or "Legal Proceedings." For example, now-bankrupt Enron Corp. disclosed some hints about its offshore partnerships in the footnotes of its SEC filings. Those footnotes generated some stories, but company officials did not disclose the true extent of the company's financial problems. In any filing, always read anything pertaining to lawsuits. That, in turn, can lead you to public documents regarding a particular suit.

All publicly traded companies now release their annual report, 10-K and proxy statement on their websites, and materials can be downloaded.

Trade Press

Beyond the newspapers and magazines you already know and read is another segment of journalism known as the *trade press.* In these journals and house organs you will find grocers talking with grocers, undertakers talking with undertakers and bankers talking with bankers. You will learn the important issues in a field, how an industry markets its products and services, and what legislation it fears and favors.

A number of trade publications are independent and objective. Among them are *Advertising Age, Aviation Week & Space Technology, Institutional Investor,*

American Banker, *Editor & Publisher*, *The Wrap* and *Variety*, the last two of which cover the entertainment industry. Many more are very pro-industry; even so, they are still valuable for learning about current issues, marketing and lobbying strategies. To find trade publications, consult the *Standard Periodical Directory* or *Ulrich's International Periodicals Directory*. Most trade publications offer online versions, like www.ogj.com, the online version of the comprehensive trade publication *Oil & Gas Journal*.

Newsletters

Newsletters, which now have morphed into subscription and fee-free topic websites, have become an important source of inside information in recent years. Some are purely ideological, but others can be valuable. Among the best are *The Energy Daily*, *Nucleonics Week* and *Education Daily*. Peter Zollman, a former reporter for United Press International, runs a subscription-only print and online newsletter, *Classified Intelligence Report*, which covers the $7 billion online classified industry, which includes such companies as Monster.com and Craigslist. Other newsletters can be found by accessing the *Oxbridge Directory of Newsletters*.

Court Records

Most companies disclose only information required by the SEC. But when a corporation sues or is sued, an extensive amount of material becomes available. Likewise, criminal action against principals in a firm can lead to a good story. It is important to check court testimony and records at all levels, including those of bankruptcy and divorce courts, all of which can be found on Pacer.gov or USCourts.gov. States also offer court records online through such sites as Iowa's www.iowacourts.state.ia.us. Journalists found information about the pay package and executive perks of former General Electric CEO Jack Welch in his divorce filing.

Local Regulators

Frequently, businesses want to enlarge their facilities or expand into new markets. To do so, they may seek funds from an industrial bond authority, which helps companies obtain large sums of money at below-market rates. When an institution such as a hospital wants to expand its services, often it must make a case for the expansion before a regional or local agency. In either case, documents filed to support the request may be revealing and may put into the public record information that previously was unobtainable. Local reporters who know how to find business plan filings in the county or city planning commission office gain insight into their area's economic development. These records are public but are often underutilized by reporters.

Other Sources

The preceding lists are certainly not exhaustive. Other relevant materials may be found at local tax and record-keeping offices, as well as in filings with the Federal Trade Commission, the Federal Communications Commission, the Food and Drug

Publicly Held Companies' SEC Filings

The following is a list of places to look for publicly held companies' SEC filings:

- **13-D.** Lists owners of more than 5 percent of the voting stock. Must report increases and decreases of holdings and be filed within 10 business days.
- **13-F.** Quarterly report of ownership by institutional investors. Includes holders of less than 5 percent of the company.
- **8-K.** Report of a significant incident.
- **10-Q.** Quarterly financial statement.
- **10-K.** Annual financial statement. Includes number of employees, major real estate and equipment holdings, significant legal proceedings. Many other important documents, such as labor contracts, are listed by reference and can be acquired through the company, a Freedom of Information Act request or a private service.
- **Proxy statement.** Contains executive salaries, director information and shareholder voting issues.
- **Annual report to shareholders.** May lack much of the data found in 10-K.
- **Securities registration statement/prospectus.** Submitted when new stock is to be issued. Usually contains same information as 10-K and proxy but is more up-to-date.

Administration, the Interstate Commerce Commission and the Bureau of Labor Statistics. In addition, various state agencies, such as the secretary of state's office, compile information on businesses registered in the state.

Don't overlook the Federal Reserve—the central bank of the U.S.—which employs scores of economic analysts at each of its 12 regional banks. Eight times a year, the Fed publishes a comprehensive book of regional statistics and analysis, nicknamed the "Beige Book," which is available online at www.federalreserve.gov. FRED, based at the St. Louis Federal Reserve Bank, continues to add business and economic data to its massive collection. The Consumer Confidence Index, a survey of 5,000 sample households by the Conference Board, gauges consumer sentiment on the U.S. economy. This is an important monthly index, followed by market watchers as well as the Federal Reserve in setting interest rates.

The Department of Commerce's Bureau of Economic Analysis (www.bea.gov) allows reporters to generate economic data by county, region or state. The BEA uses data from agencies that don't issue public reports, such as the Internal Revenue Service. The Census Bureau (www.census.gov) provides timely data on many economic functions, including business inventories and monthly retail sales. Check out the bureau's Business and Industry portal. The bureau also has a smartphone app that allows reporters to access this information in the field. Graphic artists can use the Census Bureau's data visualization tools to create information graphics.

Human Sources

Who are the people you should talk to on the business beat? Here are some who are important sources of information.

Company Executives

Although many public relations people can be helpful, the most valuable information will probably come from the head of the corporation or corporate division.
Chief executive officers are powerful people, either out front or behind the scenes,
in your community. They are often interesting and usually well informed. Not all of
them will be glad to see you, although many executives value open communication
with the press. For more than a decade companies have been releasing quarterly
financial information via electronic news services like PR Newswire and Business
Wire and discussing those results in web-based public conference calls with analysts
in which journalists can listen in, but not ask questions. Transcripts of those calls are
usually available from third parties, such as Seeking Alpha, or are on the companies'
own websites.

Public Relations Sources

Don't automatically assume the public relations person is trying to block your path.
Many people working in corporate communications are truly professional, and providing information to journalists is part of their job. Remember, though, that they
are paid to make the company look good, so they are likely to point you in the direction of the company's viewpoint. Public relations professionals aren't objective, but
that doesn't mean that the information they provide is untrue. Instead, you should
assume that it is being packaged to show the company in its best light.

Academic Experts

Your college or university has faculty members with training and experience in
business and economics. Often they are good sources for local reaction to national
developments or analysis of economic trends. If you are writing about small business or agriculture, state universities operate extension services which have regional
outreach offices that can be sources.

Trade Associations

Although trade associations clearly represent the interests of their members, they
can provide expert commentary on current issues or give explanations from the
perspective of the industry. When *The New York Times* reported on the revival of
the moving industry, the Household Goods Carriers' Bureau, a major trade group,
proved to be an important source. To find trade associations, check the federal USA.
gov site, which maintains an alphabetized list.

Chamber of Commerce Officials

Chamber of commerce officials are clearly pro-business. They will seldom make an
on-the-record negative comment about business, but they usually know who is who
and what is what in the business community. The chamber may be involved in such
projects as downtown revitalization and industry recruiting. State and regional areas
all have economic development agencies that receive tax funds and are required to
file reports of recruitment activities.

KEVORK DJANSEZIAN/AP Images

Union meetings, such as this one of the United Food and Commercial Workers in Los Angeles, can be an excellent source of labor stories.

Former Employees

Many business reporters say that their most valuable sources are former employees. Business reporter and analyst Chris Welles writes, "Nobody knows more about a corporation than someone who has actually worked there." He warns, "Many, probably most, have axes to grind, especially if they were fired; indeed, the more willing they are to talk, the more biased they are likely to be." The good reporter will exercise care in using information obtained from former employees. A quick way to search is through the social media site LinkedIn. The site offers a tutorial for journalists.

Labor Leaders

For the other side of many business stories and for pieces on working conditions, contracts and politics, get to know local union officials. The workings, legal and otherwise, of unions make good stories, too.

Other Sources

Don't overlook the value of a company's customers, suppliers and competitors. You may also want to consult with local bankers, legislators, legislative staff members, law enforcement agents and regulators, board members, oversight committee members and the like. Don't forget those ubiquitous consultants, who are usually well informed and often willing to talk, if only for background. If the company you are covering is publicly traded, investor sites like Yahoo! Finance offer a list of "peer" companies.

Announcements and Meetings

The source of much business news, and the starting point for many good stories, is an announcement by a company of a new product or the firm's reaction to some action by a government agency. News conferences can take many forms—in person or via a webcast. Companies also send out news releases via electronic outlets like PR Newswire or Business Wire, or a company PR person might send news to a reporter directly by email.

If you work in a city where one or more corporations are based, you may have the opportunity to cover an annual meeting, which invariably produces some news. Many companies will restrict those meetings to shareholders, but some do allow the media to observe, particularly Warren Buffett's company, Berkshire Hathaway.

Reporter Enterprise

As in other areas of journalism, often the best business news stories are generated by a reporter's initiative, sparked by a hunch or a tip passed along by an editor, a shareholder or a disgruntled employee or customer.

In other cases, a news release may raise questions that turn into stories. For example, a routine announcement of an executive appointment may lead a curious reporter to a story about the financial problems that produced the change in leadership. Or a stockholder's question may result in a story about a new trend in corporate financing or a shift in emphasis on operations within the company. Or a former employee's call that a company is quietly laying off workers may produce a story about the firm's declining fortunes.

Looking at the Numbers

An understanding of the numbers that a business generates is essential to any intelligent analysis of a company or an industry.

More than 100 million copies of annual reports are pumped out each year, and almost all annual reports can be downloaded from the internet, as can recent recordings of "conference calls"—or the conversations company executives have with investment analysts.

Annual reports can often be complicated, and new journalists should look first at Microsoft's reports, which feature easy-to-read financial statements. A typical annual report includes:

- An opening letter from the CEO.
- Key financial data.

- Results of continuing operations.
- Market segment information.
- New product plans.
- Subsidiary activities.
- Research and development activities or future programs.
- Summarized disclosures from the 10-K report.

Most veteran reporters, such as Diana Henriques, a contributing business writer for *The New York Times*, start with the auditor's statement, which is generally located near the back of the annual report, and also examine basic financial data, footnotes and supplementary financial information. The basic auditor's report, from one to four paragraphs long, states that the material conforms to generally accepted auditing standards and that it fairly presents the financial condition of the company. But read the report closely. Sometimes auditors hint at trouble by deviating from the standard language.

Next, move on to the footnotes, where the seeds of many fascinating stories may be germinating among the innocuous prose and numbers that follow and supplement the company's basic financial data. Then, turn to the front of the annual report to find the report from the CEO. It is usually addressed "To our shareholders" and should give an overview of the company's performance.

After that, you're ready to look at the numbers. Here are a few things to watch for:

- **Balance sheet.** This report is a snapshot of the company on one day, generally the last day of the fiscal year. The left side of the balance sheet lists the *assets*, or what the company owns. On the right side are the *liabilities*, or what the company owes, and the *shareholders' equity*, or the dollar value of what stockholders own. The two sides must balance, so the balance sheet can be summarized with the following equation: assets equal liabilities plus shareholders' equity. The balance sheet shows how the year in question compares with the previous year. Reporters should note any significant changes worth exploring for a possible story.

- **Income statement.** This report, also referred to as an *earnings statement* or *statement of profit and loss*, answers this key question: How much money did the company make for the year? Look first at *net sales* or *operating revenues* and determine if they went up or down. If they increased, did they increase faster than they did last year and faster than the rate of inflation? If sales lagged behind inflation, the company could have serious problems.

- **Return on sales (ROS).** Company management and financial analysts calculate a number of ratios to gain better insights into the financial health of an organization. One important test of earnings is the relation of net income to sales, which is obtained by dividing net income by sales and multiplying the result by 100. For example, suppose a company has sales of $150,000 and, after expenses, has a net income of $30,000.

ROS = ($30,000 / $150,000) × 100
ROS = .2 × 100 = 20 percent

Cautions When Examining an Annual Report

- Remember that the numbers on an annual report are not definite.
- Look at the company's numbers both in the context of its industry and compared with several years' performance.
- Remember that cash flow from operations, which are funds that companies get from products or services they sell, and not from the sale of assets, is the true measure of a company's performance. Earnings can also come from the sale of assets or from financing, which make the balance sheet look good but aren't sustainable.
- Use the knowledge you gain in this chapter to reach preliminary conclusions that you can pursue with experts and company officials.

The ROS will tell you how much profit after expenses was produced by each dollar of sales. Reporters should remember that average percentages can vary widely by industry, but generally the higher the percentage, the better.

■ **Return on equity (ROE).** This ratio, which shows how effectively a company's invested capital is working, is obtained by dividing net income minus preferred dividends by the common stockholders' equity for the previous year. Every year since 1997, Standard & Poor's Equity Research staff has compiled a list of the best returns on equity by U.S. companies of various sizes. ROE ratios are best compared within an industry, but generally speaking, between 15 and 20 percent is considered a good ROE.

■ **Dividends.** These payments to shareholders are declared quarterly and generally are prominently noted in the annual report. Dividends are an inducement to shareholders to invest in the company. Because companies want to see dividends rise each quarter, they sometimes go so far as to change their accounting or pension assumptions so enough funds will be available to increase dividends. Other companies, such as Berkshire Hathaway Inc., declare no dividends because they prefer to reinvest profits internally. Shareholders of Microsoft Corp. complained for years that the software giant was holding on to too much cash and urged the board to return more money to its investors through higher dividends.

Now that you have an idea of how to examine an annual report and its numbers, it is time for some important words of caution. First, the numbers in an annual report, though certified by an auditor and presented in accordance with SEC regulations, are not definite because they are a function of the accounting assumptions used in their preparation. That leads to the second and third points: Look at a company's numbers both in the context of its industry and compared with several years' performance. To understand how well a firm is performing, examine the numbers along with those of other firms in the same industry. Look at how the company has performed for the last five to 10 years. Then you will discern trends instead of basing your conclusions on one year's performance, which may be atypical.

Covering Consumer News

The phrase "consumer news" is in its broadest sense arbitrary and redundant. All economic news is, directly or indirectly, about consumers. A story about the stock market may affect or be of interest to "consumers" of stocks and bonds even though those items aren't consumed in the same sense as cornflakes. A story about the price of crude oil affects consumers of gasoline and many other products refined from crude oil. A story about a drought that may drive up the price of wheat has an impact on consumers of hamburger buns.

Many news outlets, especially local and network television, run "consumer target" features that respond to consumer complaints of alleged fraud or unfair treatment by merchants or landlords.

Where to Find Consumer News

Sources of consumer news fall into three general categories: government agencies, consumer groups and private businesses. Let's consider each of these groups.

Government Agencies

Many municipalities, especially large cities, have a consumer advocate who calls public attention to problems that affect consumers. Most county prosecuting attorneys' offices also have someone—or even a whole department—who challenges business practices of questionable legality. These offices handle cases of consumer fraud in which people pay for something they do not receive or pay for something of a certain quality and receive something less.

Most states have a consumer affairs office that investigates consumer problems and orders or recommends solutions. In addition, state attorneys general investigate and prosecute cases of consumer fraud. Most states also have regulatory commissions that represent the public in a variety of areas. The most common commissions regulate rates and practices of insurance companies, rates and levels of service of utilities and transportation companies, and practices of banks and savings and loan associations. Another source is the state auditor's office, which may also uncover fraud and wrongdoing within government or government contracts.

At the federal level, government regulatory agencies involved in consumer affairs have the power to make rules and to enforce them:

- The Federal Trade Commission oversees matters related to advertising and product safety.
- The Food and Drug Administration watches over prices and safety rules for food, drugs and a variety of other health-related items.
- The Securities and Exchange Commission oversees the registration of securities for corporations and regulates the exchange, or trading, of those securities.
- The Federal Energy Regulatory Commission regulates the rates and levels of service provided by interstate energy companies.
- The Occupational Safety and Health Administration has inspectors who routinely visit and report on safety in workplaces and factories and who investigate workplace accidents.

Consumer Groups

Nongovernment consumer groups are composed of private citizens who have organized to represent the consumer's interest. They, too, are often good sources of background information or comment.

A Business Mini-Glossary

Bonds

Governments and corporations issue bonds to raise money (capital). The bonds pay interest at a stated rate and are redeemable on a predetermined maturity date.

Constant Dollars

Because of inflation, $10 doesn't buy in 2016 what it did in 1991. Constant dollars take inflation into account by figuring their value compared with a base period.

Consumer Price Index

A measure of the relative price of goods and services, the CPI is based on the net change compared with a base period. An index of 115 means the price has increased 15 percent since the base period. Thus, to report the significance of a rise or drop in the CPI, you need to know the base year.

Dow Jones Industrial Average

The Dow is the principal daily benchmark of U.S. stock prices. It is based on the combined value of 30 major stocks, which are changed on a regular basis. Those stocks, despite the name, are no longer purely industrial, and they represent some companies listed on the NAS-DAQ and not the New York Stock Exchange. Companies on the list range from Apple to McDonald's and Exxon Mobil. Though the Dow is widely used, some prefer the accuracy of the Standard & Poor's index of 500 top U.S. companies, known as the S&P 500. Both are often expressed in terms of percentage rise and fall, which allows for comparison.

Individual Retirement Accounts

IRAs and Roth IRAs are restricted savings accounts whose earnings (as well as some contributions) are tax-free until withdrawal.

Mutual Funds

These funds are collections of bonds, stocks and other securities managed by investment companies. Individuals buy shares in them much as they buy shares of stock, but mutual funds provide more diversity.

Stocks

A share of stock represents a piece of a company. The price varies from day to day. Blue chip stocks are generally less volatile stocks that are meant for long-term investing. The price per share of blue chip stocks does not generally increase at any sort of going rate, but these stocks can give decent or large returns in the long term.

Consumer Federation of America, an advocacy and education nonprofit, and Consumers Union, an independent group that publishes the popular *Consumer Reports*, are general in nature. Many states have public-interest research groups. Other organizations, such as the Sierra Club, which concentrates on environmental matters, are such strong advocates that their information might, at times, be anti-business. Other groups may be more local in scope. They may try to enact legislation that promotes recycling, or they may fight what they perceive as discrimination in the way banks and savings and loan associations make housing loans.

Private Businesses

Almost all large corporations and many smaller ones have public relations departments, which try to present the company in the most favorable light and attempt to mask the scars as much as possible.

Because of the successes of the consumer movement, a number of companies have taken the offensive and have instituted programs they deem to be in the public interest. Oil companies tell drivers how to economize on gasoline, electric utilities tell homeowners how to keep their electric bills at a minimum and even to use solar and wind power, and credit card companies suggest ways to manage money better.

A new breed of websites, like Bankrate.com, are independent sources of information for consumers on lending rates and credit cards, though their advertising support comes from the credit industry.

How to Report Consumer Stories

Consumer stories may be exposés, bringing to light a practice that is dangerous to consumers or that increases the price of a product or service. Research for such stories can be simple and inexpensive to conduct, and the findings may arouse intense reader interest. The project can be something as simple as buying hamburger meat at every supermarket in town to see if all purchases weigh what they are marked. Theo Keith, while a reporter at WISC-TV in Madison, Wisconsin, found that 50 local gas stations with faulty meters were shorting customers on gasoline purchases.

Susan Lundine, a reporter for the *Orlando Business Journal*, scoured Florida state insurance records to detail claims from the hurricanes that crisscrossed the state in 2004: Charley, Frances, Ivan and Jeanne. Lundine found, for example, that homeowners who lived in 12 counties on Florida's east coast, 370 miles from where Ivan made landfall, claimed more than $65 million in damages from that storm. The *Business Journal* ran a county-by-county map of claims for each of the four storms, which starkly showed how ludicrous some of the claims were. The state reacted, investigating additional cases of potential insurance fraud.

Consumer stories may also be informational, intended to help readers make wiser or less expensive purchases. Other consumer stories can be cautionary, warning readers of impending price increases, quality problems with products or questionable practices of business or consumer groups. Such stories can have great impact. Dozens of magazines and books focus on consumer news, from stories on what to look for when building a new house to advice on how to select a good nursing home.

Consumer stories can put news organizations at odds with advertisers. It was a consumer story that led to a lawsuit against *The Denver Post* when it published a story about a dry cleaner that consistently lost customers' clothes.

SUGGESTED READINGS

Cohen, Sarah. *Numbers in the Newsroom: Using Math and Statistics in the Newsroom.* 2nd ed. Available in e-edition from Investigative Reporters and Editors. http://store.ire.org/products/numbers-in-the-newsroom-using-math-and-statistics-in-news-second-edition-e-version

Houston, Brant, and Investigative Reporters and Editors. *The Investigative Reporter's Handbook: A Guide to Documents, Databases and Techniques.* 5th ed. New York: Bedford/St. Martin's, 2009. This valuable guide should be on every reporter's shelf. See especially the chapter on business.

Lewis, Michael. *The Big Short: Inside the Doomsday Machine.* New York: W. W. Norton, 2010. Lewis provides a gripping explanation of the housing and credit bubbles of the 2000s.

Morgenson, Gretchen. *The Capitalist's Bible: The Essential Guide to Free Markets—and Why They Matter to You.* New York: HarperCollins, 2009. This guide offers a good discussion of business terms and concepts.

Sorkin, Andrew Ross. *Too Big to Fail: The Inside Story of How Wall Street and Washington Fought to Save the Financial System—and Themselves.* New York: Viking Adult, 2009. This is an excellent chronicle of the Wall Street collapse in 2008.

Sviokla, John, and Mitch Cohen. *The Self-Made Billionaire Effect: How Extreme Producers Create Massive Value.* New York: Portfolio, 2014. The authors studied 800 self-made billionaires, including Mark Cuban, to determine what makes them successful in adding value to their companies.

Taparia, Jay. *Understanding Financial Statements: A Journalist's Guide.* Chicago: Marion Street Press, 2004. Taparia, a popular trainer in business journalism, walks journalists through complicated financial statements.

Wilkins, Lee, Martha Steffens, Esther Thorson, Greeley Kyle, Kent Collins and Fred Vultee. *Reporting Disaster on Deadline: A Handbook for Students and Professionals.* New York: Routledge, 2012. This handbook describes how to cover disasters in today's internet age. See the chapters on economic damage and consumer fraud.

SUGGESTED WEBSITES

www.bea.gov, www.bls.gov and www.census.gov
These sites, from the U.S. Department of Commerce and the U.S. Department of Labor, offer overviews of the U.S. economy and exhaustive studies about each segment of the economy.

www.business.com
This directory of business websites offers information about individual companies and industries.

www.businessjournalism.org
This website, funded by the Donald W. Reynolds National Center for Business Journalism, at the Walter Cronkite School of Journalism and Mass Communication at Arizona State University, offers tips and tutorials for business journalism professionals and students.

www.finance.yahoo.com
This portal is an accessible and free index of corporate financial filings, stock prices and corporate news.

www.investorwords.com
This is one of many commercial sites with reliable definitions of words used in finance.

www.ire.org/nicar/database-library
The National Institute for Computer-Assisted Reporting provides access to databases and training in how to use them to analyze business, economic and regulatory information.

www.sabew.org
The Society of American Business Editors and Writers, at the Walter Cronkite School of Journalism and Mass Communication at Arizona State University, can be a good source for contacts, story ideas and student training opportunities. Students can join the organization for a modest fee.

EXERCISES

1. Jobs are the lifeblood of an economy because workers as well as businesses pay taxes. Journalists must understand unemployment rates. Go to the U.S. Bureau of Labor Statistics and find the press release on the latest monhly job numbers. Find the states with the highest and lowest rates. Now find how those statistics have changed from month to month and year to year. Now, thinking critically, what would "seasonal adjustment" mean in employment statistics? Find your state and write two paragraphs on your findings. Also think what you would do next to tell the story through people.

2. **Your journalism blog.** Find newspaper, television and internet stories on the same business topic, such as the latest employment statistics, which are released each Friday. Compare the stories in terms of their detail and sources used. Which is the most informative? Which is the most interesting? Write a blog post explaining your findings.

3. Identify a local business reporter. Study her or his work, and then interview the reporter. Ask about sources, story ideas and career opportunities.

4. Download a prospectus on a mutual fund, and study its investment rationale. Or read a prospectus on a stock offering, and study its price-earnings ratio, yield on dividends and other value indicators. Find commentary on the fund or stock on the web, and explain its performance.

5. Use LexisNexis or the SEC's EDGAR database and edgar-online.com to find the 10-K report on a publicly traded company with a local operation.

Make no mistake—in-depth reporting that uses documents and data to supplement human sources is in demand. Just look at what Mark Horvit, executive director of the global organization Investigative Reporters and Editors, reported to members about the state of investigative journalism in the summer 2014 issue of *The IRE Journal*:

> With a growing number of available news and information sources for audiences to choose from, simply reporting what is happening is not enough. Many news organizations see "investigative reporting" as the brand that can differentiate them. . . .
>
> Today, there is a greater expectation in a growing number of newsrooms that more of those on staff will know how to dig deeper and add meaning, context and value to every story of significance. Many of the managers who contact me looking for someone to fill a vacant position want reporters who know how to read a budget, comb through court records and make open records requests. We all know that hasn't always been the case.

A few examples, taken from the IRE Awards presented in 2015, show how journalists are producing exemplary, in-depth multimedia projects with human sources, documents and data.

- *The Arizona Republic* won an award in the "Print/Online-Medium" category for uncovering poor conditions and long wait times in the Phoenix Veterans Affairs Health Care System. The reporting team found that as many as 40 patients died while waiting to see VA physicians. The team also discovered that VA officials manipulated patient wait-time reports, so the delays appeared shorter than they actually were. *The Republic*'s web report included text stories, video interviews, a photo-rich timeline and an interactive map showing delays at VA facilities across the country.

- NPR and *Mine Safety and Health News* won in the "Radio/Audio" category for their reporting on how some 2,700 U.S. mining companies were allowed to skirt payment of $70 million in delinquent fines levied by federal regulators. A reporter on the project uncovered the extent of the unpaid fines by analyzing data from the U.S. Mine Safety and Health Administration, which is supposed to protect miners. NPR's reporting included traditional broadcast audio. Its web package included the broadcast audio, text stories, a table showing the 10 coal mine operators with highest unpaid fines and a bar chart showing injury rates by mine type.

- KHOU won in the "Broadcast/Video—Medium" category for its report showing how Houston Police Department officers had falsified traffic tickets so they could collect more in overtime pay resulting from court appearances. A reporter cross-referenced traffic ticket data with GPS data from the officers' locations. The investigation ran on the air and the web, with video, text and photos helping present the stories.

In this chapter you will learn:

1

How the tradition of investigative reporting grew.

2

What the process of investigative reporting is.

3

How to find and use human and written sources.

4

How reporters analyze data for their stories.

5

How investigative stories are being presented on multiple platforms and produced by teams.

**macmillanhighered.com
/newsreporting12e**
Watch **"Investigative Reporting
Resources."**

- How does investigative
  reporting differ from the usual
  reporting journalists do?
- What different challenges do
  government, nonprofit and
  commercial sources pose for
  investigative reporting?

Investigative Reporting: An American Tradition

Investigative reporting has a rich history in American journalism. The fiercely partisan editors of the Revolutionary era dug for facts as well as the mud they hurled at their opponents. In the early 20th century, investigative reporting flowered with the "muckrakers," a title bestowed angrily by Theodore Roosevelt and worn proudly by journalists. Lincoln Steffens explored the undersides of American cities, one by one, laying bare the corrupt combinations of businessmen and politicians that ran them. Ida Tarbell exposed the economic stranglehold of the oil monopoly. And Theodore Dreiser, Upton Sinclair and Frank Norris revealed the horrors of working life in factories and meatpacking plants.

Just as the work of the muckrakers appeared in magazines, nonfiction books and even novels, the work of today's investigative reporters is produced beyond traditional newsrooms. One prominent example of 21st-century muckraking is a nonprofit called ProPublica, which was established in 2007. Funded initially by foundation grants and led by a former editor of *The Wall Street Journal*, ProPublica's staff of experienced journalists tackles major investigations of national significance, often in partnership with traditional news organizations.

As economic pressures force staff cuts in traditional newsrooms, other investigative innovations are emerging at local and regional levels, too. For example, reporter Andy Hall, who decided to leave his newspaper when the staff was reduced,

Ida Tarbell, one of the original muckrakers, helped set the pattern for investigative reporting with her exposé of Standard Oil.

Courtesy of the Ida M. Tarbell Collection, Special Collections, Pelletier Library, Allegheny College

has launched the Wisconsin Center for Investigative Journalism (WisconsinWatch .org), a nonprofit cooperative that seeks to pick up where diminished newsrooms are leaving off. Another pair of veteran journalists have formed the New England Center for Investigative Reporting (necir-bu.org), another nonprofit funded by startup grants and staffed by experienced reporters. Similar efforts are under way across the country. Many of the startup news organizations rely on multimedia and interactive storytelling to connect with their primarily online audiences.

Today's investigators, like the original muckrakers, are not satisfied with uncovering individual instances of wrongdoing. They look at organizations as a whole, at entire systems, often analyzing computer databases to gain a better understanding. They seek not only to expose but to explain. In many cases, they also seek to change the problems and abuses they reveal. Many, perhaps most, investigative reporters think of themselves as more than chroniclers of fact or analysts. They also see themselves as reformers. This, too, was true of the muckrakers.

The drive to expose abuses is something the public welcomes and expects from journalists. Studies have shown that the consumers of journalism support investigative reporting when it leads to reforms. There's no conflict between investigative reporting and the journalistic standard of objectivity, either. You'll remember from Chapter 1 that objectivity doesn't have to mean neutrality. In journalism, as in science, objectivity is the method of searching for the truth. Just as scientists are not expected to be neutral about the desirability of curing disease, journalists don't have to be neutral about exposing wrongdoing. What objectivity requires of both scientists and journalists is honest, open-minded investigation and truthful reporting of the results of that investigation.

The Process

Most investigations start with a hunch or a tip that something or someone deserves a close look. If a preliminary search bears out that expectation, a serious investigation begins. When enough information has been uncovered to prove or modify the reporter's initial hunch, it's time to analyze, organize and produce the story.

Beginning the Investigation

No good reporter sets out on an investigation unless there is some basis for suspicion. That basis may be a grand jury report that leaves something untold or a tip that some public official is on the take. It may be a sudden upsurge in drug overdoses, or it may be long-festering problems in the schools. If you don't have some idea of what to look for, an investigation is too likely to turn into a wild-goose chase.

Acting on the tip or suspicion, together with whatever background material you have, you form a hypothesis. Reporters hardly ever use that term, but it is a useful one because it shows the similarity between the processes of investigative reporting and scientific investigation. In both, the hypothesis is the statement of what you think is true. Your informal hypothesis might be "The mayor is a crook" or

"The school system is being run incompetently." It is a good idea to clearly state your hypothesis when you begin your investigation. By doing so, you focus on the heart of the problem and lessen the possibility of any misunderstanding with your editor or other journalists who might be working with you.

Once the hypothesis is stated, the reporter—like the scientist—sets out to support it or show that it is not supportable. You should be open to the possibility that your first assumption was wrong. Reporters—like scientists—are not advocates. They are seekers of truth. No good reporter ignores or downplays evidence just because it contradicts his or her assumptions. In journalism, as in science, the truth about a situation is often sharply different from what is expected. Open-mindedness is an essential quality of a good investigative reporter. Remember, too, that you may have a good story even if your hypothesis is not supported.

Carrying Out the Investigation

The actual investigative work usually proceeds in two stages. The first is what Robert W. Greene, a legendary reporter and Pulitzer Prize–winning editor for *Newsday*, named the **sniff**. After you form a hypothesis, you nose around in search of a trail worth following. If you find one, the second stage, serious investigation, begins.

Preliminary checking should take no more than a day or two. Its purpose is not to prove the hypothesis but to determine the chances of proving it. You make that effort by talking with the most promising source or sources, skimming available records and data, and consulting knowledgeable people in your newsroom. The two questions you are trying to answer at this stage are these: (1) Is there a story here? and (2) Am I going to be able to get it? If the answer to either question is no, there is little point in pursuing the investigation.

When the answer to both questions is yes, the real work begins. It begins with organization. Your hypothesis tells you where you want to go. Now you must figure out how to get there. Careful organization keeps you on the right track and prevents you from overlooking anything important as you go. Many reporters take a kind of perverse pride in their illegible notebooks and cluttered desks. As an investigative reporter, you may have a messy desk, but you should arrange your files—paper and electronic—of information clearly and coherently. Begin organizing by asking yourself these questions:

- Who are my most promising sources? Who is likely to give me trouble? Whom should I go to first? Second? Last?
- What records and data do I need? Where are they? Which are public? How can I get to the ones that are not readily accessible?
- What is the most I can hope to prove? What is the least that will still yield a story?
- How long should the investigation take?

Then draw up a plan of action, such as the one shown in Figure 17.1. Experienced reporters often do this mentally. But when you are a beginner, it's a good idea to write out a plan and go over it with your editor, news director or producer. Your

2/26/16   Plan for Mayor Jane Jones story

Hypothesis: Mayor Jones accepted improper campaign contributions from Top Construction as a council member, and as mayor she later awarded the company a contract to build a new high school.

Initial source: During the course of a conversation, XX casually suggested info about the campaign contribution.

Draft: Due 3/7.

Questions
–How much of this hypothesis can I prove?
–Is XX trustworthy? What does XX have to gain? Will XX go on the record?
–Will documents or data support the hypothesis? What records are important?
–What other people should I interview—on both sides?
–Will I have at least two credible sources for each fact?
–How can I make sure the story is relevant, useful and interesting?
–Is this one story or a series?

Plan
Request and review relevant documents and data:
–Any docs from XX.
–Campaign contribution records; get Stacy to help w/ this.
–Contract bids for HS; ask Manuel how to compare.

Interview major people:
–XX, to follow up on initial info.
–Schools chancellor about bids.
–Mayor's campaign manager (Roberts?) about contributions.
–Pres. of Top Construction (Smythe?) about contributions.
–Mayor.

Write outline:
–What's the lead?
–Story structure: inverted pyramid?
–Enough facts? details? anecdotes? quotes?

Build multimedia team for presentation:
–How do we want to present the story?
–What video, audio, print and interactive elements do we need to create?
–Involve other journalists, as needed, to help with digital storytelling.

Write draft:
–Is the story complete? easy to follow? convincing? compelling?

Next steps:
–Editor? legal department?
–Need more facts? details?
–Revise and finalize draft?
–With editors, schedule print, broadcast and digital publication and social media use.

FIGURE 17.1

A plan of action lists the hypothesis and the steps the journalist will take to gather information and draft a story.

supervisor may spot some holes in your planning or have something to add. And an editor, news director or producer is more likely to give you enough time if he or she has a clear idea of what has to be done.

Allowing flexibility for the unexpected twists that most investigations take, carry out your plan. During your first round of interviews, keep asking whom else you should talk to. While you are checking records, look for references to other files or other people.

Be methodical. Many investigative reporters spend an hour or so at the end of every day adding up the score, going through their notes and searching their memories to analyze what they have learned and what they need next. Some develop elaborate, cross-indexed files of names, organizations and incidents. Others are less formal. Nearly all, however, use a code to disguise the names of confidential sources so that those sources will remain secret even if the files are subpoenaed. The method you use isn't important as long as you understand it. What is vitally important is that you have a method and use it consistently. If you fail to keep careful track of where you're going, you may go in the wrong direction, or in circles. Many investigative journalists will keep notes in a file format, such as Word, that can be easily searched.

Getting It Right

The importance of accuracy in investigative reporting cannot be overstated. It is the essential element in good journalism of any kind. But in investigative reporting especially, inaccuracy leads to embarrassment, to ruined reputations and sometimes to lawsuits. The reputations ruined are often those of the careless reporter and the newspaper. Most investigative stories have the effect of accusing somebody of wrongdoing or incompetence. Even if the subject is a public official whose chances of suing successfully for libel are slim (see Chapter 19), fairness and decency require that you be sure of your facts before you publish them in print or online.

Many experienced investigators require verification from two independent sources before they include an allegation in a story. That is a good rule to follow. People make mistakes. They lie. Their memories fail. Documents can be misleading or confusing. Check and double-check. There is no good excuse for an error.

Writing the Story

Most investigative stories require consultation with the media company's lawyer before they are published, posted online or broadcast. As a reporter, you will have little or nothing to say about the choice of your organization's lawyer. That lawyer, though, will be an important part of your investigative career. The lawyer will advise on what you can print safely and what you cannot. Most editors, producers and news directors heed their lawyers' advice. If you are lucky, the lawyer will understand and sympathize with good, aggressive journalism. If he or she does not, you may find yourself forced to argue for your story. You will be better equipped for such an argument—few reporters go through a career without several—if you understand at least the basics of the laws of libel and privacy. Chapter 19 outlines those laws, and several good books on law for journalists are listed in the Suggested Readings at the end of that chapter.

The last step before your investigation goes public is the writing and rewriting of the story. After days or weeks of intense reporting effort, the actual writing strikes some investigative reporters as a chore—necessary but unimportant. That attitude is disastrous. The best reporting in the world is wasted unless it reaches an audience. Your hard-won exposé or painstaking analysis will disappear without a trace unless your storytelling attracts the audience and maintains their interest. Most reporters who are serious about investigative reporting recognize this. They stress good storytelling almost as much as solid reporting.

Selecting an Effective Story Structure and Lead

How do you tell the results of a complicated investigation? The general rule is, as simply as you can. One approach is to use a **hard lead** (an inverted pyramid lead that reports newly discovered facts), displaying your key findings in the first few paragraphs. Another option is to adopt one of the alternative approaches to storytelling explained in Chapter 10.

C.J. Chivers, a reporter for *The New York Times*, in 2014 reported how U.S. soldiers were being harmed by abandoned chemical weapons in Iraq. Here's how he began the story:

> The soldiers at the blast crater sensed something was wrong.
> It was August 2008 near Taji, Iraq. They had just exploded a stack of old Iraqi artillery shells buried beside a murky lake. The blast, part of an effort to destroy munitions that could be used in makeshift bombs, uncovered more shells.
> Two technicians assigned to dispose of munitions stepped into the hole. Lake water seeped in. One of them, Specialist Andrew T. Goldman, noticed a pungent odor, something, he said, he had never smelled before.
> He lifted a shell. Oily paste oozed from a crack. "That doesn't look like pond water," said his team leader, Staff Sgt. Eric J. Duling.
> The specialist swabbed the shell with chemical detection paper. It turned red— indicating sulfur mustard, the chemical warfare agent designed to burn a victim's airway, skin and eyes.
> All three men recall an awkward pause. Then Sergeant Duling gave an order: "Get the hell out."

The best stories are usually about people, and this one is no exception. The drama of one event introduces readers to the bigger story. A few paragraphs later, Chivers reveals that big picture:

> From 2004 to 2011, American and American-trained Iraqi troops repeatedly encountered, and on at least six occasions were wounded by, chemical weapons remaining from years earlier in Saddam Hussein's rule.
> In all, American troops secretly reported finding roughly 5,000 chemical warheads, shells or aviation bombs, according to interviews with dozens of participants, Iraqi and American officials, and heavily redacted intelligence documents obtained under the Freedom of Information Act.

> "Go to the scene of the disaster and don't let the breaking story stop you from thinking ahead. There, you will find almost all of the sources to tell you what went wrong in responding to the disaster. Though you will have to get your proof through public-record requests, you will get your leads at the scene."
>
> — *James Grimaldi*, The Wall Street Journal
> *Source: James Grimaldi, as told to author (GK)*

GRAMMAR CHECK

What's the grammar error in this sentence?

Critics in Congress slammed the White House for what they say is its ineffective disorganized campaign to train a Syrian rebel army against ISIS.

See Appendix 1, Rule 7.

Moving from the particular to the general is both a logical progression and an effective way to show readers both the humanity and the full scope of the investigation.

Including Proof of the Story's Credibility

Notice that the last paragraph quoted above also lets readers know something about how the information was developed. That's important, too, if you want to be believed. You owe it to your audience to be as open as possible about not only what you know but how you know it. In this era of diminished credibility, it's especially important to do everything you can to be honest and open about your work.

Striving for Clear, Simple Explanations

Writing an investigative story so that it will have an impact on its audience takes the same attention to organization and detail as does any good writing. Here are a few tips that apply to all types of storytelling but especially to investigative stories:

- **Get people into the story.** Any investigation worth doing involves people in some way. Make them come alive with descriptive detail, the kind we were given in the story about abandoned chemical weapons in Iraq.

- **Keep it simple.** Look for ways to clarify and explain complicated situations. When you have a mass of information, consider spreading it over more than one story— in a series or in a main story with a sidebar. Think about how videos, photos, charts, graphs, interactives or lists can be used to present key facts clearly. Don't try to include everything you know, just enough to support your conclusions. More than that is too much. Link to documents and other source materials referenced in your reporting.

- **Tell the audience what your research means.** A great temptation in investigative reporting is to lay out the facts and let people draw the conclusions. That is unfair to both you and your audience. Lay out the facts, of course, but explain what they add up to. A team of reporters who investigated the deplorable conditions in juvenile treatment centers wrote this lead: "In residential treatment centers across Illinois, children are assaulted, sexually abused and running away by the thousands—yet state officials fail to act on reports of harm and continue sending waves of youths to the most troubled and violent facilities, a Tribune investigation found." Then the team went on to show the reality that led to that summary. If the facts are there, drawing the obvious conclusions is not editorializing. It is good and helpful writing.

- **Organize before you write.** Careful organization is as important in writing the investigative story as it is in reporting it. The job will be easier if you have been organized all along. When you are ready to write, examine your notes again. Make an outline. Pick out your best quotes and anecdotes. Some reporters, if they are writing more than one story, separate their material into individual folders, one for each story. However you do it, know what you are going to say before you start to write.

ON THE JOB Tips for Strong Investigative Work

Mark Greenblatt is an award-winning investigative reporter for Scripps Washington bureau, where he digs into high-impact national stories. Before that, Greenblatt reported in small towns and big cities, and for a major national network.

He has won the Peabody Award three times, most recently at Scripps for "Under the Radar," a 2014 series that revealed how sex offenders convicted in military courts used loopholes to evade registration when rejoining civilian society. Congress stepped in, citing the reports and passing reforms that President Barack Obama signed into law.

Greenblatt says the keys to strong investigative work are the same at every level and offers this advice:

Connect with new sources in person, not over email or phone, whenever possible. Find smart people who value public service and know the issue you are researching. Reassure them you are looking for off-the-record "tour guides," who won't necessarily be quoted, but can teach you where to look and identify documents or data that you should request.

Matt Anzur.

After you get your data, don't get lost in it. Bring it alive by highlighting the compelling people who are affected by the issue.

Most important, never give up. Agencies sometimes hunker down and try to get through a big critical story. Be relentless, though, about searching for new and strong follow-up stories to keep the pressure on and the story in the public eye. In Greenblatt's experience, the biggest reforms come only after repeated reporting to advance the original story.

At Scripps, Greenblatt has found he can advance a story by telling it online using other platforms. For instance, many local television stations may only offer three minutes for an investigative story. Scripps journalists employ platforms like podcasts and digital interactives to extend the reach of stories. They are able to connect with the audience in other ways or provide localized information

■ **Suggest solutions.** Polls have shown that readers prefer investigative stories that show how to correct the problems described in the stories. Many of today's best news organizations are satisfying readers' demands by going beyond exposure in search of solutions. Are new laws needed? Better enforcement of present laws? More resources? Better training? Remember that the early-20th-century progressive movement (of which the original muckrakers were a part) produced reforms, not just good stories.

■ **Use the web to support your story.** Your audience is skeptical. People want to be shown, not just told. So even if your story is aired first on television or radio, use your organization's website to post supporting documents, photographs, audio or transcripts of key interviews. And include any responses or defenses offered by the people or institution you're examining. Fairness is essential. In addition, use the web to visualize your data. Create news applications that allow your audience to interact with and find information that's meaningful to them.

Think of writing as the climax of a process that begins with a hypothesis, tests that hypothesis through careful investigation, checks and double-checks every fact, and satisfies the concerns of newspaper editors and lawyers. Every step in that process is vital to the success of any investigative story.

Planning the Multimedia Aspects of the Story or Series

As seen in the examples throughout this chapter, news organizations have been presenting more of their stories digitally. Traditional news organizations, such as newspapers and television, are using online platforms to build on the print or broadcast reporting that they've always done. Startup news organizations, such as ProPublica and The Center for Investigative Reporting in California, exist primarily on the web and use digital tools extensively in their storytelling.

ProPublica, for example, uses news applications to allow its audience to interact and engage with databases. The Debt by Degrees news app at https://projects.propublica.org/colleges/ lets people search to see how much colleges financially support poor students. In 2014, CIR launched a new public radio program, Reveal. Reveal is also available as a podcast, a medium that has been experiencing a surge in popularity in recent years.

News organizations that produce digital investigative journalism are relying on teams to get the job done. No one journalist—let alone an investigative reporter—has all the skills needed to create a rich interactive experience for the audience. Multimedia investigative packages often require help from videographers, digital photographers, web producers, news application developers, interactive designers, graphic artists, reporters and editors. This list is by no means comprehensive.

At least 15 journalists at *The Wall Street Journal* contributed to its Medicare Unmasked series in 2014 that won the Pulitzer Prize for investigative reporting the next year. Two editors oversaw a team of seven reporters, including some data journalists. In addition, five graphic artists contributed to the project about fraud in Medicare billing. The graphic artists created a news application that allowed audience members to look up Medicare billing data for their own doctors in addition to contributing other visual interactive charts to help show the story.

The *Chicago Tribune*, a finalist in the 2015 Pulitzer Prize for investigative reporting, also relied heavily on multimedia storytelling for Harsh Treatment, its expose of abuses in Illinois state residential treatment centers for disadvantaged children. In its contest entry questionnaire for the 2014 IRE Awards, the *Tribune* lists three reporters, a photographer, videographer, artist, graphic designer and two editors contributing to the project. Also contributing were 51 paid journalism interns from Northwestern University, who helped file open-records requests and compile information from them. Online, the *Tribune* used photo slideshows and video to help show the story. It used graphic essays, created by the artist, to show the story in yet another way (see Figure 17.2).

Successfully executing a digital investigative project takes time and planning. Early in the process, reporters should talk to their editors or producers to determine the best way to present the story or stories. Then, the editor or producer should put together the team to produce the story. Good editors will ensure that all the key players are present and able to contribute their thoughts early.

FIGURE 17.2

A graphic artist for the *Chicago Tribune* created online graphic essays to help show how children in the Illinois state system for troubled children were being harmed.

Investigative storytelling is a process that takes collaboration and teamwork. Investigative reporters need to be part of that process from the start. Because the story can change as the reporters develop more information, it's important for the team to meet regularly about any progress or obstacles.

The Sources

Investigative reporters get their information from people, documents or data. The perfect source is a person who has the pertinent documents and is eager to tell you what those documents mean. Don't count on finding the perfect source. Instead, expect to piece together the information you need from a variety of people and records. Some people will not be at all eager to talk to you, and some of the records will be difficult to obtain—and, if you do gain access to them, difficult to understand. Let's consider human sources first.

Human Sources

Suppose you get a tip that the mayor received campaign contributions under the table from the engineering firm that just got a big city contract. Who might talk?

- **Enemies.** When you are trying to find out anything bad about a person, his or her enemies are usually the best sources. More often than not, the enemies of a prominent person will have made it their business to find out as much as possible about that person's misdeeds and shortcomings. Frequently, they are happy to share what they know with a friendly reporter.

- **Friends.** Friends are sometimes nearly as revealing as enemies. In trying to explain and defend their friend's actions, they may tell you more than you knew before.

Occasionally, you may find that someone your subject regards as a friend is not much of a friend after all.

■ **Losers.** Like enemies, losers often carry a grudge. Seek out the loser in the last election, the losing contender for the contract, the loser in a power struggle. Bad losers make good sources.

■ **Victims.** If you are investigating a failing school system, talk with students and their parents. If your story is about nursing home abuses, talk with patients and their relatives. The honest and hardworking employees caught in a corrupt or incompetent system are victims, too. They can give you specific examples and anecdotes. Their case histories can help you write the story. Be wary, though. One thing enemies, losers and victims have in common is that they have an ax to grind about your subject. Confirm every allegation they make.

■ **Experts.** Early in many investigations, there may be a great deal that you don't understand. You may need someone to explain how the campaign finance laws could be circumvented, someone to interpret a contract, someone to decipher a set of bid specifications. Lawyers, accountants, engineers or professors can help you understand technical jargon or complicated transactions. If they refuse to comment on your specific case, fit the facts you have into a hypothetical situation.

■ **Police.** Investigative reporters and law enforcement agents often work the same territory. If you are wise, you will make friends with carefully selected agents. They can—and frequently will—be of great help. Their files may not be gold mines, but they have investigative tools and contacts you lack. When they get to know and trust you, they will share. Most police like seeing their own and their organizations' names in the paper. They know, too, that you can do some things they cannot. You need less proof to print that the mayor is a crook than it may take to convince a jury. Most police investigators want to corner wrongdoers any way they can. You can use that attitude to your advantage.

■ **People in trouble.** Police use this source and so can you, although you cannot promise immunity or a lesser charge, as prosecutors can. A classic case is the Watergate affair, in which members of President Richard Nixon's administration recruited five men to break into the headquarters of the Democratic National Committee to wiretap phones illegally. Once the Nixon administration started to unravel, officials trying to save their careers and images began falling all over one another to give their self-serving versions of events. People will react similarly in lesser cases.

As an investigative reporter, you cultivate sources in the same ways a reporter on a beat does. You just do it more quickly. One excellent tactic is to play on their self-interest. Losers and enemies want to get the so-and-so, and thus you have a common aim. (But don't go overboard. Your words could come back to haunt you.) Friends want their buddy's side of the story to be explained. So do you. If you keep in mind that no matter how corrupt your subject may be, he or she is still a human being. That attitude may also help ensure that you treat the subject fairly.

Experts just want to explain the problem as you present it. And you just want to understand. People in trouble want sympathy and some assurance that they still merit respect. No reporter should have trouble conveying either attitude.

Another way to win and keep sources is to protect them. Occasionally a reporter faces jail unless he or she reveals a source. Even jail is not too great a price to pay to keep a promise of confidentiality. More often, the threats to confidentiality are less dramatic. Other sources, or the subject of the investigation, may casually ask, "Where'd you hear that?" Other reporters, over coffee or a beer, may ask the same question. Hold your tongue. The only person to whom a confidential source should ever be revealed is your editor.

Human sources pose problems as well as solve them. To hurt an enemy or protect a friend, to make themselves look better or someone else look worse—and sometimes simply for fun—people lie to reporters. No reporter is safe, and no source is above suspicion. They may use you, too, just as you are using them. The only reason most people involved on any side of a suspicious situation will talk about it is to enhance their own position. That is neither illegal nor immoral, but it can trip up a reporter who fails to take every self-serving statement with the appropriate grain of salt.

Sources may change their stories as well. People forget. Recollections and situations change. Pressure is applied. Fear or love or ambition or greed intrudes. A source may deny tomorrow—or in court—what he or she told you today.

Finally, sources will seldom want to be identified. Even the enemies of a powerful person are often reluctant to see their names attached to their criticisms in print. Even friends may be reluctant to be identified. Experts, while willing to provide background information, often cite their codes of ethics when you ask them to go on the record. Stories without identifiable sources have less credibility with readers, with editors and even with colleagues.

Written Sources

Fortunately, not all sources are human. Records and documents neither lie nor change their stories, they have no axes to grind at your expense and they can be identified in print. Many useful documents are public records, available to you or any other citizen on request. Others are nonpublic but still may be available through your human sources.

Remember that most, if not all, of the relevant documents—especially the public records kept by government agencies—are likely to be accessible online. Google and other search engines shouldn't be your only tools, but they are powerful ones. Use them early and often. And don't overlook the revelations, some of them unintentional, that turn up on social networking services like Twitter, LinkedIn and Facebook.

Public Records

As the examples cited earlier show, you can learn a great deal about individuals and organizations through paper and electronic records that are available for the asking if you know where to look. Let's take a look at some of the most valuable public records and where you can find them. Most of these records can be found online in nearly every jurisdiction. Some are even available for download in a file that you can import into a spreadsheet or database manager for analysis.

- **Property records.** Many investigations center on land—who owns it, who buys it, how it is zoned, how it is taxed. You can find out all that information and more from public records. Your county recorder's office (or its equivalent) has on file the ownership of every piece of land in the county as well as the history of past owners. In most offices, the files are cross-indexed so you can find the owner of the land if you know its location, or the location and size of the property if you know the owner. Those files also will tell you who holds a mortgage on the land. The city or county tax assessor's office has on file the assessed valuation of the land, which is the basis for property taxes. Either the assessor or the local zoning agency can tell you for what use the property is zoned. All requests for rezoning are public information, too.

- **Corporation records.** Every corporation must file a document showing the officers and principal agent of the company. This document must be filed with the state in which the corporation is formed and with every state in which it does business. The officers listed may be only "dummies"—stand-ins for the real owners—but you can find out at least who the stand-ins are. But that is only the beginning.

  Publicly held corporations must file annual reports with the Securities and Exchange Commission in Washington. The reports list officers, major stockholders, financial statements and business dealings with other companies owned by the corporation. Nonprofit corporations—such as foundations and charities—must file with the Internal Revenue Service an even more revealing statement, Form 990, showing how much money came in and where it went. Similar statements must be filed with the attorneys general of many states.

  Corporations often are regulated by state or federal agencies as well. They file regular reports with the regulating agency. Insurance companies, for instance, are regulated by state insurance commissioners. Nursing homes are regulated by various state agencies. Broadcasters are overseen by the Federal Communications Commission. Labor unions must file with the U.S. Department of Labor detailed statements called *5500 forms* showing assets, officers' salaries, loans and other financial information.

  Once you have corporation records, you must interpret them. Your public library has books that tell you how. Your news organization's own business experts may be willing to help.

- **Court records.** Few people active in politics or business go through life without becoming involved in court actions of some sort. Check the offices of the state and federal court clerks for records of lawsuits. The written arguments, sworn statements and answers to questions (*interrogatories*) may contain valuable details or provide leads to follow. Has your target been divorced? Legal struggles over assets can be revealing. Probate court files of your subject's deceased associates may tell you something you need to know.

- **Campaign and conflict-of-interest reports.** Federal—and most state—campaign laws now require political candidates to disclose, during and after each campaign, lists of who gave what to whom. Those filings can yield stories on who is supporting the candidates. They also can be used later for comparing who gets what from which officeholder. Many states require officeholders to file statements of their business and stock holdings. You can check these for possible conflicts of interest or use them as background for profile stories.

- **Loan records.** Commercial lenders usually file statements showing property that has been used as security for loans. Known as *Uniform Commercial Code filings*, these can be found in the offices of state secretaries of state and sometimes in local recorders' offices.

- **Minutes and transcripts.** Most elected and appointed governing bodies, ranging from local planning and zoning commissions to the U.S. Congress, are required by law to keep minutes or transcripts of their meetings.

ON THE JOB Using Data to Drive Investigations

Steven Rich is always busy. As the database editor for investigations at *The Washington Post*, he's constantly juggling several investigations.

In the past few years, he's worked on major investigations, including stories about the sale of tax liens in the District of Columbia and police civil asset forfeiture across the United States. He's also reported on the National Security Agency, using documents leaked by Edward Snowden. These projects and others have won awards including the Pulitzer Prize for public service, the Robert F. Kennedy Award for social justice reporting and national Edward R. Murrow Award. The stories have changed laws and sparked debates in areas long overdue for conversation.

Rich's daily activities differ, depending on the tasks at hand. Data journalists typically analyze, clean and scrape—or harvest—data from around the internet. Investigative data journalists also need to file open-records requests for data.

Converting government databases into formats that can be more easily used is a big part of the job. Rich often needs to convert government databases back into their original format. In some of the worst cases, Rich has had to convert scanned PDF files that the agencies could have just as easily provided in a format like Excel.

Marvin Joseph.

The most time-consuming aspect of data journalism is the cleaning up of data. To do accurate data analysis, it's important that the data are accurate. Rich spends much of his time preparing data to be internally consistent, all the while protecting the integrity of the original data. That's why Rich tracks every change he makes.

Perhaps the biggest change in journalism since the profession is the use of multimedia storytelling in investigative journalism. From the outset, the newsroom determines how to best use video, photos and graphics in investigative projects.

Another big change at the *Post* is an increased focus on investigative journalism across beats. Much of the best investigative journalism comes from beat reporters. As a result, there's much more investigative journalism being pumped out of the *Post*, almost on a daily basis. While this means more work for Rich and the need to collaborate with more reporters, he thrives on being able to work on investigative pieces on a variety of subjects.

macmillanhighered.com
/newsreporting12e
Watch **"Shield Laws and Non-Traditional Journalists."**

- Why are shield laws important to journalists and the practice of journalism? How would journalism be different without them?
- Should citizen journalists have the same shield law protections as professional journalists working for a traditional news entity? Explain.

The states and the federal government have laws designed to ensure access to public records. Many of these laws—including the federal **Freedom of Information Act**, which was passed to improve access to government records and similar state **open-records laws**—have gaping loopholes and time-consuming review procedures. Still, they have been and can be useful tools when all else fails. Learn the details of the law in your state. You can get information on access laws and their interpretations by contacting your state's open government group.

Nonpublic Records

Nonpublic records are more difficult, but often not impossible, to obtain. To get them, you must know that they exist, where they are and how to gain access. Finding out about those things requires good human sources. You should know about a few of the most valuable nonpublic records:

- **Investigative files.** The investigative files of law enforcement agencies can be rich in information. You are likely to see them only if you have a good source in a particular agency or one affiliated with it. If you do obtain such files, treat them cautiously. They will be full of unsubstantiated allegations, rumor and misinformation. Be wary of accepting as fact anything you have not confirmed yourself.

- **Past arrests and convictions.** Records of past arrests and convictions increasingly are being removed from public scrutiny. Usually these are easier than investigative files to obtain from friendly police or a prosecuting official. And usually these records are more trustworthy than raw investigative files.

"Spotlight" on Investigative Reporting Methods

For a realistic depiction of investigative reporting, check out the 2015 film *Spotlight*, about *The Boston Globe*'s exposé of sexual abuse by Roman Catholic priests. The movie follows members of the *Globe*'s Spotlight investigative team as the journalists document the priests' rape or sexual assault of hundreds of children, crimes that were later covered up by Cardinal Bernard Law and others in the church leadership.

The movie methodically shows how the four members of the Spotlight team developed the story, initially by meeting with the leader of a group for survivors of sexual abuse by priests. Getting leads from the head of the group, a survivor himself, they slowly gather information that begins to snowball.

Reporter Matt Carroll, played by Brian d'Arcy James, has a breakthrough while looking at Archdiocese of Boston directories to research church assignments of priests. He discovers that priests who've been removed because of sexual abuse complaints no longer have church assignments in the following year. Instead, he finds their assignments are listed cryptically, such being "on leave."

Carroll, a computer-assisted reporting specialist, entered the names of the priests who had been placed on leave from 1983 to 2001 into a database, which became a key reporting tool for the team. The *Globe*'s 2002 stories won the Pulitzer Prize for public service the following year.

As part of its online package at http://www.boston.com/priestabuse/, the *Globe* produced video interviews with abuse victims and uploaded court documents that it had obtained in its reporting and through an open-records lawsuit.

- **Bank records.** Bank records would be helpful in many investigations, but they are among the most difficult types of records to get. Bankers are trained to keep secrets. The government agencies that regulate banks are secretive as well. A friend in a bank is an investigative reporter's friend indeed.

- **Income tax records.** Except for those made public by officeholders, income tax records are guarded carefully by their custodians. Leaks are rare.

- **Credit checks.** Sometimes you can get otherwise unavailable information on a target's financial situation by arranging through your newspaper's business office for a credit check. Credit reports may reveal outstanding debts, a big bank account, major assets and business affiliations. Use that information with care. It is unofficial, and companies that provide it intend it to be confidential. Plus, details about your credit check will later appear on the subject's report, for your subject to possibly see.

Problems with Written Sources

Even when you can obtain them, records and other written sources present problems. They are usually dull. Records give you names and numbers, not anecdotes or sparkling quotes. They are bare bones, not flesh and blood.

Documents and data can be misleading and confusing. Many highly skilled lawyers and accountants spend careers interpreting the kinds of records you may find yourself pondering without their training. Misinterpreting a document is no less serious an error than misquoting a person. And it's easier to do.

Documents usually describe without explaining. You need to know the "why" of a land transaction or a loan. Records tell you only the "what."

Most investigative reporters use both human and documentary sources. People can explain what documents cannot. Documents and data can help prove what good quotes cannot. You need people to lead you to documents and data and people to interpret what those mean. And you need documents and data to substantiate what people tell you. The best investigative stories combine all types of sources.

Computer-Assisted Reporting

The almost unlimited storage capacity of computers and the flexibility of digital technology enable journalists to combine text and video with links to original documents and to related information stored anywhere in the world. Journalists also use computers to analyze data and to create knowledge that nobody had before. CAR has been practiced by U.S. journalists for decades. Computers assist reporting in two main ways:

- Journalists can access digital information from databases on the internet. (See Chapter 5 for more about these resources and how to tap them.)

- Journalists can become knowledge creators by compiling and analyzing information that was previously not collected or not examined. (See Chapter 7 for more about using numbers.)

macmillanhighered.com /newsreporting12e
Watch **"The Power of Images: Amy Goodman on Emmett Till."**

- It's easy to form a mental image of Emmett Till based on Goodmann's description. Can you think of another historical image that is similarly powerful?

- Because they can evoke strong feelings, images can be used to persuade people. Think of a media image that changed your mind about something. Why was it so effective?

David Herzog, academic adviser to the National Institute for Computer-Assisted Reporting (NICAR), teaches University of Missouri students and hundreds of practicing journalists from all over the world how to use their computers as more than word processors. His students learn how to acquire data from government agencies, nonprofit organizations and other researchers. Then they place the information into a searchable database, such as an Excel spreadsheet, so they can analyze the data. Often they match information from two or more databases to find something even policymakers didn't know. To learn more, or to get help with your own reporting, go to www.ire.org/nicar. There you can benefit from computer-assisted learning.

Take, for instance, the topic of police shootings. Jo Craven McGinty was a graduate student at Missouri who mastered analytic techniques and worked part time for NICAR, helping professional journalists tell statistics-based stories. She came across an FBI database on the use of weapons by police officers. When she accepted an internship at *The Washington Post*, she took with her that knowledge and a story idea. Months later, as part of the *Post*'s investigative team, she helped tell the story that Washington police used their guns to shoot civilians more often than police in any other city. The story won a Pulitzer Prize for the *Post*. She later joined *The Wall Street Journal*, where she writes a column, "The Numbers."

Not all computer-assisted reporting leads to Pulitzers, but much of it reveals important information that otherwise would remain hidden in bureaucratic files. Sometimes those stories are hidden in plain sight, and the data must just be appropriately configured to be understood. Herzog is an expert in computer mapping, which is the use of special software programs to display information in maps to reveal significant patterns. Crimes, for example, can be mapped to show the truly dangerous areas of a city. Outbreaks of disease can be mapped to help identify sources of infection. Patterns of immigration or unemployment or voting can be demonstrated more clearly by electronic maps than words alone could describe.

SUGGESTED READINGS

Herzog, David. *Data Literacy: A User's Guide*. Los Angeles: Sage Publications, 2016. This hands-on book introduces journalism students to fundamental data skills. Herzog, an associate professor at the Missouri School of Journalism, based the book on his experience teaching student and professional journalists.

Houston, Brant. *Computer-Assisted Reporting: A Practical Guide*. 4th ed. New York: Routledge, 2015. Houston, holder of the Knight Chair in Investigative and Enterprise Reporting at the University of Illinois, has written an invaluable how-to guide for using the newest and most powerful reporting tools.

Houston, Brant, and Investigative Reporters and Editors. *The Investigative Reporters' Handbook: A Guide to Documents,* *Databases and Techniques*. 5th ed. New York: Bedford/St. Martin's, 2009. This handbook tells you how to get and how to use the most important records and documents.

The IRE Journal. Publication of Investigative Reporters and Editors Inc., 141 Neff Annex, Missouri School of Journalism, University of Missouri, Columbia, MO 65211. Every issue has articles on investigations, guides to sources and documents, and a roundup of legal developments.

Silver, Nate. *The Signal and the Noise*. New York: Penguin Press, 2012. The creator of ESPN's FiveThirtyEight blog explains how to evaluate predictions in fields ranging from politics to the weather.

SUGGESTED WEBSITES

www.icij.org

This site takes you to the work of the International Consortium of Investigative Journalists, whose ongoing Secrecy for Sale investigation has been documenting the offshore investments of powerful businessmen and politicians. The site is a great resource for examples of groundbreaking cross-border investigative projects.

www.ire.org

Begin here. Investigative Reporters and Editors, headquartered at the University of Missouri, is the world's leading source of expertise, story ideas and professional and personal support for investigative reporters.

www.ire.org/nicar

The National Institute for Computer-Assisted Reporting, a partnership of IRE and the Missouri School of Journalism, teaches the skills and provides the consulting you'll need to get and analyze the data for richer, more revealing stories.

www.opensecrets.org

The Center for Responsive Politics specializes in collecting, analyzing and making available information on money and politics in elections for federal offices. The center's handbook, *Follow the Money*, is an invaluable resource for any reporter interested in the impact of money on self-government.

EXERCISES

1. Design a project. Pick a topic to investigate and then design your project. Use the format shown in Figure 17.1 as a guide. Swap completed plans with a classmate so you can evaluate each other's work.

2. **Your journalism blog.** Use your blog to share discoveries, frustrations and lessons learned while designing your project. Invite other classmates to compare their experiences.

3. Examine three stories from Steven Rich's archives at *The Washington Post* (www.washingtonpost.com/people/steven -rich). What can you learn about the stories that he's involved with, his methods and challenges? Would you like to have a job like his? Why or why not?

4. Go to www.ire.org, and find the stories that have won recent IRE awards. Choose one story from each of at least three categories. Compare the sources and techniques used. What similarities and differences do you find in different media? Which stories seem to you most complete and most satisfying? Why?

5. School board member Doris Hart reported at last week's meeting of the board that major flaws, including basement flooding and electrical short circuits, have plagued the new elementary school. She noted that this is the third straight project designed by consulting architect Louis Doolittle in which serious problems have occurred. School Superintendent Margaret Smith defended Doolittle vigorously. Later,

Hart told you privately that she suspects Doolittle may be paying Smith off to keep the consulting contract, which has earned the architect more than $100,000 per year for the past five years. Describe how you will investigate the following:

a. The sniff.
b. Human sources. Who might talk? Where should you start? Whom will you save for last?
c. What records might help? Where are they? What will you be looking for?
d. What is the most you can hope to prove? What is the least that will yield a story?

6. Choose a public official in your city or town, and compile the most complete profile you can, using only public records.

7. Use one or more of the computer databases described here and in Chapter 5 to learn as much as you can about your representative in Congress. Write the most complete investigative profile you can from the databases. In a memo, explain what additional information you'd need to complete your story and where it might be found.

8. Visit the open-data portal for the federal government (www .data.gov) and the one for your state. Identify one database on each site, and write a few paragraphs about how you could use each for further reporting.

Getty Images Sport/Getty Images

"Alex Rodriguez is the saddest $275-millionaire in the history of the world."

So wrote Fraser Seitel, a noted author and opinion writer for *O'Dwyer's* in March 2014. Seitel reports that after a year trying, A-Rod withdrew his lawsuits against Major League Baseball, the players' union and the New York Yankees and accepted his punishment for taking performance-enhancing drugs.

He would miss the entire 2014 season.

"A-Rod's capitulation was a complete and utter defeat for himself and his high-powered team of legal and public relations consultants," Seitel wrote. Rodriguez thought it was unclear whether the Yankees would take him back (he had suffered injuries), and he was not at all sure that Yankee fans ("a good portion of whom never liked Rodriguez anyway and now abhor him") would accept him back.

"One thing, however, in the sad story of Rodriguez is clear," Seitel wrote. "By choosing to take guidance from a publicity-hungry attorney rather than seeking out sound public relations advice, Rodriguez has ruined his reputation, his legacy and most likely the remainder of his life."

Except it didn't.

In his first at-bat in Yankee Stadium the following season, A-Rod was "warmly cheered." Supporters easily drowned out a "smattering of boos." His No. 13 was the most popular on jerseys in the stadium. Other jerseys spelled out #FORG1V3, combining his uniform number with the word "forgive."

On July 28, 2015, his 40th birthday, A-Rod hit his 24th home run. He had hit three home runs two days earlier. He was hitting an excellent .272. (A player who gets a hit one out of three times is batting .333—which is rarely done. In 2015, the average for all major league players was .254.) Rodriguez already had 59 RBIs, or runs batted in. His Yankee teammate Brian McCann had 94 for the entire season to lead the team.

Seitel wrote that Rodriguez "lacked public relations instincts . . . ." Yet, he wrote, "Most who know him say that Alex Rodriguez truly loves to play baseball and respects the game. If anyone could be 'coached' to present a fuller, more truthful, more sympathetic portrait of himself, it was A-Rod."

Was he coached? We know only that after lying to Katie Couric in December 2007 about taking forbidden substances, in an interview with Peter Gammons in February 2009, Rodriguez said:

> It was time to grow up, stop being selfish, stop being stupid and take control of whatever you're ingesting. And for that, I couldn't be—I couldn't feel more regret and feel more sorry because I have so much respect for this game, and, you know, the people that follow me and respect me. And I have millions of fans out there that are, you know, will never look at me the same.

You and all public relations professionals can learn something from A-Rod. The whole incident clearly demonstrated the need for those who have committed transgressions to admit them, to apologize and to act to repair any damage caused. And the longer you wait to do that, the more difficult it is to do.

If you intend to work in any area of public relations, you need to have expertise in the media and in the use of social media. Social media are not just for people who represent celebrities or who handle management or crisis communications. Internal public relations and corporate communicators want their employees to monitor social media for potential public relations crises and opportunities and to report them immediately. They also use the social media to spread the good word about their organizations.

If you are planning to work in the public relations field, you need to be prepared to use all types of media—not just print, television and radio, but also digital media, including social media networks—to get your job done.

Public Relations: A Different Approach to News

Professionals agree that the skill most required of public relations people is good writing. Journalism schools traditionally require a course in news writing for students interested in public relations, and many public relations professionals like to hire people with some news writing experience. Only by studying news and how news organizations operate will you be successful in public relations or in offices of public information. For example, knowing how reporters deal with news releases will help you write better releases. Of course, studying the news also helps you enormously in the advertising world and in what is now frequently called *strategic marketing* or *strategic communication*.

Not only do skilled public relations or public information practitioners know how to write news, but they also apply all the principles of good news writing in their news releases. Thus, a good news release meets the criteria of a good news story. Like a good story, it should have some staying power, as organizations often keep recent news releases available on their websites. You can see a typical news release in Figure 18.1. Notice that the release begins with the name of the organization putting out the release and includes the contact person's name, title, phone number and email address. If the news is for immediate release, say so. Otherwise, indicate a release date.

Public relations professionals also know that doing internal and external communications for an organization demands a specific perspective and, in many cases, a specific kind of writing. Of course, good writing is good writing, and what you have learned so far applies to public relations writing. But you also will be called on to do writing that is different from the kinds of writing journalists do.

Defining Public Relations

Rex Harlow, called by some the "father of public relations research" and perhaps the first full-time public relations educator, claimed to have found 472 definitions of public relations. One definition, in use from 1982 to 2012 according to the Public

NEWS RELEASE

FOR IMMEDIATE RELEASE: December 7, 2015   No. 15-26
MEDIA CONTACT: GARY SOMERSET 202.512.1957   mb 202.355.3997 | gsomersst@gpo.gov

NEW MEXICO LIBRARY JOINS GPO PROGRAM AS ALL-DIGITAL MEMBER

WASHINGTON—The U.S. Government Publishing Office (GPO) designates The Institute of American Indian Arts (IAIA), a land-grant institution of higher learning in Santa Fe NM, as the newest all-digital member of GPO's Federal Depository Library Program (FDLP). The Institute will provide patrons with digital-only access to Federal Government publications at no cost.

###

U.S. GOVERNMENT PUBLISHING OFFICE | KEEPING AMERICA INFORMED | OFFICIAL | DIGITAL | SECURE
732 North Capitol Street, NW, Washington, DC 20401-0001 | **www.gpo.gov** | **www.fdsys.gov**

Follow GPO on **Facebook** http://www.facebook.com/USGPO, **Twitter** http://twitter.com/USGPO,
Pinterest http://pinterest.com/usgpo/, and on **YouTube** http://www.youtube.com/user/gpoprinter.

Relations Society of America, was simple: "Public relations helps an organization and its publics adapt mutually to each other."

In 2012, PRSA selected this definition by a public vote: "Public relations is a strategic communication process that builds mutually beneficial relationships between organizations and their publics."

Not that the new definition—or any definition—will stop the critics of public relations. Rick Rice, an independent consultant with more than 35 years of experience in public relations, says, "It takes more than a new definition to change the way people perceive the public relations industry." The public "has a fundamental lack of respect for PR practitioners," he says. This lack of respect can only be corrected in two ways:

1. By focusing on measurement and accountability.
2. By improving training and development.

This chapter will help you with your training and development. It will be up to you to increase the respect people have for what you do.

FIGURE 18.1

A traditional news release follows AP style. Note that this release includes the line "For immediate release" at the top. The release also indicates whom to contact, and how, for more information and gives social media links. This release is distributed both as a PDF (shown) and in a text (HTML) version on the organization's website.

We've looked at the new definition of public relations. In *Public Relations: Strategies and Tactics*, Dennis Wilcox, Glen Cameron, and Bryan Reber write that these key terms are essential to understand:

- **Deliberate:** The "activity is intentional . . . designed to influence, gain understanding, provide feedback, and obtain feedback."
- **Planned:** "organized . . . systematic, requiring research and analysis."
- **Performance:** "based on actual policies."
- **Public interest:** "mutually beneficial to the organization and to the public."
- **Two-way communication:** "equally important to solicit feedback."
- **Management function:** "an integral part of decision-making by top management."

Public relations, then, is not just publicity, which seeks to get the media to respond to an organization's interests. Nor is it advertising or marketing, which are more directly concerned with sales. Through advertising, an organization pays to get the attention of the public, and marketing combines a whole host of activities to sell a product, service or idea.

A Range of Interests

If you wish to write in the field of public relations, you have many areas from which to choose.

- **Media relations:** seeking publicity and answering questions posed by the media.
- **Government affairs:** spending time with legislatures and regulatory agencies and doing some lobbying.
- **Public affairs:** engaging in matters of public policy.
- **Industry relations:** relating to other firms within the industry and to trade associations.
- **Investor, financial or shareholder relations:** working to maintain investor confidence and good relationships with the financial world.

More and more today, the term **strategic** communication is replacing "public relations," perhaps because the demands made of public relations professionals are greater today than they were a generation ago. As Ronald Smith explains in *Strategic Planning for Public Relations*:

> No longer is it enough merely to know *how* to do things. Now the effective communicator needs to know *what* to do, *why* and how to *evaluate* its effectiveness. Public relations professionals used to be called upon mainly for tasks such as writing news releases, making speeches, producing videos, publishing newsletters, organizing displays and so on. Now the profession demands competency in conducting research, making decisions and solving problems. The call now is for strategic communicators.

Social media came as an enormous boon to public relations. Agencies are now able to make available "social media platforms, creative-digital services, content development, website and app design, logo design and naming, experiential marketing, licensing, business results measurement and market research."

In short, the strategic communicator must take a more scientific approach, do some research, make careful choices and, when finished, evaluate the effectiveness of the completed program. Such a communicator would certainly be expected to write clearly and precisely, but differently from reporters.

Objectivity and Public Relations Writing

In traditional reporting, journalists strive to remain unbiased. They should not set out to prove something. Certainly, they should not be advocates for a point of view. They should get the facts, and let the facts speak for themselves.

By contrast, columnists do have a point of view, and good ones find ways to support it convincingly. Editorial writers use facts to persuade people to change their minds, to confirm their opinions, or to get people to do something or to stop doing something. (See Figure 1.1 in Chapter 1 for a comparison of how reporters and commentators approach accuracy, fairness and bias in writing.)

That's also what public relations writers do. Though sometimes they wish only to inform their audiences, they most often want to do what editorial writers do: persuade the audience to accept a particular position.

However, there's one major difference. News commentators serve the public. Public relations writers work for an organization or for a client other than a news operation. Their job is to make that organization or client appear in the best possible light. Effective public relations writers dare not ignore facts, even when the facts are harmful or detrimental to the cause they are promoting. But because they are promoting a cause or looking out for the best interests of the people for whom they are working, they will interpret all news, even bad news, in the most favorable light.

Public relations writers work much the way attorneys work for clients—as advocates. They should not lie or distort, but they might play down certain facts and emphasize others. In its "Official Statement on Public Relations," the Public Relations Society of America says:

> Public relations helps our complex, pluralistic society to reach decisions and function more effectively by contributing to mutual understanding among groups and institutions. It serves to bring private and public policies into harmony. . . . The public relations practitioner acts as a counselor to management and as a mediator, helping to translate private aims into reasonable, publicly acceptable policy and action.

The PRSA has a code of ethics for the practice of public relations. The code, given in full on its website (www.prsa.org), requires members to "adhere to the highest standard of accuracy and truth," avoiding extravagant claims or unfair comparisons and giving credit for ideas and words borrowed from others. It also requires members not to "knowingly disseminate false or misleading information."

macmillanhighered.com /newsreporting12e
Watch **"Give and Take: Public Relations and Journalism."**

- What are the pros and cons for the public if journalists become more trusting of PR practitioners than have been in the past?
- The PR practitioner in the video talks about putting a positive spin on negative events. Can you think of a time you thought someone was putting a "spin" on an event? How credible did the report seem?

The Main Focus of Public Relations Writing

Public relations personnel are concerned with three things: the message, the audience and the media used to deliver the message.

The Message

To be an effective public relations professional, you must know the message your organization wants to send. That message might focus on a product, a program or the organization itself. For every message you work on, you must first know what you hope to accomplish, even if your purpose is just to inform.

The following news release is typical for an association of administration that exists to keep its members informed:

> **Do You Know the Difference Between Your Company's Disaster Risk and Its Preparedness Level?**
> **Advisory Date:** Wednesday, July 22, 2015
> **Advisory Number:** MA15-42
> **Contact:** Carol Chastang (202) 205-6987
>
> WASHINGTON—Human nature—the tendency to believe that a natural or man-made disaster will never occur—often undermines the clear-headed work needed to create a business continuity plan. In a recent study done by Staples, less than half of small businesses said they were prepared for severe emergencies.
>
> Each year, lack of disaster preparedness takes a severe financial toll on small businesses. Meanwhile, with solid planning, a business owner can protect both financial and human capital, developing an organization resilient enough to withstand any kind of threat.
>
> Learn how preparedness affects your company's bottom line at a free webinar on Wednesday, August 5, hosted by the U.S. Small Business Administration and Agility Recovery.
>
> SBA has partnered with Agility to offer business continuity strategies at its "PrepareMyBusiness" website. Visit www.preparemybusiness.org to access past webinars and get additional preparedness tips.
>
> The SBA provides disaster recovery assistance in the form of low-interest loans to homeowners, renters, private nonprofits and businesses of all sizes. To learn more, visit www.sba.gov/disaster.
>
> **WHAT:** "The Impact of Preparedness on the Bottom Line"
> A live presentation, followed by a question and answer session.
> **WHEN:** Wednesday, August 5, 2015—2 p.m. to 3 p.m. ET
> **HOW:** Space is limited. Register at http://agil.me/prep4bottomline

The release is clear, concise and complete. The final paragraph reminds readers of the help available to them on the SBA website.

The Audience

Almost as important as knowing all you can about the message is knowing the audience to whom you are directing the message. The better you target your audience, the more effective you will be. As in advertising, the demographics and psychographics (the interests, attitudes and opinions) of your target audience determine the way you write your message, the language you choose and the simplicity or complexity of the piece you create.

Who are these people, what are their attitudes, and what do they do for work and recreation? You will answer these questions somewhat differently if you write for internal audiences (employees or managers) or external audiences (the media, shareholders, constituents, volunteers, consumers or donors).

Ford Motor Company did more than use public relations to target its audience—it truly involved its audience. In a news release about the new Ford Fiesta, Jim Farley, Ford Motor Company executive vice president of global marketing, said, "Fiesta was designed to reflect the individuality of the customer, so we feel the marketing efforts should give the reins to the people who will be driving it."

The release says that "Ford was the first automaker to truly introduce social media and now, the evolution of the Fiesta Movement" took them to a new level.

Ford advertising and media manager Keith Koeppen added, "Consumers—Millennials in particular—like being a part of the brands they feel represent them. This demographic is accustomed to creating content about their lives, so it just makes sense to give their creativity a bigger platform with greater scale.

"It's all part of the democratization of the media," he said.

At a career forum at Boston University, Professor Edward Boches said Ford conducted "a brilliant PR social campaign to launch the Fiesta by giving the car to 100 socially savvy content creators."

He went on to say that the promotion generated hundreds of stories, millions of views, thousands of new customers and gave Ford "valuable learning about a generation it hopes to win over."

When JCPenney chose Ellen DeGeneres for its spokesperson, the conservative anti-gay group One Million Moms thought the company made a big mistake. It threatened a boycott. JCPenney trusted its choice and continued letting the popular talk-show host do the talking in ads nationally. The ads were a great success, and the boycott ended as quickly as it began.

Other groups used public relations over the JCPenney issue to their advantage. The Gay and Lesbian Alliance Against Defamation used the controversy to call attention to the fact that in 29 states a person could be fired just for being gay. Membership in GLAAD increased by 50,000. A Facebook group called "1 Million People Who Support Ellen for JCPenney" quickly attracted more members than One Million Moms.

The Media

Once you have mastered the message or product and targeted the audience, you have to choose the media through which to deliver that message.

Research shows that the more media you use, the better chance you have to succeed. That's why effective public relations people, like those in advertising, think in terms of campaigns and strategies. A campaign assumes that you can't just tell an audience once what you want them to learn, retain and act on. It's far more effective to send the message in a mix of media in a carefully timed or orchestrated way. To do this, you must learn what each medium does best.

ON THE JOB Know Why You Are Communicating

When **Mary Ann McCauley** left college with a journalism degree, she never expected to be practicing public relations. Her career has taken her from the police- and fire-beat on a daily in Mason City, Iowa, to ownership of a southern Kansas weekly (where she learned about illiteracy in America), to Hallmark, United Technologies and ultimately to her own consultancy.

The journalism training prepared her for two important skills. One, she learned to quickly grasp new information and turn it into concise and clear content. Two, she developed the skill to deliver that content to the right audience in a format that reached the audience most effectively.

"One of the things I've learned to be true is that before you touch the keyboard you need to ask: 'What do we want readers/viewers/listeners to do?'" she says. "The answer to that question always leads me to the right communication tool delivered through the most effective channel.

"You can be the best writer in the room," says Mary Ann. "But if you don't align the content with the audience's expectations and deliver it through a medium where they seek key information about the topic, you have not completed the circle of communication."

A good example is a situation Mary Ann faced early in her consultancy when a prospective client wanted to take on a local business for what he saw as an unfair business practice. "He believed that going to the local TV station's investigative crew was the answer," she says. "When I asked what he wanted to have happen as a result of the story, he realized that TV exposure wasn't the solution." He chose another non—public relations approach because Mary Ann helped him see that seeking publicity about the issue wasn't going to get the result he desired. He took a more diplomatic approach suggested by Mary Ann and got the outcome he wanted.

In the short term, Mary Ann talked herself out of acquiring the client by offering the right advice and not just doing as he suggested to gain a client. The end result, however, was a long relationship that began a few months later during which she provided several levels of counsel and secured referrals to his associates and family members.

The moral—always know why you are communicating and what outcomes you desire before you choose the tool. A single phone call or email may get you the desired result where a mass-distributed news release just gets you a two-sentence brief buried someplace.

"That's good communication; that's good public relations," she says.

Television, Radio and Newsstand Publications

For a message that nearly everyone wants or needs to know, television might be your best medium. Television offers color and motion; television can show rather than tell.

Radio listeners usually are loyal to one radio station. They will listen to your message over and over. The more often they hear it, the more likely they are to retain it.

Print media such as newspapers and magazines are better for complicated messages and sometimes for delicate messages. People can come back again and again to a print message. Some argue that print still has more credibility than other media.

The Internet: An All-in-One Medium

Perhaps the best way to do public relations today is through digital media. More and more people are getting the information and products they need online—from their laptop, desktop computer, smartphone or tablet. Here you have the advantages of every medium—print, video and audio—all in one. Remember, people who spend a lot of time online generally are better educated and more affluent than those who do not. They love the control they have over the messages they find online. They can click on only the information they want, and they can do so in any order they choose. They can be involved and engaged and can respond to one another.

What is so challenging about digital media is the high degree of individualization; the online world is one of "mass customization." You must present the message at different levels to different people so that every person feels as if you are writing only to him or her. It's all about individual choices and involving your readers so they will interact with you. As web usability expert Jakob Nielsen puts it, online readers are "selfish, lazy and ruthless." Just remember, successful communication online means ideally making use of video and audio, as well as print, to get your story across. (For more about writing for the digital media, review Chapter 11.)

Social Media

It is no exaggeration to say that social media have radically changed the way professionals do public relations. David Avitabile, president of JFK Communications, writes, "In many ways, social media was made for public relations and vice versa."

The advantages are enormous. As Avitabile notes, "The ability to develop a story over time, to weave in new messages, to engage with customers in meaningful ways and respond to their feedback are all features of social media."

According to recent studies, 88 percent of companies surveyed use social media outlets for PR purposes. Social media coach Sally Falkow says, "If you are looking for a job in PR or marketing, social media training and experience would be your best bet."

Nearly every area of our lives is under the influence of social media. For example, Steve Bryant and Laurie Demeritt, in a joint study "Clicks and Cravings: The Impact of Social Technology on Food Culture," found that social media are now "replacing mom as the go-to culinary source." Almost half of consumers are learning about food through social networks such as Twitter and Facebook, and 40 percent through websites, apps or blogs, they report.

Everything has become personal in today's public relations world. For example, Bryant and Demeritt report that "today's consumers want to hear from people who eat and cook food more than they want to hear from the entities who sell."

Twitter, Tumblr and other microblogging sites make it possible to send short text messages and internet links to large groups of subscribers instantaneously. In addition, social media giants like Facebook, Google+ and LiveJournal have the capacity to reach large groups with targeted messages.

All of this developed rapidly, and most experts believe that we've seen only the beginning. Print will not disappear, but the arrival of the microblog might change the way we write nearly everything.

TIPS

The 15 Most Popular Social Networking Sites

These sites ranked highest in unique monthly visitors, as of December 2015:

- Facebook
- Twitter
- LinkedIn
- Pinterest
- Google+
- Tumblr
- Instagram
- VK
- Flikr
- Vine
- Meetup
- Tagged
- Ask.fm
- MeetMe
- ClassMates

—eBizMBA

TIPS

Avoid Overused Words

Some PR workers consider certain words and phrases overused in news releases. Here are some examples you might want to avoid:

- Announcement
- Award-winning
- Cutting edge
- Exciting
- Exclusive
- Groundbreaking
- Innovative
- Proactive
- Revolutionary
- Unprecedented

And, of course, the arrival of social media teams sometimes helps do amazing things quickly. Oreo cookies had a 15-person social media team ready to respond to whatever could happen at Super Bowl XLVII.

Good thing.

The Superdome lights went out for 34 minutes. The team sprang into action and tweeted a picture of a single Oreo with the words: "Power Out? No problem. You can still dunk in the dark."

As *Wired* reporter Angela Watercutter wrote: "Touchdown Oreo."

Internal Publications, Brochures and Billboards

If you work in internal communications, you might decide to publish a newsletter or magazine for employees. A large number of corporations are now communicating with employees throughout the day using an **intranet**, an internal online service accessible only to employees. They are also using social media. As a result, most organizations have abandoned their regularly published, internal print publications.

For messages that need more explanation or study, such as health-care matters, perhaps a printed brochure will do the job best. Externally, for matters that might concern the community, you might want to use billboards in addition to paid print ads or radio and television ads. Or you might choose to write news releases and leave it to others to interpret your message.

Sometimes, however, there's no quick fix. What took a long time to build can come tumbling down quickly, and then a long rebuilding process is necessary.

Persuasive Writing

Most of the time, you will write to try to persuade people. To succeed, you must study the techniques of persuasion and use them carefully.

Your Attitude

To persuade people, you need to believe three things:

■ **People are essentially good.** If you are convinced of this, you will appeal to people's basic goodness and fairness.

■ **People are intelligent or at least educable.** Don't talk down to people; don't assume that you can trick or fool them. Of course, don't assume that just because they are intelligent and educated, they know the subject matter as well as you do. A good rule: Never underestimate the intelligence of your audience, and never overestimate what they know. A college professor with a Ph.D. in philosophy might be brilliant in that area but might know nothing about the financial markets.

■ **People are changeable.** You must believe not only that people are changeable but also that you can change them.

Six Alternatives to Sending a News Release

PR professional Claire Celsi suggests you write a news release to gather your thoughts but then not send it. Instead, do one of the following:

1. Send an email pitch. More than 90 percent of reporters say they want email pitches.
2. Make a website posting.
3. Send a tweet.
4. Send a Facebook message.
5. Pick up the phone.
6. Offer to meet the reporter for coffee if you're in the same city.

—Public Relations Princess

Credibility and Trust

More than anything else, you need to establish and maintain your credibility and the credibility of the organization you represent. Aristotle wrote that the character of the speaker is the most essential and powerful component of persuasion. Without a doubt, character is the most important attribute public relations people need to have and to develop. A sterling reputation takes a long time to build—and it can be lost in an instant.

In addition, you must assume good will on the part of your audience. You cannot persuade people by abusing them or by calling them names. You are foolish to look at a client or the public as your enemy. This is particularly true regarding your attitude toward the press. Too many public relations professionals consider the press to be the enemy, not to be trusted with the truth, to be stonewalled at every opportunity.

Executives and politicians continue to avoid answering questions and discussing issues by attacking the press. Some say Newt Gingrich won the CNN Republican presidential primary debate in South Carolina in January 2012 by doing just that. When asked about what his ex-wife said was his request for an open marriage, Gingrich replied to moderator John King:

> I think the destructive, vicious, negative nature of much of the news media makes it harder to govern this country, harder to attract decent people to run for public office. And I am appalled that you would begin a presidential debate on a topic like that.

For those words, Gingrich received a standing ovation.

Some called it good public relations. It was not. Even though he won the debate, Gingrich did not win the Republican nomination. A better approach might have been for him to use the question to explain his side of the story in a way that would help him with his longer-term goal of gaining the nomination.

> "The next time you become incensed about something the media has done—or you want to go on a crusade—call your travel agent and go on a golfing vacation instead."
>
> — Bill Huey, president of Strategic Communication, O'Dwyer's PR Report

News Releases That Get Attention

Perhaps nothing that you will be called on to write is more important than news releases. This is true, in spite of what people such as Simon Dumenco, the "Media Guy" columnist for *Advertising Age*, have written: "The long-suffering, much-maligned press release, I'd argue, finally died this summer, thanks particularly to JetBlue and BP, with a little moral support from Kanye West and just about every other celebrity with thumbs."

For what it's worth, a Google search for "Is the press release dead" shows about 99,600,000 results. But don't be deceived. Not all of those results are about its death.

In an article entitled "Not So Fast" on WiredPen.com, Kathy Gill wrote, "What press releases—or blog posts—can do is provide an accessible back story that cannot or will not be included in a 30-second TV news story or a six-column-inch news story. One thing tweets do well is provide a link to more detailed information: the press release, whether its form is a classic release or the modern blog post."

> **❝**If you don't understand good journalistic style and format (who, what, when, where and why) for writing a press release, you harm your company and yourself.**❞**
>
> — *G.A. Marken, president of Marken Communications,* Public Relations Quarterly

A "2014 Disrupting the Press Release" study by Green Target that surveyed 100 journalists and a series of focus groups with reporters and editors in Chicago and New York found that 41 percent of journalists considered news releases "sometimes valuable," 25 percent "valuable," and 22 percent "very valuable." Remarkably, that means that 88 percent of journalists find some value in news releases.

Journalists indicated that the news releases had three seconds to get their attention, and nearly 70 percent said they spent less than one minute reading them. Not surprisingly—but seldom seen in news releases—53 percent of the journalists said they would find it helpful if the key information would be presented in the form of bullet points. Another 36 percent were open to the idea. Sixty-eight percent want only the facts. Seventy-nine percent say a good subject line gets them to open your news release.

Even the smallest newspaper or radio or television station gets dozens of news releases weekly. Myriads of print and electronic publications such as those in the American Business Media and the Specialized Information Publishers Association also receive dozens of public relations releases weekly. Most releases are now sent electronically or through public relations wire services. Regardless of how you send your news, your problem is still the same: How do you break through the clutter and attract the attention of the gatekeepers at these publications?

Here are some guidelines to help you get your message to your intended audience.

Know What News Is and How to Write It

The news media will not pay attention to fluff—copy that is laced with opinion or self-serving quotations. Worse, they will ridicule your work and discard it immediately. Avoid statements such as this: "Moonfield College is recognized as the foremost and most prestigious college of liberal arts in the entire Midwest." Who says?

ON THE JOB Public Relations Writing

After **Brad Whitworth** received his journalism degree, he joined the staff of a small magazine covering Illinois politics. When the magazine abruptly folded six months later, he moved into corporate communications, where he worked first for a small association and then for a large insurance company.

Whitworth has spent the past 35 years doing public relations, speechwriting and internal communications for Silicon Valley companies, including high-tech giants HP and Cisco. For 10 of those years, business travel took him to Asia Pacific, Latin America and Europe.

"For global audiences, it's important to keep your words and sentences as simple as possible," says Whitworth. "In fact, the more complex or technical your subject, the simpler your words need to be.

"Everything I learned in journalism school about making communications clear, concise, consistent and complete is even more critical when connecting with customers or co-workers halfway around the world. For most of them, English is their second language."

Today he is connected around the clock with his Cisco colleagues using technology: everything from high-definition video conferencing in his home office to hand-held instant messaging on the road. "Technology is constantly changing the ways we communicate and the way we live our lives." In addition to the latest gadgets and applications, Whitworth relies on a human network: the International Association of Business Communicators.

"I landed my job at HP through IABC's job bank and have hired dozens through the network." He's given back to IABC, too, serving as president of local chapters in Illinois and California and as the youngest chairman ever of the 16,000-member global not-for-profit organization.

"A professional association like IABC can keep you plugged in with others who do the same kind of work," he says. "You can share best practices, learn about job opportunities and take part in seminars, conferences and workshops. The profession is constantly evolving, so your learning should never stop. That's especially true after you've left campus."

Brad Whitworth.

To write for most publications, certainly for news media and the majority of print and electronic publications, you need to know Associated Press style. (See Appendix 2 for a summary of the style that is followed by most news publications.) Correct spelling, usage and grammar are essential of course, but adhering to AP style is just as important. Why should news editors take you seriously if you don't bother to write in the style of their publications? That includes knowing how to write in the inverted pyramid format (see Chapter 8). Later in this chapter you will learn different approaches to writing news releases.

Some newspapers and magazines have their own stylebooks. Quite a few magazines follow *The Chicago Manual of Style*. Be sure you know what you're doing.

Know the Structure and Operations of Newsrooms

If you do not get actual experience in a television, radio, newspaper or convergence newsroom in college, find ways to spend some time in at least one of these. Use your public relations skills to get inside and to experience what goes on there.

GRAMMAR CHECK

What's the grammar error in this sentence?

New York hedge fund manager Martin Shkreli increased the price of his newly-acquired drug, Daraprim, by 5,455 percent.

See Appendix 1, Rule 11.

The simplest and most important thing you can learn about newsrooms is that they have deadlines. Learn the deadlines of the media in your area, and respect them. This means that you should not call in a story to a television news station a half-hour before airtime. Not only will the station not use your story, but station employees will resent you and not forget the interruption at a critical time. News organizations will tell you what time you must submit a story to make the news that day.

Be sure that you make yourself available—by phone, email, fax, online, or in person—24 hours a day. Nothing is more important for a public relations practitioner. A reporter on deadline will write the story with or without you. It's *always* best that you talk to the reporter.

Know the People in the News Media and the Jobs They Hold

It's especially important to know who does what at the newspapers you contact. Sending a release addressed simply to a newspaper can be a waste of time and make you look as if you do not know what you are doing. Sending a release to the business editor or to the features editor makes more sense. Addressing by name the editor of the section in which you wish the story to appear works best.

Read what Chris Anderson, former editor-in-chief of *Wired* magazine, had to say on this subject in his blog:

> Sorry, PR people: you're blocked.
> I've had it. I get more than 300 e-mails a day and my problem isn't spam . . . it's PR people. Lazy flacks send press releases to the Editor in Chief of *Wired* because they can't be bothered to find out who on my staff, if anyone, might actually be interested in what they're pitching. . . . So fair warning: I only want two kinds of e-mail: those from people I know, and those from people who have taken the time to find out what I'm interested in and composed a note meant to appeal to that (I love those e-mails; indeed, that's why my e-mail address is public).

> "Employers want people who can write and communicate ideas—who can pull complex or fragmented ideas together into coherent messages. This requires not only technical skill but also intelligence. It also requires a love of writing."
>
> — *Thomas H. Bivins,* Public Relations Writing

News Releases That Get Used

Fraser P. Seitel, author, communications consultant and teacher, identifies the following as the eight news release topics that are most likely to be used:

1. New products or projects.
2. Personnel promotions—at least of important people.
3. Trends.
4. Conflict.
5. Topicality—"relating your news to pressing issues of the day."
6. Local heritage—tying news to community roots or history.
7. Human interest.
8. Insanity—the truly bizarre or unusual.

If the people to whom you send news releases know and trust you, they are more likely to pay attention to your releases. Sometimes you can call them with a story idea and let them write their own stories. There's nothing writers like more than to get wind of good stories. Remember, your job is to help reporters write good stories. If you can help them do that and at the same time serve your client's interests, you will be a successful public relations practitioner.

Know the Style of Writing That Fits the Medium

Do not make the mistake of sending to a radio or television station the same news release that you send to a newspaper. Do not expect busy journalists to translate your newspaper release into broadcast copy. If you can write radio or television copy (see Chapter 12), you have a much better chance of getting the copy read over the air. Remember, too, that writing for digital media (see Chapter 11) differs from writing for print.

In our social media world, sometimes you can tweet a news release. Your headline must inform and grab, but keep it well below 140 characters so that people can retweet it with a brief comment.

Wendy's used only 84 characters to win the 2011 Twitter Golden Tweet Award for the most retweeted post of the year. Wendy's paid for the promotional ad. All it said was this: "RT for a good cause. Each retweet sends 50¢ to help kids in foster care. #tweetItFwd." The ad ran on Father's Day as part of the company's annual promotion for the Dave Thomas Foundation for Adoption, and it raised $50,000.

Become acquainted with Google Insights, Google AdWords, Keyword Discovery and Wordtracker for help with choosing the right words. Vanessa Bugasch, of the PR software and services company Cision, warns against overlinking, which might cause confusion. But she does advise writers to use one or two key words in the headline or subhead. She tells us that using them in the first two paragraphs has more impact than placing them lower in the release and cites research that shows that news releases "with pictures, video and other multimedia get at least 80 percent more search traffic than text-only releases."

You must be aware that just as some newspapers will use your news releases almost verbatim—some have sections of verbatim releases about events, promotions and so on—some radio and television stations will use your audio and video releases without editing them. In 2005, a *New York Times* investigation found that during the Bush administration at least 20 federal agencies, including the Defense Department, were distributing video news releases (VNRs) that made everyone and everything in government look good—including the war in Iraq. The government paid private public relations firms millions to produce messages that looked like traditional reporting—and stations used them.

The nonprofit group Center for Media and Democracy reported in 2006 that over a 10-month period at least 77 television stations used VNRs. Not one told viewers who had produced them. In some VNRs, publicists acted as news reporters.

In a 2009 hearing of the Consumer Protection, Product Safety, and Insurance Subcommittee of the Commerce Committee, Sen. Claire McCaskill (D–Mo.) called the use of VNRs "unconscionable." She said, "Our news folks have enough problems with credibility right now without fake news being aired." But VNRs continue to be broadcast without explanation. In 2012, for example, CNN ran a VNR for vaccines before the start of the school year.

Up until 2012, the Public Relations Society of America awarded Bronze Anvils for the best VNR. In 2013, the society changed the category's name from VNRs to "Online videos." It's really the same award.

Know How to Distribute Information Online

Of course, not even the largest newspapers or radio or television networks can reach as many people as digital media can. With millions of websites, there are practically no limits to the audiences that can be reached on the internet. First, you must establish your own credible, up-to-date, interactive website. Second, you must be thoroughly familiar with websites such as Online Public Relations, PR Newswire and Synaptic Digital so that you can distribute your releases online and keep up with what's happening in public relations. Third, you must become expert at using digital media to get across your organization's messages (see Chapter 11).

Digital News Releases

To be effective in their jobs, writers of news releases need to learn all the techniques that journalists use in writing news stories.

The straight, no-nonsense inverted pyramid news release remains the staple of the public relations professional. Many believe that news professionals will not take any other approach seriously. (See Chapter 8 for more on the inverted pyramid.) For an example of a traditional news release, see Figure 18.1 earlier in this chapter.

A less traditional news release, written in a lighter style, can be more engaging. Take a look at the news release, shown in the annotated model "News Release Responding to a Crisis," on page 405, that the Contemporary Jewish Museum released in connection with an incident that had recently occurred. Notice the excellent first sentence, in which the emphasis on "hands" turns a negative occurrence at the museum into an occasion for celebration. The release goes on to acknowledge the "widely publicized incident" to which the museum is responding and to give details about the upcoming Hand Holding Day events. The ending—which ties back to the hand theme and adds "so shake a leg"—is an unexpected and delightful ending for a news release.

Despite the continued use of traditional news releases, today's savvy public relations professionals are sending social media news releases. Here are some of the steps, summarized and condensed, that digital PR expert Sally Falkow recommends for successful social media news releases:

■ Write a short, concise headline.
■ Answer the five W's in the first paragraph.
■ List the core news facts in bullet points.

Press Release
HAND HOLDING DAY at the CJM
Sunday, July 24, 2011
9 AM–5 PM

San Francisco, CA, July 21, 2011—It's time for a show of hands this Sunday, July 24 at the Contemporary Jewish Museum as we celebrate Hand Holding Day! In the aftermath of a widely publicized incident in our galleries in which a contract security guard, acting in his individual capacity, told two women holding hands that it was not allowed,* the Museum demonstrates its ongoing commitment to diversity by encouraging visitors to come stroll hand in hand through the galleries no matter who you love and to celebrate the LGBT families in our community.*

"We are excited about welcoming everyone to the Museum for a day of celebration," says CJM Director and CEO Connie Wolf. "When we learned that a contract security officer was not in alignment with the Museum's values and policies, he was immediately removed from the Museum and reprimanded. The Museum is dedicated to engaging all visitors in the diversity of culture, history, art, and ideas. Sunday at the Museum will be an extraordinary opportunity to share in the diversity of people, ideas, and community."

The morning features several previously scheduled activities just for families with young children in conjunction with the current Seeing Gertrude Stein: Five Stories exhibition including special art-making activities, tours of the exhibition, and performances by the SF Lesbian/Gay Freedom Band, the Voices Lesbian Choral Ensemble, and Lesbian/Gay Chorus of San Francisco. The LGBT Family Morning of Stein takes place 9 AM to 12 PM and is appropriate for young children (preschool through nine years old) and their families. All families are welcome, and youth 18 and under are always free. Learn More.

Later that day, loved ones can hold hands as they enjoy a special free performance by actress Laura Sheppard entitled Paris Portraits: Stories of Picasso, Matisse, Gertrude Stein and their Circle, her one-woman show based on the new memoir of Gertrude Stein by Harriet Levy from Heyday Books. The 30-minute performance starts at 2 PM and is followed by a conversation with Sheppard and historians Frances Dinkelspiel and Fred Rosenbaum. Get Tickets.

(continued)

News release publicizes an event designed to respond to a negative incident.

The museum's swift corrective action is highlighted.

The release restates the museum's position on the issue.

Details of the event make the museum's position clear.

This link enables the reporter to get more information.

This link provides a service to the reader.

A fun day is at hand so shake a leg and come join us! It's all free with regular admission.

*For more information, view "The Contemporary Jewish Museum Responds to Incident in Gallery" press release.

This link to an earlier release about the incident provides background.

About the Contemporary Jewish Museum

With the opening of its new building on June 8, 2008, the Contemporary Jewish Museum (CJM) ushered in a new chapter in its twenty-plus year history of engaging audiences and artists in exploring contemporary perspectives on Jewish culture, history, art, and ideas. The facility, designed by internationally renowned architect Daniel Libeskind, is a lively center where people of all ages and backgrounds can gather to experience art, share diverse perspectives, and engage in hands-on activities. Inspired by the Hebrew phrase "L'Chaim" (To Life), the building is a physical embodiment of the CJM's mission to bring together tradition and innovation in an exploration of the Jewish experience in the 21st century.

For media information or visuals visit our online press gallery or please contact:

Contemporary Jewish Museum

Nina Sazevich
Public Relations
415.752.2483
Nina911@pacbell.net

Full contact info makes the journalist's job easier.

Daryl Carr
Director of Marketing & Communications
415.655.7834
dcarr@thecjm.org

Online: thecjm.org/press | thecjm.org/imagegallery

This news release confronts negative publicity head-on and promotes the organization's corrective actions.

ANNOTATED MODEL   Social Media News Release

Eye-catching design makes use of strong graphic elements.

Social Media Release – Faces of Diversity 2011

April 13, 2011

Heading and deck use terms easily found in an Internet search.

National Restaurant Association's 2011 Faces of Diversity Awards Winners Illustrate the American Dream of Entrepreneurship

CONTACT INFORMATION

Annika Stensson | (202) 973-3677 | astensson@restaurant.org | Twitter@WeRRestaurants

Contact info is prominent.

2011 FACES OF DIVERSITY AWARDS

Theme gives the "so what."

The Faces of Diversity Awards, created by the National Restaurant Association in partnership with PepsiCo Foodservice, celebrate diversity in the restaurant and foodservice industry and among the industry's nearly 13 million employees.

Beautifully presented logo.

NEWS HIGHLIGHTS

Key news points are given in a bulleted list.

- The National Restaurant Association today honored four restaurant entrepreneurs and a renowned culinary college with its 2011 Faces of Diversity awards.

- The award celebrates members of the restaurant and foodservice industry who have embraced diversity and inclusion at their own business operations and achieved the American dream in the process. . . .

Important news here of American Dream Award winners, briefly stated and again bulleted.

- This year's American Dream Award winners are:
  - **Berekti and Akberet Mengistu, Mesob restaurant, Montclair, N.J.:** These Ethiopian-born sisters . . .
  - **Amporn Vasquez, Pizza by Elizabeths, Greenville, Del.:** This executive chef . . .
  - **Richard Castro, McDonald's franchisee, El Paso, Texas:** As a child . . .

A special award.

- The Inspiration Award winner is:
  - **The Culinary Institute of America, Hyde Park, N.Y., and Silver Ventures Inc., San Antonio:** In an attempt to increase the number of Hispanic managers and restaurant owner-operators in business . . .

Link to a longer, more detailed news release.

- Read the full news release.

(continued)

A nontraditional news release makes the most of what the digital media offer.

ANNOTATED MODEL Social Media News Release (*continued*)

QUOTE

Relevant quote is labeled and clearly displayed.

- "The restaurant industry is one of the most diverse industries in the United States, and we are celebrating that by honoring these individuals and companies with our 2011 Faces of Diversity awards. It is a true pleasure to recognize their personal and professional achievements, which underscore how hard work and determination lead to success in our industry."

  — *Dawn Sweeney, president and CEO for the National Restaurant Association*

VIDEO: 2011 FACES OF DIVERSITY WINNERS

You may also watch each winner's video individually:

The release gives video links that can be embedded into a story.

- The Culinary Institute of America
- Richard Castro
- Amporn Vasquez
- Berekti and Akberet Mengistu

FACES OF DIVERSITY IMAGE GALLERY

Download photos of the 2011 Faces of Diversity award winners, and the Faces of Diversity logo.

The release gives photos and graphics that journalists can use.

Berekti and Akberet Mengistu

Logo

The Culinary Institute of America

LINKS

Links to other sources give reporters access to more info.

- News release on the 2011 Faces of Diversity winners
- News release on 2011 Inspiration Award winner The Culinary Institute of America
- The Culinary Institute of America San Antonio campus . . .

BOILERPLATE

- Founded in 1919, the National Restaurant Association is . . . For more information, visit our website at www.restaurant.org.

The history of the organization is also included, with its URL.

- List the core news facts in bullet points.
- Add approved quotes.
- Write the rest in narrative form; use relevant keywords so that journalists and others can find the release through search engines or social sites.
- Add links to research, facts, statistics or trends.
- Include an original, high-quality image that tells the story.
- Provide the source URL for the image so that bloggers and journalists can use it easily and quickly.
- Add more images, icons and, if possible, a short video, plus more supporting materials, such as charts and infographics.
- Provide an embed code with these items so that they can be easily republished. (An embed code acts like a link to video content.)
- Add the "About Us" boilerplate and contact person.
- Make the release available in an RSS news feed.
- Add sharing buttons so that the release can be shared through social networking sites.

Study the annotated model "Social Media News Release" on page 407 for an example. Notice how the information leaps out at you, and note how many choices the release gives the readers and how many connections it provides.

The social media news release has changed the way public relations professionals think about doing news releases. And the social media have changed the way they think about doing public relations.

Some Final Advice

In addition to writing news releases, public relations professionals are involved with many other important functions that increase the value of public relations, including planning and carrying out successful press conferences and dealing with the foreign press.

You might be hired as a speechwriter or to do something as specialized as write an organization's annual report. Corporations and institutions such as hospitals and universities hire thousands of communicators to get their messages out to the public. Or you might work for a public relations agency that is hired to do this work for organizations. Many people make a good living working out of their homes for just a half dozen or fewer clients. No matter where you work, public relations demands that you never stop developing your skills and continuing your education.

SUGGESTED READINGS

Bivins, Thomas H. *Public Relations Writing: The Essentials of Style and Format*. 8th ed. New York: McGraw-Hill, 2013. Bivins covers the wide variety of writing expected of public relations professionals.

Brown, Rob. *Public Relations and the Social Web: How to Use Social Media and Web 2.0 in Communications*. Philadelphia: Kogan Page, 2009. This book discusses the whole range of social media, including social media releases, Twitter and wikis.

Carnegie, Dale. *How to Win Friends and Influence People*. Revised Edition. New York: Pocket Books, 1982. The classic: absolutely guaranteed worthwhile reading for anyone in public relations.

Holtz, Shel. *Public Relations on the Net*. 2nd ed. New York: Amacom, 2002. Anything Holtz says or writes about online subjects is worth paying attention to. See also www.holtz.com/blog.

Howard, Carole, and Wilma Mathews. *On Deadline: Managing Media Relations*. 5th ed. Prospect Heights, Ill.: Waveland Press, 2013. This excellent practical book shows how organizations should deal with the news media.

Lattimore, Dan, Otis Baskin, Suzette Heiman and Elizabeth Toth. *Public Relations: The Profession and the Practice*. New York: McGraw-Hill, 2011. This good survey is divided into four parts covering the profession, the process, the publics and the practice.

Newsom, Doug, and Jim Haynes. *Public Relations Writing: Form and Style*. 9th ed. Belmont, Calif.: Wadsworth, 2010. A truly thorough classic, this book even has a section on grammar, spelling and punctuation.

Ogilvy, David. *Ogilvy on Advertising*. Toronto: John Wiley, 1983. Get a copy; read it. A must.

Phillips, David, and Philip Young. *Online Public Relations: A Practical Guide to Developing an Online Strategy in the World of Social Media*. 2nd ed. Philadelphia: Kogan Page, 2009. The authors discuss many new ways for creative people to reach large audiences.

Reis, Al, and Jack Trout. *Positioning: The Battle for Your Mind*. New York: McGraw-Hill, 2000. The incredibly simple advice that told industry that, to be successful, all it had to do was to find its niche. A classic that you will use and never forget.

Seitel, Fraser P. *The Practice of Public Relations*. 10th ed. New York: Prentice Hall, 2006. You can tell Seitel has been a teacher. He writes simply, clearly and engagingly.

Smith, Ronald. *Strategic Planning for Public Relations*. New York: Routledge, 2009. This book explains well the shift from public relations to strategic communications.

Wilcox, Dennis L., Glen T. Cameron and Bryan H. Reber. *Public Relations: Strategies and Tactics*. 11th ed. Boston: Allyn & Bacon, 2014. These outstanding professors keep you up-to-date in the field.

SUGGESTED WEBSITES

www.instituteforpr.org

This website offers information about public relations research, measurement, programs, seminars, publications, scholarship and so on from the Institute for Public Relations, which explores "the science beneath the art of public relations."

macmillanhighered.com/newsreporting12e

When you visit LaunchPad Solo for Journalism, you will find research links, exercises, and LearningCurve adaptive quizzing to help you improve your grammar and AP style usage. In addition, the site's video collection hosts the videos highlighted in this and other chapters as well as additional clips of leading professionals discussing important media trends.

www.odwyerpr.com

On this website, you can also find *O'Dwyer's PR Report*, an excellent monthly publication that devotes each issue to a public relations specialty field. This independent website and publication is often highly critical of the profession.

www.prsa.org

The website of the Public Relations Society of America has general information about the society, lists its chapters and sections, and offers information on publications, membership and accreditation, recognition and awards, conferences and seminars.

www.prwatch.org

This website, from the Center for Media and Democracy, investigates "public relations spin and propaganda." It sends out more than 1,000 news releases each day.

EXERCISES

1. Imagine that a classmate is killed in a car accident. A few thousand dollars are raised to set up a scholarship to honor his memory but much more money is needed to endow the scholarship. A group of students who have been training to run in the Chicago Marathon decide to solicit money for each mile the runners complete. The proceeds will help support the scholarship. You decide to get involved. How would you advise them?

    a. Who is your target audience or audiences?
    b. Which medium would be most effective in reaching your audience?
    c. How will you make use of social media throughout your fundraising campaign?

    Write a detailed report of your plan.

2. **Your journalism blog.** On your blog, write a post explaining why you would like to work in public relations—or why you would not.

3. Visit with your college sports information director. Interview him about the most difficult aspects of his job. Write a report.

4. Interview a student from a small town. Then write a news release about his or her life and activities at the university, and email it to the town's newspaper.

5. Visit a local hospital. Interview the head of public relations there about their responsibilities. Write a story that includes anecdotes and stories that the person shared with you.

The First Amendment states:

> Congress shall make no law respecting an establishment of religion, or prohibiting the free exercise thereof; or abridging the freedom of speech, or of the press; or the right of the people peaceably to assemble, and to petition the Government for a redress of grievances.

That's it: 45 words setting forth the basis for a free press in the U.S. It's deceptively simple.

The First Amendment: Journalists' Rights and Responsibilities

The first five words of the First Amendment tell us a great deal about the Founding Fathers' intent: "Congress shall make no law. . . ." Rather than enumerate an array of rights granted, the amendment begins instead with a clear prohibition on the reach of the state into our ability to express ourselves.

But surely the framers of the Constitution did not mean literally "no law" under any circumstances, did they? The U.S. Supreme Court has never thought so, upholding a wide variety of restrictions on speech through the years. Still, by imposing broad limits on the power of the government to restrict speech and expression, the First Amendment creates a system that protects the vast majority of speech in the U.S.

Such powerful protection is justified by the importance of free speech. The philosopher Alexander Meiklejohn provided the strongest explanation for free speech in a democratic society. Meiklejohn wrote that the Constitution is based on a two-tiered political agreement. First, all authority, whether to exercise control or determine common action, belongs to the people. Second, free people govern themselves, and to do so effectively, they must have access to a free flow of accurate information. When people govern themselves, "it is they—and no one else—who must pass judgment upon unwisdom and unfairness and danger," he wrote.

So the free flow of ideas is necessary in a democracy because people who govern themselves need to know about their government and about those who run it, as well as about the social and economic institutions that greatly affect their day-to-day lives. Most people get that information through newspapers, the internet, social media, radio and television. Increasingly, citizen journalists are communicating through blogs. While professional journalists debate whether blogs should be considered "real" journalism, the legal system is grappling with the issue of how to apply constitutional precedents to them.

The speed with which information can spread across social networks makes it more important than ever to understand the basics of media law. You don't have to be an expert. You just need to know when it's time to slow down and think a bit before hitting the "send" button.

1

What rights you have as a journalist and the source of those rights.

2

How to spot potentially libelous situations and what to do about them.

3

When you might be invading someone's privacy.

4

What kinds of problems you may face when protecting confidential sources.

5

What rights you have when obtaining access to courtrooms and court documents.

6

What you should know about copyright and fair use.

GRAMMAR CHECK

What's the grammar error in this sentence?

Pakistani human rights activist Malala Yousafzai was almost killed by a Taliban assassin in October 2012; but she remains a dedicated advocate for girls' education.

See Appendix 1, Rule 9.

Digital publishing raises all kinds of issues that journalists never had to consider before as well as new challenges to government transparency. In 1966, Congress passed the Freedom of Information Act to assist the public in finding out what is happening in federal agencies. The act was amended in 1996 by the Electronic Freedom of Information Act to improve access to computerized government records and was amended again in 2008 to ease the process of making requests. All 50 states have similar open-records laws. Though of great assistance to the press, these laws are also used by individuals and businesses to gain information previously kept secret by the government. Other laws ensure access to government transactions. The federal government and all the states have **open-meetings laws**—often called *sunshine laws*—requiring the public's business to be conducted in public. However, all of these access laws contain exemptions that keep some records and meetings private.

The First Amendment, the Freedom of Information Act and the sunshine laws demonstrate America's basic concern for citizen access to information needed for the "unfettered interchange of ideas." Nevertheless, some laws do reduce the scope of freedom of the press.

Libel

Traditionally, most of the laws limiting the absolute principle of freedom of the press have dealt with libel. These laws result from the desire of legislatures and courts to help individuals protect their reputations. Their importance was explained by U.S. Supreme Court Justice Potter Stewart in a 1966 libel case:

> **The right of a man (or woman) to the protection of his (or her) own reputation from unjustified invasion and wrongful hurt reflects no more than our basic concept of the essential dignity and worth of every human being—a concept at the root of any decent system of ordered liberty.**

Protection for reputations dates back centuries. In 17th-century England, individuals were imprisoned and even disfigured for making libelous statements. One objective was to prevent criticism of the government. Another was to maintain the peace by avoiding duels. Duels have fallen by the wayside, and government is freely criticized, but the desire to protect an individual's reputation is just as strong.

Identifying Libel

A case concerning Israeli Gen. Ariel Sharon (sha-RONE) is helpful in understanding libel. The extensively covered trial was held in the winter of 1984–1985 in the federal courthouse in Manhattan. The case was based on a 1983 *Time* magazine cover story, "Verdict on the Massacre," about Israel's 1982 judicial inquiry into the massacre of several hundred civilians in two Palestinian refugee camps in Lebanon.

The *Time* article suggested that Sharon, then Israel's defense minister and later its prime minister, had ordered the massacre. The general sued *Time*. His attorneys knew they would have to show that their client had suffered hatred, contempt or ridicule because these statements were serious attacks on his reputation and not just unpleasant comments.

The jury's decision was in three parts. The first part of the verdict was in answer to this question: Was the paragraph concerning Sharon defamatory? The jury said it was. This meant the *Time* article had damaged Sharon's reputation and had exposed him to hatred, contempt or ridicule.

The second question for the jury was this: Was the paragraph concerning Sharon false? Again the jury answered affirmatively. If the answer had been no, the case would have ended there. Truth is a complete defense for libel.

The third question for the jury concerned whether the paragraph was published with "actual malice"—with knowledge that it was false or with reckless disregard of whether it was false ("serious doubt" that it was true). The jury answered no. Thus the trial ended in favor of *Time* magazine, despite the jury's ruling that the article was defamatory.

Courts often rely on four categories of statements to help jurors like those in the Sharon case decide if someone's reputation has been damaged because he or she has been brought into hatred, contempt or ridicule:

> "The Government's power to censor the press was abolished so the press would remain forever free to censure the Government."
>
> — *Hugo Black, U.S. Supreme Court Justice*

1. **Accusing someone of a crime.** This category may have been the basis for the Sharon suit.
2. **Damaging a person in his or her public office, profession or occupation.** If the statements by *Time* against Sharon did not accuse him of crimes, they did damage him in his profession as a military man.
3. **Accusing a person of serious immorality.** The example lawyers often use is accusing a woman of being unchaste. Many states have statutes that make an accusation of unchastity a cause of action in a libel suit.
4. **Accusing someone of having a loathsome (that is, contagious) disease.** This category was fading as a source of defamation until the AIDS epidemic gave it new life.

This does not mean you can never say a person committed a crime, was unethical in business, was adulterous or had a loathsome disease. It does mean you must be certain that what you write is true.

Libel Suit Defenses

There are three traditional defenses against libel: truth, privilege, and fair comment and criticism. Two other constitutional standards—the actual malice and negligence tests—also help libel defendants. The court case clarifying these standards involved traditional media—newspapers, magazines and broadcast outlets that provide news and information to general audiences—but the principles are now being applied to the internet, including blogs and social media. In 2006, a blogger in Georgia lost the first of these electronic libel cases. He was ordered to pay $50,000 to a lawyer he had criticized. The diagram in Figure 19.1 shows the various defenses to a libel suit.

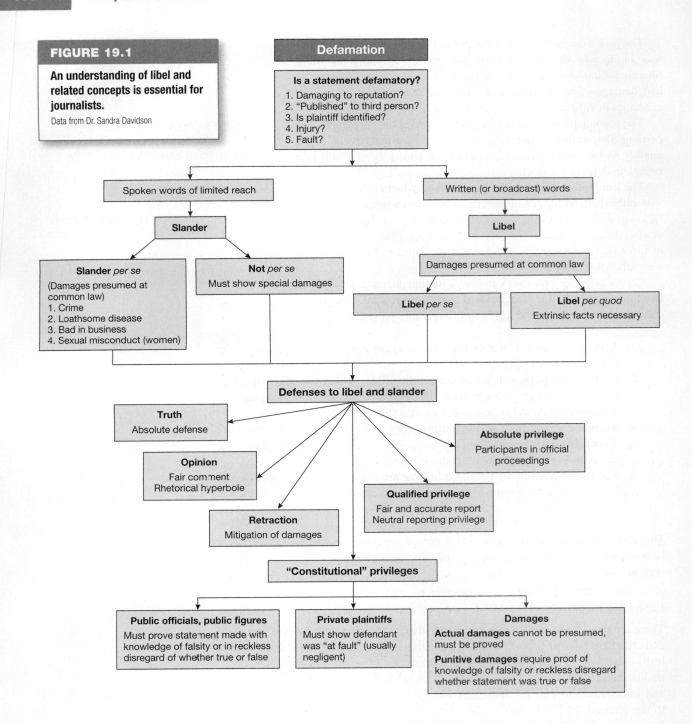

FIGURE 19.1

An understanding of libel and related concepts is essential for journalists.

Data from Dr. Sandra Davidson

Defamation

Is a statement defamatory?
1. Damaging to reputation?
2. "Published" to third person?
3. Is plaintiff identified?
4. Injury?
5. Fault?

Spoken words of limited reach

Written (or broadcast) words

Slander

Libel

Slander *per se*
(Damages presumed at common law)
1. Crime
2. Loathsome disease
3. Bad in business
4. Sexual misconduct (women)

Not *per se*
Must show special damages

Damages presumed at common law

Libel *per se*

Libel *per quod*
Extrinsic facts necessary

Defenses to libel and slander

Truth
Absolute defense

Opinion
Fair comment
Rhetorical hyperbole

Retraction
Mitigation of damages

Absolute privilege
Participants in official proceedings

Qualified privilege
Fair and accurate report
Neutral reporting privilege

"Constitutional" privileges

Public officials, public figures
Must prove statement made with knowledge of falsity or in reckless disregard of whether true or false

Private plaintiffs
Must show defendant was "at fault" (usually negligent)

Damages
Actual damages cannot be presumed, must be proved
Punitive damages require proof of knowledge of falsity or reckless disregard whether statement was true or false

Truth

Truth is the best defense against libel. In libel cases involving matters of public concern, the burden of proof is on the plaintiff—the person who is suing. This placement of the burden, however, does not change the reporter's responsibility to seek the truth in every possible way.

You cannot be certain, for example, whether a person charged with arson actually started the fire. Who told you that Joe Jones started the fire? The first source to check is the police or fire report. If a police officer or fire marshal says that Jones started a fire, you can report not that Jones did it but that he has been *accused* of doing it. Unless you have information you would be willing to present in court, you should go no further. Be sure you report no more than what you *know* is true. And if you have a document in your hands that proves what you write, you're in even better shape.

When a newspaper in Oklahoma reported that a wrestling coach had been accused of requiring a sixth-grader, who wanted to rejoin the team, to submit to a whipping by his fellow students while crawling naked through the legs of team members, the coach sued. He claimed damage to his reputation.

In cases like this, the reporter has to be certain not just that one or more participants told of the incident but also that the statements were true. In court, some participants might testify to an occurrence, and others might testify the incident never took place. A jury would have to decide on the credibility of the participants.

Although you must always strive for absolute truth in all of your stories, the courts will settle for what is known as **substantial truth** in most cases. This means that you must be able to prove the essential elements of all you write.

The Georgia case and others show that the courts are holding bloggers to the same standard established for traditional media. In the Georgia case, a disappointed client accused his former attorney, in a blog, of bribing judges. The lawyer sued and won when the blogger couldn't show that his charge was true.

Privilege

In addition to truth, the courts traditionally have allowed another defense against libel: **privilege**. This defense applies when you are covering any of the three branches of government. The courts allow legislators, judges and government executives the **absolute privilege** to say anything—true or false—when acting in their official capacities. The rationale is that the public interest is served when an official is allowed to speak freely and fearlessly about making laws, carrying them out or punishing those who do not obey them. Similarly, a participant in a judicial proceeding, such as an attorney, court clerk or judge, is absolutely privileged to make false and even defamatory statements about another person during that proceeding.

In the executive branch it isn't always clear whose statements are privileged and when. The head of state and the major officers of executive departments of the federal and state governments are covered. However, minor officials might not enjoy the protection of absolute privilege.

> " Journalists don't believe . . . the FOIA (Freedom of Information Act) was created to be turned on us as an excuse to hide information. "
>
> — *Sarah Overstreet, columnist*

As a reporter, you have a **qualified privilege**, sometimes called *neutral reporting* or *conditional privilege*, at the federal level and in some states, to report what public officials say. Your privilege is conditioned on your report's providing full, fair and accurate coverage of the court session, the legislative session or the president's press conference, even if any one of the participants made defamatory statements. You can quote anything the president of the U.S. says without fear of losing a libel suit, even if the president is not acting in an official capacity. Reporters have a qualified privilege to report unofficial statements.

But there are many other levels of executives in federal, state and local governments. Mayors of small towns, for instance, often hold part-time positions. Although you are conditionally privileged to report on what those officials say when they are acting in their official capacities, a problem can arise when the part-time mayor says something defamatory when not acting in an official capacity. Courts in some jurisdictions might grant a qualified privilege; other courts might not.

Fair Comment and Criticism

In some types of writing, you may be commenting or criticizing rather than reporting. The courts have protected writers who comment on and criticize the public offerings of anyone in the public eye. Included in this category are actors and actresses, sports figures, public officials and other newsworthy people. Most often, such writing occurs in reviews of plays, books or movies, or in commentary on service received in hotels and restaurants.

The courts call this **fair comment and criticism**. You are protected as long as you do not misstate any of the facts on which you base your comments or criticisms and as long as you do not wrongly imply that you possess undisclosed, damaging information that forms the basis of your opinion. Merely labeling a fact as an opinion will not result in opinion protection, the U.S. Supreme Court ruled in 1990.

The Actual Malice Test and Public Officials

It was a small but momentous step from fair comment and criticism to the case of *The New York Times Co. v. Sullivan*. In 1964, the U.S. Supreme Court decided that First Amendment protection was broader than just the traditional defenses of truth and privilege and that the press needed even greater freedom in its coverage of public officials.

The case started with an advertisement for funds in *The New York Times* of March 29, 1960, by the Committee to Defend Martin Luther King Jr. and the Struggle for Freedom in the South. The advertisement contained small, inconsequential factual errors concerning the police, according to Montgomery, Alabama, Commissioner L.B. Sullivan. He thought the errors damaged his reputation, and he won a half-million-dollar judgment against *The New York Times* in an Alabama trial court.

The Supreme Court said it was considering the case "against the background of a profound national commitment to the principle that debate on public issues should be uninhibited, robust and wide open." Thus Justice William Brennan wrote that the Constitution requires a federal rule prohibiting a public official from recovering damages from the press for a defamatory falsehood relating to his or her official conduct, unless the public official can prove the press had knowledge that what was printed was false or that the story was printed with reckless disregard of whether it was true or not. The justices called this the **actual malice test**.

The actual malice test was applied later in a case involving a story on CBS's *60 Minutes* about a retired U.S. Army officer. Col. Anthony Herbert contended the broadcast falsely portrayed him as a liar. He tried to prove that producer Barry Lando recklessly disregarded whether it was a false broadcast. Herbert asked some questions that Lando claimed were protected by the First Amendment because they inquired into his state of mind and into the editorial processes during the production of the program. Eventually, the U.S. Supreme Court decided the "state of mind" case in Col. Herbert's favor.

The decision in the Sharon case discussed earlier in this chapter is an example of the burden of proving actual malice against the press. The jury decided that when the article in question was printed, *Time* did not know that its statement about Gen. Sharon was false.

In 1991, the Supreme Court decided *Masson v. New Yorker Magazine*, the so-called fabricated quotes case. Jeffrey Masson, a psychologist, had sued the magazine and journalist Janet Malcolm, accusing them of making up quotes he never said. Overruling a lower court's decision that journalists could fictionalize quotations by making rational interpretations of speakers' remarks, the Supreme Court protected the sanctity of quotation marks. But the court also made clear that not every deliberate change in a quotation is libelous. Only a "material change in the meaning conveyed by a statement" poses a problem. Although Masson won the right to try his case, he lost against all defendants in 1994.

The Actual Malice Test and Public Figures

The actual malice protection was expanded in two cases in 1967 to include not only public officials but also *public figures*—people in the public eye but not in public office.

The first case stemmed from a *Saturday Evening Post* article that accused Coach Wally Butts of conspiring to fix a 1962 college football game between Georgia and Alabama. At the time of the article, Butts was the athletic director of the University of Georgia. The article, titled "The Story of a College Football Fix," was prefaced by a note from the editors of *The Post* stating:

> Not since the Chicago White Sox threw the 1919 World Series has there been a sports story as shocking as this one. . . . Before the University of Georgia played the University of Alabama . . . Wally Butts . . . gave (to Alabama's coach) . . . Georgia's plays, defensive patterns, all the significant secrets Georgia's football team possessed.

The Post reported that, because of an electronic error about a week before the game, George Burnett, an Atlanta insurance salesman, had accidentally overheard a telephone conversation between Butts and the head coach of Alabama, Paul Bryant.

ON THE JOB The Keys to Avoiding Libel

Ken Paulson earned a law degree after graduating from journalism school. He then practiced journalism for 18 years. After serving as senior vice president of the Freedom Forum and executive director of the First Amendment Center at Vanderbilt University, he returned to the newsroom as editor of *USA Today*. He then moved to head the Newseum in Washington, before returning to the First Amendment Center. He is now dean of journalism at Middle Tennessee State University.

"Having a law degree has been helpful as a journalist," Paulson says, "but the key to avoiding libel suits really boils down to a few fundamentals."

Those fundamentals are rooted in professionalism and common sense. Paulson suggests that journalists ask themselves these questions:

- Have I reported fully?
- Have I reported factually?
- Have I reported fairly?
- Have I reported in good faith?

First Amendment Center.

"If you can answer those four questions in the affirmative, the law will take care of itself," he says.

Coach Butts sued Curtis Publishing Company, publishers of *The Saturday Evening Post*, and won a verdict for $60,000 in general damages and $3 million in punitive, or punishment, damages. Curtis Publishing appealed the case to the Supreme Court and lost. The trial judge reduced the amount of the damages to $460,000.

The second case was decided the same day. Gen. Edwin Walker sued the Associated Press for distributing a news dispatch giving an eyewitness account by an AP staffer on the campus of the University of Mississippi in the fall of 1962. The AP reported that Gen. Walker personally had led a student charge against federal marshals during a riot on the Mississippi campus. The marshals were attempting to enforce a court decree ordering the enrollment of a black student.

Walker was a retired general at the time of the publication. He won a $2 million libel suit in a trial court, but the Supreme Court ruled against him.

In both cases, the stories were wrong. In both, the actual malice test was applied. What was the difference between the Butts and Walker cases?

The justices said the football story was in no sense "hot news." They noted that the person who said he had heard the conversation was on probation in connection with bad-check charges and that *Post* personnel had not viewed his notes before publication. The court also said, as evidence of actual malice on the part of *The Post*, that no one looked at the game films to see if the information was accurate; that a regular staffer, instead of a football expert, was assigned to the story; and that no check was made with someone knowledgeable in the sport. In short, *The Post* had not done an adequate job of reporting.

The evidence in the Walker case was considerably different. The court said the news in the Walker case required immediate dissemination because of the riot on campus. The justices noted that the AP received the information from a correspondent who was present on the campus and gave every indication of being trustworthy and competent.

In the Butts and Walker cases, the court used two definitions of public figure. The first is a person like Butts who has assumed a role of special prominence in the affairs of society—someone who has pervasive power and influence in a community. The second is a person like Walker who has thrust himself or herself into the forefront of a particular public controversy in order to influence the resolution of the issues involved.

In the 1970s, the Supreme Court decided three cases that help journalists determine who is and who is not a public figure. The first case involved Mrs. Russell A. Firestone, who sued for libel after *Time* magazine reported that her husband's divorce petition had been granted on grounds of extreme cruelty and adultery. Mrs. Firestone, who had married into the Firestone Tire and Rubber Co. family, claimed that those were not the grounds for the divorce. She also insisted that she was not a public figure with the burden of proving actual malice.

The Supreme Court agreed. Even though she had held press conferences and had hired a clipping service, the court ruled that she had not thrust herself into the forefront of a public controversy in an attempt to influence the resolution of the issues involved. The court admitted that marital difficulties of extremely wealthy individuals may be of some interest to some portion of the reading public but added that Mrs. Firestone had not freely chosen to publicize private matters about her married life. The justices said she was compelled to go to court to "obtain legal release from the bonds of matrimony." They said she assumed no "special prominence in the resolution of public questions." The case was sent back to Florida for a finding of fault, and a new trial was ordered. Eventually, the case was settled out of court.

The second case involved Sen. William Proxmire of Wisconsin, who had started what he called the Golden Fleece Award. Each month he announced a winner who, in his opinion, had wasted government money. One such winner was Ronald Hutchinson, a behavioral scientist who had received federal funding for research designed to determine why animals clench their teeth. Hutchinson had published articles about his research in professional publications. In deciding that Hutchinson was not a public figure, the court ruled that he "did not thrust himself or his views into public controversy to influence others." The court admitted there may have been legitimate concerns about the way public funds were being spent but said this was not enough to make Hutchinson a public figure.

The third case concerned an individual found guilty of contempt of court in 1958 for his failure to appear before a grand jury investigating Soviet espionage in the U.S. Ilya Wolston's name had been included in a list of people indicted for serving as Soviet agents in a 1974 book published by the Reader's Digest Association. In fact, Wolston had not been indicted on that charge, and he sued.

The Supreme Court, in deciding that Wolston was not a public figure, found that he had played only a minor role in whatever public controversy there may have been concerning the investigation of Soviet espionage. The court added that a private individual is not automatically transformed into a public figure merely by becoming involved in or being associated with a matter that attracts public attention.

As a journalist, do you have the same protection from a libel action when you write about a person somewhat connected with a news event as you do when you are certain a person is a public figure or public official? A 1974 Supreme Court decision says the answer is usually no. In the landmark *Gertz v. Robert Welch, Inc.* case, the justices said states may give more protection to private individuals if a newspaper or radio or television station damages their reputations than if the reputations of either public officials or public figures are damaged. Generally, you have protection from a libel action when you write about people who have thrust themselves into the forefront of a controversy or event. More recent cases have cemented this rule, as the courts tend to look broadly at those involved in newsworthy events as public figures.

The Negligence Test and Private Citizens

Private citizens who sue for punitive damages must meet the same actual malice test as public officials and public figures do. Because of the Gertz case, states have been allowed to set their own standards for libel cases involving private citizens who sue only for actual damages. A majority of states and the District of Columbia have adopted a **negligence test**, which requires you to use the same care in gathering facts and writing your story as any reasonable reporter would use under the same or similar circumstances. If you make every effort to be fair and answer all the questions a reasonable person may ask, you probably would pass the negligence test.

One state, New York, has adopted a gross irresponsibility test. A few states have established a more stringent standard that requires private citizens to prove actual malice. Some states simply require a jury to find "fault."

Libel Remains a Danger

Despite all the available defenses, libel remains a serious risk to journalists' financial health, as the following example demonstrates. In 1997, a Texas jury awarded a record $222.7 million to a defunct bond-brokerage firm against Dow Jones & Co., which owns *The Wall Street Journal*. The judge threw out $200 million in punitive damages but let stand the $222.7 million in actual damages for a *Journal* story about "bond daddies."

For citizen journalists, such as bloggers, even awards that are much smaller could be devastating. If you blog, you should meet the same standards of fairness and accuracy that are expected of traditional media. (See "Citizen Journalists, Social Media and the Law" on p. 427.)

Libel and the Internet

As we have seen, individuals who libel others over the internet can be held responsible. But the internet raises the interesting question of whether an online service provider like AOL or MSN can be held responsible for the libelous messages of their users.

In 1991, CompuServe successfully defended itself against a libel suit in a New York federal trial court. CompuServe had entered a contract with another company to provide an electronic bulletin board in the form of a newsletter about journalism. The second company then used a third company to create the newsletter. Because CompuServe did not try to exercise any editorial control over the newsletter, the court let CompuServe off the hook for libel. The court also reasoned that no library can be held responsible if a book that the librarian has not reviewed contains libel. CompuServe, the court said, was providing an "electronic, for-profit library."

In 1995, however, another online service provider, Prodigy, lost a similar libel case. To promote itself as a family-oriented internet company, Prodigy controlled the content of its computer bulletin boards by using screening software to look for forbidden words, and its editorial staff blocked allegedly offensive posts. Unfortunately for Prodigy, no screening software could identify libelous material. A New York trial court said that by holding itself out as exercising editorial control, Prodigy was "expressly differentiating itself from its competition and expressly likening itself to a newspaper." Thus the court treated Prodigy like a newspaper and held it liable for libel posted on one of its bulletin boards.

Congress did not agree with the Prodigy decision, however, and effectively overruled the case in 1996 by passing "protection for 'Good Samaritan' blocking and screening of offensive material." Congress obviously did not support the idea that the failure to screen meant protection from libel but that limited screening could lead to liability. Federal courts have uniformly upheld the rule.

Invasion of Privacy

Libel is damage to an individual's reputation. **Invasion of privacy** is a violation of a person's right to be left alone.

As a reporter, you may be risking an invasion of privacy suit under any of these circumstances:

- You physically intrude into a private area to get a story or picture—an act closely related to trespass.
- You publish a story or photograph about someone that is misleading, and thus you portray that person in a "false light."
- You disclose something about an individual's private affairs that is true but that is also offensive to a person of ordinary sensibilities.

Invasion of privacy may also be claimed if someone's name or picture is used in an advertisement or for similar purposes of trade. Such *appropriation* will not affect you when you are performing your reporting duties.

Consent is a basic defense in invasion of privacy suits. Make sure, however, that your use of the material does not exceed the consent given.

TIPS

You May Be Committing Invasion of Privacy By:

- Trespassing on private property.
- Portraying someone in a "false light."
- Causing unwanted publicity that is offensive to a person of ordinary sensibilities.

Another basic defense in an invasion of privacy suit is that you're a reporter covering a newsworthy situation. The courts usually protect members of the press against invasion of privacy suits when they are reporting matters of legitimate public interest. There are the three exceptions listed earlier, however: trespassing, portraying in a "false light," and causing unwanted publicity.

Trespassing

The first exception arises when you enter private property without permission to get a story. You cannot trespass on private property to get a story or to take a picture, even if it is newsworthy. The courts will not protect you when you are a trespasser.

Two *Life* magazine staffers lost an invasion-of-privacy suit because, posing as patients, they went into a man's home to get a story about a faith healer. They lost the case even though they were working with the district attorney and the state board of health.

You may enter private property only when you are invited by the owner or renter. And you should never use deception to gain entry to property you otherwise have no legal right of access to.

Portraying in a "False Light"

The courts also will not protect you if you invade someone's privacy by publishing misleading information about that person. For example, a legal problem arises if a photograph or information from a true story about a careful pedestrian struck by a careless driver is used again in connection with a story about, say, careless pedestrians. The pedestrian who was hit could file a lawsuit charging libel, "false light" invasion of privacy or even both in some states.

Some states do not recognize "false light" invasion of privacy and insist that libel is the appropriate form of suit. But "false light" suits can cover situations in which a picture or story is misleading but not defamatory. Even flattering material can place a person in an unwanted, false light.

Causing Unwanted Publicity Offensive to a Person of Ordinary Sensibilities

The third type of invasion of privacy that the courts recognize—unwanted publicity—arises from stories about incidents that, because they are true, are not defamatory but can be offensive to a person of ordinary sensibilities. The courts say that in order for privacy to be invaded, there must be a morbid and sensational prying into private lives. Merely being the subject of an unflattering or uncomfortable article is not enough. An example is a picture published by *Sports Illustrated* in which a football fan's pants zipper was open. The fan sued for invasion of privacy but lost.

Also in the area of unwanted publicity, the Supreme Court held in 1975 and again in 1989 that truthfully reporting the name of a rape

> "There are only two occasions when Americans respect privacy. . . . Those are prayer and fishing. "
>
> — *Herbert Hoover, 31st U.S. president*

victim is permitted. In 1976 and in 1979 the justices upheld the right of the press to publish the names of juveniles involved with the law because the information was truthful and of public significance.

Protection of Sources and Notes

Another area you must know about is your ability—or inability—to protect your sources and notes. The problem might arise in various situations. A grand jury that is investigating a murder might ask you to reveal the source of a story you wrote about the murder. Or you may be asked to testify at a criminal or civil trial.

The conflict that arises is between a reporter's need to protect sources of information and the duty of every citizen to testify to help the courts determine justice. Your work as a reporter will take you to events that are important and newsworthy. Anyone wanting the facts about an event can subpoena you to bring in all the details. Journalists usually resist. They work for their newspaper or radio or television station, not a law enforcement agency. Their ability to gather information would be compromised if sources knew that their identities or their information could go to the police.

Some protection against testifying—shield laws—has been adopted by these 40 states and the District of Columbia:

Alabama	Kentucky	North Dakota
Alaska	Louisiana	Ohio
Arizona	Maine	Oklahoma
Arkansas	Maryland	Oregon
California	Michigan	Pennsylvania
Colorado	Minnesota	Rhode Island
Connecticut	Montana	South Carolina
Delaware	Nebraska	Tennessee
Florida	Nevada	Texas
Georgia	New Jersey	Utah
Hawaii	New Mexico	Washington
Illinois	New York	West Virginia
Indiana	North Carolina	Wisconsin
Kansas		

Shield law protection is important because without it, journalists do go to jail. In 2001–2002, Vanessa Leggett, a freelance journalist in Houston, spent 168 days in jail for refusing to hand over notes and interview tapes she had made while writing a book about the murder of a Houston socialite. Texas had no shield law at the time. In 2004–2005, Jim Taricani, a broadcast reporter in Providence, Rhode Island, spent four months under house arrest for refusing to tell who gave him an FBI videotape that showed a Providence official taking a bribe from an undercover FBI agent. A federal judge had ordered Taricani to reveal his source. Although Rhode Island has a shield law, the federal government does not.

macmillanlearning.com
/newsreporting12e

Watch **"Bloggers & Legal Rights."**

- How do the legal protections and responsibilities of bloggers compare with those of print or television journalists?
- Should professional journalists have different rights and more protection than bloggers? Explain.

Perhaps *New York Times* reporter Judith Miller has garnered the most publicity for being jailed to protect a source. Her saga started when conservative columnist Robert Novak revealed the name of a CIA undercover agent, Valerie Plame. Plame's husband, retired diplomat Joseph Wilson, had said the Bush administration misrepresented the facts when it claimed that President Saddam Hussein of Iraq had tried to buy depleted uranium from Niger. The disclosure about Plame came after Wilson's assertions.

Miller did not use Plame's name in her stories, but she went to jail on July 6, 2005, for refusing to reveal the source who had provided her with information about the agent. Because it is a violation of federal law for an official to reveal the identity of an undercover CIA agent, a special prosecutor was assigned to investigate that leak. Several other journalists did testify after receiving permission from their sources. Miller and her bosses at *The Times* took the position that her promise to hold confidential her sources' names was not one she could break. The U.S. Supreme Court refused to hear her appeal. Although her imprisonment inspired bills in Congress calling for a federal shield law, Congress has not yet passed such a law.

Miller was released after serving 85 days in jail when her source gave her permission to reveal his identity. The only criminal charge to result from the investigation was a charge against Lewis "Scooter" Libby, assistant to Vice President Dick Cheney, of lying to investigators. Libby was convicted in federal court.

In 1980, Congress did pass the Privacy Protection Act. Under that act, federal, state and local law enforcement officers generally may not use a search warrant to search newsrooms. Instead, they must get a subpoena for documents that instructs reporters and editors to hand over the material. Officers may use a warrant to search newsrooms only if they suspect a reporter of being involved in a crime or if immediate action is needed to prevent bodily harm, loss of life or destruction of the material.

The difference between a search warrant and a subpoena is great. Officers with a search warrant can knock on the door, enter the newsroom and search on their own. A subpoena does not permit officers to search the newsroom. A subpoena for specific documents requires reporters to turn over the material to authorities at a predetermined time and place. In addition, it gives reporters time to challenge in court the necessity of surrendering the material.

Even in states with shield laws, judges in most criminal cases involving grand juries will not allow you to keep your sources secret. In other criminal cases, courts may allow confidentiality if a three-part test is met. Supreme Court Justice Potter Stewart suggested this test in his dissent in *Branzburg v. Hayes*, decided in 1972:

> Government officials must, therefore, demonstrate that the information sought is clearly relevant to a precisely defined subject of government inquiry.... They must demonstrate that it is reasonable to think the witness in question has that information.... And they must show that there is not any means of obtaining the information less destructive of First Amendment liberties.

In civil litigation, you may be permitted to keep sources confidential in most cases unless the court finds that the information sought is unavailable from other sources and highly relevant to the underlying litigation or of such critical importance to the lawsuit that it goes to the heart of the plaintiff's claim.

If you are sued for libel, you will find it difficult both to protect your sources and to win the lawsuit. The court might well rule against you on whether a statement is true or false if it came from a source you refuse to name.

The best way to avoid such confrontation with the courts is not to promise a source you will keep his or her name confidential. Only for the most compelling reason should you promise confidentiality.

In 1991, the U.S. Supreme Court ruled in *Cohen v. Cowles Media Co.* that the First Amendment does not prevent a source from suing a news organization if a reporter has promised the source confidentiality but the newspaper publishes the source's name anyway.

The latest controversy over journalistic privilege involves the status of bloggers and other digital authors under state shield laws. Shield laws for the most part were written before blogs existed, and thus often limit protection to members of bona fide news organizations. The law struggles to keep pace with emerging digital news operations and independent bloggers, with predictable results.

A New Jersey Superior Court judge ordered a blogger to defend her status as a journalist and explain why the state's shield law applied to her in her effort to avoid revealing the names of government officials she accused of wrongdoing.

Union County prosecutors subpoenaed blogger Tina Renna for the names of 16 government officials she accused of misusing county generators after Hurricane Sandy. Renna, who runs the website The County Watchers, claimed her sources would be revealed if she handed over the officials' names. A similar suit in Oregon raised the same issue: Are bloggers "journalists" and entitled to the protection of shield laws? In many states, the answer is far from clear.

Citizen Journalists, Social Media and the Law

The general rule is to apply old law to new technology. Libel law developed over the centuries in England and then in the United States. Truth developed as a libel defense in U.S. law primarily during the 19th century—well before the advent of radio, television, or the internet and social media. But the medium of transmission does not make a difference. The question is whether the message is true. Courtney Love found that out the hard way when she settled two suits in 2015 for Twitter-based libel by paying fashion designer Dawn Simorangkir first $430,000 and then $350,000.

Yet new technologies do bring some novel questions. As mentioned earlier, in 1966 Congress enacted legislation clarifying that online service providers, even those who screen content, are not responsible for libel posted by third parties. This protection is broad enough to cover news organizations that permit comments on their websites, and even to protect sites like Craigslist. But the people who do the posting are liable for libelous comments.

Those who post comments on the internet or other social media need to beware. They are responsible not only for their own defamatory words but also for repeating the defamatory words of others. This repetition is called "republication" of a libel, and it can lead to a successful defamation suit. Reposting or retweeting fall under the old republication-of-libel law.

Commentators can also be lulled by a false sense of security into posting or otherwise communicating defamatory comments "anonymously." Anyone using electronic means of communication is creating an electronic trail. Yes, computer experts can follow these electronic bread crumbs right to the perpetrator. In libel cases, subpoenas to the companies providing the electronic-communications services can lead to discovery of the source of the libel. Even the popular social media app Yik Yak leaves users vulnerable to discovery, as a college student posting racist threats at the University of Missouri found out in 2015.

Because anything posted on the internet has international reach, libel suits might possibly be filed in foreign countries. In 2004 in *Gutnick v. Dow Jones & Co.*, Australia's Canberra High Court unanimously affirmed jurisdiction in a case involving an article on *The Wall Street Journal*'s website by ruling that the place of publication was where the article was downloaded (Australia), not uploaded (New Jersey). Dow Jones then settled out of court for $580,000.

Of course, libel is not the internet journalist's only concern. The full spectrum of legal liability falls equally on anyone who, for example, invades privacy. Again, the message, not the medium of transmitting the message, is what matters.

To avoid copyright problems, instead of quoting large sections of other people's work without permission, use a link to the original source.

For bloggers who want to extol the virtues of products, the Federal Trade Commission has "Guides." Bloggers must disclose meaningful relationships with companies and products that they blog reviews about. Is a blogger being paid to do so or getting free samples or other benefits? The FTC can take violators to court and get injunctions against them.

A blogger who promises confidentiality to anonymous sources must also be aware that even if he or she lives in a state with a shield law, the definition of who is covered by the shield law may not be broad enough to cover the blogger. In 2006 and 2007, blogger Josh Wolf spent 226 days in jail in California. Josh's offense was his refusal to testify before a federal grand jury and hand over his raw videotape of a G-8 Summit protest that left a San Francisco police officer injured in 2005.

In short, a little "tweaking" of the law is sometimes necessary to accommodate new technology. But remember that new methods of transmitting messages come with all the same old legal baggage that encumbers older forms of communication.

Access to Courts

The Supreme Court held in 1979 that "members of the public have no constitutional right" under the Sixth Amendment to attend criminal trials. In a reversal exactly one year later, the justices held that the public and the press have a First Amendment right to attend criminal trials. The justices said the right was not absolute but trial judges could close criminal trials only when there was an "overriding interest" to justify such closure. The basic concern of judges when they close trials is to protect the accused person's Sixth Amendment right to an "impartial jury"—often translated by attorneys as "a fair trial."

In addition, the First Amendment prevents the government from conducting business—even trials—in secret. In the Richmond Newspapers case in 1980, Chief Justice Warren Burger traced the unbroken and uncontradicted history of open judicial proceedings in England and the U.S. He concluded that there is a "presumption of openness" in criminal trials and pointed out the important role of the news media as representatives of the public.

By 1984, the Supreme Court had decided that openness in criminal trials "enhances both the basic fairness of the criminal trial and the appearance of fairness so essential to public confidence in the system." Public proceedings vindicate the concerns of victims and the community in knowing that offenders are being brought to account for their criminal conduct "by jurors fairly and openly selected." Proceedings of jury selection can be closed, the chief justice said, only when a trial judge finds that closure preserves an "overriding interest" and is narrowly tailored to serve that interest.

Judges are using that option. For instance, when John Gotti was convicted of organized crime activities in New York, the jurors' names were kept secret. Gotti's attorneys unsuccessfully challenged their anonymity. Jurors' names in the Rodney King case, which resulted in riots in Los Angeles in 1992, also were withheld.

In 1986, the Supreme Court said that only an overriding interest found by a trial judge can overcome the presumption of openness of criminal proceedings. Today, 47 states allow cameras in at least some state courtrooms. Cameras are permitted in some lower federal courts but are excluded from the U.S. Supreme Court.

Copyright and Fair Use

The purpose of copyright law is to ensure compensation to authors for contributing to the common good by publishing their works. The Constitution provides for this in Article 1, Section 8, by giving Congress the power to secure "for limited times to authors and inventors the exclusive right to their respective writing and discoveries." The same section indicates that this provision is intended "to promote the progress of science and useful arts" for the benefit of the public. Copyright laws both protect your work and prohibit you from using significant amounts of others' writings without permission, which may in some cases require payment of a fee.

Key elements of copyright law include the following:

- Copyrightable works are protected from the moment they are fixed in tangible form, whether published or unpublished.

- Copyright protection begins with a work's "creation and . . . endures for a term consisting of the life of the author and 70 years after the author's death."

- Works for hire and anonymous and pseudonymous works are protected for 95 years from publication or 120 years from creation, whichever is shorter.

- There is a "fair use" limitation on the exclusive rights of copyright owners. In other words, it may be permissible to quote small excerpts from a copyrighted work without permission. According to the Supreme Court, these factors govern fair use:

   1. The purpose and character of the use.
   2. The nature of the copyrighted work.
   3. The size and significance of the portion used in relationship to the copyrighted work as a whole.
   4. The effect on the potential market for or value of the copyrighted work.

Although a work is copyrighted from the moment it is fixed in tangible form, the copyright statute says certain steps are necessary for the work to receive statutory protection. The author or publisher must:

- Publish or reproduce the work with the word "copyright" or the symbol ©, the name of the copyright owner and the year of publication.

- Register the work at the Library of Congress by filling out a form supplied by the Copyright Office and sending the form, the specified number of copies (usually one copy of an unpublished work and two copies of a published work), and a fee to the Copyright Office. The copies and registration fee may be sent together and usually are.

Copyright law has a special provision for broadcasters of live programs. Broadcasters need only make a simultaneous tape of their live broadcasts in order to receive copyright protection. The tape fulfills the requirement that a work be in a "fixed" form for copyright protection. Because a digital form is a "fixed" form, editors of online newspapers already meet that copyright requirement.

Some aspects of U.S. copyright law changed in 1989, when the U.S. finally joined the 100-year-old Berne Convention, an international copyright treaty, primarily to prevent the pirating of American film productions in other countries. The changes include the following:

- Placing a copyright notice on a work is no longer necessary to protect a copyright after publication. This is in line with the Berne Convention principle that copyright protection should not be subject to formalities. The copyright notice, however, is still widely used because it acts as a bar to an infringer's claim of innocent infringement.

- Copyright registration is generally a prerequisite for access to the federal courts for an infringement action. Registration prior to infringement is required for a copyright owner to recover statutory damages or attorney fees. The amount of statutory damages is determined by the judge.

Online journalism has created new copyright concerns. Using online content from others without permission can raise significant copyright issues, as the courts are still wrestling with the extent of the fair-use doctrine when it comes to online usage. The safe route, and the ethical choice, is to seek permission before using the work of others and to link to other news sites if you wish to direct readers to other content online.

The digital media also have changed the rules of the game for freelancers and other content providers. In 2001, the U.S. Supreme Court, ruling against media companies, said freelance writers have the power to decide whether the articles they sold to print publications may be reproduced in an electronic form. In a 7-2 decision, the justices ruled that *The New York Times* must either pay its freelance authors when redistributing their articles online or negotiate other conditions for republication.

SUGGESTED READINGS

Carter, T. Barton, Marc A. Franklin and Jay B. Wright. *The First Amendment and the Fourth Estate*. 8th ed. Westbury, N.Y.: Foundation Press, 2000. This text focuses on the relationship between the First Amendment and the press itself.

Middleton, Kent R., Robert Trager and Bill F. Chamberlin. *The Law of Public Communication*. 6th ed. Boston: Allyn & Bacon,

2003. This is a valuable and authoritative treatment of free-speech and free-press issues.

Overbeck, Wayne. *Major Principles of Media Law*. Toronto: Thomson Wadsworth, 2004. This standard text covers all important aspects of law as it applies to the mass media.

SUGGESTED WEBSITES

www.firstamendmentcenter.org
At this Freedom Forum site, you'll find the "State of the First Amendment" report by Donna Demas, which discusses the public's ambivalence about First Amendment issues.

www.medialaw.org
This is the site of the Media Law Resource Center, "a nonprofit information clearinghouse" organized in 1980 by leading media groups "to monitor developments and promote First Amendment

rights in the libel, privacy and related legal fields." The site features a 50-state survey of media libel law.

www.rcfp.org
The Reporters Committee for Freedom of the Press maintains online publications and guides on First Amendment and freedom-of-information issues. Here you'll find current hot stories, plus archives and much more.

EXERCISES

1. Using a search engine, identify a current First Amendment controversy of local interest. What are the issues? Write a two-page essay outlining the arguments and predicting the outcome of the controversy based on First Amendment analysis.

2. *The New York Times Co. v. Sullivan*, 376 U.S. 254 (1964), was a landmark decision in favor of the press. Discuss, in a short essay, the consequences for the press if the decision had been different.

3. Using the LexisNexis database, determine how the U.S Supreme Court has used *Richmond Newspapers v. Virginia* 448 U.S. 555 (1980), in later cases dealing with openness in criminal proceedings.

4. **Your journalism blog.** Find a news story generated by a public records request. One way to do this is by searching

the "FOI-at-work" tag at www.theartofaccess.com, a blog dedicated to freedom-of-information news. Write a blog post summarizing the story and explaining why access to governmental information was important to the story.

5. A group of students in your journalism class has decided to start a blog that focuses on campus issues of interest to the student body. The blog will welcome comments from students. Draft a set of principles for blog users to follow to avoid legal missteps.

6. What the law allows and what journalism ethics require can be quite different. Discuss the differences and similarities between those two guiding principles.

CHAPTER 20 ETHICS

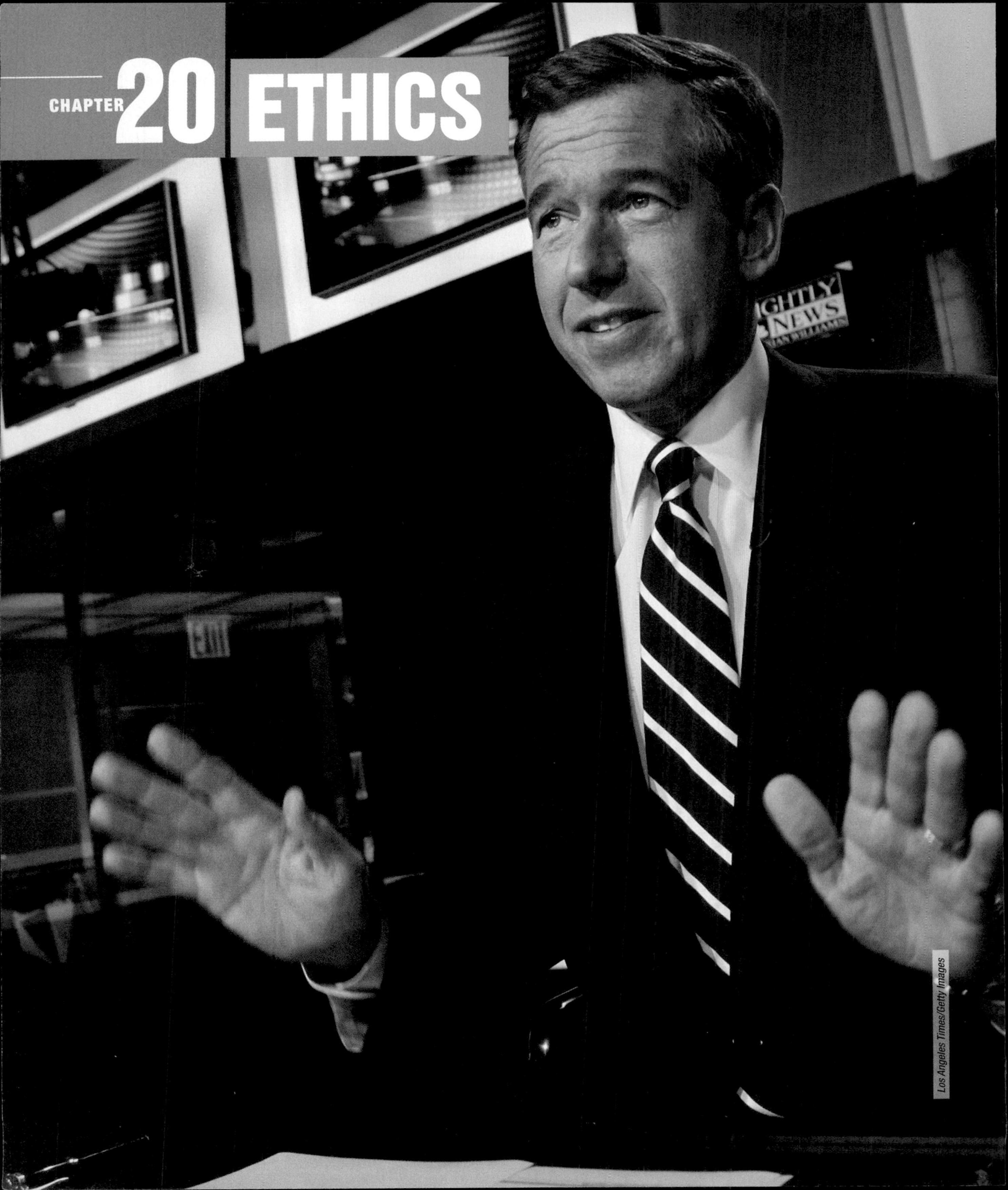

Los Angeles Times/Getty Images

For all those who heard him tell the story, it sounded like a chilling experience for NBC managing editor and news anchor Brian Williams—being in a helicopter in Iraq in 2003 that came under fire by a rocket-propelled grenade.

It was probably more chilling for Williams when he learned that military personnel said they witnessed him arrive on a helicopter that trailed the one that had been hit.

Williams had not only told his story on the Nightly News on Jan. 30, 2015, but he had also recounted the incident in other places at other times. Originally, in 2003, during the year the incident occurred, Williams told the truth about what happened. In 2007, his version of the truth began to change.

Some predicted that if Williams made up this story, he probably invented or enhanced others. Not surprisingly, it did not take NBC investigators long to uncover 11 instances in which he had exaggerated the truth or misled viewers in his reporting.

What a calamitous fall for the credibility of one of the nation's leading, most trusted journalists. Williams had failed in the most fundamental duty of journalists, the ethical requirement every citizen has the right to expect and demand of journalists—telling the truth.

It would be bad enough if only the reputation of Williams was damaged by his actions. However, because of his position, it was trust in journalism itself that took a serious blow.

Again we turn to the classic work, *The Element of Journalism*, by Bill Kovach and Tom Rosenstiel:

> If those doing journalism are truth seekers, it must follow that they be honest and truthful with their audiences, too—that they be truth presenters. . . . , If nothing else, this responsibility requires that those engaged in journalism be as open and honest with audiences as they can about what they know and what they don't. How can you claim to be seeking to convey the truth when you're not truthful with the audience in the first place?

"Truth matters," Richard Gingras and Sally Lehrman wrote in *The Trust Project* in October 2014. "Without it, both the news enterprise and our collective state of knowledge suffer. We live in an ever more challenging and complex world. Holding government, corporations and institutions accountable is increasingly vital. A working democracy relies on fair, accurate and thorough information that is distributed widely, consumed widely and respected for its credibility."

The authors cited a 2012 Pew Research Center survey that said Americans "simply did not expect a fair, full and accurate account of the days' events and issues." And 26 percent said "they did not trust the news to get facts right."

Does that mean journalists are unethical or are they simply incompetent? Or both?

Confusing the debate is the question of who is a journalist. Journalists work in the mass media, but in no way should journalism be identified as the mass

1
How the public perceives journalism ethics.

2
Three philosophical approaches that can help you find answers to ethical questions.

3
How to apply a method of principled reasoning to ethical problems.

4
What ethical questions are of special importance to journalists.

5
How to recognize and avoid plagiarism.

6
How to apply ethics to Twitter messages.

macmillanhighered.com
/newsreporting12e
Watch **"Journalism Ethics: What News Is Fit to Print?"**

- Who decides what news is fit to publish, post or broadcast? Who decides issues such as whether to publish the names of sexual assault victims? Who should decide, and why?
- How might convergence make it harder for journalists to maintain long-held ethical standards?

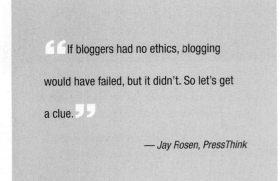

> **"** If bloggers had no ethics, blogging would have failed, but it didn't. So let's get a clue. **"**
>
> — *Jay Rosen, PressThink*

media. The mass media include movies, fictional television series and music—none of which purport to be journalism.

You can, of course, find journalism in blogs, in Twitter messages and in every other form of social media. And the principles and guidelines for being ethical apply to all media that can correctly be categorized as journalism. But journalism ethics do not necessarily apply to shows featuring political satirists, activist TV commentators or celebrity watchers, for example. Such shows may have the veneer of journalism, but they use current events only for entertainment purposes or commentary.

The Public Perception of Journalism Ethics

U.S. citizens have never had much regard for journalists' ethics. In a Gallup poll published on Dec. 21, 2015, 27 percent of respondents rated the honesty and ethics of journalists high or very high and 30 percent low or very low.

However, often people who accuse the news media of being unethical have no clear notion of what journalism and journalism ethics are all about. Yet most of these people will say they have no trust in the press because they consider journalism ethics to be an oxymoron (a contradiction in terms). Despite this public perception, journalism has never been practiced in a more ethical way in this country and in a host of other countries around the globe. How can that be? Let's look at two factors influencing the theory and practice of journalism today.

Bloggers as Watchdogs

Some of the credit for the increased ethical behavior of journalists belongs to bloggers and many others on the internet who are serving as watchdogs of the press and calling attention to every irregularity they see. Twitter users are quick to find errors, exaggerations and other problems with news coverage. As a result, journalists have responded by becoming much more transparent and by discussing their mistakes and failings.

David Leonhardt, Washington bureau chief for *The New York Times*, wrote in his Reddit chat: "I think the web has created a more responsible press, with higher standards. Think how much easier it is for readers to point out flaws (or perceived flaws!) in a story today than in the past."

Journalism Codes of Ethics

Like many other professions, journalism in its many forms has codes of ethics. Some professions have the power to keep people from practicing unless they have membership or a license to practice. These professions can also censure practitioners in a meaningful way, perhaps even keeping members from practicing if they violate the code of the profession.

Despite journalists' increased accountability, journalism as a profession has not established a mandatory and enforced code. Although there are voluntary societies in journalism, no association has the authority to enforce restrictions on journalists' behavior. That's because of a fear that such an association and such a code might in some way infringe upon freedom of the press or freedom of speech.

Examples of journalistic professional societies that have codes include the Society of Professional Journalists, the Public Relations Society of America, the International Association of Business Communicators, the American Society of Business Press Editors, the American Society of Magazine Editors and the American Business Media. However, journalists do not *have* to belong to such organizations to practice their profession.

Some critics condemn codes of ethics either for being hopelessly general and therefore ineffective or for being too restrictive. Some argue that strict codes help improve journalists' credibility; others say they merely make journalists easy targets for libel suits. Still, a majority of news organizations have established and enforced codes that restrict employees in their work. Journalists who have plagiarized, for example, have been suspended or fired from their news organizations.

Your employer might or might not have a code of ethics. Either way, you should devise your own ethical values and principles. Your upbringing, your education, and perhaps your religious training have already helped prepare you to do this.

Journalists too often and too easily justify all of their actions by citing the First Amendment. Because of the wide range of the First Amendment and the relatively few legal restraints on journalism, journalists need to discuss proper conduct—perhaps more than members of any other profession. As the famous Commission on Freedom of the Press, also known as the Hutchins Commission, concluded in 1947, unless journalists set their own limits on what is acceptable and responsible, government will eventually and inevitably do it for them.

Three Ethical Philosophies

Your personal ethics might derive from the way you answer one fundamental question: Does the end justify the means? In other words, should you ever do something that is not good in itself in order to achieve a goal that you think is good? Here's how adherents to three different ethical philosophies would answer that question.

The Ethics of Duty

Some ethicists hold quite simply that we have a duty to do what is right. They believe that some actions are always right and some always wrong; that is, there exists in nature (or, for those with religious faith, in divine revelation) a fixed set of principles or laws from which we should not deviate. For these people, the end *never* justifies the means.

That belief is why some refer to this ethical philosophy as **absolutism** or *legalism*. An absolutist sees one clear duty: to discover the rules and to follow them. For example:

- Suppose you believe that it's always wrong to lie. If you learn that a friend cheated on an exam and you are asked about your friend's actions by a college administrator, you would answer truthfully. You might be torn by loyalty to your friend, but you would not lie.

- Suppose you believe that it's wrong to keep someone else's property without permission. If you find a wallet with $500 in it, you would make every effort to return the wallet to its rightful owner.

One such absolutist was Immanuel Kant (1724–1804). Kant proposed the "categorical imperative," a moral law that obliges you to do only those things that you would be willing to have everyone do as a matter of universal law. Once you decide what the correct action is, you must regard your decision as unconditional and without exception, and you must do what you decide.

Many people draw support for their rigid sense of duty from their religious beliefs. They cite the Bible, the Quran or another religious source. If they themselves cannot resolve an ethical problem, they might turn to a minister, priest, rabbi, imam or guru for the answer. The absolutist is concerned only with doing what is right and needs only to discover what the right action is.

The journalist with this sense of duty is concerned only with whether an event is newsworthy. If an event is interesting, timely, significant or important, it is to be reported, regardless of the consequences. The duty of the journalist is to report the news. Period. Newscaster Walter Cronkite once said that if journalists worried about all the possible consequences of reporting something, they would never report anything.

Journalists who believe they have a duty to tell the news discount any criticism of the press for any stories it delivers to the public. Stop blaming the messenger, they say. We don't make events happen; we just report them.

The Ethics of Final Ends or Consequences

Many people believe that what makes an act ethical is not the act itself but the consequences of the act. In other words, they believe that the end can and often does justify the means. Actions that have "right consequences" are ethical actions. In this philosophy, ethics are more *relativistic* than absolutist. For example:

- Suppose your sister tells you that her husband is abusing her and she is moving to a shelter for battered women. If the husband asks you where your sister is, you would be justified, as one who practices relativism, in lying to protect her from him.

- Suppose a friend swears you to secrecy before telling you that he is feeling suicidal. If you believe that the consequences of an action determine its ethics, you would be justified in breaking your promise and getting help for your friend from a counselor or the friend's family.

An important consideration in relativism, the belief that nothing is objectively right or wrong, is the intention of the person performing the act. What one person would declare unethical, another person would do for a good purpose or a good reason. For example, police often work undercover, concealing their identity in order to apprehend criminals. In the course of this work, if they must lie or even get involved in criminal activity, they would accept that. Their purpose is to protect the public; their intention is to work for the good of society. The end justifies the means.

Some journalists would not hesitate to do the same. Some might require that certain conditions be in place before they would steal or use deceit, but then they would proceed. They believe their purpose is to be the watchdog of government, to protect the common good, to keep the public fully informed. Whatever they must do to accomplish these goals, they argue, is clearly ethical.

Situation Ethics: The Ethics of Specific Acts

When asked whether the end justifies the means, a person subscribing to **situation ethics** would reply, "It all depends." Here are four philosophies that make use of some form of situation ethics.

ON THE JOB Develop Your Ability to Identify Ethical Situations

Jean McHale earned her bachelor's degree in journalism and began her career in editorial roles at employee newsletters and trade publications. She transitioned to public relations and media-relations roles in government, higher education, and association management. She recently became accredited in public relations and continues to adopt new tools and technologies to develop and deliver messages and information. McHale says she has faced ethical choices throughout her career, but few situations presented themselves as neatly packaged defining moments.

"I've learned to recognize when my internal caution light is flashing," she says. "It is often a time when I cannot muster the energy to start a simple task, or when I feel the urge to rush through an assignment to get it off my plate."

Throughout her career, McHale has been asked to demonstrate ethical reasoning skills—often even before landing the job. "In most every job interview I've had, I've been asked to describe an ethically challenging situation and how I handled it."

Tim Trumble Photography.

When responding to this question, McHale says it isn't necessary to have a heroic watchdog story or to embellish your role in past situations. "Employers use this question to understand how you translate ethical principles into practice," she says. "It's fine to describe everyday situations and to explain why you chose to take action or why you elected not to take action.

"Being able to articulate your process for recognizing ethically challenging situations and working through them will show employers and colleagues that you strive to be transparent and are capable of critical thinking when evaluating a situation."

McHale offers this final advice: "I can't overemphasize the importance of trusting your unique values, education and experiences to guide the professional and ethical decisions you will encounter throughout your career."

TIPS

Ask These 10 Questions to Make Good Ethical Decisions

1. What do I know? What do I need to know?
2. What is my journalistic purpose?
3. What are my ethical concerns?
4. What organizational policies and professional guidelines should I consider?
5. How can I include other people, with different perspectives and diverse ideas, in the decision-making process?
6. Who are the stakeholders—those affected by my decision? What are their motivations? Which are legitimate?
7. What if the roles were reversed? How would I feel if I were in the shoes of one of the stakeholders?
8. What are the possible consequences of my actions? Short term? Long term?
9. What are my alternatives to maximize my truth telling responsibility and minimize harm?
10. Can I clearly and fully justify my thinking and my decision? To my colleagues? To the stakeholders? To the public?
—Bob Steele, Nelson Poynter Scholar for Journalism Values

No Moral Absolutes

Some believe there are no moral absolutes and that there is only one operative principle: Every person or every situation is unique, and to resolve an ethical problem by applying principles held by others or principles that apply in other cases is unethical. They believe that because each situation is unique, each ethical problem must be judged entirely on its own merits.

Love of Neighbor

Another type of situation ethics is based on the golden rule, essentially "You shall love your neighbor as yourself." This ethic holds that all principles are relative to one absolute: love of neighbor. Many think of love of neighbor as an essential Judeo-Christian value, but the fact is that most religions, as well as secular humanism and other creeds, hold human values as the highest good.

To state it simply, this form of situation ethics always places people first. In every ethical dilemma, you must always do what is best for people. Sometimes you must choose between love for one person and love for a larger community of people.

The Greatest Good for the Greatest Number

Love of neighbor can lead you to choose the action that is most likely to yield the greatest good for the greatest number. Some people add the words "over a long period of time" because some actions might seem wrong if one looks merely at the present situation.

Most journalists probably subscribe to this ethic. They know, for example, that publishing a story about the infidelities of a public official might destroy the person's reputation or hurt his or her family, but taking a greatest-good-for-the-greatest-number view, they decide that for the greater good, the public should have this information. The decision to publish will seem even more justifiable if the public official is involved in embezzlement or bribery or a possible threat to national security.

Ayn Rand's Rational Self-Interest

Ayn Rand's ethical philosophy of rational self-interest is the opposite of the greatest good for the greatest number and certainly of any form of altruism. Someone subscribing to her notion of ethical egoism would never sacrifice himself or herself for the good of others. An ethical egoist always looks out for his or her own self-interest first, believing that if everyone acted in this manner, we all would be better off.

Journalists who are ethical egoists do not mind using people for stories (for example, asking crime victims questions like "What did you feel when you were being shot at?"), even if the people they use have no idea how embarrassing the story might be to them. Photographers might take pictures of dying or dead children and of their grieving parents. Newscasters might not hesitate to show people committing suicide. In their opinion, whatever helps them get good stories and thus advance in the profession is ethical.

Some critics accuse journalists of embracing rational self-interest merely to sell publications or to increase traffic or ratings. However, on many occasions journalists report stories that anger both their readers and their advertisers.

Resolving Ethical Issues

Far too often, newsroom decisions are made on the basis of what will get the most views on the web or what will get the viewers' attention. If you subscribe to the ethics of duty, you have no decisions to make. If you know the news, report it. But most ethicists believe that reasonable people must make reasoned or principled decisions. These must be based on principles that will help you decide on proper or moral ways to act.

Principled reasoning assumes that you are not acting ethically if you do something simply because you have been told to do it or because that's what everyone else does. You are not ethical if you report a story just to beat the competition.

To help journalists and others make ethical decisions, ethicists Clifford Christians, Kim Rotzoll and Mark Fackler adapted a model of moral reasoning devised by Dr. Ralph Potter of Harvard Divinity School. Called the Potter Box (Figure 20.1), the model has four elements:

■ **Appraising the situation.** Making a good ethical decision begins with good reporting. You cannot make an ethical decision unless you know all the facts. Sometimes when you don't appraise a situation fully and get all of the facts, you end up being highly embarrassed. The same can happen when you edit out facts so as to change a story.

Neglecting to report the facts or to do any real reporting can result in great embarrassment for the media. Who would not like to believe that eating chocolate every day would help you lose

> ❝I tell the honest truth in my paper, and I leave the consequences to God.❞
>
> —*James Gordon Bennett,*
> *newspaper publisher, 1836*

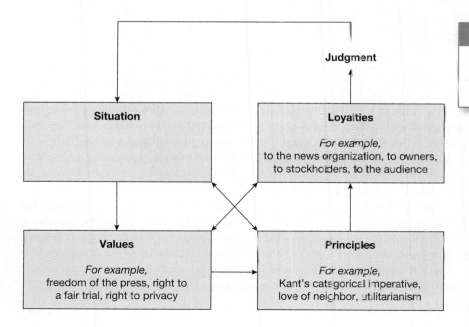

FIGURE 20.1

The Potter Box can help journalists analyze and resolve ethical problems.

Judgment

Situation

Loyalties

For example,
to the news organization, to owners,
to stockholders, to the audience

Values

For example,
freedom of the press, right to
a fair trial, right to privacy

Principles

For example,
Kant's categorical imperative,
love of neighbor, utilitarianism

weight? Science writer John Bohannon conducted a pseudo experiment to prove just that and then attempted to have certain results he and his cohorts chose published. Their website, Institute of Diet and Health, helped the process. Also, Bohannon said, "Since it was such bad science, we needed to skip peer review altogether."

The "study" appeared in numerous newspapers, on a couple of TV stations, and in *Shape* and *Prevention* magazines. Bohannon had to pay a fee to have it published in the *International Archives of Medicine*, apparently a normal practice. The publisher told him he had produced "an outstanding manuscript." It was published there in two weeks without a word changed.

Bohannon, who has a Ph.D. in molecular biology, says few reporters asked about how the research was conducted or about why the Institute of Diet and Health had done nothing previously. He says he doesn't blame reporters who picked up the chocolate study as much as the editors and media owners: "I know the pressure they're under. The blame really rests with the editors and owners of these media outlets—they're the ones who are profiting on this information, and they're pushing their reporters relentlessly with this daily grind of getting headlines out.

"You have to start by shaming them."

■ **Identifying values.** What are your personal values, your news organization's values, your community's values, the nation's values? For example, you might place high value on your personal credibility and on that of your news organization.

When 27-year veteran and three-time Pulitzer Prize–winning *Washington Post* reporter Sari Horwitz was caught copying and pasting material from *The Arizona Republic* twice in six days, it wasn't just *The Post* that was harmed. As Dennis Wagner, the reporter who did most of the work on the original story, said, "It's bad because it undermines the credibility not just of *The Washington Post* but of journalists in general. People think we take shortcuts and cheat, and it's hurtful to all of us."

Horwitz blamed deadline pressures for her actions and apologized. "It was wrong. It was inexcusable," she said. "And it is one of the cardinal sins in journalism. I apologize to *The Arizona Republic* and its reporters and editors."

■ **Appealing to ethical principles.** Look at the various ethical principles discussed previously. Contrary to what many believe, it's not always sufficient to follow your gut. If that were true, the world would have only ethical people in it. Nor are the principles meant to be a shopping list from which you choose items that serve your personal interest. To be ethical, you might have to choose a principle or principles that are far from expedient.

It might be expedient to make up sources to fit a story you are reporting, but expedience is rarely if ever a good ethical principle. Madison Roberts, a freshman majoring in journalism at the University of Alabama, created names, years and majors for sources in her stories in *The Crimson White,* the university newspaper. She had quoted nearly 30 students and a professor, none of whom existed, and wrote a number of stories with only fabricated sources.

"I was overwhelmed and succumbed to a lot of pressure I'd been under," Roberts wrote. "I did it because *The Crimson White* had become so important to me that I didn't want to lose it."

■ **Choosing loyalties.** Without question, your most important loyalty must be to your own principles and values. You must be able to look yourself in the mirror; you must be able to sleep at night. Your second most important loyalty is to your readers, listeners or viewers. You have a bond with them, and you dare not break their trust. Third, be loyal to the news organization for which you work. Sometimes this involves a bit of compromise, but you must consider seriously what your boss wants from you. You do need a job. Fourth, you must be loyal to your sources and to the people about whom you are reporting.

Sometimes being loyal to yourself and your principles gets you thrown in jail or fired. Caitlin Curran believed that it was wrong for brokerage houses to sell worthless mortgage-backed securities. A photo of her carrying a sign of her belief went viral on the web, and she was fired from her part-time job as a web producer with a Public Radio International show on WNYC in New York. Curran knew the rules against activism, and she chose to do something she deemed more important.

You need not consider the four elements in the Potter Box in any particular order. Also, don't stop reasoning after you have touched upon the four elements. Principled reasoning should continue, and be sure to use it in the discussion of other ethical problems. The main objection to the Potter Box is that using it takes too much time and is impractical in the deadline-driven business of journalism. However, as you become better acquainted with ethical principles and more practiced at principled reasoning, you will be able to make ethical decisions much more quickly and reasonably.

Ethical Problems for Journalists

Because of the First Amendment, American society has relatively few "rules" for journalists despite the special problems they face. The web has introduced new ethical issues for journalists and, many times, those who write news for the web have had no training in journalism ethics.

Without a doubt, the news often is not vetted the way it used to be before appearing in a newspaper or in a regular newscast. Cutbacks in newsroom staffs have also added to the difficulty of maintaining accuracy and credibility. Reporters are now expected to be involved in social media, and that, too, takes precious time.

All of this does not excuse the ethical violations discussed here. If anything, journalists need to be more versed in applying ethical principles than ever before.

> "Journalists are becoming the de facto peer review system. And when we fail, the world is awash in junk science."
>
> — *John Bohannon, science writer*

> "Ethics is a system of principles, a morality or code of conduct. It is the values and rules of life recognized by an individual, group or culture seeking guidelines to human conduct and what is good or bad, right or wrong."
>
> — *Conrad C. Fink, professor and author*

Deceit

When is it permissible to lie, misrepresent yourself or use a hidden audio recorder or camera? When may you steal documents? For those subscribing to the ethics of duty, the answer is simple: Never! The simple reason is that they would never want lying or concealing one's identity to become a universal law. For others, the answer is not easy.

> **"**Journalists demean themselves and damage their credibility when they misrepresent themselves and their work to news sources and, in turn, to the public at large.**"**
>
> — *Everette E. Dennis, Dean and CEO of Northwestern University in Qatar*

Journalists and other writers have often concealed their identity in pursuit of a story. One reporter got a job in a grocery store to expose it for selling bad meat; an atheist became close to churchgoers to write a book about the evangelical church. Yet Fred Barnes, an editor at *The Weekly Standard*, says that if you're a journalist, it's dishonest to profess to be someone you're not.

Former *Los Angeles Times* writer and now Washington editor of *Harper's Magazine* Ken Silverstein misrepresented his identity "pretending to be the representative of a London-based energy company with business interest in Turkmenistan." He was reporting on Washington lobbyists who were doing their usual work of selling their services for any reason to any client. In an essay in *Harper's*, Silverstein takes the Washington press corps to task for being too timid for not using deception as a reporting tool.

A group of journalists in an ethical decision-making seminar at the Poynter Institute devised a list of criteria to justify the use of deceit. The box "Conditions Justifying the Use of Deceit by Journalists" below synthesizes their conclusions. All the conditions listed there must be present to justify deceit.

Conditions Justifying the Use of Deceit by Journalists

- An issue of profound public importance:
  - Of vital public interest, revealing system failure at high levels.
  - A preventive measure against profound harm to individuals.
- All other alternatives exhausted.
- Eventual full disclosure of the deception and the reason for it.
- Full commitment to the story by everyone involved.
- The harm prevented outweighs any harm caused.
- A meaningful, collaborative and deliberative decision-making process that takes into account:
  - Short- and long-term consequences of the deception.
  - The impact on credibility.
  - Motivations for actions.
  - Congruence between the deceptive act and the organization's editorial mission.
  - Legal implications.
  - Consistency of reasoning and action.

Conflicts of Interest

Conflicts of interest can crop up anywhere, especially in the area of politics. On his MSNBC show, José Diaz-Balart once broadcast from a National Council of La Raza (NCLR) conference in Los Angeles. When hosting an illegal immigrant activist who was calling for legalization and citizenship, Diaz-Balart responded favorably. He also used the program to support the NCLR agenda. Diaz-Balart did not mention that at the conference, he had received an award, the Ruben Salazar Award for Communication, given "each year to an outstanding communications professional dedicated to portraying news relevant to U.S. Hispanics." Even when a guest congratulated him for the award, he did not explain what the guest what talking about.

José Diaz-Balart probably knew he would receive an award at the NCLR convention. Broadcasting his program from there and expressing views supporting the NCLR agenda demonstrated a clear conflict of interest. Also, once a guest congratulated him on the reward, he certainly should have acknowledged it.

Conflicts of interest can occur outside the political arena, too. The Public Relations Society of America's Member Code of Ethics states that a member shall "disclose financial interest (such as stock ownership) in a client's organization." Should business reporters be allowed to cover companies in which they own stocks? Should all reporters be required to list the companies in which they hold stocks? Should religion writers cover news and events of the religion to which they belong?

Friendship

Friendship might be the greatest obstacle to the flow of information. No one knows whether friendship causes more stories to be reported or more stories to be killed. Either way, it sets up a powerful conflict of interest. If you are ever assigned to a story that involves a personal acquaintance, ask your supervisor to give the assignment to someone else.

Payola

Payola is a contraction of "pay" and "Victrola" (an early phonograph for playing LP records). That etymology tells you that payola began in the music industry in radio in the 1960s. It soon became illegal in that industry, and it was never permitted in journalism. Journalists may not accept payment for a story other than from their employer. Also, news organizations frown upon reporters doing promotional work for people they cover.

Not being permitted does not mean it's not happening. The line between demanding pay, favors or gifts and simply accepting them without asking for them is quite thin. That line is frequently being crossed in the world of blogging these days. As Jonathan Strong of *The Daily Caller* wrote in 2010:

> [I]ncreasingly, many bloggers are also secretly feeding on cash from political campaigns, in a form of partisan payola that erases the line between journalism and paid endorsement.
>
> "It's standard operating procedure" to pay bloggers for favorable coverage, says one Republican campaign operative. A GOP blogger-for-hire estimates that "at least half the bloggers that are out there" on the Republican side "are getting remuneration in some way beyond ad sales."

And it's not just in the world of politics. Pete Brown, who writes a blog about beer, tells us about an agency that contacted him with this message:

> I was wondering what the cost would be for me if I wanted to seed 1 story a week for a month. Basically, what I mean by seeding is that you'd blog or someone would write something saying . . . "I heard this beer is X% alcohol content," etc. . . . Let me know if this is something you'd be interested in doing and again, if so, what is the price tag associated with that.

Brown states it simply. By taking money it becomes advertising, and he would be presenting the information as if it were not—"clearly misleading my readers, and being dishonest in my writing."

That, he says, he would never do—for three reasons: "One—integrity—I have some. Two—career practicality—if I did this, and someone found out that I'd done it, no one would ever trust anything I wrote ever again. My writing career would be over. And three—it is probably illegal. It certainly breaks any general journalistic and blogging standards of behavior."

Actually, of course, it is not illegal, but you have to admire Brown's "standards of behavior."

Some conflicts of interest are perhaps not so obvious. Should news agencies prohibit journalists from accepting speakers' fees? Should Congress attempt to legislate full disclosure of journalists' income and associations?

Freebies

When journalists accept freebies from people they cover, the gifts always come with a price. They raise these questions:

- Can reporters remain objective?
- Do gifts cause reporters to write stories they otherwise would not write?
- Does the public perceive the reporter who accepted or is suspected of accepting freebies as objective?

As with other conflicts of interest, it's the perception that is paramount. Some argue that the least reporters must do is disclose prominently in their stories any freebies they accepted. As in any case of deceit, reporters must disclose how they were able to get the story and why accepting freebies was necessary.

For example, travel writers are offered free trips, free cruises, free hotel accommodations and other freebies by companies that expect them to write about what they experience. Many small news outlets cannot afford to send their travel writers on expensive tours. Travel writers who accept freebies must mention doing so in their stories and allow readers to decide whether to trust the reporting.

After a lecture on this topic to travel writers, a participant approached the speaker and asked, "Are you saying that if a company gives you a free trip somewhere and you find some things to criticize, you're supposed to write about the negative aspects of the trip?"

Yes.

Most news organizations have rules against accepting freebies. The Society of Professional Journalists says, "Nothing of value shall be accepted." Is a cup of coffee something of value? The Associated Press expects its staff members to return gifts of "nominal value." Is a baseball cap of nominal value?

Checkbook Journalism

Paying a source for information brings up a number of ethical questions.

- Must you always report that you had to pay a source for information?
- Should reporters be in the business of keeping other reporters from getting a story?
- Are paid sources likely to have an ax to grind?
- Do paid sources come forward only for financial gain?
- Will the audience believe your story if you paid your source for it?
- If you pay some sources for information, will others start to demand pay for information?

ABC News first denied and then admitted paying $200,000 to accused murderer Casey Anthony for "exclusive rights to an extensive library of photos and home video for use by our broadcasts, platforms, affiliates and international partners." Less than two weeks later, ABC abandoned checkbook journalism altogether. According to *The Daily Beast*/Poynter on www.poynter.com, the new president of ABC News, Ben Sherwood, "concluded that the cash-register approach to journalism was starting to tarnish the network's credibility, even though the practice was relatively infrequent."

Surely, good reporting demands that you pay sources only when necessary and only if you can get other sources to corroborate your findings. You'd also better be sure that your bosses know that you're doing it.

As he always does, Evan Rosenblum, an executive producer for the celebrity website TMZ, paid for the video showing Baltimore Ravens star running back Ray Rice knocking out his then fiancée Janay Palmer in an elevator in an Atlantic City hotel. The video caused Rice to be suspended indefinitely from the NFL.

Participation in the News

At times, journalists receive severe criticism for doing what seems to be right and humane. When network correspondents were seen on television performing medical treatment in Haiti, Dr. Carl Elliott of the University of Minnesota Center for Bioethics called it "a classic PR tactic using humanitarian aid as a public relations device, in order to drive up ratings for their network."

> "Conflict of interest is practically the only place in ethics where perceptions matter almost as much as what is the case."
>
> — *Lee Wilkins, co-author of* Media Ethics: Issues and Cases *and editor of the* Journal of Mass Media Ethics

ON THE JOB Nurturing a Healthy Ethical Process in an Ever-Changing Environment

Poynter Institute.

Every morning **Kelly McBride** walks into her office at the Poynter Institute, clicks on ESPN, boots up TweetDeck, Facebook and a dozen aggregation sites, and scans the developments of the day.

Then her phone starts to ring. Eight years ago, the calls came from professional journalists working in newsrooms. Now many come from bloggers, freelancers and political activists. Although the callers differ widely, they have one thing in common: They're all making ethical choices that have significant consequences.

"Every journalist must 'do ethics' in every story," McBride says. "Young journalists make a common mistake when they fail to identify everyday decisions as ethical choices. Journalists of all experience levels make an even bigger mistake: They assume they should know the answer to every ethical question. Both mistakes undermine a healthy ethical process."

McBride spent 14 years as a reporter at *The Spokesman-Review* in Spokane, Washington. As the journalism landscape has dramatically changed in recent years, McBride has often been the champion of ethical reasoning in an environment that seems to have few widely accepted notions of right and wrong.

"I've stopped trying to figure out who is a journalist and who isn't. Instead, I focus on information that acts like journalism," she says. "If a certain piece of information acts like journalism, then there should be an ethical process behind it because it affects the democratic process.

"Young journalists and small bloggers have more power than they imagine in growing this process," McBride says.

She learned that in a healthy newsroom, reporters constantly turn to one another for exchanges. The pathways between the editors' and reporters' desks are busy, two-way streets. At the intersections, journalists cluster in conversation. The most encouraging sign of all occurs when a huddle briefly loosens up and more people are invited into the discussion.

"When a culture is sick, decisions are made in secret, behind closed doors," McBride says. "Surprises show up in the paper or on the air without explanation, and no one knows how the decisions were made. People are afraid to ask questions. There is very little talking."

The same ethical process occurs in new forms of media, but often the conversations happen in virtual spaces like Twitter.

From the Poynter Institute, McBride gets a larger view. "The underlying values of journalism are becoming more and more diffuse, the further we get along in this revolution. In the future, we will get journalism from a variety of sources, including but not limited to professional journalists. The prevailing values of truth and accuracy are going to look different, depending on the source creating the story. I worry about the effect that will have on democracy."

McBride is vice president of academic programs at the Poynter Institute. You can send her questions at Kelly@poynter.org and read her regular column at www.poynter.org.

Bob Steele, who taught journalism ethics at DePauw University, concurs. He told blogger Matea Gold of the *Los Angeles Times*: "If it's imperative that (a reporter) intervene and help medically, then take him out of his journalistic role and do that. But don't have him covering the same stories in which he's a participant. It muddles the journalist reporting. It clouds the lens in terms of the independent observation and reporting."

Must journalists be passive citizens? Must they give up all activity that advocates or shows a point of view? Must a religion reporter be an atheist? Richard Harwood, *Washington Post* ombudsman at the time, told a conference of journalists: "You have every right in the world to run for office, or participate in a political activity or lobbying activity. You don't have the 'right' to work for *The Washington Post*."

Wisconsin State Journal editor John Smalley told his staffers:

> People accept work-related policies and restrictions all the time. If you want to sell high-end clothing, you can't wear cut-off jeans to work. If you want to deliver Coca-Cola, you can't drink Pepsi in your truck.
>
> And if you want to be a journalist, you keep your politics to yourself. That's just the way it is, and it's a deal every journalist accepts when he or she joins the profession.

Advertising Pressure

It's likely you won't work long at a news organization before you realize some subjects are taboo to write about and others are highly encouraged. If you are lucky, you will work for a paper, station or magazine with a solid wall of separation between editorial and advertising, sometimes referred to as "the separation of church and state."

However, in some places, advertising salespeople are allowed to peek over that wall and see what stories the publication or station is planning to run. That information might help sell some advertising. Some say, what could be wrong with that?

The next step is for the advertising department to climb over the wall and suggest that editorial do a story on some subject so that advertising can be sold.

And then the next step isn't too far away. Advertising salespeople begin to suggest or even to dictate what must and must not be printed in the newspaper, said on radio or shown on television, or even displayed on the website. In print media, advertisers might want the layout, design and type of their ads or sections to look like the publication's normal layout and design. They might also insist that the word "advertising" appear in small print or at the bottom of the page, or that it be dropped altogether. Some advertisers prefer the term "sponsored by," which they believe softens the pure sales pitch of their message.

In early 2010, newspaper consultant Alan Mutter reported in his blog that 17 percent of newspapers had returned to an earlier practice of placing ads on their front pages, including the venerable *New York Times* that began the practice a year earlier.

Newspapers have also used colorful "sticky notes" above the fold to advertise. Magazines are doing the same.

Frank Anderson, writing under the head "Magazine Cover Advertisements: A Necessary Evil—Or Just Evil," wonders why anyone would believe a magazine with an ad on the cover. He writes that cover ads do not set the right tone for publication. To him they shout, "Hey, our magazine has sold out."

> "But I don't believe that paying sources is unethical, as long as it's disclosed to the reader; in some cases I think it makes for better journalism. It gives a fair share of the profits to sources who spend time and take risks."
>
> — *John Tierney, from "Newsworthy," reprinted from the New York Times Company*

> " If you're not involved in the community at all and you're totally neutralized, you end up not knowing enough about the community, not being able to get enough leads and so on in order to do your job. "
>
> — *Ethicist Louis W. Hodges, quoted by Tony Case in* Editor & Publisher

Magazines and "New Financial Pillars"

The Atlantic Monthly has brought journalists and policymakers together for off-the-record conversations for years, with each meeting sponsored by a different corporation. Eric Alterman, a senior fellow at the Center for American Progress, quotes *Atlantic Monthly* Media Chairman David Bradley as saying such meetings are necessary because "the economic foundation beneath journalism is falling away." The article quotes Bradley further: "The imperative, as I see it, is to rebuild journalism on different financial pillars. One of them, and not inconsequential to us, is events—of all types."

The dangers in these practices are twofold. The policymakers involved in these friendly chats are more likely to demand friendly stories from the writers or, perhaps worse, no stories at all. No stories would deprive readers of information they need or should have.

Invasion of Privacy

Most journalists would cry out against an invasion of their own privacy. Yet many of them argue for a vague "right to know" when they report on others, especially if those others are public officials or public figures. The head-on collision of the right to know and the right to privacy will confront you every day of your reporting life. The Constitution mentions neither "right."

There are many ways to invade people's privacy with hidden cameras and microphones. Now nearly everyone with a cellphone has become a photographer, and no place is private outside one's home.

One thing we know for sure. Nothing you write on the internet is secure. *New York Times* reporter Nicole Perlroth quotes internet security researcher Dan Kaminsky:

> What people don't realize is that hacking and spying went mainstream a decade ago. They think hacking is some difficult thing. Meanwhile, everyone is reading everyone else's emails—girlfriends are reading boyfriends', bosses are reading employees'— because it's just so easy to do.

True, there are some ways to slow people down from reading your emails, but Kaminsky says, "The reality is if you don't want something to show up on the front page of *The New York Times*, then don't say it." The ethical question that remains for you is this: Is it ever ethical to quote someone's personal email? If doing so would prevent a serious evil from occurring (stopping the bombings at the 2013 Boston Marathon), a teleological ethicist would justify it. Otherwise, privacy would demand refraining from using it.

Crime Victims

The most obvious and talked-about issue related to the right to privacy is naming crime survivors, especially rape and sex-crime survivors. The U.S. Supreme Court has held that news agencies cannot be punished for publishing lawfully obtained information or information from a public record. Meanwhile, legislators in many states are looking for ways to close the records on rape and to punish police, hospitals, court clerks and other officials who release survivors' names.

So the issue comes down to a matter of ethics, and as usual, there is not complete agreement. Not publishing the name continues the stigma that somehow the rape was the survivor's fault. Publishing the survivor's name heaps more suffering upon that person. Few news outlets would publish a rape survivor's name without the person's approval.

And there's always the possibility that the accusation is false.

Solving ethical questions is not easy. Suppose you had been the editor in Kennebunk, Maine, a town of 10,500, and were handed a list of more than 150 names of residents, including some prominent community figures, who were secretly taped having sexual encounters with 29-year-old Zumba instructor Alexis Wright.

- Would you publish all of the names? What is your policy for publishing misdemeanors?
- Would you publish only the names of the prominent community figures?
- Would it make a difference if your paper publishes a police log as a matter of routine?
- What if you know other papers in the area will publish the names?
- If you do not publish the names, are you concerned that innocent men might be thought to be among the 150?

Juvenile Offenders

Another ethical issue concerns publishing the names of juvenile offenders. News agencies traditionally have not published them because they have held that juveniles are entitled to make juvenile mistakes, even if those mistakes are crimes. After all, juvenile court records are sealed. Again, the courts have upheld the right to publish juvenile offenders' names that are on the public record.

Some media critics have applauded the publication of the names of juvenile offenders. However, in addition to the stigma forever attached to the juvenile offender's name and the embarrassment to his or her parents and family, some worry that in some groups a youth's notoriety will encourage other young people to violate the law. Others argue that shame will stop other juveniles from committing crimes.

Victims of Child Abuse and Their Families

"Prison for Subway's Jared." Front-page *USA Today* headline. Anyone who had kept up with the news was not too surprised, but it was still shocking. The subhead gave some news: "Fogle sought teen sex, child porn; will pay 14 victims."

Child abuse is news, and it should be, especially if it involves well-known celebrities such as Fogle whose foundation arranged for him to visit schools and urge children to adopt good eating habits and to exercise.

The victims of Fogle's abuse, both those he abused physically and those in pornographic videos he viewed, apparently did not report his actions. Victims of child abuse are often ashamed to talk about it, even to their parents, and their parents are even more ashamed. But once one victim has the courage to speak, others often follow. The lessons of the child abuse accusations at Penn State University are obvious.

The Philadelphia Inquirer reported that, after the Penn State scandal broke, the hotline of the Rape, Abuse and Incest National Network had its busiest month since it started in 2006. The average number of sessions a month jumped from 2,500 to 3,100. A lawyer in Miami who represents victims of sexual abuse reported that his website, which ordinarily receives 5,000 hits a month, received 15,000 in one month after the scandal broke. In the six weeks after the scandal became public, the Survivors Network of Those Abused by Priests said that "it had been deluged with emails and phone calls from survivors, many breaking their silence for the first time."

Perhaps reporters have inborn respect and admiration for certain people and professions. Are they too prone to see only the heroics of sports stars? Is that why not a single reporter checked on anything that Notre Dame's Manti Te'o was saying about his fictional girlfriend? How could Father Lawrence Murphy have sexually abused as many as 200 boys in a school for the deaf in St. Francis, Wisconsin, without anyone in the press knowing about it? How could so much sexual abuse by Roman Catholic priests have gone on for so long without more investigations from the news media?

Is there any class or profession or institution that journalists should not be skeptical of? Should the news media pay more attention to rumors?

And how far, how graphic, should the news media go in describing what victims are made to suffer? Should reporters visit their parents?

Sexual Orientation

Perhaps no issue is as muddled and contentious as when to reveal someone's sexual orientation. Not even the members of the National Lesbian and Gay Journalists Association have agreed on a policy. However, when a public figure or a religious leader has made a point of attacking gays or opposing same-sex marriage and that person is secretly leading a gay life, most would agree it is ethical to out that person.

Public Figures

These are just a few of the myriad privacy issues you will face. Journalists are still protected when writing about public officials and public figures—most of the time. But what about the children of politicians or celebrities?

Websites exist that have files on nearly everyone. Some allow you to see what anyone has ever posted in a chat room. What may journalists use? Legitimate, respectable journalism does not permit, let alone use, material obtained by hacking. Some corporations, however, claim the right to know what employees write on company computers during work time. The federal government sometimes claims the right to capture emails for national security reasons.

Photos and Video

The Associated Press Statement of News Values could not be clearer: "AP pictures must always tell the truth. We do not alter or digitally manipulate the content of a photograph in any way."

The National Press Photographers Association Code of Ethics states: "Treat subjects with respect and dignity. Give special consideration to vulnerable subjects and compassion to victims of crime or tragedy. Intrude on private moments of grief only when the public has an overriding and justifiable need to see."

Those two rules are the primary ethical concerns of photojournalists of all media. Photomanipulation is so simple with Photoshop or other editing devices, and privacy is too easily and too often violated.

Photographers for print and video journalists must respect people's dignity at crime and disaster scenes, and they need to be invited to a funeral unless it is for a public figure. With permission of the family, they may now photograph coffins containing deceased soldiers from U.S. military actions.

Judgments about using photos are often a matter of taste more than ethics. Here are some examples.

Perhaps you would not expect the New York *Daily News* to doctor a photograph to make it appear less gory, but that's what the paper did to its front-page picture in its coverage of the 2013 Boston marathon tragedy. The man on the back page of a wrap-around cover had a badly mangled, bloodied leg. You see a normal leg in the *Daily News* photo.

"The *Daily News* edited that photo out of sensitivity to the victims, the families and the survivors," *Daily News* spokesperson Ken Frydman said. "There were far more gory photos that the paper chose not to run, and frankly I think the rest of the media should have been as sensitive as the *Daily News*."

Photo by: NY Daily News via Getty Images.

The New York Daily News *altered this photo of the aftermath of the Boston Marathon bombing to make the scene less disturbing to readers.*

The New York *Daily News* did not show similar sensitivity telling the news about the slaying of WBDJ reporter Alison Parker and her cameraman Adam Ward in Roanoke, Virginia, Aug. 26, 2015. In three panels, the paper printed close-up images of the gunman's execution on its front page.

A half dozen or more tabloids from around the world were equally insensitive with the photos and headlines emphasizing that the two victims were shot dead on "live TV." The (London) *Daily Mail*'s headline said a "gunman with a grudge shot news girl on live TV."

Some argued that there's a blurry line between showing and not showing the photos taken by the murderer. How else would we witness the horror?

"The line is pretty clear to me. It is the moment when information becomes exploitation," said Ken Paulson, a former *USA Today* editor in chief, president of the First Amendment Center and dean of communications at Middle Tennessee State University.

Freelance photographer R. Umar Abbasi was waiting for a train on the platform of the 49th Street subway station in Manhattan when he saw a man on a subway track about to be killed by an oncoming train. Jeff Sonderman quotes the photographer in *Poynter* as saying, "I just started running, running, hoping that the driver could see my flash." What his flashes did capture were pictures of a desperate man trying to save his life. The engineer saw the flashes but said he could not stop.

The *New York Post* could have stopped. It did not have to run the resulting photo—at least not on a full front page—but it did. It's one thing to ask whether the photographer should have dropped his camera and tried to save the man's life. There were others present who could have done so. Some people defended the photographer. But it is another question to ask whether the *Post* had any reason to run the photo—and on the front page.

Some people defended the newspaper's decision. But most people, including journalism professors and scholars, condemned the *Post* for being sensationalistic and insensitive. *USA Today* quoted Poynter's Kelly McBride as saying that printing the picture had no "journalistic purpose." She explained that it did "not bear witness to something people need to know about."

Withholding Information

A journalist's job is to report the news. The public expects it—even demands it. To deliberately withhold news from the public becomes a matter of ethics.

Donald J. Trump once told President Barack Obama he would make a $5 million donation to a charity if the president would release his college records and passport information. In response, Lloyd Grove, editor of *The Daily Beast*, wrote in his paper: "Effective immediately, in light of your latest foolish attempt at seeming important, we will ignore you and your hot air for the foreseeable future—or at the very least, until after the Nov. 6 election."

Another blackout of the news was announced by *The Huffington Post:*

> After watching and listening to Donald Trump since he announced his candidacy for president, we have decided we won't report on Trump's campaign as part of *The Huffington Post*'s political coverage. Instead, we will cover his campaign as part of

our Entertainment section. Our reason is simple: Trump's campaign is a sideshow. We won't take the bait. If you are interested in what The Donald has to say, you'll find it next to our stories on the Kardashians and The Bachelorette.

The Huffington Post's decision was roundly criticized by many who already questioned its legitimacy as a news agency. Even five-time independent candidate for president Ralph Nader condemned the decision: "If [*The Huffington Post*] existed in the 1980s, would they have done this to that B-list actor, Ronald Reagan?"

However, sometimes withholding information is the ethical course. Few knew that Richard Engel, the chief foreign correspondent for NBC news, and his TV crew had spent five days in captivity in Syria. Their kidnapping was a secret because NBC, the other major television networks, and newspapers such as *The New York Times*, agreed to keep the facts quiet until the safe return of the journalists.

Is it ever permissible to withhold information from the news organization for which you work? If you are a working journalist writing what you hope will be a best-selling book, may you save some "news" until after the book is published?

If you work as a journalist, are you ever off-duty? A doctor isn't. Doctors take an oath to treat the sick. If you witness something at a friend's house or at a party, do you tell your news director about it? One reporter was fired when his boss discovered that he had attended a rock band's post-concert party, where lines of cocaine were openly available. The reporter did not include this information in his coverage of the band. His defense was that if he reported the illegal drug use, he would never get interviews with or access to other rock groups, and he would be finished as a music critic. His excuse didn't save his job.

When should you withhold information because the police ask you to or because it may jeopardize a case? McBride says, "Cutting deals to withhold information is dangerous. It should be done with great caution, much forethought and only in rare circumstances." She also warns that "we too readily agree with police and keep information from the public."

Incorrect and Incomplete Information

One situation in which some media organizations withhold information occurs when they have published incorrect information. Print publications that get the news wrong customarily inform readers of these mistakes in a corrections column, usually on the second page of the publication. Some online news sites, however, act as if they never make mistakes. They simply post new stories with updated information or act as if the first stories never appeared. The Canadian Association of Journalists has these recommendations for online corrections:

- Be transparent with your online audience, telling them when you've made an error—be it a spelling mistake or new information in a developing story.

- Engage your readers: Ask them to point out mistakes, verify the information they provide in corrections and make this an easy process.

- Be timely with your corrections.

- Place your corrections with or as part of the article. There's no real "Page 2" online that mirrors the newspaper tradition when it comes to corrections.

- Have the same standard for accuracy and corrections across all platforms. If people clicked through via Twitter, Facebook, LinkedIn or Google+, the correction and corrected items should also be found in these spots.

Online journalists often make up for incomplete information by using links to external sites. Are raw data journalism? How much and how often may you link to raw data, and with what warnings or interpretations? There's little doubt that readers appreciate links to source data so they can make judgments for themselves. At the same time, good websites help readers navigate that information. Journalists are still trying to find the right balance between the two.

Plagiarism

No one wants you to use his or her work as your own. Everyone condemns **plagiarism**—journalism's capital offense.

Plagiarism regularly raises its ugly head everywhere. Rookies and veterans in every area of journalism ruin their personal reputations and sully the reputations of the news organizations for which they work.

It's not that writers don't realize the wrong they are doing. BuzzFeed's political editor was fired after it was discovered that in 41 instances in his 500 stories there were "sentences or phrases copied word for word from other sites."

The week the news broke about his plagiarism, Benny Johnson expressed his disapproval of plagiarism. He accused another site of using language from one of his stories, and he wrote, "Repeat after me, copying and pasting someone's work is called 'plagiarism.'"

CNN received no complaints about plagiarism, and yet one of its London bureau news editors had published about 50 stories containing 128 separate instances of plagiarism. Most of the material Marie-Louise Gumuchian had lifted came from "an

Beware of Plagiarism!

Roy Peter Clark of the Poynter Institute cautions against the following acts of plagiarism:

- Taking material verbatim (word for word) from the newspaper library.
- Using material verbatim from the wire services.
- Using material from other publications.
- Using news releases verbatim.
- Using the work of fellow reporters.
- Using old stories over again.

extensive archive" of work she had done at Reuters. The plagiarism was discovered in a routine editing check by a single copy editor. CNN then ran it through plagiarism-flagging software that turned up "two or three things" that caused a deeper look at "all of her work."

A Reuters spokesperson said, "While employed by Reuters we were not aware of any concerns raised about Ms. Gamuchian's work. However in light of press reports we are reviewing her stories."

Perhaps the greatest temptation is to plagiarize material published online. But you also might be tempted to lift words from your own news organization's stories or from a wire report. Some reporters have felt justified taking quotes and verbatim sentences from news releases and inserting them into their stories. Make sure you're not plagiarizing when you think you're paraphrasing (Figure 20.2). And attribute, attribute, attribute. You always serve your readers best when you get your own quotations. Don't even reuse your own material or stories or columns without letting your readers know what you are doing. Remember, internet users are quite effective at spotting many of these practices. Bloggers and Twitter users will catch and expose you!

Though it might seem impossible, some people believe writers can plagiarize and have absolutely no idea they are doing so. They say that sometimes something you have read becomes so familiar that you later consider it your own. Sometimes plagiarism results from sloppy note taking.

You must fight every impulse to use others' work, question everything, check any doubts, and avoid any hint of plagiarism. And just as certainly you must resist temptations to make up people, to fabricate events and to invent quotations.

Social Media Ethics

News appears not just on news organization websites but also on social media like Instagram, Facebook and YouTube. Twitter, for example, has become a most useful and even necessary tool for obtaining tips and leads to stories. All the guidelines of journalism ethics apply to reporters' use of Twitter. Journalist and media strategy consultant David Brewer summarizes the main ethical issues as they apply to Twitter:

- **Accuracy:** well-sourced information based on solid evidence.
- **Impartiality:** fair and open-minded, exploring of all significant views.
- **Fairness:** transparent, open and honest, based on straight dealing.
- **Offense:** delivering challenging journalism that is sensitive to audience expectations.
- **Integrity:** dealing with groups keen to use the media for their own advantage.
- **Privacy** must be respected and not invaded unless it is in the public interest.

All of this within 140 characters. If Twitter does nothing else for you, it forces you to think ethically while being concise. Journalists using other social media can take these guidelines to heart too.

TIPS

Three Final Guidelines

- Be free of obligations to anyone or to any interest except the truth. The primary obligation of the journalist is to be free.
- Be fair. Even children know when you treat them unfairly or when they are being unfair. So do you.
- Remember good taste. Some actions and stories might be ethical, but they might be in bad taste.

Plagiarism, Quotation and Paraphrase

Using an Attributed Quotation—Acceptable

The journalist fully identifies the source of the quotation and puts the source's exact words in quotation marks.

As William A. Henry III writes in *Time* magazine, reporters have a "First Amendment bond" with their readers. "Plagiarism," he writes, "imperils that bond, not because it involves theft of a wry phrase or piquant quote, but because it devalues meticulous, independent verification of fact—the bedrock of a press worth reading."

Paraphrasing a Quotation—Acceptable

The journalist identifies the source and restates the source's original idea in the journalist's own words.

William A. Henry III writes about the destructive effect on journalism that plagiarism can have, suggesting that it compromises the integrity of the reportorial research process.

Plagiarizing—Unacceptable

Even though the source is identified, the journalist errs by using the source's original words (in bold) without putting them in quotation marks. Simply using distinctive words and phrases without quotation marks can constitute plagiarism.

In writing about how plagiarism **imperils** a reporter's **bond** with readers, William A. Henry III says the practice goes beyond stealing **a wry phrase or piquant quote**. It **devalues the meticulous, independent verification of fact** that journalism depends on.

Plagiarizing—Unacceptable

The journalist has not identified the source and has not put the source's original words (in bold) in quotation marks. Changing the occasional word (for example, "striking" rather than "piquant") or the structure of a sentence is not sufficient to avoid plagiarism.

Plagiarism damages the reporter's **bond** with his or her readers. It goes beyond the **theft of a wry phrase or** striking **quote** and diminishes the foundation of journalism—**the meticulous, independent verification of facts**.

SUGGESTED READINGS

Christians, Clifford G., Mark Fackler, Kathy Richardson, Peggy Kreshel and Robert H. Woods Jr. *Media Ethics: Cases and Moral Reasoning*. 9th ed. Boston: Allyn Bacon, 2016. The authors apply the Potter Box method of principled reasoning to dozens of journalism, advertising and public relations cases.

Fletcher, Joseph. *Situation Ethics: The New Morality*. Louisville, Ky.: Westminster John Knox Press, 1997. First published in 1966, this classic work on Christian situation ethics is for some a breath of fresh air, for others pure heresy.

Kovach, Bill, and Tom Rosenstiel. *The Elements of Journalism: What Newspeople Should Know and the Public Should Expect*. New York: Crown Publishers, 2007. This book should be required reading for every journalism student and journalist.

Meyers, Christopher, ed. *Journalism Ethics: A Philosophical Approach*. New York: Oxford Univ. Press, 2010. Even a quick look at this book's table of contents tells you it brings together the best journalism scholars writing about journalism's most vital topics.

Patterson, Philip, and Lee Wilkins. *Media Ethics: Issues and Cases*. 8th ed. Burr Ridge, Ill.: McGraw-Hill Humanities, Social Sciences and World Languages, 2014. This book offers an excellent discussion of journalism ethics with up-to-date cases.

Wilkins, Lee, and Clifford G. Christians, eds. *The Handbook of Mass Media Ethics*. New York: Routledge, 2009. In this handbook, scholars look at the intellectual history of mass media ethics over the past 25 years and summarize past and possible future research.

SUGGESTED WEBSITES

www.ijnet.org

This is the website of the International Journalists' Network. Here you can find the codes of ethics of nearly every country or press association that has one. It also reports on the state of the media around the world and contains media directories.

www.journalism.indiana.edu/resources/ethics

This site, from Indiana University's School of Journalism, contains a large set of cases to help you explore ethical issues in journalism. The initial cases were published in *FineLine*, a newsletter by Barry Bingham Jr.

macmillanhighered.com/newsreporting12e

When you visit LaunchPad Solo for Journalism, you will find research links, exercises, and LearningCurve adaptive quizzing to help you improve your grammar and AP style usage. In addition, the site's video collection hosts the videos highlighted in this and other chapters as well as additional clips of leading professionals discussing important media trends.

www.spj.org

(Click on "Resources, Training & Career" on the top of the screen. Then scroll down to "Ethics.") The ethics site of the Society of Professional Journalists provides the SPJ code of ethics, ethics news, an ethics hotline, an SPJ ethics listserv, ethics case studies and other ethics resources.

EXERCISES

1. Search for at least two articles on whether to publish the names of one of the following:

   a. Juvenile criminal suspects and defendants.
   b. Victims of rape, molestation or other sex crimes.
   c. Gay men and lesbians who have not publicly stated their sexual orientation.

   Write a brief essay about your findings.

2. Using what you have learned in this chapter, answer this question: Does the end ever justify the means? Give at least two examples.

3. You've learned that the daughter of a local bank president has been kidnapped. The kidnappers have not contacted the family, and police officials ask you to keep the matter secret for fear the abductors might panic and injure the child. Describe how an absolutist, a person who believes the end

justifies the means, and a situation ethicist would make their decisions about how to handle the situation.

4. You're assigned to write a piece on a new bus service from your town to Chicago. Your editor tells you to ask the bus company for a free round-trip ticket. What will you do, and why?

5. For at least a year, reporters on your paper have heard rumors that a retirement home is negligent in its care of the elderly. Your editor asks you to get a job there as a janitor and to report what you find. How will you respond, and why?

6. You are a photographer. Your editor has told you to keep an eye out for any instances of police brutality. You happen to see a policeman knock down a homeless man and begin kicking him. Will you take photos, or will you attempt in some way to discourage the policeman from hurting the homeless man? Explain.

7. **Your journalism blog.** You are the theater critic for your news organization. A producer has offered you free tickets to an upcoming premiere performance. Should you accept the tickets? Why or why not? Write a blog post explaining your conclusions, and invite others to comment on your blog.

20 Common Errors of Grammar and Punctuation

Grammar provides our language's rules of the road. When you have a green light, you proceed on faith that other drivers will not go through their red light. That's because drivers have a shared understanding of the rules of the road. Similarly, writers have a shared understanding of the grammar rules that ensure we understand what we are reading. Occasionally, as on the road, there is a wreck. We dangle participles, misplace modifiers and omit commas. If we write "Running down the street, his pants fell off," we are saying a pair of pants was running down a street. If we write "He hit Harry and John stopped him," the missing comma makes the meaning, on first reading, "He hit Harry and John."

To say what you mean—to avoid syntactic wrecks—you must know the rules of grammar. We have compiled a list of 20 common errors that we find in our students' stories and in the stories of many professionals. Avoid them and you'll write safely.

To take quizzes based on this list of 20 common errors of grammar and punctuation, go to LearningCurve for AP Style on LaunchPad for Journalism: **macmillanhighered .com/newsreporting12e**. There you will find advice and activities that go beyond grammar; LearningCurve offers exercises on Associated Press style—the style that makes news writing distinctly journalistic.

1. Incorrect comma in a series in Associated Press style

Use commas to separate the items in a series, but do not put a comma before *and* or *or* at the end of the series unless the meaning would be unclear without a comma.

Incorrect comma before *and*	The film was fast-paced, sophisticated, and funny.
Clear without comma	The film was fast-paced, sophisticated and funny.

A comma before *and* or *or* can prevent confusion.

Unclear without comma	He demanded cheese, salsa with jalapeños and onions on his taco.

Adding a comma before *and* prevents readers from wondering if he demanded salsa containing both jalapeños and onions or if the salsa and the onions were two separate toppings.

Clear with comma   He demanded cheese, salsa with jalapeños, and onions on his taco.

The sentence can be revised to mean salsa with both jalapeños and onions.

Clear revision   He demanded cheese and salsa with jalapeños and onions on his taco.
without comma

2. Run-on sentence

An independent clause contains a subject and a predicate and makes sense by itself. A run-on sentence—also known as a *comma splice*—occurs when two or more independent clauses are joined incorrectly with a comma.

Run-on   John Rogers left the family law practice, he decided to become a teacher.

You can correct a run-on sentence in several ways. Join the clauses with a comma and one of the coordinating conjunctions—*and, but, for, nor, or, yet* or *so*—or join the clauses with a semicolon if they are closely related. Use a subordinating conjunction such as *after, because, if* or *when* to turn one of the clauses into a dependent clause. Or rewrite the run-on as two separate sentences.

Correcting a run-on with a comma and a coordinating conjunction
John Rogers left the family law practice, for he decided to become a teacher.

Correcting a run-on with a semicolon
John Rogers left the family law practice; he decided to become a teacher.

Correcting a run-on by making one independent clause a dependent clause
John Rogers left the family law practice when he decided to become a teacher.

Correcting a run-on by writing two separate sentences
John Rogers left the family law practice. He decided to become a teacher.

3. Fragment

A fragment is a word group that lacks a subject, a verb or both yet is punctuated as though it were a complete sentence. Another type of fragment is a word group that begins with a subordinating conjunction such as *because* or *when* yet is punctuated as though it were a complete sentence.

Fragments   After she had placed her watch and an extra pencil on the table. Without feeling especially sorry about it.

Correct a fragment by joining it to the sentence before or after it or by adding the missing elements so that the fragment contains a subject and a verb and can stand alone.

Correcting a fragment by joining it to another sentence

After she had placed her watch and an extra pencil on the table, the student opened the exam booklet.

Correcting a fragment by turning it into a sentence

She apologized to her boss for the outburst without feeling especially sorry about it.

4. Missing comma(s) with a nonrestrictive element

A nonrestrictive element is a word, phrase or clause that gives information about the preceding part of the sentence but does not restrict or limit the meaning of that part. A nonrestrictive element is not essential to the meaning of the sentence; you can delete it and still understand clearly what the sentence is saying. Place commas before and (if necessary) after a nonrestrictive element.

Unclear	The mayor asked to meet Alva Johnson a highly decorated police officer.
Clear	The mayor asked to meet Alva Johnson, a highly decorated police officer.

Unclear	His wife Mary was there.
Clear	His wife, Mary, was there.

5. Confusion of *that* and *which*

The pronoun *that* always introduces restrictive information that is essential to the meaning of the sentence; do not set off a *that* clause with commas. The pronoun *which* introduces nonrestrictive, or nonessential, information; set off a nonrestrictive *which* clause with commas.

Incorrect	The oldest store in town, Miller and Co., that has been on Main Street for almost a century, will close this summer.
Correct	The oldest store in town, Miller and Co., which has been on Main Street for almost a century, will close this summer.

Incorrect	The creature, which has been frightening residents of North First Street for the past week, has turned out to be a screech owl.
Correct	The creature that has been frightening residents of North First Street for the past week has turned out to be a screech owl.

6. Missing comma after an introductory element

A sentence may begin with a dependent clause (a word group that contains a subject and a verb and begins with a subordinating conjunction such as *because* or *when*), a prepositional phrase (a word group that begins with a preposition such as *in* or *on* and ends with a noun or pronoun), an adverb such as *next* that modifies the whole sentence, or a participial phrase (a word group that contains a past or present participle, such as *determined* or *speaking*, that acts as an adjective). Use a comma to separate these introductory elements from the main clause of the sentence.

Dependent clause	<u>After the applause had died down,</u> the conductor raised his baton again.
Prepositional phrase	<u>Without a second thought,</u> the chicken crossed the road.
Adverb	<u>Furthermore,</u> the unemployment rate continues to rise.
Participial phrases	<u>Waiting in the bar,</u> José grew restless.
	<u>Saddened by the news from home,</u> she stopped reading the letter.

Although it is always correct to use a comma after an introductory element, the comma may be omitted after some adverbs and short prepositional phrases if the meaning is clear.

Suddenly it's spring.

In Chicago it rained yesterday.

Always place a comma after two or more introductory prepositional phrases.

In May of last year in Toronto, Tom attended three conventions.

Here are more examples:

Incorrect	Shaking her head at the latest budget information the library administrator wondered where to find the money for new books.
Correct	Shaking her head at the latest budget information, the library administrator wondered where to find the money for new books.

Incorrect	After a week of foggy, rainy mornings had passed he left Seattle.
Correct	After a week of foggy, rainy mornings had passed, he left Seattle.

7. Missing comma(s) between coordinate adjectives

Adjectives are coordinate if they make sense when you insert *and* between them or place them in reverse order.

Coordinate	The frightened, angry citizens protested the new policy.
adjectives	The frightened and angry citizens protested the new policy.

The adjectives make sense with *and* between them, so they are coordinate.

The angry, frightened citizens protested the new policy.

The adjectives make sense in reverse order, so they are coordinate. Separate coordinate adjectives with commas.

Incorrect	The gaunt lonely creature was also afraid.
Correct	The gaunt, lonely creature was also afraid.

8. Missing comma(s) in a compound sentence

Two or more independent clauses—word groups containing a subject and a verb and expressing a complete thought—joined with a coordinating conjunction (*and, but, for, nor, or, yet* or *so*) form a compound sentence. Place a comma before the conjunction in a compound sentence to avoid confusion.

| Unclear | She works as a pharmacist now and later she plans to go to medical school. |
| Clear | She works as a pharmacist now, and later she plans to go to medical school. |

9. Misused semicolon

In a compound sentence that has a coordinating conjunction joining the clauses, place a comma before the conjunction, not a semicolon.

| Incorrect | The Chicago Cubs did not play in the World Series; but they did win their division. |
| Correct | The Chicago Cubs did not play in the World Series, but they did win their division. |

10. Misplaced or dangling modifier

Modifiers are words or phrases that change or clarify the meaning of another word or word group in a sentence. Place modifiers immediately before or directly after the word or words they modify. A *misplaced modifier* appears too far from the word or words it is supposed to modify in the sentence. A *dangling modifier* appears in a sentence that does not contain the word or words it is supposed to modify. A modifier at the beginning of a sentence should refer to the grammatical subject of the sentence.

	subject
Misplaced modifier	Having predicted a sunny morning, the downpour surprised the meteorologist.
	subject
Correct	Having predicted a sunny morning, the meteorologist did not expect the downpour.
	subject
Dangling modifier	Working in the yard, the sun burned her badly
	subject
Correct	Working in the yard, she became badly sunburned.

11. Missing or misused hyphen(s) in a compound modifier

A compound modifier consists of two or more words used to modify a single noun. When a compound modifier precedes a noun, hyphenate the parts of the compound unless the compound consists of an adverb ending in *-ly* followed by an adjective.

| Incorrect | His over the top performance made the whole film unbelievable. |

The <u>freshly-printed</u> counterfeit bills felt like genuine dollars.

The local chapter of Parents Without Partners will sponsor a <u>come as you are</u> party on Saturday.

Correct   His <u>over-the-top</u> performance made the whole film unbelievable.

The <u>freshly printed</u> counterfeit bills felt like genuine dollars.

The local chapter of Parents Without Partners will sponsor a <u>come-as-you-are</u> party on Saturday.

12. Missing or misused apostrophe

Do not confuse the pronoun *its*, meaning "belonging to it," with the contraction *it's*, meaning "it is" or "it has." Although the possessive form of a noun uses an apostrophe (*Tom's*), possessive pronouns (*its*, *hers*, *his*, *ours*, *yours*, *theirs*) never take apostrophes.

Incorrect   The car is lying on <u>it's</u> side in the ditch.

<u>Its</u> a blue 2009 Ford Taurus.

That new car of <u>her's</u> rides very smoothly.

Correct   The car is lying on <u>its</u> side in the ditch.

<u>It's</u> a blue 2009 Ford Taurus.

That new car of <u>hers</u> rides very smoothly.

For clarity, avoid using the contraction ending in -*'s* to mean "has" instead of "is."

Unclear   <u>She's</u> held many offices in student government.

Clear   <u>She has</u> held many offices in student government.

13. Incorrect pronoun case

A pronoun that is the subject of a sentence or clause must be in the subjective case (*I*, *he*, *she*, *we*, *they*). A pronoun that is the direct object of a verb, the indirect object of a verb, or the object of a preposition must be in the objective case (*me*, *him*, *her*, *us*, *them*). To decide whether a pronoun in a compound construction—two or more nouns or pronouns joined with *and* or *or*—should be subjective or objective, omit everything in the compound except the pronoun and see whether the subjective or objective case sounds correct.

Incorrect   He took my wife and <u>I</u> to dinner.

Try that sentence without the first part of the compound, *my wife and*. It sounds incorrect.

Correct   He took my wife and <u>me</u> to dinner.

Here's another example.

Incorrect   <u>Her</u> and her family donated the prize money.

Try that sentence without the second part of the compound, *and her family*. It sounds incorrect.

> **Correct**   <u>She</u> and her family donated the prize money.

The pronouns *who* and *whom* often cause confusion. *Who* (or *whoever*) is subjective; *whom* (or *whomever*) is objective. If the pronoun appears in a question, answer the question using a pronoun (such as *I* or *me*) to determine whether to use the subjective or objective form.

> **Incorrect**   <u>Who</u> does Howard want to see?

Answering the question—*Howard wants to see <u>me</u>*—reveals that the pronoun should be objective.

> **Correct**   <u>Whom</u> does Howard want to see?

When *who* or *whom* is not part of a question, it introduces a dependent clause. Determine the case of the pronoun in the clause by removing the clause from the sentence and replacing *who* or *whom* with *I* and *me* to see which form is correct.

> **Incorrect**   She welcomed <u>whomever</u> knocked on her door.

The dependent clause is *whomever knocked on her door.* Replacing *whomever* with *I* and *me*—*I knocked on her door; me knocked on her door*—reveals that the subjective form, *whoever*, is correct.

> **Correct**   She welcomed <u>whoever</u> knocked on her door.

14. Lack of agreement between pronoun and antecedent

Pronouns must agree in number (singular or plural) and person (first, second or third) with their *antecedents*—the nouns or pronouns to which they refer. Do not shift, for example, from a singular antecedent to a plural pronoun, or from a third-person antecedent to a first- or second-person pronoun.

> **Incorrect**   The <u>class</u> meets on Thursdays to check <u>their</u> work.
>
> **Correct**   The <u>class</u> meets on Thursdays to check <u>its</u> work.
>
> Class <u>members</u> meet on Thursdays to check <u>their</u> work.

15. Biased language

Avoid stereotypes and biased language. Take special care to avoid gender-specific pronouns.

> **Biased**   A reporter must always check <u>his</u> work.
>
> **Acceptable**   Reporters must always check their work.
>
> If you are a reporter, you must always check your work.
>
> **Biased**   Local politicians and their <u>wives</u> attended a dinner in honor of the visiting diplomat.
>
> **Acceptable**   Local politicians and their spouses attended a dinner in honor of the visiting diplomat.

Biased	Dr. Jones, a <u>deaf-mute</u>, spoke about the challenges she faced in medical school.
Acceptable	Dr. Jones, who cannot hear or speak, spoke about the challenges she faced in medical school.

16. Lack of agreement between subject and verb

Subject and verb must agree in number. Use the form of the verb that agrees with a singular or plural subject. Be especially careful to identify the subject correctly when words, such as a prepositional phrase, separate subject from verb.

Incorrect	The bag with the green stripes <u>belong</u> to her.
Correct	The bag with the green stripes <u>belongs</u> to her.

A compound subject with parts joined by *and* is always plural.

Incorrect	A mystery writer and her daughter <u>lives</u> in the house by the river.
Correct	<u>A mystery writer and her daughter live</u> in the house by the river.

When parts of a compound subject are joined by *or*, make the verb agree with the part of the compound closest to the verb.

Incorrect	Either Mike or his sisters <u>has</u> the spare key.
Correct	Either Mike or <u>his sisters have</u> the spare key.

17. Incorrect complement with linking verb

A linking verb such as *be, appear, feel* or *become* links a subject with a word or words that identify or describe the subject. When the identifying word—called a *subject complement*—is a pronoun, use the subjective case for the pronoun.

Incorrect	That was <u>him</u> on the telephone five minutes ago.
Correct	That was <u>he</u> on the telephone five minutes ago.

A word or words that describe the subject and follow a linking verb must be adjectives.

Incorrect	She feels <u>terribly</u> about the things she said.
Correct	She feels <u>terrible</u> about the things she said.

18. Incorrect use of subjunctive mood

Conditions contrary to fact require a verb to be in the subjunctive mood. Apply this rule in stories about all pending legislation at all levels of government. Use the subjunctive mood in "that" clauses after verbs of wishing, suggesting and requiring; in other words, use the subjunctive in clauses, dependent or independent, that do not state a fact.

Incorrect	The bylaws require that he <u>declares</u> his candidacy by April 10.
Correct	The bylaws require that he <u>declare</u> his candidacy by April 10.

Incorrect	The bill <u>will</u> require everyone to register for the draft at age 18.
Correct	The bill <u>would</u> require everyone to register for the draft at age 18.

19. Wrong word

Wrong-word errors include using a word that sounds similar to, or the same as, the word you need but means something different (such as writing *affect* when you mean *effect*) and using a word that has a shade of meaning that is not what you intend (such as writing *slender* when you want to suggest *scrawny*). Check the dictionary if you are not sure whether you are using a word correctly.

Incorrect	Merchants who appear <u>disinterested</u> in their customers may lose business.
Correct	Merchants who appear <u>uninterested</u> in their customers may lose business.

Incorrect	The guests gasped and applauded when they saw the <u>excessive</u> display of food.
Correct	The guests gasped and applauded when they saw the <u>lavish</u> display of food.

20. Incorrect verb form

Every verb has five forms: a base form (*talk*; *see*), a present-tense form (*talks*; *sees*), a past-tense form (*talked*; *saw*), a present-participle form used for forming the progressive tenses (*is talking*; *is seeing*), and a past-participle form used for forming the passive voice or one of the perfect tenses (*has talked*; *has seen*).

Dropping the ending from present-tense forms and regular past-tense forms is a common error.

Incorrect	The police are <u>suppose</u> to protect the public.
Correct	The police are <u>supposed</u> to protect the public.

Incorrect	The city <u>use</u> to tax all clothing sales.
Correct	The city <u>used</u> to tax all clothing sales.

Regular verbs end in *-ed* in the past tense and past participle, but irregular verbs do not follow a set pattern for forming the past tense and past participle (for example, *saw*, *seen*), so those forms of irregular verbs are frequently used incorrectly. Look up irregular verbs if you are uncertain of the correct form.

Incorrect	The manager was not in the restaurant when it was robbed because he had <u>went</u> home early.
Correct	The manager was not in the restaurant when it was robbed because he had <u>gone</u> home early.

Incorrect	The thieves <u>taked</u> everything in the safe
Correct	The thieves <u>took</u> everything in the safe.

ANSWERS TO GRAMMAR CHECK ACTIVITIES

Chapter 1: The U.S., the U.K., Germany, China, <u>Russia and</u> France all agreed to the historic Iran nuclear deal.

Chapter 2: After arriving at the Greek island of <u>Lesbos</u>, thousands of refugees find themselves with insufficient food and medical care.

Chapter 3: Guatemalan President Otto Pérez Molina resigned from office after an investigation into his regime's corruption over the past three <u>years</u>, and now he awaits trial in Matamoros Prison.

Chapter 4: In September 2015, Pope Francis delivered an evening prayer at St. Patrick's Cathedral, <u>which</u> has stood in midtown Manhattan for more than 100 years.

Chapter 5: Donald <u>Trump</u>, the real estate <u>magnate</u>, says he hopes to become "the greatest jobs president that God ever created."

Chapter 6: Ballot selfies, which may reveal <u>whom</u> a person voted for, could prompt the return of vote-buying, according to a prominent elections expert.

Chapter 7: The Alaskan peak known as Mount McKinley was officially restored to <u>its</u> original Koyukon name, Denali.

Chapter 8: The growth of gambling in New York, Pennsylvania, Maryland and Delaware <u>has</u> cut into casino revenue in Atlantic City.

Chapter 9: Formerly flying outside the State House in Charleston, S.C., <u>the Confederate flag</u> was taken down by state troopers after a vote in the state assembly.

Chapter 10: <u>After</u> Rowan County clerk Kim Davis refused to issue marriage licenses to same-sex couples, she spent five days in jail for contempt of court.

Chapter 11: In September 2015, Russia deployed half a dozen tanks and 35 armored carriers to Syria in a move to build up <u>its</u> military presence in the region.

Chapter 12: China's stock market crisis in August 2015 had a substantial <u>effect</u> on international markets.

Chapter 13: Since the U.S. Supreme Court's decision in *Obergefell v. Hodges,* federal law requires that every state <u>issue</u> marriage licenses to same-sex couples.

Chapter 14: It was Barack Obama who became the first African-American president in 2009, and it was <u>he</u> who won reelection in 2012.

Chapter 15: After Russian troops invaded Crimea in February <u>2014,</u> President Vladimir Putin claimed that Russia's annexation of the region complied with international law.

Chapter 16: Relations between North and South Korea, increasingly testy in recent months, <u>used</u> to allow for occasional "reunion" meetings for families separated during the 1950-53 Korean War.

Chapter 17: Critics in Congress slammed the White House for what they say is its <u>ineffective</u>, disorganized attempt to train a Syrian rebel army against ISIS.

Chapter 18: New York hedge fund manager Martin Shkreli increased the price of his <u>newly acquired</u> drug, Daraprim, by 5,455 percent.

Chapter 19: Pakistani human rights activist Malala Yousafzai was almost killed by a Taliban assassin in October 2012, <u>but</u> she remains a dedicated advocate for girls' education.

Chapter 20: A candidate for the office of U.S. president must be a natural-born citizen of the U.S. <u>and at least</u> 35 years old.

Wire-Service Style Summary

Most publications adhere to rules of style to avoid annoying inconsistencies. Without a stylebook to provide guidance in such matters, writers would not know whether the word *president* should be capitalized when preceding or following a name, whether the correct spelling is *employee* or *employe* (dictionaries list both), or whether *Twelfth Street* or *12th Street* is correct.

Newspapers use stylebooks to provide such guidance. For consistency, most newspapers follow rules in *The Associated Press Stylebook*. Many also list their own exceptions to AP style in a separate style sheet. There often are good reasons for local exceptions. For example, AP style calls for spelling out *First Street* through *Ninth Street* but using numerals for *10th Street* and above. But if a city has only 10 numbered streets, for consistency it might make sense to use *Tenth Street*.

This appendix is an abbreviated summary of the primary style rules. (See Chapter 12 for more on radio and television style.) This summary should be helpful even for those without a stylebook, but we provide it assuming that most users of this book have one. Why? Because this section includes only the rules used most frequently, arranged by topic to make them easier to learn. Only about 10 percent of the rules in a stylebook account for 90 percent of the style you will use regularly. You will use the rest of the rules about 10 percent of the time. It makes sense, therefore, to learn first the rules you will use most often.

Abbreviations and Acronyms

Punctuation of Abbreviations

■ Generally speaking, abbreviations of two letters or fewer have periods:
600 B.C., A.D. 1066
8 a.m., 7 p.m.
UN, US, R.I., N.Y.
8151 Yosemite St.
EXCEPTIONS: *AM radio, FM radio, 35 mm camera, the AP Stylebook, LA smog, D-Mass., R-Kan., IQ, TV, EU*
■ Most abbreviations of three letters or more do not have periods:
CIA, FBI, NATO
mpg, mph
EXCEPTION: *c.o.d.* for *cash on delivery* or *collect on delivery*

Symbols

- Always write out % as *percent* in a story, but you may use the symbol in a headline.
- Always write out & as *and* unless it is part of a company's formal name.
- Always write out ¢ as *cent* or *cents*.
- Always use the symbol $ rather than the word *dollar* with any actual figure, and put the symbol before the figure. Write out *dollar* only if you are speaking of, say, the value of the dollar on the world market.

Dates

- Never abbreviate days of the week except in a table.
- Don't abbreviate a month unless part of a specific date:
  August 2016; *Aug. 17*; *Aug. 17, 2016*
- The five months spelled with five letters or fewer are never abbreviated:
  March; *April 20*; *May 13, 2016*; *June 1956*; *July of that year*
- Never abbreviate *Christmas* as *Xmas*, even in a headline.
- *Fourth of July* is written out.
- *Sept. 11* and *9/11* are both acceptable.

People and Titles

- Some publications still use courtesy titles (*Mr.*, *Mrs.*, *Ms.*, *Miss*) on second reference in stories, although most seem to have moved away from them as sexist. Many publications use them only in quotations from sources. Others use them only in obituaries and editorials, or on second reference in stories mentioning a husband and wife. In the last case, some newspapers prefer to repeat the person's whole name or, especially in features, use the person's first name. The Associated Press suggests using a courtesy title when someone requests it, but most journalists don't bother to ask.
- Use the abbreviations *Dr.* (for a medical doctor, not someone with a Ph.D. degree), *Gov.*, *Lt. Gov.*, *Rep.*, *Sen.* and *the Rev.*, as well as abbreviations of military titles, on first reference; then drop the title on subsequent references. Some titles you might expect to see abbreviated before a name are not abbreviated in AP style: *Attorney General*, *District Attorney*, *President*, *Professor*, *Superintendent*.
- Use the abbreviations *Jr.* and *Sr.* after a name on first reference if appropriate, but do not set them off by commas as you learned to do in English class.

Organizations

- Write out the first reference to most organizations in full rather than using an acronym: *National Organization for Women*. For *GOP*, *CIA* and *FBI*, however, the acronym may be used on the first reference.
- You may use well-known abbreviations such as *FCC* and *NOW* in a headline even though they would not be acceptable on first reference in a story.
- Do not put the abbreviation of an organization in parentheses after the full name on first reference. If an abbreviation is that confusing, don't use it at all. Instead, call the organization something like "the gay rights group" or "the bureau" on second reference.

■ Use the abbreviations *Co., Cos., Corp., Inc.* and *Ltd.* at the end of a company's name even if the company spells out the word; do not abbreviate these words if followed by other words such as "of America." The abbreviations *Co., Cos.* and *Corp.* are used, however, if followed by *Inc.* or *Ltd.* (These latter two abbreviations are not set off by commas even if the company uses commas.)

■ Abbreviate political affiliations after a name in the following way:
Sen. Claire McCaskill, D-Mo., said . . .
　　Note the use of a single letter without a period for the party and the use of commas around the party and state abbreviations.

■ Never abbreviate the word *association*, even as part of a name.

Places

■ Abbreviate state names in lists, tables, credit lines, political party affiliations and photo captions. In the body of a story, don't abbreviate a state name that follows the name of a city in that state:
Nevada; Brown City, Michigan

■ Never abbreviate the six states spelled with five or fewer letters or the two noncontiguous states:
Alaska, Hawaii, Idaho, Iowa, Maine, Ohio, Texas, Utah

■ Use the traditional state abbreviations, not the Postal Service's two-letter ones:
Miss., not *MS*
EXCEPTION: Use the two-letter postal abbreviations when a full address is given that includes a ZIP code.

Here are the abbreviations used in some places, including party affiliations (R-Ohio).

Ala.	Fla.	Md.	Neb.	N.D.	Tenn.
Ariz.	Ga.	Mass.	Nev.	Okla.	Vt.
Ark.	Ill.	Mich.	N.H.	Ore.	Va.
Calif.	Ind.	Minn.	N.J.	Pa.	Wash.
Colo.	Kan.	Miss.	N.M.	R.I.	W.Va.
Conn.	Ky.	Mo.	N.Y.	S.C.	Wis.
Del.	La.	Mont.	N.C.	S.D.	Wyo.

■ Use state names with domestic towns and cities unless they appear in the wire-service list of cities that stand alone in datelines. Many publications add to the wire-service list their own list of towns well-known in the state or region. Use a nation's full name with foreign towns and cities unless they appear in the wire-service list of cities that stand alone in datelines. Once a state or nation has been identified in a story, it is unnecessary to repeat the name unless clarity demands it. The lists of cities in the U.S. and the rest of the world that the wire services say may stand alone without a state abbreviation or nation are too lengthy to include here. Consult the appropriate stylebook. A handy rule of thumb is if it's an American city that has a major sports franchise, it probably stands alone. Likewise, if it's a foreign city most people have heard of, it probably stands alone.

■ Don't abbreviate the names of thoroughfares if there is no street address with them:
Main Street, Century Boulevard West

■ If the thoroughfare's name has the word *avenue, boulevard, street* or any of the directions on a map, such as *north* or *southeast*, abbreviate those words with a street address:
1044 W. Maple St., 1424 Lee Blvd. S., 999 Jackson Ave.

■ In a highway's name, always abbreviate *U.S.*, but never abbreviate a state's name. In the case of an interstate highway, the name is written in full on first reference, abbreviated on subsequent ones:
U.S. Highway 63, *Massachusetts 2*
Interstate 70 (first reference), *I-70* (second reference)

■ Never abbreviate *Fort* or *Mount*.

■ Always use the abbreviation *St.* for *Saint* in place names.
EXCEPTIONS: *Saint John* in New Brunswick, *Sault Ste. Marie* in Michigan and Ontario

■ Abbreviate *U.S.*, *U.K.* and *U.N.* as both nouns and adjectives in text.

Miscellaneous

■ Use the abbreviation *IQ* (no periods) in all references to *intelligence quotient*.

■ Abbreviate and capitalize the word *number* when followed by a numeral: *No. 1*.

■ Use the abbreviation *TV* (no periods) as an adjective or noun as an abbreviated form of *television*.

■ Use the abbreviation *UFO* in all references to an *unidentified flying object*.

■ Generally, spell out *versus*, but use the abbreviation *vs.*, not *v.*, for *versus* in short expressions: *guns vs. butter*. Use *v.* for court cases: *Marbury v. Madison*.

Capitalization

■ Proper nouns are capitalized; common nouns are not. Unfortunately, this rule is not always easy to apply when the noun is the name of an animal, food or plant or when it is a trademark that has become so well-known that people mistakenly use it generically.

■ Regions are capitalized; directions are not: *We drove east two miles to catch the interstate out West.*

■ Adjectives and nouns pertaining to a region are capitalized: *Southern accent, Southerner, Western movie.*

■ A region combined with a country's name is not capitalized unless the region is part of the name of a divided country: *eastern U.S., North Korea.*

■ A region combined with a state name is capitalized only if it is famous: *Southern California, southern Colorado.*

■ When two or more compound proper nouns are combined and have a word in common, the shared plural is lowercased: *Missouri and Mississippi rivers, Chrisman and Truman high schools.*

■ Government and college terms are not always consistent.
  ▪ *College departments* follow the animal, food and plant rule: Capitalize only words that are already proper nouns in themselves: *Spanish department, sociology department*. By contrast, always capitalize *a specific government department*, even without the city, state or federal designator and even if it's turned around with *of* deleted: *Police Department, Fire Department, Department of State, State Department.*
  ▪ *College and government committees* are capitalized if the formal name is given rather than a shorter, descriptive designation: *Special Senate Select Committee to Investigate Improper Labor-Management Practices*; *rackets committee.*
  ▪ *Academic degrees* are spelled out and lowercased: *bachelor of arts degree, master's degree.* Avoid the abbreviations *Ph.D., M.A., B.A.*, etc., except in lists.

- Always capitalize (unless plural or generic) *City Council* and *County Commission* (but alone, *council* and *commission* are lowercased). *Cabinet* is capitalized when referring to advisers. *Legislature* is capitalized if the state's body is formally named that. *Capitol*, the building, is capitalized, but *capital*, the city, is not. Capitalize *City Hall* even without the city name but not *county courthouse* without the name of the county.

- Never capitalize *board of directors* or *board of trustees* (but formal governing bodies, such as *Board of Curators* and *Board of Education*, are capitalized). *Federal*, *government* and *administration* are not capitalized. *President* and *vice president* are capitalized only before a name and only when not set off with a comma:

  President Barack Obama

  Vice President Joe Biden

  the president, Barack Obama, said . . .

- *Military titles (Sgt., Maj., Gen.)* are capitalized before a name, as are *Air Force, Army, Marines* and *Navy* if referring to U.S. forces.

- *Political parties* are capitalized, including the word *party*: *Democratic Party, Socialist Party*. However, capitalize words such as *communist, democratic, fascist* and *socialist* only when they refer to a formal party rather than a philosophy.

- Terms related to the internet are not always consistent.

  - *Internet* is lowercase. Some other internet and technology terms are capitalized; some are not: *BlackBerry(s), blog, cellphone, chat room, click-thru(s), crowdsourcing, home page, IP* address, *Listserv* (trademarked software), *retweet, smartphone, social media* (n., adj.), *tweet* (n., v.), *VoIP, Wi-Fi*.

  - *World Wide Web* is capitalized. But *web website, webcam, webcast* and *webmaster* are lowercased.

  - *Email* (note lack of hyphen) and other similar terms (*e-book, e-commerce, e-business*) are lowercased.

  - *IM* is acceptable for a second reference to *instant message*; also *IM'ing, IM'd*.

  - The proper names *iPad, iPhone* and *iPod* should be capitalized at the start of a sentence or headline (*IPad, IPhone, IPod*).

- Some religious terms (including holidays) are capitalized; most are not: *bar mitzvah, nirvana, Hanukkah, Ramadan*.

  - *Pope* is lowercased except before a name: *the pope, Pope Francis*.

  - *Mass* is always capitalized.

  - Pronouns for *God* and *Jesus* are lowercased.

  - Names of religious figures are capitalized: *Prophet Muhammad, Buddha*.

  - Names of holy books are capitalized: *Talmud, Quran* (preferred to *Koran*). *Bible* is capitalized when meaning the Holy Scriptures and lowercased when referring to another book: *a hunter's bible*.

  - Sacraments are capitalized if they commemorate events in the life of Jesus or signify his presence: *Holy Communion* but *baptism, communion*.

- Proper names and adjectives for races, ethnicities, and nationalities and religions are capitalized, but color descriptions are not: *African American, Arab, Asian* (preferred to *Oriental* for people), *Caucasian, Cherokee, Chinese* (singular and plural), *French Canadian, Muslim, Negro* (used only in names of organizations and quotations), *white, black*. (Note that *Arab*, which denotes ethnicity, and *Muslim*, which refers to religion, are not interchangeable. For example, many Arabs are Christian, and Muslims may be Indian, Indonesian, Turkish, American, etc.)

- *Illegal immigration* is an acceptable usage, but do not use *illegal immigrant, illegal alien* or *an illegal* as a noun to refer to a person: *he entered the country illegally*
- Formal titles of people are capitalized before a name, but occupational names are not:
  President Barack Obama, Mayor Laura Miller, Coach Roy Williams, Dean Jaime Lopez, astronaut Ellen Ochoa, journalist Fred Francis, plumber Phil Sanders, pharmacist Roger Wheaton
  Some titles are not easy to recognize: *managing editor, chief executive officer.* When in doubt, put the title after the name, set it off with commas, and use lowercase.
- Formal titles that are capitalized before a name are lowercased after a name:
  Barack Obama, president of the U.S.; Mike Rawlings, mayor of Dallas; Roy Williams, coach of the North Carolina Tar Heels; Fred Wilson, dean of students
- Formal titles that are abbreviated before a name are written out and lowercased if they follow a name:
  Gov. Andrew Cuomo; Andrew Cuomo, governor of New York
  Sen. Lindsey Graham of South Carolina; Lindsey Graham, senator from South Carolina
- The first word in a direct quotation is capitalized only if the quote meets both of these criteria:
  - It is a complete sentence. Don't capitalize a partial quote.
  - It stands alone as a separate sentence or paragraph, or it is set off from its source by a comma or colon.
- A question within a sentence is capitalized:
  My only question is, When do we start?

Numbers

- Cardinal numbers (numerals) are used in:
  - Addresses. Always use numerals for street addresses: *1322 N. 17th St.*
  - Ages. Always use numerals, even for days or months: *3 days old*; *John Burnside, 56.*
  - Aircraft and spacecraft: *F-4, DC-10, Apollo 11.* Exception: *Air Force One.*
  - Clothes sizes: *size 6.*
  - Dates. Always use the numeral alone—no *st, nd, rd* or *th* after it: *March 20.*
  - Decades: *the 1980s, the '80s, the early 2000s* (or *first decade of the 21st century*).
  - Dimensions: *5-foot-6-inch guard* (but no hyphen when the word modified is one associated with size: *3 feet tall, 10 feet long*).
  - Highways: *U.S. 63.*
  - Millions, billions and trillions: *1.2 billion, 6 million.*
  - Money. Always use numerals, but starting with a million, write like this: *$1.4 million.*
  - Numbers: *No. 1, No. 2.*
  - Percentages. Always use numerals except at the beginning of a sentence: *4 percent.*
  - Recipes. All numbers for amounts take numerals: *2 teaspoons.*
  - Speeds: *55 mph, 4 knots.*
  - Sports. Use numerals for just about everything: *8-6 score, 2 yards, 3-under-par, 2 strokes.*
  - Temperatures. Use numerals for all except *zero.* Below zero, spell out *minus*: *minus 6*, not *-6* (except in tabular data).
  - Times: *4 a.m., 6:32 p.m., noon, midnight, five minutes, three hours.*
  - Weights: *7 pounds, 11 ounces.*
  - Years: Use numerals without commas. A year is the only numeral that can start a sentence: *1988 was a good year.*

- Numerals with the suffixes *st*, *nd*, *rd* and *th* are used for:
  - Political divisions (precincts, wards, districts): *3rd Congressional District.*
  - Military sequences: *1st Lt., 2nd Division, 7th Fleet.*
  - Courts: *2nd District Court, 10th Circuit Court of Appeals.*
  - Streets after *Ninth.* For *First* through *Ninth*, use words: *Fifth Avenue, 13th Street.*
  - Amendments to the Constitution after *Ninth.* For *First* through *Ninth*, use words: *First Amendment, 16th Amendment.*
- Words are used for:
  - Numbers less than 10, with the exceptions noted above: *five people, four rules.*
  - Any number at the start of a sentence except for a year: *Sixteen years ago . . .*
  - Casual numbers: *about a hundred or so.*
  - Fractions less than one: *one-half.*
- Mixed numbers are used for fractions greater than one: *1 1/2.*
- Roman numerals are used for a man who is the third or later in his family to bear a name and for a king, queen, pope or world war: *John D. Rockefeller III, Queen Elizabeth II, Pope John Paul II, World War I.*

Suggested Website

www.apstylebook.com
The Associated Press provides its stylebook in several formats, including as a traditional printed book, an online subscription and a mobile device (smartphone or tablet) application.

Society of Professional Journalists' Code of Ethics

Preamble

Members of the Society of Professional Journalists believe that public enlightenment is the forerunner of justice and the foundation of democracy. Ethical journalism strives to ensure the free exchange of information that is accurate, fair and thorough. An ethical journalist acts with integrity.

The Society declares these four principles as the foundation of ethical journalism and encourages their use in its practice by all people in all media.

Seek Truth and Report it

Ethical journalism should be accurate and fair. Journalists should be honest and courageous in gathering, reporting and interpreting information.

Journalists should:

- Take responsibility for the accuracy of their work. Verify information before releasing it. Use original sources whenever possible.
- Remember that neither speed nor format excuses inaccuracy.
- Provide context. Take special care not to misrepresent or oversimplify in promoting, previewing or summarizing a story.
- Gather, update and correct information throughout the life of a news story.
- Be cautious when making promises, but keep the promises they make.
- Identify sources clearly. The public is entitled to as much information as possible to judge the reliability and motivations of sources.
- Consider sources' motives before promising anonymity. Reserve anonymity for sources who may face danger, retribution or other harm, and have information that cannot be obtained elsewhere. Explain why anonymity was granted.
- Diligently seek subjects of news coverage to allow them to respond to criticism or allegations of wrongdoing.
- Avoid undercover or other surreptitious methods of gathering information unless traditional, open methods will not yield information vital to the public.

The SPJ Code of Ethics is a statement of abiding principles supported by additional explanations and position papers that address changing journalistic practices. It is not a set of rules, rather a guide that encourages all who engage in journalism to take responsibility for the information they provide, regardless of medium. The code should be read as a whole; individual principles should not be taken out of context. It is not, nor can it be under the First Amendment, legally enforceable.

Sigma Delta Chi's first Code of Ethics was borrowed from the American Society of Newspaper Editors in 1926. In 1973, Sigma Delta Chi wrote its own code, which was revised in 1984, 1987, 1996 and 2014.

■ Be vigilant and courageous about holding those with power accountable. Give voice to the voiceless.

■ Support the open and civil exchange of views, even views they find repugnant.

■ Recognize a special obligation to serve as watchdogs over public affairs and government. Seek to ensure that the public's business is conducted in the open, and that public records are open to all.

■ Provide access to source material when it is relevant and appropriate.

■ Boldly tell the story of the diversity and magnitude of the human experience. Seek sources whose voices we seldom hear.

■ Avoid stereotyping. Journalists should examine the ways their values and experiences may shape their reporting.

■ Label advocacy and commentary.

■ Never deliberately distort facts or context, including visual information. Clearly label illustrations and re-enactments.

■ Never plagiarize. Always attribute.

Minimize Harm

Ethical journalism treats sources, subjects, colleagues and members of the public as human beings deserving of respect.

Journalists should:

■ Balance the public's need for information against potential harm or discomfort. Pursuit of the news is not a license for arrogance or undue intrusiveness.

■ Show compassion for those who may be affected by news coverage. Use heightened sensitivity when dealing with juveniles, victims of sex crimes, and sources or subjects who are inexperienced or unable to give consent. Consider cultural differences in approach and treatment.

■ Recognize that legal access to information differs from an ethical justification to publish or broadcast.

■ Realize that private people have a greater right to control information about themselves than public figures and others who seek power, influence or attention. Weigh the consequences of publishing or broadcasting personal information.

■ Avoid pandering to lurid curiosity, even if others do.

■ Balance a suspect's right to a fair trial with the public's right to know. Consider the implications of identifying criminal suspects before they face legal charges.

■ Consider the long-term implications of the extended reach and permanence of publication. Provide updated and more complete information as appropriate.

Act Independently

The highest and primary obligation of ethical journalism is to serve the public.

Journalists should:

■ Avoid conflicts of interest, real or perceived. Disclose unavoidable conflicts.

■ Refuse gifts, favors, fees, free travel and special treatment, and avoid political and other outside activities that may compromise integrity or impartiality, or may damage credibility.

■ Be wary of sources offering information for favors or money; do not pay for access to news. Identify content provided by outside sources, whether paid or not.
■ Deny favored treatment to advertisers, donors or any other special interests, and resist internal and external pressure to influence coverage.
■ Distinguish news from advertising and shun hybrids that blur the lines between the two. Prominently label sponsored content.

Be Accountable and Transparent

Ethical journalism means taking responsibility for one's work and explaining one's decisions to the public.

Journalists should:

■ Explain ethical choices and processes to audiences. Encourage a civil dialogue with the public about journalistic practices, coverage and news content.
■ Respond quickly to questions about accuracy, clarity and fairness.
■ Acknowledge mistakes and correct them promptly and prominently. Explain corrections and clarifications carefully and clearly.
■ Expose unethical conduct in journalism, including within their organizations.
■ Abide by the same high standards they expect of others.

Glossary

absolute privilege   The right of legislators, judges and government executives to speak without threat of libel when acting in their official capacities.

absolutism   The ethical philosophy that holds that there is a fixed set of principles or laws from which there is no deviation. To the absolutist journalist, the end never justifies the means.

actual malice test   Protection for reporters to write anything about an officeholder or candidate unless they know that the material is false or they recklessly disregard the truth.

advance   A report covering the subjects and issues to be dealt with in an upcoming meeting or event.

anecdote   An informative and entertaining story within a story.

annual percentage rate (APR)   The annual cost of a loan expressed as a percentage. The basic method for computing APR is set forth in the Truth in Lending Act of 1968.

assessed value   The amount that a government appraiser determines a property is worth.

attribution   Identification of the source of the information or quotation.

average   (1) A term used to describe typical or representative members of a group. (2) In mathematics, the result obtained when a set of numbers is added together and then divided by the number of items in the set.

background   Information that may be attributed to a source by title but not by name; for example, "a White House aide said."

beat   A reporter's assigned area of responsibility. A beat may be an institution, such as a courthouse; a geographic area, such as a small town; or a subject, such as science. The term also refers to an exclusive story.

blotter   An old-fashioned term for the arrest sheet that summarizes the bare facts of an arrest. Today this information is almost always stored on a computer.

bonds   Governments and corporations issue bonds to raise money (capital). The bonds pay interest at a stated rate and are redeemable on a predetermined maturity date.

change of venue   The transfer of a court proceeding to another jurisdiction for prosecution. This often occurs when a party in a case claims that local media coverage has prejudiced prospective jurors.

citizen journalism   A new form of media in which citizens actively participate in gathering and writing information, often in the form of news. Also called *participatory journalism*.

click-through rate   The measurement of how often online readers open individual links/stories.

closed-ended question   A direct question designed to draw a specific response—for example, "Will you be a candidate?"

commentary   An essay, column or blog that comments on rather than just reports the news.

compound interest   Interest paid on the total of the principal (the amount borrowed) and the interest that has already accrued.

constant dollars   Monetary amounts adjusted for inflation.

Consumer Price Index   A tool used by the government to measure the rate of inflation. CPI figures, reported monthly by the Bureau of Labor Statistics of the U.S. Department of Labor, compare the net change in prices between the current period and a specified base period. Reporters should use these data to accurately reflect the actual costs of goods and services.

content aggregator   A company that collects and distributes news from traditional media sources but does little or no independent news gathering.

convergence   A term defined in different ways by different people in the media industry but generally used to describe the coordination of print, broadcast and online reporting in a news operation.

crowdsourcing   The practice of inviting unpaid readers and viewers to submit their own stories, photographs and video and sometimes to lend their expertise to help solve community problems.

deep background   Information that may be used but that cannot be attributed to either a person or a position.

delayed-identification lead   The opening paragraph of a story in which the "who" is identified by occupation, city, office or any means other than by name.

dialogue   A conversation between two or more people, neither of whom normally is the reporter.

direct quote   A quote inside quotation marks that captures the exact words of the speaker.

documentary   In-depth coverage of an issue or event, especially in broadcasting.

Dow Jones Industrial Average   The principal daily benchmark of U.S. stock prices. It is based on the combined value of 30 major stocks, which are changed on a regular basis.

explanatory journalism   Journalism that explains not only what happened but how. The use of this technique often distinguishes professional journalism from citizen journalism.

Facebook   The world's most-used social networking website, which allows people to share updates, photos and news in a series of personalized feeds.

fair comment and criticism   Opinion delivered on the performance of someone in the public eye. Such opinion is legally protected as long as reporters do not misstate any of the facts on which they base their comments or criticism, and it is not malicious.

feature   A story that includes little or no breaking news.

flat-file database   A simple database program that allows users to keep track of almost any type of data. A simple address book is an example.

Freedom of Information Act   A law passed in 1966 to make it easier to obtain information from federal agencies. The law was amended in 1974 to improve access to government records.

free press/fair trial controversy   The conflict between a defendant's right to an impartial jury and a reporter's responsibility to inform the public.

gatekeepers   Editors who determine what readers or viewers read, hear and see.

hard lead   A lead that reports a new development or newly discovered fact.

hard news   Coverage of the actions of government or business, or the reporting of an event, such as a crime, an accident or a speech. The time element often is important. See also *soft news*.

hashtag   A phrase consisting of a number sign (#) and a word or words, used to identify topics on social media, especially Twitter.

hyperlink   A connection between two places on the web.

hypermedia   Web links to audio, video and pictures.

hypertext   A web document coded in HTML.

immediate-identification lead   The opening paragraph of a story in which the "who" is reported by name.

indirect quote   A paraphrase of the speaker's words. Because it is a paraphrase, the words are not in quotation marks.

individual retirement accounts   Restricted savings accounts whose earnings (as well as some contributions) are tax-free until withdrawal.

inflation   The rising cost of living as time goes by. See also *Consumer Price Index*.

interviewing   Having conversations with sources.

intranet   An internal online service accessible only to employees of a particular company or organization.

invasion of privacy   Violation of a person's right to be left alone.

inverted pyramid   The organization of a news story in which information is arranged in descending order of importance.

investigative reporting   The pursuit of information that has been concealed, such as evidence of wrongdoing.

lead   (1) The first paragraph or first several paragraphs of a newspaper story (sometimes spelled *lede*). (2) The story given the best display on Page 1. (3) A tip.

lead-in   An introduction to a filmed or recorded excerpt from a news source or from another reporter.

legacy media   Traditional media outlets such as newspapers, magazines, broadcast television and the like.

libel   Damage to a person's reputation caused by a false written statement that brings the person into hatred, contempt or ridicule or injures his or her business or occupational pursuit.

line-item budget   A budget showing each expenditure on a separate line.

listicle   An online article structured primarily as a numbered or bulleted list.

margin of error   The difference between results from the entire population (all registered voters in your county, for example) and a random sample of the population. It is usually expressed as plus or minus x points. The x depends on the size of the sample. The larger the sample, the smaller the margin of error.

median   The middle number in a series arranged in order of magnitude; it is often used when an average would be misleading. (If the series has an even number of items, the median is the average of the two "middle" numbers.) See also *average*.

millage rate   The tax rate on property, determined by the government.

moblog   A type of internet blog in which the user publishes blog entries directly to the web from a smartphone or other mobile device.

morgue   The newsroom library, where published stories, photographs and resource material are stored for reference.

multiple-element lead   The opening paragraph of a story that reports two or more newsworthy elements.

mutual funds   A collections of bonds, stocks and other securities managed by investment companies.

negligence test   The legal standard that requires reporters gathering facts and writing a story to use the same degree of care that any reasonable individual would use in similar circumstances.

news hole   The amount of space (in print) or time (in broadcast) available for news reporting.

news narrative   A story that sums up the news in the first paragraph or two and then describes events chronologically rather than ranking them in descending order of importance.

not for attribution   An expression indicating that information may not be ascribed to its source.

nut paragraph   A paragraph that summarizes the key element or elements of a story. Nut paragraphs usually are found in stories not written in inverted pyramid form. Also called a *nut graf*.

off the record   An expression that usually means "Don't quote me." Some sources and reporters use it to mean "Don't print this." Phrases with similar, and equally ambiguous, meanings are "not for attribution" and "for background only."

online videoconferencing   An internet-enabled, real-time communication where participants can both see and hear each other.

open-ended question   A question that permits the respondent some latitude in the answer—for example, "How did you get involved in politics?"

open-meetings law A state or federal law, often called a *sunshine law*, guaranteeing public access to meetings of public officials.

open-records law A state or federal law guaranteeing public access to many—but not all—kinds of government records.

parallelism A technique of presenting ideas in similar grammatical forms.

paraphrase A technique that digests, condenses or clarifies a quotation to convey the meaning more precisely or succinctly than the speaker's words do; an indirect quotation. Quotation marks are not used with paraphrases.

PDF file A computerized document that preserves formatting.

percentage change A number that explains by how much something goes up or down.

percentage point A unit of measure used to express the difference between two percentages. For example, the difference between 25 percent and 40 percent is 15 percentage points.

phablet A smartphone, such as an iPhone 6 Plus, with a screen that is larger than usual for a phone but not quite as large as a that of a tablet.

plagiarism The act of using any part of another person's writing and passing it off as your own.

play A shortened form of *display*. A good story may be played at the top of Page 1; a weak one may be played inside.

podcast A method of distributing multimedia files, usually audio or video, to mobile devices or personal computers so that consumers can listen or watch on demand. The term is derived from Apple Computer's iPod, but podcasts may be received by almost any music player or computer.

population In scientific language, the whole group being studied. Depending on the study, the population may be, for example, voters in St. Louis, physicians in California or all residents of the U.S.

primary source A person who witnesses or participates in an event, or an authentic document from an event.

principal The amount of money borrowed.

privilege A defense against libel that claims journalists have the right to repeat what government officials say or do in their official capacities.

profile A story intended to reveal the personality or character of an institution or person.

program budget A budget that clearly shows what each agency's activities cost.

proportion An explanation that relates one specific number to another or to the quantity or magnitude of a whole.

qualified privilege The right of journalists to report what government officials say or do in their official capacities if the report is full, fair and accurate.

question-and-answer A news story format that is a nearly verbatim transcript of an interview.

quote As a noun, a source's exact words, as in "I have a great quote here." As a verb, to report a source's exact words inside quotation marks.

rate The amount or degree of something measured in relation to a unit of something else or to a specified scale. In statistics, rate often expresses the incidence of a condition per 100,000 people, such as a murder or suicide rate. Rate also can reflect the speed at which something is changing, such as inflation or the percentage increase in a budget each year.

records column A regular newspaper feature that contains such information as routine police and fire news, births, obituaries, marriages and divorces.

relational database program A database program that permits users to determine relationships between two or more dissimilar databases. For example, a relational database program would enable a reporter to compare one database of people convicted of drunken driving with another database of school-bus drivers. The result would show how many bus drivers had drunken-driving convictions.

rundown A line-up of stories to appear in a newscast.

sample A portion of a group, or population, chosen for study as representative of the entire group.

secondary source A source who talked to a witness, such as a public safety official investigating a crime. The witness would be a primary source.

service journalism An aspect or type of journalism that recognizes usefulness as one of the criteria of news. Taking into consideration content and presentation, service journalism presents useful information in a usable way—for instance, by placing key information in a list or graphic box.

setup In broadcasting, an introductory statement to pique the interest of listeners or viewers. In written accounts, the material between the opening of a narrative story and the body. It generally consists of the transition to the theme paragraph, the nut paragraph, and, when appropriate, the "so what" and "to be sure" statements and foreshadowing.

shovelware Stories posted on the web exactly as they appeared in print.

sidebar A secondary story intended to be run with a major story on the same topic. A story about a disaster, for example, may have a sidebar that tells what happened to a single victim.

simple interest Interest paid on the principal (the amount borrowed).

situation ethics The philosophy that recognizes that a set of rules can be broken if circumstances indicate that the community would be served better by breaking them. For example, a journalist who generally believes that deceiving a news source is unethical may nevertheless be willing to conceal his or her identity to infiltrate a group operating illegally.

slug A word that identifies a story as it is processed through the newspaper plant or at a broadcast news station. A slug is usually placed in the upper left-hand corner of each take of a newspaper story.

sniff   The preliminary phase of an investigation.

social media   Online sites and apps designed to enable content-sharing and networking. As opposed to the mass media, social media allow people to communicate with friends informally; for example, using Twitter, Facebook or Instagram.

soft news   Stories about trends, personalities or lifestyles. The time element usually is not important. See also *hard news*.

sound bite   An audio recording that accompanies a story in radio or television news or, more recently, that is available even on newspaper websites as a supplement to the printed product.

spot news   A timely report of an event that is unfolding at the moment.

stocks   Shares in a piece of a company.

strategic communication   An approach that uses research-based evidence to create strategies and tactics aimed at achieving a desired response from a given audience. Communicators seek to maximize effects by coordinating the best combination of media, social, digital, or interpersonal tactics to accomplish organizational or marketing goals.

substantial truth   The correctness of the essential elements of a story.

summary lead   The first paragraph of a news story in which the writer presents a synopsis of two or more events rather than focusing on any one of them.

tablet   A self-contained, flat-panel computer, like an iPad, that is portable. Most tablets are about the size of a book.

teleprompter   A mechanical or electronic device that projects broadcast copy next to the television camera lens so that a newscaster can read it while appearing to look straight into the lens.

tickler   A file of upcoming events kept on paper or stored electronically at the assignment desks of most news organizations.

tie-back   (1) The sentence or sentences relating a story to events covered in a previous story. Tie-backs are used in follow-up or continuing stories or in parts of a series. (2) The technique of referring to the opening of a story in the story's ending.

"to be sure" paragraph   In stories focusing on one person or perspective, a statement reflecting the opinions of those who disagree with the person featured, as in "To be sure, not everyone agrees."

Twitter   A microblogging site that allows users to post short status updates in 140 characters or fewer, and follow the updates of friends, celebrities, news organizations and others.

URL   Short for *uniform resource locator*, the address of an internet site.

webcast   An audio or video report available on a website.

"you" lead   The first paragraph of a story, written using the informal, second-person pronoun "you."

Acknowledgments *(continued from page iv)*

Chapter 2

"Engaging Communities: Content and Conversation," by Joy Mayer, June 27, 2011. *Nieman Reports*, Summer 2011. Reprinted by permission of the Nieman Foundation for Journalism at Harvard.

Chapter 4

Horovitz, Bruce, "Ads Put Obese People in Spotlight," *USA Today*, October 4, 2012 © 2012 Gannett-USA Today. All rights reserved. Used by permission and protected by the Copyright Laws of the United States. The printing, copying, redistribution, or retransmission of this Content without express written permission is prohibited.

Barnard, Anne, "A Stirring in St. Albans: Emboldened by '08 Race to Roil Waters at Home," *The New York Times*, Sept. 4, 2009. © 2009 The New York Times. All rights reserved. Used by permission and protected by the Copyright Laws of the United States. The printing, copying, redistribution, or retransmission of this Content without express written permission is prohibited.

"Terror Sting Thwarts Car Bomb Attempt," The Associated Press, October 18, 2012. Reprinted by permission.

Chapter 5

"Chemical Fallout: Bisphenol A Is in You," by Susanne Rust, Cary Spivak, and Meg Kissinger, *Milwaukee Journal Sentinel* article © Milwaukee Journal Sentinel and reprinted with permission.

Stan Ketterer "Evaluating Links" Reprinted by permission.

Chapter 6

Ayesha Sitlani. http://www.merck.com/about/featured-stories/Ayesha_Sitlani.html. Copyright © Merck Sharp & Dohme Corp, a subsidiary of Merck & Co., Inc. Used with permission.

"Celebrating Grand Opening Today for Mayo Clinic Square: Mayo Clinic, Minnesota Timberwolves, Minnesota Lynx." Reprinted by permission.

News release: "Emerging Health Risk: Every Day More Than 30 Children Get into Liquid Laundry Packets." Reprinted by permission of Safe Kids Worldwide.

New Release: Ayesha Sitlani. Reprinted by permission of Merck National Service Center.

News release: "Humane Society of Missouri Confirms: Guilty Pleas Entered in Federal Court to Charges from Largest Dog Fighting Raid and Rescue in U.S. History." Reprinted by permission of the Humane Society of Missouri.

News release: "Concussion Assessment Tool Wins Notre Dame Business Plan Competition," University Alliance. Reprinted by permission of Notre Dame News.

Chapter 8

Phillips, Elizabeth, "Man Arrested in Attack, Charged with Child Endangerment," *Columbia Missourian*, November 17, 2006. © The Columbia Missourian. Reprinted by permission.

Lakhani, Asif, "Parks and Recreation, City Council Discuss Plans for Parks Tax," *Columbia Missourian*, November 29, 2010. © The Columbia Missourian. Reprinted by permission.

"UPDATE: Man dies in afternoon car accident," *Columbia Missourian*, Jun 21, 2015. © The Columbia Missourian. Reprinted by permission.

Chapter 9

Marcum, Diana, "Sinking land and hearts: For the Central Valley town of Stratford, where the water table has fallen 100 feet, survival isn't a given," *Los Angeles Times*, Oct. 24, 2014. Reprinted by permission.

Kiernan, Louise, "A Conversation with Pulitzer Prize Winner Diana Marcum," *Nieman Storyboard*, April 30, 2015. Reprinted by permission of the Nieman Foundation for Journalism at Harvard.

Linda Keene, "San Diego didn't report earlier E. coli outbreak," *The Seattle Times*, March 11, 1993. Copyright © 1993 The Seattle Times. Reprinted with permission.

Mezz, Dave, "Booby Prize: Although It Was Curtains for Her Breasts . . . Heather Carver's Sense of Humor Remains Center Stage," *Vox*, Jan. 25, 2007. Reprinted by permission of the author.

Student essay excerpt: "Opportunity would take Millard away [. . .]. Reprinted by permission of Sara Trimble.

Student essay excerpt: "But Overeem is more than a music fanatic. [. . .]. Reprinted by permission of Megan Farokhmanesh.

Chapter 10

Gelineau, Kristen and Nessman, Ravi, "Ill-Fated Train Ride Tears Indian Boy from Mother, Sparks 25-Year Worldwide Hunt for Home," The Associated Press, June 9, 2012. Reprinted by permission.

Meinhardt, Jane, "Mother Accused of Being Criminal Ringleader," *Tampa Bay Times*, October 21, 1994 © 1994 Tampa Bay Times. All rights reserved. Used by permission and protected by the Copyright Laws of the United States. The printing, copying, redistribution, or retransmission of this Content without express written permission is prohibited.

Tully, John, "Horse Power," *Columbia Missourian*, Nov. 27, 2006. Reprinted by permission.

Student essay excerpt: "Karen Elliott, 44, remembers the phone call [. . .]. Reprinted by permission of Karen Elliott.

Student essay excerpt: "Anita Poore hit the rough pavement of the parking lot with a thud. [. . .]. Reprinted by permission of Anita Poore.

Student essay excerpt: "She's 73 and has been teaching for 53 years. [. . .]." by Bailey Otto.

Index

*Note: Page numbers in *italics* indicate material presented in boxes. Page numbers followed by *f* indicate figures. **Boldface** page numbers indicate glossary terms.

Annotated Models

Copy Editing and Proofreading Symbols

Writing and editing for today's media are done almost exclusively on computers. Only in the book industry are some manuscripts still prepared on paper. Nevertheless, at some small newspapers and magazines, editors prefer to edit on paper. For that reason, failure to learn the copy editing symbols used in manuscript preparation is a mistake. There is a good chance you will need to use those symbols at some point in your career, if only to satisfy the occasional editor who prefers doing things the old-fashioned way.

You are even more likely to use proofreading symbols, which are used on galley proofs and page proofs to correct typeset copy. While there are some similarities in the two sets of symbols, there also are differences. The chart below illustrates the most common proofreading symbols (used to correct typeset copy), and the adjacent chart shows the most common copy editing symbols (used in manuscript preparation).

Proofreading Symbols

Symbol	Meaning	Symbol	Meaning
∧	Insert at this point.	✓✓	Space evenly.
⊥	Push down space.	◠	Close up entirely.
ℯ	Take out letter, letters or words.	⊏	Move to left.
ꓯ	Turn inverted letter.	⊐	Move to right.
(lc)	Set lowercase.	⊔	Lower letter or word.
(wf)	Wrong font letter.	⊓	Raise letter or word.
(ital)	Reset in italic type.	(out see copy)	Words are left out.
(rom)	Reset in roman (regular) type.	//=	Straighten lines.
(bf)	Reset in boldface type.	¶	Start new paragraph.
⊙	Insert period.	(no ¶)	No paragraph. Run together.
⌄	Insert comma.	(tr)	Transpose letters or words.
⌄;	Insert semicolon.	(?)	Query; is copy right?
⊨	Insert hyphen.	⊢⊣	Insert dash.
⌄	Insert apostrophe.	☐	Indent 1 em.
⌄⌄	Enclose in quotation marks.	☐☐	Indent 2 ems.
≡	Replace with a capital letter.	☐☐☐	Indent 3 ems.
#	Insert space.	(stet)	Let it stand.

Copy Editing Symbols

Indent for new paragraph

no ¶   No paragraph (in margin)

Run in or bring

copy together

Join words: week end

Insert a word or phrase   *single*

Insert a missing letter

Take out any extra letter

Transpose tow letters

Transpose words two

Make letter lower case

Capitalize columbia

Indicate boldface type   bf

Abbreviate January 30

Spell out abbrev.

Spell out number 9

Make figures of thirteen

Separate run together words

Join letters in a w ord

Insert period

Insert comma

Insert quotation marks

Take out some word

Don't make this correction   stet

Mark centering like this

Indent copy from both sides by using these marks

Spell name Smyth as written

or   fc

Spell name Smyth as written

There's more story: More

This ends story: # 30

Do not obliterate copy; mark it out with a thin line so it can be compared with editing.

Mark in hyphen: =

Mark in dash: ⊢

a and u

o and n

515

LaunchPad Solo
macmillan learning

Where Students Learn

Videos
macmillanhighered.com/newsreporting12e

Throughout *News Reporting and Writing*, the book directs you to **LaunchPad Solo for Journalism**, where videos complement the material in the text. Here is a list of all the videos featured in the book, sorted by chapter. For directions on how to access these videos online, please see the instructions on the facing page.